ADDITIONAL PRAISE FOR *THE NEW EVIL*

"Dr. Michael Stone's classic book *The Anatomy of Evil* has provided the most detailed and comprehensive description of psychopathic behavior available in contemporary psychiatric literature. The present volume, written by him in collaboration with Dr. Gary Brucato, further deepens and expands the precise presentation of the entire spectrum of psychopathy, proposes a comprehensive set of a 'Gradations of Evil' scale, and thus makes a fundamental contribution to the diagnostic and prognostic evaluation of this pathology. A major, disturbing finding emerges from this study: the increase of extremely destructive, violent individual criminal behavior since the 1960s in this country and, to a lesser degree, in other parts of the world. This book challenges the reader to become concerned about the increase of evil that we are witnessing, to reflect on its causes, and to recognize our collective responsibility to confront this development. It is a must-read for all mental health professionals and for the educated citizen alert to our social problems."

> —Otto Kernberg, MD, professor of psychiatry at the Weill Cornell Medical College, and training and supervising psychoanalyst at the Columbia University Center for Psychoanalytic Training and Research

"*The New Evil* is a fascinating and disturbing addition to the study of violent crime and its motivations. Stone and Brucato explore the twenty-two gradations of evil and compare earlier felonious acts to the abrupt escalation and broadened diversity of the new era of violence that arrived in the 1960s. *The New Evil* merits inclusion on the reference shelf alongside the classics by Hare and Cleckley."

> —Diane Fanning, author of *Bitter Remains* and Edgar® Award finalist

"In this impressive book, Stone and Brucato provide one of the most comprehensive, conceptually clear frameworks on the typology of violence. Using extensive case studies, they explore and offer insight into different motives and patterns of homicides and other violent behavior. This book sharpens and enhances our understanding of violence and psychopathology of evil acts like no other resource."

> —Ali Khadivi, PhD, clinical and forensic psychologist and professor of psychiatry and behavioral sciences, Albert Einstein College of Medicine

"The varieties of evil encountered in the commission of serious crimes can easily defy understanding. The first step toward making sense of all of this is through the process of classification. Identifying the critical elements that things have in common in order to classify them into categories helps to impose order on a chaotic, mystifying, and often horrifying aspect of human behavior. By dividing motivations for murder and other serious crimes into twenty-two well-defined gradations that range from the least evil (killing in self-defense) to evil at its most extreme (murder in the context of torture), Stone and Brucato's excellent book *The New Evil* provides readers with the tools to tease apart the motivations underlying violent crime acts and to help make the unfathomable more understandable."

—Michael B. First, MD, editorial consultant on the
fifth edition of the American Psychiatric Association's
Diagnostic and Statistical Manual of Mental Disorders

THE NEW EVIL

THE NEW
EVIL

Understanding the Emergence of
MODERN VIOLENT CRIME

MICHAEL H. STONE, MD
AND GARY BRUCATO, PHD

Afterword by Dr. Ann Burgess
Forensic psychiatric nurse, Connell School of Nursing,
Boston College, and coauthor of
Sexual Homicide and the *Crime Classification Manual*

Prometheus Books
59 John Glenn Drive
Amherst, New York 14228

Inquiries should be addressed to
Prometheus Books
59 John Glenn Drive
Amherst, New York 14228
VOICE: 716–691–0133 • FAX: 716–691–0137
WWW.PROMETHEUSBOOKS.COM

23 22 21 20 19   5 4 3 2 1

Library of Congress Cataloging-in-Publication Data

Names: Stone, Michael H., 1933- author. | Brucato, Gary, 1978- author.
Title: The new evil : understanding the emergence of modern violent crime / Michael H. Stone, MD, Gary Brucato PhD.
Description: Amherst : Prometheus Books, 2019. | Includes index.
Identifiers: LCCN 2018046789 (print) | LCCN 2018061766 (ebook) |
    ISBN 9781633885332 (ebook) | ISBN 9781633885325 (paperback)
Subjects: LCSH: Criminal psychology. | Good and evil. | BISAC: TRUE CRIME /
    Murder / General. | PSYCHOLOGY / Forensic Psychology.
Classification: LCC HV6080 (ebook) | LCC HV6080 .S834 2019 (print) |
    DDC 364.3—dc23
LC record available at https://lccn.loc.gov/2018046789

Printed in the United States of America

CONTENTS

PART I: THE TWENTY-TWO DEGREES OF EVIL

PART II: THE ERA OF "NEW" EVIL

THE TWENTY-TWO DEGREES OF EVIL

Gary Brucato, PhD

Edited by Michael Stone, MD

CHAPTER ONE

INTRODUCTION TO THE GRADATIONS OF EVIL SCALE

In April of 1996, forty-nine-year-old James Patterson Smith entered a police station in the Gorton area of Manchester, England, to report the death of his seventeen-year-old girlfriend, Kelly Anne Bates. He explained that, during a fight in a shared bath, she somehow inhaled water and asphyxiated, despite his gallant attempts to revive her. Upon investigation, police found blood on the walls and floor of virtually every room of Smith's house, belying his dubious tale of a lover's quarrel gone badly awry.[1]

Dr. William Lawler, a seasoned pathologist who had previously examined nearly six hundred cases of homicide, remarked that the wounds Bates sustained were the most extensive he had ever encountered.[2] She had been found naked in Smith's bedroom, covered in over 150 distinct injuries. She spent the last month of her young life bound in the house with a ligature around her neck, or tied by her hair to chairs or radiators. She had lost about forty-four pounds due to starvation and was deprived of water for days before her death. Smith had systematically tortured and disfigured her, singeing her with a hot iron and boiling water; repeatedly piercing her with multiple sharp implements; crushing her hands and kneecaps; and mutilating her face, mouth, and body. Her scalp was partially removed. As much as three weeks before her death, Smith had blinded her by gouging out both of her eyes. Finally, he bludgeoned her with a showerhead and fatally drowned her in a bathtub filled with water.[3] Throughout the subsequent murder trial, Smith accepted no responsibility, claiming that, before her purely "accidental" death, Bates had routinely harassed him, dared him to hurt her, and inflicted injuries upon herself to falsely suggest abuse and to impugn his reputation.[4] Remarking upon the sadistic killer's "catalog of depravity," the judge in the case sentenced him to life imprisonment, with a minimum of twenty years.[5]

How are we to make sense of a tragedy so utterly grotesque and heartbreaking? What psychiatric, psychological, or medical diagnosis could possibly account for the actions of a man like James Patterson Smith, who had a long history of aggression toward women, including beating a pregnant girlfriend and trying to drown two others during violent attacks?[6] Is there anyone among us who would not view his actions as a moral evil, beyond all human understanding? Indeed, the victim's father, who had the terrible task of identifying her brutalized body, remarked of her killer, "People called him an animal, but an animal wouldn't do that to another animal. He is a very evil man."[7]

Dr. Stone and I contend that the concept of evil, which is universally sensed on a basic level, and yet extremely difficult to articulate and comprehend, is worthy of serious inquiry. We have dedicated significant portions of our careers to this area, spending years evaluating, studying, and sometimes even treating violent killers, rapists, child abusers, and other offenders—people whose crimes few would hesitate to call "evil"—in prisons, hospitals, and other settings. Within this larger context, Dr. Stone has made a specialty of what are known as personality disorders, characterized by inflexible, maladaptive patterns of behavior, thought, and inner experience, which, as we shall see, constitute a key aspect of violent behavior. My own area of expertise, following forensic training and experience, has been psychosis, or abnormal states of the mind, in which perceptions, thoughts, and emotions are impaired to the point that one loses contact with reality. In my clinical work, as well as in my research with a team of investigators, I explore the relationship between violent thoughts and behaviors, and psychotic illness, especially as the latter first emerges in adolescents and young adults.

By "evil," we are not referring to spiritually sinful or societally forbidden acts, per se, since what is deemed abominable by one religion or culture might be fully accepted by another. Rather, we refer to the types of actions that virtually anyone, regardless of faith, time, or place, would find unspeakably horrible and utterly depraved. Moreover, we note that acts commonly called "evil" share three other core elements, in that they are generally preceded by *malice aforethought* or premeditation, inflict wildly excessive degrees of suffering, and would be considered altogether incomprehensible to the average individual. We find that, whatever one maintains to be the cause or origin of evil, on a psychological, biological, or spiritual level, atrocities to which this term is applied will universally possess these four fundamental features. Indeed, each can be readily observed in the methodical, protracted torture and murder of Kelly Anne Bates and in the ensuing reaction of the shocked and bewildered public. It should be noted that, when, in common parlance, the word "evil" is used to describe someone, the implication is that the individual has habitually and often committed evil acts. We find, however, that even the most egregious repeat offenders do not spend from dusk to dawn of each and every day perpetrating evil deeds. Some persons of the latter type demonstrate pleasant and innocuous relationships with family, neighbors, coworkers, and others for years, while leading "double lives" in which terrible crimes are secretly committed. Thus, the term "evil," as we will be using it, will not generally refer to people themselves but rather to actions that are so violent and horrifying as to evoke the typical emotional reaction we have just described. Only in rare instances do certain persons commit heinous, sadistic offenses with such frequency and regularity as to perhaps justify being called evil people, and not merely individuals who perpetrate evil acts.

With these key concepts in mind, we turn to the basic questions of whether some individuals' acts and core drives are more evil than others' and, if so, how we might classify them into distinct, meaningful categories that can then be ranked by severity. In *The Anatomy of Evil*, Dr. Stone proposed a Gradations of Evil scale, whereby, for the first time, we might endeavor to quantify the degree of evil associated with an individual's violent and/or homicidal actions.[8]

Using a twenty-two-point continuum, the instrument takes into account the morality of the prime motivation underpinning an individual's crime or repeated criminal acts, ranging from the justifiable to the groundlessly cruel. While the rankings cover a wide array of offenses, murder, within a number of contexts and associated with a variety of motivations, is particularly emphasized. The scale weighs, for instance, whether a homicide is driven by self-defense or feelings of helplessness in the context of abuse. It captures those who take lives due to feelings of jealousy or rage that are intense and difficult to control. It considers those who kill out of blind loyalty to another person or party, or who aim to eliminate anyone impeding the achievement of some selfish end. As it moves into its upper limits, the scale ranks individuals who commit murders for sport, to conceal evidence of a crime, due to loss of contact with reality, or for perverse sexual gratification. At the extreme end are those who subject victims to prolonged, unimaginable torment, without a hint of compassion or regret, sometimes followed by killing and sometimes not. Stated another way, higher rankings reflect more severe levels of *psychopathy*—a constellation of personality traits and tendencies, such as deceit, callousness, lack of remorse, manipulation, grandiosity, glibness, and superficial charm, while the highest levels also involve *sadism*, the derivation of pleasure from the pain and humiliation of others. In addition to these often overlooked distinctions, the scale's categories delineate "evil" actions to which the average onlooker might respond less strongly, perhaps even with a measure of understanding and sympathy, and ones that are likely to elicit horror, bafflement, and disgust, such as intentionally drawn-out torture, necrophilia, or the sexual assault or killing of children.

Thus, Dr. Stone's scale has real value for understanding why murderers, for instance, should not be grouped into a single category merely because they have killed. This is especially true of those we call *serial killers*, a topic we will discuss at some length. Serial murder is presently defined by the Federal Bureau of Investigation as "the unlawful killing of two or more victims by the same offender(s), in separate events."[9] As we shall see, this definition is problematic, in that it disregards entirely the notion of motive, such that an individual who has shot to death two homeowners during separate burglaries would be grouped alongside double murderer Ed Gein, who exhumed corpses from graveyards and created articles of clothing and household items from their bones and skin. It also disregards the time frame between homicides, which eliminates a key distinction between serial killers and what we call *mass* or *spree murderers*, classifications we will define later in this book. According to an earlier definition, a serial killer is one who murders three or more individuals, usually in the service of abnormal psychological gratification, with the killings occurring over more than a month and with a significant period of time between them.[10] Here, the issue is that "abnormal psychological gratification" is vague, failing to distinguish between what specific drives one might be satisfying when one kills, such that John Wayne Gacy, the sexually sadistic torturer, rapist, and murderer of thirty-three boys and young men,[11] might be categorized alongside Dorothea Puente, who swindled social security checks from elderly and developmentally disabled guests in her boarding home, killing nine of them with poison.[12] We shall see that, in fact, serial murderers can be motivated by several different psychological processes or exhibit highly distinct personality profiles. Dr. Stone's categories help elucidate these important disparities.

It is critical to note that the scale's focus is isolated to crimes that occur in peacetime, since wartime can alter the justifiability of an "evil" act in an individual's mind. For instance, someone who detonates an explosive device during a military conflict, causing untold destruction and death, may later, in civilian life, experience pangs of conscience at the thought of swatting a fly. Acts of terrorism, which tend to be committed by persons who view themselves as parts of religiously or philosophically motivated armies, are also not evaluated by the scale. Similarly, organized crime activity is excluded, in that it constitutes routine business within some wider enterprise, in which one criminal syndicate is at constant "war" with various others.

Throughout our first several chapters, we will discuss each ranking in the scale, describing the key distinctions between them in detail. The twenty-two categories are as follows:

Killing in Self-Defense or Justified Homicide
1. Justifiable homicide (killing was in self-defense, not psychopathic)
Impulsive Murders in Persons without Psychopathic Features
2. Jealous lovers; egocentric, immature people committing crimes of passion
3. Willing companions of killers, impulse-ridden, some antisocial traits
4. Killing in self-defense, but extremely provocative toward the victim
5. Traumatized, desperate persons who kill relatives or others, yet have remorse
6. Impetuous, hotheaded murderers, yet without marked psychopathic traits

Persons with a Few or No Psychopathic Traits; Murders of a More Severe Type
7. Highly narcissistic persons, some with a psychotic core, who murder loved ones
8. Murders sparked by smoldering rage, resulting sometimes in mass murder
Psychopathic Features Marked; Murders Show Malice Aforethought
9. Jealous lovers with strong psychopathic traits or full-blown psychopathy
10. Killers of people who were "in the way" (including witnesses); extreme egocentricity
11. Fully psychopathic killers of people who were "in the way"
12. Power-hungry psychopaths who murder when "cornered"
13. Inadequate, rageful psychopaths, some committing multiple murders
14. Ruthlessly self-centered psychopathic schemers
Spree or Multiple Murders; Psychopathy Is Apparent
15. Psychopathic, cold-blooded spree or multiple murderers
16. Psychopathic persons committing multiple vicious acts (including murder)
Serial Killers, Torturers, Sadists
17. Sexually perverse serial killers; killing is to hide evidence, no torture
18. Torture-murderers, though the torture element is not prolonged
19. Psychopaths driven to terrorism, subjugation, intimidation, rape, etc., short of murder
20. Torture-murderers, but in persons with distinct psychosis, such as schizophrenia
21. Psychopaths committing extreme torture, but not known to have killed
22. Psychopathic torture-murderers, with torture as the primary motive; the motive need not always be sexual

Experience tells us that those using the scale typically grasp, with no difficulty, the first eight categories, in which non-psychopathic persons commit murder or other serious acts of violence in self-defense, or in the contexts of abuse, impulsiveness, or intense feelings of jealousy or anger. Categories 9 through 22 tend to prove more challenging, since they require moving beyond motivations that are clear-cut, situational, and human in tone to ones that are selfish, perverse, and cruel to degrees generally unfathomable by the average individual. Moreover, understanding of these categories requires familiarity with and the ability to distinguish between psychological concepts such as *psychopathy*, *narcissism*, *psychosis*, and *sadism*, all of which we will define and discuss in the coming chapters.

To clarify the distinctions between the scale's sometimes complicated categories, we have provided highly detailed case histories of a number of individuals designated to each. The names and facts provided are all matters of public knowledge, having been openly reported by the media, including, in some instances, offenders' specific psychiatric diagnoses. These are interwoven with insights regarding the respective individuals' established motivations and how these may have related to formative experiences, as well as *signature* elements of their crimes—that is, features that were not necessary components of their modi operandi but, rather, psychologically required by the perpetrators for personal, psychological reasons. For example, a killer's method might be to murder women by strangulation, but his signature might be to do so with a black nylon stocking, constituting a sort of "calling card." Such elements in crimes provide key clues as to a given repeat murderer's underlying needs and drives, and are sometimes so idiosyncratic as to facilitate criminal profiling, establishment of a suspect in a series of linked homicides, and, ultimately, apprehension by authorities. We will also review points drawn from the academic literature on the genetic, dispositional, and environmental antecedents to violence, as well as various systems for categorizing criminal behavior. Wherever possible, we will include samples of offenders' actual written or spoken language, culled from published interviews and personal writings. Some examples of the latter have been reproduced alongside original artworks by various serial murderers, in a selection of illustrations elsewhere in this book. At the close of part I, which constitutes the most comprehensive exposition of Dr. Stone's ranking system published to date, we will introduce an algorithm we have developed, which greatly facilitates the process of determining a violent individual's most appropriate ranking in the Gradations of Evil scale.

In part II, Dr. Stone will discuss the increased frequencies and unprecedented heinousness of rapes, serial murders, and other violent crimes since the turbulent era of the 1960s, illuminating a number of cultural, psychological, and philosophical factors that we feel may have fundamentally contributed to these disturbing trends. He will also catalog several types of violence that have first emerged during this era of "new evil," as we have termed it, including mass shootings by civilians involving semiautomatic weapons, internet-related crimes, fetus-snatching, and other contemporary atrocities.

As we move along Dr. Stone's continuum, it moves upward through higher numbers, but it might best be envisioned as traveling downward, the way Dante Alighieri, in his immortal *Inferno*, is escorted by the poet Virgil lower and lower into the bottommost circle of hell, where the devil, himself, resides. Indeed, Dante's depiction of the netherworld, with its nine circles of torment for various moral abominations, inspired Dr. Stone to create the instrument. Readers are forewarned that, as we make this descent, some of the details of the crimes we describe will be difficult to read. It is important to hold in mind the relative rareness of cases of extreme evil, especially serial killing. Across time and space, and billions of people, past and present, it has always been the worst of human behavior that garnered the most attention. Let us never forget that there are wonderful, selfless people in the world, who are worthy of their own scale, circling through the heights of heaven, as Dante ultimately did.

Finally, let us pause a moment to remember the men, women, and children who have fallen victim to the monstrous behaviors of the offenders we will encounter here. We will meet young people, sleeping in their beds or playing in public places, who were suddenly snatched up and carried away into unimaginable darkness. We will encounter women who happened to cross the paths of sexually depraved predators who took away their choices, and yanked them from their lives and loves and other destinies. We will discuss people who had never harmed a hair on a single head, no less those of their torturers or killers. These stories will force us to reflect on the stark reality that these victims were real people who could have been our own children, grandchildren, parents, siblings, spouses or significant others, friends, or neighbors—you or I. Any of us. Let us remember, still, that the existence of evil proves, incontrovertibly, its counterpart, which is goodness, motivated by denial of the self and by love.

CHAPTER TWO

CATEGORIES 1–6

I and the public know
What all schoolchildren learn,
Those to whom evil is done
Do evil in return.

—W. H. Auden, "September 1, 1939," *Another Time*

In Sir Arthur Conan Doyle's classic Sherlock Holmes tale "The Adventure of the Devil's Foot," the sleuth determines that a celebrated explorer and huntsman, Dr. Leon Sterndale, has avenged the murder of his mistress by fatally poisoning her killer with a vaporized toxin. Holmes empathizes with Sterndale's decidedly human motivation and is unable to condemn him as a basically evil man, remarking to his friend and biographer, "I have never loved, Watson, but if I did and the woman I loved had met such an end, I might act even as our lawless lion-hunter has done. Who knows?"[1]

Dr. Sterndale's crime is a plausible example of the type of violence generally designated to the first six categories of the Gradations of Evil scale—and the reaction evoked in Holmes is precisely the type typically experienced by those who hear about such acts. Individuals ranked at this low end of the spectrum will all have felt driven to kill or commit other heinous acts in the contexts of specific situational factors, such as the need to escape abuse or defend oneself, or under the duress of intense emotions, such as jealousy or rage. Scattered narcissistic or antisocial traits may be present in such persons but never to degrees associated with psychopathy—again, a concept we will discuss in some detail in the coming chapters. These types rarely progress to commit murder or other serious crimes on separate occasions, and tend to subsequently exhibit sincere remorse and amendment of life, although these moral prognoses must be examined on a case-by-case basis. Let us now individually touch upon these first six categories, providing case examples as we go.

CATEGORY 1

Individuals ranked here have killed, but solely in self-defense during an attempted manslaughter, murder, rape, or armed robbery. Such homicides are deemed to be "justified" in the eyes of the law and are, therefore, categorized on the scale as "non-evil" acts. They do not involve malice aforethought, are not vicious or wildly extreme in nature, are committed by persons with no psychopathic or sadistic personality features, and are followed by genuine contrition. Thus, such homicides are included in the scale merely to establish a point of distinction from the types of actions associated with the twenty-one other categories, which will, by contrast, involve, to increasing degrees, the characteristics of "evil" proposed in our introduction. The following example received considerable media attention in 2009.[2]

John Pontolillo, a twenty-year-old chemistry student at Johns Hopkins University, filed a police report after discovering that two laptops and a video game system had been stolen from a home he shared with three friends. Deciding that he should check on his car, Pontolillo stepped outside with a samurai sword he kept in his bedroom, where he noticed forty-nine-year-old Donald Rice hiding under a porch behind the house. Rice, who had just been released from jail two days prior, was a career criminal who had been arrested more than two dozen times for breaking and entering, burglary, and car theft.

Pontolillo raised the sword and shouted at Rice to remain in place, calling for his roommates to alert the police. Rice instead raised his arms and hurled himself at the student, backing him up against a wall. Pontolillo, fearing for his safety, struck Rice with a single blow of the sword, creating a large gash in his chest and nearly severing his left hand. The attacker expired at the scene.

It was ultimately determined that Pontolillo legitimately believed he was in danger of death or suffering some serious bodily injury, such that he was fully justified in defending himself as he did. He was not charged in Rice's death.

A second example is the case of twenty-six-year-old Faith Martin of Illinois. In November of 2010, she had a squabble with her abusive, hard-drinking, forty-four-year-old boyfriend, Willie Arrington, with whom she had a young son. Arrington had a history of several violent assaults on other people, including kicking his best friend down a flight of stairs and biting off a chunk of a man's cheek during a brawl. She compared him to "a freight train going 1,000 miles per hour" when he was drunk and enraged. The day after their blowup, he visited her apartment and began punching and choking her, and the two wound up in her kitchen. Certain that he was hell-bent on taking her life, she grabbed a knife from the sink and fled into another room. Arrington pursued her, slamming her into a closet door and pushing her to the ground. She plunged the blade into his chest, piercing his aorta. Martin, horrified at what she had done, raced to a friend's apartment to seek help, but Arrington died at the scene. "I loved him, I didn't want to hurt him," she would later say. "I wanted to scare him—I wanted him to stop." Martin was initially charged with first-degree murder and held in prison for over a year. She was, however, subsequently acquitted on the grounds that Arrington had been a brutally abusive partner and that, during his violent assault, she fatally stabbed him in the context of very real fear for her own safety. According to the *Chicago Tribune*, "The judge called it the best case of self-defense that he had ever seen."[3]

CATEGORY 2

Here, we shift into the portion of the scale, ranging from Categories 2 through 6, associated with homicides committed by non-psychopathic individuals who act out of impulse. The specific impulse that serves as the impetus in Category 2 is jealousy within the context of spurned or unrequited romantic love. Sometimes called *crimes of passion*, these killings are generally carried out by egocentric and immature, but otherwise reasonably "normal" individuals with no criminal backgrounds, who suddenly act out in moments of blind, murderous rage. These are typically followed by feelings of sincere remorse. We find an example of this type of homicide in the case of Samuel Collins of Maine.[4] In 1996, Collins, who was then forty-two, made a surprise visit to the supermarket where his beloved wife of ten years, Lucinda, was employed. After discovering her kissing a coworker, he traveled home, shocked and consumed by overwhelming jealousy. Upon her return from work, he attacked her, dragging her across the floor by the hair, beating her and fatally stabbing her at least a dozen times with a knife. He then turned the blade on himself, slashing his wrists and chest, and phoned his mother to announce the intended murder-suicide, saying, "I can't live without her, she can't live without me, and this is the best way of doing it." Police found Collins lying alongside his wife's bloody corpse on the floor of their bathroom. They were able to save his life, and, two years later, he was found guilty of the grisly homicide.

Notably, some jealousy-related murders require higher rankings on the Gradations of Evil scale, due to narcissism, premeditation, unusual degrees of violence, or lack of subsequent remorse. Consider, for instance, the widely publicized Belgian "Parachute Murder" case, in which a woman was convicted of killing a romantic rival in a methodical, ruthless, less impulsive manner.

Els "Babs" Clottemans, a twenty-two-year-old elementary school teacher, and Els Van Doren, a thirty-eight-year-old married mother of two, both met and fell in love with Marcel Somers at a parachute club in Zwartberg. The three drank together, and the handsome twenty-five-year-old arranged to sleep with the two women on a strict schedule: Clottemans saw him on Fridays, and Van Doren on Saturdays. In November of 2006, while Clottemans was spending a night on Somer's couch, she overheard him and Van Doren making love in the bedroom. It is believed that, having noticed Van Doren's parachute nearby, she severed the release cords. When the trio went skydiving the following week, Van Doren's primary and reserve parachutes both failed to deploy, and she plummeted, while frantically fumbling, two miles to her death, landing in a garden in the town of Opglabbeek. Horrifying footage of the tragedy was captured on a camera mounted atop the victim's helmet. Investigators noted that, while the three would normally jump together to create a formation, Clottemans remained on the plane a few extra seconds and watched her rival's dive from above. Protesting her innocence, she attempted suicide during questioning by police. She was sentenced to thirty years in prison in 2010.[5]

In this case, the motive was, indeed, jealousy, but, even after a week of contemplation, the apparent murder plot by Clottemans was not aborted, and Van Doren's demise seems to have been designed to be particularly cruel in nature, with no chance of survival. Since the more sudden impulsivity and blind rage components seen in the Collins case are not present here, a ranking of 2 would not sufficiently characterize the nature of this crime. As we shall see, it would instead be assigned to Category 9 of the Gradations of Evil scale.

CATEGORY 3

This uncommon ranking is for impulsive, sometimes somewhat antisocial individuals who participate in the depraved acts of a killer or the leader of a murderous cult, either through passivity, fear, brainwashing, or some other factor. Typically, a blend of dread, adoration, or personal need leads them to blindly follow some master manipulator. When the trancelike hold is ultimately broken, such persons generally experience sincere remorse and accept responsibility for their actions—unlike those whose horrible crimes they aided and abetted. Let us consider, in some detail, the story of Leslie Van Houten, who participated in the two-day murder spree perpetrated by Charles Manson's mind-controlled cult in 1969.

It would be difficult to overstate the hold Manson—a grungy, diminutive ex-convict with a psychopathic, highly charismatic personality—maintained over his so-called "family." Manson's followers, people in their teens and early twenties who were dealing with various family conflicts, viewed him as an authority figure who, unlike their parents, understood their true needs and desires. In exchange, they were required to undergo "ego-death," a complete abandonment of the sense of self.[6] A misogynist who believed women to be lesser beings, Manson commanded them to participate in orgies at the isolated ranch where they lived a communal existence, sometimes involving male visitors who were strangers to them.[7]

Manson further disintegrated his followers' personal identities by drugging them with LSD and constantly barraging them with pseudo-spiritual rhetoric,[8] claiming, at various points, that he was Jesus, God, and the devil,[9] and that all aspects of traditional society, including the nuclear family, law, and morality, should be disregarded or dismantled.[10] He convinced them that, when the great race war he called Helter Skelter finally arrived, they would survive it by going underground and building up a population of 144,000 cult members, who would later reemerge and dominate the world.[11] The Beatles, he claimed, were the Four Horsemen of the Apocalypse described in the New Testament book of Revelations, and, through their *White Album*, they were directly communicating with him.[12] Although, to someone encountering him for the first time, he may have seemed utterly deluded and disorganized as he rambled on about such things, he was, in fact, an adept con artist who, while in McNeil Island Penitentiary in the 1960s, had absorbed ideas about interpersonal influence and manipulation from inmates steeped in hypnotism, Scientology, psychology, and the ideas of Dale Carnegie about how to win over other people.[13] His paranoia and other psychotic-like traits were firmly embedded within a wider picture of psychopathy and mind-altering drug use—concepts we will discuss in detail later in this book.

Manson reasoned that, if the family were to commit high-profile crimes against wealthy whites, African Americans would be blamed for them and his prophesied race war would rapidly erupt. On August 9, 1969, cult members Charles "Tex" Watson, Linda Kasabian, Susan Atkins, and Patricia Krenwinkel were sent to the friend-filled home of pregnant actress Sharon Tate, wife of director Roman Polanski, and instructed to "totally destroy" the inhabitants, "as gruesome as you can."[14] Steven Parent, a friend of the property's caretaker, was immediately stabbed and shot to death. Watson announced himself as the devil and kicked sleeping houseguest Wojciech Frykowski in the head. Watson bound Tate and Jay Sebring together with ropes, which were tied around their necks and slung over the ceiling beams, before Sebring was fatally shot for his protestations. Frykowski and coffee heiress Abigail Folger, who were brutally stabbed twenty-eight and fifty-one times, respectively, were both killed. Watson and/or Atkins stabbed Tate sixteen times.[15] An "X," believed by some to signify removal from society, was carved into her pregnant belly.[16] Having been told by Manson to "leave a sign . . . something witchy,"[17] Atkins wrote the word "pig" in Tate's blood on the front door of the house.[18]

The following night, after the cult celebrated its "triumph" with an orgy of sex and marijuana, Manson instructed the same cult members to kill anew, this time adding Van Houten and Steve Grogan and accompanying the group himself. They randomly selected the Los Angeles home of forty-four-year-old grocery store chain owner Leno LaBianca and his thirty-eight-year-old wife, Rosemary LaBianca, who operated a fashionable dress shop. After Manson and Watson tied up the couple, assuring them they would only be robbed, Atkins, Grogan, and Kasabian departed the scene with their leader and the others went straight to work, like so many obedient drones. Watson placed pillowcases over the heads of the victims, who were in separate rooms, before wrapping pieces of electrical cord, torn from a lamp, around their necks.[19] He then stabbed Mr. LaBianca to death. The deceased would later be found with a knife and a fork jutting out of his body, and the word "war" carved into his stomach.[20] His screams prompted his wife, who was with Van Houten and Krenwinkel, to thrash out in self-defense. Van Houten held her down while Krenwinkel unsuccessfully attempted to stab her in the chest with a knife taken from the kitchen. The blade bent on the victim's clavicle. Watson then entered the room and stabbed Mrs. LaBianca numerous times. When he reminded Van Houten that she had been instructed by Manson to "do something" that night, she stabbed Mrs. LaBianca, who was already dead, over a dozen times, in the lower back and buttocks. A subsequent autopsy would tally forty wounds in all. Krenwinkel then wrote on the walls with Mrs. LaBianca's blood, and Van Houten attempted to remove possible fingerprints, after which the trio ate cheese and drank milk from the victims' refrigerator.[21]

By October of 1969, Manson and several of his followers, including Van Houten, were in police custody.[22] In the months following the killings, Van Houten and the other cult members who participated in the various parts of the murder spree were tried in Los Angeles. Because Van Houten was the youngest and considered to be the least devoted to Manson, it was anticipated by some that she would likely receive a lenient sentence. However, she repeatedly disrupted trial proceedings with giggling, particularly during discussion of the murders. She also showed little remorse at the time, saying, "Sorry is only a five-letter word." In 1971, all of the defendants were convicted and sentenced to be executed, but all of the death sentences were ultimately commuted.[23]

By the late 1970s, Van Houten was considered to have undergone a significant personal change. In 2002, a superior court judge described her as having been a model prisoner for thirty years. She completed all available programs for inmates and assisted other incarcerated people.[24] She underwent decades of psychotherapy, to attempt to learn how she fell under Manson's mind control. Van Houten has long expressed remorse and renounced Manson, who, by contrast, took no real responsibility for his role in the killings.[25] He died of cardiac arrest in 2017, at the age of eighty-three.

Manson, Atkins, Krenwinkel, and Watson might best be ranked in Category 15 of the Gradations of Evil scale, designated for psychopathic, cold-blooded spree killers or multiple murderers. In Manson's unique case, murders were carried out through willing participants, at his behest. Van Houten, by contrast, is ranked here, in Category 3. She was not at the scene of the Tate murders. While she helped to subdue the LaBiancas, she only stabbed the latter alongside Watson after Mrs. LaBianca had already expired. Moreover, with time, reflection, and the lifting of Manson's spell, Van Houten has displayed contrition, devoting her years in prison to altruistic behaviors and personal healing.

CATEGORY 4

Similar to Category 1, Category 4 is associated with individuals who kill in self-defense. However, they are not generally exonerated when legally tried, due to the critical difference that, here, the threat in which self-defense efforts are carried out is the result of what is demonstrated to be extreme provocation on the attacked person's own part. Consider the following example.

On August 9, 2010, thirty-one-year-old Jose Rodriguez Elizondo, an off-duty US Customs and Border Protection (CBP) officer, visited the Punto 3 nightclub in Texas with his wife and brother. His wife alleged that, while they were being ejected from the club following a disagreement, she was pushed by bouncer Fermin Limon Jr., who was the son of the establishment's owner. Elizondo and Limon began arguing, and several security guards came over to assist. Elizondo broke free and ran nearly seventy yards to his truck, where his CBP-issued firearm and badge were located. He had his gun in hand as the men banged on the windows and forced him out of the vehicle. When Limon grabbed him, Elizondo began to pistol-whip him. He was suddenly approached by forty-nine-year-old Limon Sr., who was holding a 9mm pistol. Elizondo claimed that he told the elder Limon to put down his weapon at least twice before feeling compelled to shoot him in self-defense. Bar security saw it differently, reporting that Elizondo fired instantly as Limon was trying to calm the escalating situation. Following shots to his leg and chest, Limon Sr. hid behind a vehicle while a bouncer, who had taken over the pistol, fired several shots at Elizondo. The club owner later died as a result of his injuries. The following year, Elizondo, who it was felt provoked and did not abandon the encounter, was convicted of murder and sentenced to twenty-five years in prison. Later the defense appealed, and Elizondo was granted a new trial, due to an error related to the charge. He pled guilty and accepted a sentence of five years, of which he had already served a substantial portion.[26]

We would also categorize here the case of Susan Cummings, one of two fraternal twin sisters born in Monaco in 1962 to a billionaire arms dealer and his Swiss wife, Samuel and Irma Cummings. In 1984, the twins' father purchased for them a lavish estate in Warrenton, Virginia, named Ashland Farms, complete with a stone and frame manor house, two cottages, twenty-two horse stalls, and a two-hundred-foot indoor riding arena.[27] In 1995, Susan Cummings began dating Roberto Villegas, a dashing Argentine polo player. He had recently left a long-term relationship with a Floridian woman, who was pregnant with their son. Shortly after the child's birth, Villegas began spending his summers in Virginia to ride the polo circuit, where he was hired by Cummings as an instructor.[28] Before long, he moved into the estate, and, by the following year, their dynamic had become a stormy one. He was reportedly ill-tempered and verbally aggressive, and Cummings grew increasingly detached. Her alleged frugality, despite immense wealth, was a further point of contention.[29] Villegas was not paid for his work and came to greatly resent his financial dependency upon her.[30] Rumors swirled that he was engaging in affairs with other women.[31] Their relationship ultimately became explosive, and, on September 7, 1997, Cummings fatally shot him four times with a Walther 9mm semiautomatic—one of the guns imported by her father—as he sat eating breakfast at their kitchen table.[32]

Following her confession to police, she was arrested and charged with homicide. She claimed that Villegas had become physically abusive, grabbing her by the throat and slowly cutting her arm with a knife, saying he was going to teach her a lesson. She explained that she begged him to stop and suggested they have some coffee and talk. When she went over to the sink, she heard his chair move and believed him to be coming toward her.

Thinking quickly, she grabbed the gun she kept in a nearby cabinet and repeatedly fired at him.[33] An attorney defending Cummings noted that, two weeks before the shooting, she had filed a statement with local deputies, in which she called him "overpowering, short-fused and the crazy type." She described how he refused to allow her to leave him and that, in the prior month, he had begun to show signs of aggression, allegedly telling her, "I will put a bullet in your head and hang you upside-down to let the blood pour on your bed." A 1987 battery charge against him was also noted.[34] Villegas was quoted as once saying, "I treat my women and my horses the same way. . . . If I can't break them, I kill them."[35]

Prosecutors, by contrast, posited that the killing was premeditated and that Cummings had cut herself before staging a self-defense scenario. In the end, despite being convicted of voluntary manslaughter, she was sentenced to only sixty days in jail and a $2,500.00 fine.[36] In this case, we do not encounter a situation in which one inoffensive person is maltreated by someone else in a totally one-sided manner, as observed in Category 1. This case involved two individuals in a tense, negative dynamic, to which they both contributed to some degree, and it flared up into an incident in which one party then felt the need to defend herself against threat of bodily harm or even death. Hence, we feel that Category 4 is the most appropriate ranking for the slaying of Villegas on the Gradations of Evil scale.

CATEGORY 5

Individuals in Category 5, who show no signs of psychopathy, feel driven to homicide by traumatic or desperate circumstances, followed by bona fide guilt and remorse. These killings are generally impulsive, without much deliberation. The victims are typically family members or significant others, but other people perceived as contributing to the individual's negative circumstances might instead be targeted. Looking over a variety of cases classified here, we note that the emotions involved are more often than not about a sense of weakness or helplessness, arising due to the convergence of two forces: First, there is some external problem, such as aggression or maltreatment by a spouse or partner, financial difficulties, or some other adverse condition in the home. Second, there is an internal, psychological factor, such as intense anxiety, trauma related to prior abuse, or profound depression, sometimes with transient psychotic thinking. The individual consequently feels hopeless, lost, and driven over the proverbial edge, before a period of returning to his or her baseline level of functioning. We also note that these homicides can sometimes be especially violent in intensity, as if the individual has focused long pent-up hurt, resentment, and frustration into one explosive emotional expression.

We see these elements in the case of Diane Clark of England, who, at the age of forty-two, had suffered the final straw in an abusive marriage, brutally stabbing her forty-six-year-old husband Graham Clark to death.[37] Mr. Clark, who was a heavy gambler and drinker, had a history of convictions for criminal behavior dating back to adolescence. The two were married in 1974, after a courtship of only two months, and, almost immediately, Mrs. Clark found herself subjected to her husband's violent outbursts, especially when he was intoxicated. Within three years, she had grown drawn, thin, and anxious. Mr. Clark hardly worked, forcing her to be the sole breadwinner for their five children, for whose sake she felt obliged to remain with her husband. He beat her, so she had to wear long-sleeved jumpers all year long to conceal bruises, and he forced her to engage in sex, first when drunk, and eventually even when sober. Mr. Clark falsely accused her of extramarital affairs and once flew into a rage when she said she wished to consult a physician who simply happened to be male.

In September of 1997, Mr. Clark demanded that his wife leave their home, and she sought refuge in a hotel, where she worked as a waitress. Making her mind up to tell her husband that she wished to leave the marriage, Mrs. Clark came home to find the house vandalized with paint and her husband in an alcohol-fueled rage. He suddenly punched her in the face, tore buttons from her blouse, and shredded a bouquet of roses he had brought home as a peace offering. Mr. Clark demanded that she leave again, and, as he searched around for a suitcase, she grabbed a kitchen knife and stabbed him four times in the back and left shoulder. He expired in their hallway. Mrs. Clark, who was arrested, told authorities that she simply could not take any more of her husband's maltreatment.

At her trial, it was made clear that Mrs. Clark, who felt authentic contrition for what she had done, had no indications of a psychopathic personality. The judge spoke of a "smoking fuse of provocation" that led her to act in a way "totally out of character."[38] Following her guilty plea to manslaughter, she was set free and returned to her children to begin her life anew.

A second example, also from England, is the case of fifty-nine-year-old former plumber Dennis Long, who killed his sixty-two-year-old longtime romantic partner, Judith Scott.[39] According to Long, he was routinely both emotionally and physically abused by Scott throughout their three decades together, during which they raised two daughters she had from a prior relationship. She also had four grandchildren. Scott ridiculed and shamed Long, repeatedly beat him with a poker, and once left him with a broken thumb. On occasion, he would walk away from the relationship, only to return shortly thereafter. In March of 2010, Long was assaulted by a local bully as he and Scott made their way home from a pub, and, in addition to not defending himself, he refused to inform the police. Enraged, Scott mocked him for lacking backbone, said she should wear trousers and he a dress, and called him a "pansy" and a "poof." With that, Long explained, he snapped. After taking up a knife, he fatally stabbed her in the arm and twice in the chest. He immediately called emergency services and told the dispatcher, "I just lost it—She gave me grief, so I knifed her." He was subsequently arrested and tried for murder.

Long was ultimately cleared of the charge, on the grounds of "cumulative provocation" over the course of years, but convicted of manslaughter. He was sentenced to four years and eight months in prison for the killing. It should be emphasized that, as his trial progressed, there were no indications of psychopathy across his lifetime. He was described as a kind, hardworking person of previously good character, who abhorred violence, avoiding even swear words. The judge described him as "a placid, unassertive, rather weak man," and he was found to be filled with bona fide remorse about the killing of Scott.

CATEGORY 6

Category 6 is the designation for a hotheaded individual who commits homicide in an entirely impetuous manner. There is no self-defense involved. Because the person's temperament is an aggressive one, it is possible for there to be a prior history of violent behavior or even criminal acts. However, these temper-related incidents would not be of the type associated with an underlying psychopathic personality. The spur-of-the-moment, totally unplanned crimes assigned to this category can be set off by essentially any overpowering emotion or experience—for instance, some severe humiliation. If the trigger is jealousy, the violent act is so unusually extreme that a ranking of Category 2 is insufficient.

It is noteworthy that the violence associated with this ranking can extend to the killing of multiple individuals at one time. Thus, it is technically possible for an individual categorized here to have committed *mass murder*. Until recently, this was described by the FBI as "four or more victims slain, in one event, in one location," but, as a result of a federal statute, the definition changed to "three or more killings in a single event" in 2012.[40] Either criterion would categorize Coy Wayne "Elvis" Wesbrook, whose case we will now discuss, as a mass murderer.[41]

On November 13, 1997, Houston-area police responded to numerous reports from the same apartment complex of what sounded like five gunshots fired during a span of about forty seconds. There were also descriptions of a man standing near his pickup truck in the parking lot, saying things like, "I did it" and "I did what I had to do." There, authorities found Wesbrook, thirty-nine years of age at the time and, on the ground nearby, the body of forty-one-year-old Anthony Rogers. Wesbrook explained that he had just killed his ex-wife, thirty-two-year-old Gloria Coons. The two had been married for a year before divorcing in 1996, due to the rockiness of their relationship. Thereafter, they continued to see one another and even lived together for a time. He moved out of their shared apartment about three months prior to the current incident.

In the living room of one of the apartments, deputies found the bodies of thirty-five-year-old Antonio Cruz and forty-three-year-old Ruth Money. A third person, thirty-two-year-old Kelly Hazlip, was on the floor and still alive. In the bedroom, they found his ex-wife, also living. All had been shot once at close range in the head, chest, or abdomen. Coons died shortly after the arrival of emergency workers, and Hazlip expired five days later.

According to Wesbrook, he and Coons had lunch the night before the shooting, during which she expressed interest in possible reconciliation. Still in love with his ex-wife, he was elated by this development. He went to her apartment that evening, finding her with her roommate, Money, as well as two men, Rogers and Hazlip. They all appeared to have been drinking heavily. He was uncomfortable with the situation but agreed to join the group. Cruz appeared a short while later. Wesbrook had several beers and felt "buzzed." Then, when Coons suddenly flashed her breasts to all present, Wesbrook felt humiliated. She proceeded to escort Hazlip into her bedroom, and the two were joined by Rogers several minutes later. Wesbrook would later report that, when Rogers emerged with his pants open, Coons announced that she had just performed oral sex on him and was about to have intercourse with Hazlip.

Wesbrook's account continued that, feeling distraught and crestfallen, he got up to leave but was followed outside by Cruz, who grabbed the keys to Wesbrook's truck to prevent his departure. Gabbing a .36-caliber hunting rifle from his truck, he followed Cruz back into the apartment with the goal of retrieving his keys, which were, indeed, later found in the pocket of Cruz's pants. Once inside, all hell broke loose. The group began to verbally harass, threaten, and physically assault him. Money hurled a beer at him, reportedly causing the rifle to discharge, killing her instantly. When Cruz and Rogers rushed toward him, he fired at both. Then, walking into the room where Coons and Hazlip were having sex, he shot them both, blinded with rage. He then walked outside and patiently waited for the police. Rogers apparently managed to exit the apartment building and expired in the parking lot.

At his trial, Wesbrook explained that he had no intention of killing anyone that night but that he "lost it."[42] A psychologist for the defense described him as having been "very much at the end of his rope" at the time of the murders. It emerged that, not long before the shootings, he learned that his nine-year-old daughter with a previous wife had allegedly been sexually molested. There was also some question of whether he was intellectually disabled. Wesbrook did not have a criminal record. However, the state alleged a history of acts in the context of hotheadedness that had never been reported to police, including threatening to burn down the home of his first wife, attempting to torch the home of his ex-landlords following an eviction, and intimidating Coons and her friends on another occasion.[43]

In 1998, Wesbrook was found guilty of capital murder and sentenced to death. He expressed deep remorse, stating, "I've regretted everything a trillion times. . . . If I could bring those people back to life, I would." He was nevertheless executed for his rampage by lethal injection in 2016.[44]

CHAPTER THREE

CATEGORIES 7 AND 8

I wonder if the course of narcissism through the ages would have been any different had Narcissus first peered into a cesspool. He probably did.

—Frank O'Hara, *Early Writing*, 1977

Categories 7 and 8 of the Gradations of Evil scale shift us away from unplanned, impetuous aggression related to self-defense, jealousy, rage, or adverse circumstances. Here, we first encounter individuals whose basic underlying personality structures—not merely proclivities to be hot-headed or impulsive—partially set the stage for murder or other acts of extreme violence. As we shall see, there are key distinctions between the types of individuals assigned to Categories 7 and 8. However, both involve persons who, after a period of chronically feeling overlooked or slighted, and possibly nursing long-term grudges, feel driven to violence. The killing is generally more severe in nature than would be associated with the earlier categories, and—critically—there is some scheming and planning involved. Furthermore, while some aberrant personality traits are present, these individuals do not exhibit full-blown psychopathy.

CATEGORY 7

Individuals ranked here are driven to kill by intense degrees of narcissism—that is to say, grandiosity, extreme self-centeredness, and a constant craving for the admiration of other people. Such needs can sometimes lead these types to become caught up in grandiose ideas that are partially or even fully delusional, such as thoughts of having a special bond with a celebrated person or God, or being the center of other people's attention. They are also sometimes capable of killing or acting out aggressively for no reason other than the satisfaction of their own egotistical needs. For instance, the objective may be to gain notoriety or, in some cases, the staging of a victimization situation in order to draw the sympathies of other people. This lends them a quasi-psychopathic quality. When individuals ranked in this category kill in the context of intense jealousy, it is generally due to wounded pride and resentment associated with feeling less desirable than someone else. Let us consider the following widely publicized case.

In October of 1980, twenty-five-year-old Mark David Chapman purchased a .38-caliber revolver, leaving his wife and their Hawaii home to travel to New York City. His aim was to kill the singer and songwriter John Lennon, whose 1966 remark that his band, the Beatles, was "more popular than Jesus" offended Chapman's Christian sensibilities.[1] Additionally, over the past two years, the disturbed loner had become fixated upon J. D. Salinger's 1951 novel *The Catcher in the Rye*, in which an angst-ridden teenager tackles feelings of alienation, existential confusion, and the loss of childhood innocence.[2] Lennon had begun to seem to him like one of the "phonies" bemoaned in the book, the type who spouts platitudes about simplicity and fairness but lives a lavish lifestyle while other people struggle and starve.[3] Chapman's identification with the novel's young protagonist, Holden Caulfield, had grown so intense that he tried to legally adopt the character's name as his own.[4]

On December 7, 1980, Chapman spent several hours staking out the Dakota, the fabled Manhattan apartment building where Lennon; the singer's wife, Yoko Ono; and their five-year-old son, Sean, resided. When his target failed to appear, Chapman mimicked the actions of his beloved Holden in Salinger's book by heading back to his hotel and contacting an escort service, paying his female companion $190 to merely listen as he spoke. The following day, he opened up the Bible to the Gospel of John and wrote the surname Lennon after the name of the evangelist. Resolving to kill the star, he headed back to the Dakota, picking up fresh copies of the Bible and *The Catcher in the Rye* on his way.[5] In the latter, he wrote, "To Holden Caulfield, This is my statement. Holden Caulfield."[6]

Later that day, Chapman met Lennon's housekeeper and young Sean on the street.[7] Around five in the evening, Lennon and Ono left the Dakota for a recording session, and, as they made their way to their limousine, Chapman shook Lennon's hand and acquired his autograph on a record sleeve. When the couple returned nearly six hours later, Chapman was still there. Waiting until they had turned away from him, he shot Lennon four times in the back and shoulder. When police arrived at the scene, they found Chapman reading *The Catcher in the Rye*. Lennon was pronounced dead at a nearby hospital,[8] and the world, plunged into mourning, struggled to fathom what type of man could wish to silence such a beloved musical icon.

The killer was born in May of 1955 in Fort Worth, Texas. His reportedly "unemotional" but occasionally volatile father was a US Air Force staff sergeant, alleged to have been abusive toward Chapman's mother. The latter, described as "dreamish" and "moody," worked as a nurse. He had one younger sister.[9] His family lived for a period in Purdue, Indiana, before settling in Decatur, Georgia, where Chapman had a few meaningful friendships. When Chapman was eleven, his IQ was found to be in the superior range. An intellectually curious, active adolescent, he worked in a library, collected coins, started a local newspaper, and earned money by washing bicycles. He enjoyed burying time capsules and sent up helium balloons containing messages he hoped would reach distant places. Chapman also became an avid Beatles fan in his youth, charging friends a fee to watch him perform a lip-synched version of "She Loves You." His father taught him how to play the guitar.[10]

From childhood through early adolescence, Chapman had a tendency to shake and rock his body, sometimes resulting in head injuries. Starting in the third or fourth grade, when he experienced some bullying at school surrounding his poor athletic abilities, he retreated into a vivid fantasy world in which he was not a misfit but a figure of great admiration. He would later say that he fantasized about being the king of a world of "little people" whom he imagined lived in the walls of his home. He explained, "I was their hero and was in the paper every day, and I was on TV, their TV, and that I was important." By age fourteen, Chapman was sniffing glue and lighter fluid, and abusing marijuana, cocaine, and heroin. He began skipping school and stopped bathing, adopting an "anti-parent, anti-everything" stance. He once ran away from home to live on the streets of Miami for two weeks. He spent one night in jail during an LSD trip.[11]

In 1971, Chapman joined a Christian group geared toward healing drug addiction, and he began disseminating tracts, wearing a large cross around his neck and proselytizing to friends. At seventeen, he was once again a diligent student and found work as a camp counselor for the YMCA. Seeking to restore his sullied innocence—a theme that he would find echoed in *The Catcher in the Rye*—he refused to play the Beatles anymore, considering Lennon's statement regarding the fame of the band blasphemous. In 1975, Chapman worked overseas in Beirut and then at an Arkansas resettlement camp for refugees from Vietnam. There, he met and began dating Jessica Blankenship, and the couple became involved with a charismatic Christian group that performed exorcism rituals and spiritual healings.[12]

At this time, Blankenship began noticing a peculiar division in Chapman's personality. Part of the time, he was morally rigid, refusing to be flirtatious, play the guitar, or consume junk food. Elsewhere, he enjoyed performing music, drank, and lost his virginity with a coworker behind Blankenship's back. He depicted these as a battle between his flesh and his spirit, which gave rise to intense feelings of guilt. Then, after he enrolled in a conservative Presbyterian college in Tennessee, he became preoccupied with thoughts about death and suicide, cried after making any sort of physical contact with Blankenship, and described a fantasy about having sex with a prostitute while his girlfriend looked on. He took a job as a security guard, which led to firearm training. Eventually, he outfitted his car with a spotlight, some tear gas, a club, and a gun. By this point, Chapman had become so on edge that even a minor provocation could set off explosive anger. Profound despair overtook him, and he made up his mind to commit suicide in Hawaii, relocating there in 1977. He phoned a suicide hotline and entered psychotherapy, but not long thereafter, he drove to a deserted area and used a vacuum cleaner hose attached to his car's exhaust pipe to try to end his life by carbon monoxide inhalation. A fisherman found him before he succeeded, and, furthermore, the exhaust had burned through the hose, all of which he interpreted as signs of God's will. He was treated in a hospital and, following discharge, took up a job there. Around this same time, his parents divorced and his mother came to join him in Hawaii.[13]

In 1978, Chapman took a six-week trip around the world, entering into a relationship with his travel agent, Gloria Abe. They married the following year. In the course of his hospital work, he was isolative and argumentative, and began to drink heavily. It was then that he became fixated on Salinger's novel and the idea of killing a celebrity. John Lennon was only one name on his list of possible victims, which also included actress Elizabeth Taylor and TV host Johnny Carson, among several others.[14]

At Chapman's murder trial in 1981, back-and-forth between the defense and prosecution surrounding his mental state at the time of the killing came to a halt when he entered a guilty plea. Although he framed his desire to kill in spiritual terms, there was some indication that he believed that murder, especially of an eminent person, would make him "somebody," forever elevating him from invisibility and anonymity. Indeed, when an assassin kills a celebrated individual, the two become permanently conjoined in history, such that it becomes impossible to tell the story of one without making mention of the other. Chapman received a sentence of twenty years to life.[15] When later asked by a parole board what motivated him to kill the beloved Beatle, he replied, "Attention, bottom line."[16] Here, laid bare, we find the narcissistic brand of motive underlying murders categorized at level 7 of the Gradations of Evil scale.

We encounter a disturbing second example of attention seeking at the high cost of homicide in the case of Marybeth Tinning, born Marybeth Roe in Duanesburg, New York, in 1942. Little is known about her early childhood, beyond that she had one younger brother and that her mother worked while her father fought overseas in the Second World War. This resulted in her being placed in the care of various relatives, one of whom callously informed her that she was an accidental, unwanted child. This led her to feel that her parents were happier about her brother's birth than her own. When her father returned from duty, taking up work as a press operator, he reputedly beat Tinning, smacked her with a flyswatter, and locked her in a closet.[17]

Tinning was an average student and considered plain, temperamental, and attention starved by her schoolmates, who shunned her en masse, such that a former teacher would remember her as "almost a nonentity." In an effort to gain other people's interest, she took to concocting outlandish stories. Tinning graduated from high school in 1961 and worked various odd jobs until she found steadier work as a nursing assistant at a Schenectady hospital. She married Joe Tinning, a man in the same field as her father. In 1971, her father died, never having supplied the attentiveness and loving concern she long desired. She found his passing emotionally overwhelming.[18]

The Tinnings would have thirteen children between 1972 and 1985, but nine would tragically die in infancy or early childhood, beginning with her daughter Jennifer, who succumbed to acute meningitis at just eight days old. Three weeks later, two-year-old Joseph Jr. died of an unconfirmed virus and a "seizure disorder." Then, after six more weeks, four-year-old Barbara died of what was believed to be cardiac arrest. Two-week-old Timothy died of sudden infant death syndrome (SIDS) in 1973, five-month-old Nathan of "pulmonary edema" in 1975, two-and-a-half-year-old Mary of SIDS in 1979, three-month-old Jonathan of undetermined causes in 1980, and three-year-old Michael of "bronchial pneumonia" in 1981.[19]

In December of 1985, the Tinnings' three-month-old, Tami Lynne, was found unconscious in her bed, which was covered with blood. The child's death was attributed to SIDS, but police caught on. Mrs. Tinning ultimately confessed to smothering the baby with a pillow and was suspected of seven other infanticides. She was believed by some to display symptoms of Munchausen syndrome by proxy, a psychiatric condition in which someone caring for a child, or elderly or disabled person, intentionally harms his or her charge as a means of gaining sympathy and personal attention. It emerged that Mrs. Tinning would primp herself and soak up the condolences at her children's funerals, playing up the role of a mother repeatedly bearing intense grief, and it was suggested that the focus upon her following the natural death of her first child in 1972—arguably the only meaningful attention she ever received—became something of an addiction for her. In 1987, Mrs. Tinning was convicted of second-degree murder for "depraved indifference to human life" in the murder of Tami Lynne and sentenced to twenty years to life.[20] She was released on parole in 2018, at the age of seventy-five, long unable to bear any additional children.[21]

It is worth noting that, if she did, indeed, commit at least two homicides in separate events, Tinning would be the first murderer we have thus far described who meets the previously mentioned FBI criteria for serial murder. As we shall discuss later in this volume, mothers who commit repeat infanticide constitute a subcategory of serial killing that is not necessarily associated with a marked degree of psychopathy or sadism, and such cases can sometimes be ranked at the lower end of the Gradations of Evil scale.

We conclude our description of Category 7 with the truly disturbing case of Armin Meiwes of Rotenburg, Germany. Born in Kassel in December of 1961, he was considered an average child prior to age eight, enjoying the picturesque vistas of his Hessian hometown on the Fulda River and playing with animals. This happier time was shattered when his father, described as stern and detached, abandoned his overbearing, thrice-married mother. In short order, one of his brothers became a priest and another permanently moved away. His mother made him perform grueling chores; forced him to wear traditional lederhosen to school, which made him the butt of constant gibes; insisted upon accompanying him everywhere; and admonished him publicly, sometimes calling him "worthless." Gradually slipping into a world of pure fantasy, Meiwes created an imaginary brother named Franky whom he envisioned as a very good listener, and became fixated on the story of "Hansel and Gretel"—especially the part in which the cannibalistic witch fattens up Hansel to eat him. Telling Franky that he was becoming increasingly fascinated by the subject of devouring a human being, he tore apart a Barbie doll and cooked the plastic parts on a grill. He also read heavily about infamous serial killer Fritz Haarmann, dubbed "the Vampire of Hanover," who butchered his young male victims and consumed their blood. At twelve, Meiwes began fantasizing about eating his friends so that they could become permanent parts of himself and never abandon him—a strange, symbolic solution for a lonely boy who had suffered the loss of the majority of his family.[22]

In adulthood, Meiwes worked as a computer engineer and served in the military. He was engaged to a woman for nine months, whom he ultimately found just as unbearable as his mother. "It was like going from the shower to the storm," he would later say. He would also admit that he did not feel it was possible to marry as long as his mother was still living. She developed cancer, and Meiwes was her ever-attentive caretaker, until she succumbed to the disease. He was thirty-eight at the time. Again, he found himself unable to tolerate loss in a mature and realistic manner. Meiwes reportedly constructed a shrine in her honor in the forty-three-room mansion she left behind, ritualistically placing one of her wigs on the head of a doll each night before going to bed. He boarded up the window to her room, allowing no light to enter. Free of his mother's restraints, he became fascinated by pornography with sadomasochistic themes, and embraced an emergent homosexuality, frequenting gay bars and enjoying dalliances with male army buddies. His cannibalistic fantasies resurfaced, and, on one occasion, he fashioned pieces of pork into the shape of a dismembered penis and devoured it. It was in 2001 that Meiwes made up his mind to at last play out his lifelong fantasy of killing and eating an actual person.[23]

After Meiwes had posted an advertisement on the internet, recruiting a "young, well-built 18–30 year-old to be slaughtered and then consumed," he heard from several applicants who met him in hotel rooms and role-played cannibalistic acts, but, to his disappointment, no one had taken him literally. His luck changed when he stumbled across an ad placed by a forty-three-year-old engineer and masochist named Bernd Brandes, entitled "Dinner—or Your Dinner," offering, "the chance to eat me alive."[24] When Meiwes enthusiastically invited him to a farmhouse he owned, Brandes responded, "I hope you find me tasty."[25] The collective term for these erotic wishes to either eat or be eaten by another person is *vorarephilia*, from the Latin *vorare*, which means to "devour" or "swallow."

The two men met, and, after sex, Meiwes felt the desire to consume his new partner, like the female praying mantis, which will sometimes feast upon the head of a male after copulation, gradually working its way through the rest of the carcass. For an analgesic, he fed Brandes a half a bottle of schnapps blended with twenty sleeping pills. Note that this fact lowers the ranking for Meiwes on the Gradations of Evil scale, since a more psychopathic or sadistic individual would have disregarded or even relished the victim's pain. After the sedatives took effect, it was mutually agreed that Meiwes would sever his companion's penis and that he would fry it for the two of them to eat. As captured on a profoundly disturbing home video, Meiwes first unsuccessfully attempted to bite off the appendage before removing it with a knife amid a loud scream from his willing victim. Brandes then tried to eat some of his own penis but found it unappealingly "chewy." Meiwes fried it in a pan with salt, pepper, garlic, and wine, but it proved too burnt for consumption, so he fed it to his dog. At this point, Meiwes helped the victim into a bath, where he could slowly "bleed out" while Meiwes watched a Disney film. After trying to stand up, Brandes collapsed and slipped into unconsciousness, at which time Meiwes dragged him to an upper level of the house.[26]

After a period of prayer to both God and the devil, Meiwes killed his new lover by stabbing him in the throat. He then suspended him from a meat hook. Freezing forty-four pounds of meat from the painstakingly dismembered corpse in his refrigerator, he spent ten months savoring Brandes over the course of a variety of candlelit meals. Of the experience of devouring a piece of the victim's back in the form of a rump steak, prepared with potatoes and sprouts, Meiwes would later remark, "The first bite was, of course, very strange. It was a feeling I can't really describe. I'd spent over 40 years longing for it, dreaming about it. And now I was getting the feeling that I was actually achieving this perfect inner connection through his flesh." It tasted to him much like pork—an opinion often rendered by cannibals. It is intriguing to observe that, in addition to providing Meiwes sexual gratification, the experience gave him the pleasure of merging with another person and having the victim's body become, quite literally, part of his own. The victim's skull was buried in the killer's garden. Meiwes came to the attention of authorities in December of 2002 when he posted new advertisements in an effort to locate a second victim. He informed police that the stockpile of flesh in the refrigerator had been removed from a wild pig. Two years later, expressing remorse for his heinous crime, he was convicted of manslaughter, but a 2006 retrial for murder led to life imprisonment. He has since become a strict vegetarian.[27]

As noted, Meiwes was not a torturer or a sadist. Moreover, no significant history of psychopathic behaviors or traits was noted at his trial. Instead, his crime appears to have been related to loneliness and an intense sensitivity to abandonment. From these feelings sprung forth a rich but terrifying world of fantasy and the egocentric need to eliminate the boundaries between himself and a love object, even if it meant taking advantage of an apparently vulnerable, self-loathing individual.

CATEGORY 8

Category 8 is the highest ranking on the Gradations of Evil scale in which one can place a killer who is not markedly psychopathic. The hallmark of these types is an underlying, slowly growing rage, rooted in resentment surrounding past maltreatment, bigotry, misogyny, rejection, or some other interpersonal factor. This eventually becomes ignited and prompts them to plan out acts of unmitigated, oftentimes spectacular violence. This is also the first point on the scale in which we might expect an individual to commit murder on a shockingly large scale and to target strangers who have not, specifically, done the killer any harm. This represents a manifestation of the enormity and universality of their deep-seated anger. The case of George "Jo Jo" Hennard, one of the worst mass shooters in American history, provides a quintessential example of this type of offender.

Hennard's abbreviated life began in Sayre, Pennsylvania, in 1956 and ended by suicide in 1991, just one day after his thirty-fifth birthday. His father was a prosperous orthopedics expert whose work in various international hospitals forced their family to relocate constantly, leaving Hennard feeling overlooked and unsettled as a boy. In adolescence, he was quiet and angry, and after high school he joined the US Navy, where he was suspended due to a racially heated argument with a shipmate and later arrested for cannabis possession. In 1983, his parents divorced for unclear reasons. Six years later, he lost a job as a merchant seaman, after marijuana was found in his room on a ship, prompting loss of his seaman's license and a period of treatment for substance abuse.[28]

Hennard drifted from job to job across the United States, described by coworkers and those who knew him around this time as a "loner," "combative," "rude," "impatient," and "troubled,"[29] with "the Devil in his eyes."[30] All the while, he was growing increasingly lonely and resentful of women. As the drummer for a musical group called Missing Links, he was disliked by his bandmates for his insufferable attitude and bitter hatred of the female sex.[31] Having settled in Texas, he sent two young adult sisters residing near his home a bizarre five-page diatribe, saying that while he viewed the women in his local area as "mostly white treacherous female vipers," he saw the "best" of womanhood in them. He also asked to get together with his "two teenage groupies fans" for a long talk, failing to realize that they wanted nothing to do with him.[32] A psychiatrist friend of their father analyzed the missive, noting "pent up anger" and a "grandiose sense of power."[33] Hennard was also known to have had strong resentments of African Americans, Hispanics, and gays.[34]

By the early 1990s, Hennard had grown paranoid with thoughts that his phone might be bugged,[35] and highly obsessive, compulsively cleaning his furniture and car, and making endless notes to himself in journals and on a tape recorder. Over and over, at all hours of the night, he could be heard performing Steely Dan's song "Don't Take Me Alive," about an armed individual holed up against his enemies. It became something of a personal anthem for him. He also began standing beneath the bedroom window of the two sisters to whom he had penned his lengthy letter, staring and chain-smoking for long periods. When the girls' family Shih Tzu began barking at something or someone in the night, it was mysteriously found poisoned to death.[36]

In early October of 1991, Hennard found himself inspired by a documentary about James Huberty, a disgruntled man who killed twenty-one people at a California McDonald's eatery in 1984. He was also impressed by Terry Gilliam's 1991 film *The Fisher King*, in which a radio host's insensitive remarks prompt a disturbed listener to visit a busy bar with a rifle and open fire.[37]

Weeks later, on October 16, 1991, Hennard enjoyed a pleasant breakfast and drove seventeen miles to a Luby's Cafeteria in Killeen. He intentionally crashed his pickup truck into the dining area, injuring an elderly man, and, seizing upon the pandemonium this created, shot two random people with Ruger P89 and Glock 17 semiautomatic pistols he had recently legally acquired. Stepping out of the truck, he shouted, "This is what Bell County has done to me!" At point-blank range, he shot people hiding under tables, killing twenty-three and injuring twenty. Survivors reported seeing him smirk while spouting misogynistic statements at the women before firing at them. He was quoted as shouting, "All women of Killeen and Belton are vipers! This is what you've done to me and my family! This is what Bell County did to me. . . . This is payback day!"[38] Indeed, he had passed over men to focus on shooting women, who constituted the majority of those he killed and wounded.[39]

During a pause in the rampage, one patron heroically hurled himself through the glass window of the establishment, allowing about a third of the survivors to escape. For some unclear reason, Hennard permitted a woman with a four-year-old child to leave the scene.[40] About eighty others remained trapped inside. The killer then engaged in a heated shootout with police, who struck him four times. He took cover in a restroom, pressing one of his pistols to his head and using his final bullet to end his life, perhaps while calling to mind the lyrics to "Don't Take Me Alive." The entire tragedy lasted fifteen minutes.[41]

This case seems almost archetypical in the current climate of routine mass shootings in the United States, in which emotionally troubled young males enter public places with firearms and take the lives of high numbers of random citizens. We must emphasize, however, that it is not the method of the killing or the types of individuals Hennard targeted that place him in Category 8 of the Gradations of Evil scale. Rather, his ranking reflects his smoldering anger, which, when ignited, led to a furious, yet painstakingly planned-out explosion of rage. Although he despised people from several demographic groups, his extreme anger seemed especially focused upon women, who likely found him intense, off-putting, or even frightening.

Mention should be made of Suzanna Gratia Hupp, who survived Hennard's murderous rampage. She watched in horror as her sixty-seven-year-old mother was shot in the head while cradling her seventy-one-year-old father, whom Hennard had fatally struck in the chest. Five years later, Hupp, who regretted not being able to carry her handgun into the restaurant due to state safety statutes, was elected as a Republican member of the Texas House of Representatives. There, she helped establish a law to permit her state's citizens to carry concealed weapons.[42]

CHAPTER FOUR

CATEGORIES 9–14

From childhood's hour I have not been
As others were—I have not seen
As others saw—I could not bring
My passions from a common spring—
From the same source I have not taken
My sorrow—I could not awaken
My heart to joy at the same tone—
And all I lov'd—I lov'd alone—
Then—in my childhood—in the dawn
Of a most stormy life—was drawn
From ev'ry depth of good and ill
The mystery which binds me still—
From the torrent, or the fountain—
From the red cliff of the mountain—
From the sun that 'round me roll'd
In its autumn tint of gold—
From the lightning in the sky
As it pass'd me flying by—
From the thunder, and the storm—
And the cloud that took the form
(When the rest of Heaven was blue)
Of a demon in my view.

—Edgar Allan Poe, "Alone"

As we move along the continuum to Category 9, we traverse an important threshold. The remainder of the scale encompasses persons who commit "evil" acts partly or wholly as the result of varying degrees of psychopathy, a key concept we will now explore in some detail. From this point onward, we will no longer encounter individuals who feel driven to homicide or other acts of violence by situational duress. Rather, the remainder of the scale is populated by methodical types who are motivated by self-serving personal objectives, which we will individually discuss: desires to eliminate those who pose obstacles to the attainment of romantic love or power, or who threaten one's freedom; to pilfer other people's assets; to dispel ennui with some twisted form of stimulation; to satisfy perverse sexual desires; to intimidate and subjugate; and to sadistically torture, in ways unimaginable to the average person. In some cases, as we shall see, the psychopathic individual is further influenced by symptoms of psychotic illness, reviewed in depth in the chapter dealing with Category 20, or by the disinhibiting effects of drugs or alcohol.

The concept of psychopathy was first systematically defined by psychiatrist Dr. Hervey M. Cleckley in his groundbreaking 1941 book *The Mask of Sanity*.[1] The term refers to egocentric, grandiose individuals who feel little to no compassion for other people, manifested by persistent asocial and amoral behaviors, such as deceiving, manipulating, abusing, or even killing. Such persons display minimal, if any, remorse, guilt, or sense of responsibility following such acts, and they do not generally learn from previous mistakes. Psychopaths tend to be impulsive and fearless, with poor behavioral controls and a high need for excitement and stimulation. Interpersonally, they are often superficially charming and typically experience emotions on a shallow level. This pattern of behavior, motivations, and internal experiences tends to originate in childhood and persists across the whole of one's lifetime, constituting a disturbance of the personality structure itself. They are about eight times more likely to be male than female.

It is important to note that psychopathic traits and behaviors occur on a spectrum, such that it is possible for an individual to possess only a handful of the characteristics, associated with occasional social and/or occupational issues, but not resulting in any major impact upon his or her day-to-day functioning. This fact is often ignored by the general public, which often erroneously imagines every psychopathic individual to be the extreme, serial killing type when, in fact, some psychopaths have interpersonal difficulties that never amount to serious crime. Moreover, not everyone who commits murder or some other act of extreme violence should automatically be deemed a psychopath. As our prior points about Categories 1 through 8 on the Gradations of Evil scale have hopefully made clear, individuals can feel driven to such crimes by a number of factors other than psychopathy.

Unfortunately, the bulk of research on the subject has been conducted in prisons and forensic psychiatric settings, where one tends to encounter only those with the most serious degrees of psychopathy. Even within such populations, identifying psychopathic persons is challenging, in that they sometimes minimize or flatly deny certain traits and past behaviors, either in the hopes of securing lighter sentences or certain privileges, or else for the amusement of outwitting those who are endeavoring to study them.

The identification of psychopathic persons has been greatly advanced by the Psychopathy Checklist-Revised (PCL-R), developed by psychologist Dr. Robert Hare. The twenty-question measure employs an in-person interview, as well as review of collateral information, such as one's treatment or legal records. It examines personality traits within two factors: Factor 1 explores interpersonal and affective deficiencies, such as superficial charm, shallow affect, manipulativeness, and lack of empathy, while Factor 2 captures antisocial behaviors, including irresponsibility, poor behavior controls, impulsiveness, juvenile delinquency, and *criminal versatility*. The latter refers to a propensity of an individual to commit several different types of crime. For example, we might observe murder, sexual assault, theft, and forgery in the same offender's history. Each item is scored on a three-point scale, with a rating of 0 if it does not apply, 1 if there is a partial match or mixed information, and 2 if there is a reasonably good match. The maximum score is 40. A score of 30 is considered indicative of psychopathy.[2]

Another area of confusion concerns the inconsistent use of the terms *psychopathy*, *sociopathy*, and *antisocial personality disorder*, even among professional clinicians and academics. In reality, these terms have somewhat different meanings and should not be used interchangeably. The words *sociopathy* and *psychopathy* reflect, in the Latin prefix *socio-* and the Greek prefix *psycho-*, distinct hypotheses about the origins of antisocial behavior. *Sociopathy* deemphasizes abnormal psychological states, suggesting that antisocial persons are not mentally disturbed to the point of not recognizing right from wrong.

Furthermore, it conceptualizes antisocial behavior as stemming from social and environmental factors, particularly during one's formative years. *Psychopathy*, by contrast, conveys the notion that antisocial behavior may be partially attributable to genetic, physiological, and cognitive factors, in addition to social and environmental influences.[3] Notably, neither term constitutes a diagnostic category in the current edition of the *Diagnostic and Statistical Manual of Mental Disorders (DSM-5)*, which delineates the classification system and specific criteria for psychiatric pathologies within the field of mental health. Instead, the *DSM* nosology contains the diagnosis of antisocial personality disorder,[4] associated with the following symptoms:

A. A pervasive pattern of disregard for and violation of the rights of others, occurring since age 15 years, as indicated by three (or more) of the following:

1. Failure to conform to social norms with respect to lawful behaviors, as indicated by repeatedly performing acts that are grounds for arrest.
2. Deceitfulness, as indicated by repeated lying, use of aliases, or conning others for personal profit or pleasure.
3. Impulsivity or failure to plan ahead.
4. Irritability and aggressiveness, as indicated by repeated physical fights or assaults.
5. Reckless disregard for safety of self or others.
6. Consistent irresponsibility, as indicated by repeated failure to sustain consistent work behavior or honor financial obligations.
7. Lack of remorse, as indicated by being indifferent to or rationalizing having hurt, mistreated, or stolen from another.

B. The individual is at least age 18 years.
C. There is evidence of conduct disorder with onset before age 15 years.
D. The occurrence of antisocial behavior is not exclusively during the course of schizophrenia or bipolar disorder.

Notably, as per Criterion B, the condition is not diagnosed in individuals under eighteen years of age. Yet, antisocial traits and behaviors are known to generally date to childhood. Thus, conduct disorder, which involves the habitual violation of the rights of others and nonconformity with the law or age-appropriate social norms, serves as a sort of childhood equivalent or precursor to antisocial personality disorder. Of note, the *DSM-5* diagnostic criteria for conduct disorder include a "with limited prosocial emotions" specifier when two or more of the following characteristics are present over at least twelve months and in multiple relationships or settings: lack of remorse or guilt, callousness / lack of empathy, lack of concern about performance in important activities, and shallow or deficient affect.[5] While the diagnostic criteria for conduct disorder weigh an individual's actions, this specifier involves the emotional aspects of such behavior, as well as how these features are experienced by other people.

Notably, the *DSM* description of antisocial personality disorder fails to capture several well-established aspects of psychopathy examined by Hare and others, such as glib charm and superficiality, egocentricity and grandiosity, shallow emotionality, and the need for excitement. When the *DSM* diagnosis was altered for the manual's fourth edition, published in 1994, the new criteria had the effect of excluding psychopathic traits that would have to be subjectively determined by clinicians, instead emphasizing socially deviant behaviors that one can objectively observe.[6] Consequently, as noted by Hare, the vast majority of criminals—an estimated 80 to 85 percent—will meet antisocial personality disorder criteria, but only about 20 percent would qualify for what he would consider bona fide psychopathy.[7] Furthermore, this 20 percent is thought to account for about half of all of the most serious crimes committed, including 50 percent of all repeat rapists.[8] These disagreements surrounding terminology, features, and etiology not only make it difficult to study psychopathy but also to formulate appropriate methods of treatment—if the latter is even possible.

Indeed, one could make a solid case that psychopaths—true psychopaths, of the ilk defined by Hare—are essentially an untreatable population, partially because they do not generally feel they require clinical care or seek it out.[9] When they do participate in treatment—sometimes due to court mandates, following criminal offenses—they tend to make little to no meaningful change, sometimes simply going through the motions of participating in psychotherapy and other interventions, with no real effort to improve themselves or their relationships. A clinician might attempt strategies that target specific antisocial behaviors, such as stealing, manipulation of others, or physical aggression, or which build up empathy and compassion. It may well be, however, that true psychopaths possess abnormal brains, which render them basically incapable of being taught or conditioned to experience such emotions, or to better evaluate the long-term consequences of their actions. For instance, there is some evidence that, among such persons, there may be fewer connections between the amygdala, which mediates fear and anxiety, and the ventromedial prefrontal cortex, believed to be involved in feelings of guilt and empathy.[10] It has elsewhere been demonstrated that individuals with greater numbers of psychopathic traits show increased activity in a brain area known as the ventral striatum, which is involved in evaluating subjective rewards, when the latter are more immediate. That is to say, the brains of psychopaths may be prone to overvalue instantaneous gratification, such that they pay less mind to future consequences of immoral or possibly dangerous behaviors. Thus, psychopathy might be seen as involving impulsive, shortsighted decision-making processes, similar to those associated with abuse of illicit substances or binge-eating disorders.[11] As we shall later discuss, however, a distinction is sometimes made between *primary psychopathy*, in which traits such as lack of empathy and fear are genetically determined, and *secondary psychopathy*, in which individuals are so humiliated, traumatized, and badly maltreated during their younger years that they emerge with boundless feelings of hatred of other people, displaying traits and behaviors that resemble those of persons with primary psychopathy. By contrast, however, secondary psychopathy may involve more remorse and less fearlessness than the primary type.[12]

Furthermore, teaching individuals who meet criteria for psychopathy which aspects of themselves they should and should not display to others sometimes helps them to better "pass" for "normal" and gain the trust of those upon whom they wish to prey.[13] Additionally, the treatment of antisocial traits and behaviors after adolescence, when full-blown psychopathy has generally become "locked in," would likely prove an especially fruitless endeavor. Perhaps it is best to either hope for short-lived behavioral improvements or to wait for the intensity and rate of antisocial behavior to decrease as one ages over time, which is generally the case.

Having established this critical concept, we can now proceed with our characterizations of Categories 9 through 14 of the Gradations of Evil scale. Individuals ranked in these six categories do not necessarily exhibit full-blown psychopathy, but they do display at least marked traits. The distinctions among the six types captured here are chiefly related to their specific motivations for murder or other acts that are commonly called "evil." We will encounter individuals whose jealousy makes them capable of coolly planned acts of retaliation; who wish to eliminate other people who pose obstacles to freedom, some romantic interest, or power; and who guiltlessly swindle other people's assets. Note that we have not yet arrived at the level of scale associated with fully psychopathic persons who commit rape, torture, and/or murder for less "pragmatic" and more self-indulgent purposes, such as to dispel ennui with some perverse form of stimulation, satisfy depraved sexual desires, intimidate and subjugate others, and/or sadistically inflict pain.

CATEGORY 9

Fully or semi-psychopathic individuals who kill with methodical, malicious intentions arising from jealousy are assigned to Category 9 of the scale. The non-impetuous quality of these homicides distinguishes them at once from the spur-of-the-moment brand encountered in Category 2. Even Category 6, with its emphasis on more extreme violence in the context of hotheadedness, which can certainly be set off by jealousy, is not an adequate ranking for this type. This is because a ranking of 6 does not convey the degree of detachment and planning that we encounter here, nor the perpetrator's typically vindictive and unremorseful nature. The reader is reminded of the "Parachute Murder" case described earlier, in which we observed cold-blooded, calculated homicide, in contrast to the more impetuous "crime of passion" perpetrated by Samuel Collins after he learned of his wife's infidelity. As noted, the former belongs here, in Category 9, due to the extreme cruelty of the homicide and the significant degree of premeditation, with no change of mind or remorse despite time and deliberation.

We find another example of this type of jealousy killing in the case of Paul Snider, who in 1980 brutally raped and murdered his wife, the stunningly beautiful *Playboy* playmate and film actress Dorothy Stratten. Snider was born to Jewish parents in Vancouver, British Columbia, in 1951, growing up in a rough neighborhood in which machismo was prized and nurtured. His parents separated when he was a boy, and he was left to fend for himself, leaving school in the seventh grade. He emerged from these unstable, impoverished early years with a personality characterized by psychopathic, narcissistic, and paranoid features. Insecure about his undeveloped physique in adolescence, he took up bodybuilding and aimed to always be well-groomed and stylishly dressed in public. Money and sex quickly became his twin obsessions. By the mid-1970s, Snider was working as a car show and nightclub promoter, but it was thought he was also earning income as a pimp. A man of expensive tastes, which were well beyond his financial means, he drove a Corvette, strolled about town swathed in mink, and wore a jewel-encrusted Star of David around his neck. He owed a fortune to loan sharks, who once suspended him by his ankles from the thirtieth floor of a hotel, prompting him to flee to the United States.[14]

With grand aspirations of becoming an actor, director, or producer, Snider headed to Los Angeles, where he struggled to find acceptance in Hollywood's inner circles. He oversaw prostitution activity in LA, insisting that his band of streetwalkers dress in glamorous 1950s fashions. Feeling like something of a failure, he returned to Canada in 1977, making his mind up to avoid trouble and never wind up in jail—a concept that terrified him.[15] It was back in Vancouver that, during a visit to a Dairy Queen with a friend, he first encountered seventeen-year-old counter girl and high school student Dorothy Ruth Hoogstraten. Turning to his companion, he remarked, "That girl could make me a lot of money." He obtained her phone number from an acquaintance and relentlessly pursued her until they entered into an affair several months later. It has been suggested that Hoogstraten, whose father left her family when she was quite young, leaving them in financially dire straits, was taken by the older, streetwise schemer, who bedecked her in jewels and wined and dined her in his posh apartment. He escorted her to her high school graduation dance and had her sit for professional modeling shoots. Shy and insecure with no ambitions beyond secretary work, Hoogstraten was enthralled by his constant compliments and gradually became swept up in Snider's ambitious plans for their future.[16]

Just after Hoogstraten's eighteenth birthday, Snider began pressuring her to sit for another round of photographs, this time in the nude, which he hoped to enter in *Playboy* magazine's twenty-fifth anniversary Playmate contest. Convincing her that this was a critical first step toward an acting career, he was chagrined to note that women in Canada had to be at least nineteen years of age to appear nude in a magazine without parental consent. He got around this by forging her mother's signature on a release form. Following the shoot, Snider explained that, should they meet Hugh Hefner, she might have to tolerate his sexual advances in order for her career to progress as they were hoping.[17]

Hoogstraten lost the *Playboy* contest but was invited to spend time at Hefner's mansion. She was ultimately named Playmate of the Month for August of 1979, rechristened Dorothy Stratten. As soon as word of her magazine appearance reached his ears, Snider proposed marriage and flew to LA to join her, hoping to hitch himself to a rising star who might financially support the two of them. By 1979, the couple was married and Stratten was trying her hand at acting. She began taking small roles on television programs and played the title role in the 1980 science fiction B movie *Galaxina*. In the meantime, Snider used some of her earnings to operate sleazy wet T-shirt and underwear contests, and to invest in a male strip club, which later became the popular Chippendales franchise. He purchased a new Mercedes with vanity plates reading "Star-80" and mused about their forthcoming life in the estates of Bel Air. Despite having numerous extramarital affairs, Snider was intensely jealous and possessive of his wife. He carefully monitored whether she smoked, drank, or used drugs, and dictated how she should behave around men, teaching her to take advantage of the interests of would-be suitors, while turning down their sexual passes.[18]

In 1980, Stratten befriended the movie director Peter Bogdanovich, who cast the ravishing starlet in his then forthcoming film *They All Laughed*, released the following year. The two hit it off and embarked upon a highly secretive affair in New York City. She was selected as *Playboy*'s Playmate of the Year and was finding herself constantly surrounded by fans, photographers, and the press—a lifestyle that likely filled Snider with unbearable envy, above all else. When he began detecting a chill in her voice during telephone conversations, he became increasingly enraged and controlling, having her private phone calls screened. By June of 1980, Stratten had become estranged from Snider, severing their financial ties. He groomed another seventeen-year-old girl to look just like his wife and tried to pitch her to *Playboy*, which promptly turned him down. He then got the idea of suing Bogdanovich for "enticement to breach management contract," in stealing away the woman he primarily viewed as a cash cow, and hired a private eye to trail Stratten and her new lover.[19]

Regretting the bad blood developing between her and Snider, Stratten suggested that they get together for lunch on August 8, 1980, which he viewed as an indication that they were on the verge of reconciliation. Instead, there was only iciness between them, and they wound up in their apartment, where Stratten at last confessed her affair with Bogdanovich before gathering up some clothes. Snider sank into a black mood, during which he acquired a twelve-gauge shotgun. On August 14, the day before his twenty-ninth birthday, they got together to discuss a formal divorce and how they would handle financial matters. Prior to this second meeting, Snider had considered hiding a recording device, hoping Stratten would make some legally actionable promise to provide for him.[20]

No one knows for certain what was said between Snider and Stratten that day, or whether he had plotted in advance to murder or simply frighten her. What ultimately transpired was truly horrendous. Snider strapped his estranged wife into a homemade bondage device and savagely raped and sodomized her—both before and after pressing the rifle to her face and pulling the trigger. Stratten was only twenty years old. He then fatally shot himself in the head.[21]

In 2014, Bogdanovich, who was reportedly emotionally devastated by Stratten's murder, shared a poignant story with the website UPROXX. One night while they were browsing a bookshop, Stratten found herself caught up in a book about Joseph Merrick, the severely deformed nineteenth-century figure dubbed the "Elephant Man," who was also the subject of a 1977 play by Bernard Pomerance and a 1980 film by David Lynch. As she glanced over the horrifying photos of the misshapen, tumor-ridden man, Bogdanovich found himself puzzled by her interest in so morbid a subject. After her death, while directing his 1985 film *Mask*, a biopic about Rocky Dennis, another victim of extreme physical deformity, he came to a realization: great beauty and great ugliness have something in common, in terms of the limitations they impose upon an individual.[22] Perhaps there is some truth to the notion that people will sometimes struggle to relate to those at either end of the spectrum of physical beauty as whole and complex human beings. Certainly, Paul Snider felt that if he could not possess the wife he viewed as a financially beneficial trophy, he would permit nobody else to do so. It is perhaps no coincidence that he chose to annihilate the face that had instantly ensnared him in 1977 and that had afforded her a lifestyle he probably desired more than he yearned for Stratten herself. In a sense, he shot her with a rifle the way he had once shot her with a camera—both as aggressive means of possessing her. It is also tremendously symbolic that Snider engaged in sexual acts with his wife after he had savagely taken her life, having now quite literally reduced her to a body without a soul to animate it.

CATEGORY 10

Individuals in Category 10 do not necessarily harbor specific ill will toward those they kill. Rather, they are motivated to eliminate them simply because they are "in the way." A victim might have known too much about one's past, posed a burden, or constituted an impediment to some selfishly desired objective. These murderers are extremely egocentric and typically meet some, but not full, criteria for psychopathy. Such killers might stage aspects of crime scenes, fabricate details, or intentionally injure themselves to mislead authorities, and there may be little to no subsequent remorse.

Moreover, Category 10 offenders are capable of rather shocking murders that draw significant media coverage and are invariably called "evil." In some individuals assigned to this place on the scale, crimes are sensational in nature, related to cravings for wide-scale attention. Others, for various self-centered "practical" reasons, might kill their own children, murder an elderly or physically impaired person, systematically eliminate an entire family, or slay a pregnant woman in order to steal the infant from her womb and raise it as one's own. While these types do not generally demonstrate full histories of psychopathic traits and behaviors, their crimes demonstrate a disturbing capacity for cold-bloodedness when faced with some significant challenge to their personal needs or desires.

Consider the story of Susan Smith, who was found frantically crying on the doorstep of a stranger's Union, South Carolina, home in October of 1994, claiming she had been carjacked by an African American male who kidnapped her fourteen-month-old son Alex and three-year-old son Michael. She described how she and her boys were stopped at a red light when an armed man jumped into the car and demanded that she drive off, before ejecting her from the vehicle, claiming he would not hurt the children. She described hearing them cry out for her as he sped away. For nine days, she and her ex-husband, David Smith, pleaded with the public for the safe return of their sons, and the nation grieved along with them.[23] When speaking to the press, she spoke repeatedly of her unwavering faith in God.

It was noticed that as Smith repeated the details of the tragedy on several occasions, they were sometimes markedly inconsistent. She and her ex-husband underwent polygraph tests, and only he passed. Moreover, Smith kept telling friends that she hoped she would receive a visit from a man named Tom Findlay, with whom she had recently been having an affair. He broke it off by means of a "Dear John" letter, allegedly due to not wanting a relationship with a woman who had two young children. It was striking to friends that her mind would be wandering to her ex-boyfriend, during the frantic search for her two missing children. She also seemed overly concerned with how she appeared on television, and it was observed that, following sobbing attacks in public, her eyes were, in fact, completely dry.[24]

Soon enough, Smith's dark secret emerged. She confessed that, on October 25, 1994, she strapped her two sons into car seats in the back seat of her Mazda, drove to John D. Long Lake, lowered the hand brake, and rolled the car down a boat ramp. She watched as the children drowned, crying and calling for her as the vehicle was slowly swallowed up by the water. The hijacking tale was a contrivance of Smith's to cover up a crime aimed at winning back her ex-boyfriend. Later that day, divers recovered the bodies of her boys, eighteen feet beneath the surface of the lake, in the upside-down car, dangling from their car seats. Findlay's letter was also recovered from the vehicle. Smith was subsequently charged with two counts of first-degree murder, to which she pled not guilty.[25] At her 1995 trial, she claimed she had been battling depression, with periods of suicidality, for years. Her defense team described her as having a dependent personality, such that her need for a relationship with Findlay overcame her better judgment. The prosecution presented her as a cold-blooded killer, who murdered her own children simply because they were impediments to a new romance.[26]

Smith was born in September of 1971 in the same town in which she would commit her double homicide twenty-three years later. She had two older brothers. When she was six, their parents divorced, and, five weeks later, their father committed suicide. Shattered by this loss, Smith kept an audiotape of his voice in her bureau drawer and was thought to be detached and odd in the wake of his death. About two years later, in 1979, their mother married a wealthy local businessman, Beverly C. Russell Jr., a divorced father of three who gained prominence in the state Republican Party and the Christian Coalition. At thirteen, Smith attempted suicide for unclear reasons. She was considered a good student in adolescence and was well-liked by her peers. At sixteen, she alleged that she was sexually assaulted by her stepfather, to which he reportedly confessed, expressing remorse. The family attended therapy, and her stepfather moved out of the house, but Smith claimed that the abuse continued. Years later, she reportedly told a psychiatrist that she felt she had willingly consented to Russell's advances, admitting to jealousy of the attention Russell lavished upon her mother.[27]

Around age seventeen, Smith, who had been working at a local supermarket, was impregnated by a coworker with whom she was having an affair, and underwent an abortion. When he ended the relationship, she attempted to overdose on aspirin, resulting in hospitalization.[28] She was diagnosed with an adjustment disorder, based upon the notion that she was struggling to accept her recent breakup. She then began dating another coworker, the aforementioned David Smith, whom she married in 1990 and with whom she had the two sons she drowned in the lake. The marriage was a stormy one, with accusations of infidelity on both sides and numerous blowups at work, followed by short-lived reconciliations. In 1993 or 1994, Smith took a new job at Conso Products, where she began dating Findlay, the handsome twenty-seven-year-old son of the boss. They called off the affair after several months, when it was discovered by her husband. Around September of 1994, however, when Smith and her husband decided to divorce, Findlay and Smith reconnected. A month later, she received Findlay's letter, of which she would later remark, "I had never felt so lonely and sad in my entire life."[29] In reality, this was the second great abandonment by a male figure in her lifetime, with the first being the loss of her father, due to his emotionally devastating suicide, when she was six years old.

In 1995, Smith was found guilty of murdering her young sons and was sentenced to life in prison with a minimum of thirty years. During her incarceration, she has been accused of engaging in sexual relations with two correctional officers, as well as possession of marijuana and narcotics. It was also alleged that, in 2012, she almost fatally slashed her wrists with a razor blade, which had been smuggled into the prison.[30]

For Smith, the wish to eliminate people who were "in the way" was related to desiring a certain relationship. In the blood-chilling case of Ronald Gene Simmons, it was associated with preventing his family from leaving him and a dark, humiliating secret from becoming public knowledge.

Simmons was born in July of 1940 in Chicago, Illinois. At the age of three, he lost his father to a stroke, and, a year later, his mother remarried. In 1946, his family relocated to Little Rock, Arkansas, for reasons related to his stepfather's work as a civil engineer, and they would move several times across the state until Simmons was in early adolescence. At seventeen, Simmons dropped out of high school and joined the navy. While stationed at Bremerton Naval Base in Washington State, he met Bersabe Rebecca "Becky" Ulibarri, whom he married in New Mexico in 1960. Over the next eighteen years, they would have seven children. In 1963, Simmons left the navy, joining the air force in 1965. During his military career, he earned a Bronze Star, the Republic of Vietnam Cross, and the Air Force Ribbon for his superb marksmanship. When he retired in 1979, he had earned the rank of master sergeant.[31]

In 1981, Simmons found himself under investigation by the Department of Human Services in Cloudcroft, New Mexico, for allegations of incest with his seventeen-year-old daughter, Sheila, by whom he fathered a child. To evade arrest, he gathered up his family and fled to Ward, Arkansas, in 1981 and then to Dover, elsewhere in the state, in 1983. Simmons worked various odd jobs, leaving one position as an accounts receivable clerk at a motor freight company due to reports of making inappropriate sexual advances toward a female employee. He subsequently worked at a convenience store.[32] All the while, Simmons, who was described as a repressive, abusive loner, tried to sequester his family from the world and continue to protect his humiliating secret and evade capture. He refused any heat or air-conditioning, or indoor toilets, and the children were forced to perform intense manual labor. When his wife decided she could no longer accept his behavior, she indicated that she might wish to move to Texas with the children, where they could potentially leak word about his misdeeds and whereabouts. Authorities believed this might have triggered the nightmare that unfolded across a week-long period in 1987.[33]

Shortly before Christmas of that year, Simmons made up his mind that his safest bet was to eliminate his entire family. He had several of his children dig a ditch, four feet deep, telling them he had decided to install an outhouse. They were, in reality, digging what would later be their own mass grave.[34] On the morning of December 22, he began the slaughter by shooting his wife and their twenty-nine-year-old son, Gene, with a .22-caliber pistol. He then fatally strangled a three-year-old granddaughter, Barbara. After a drink, he callously dumped the bodies in a cesspit on their property. When his children, eight-year-old Becky, eleven-year-old Mari-anne, fourteen-year-old Eddy, and seventeen-year-old Loretta, returned home, Simmons told them he wanted to give them their Christmas presents one by one. Once alone with the victims, he strangled them while holding their heads underwater in a rain barrel.[35]

On the afternoon of December 26, he murdered seven more family members who came for a holiday visit. He fatally shot his twenty-three-year-old son Billy and his twenty-two-year-old daughter-in-law Renata. He then proceeded to strangle and drown their twenty-month-old son Trae. Later the same day, he shot and killed twenty-four-year-old Sheila—the daughter whom he had been accused of abusing—and her twenty-three-year-old husband, Dennis McNulty. Simmons then strangled the child he had incestuously fathered—seven-year-old Sylvia Gail—and his twenty-one-month-old grandson Michael. He covered all of the bodies with coats, except for that of Sheila, which he draped with the best tablecloth in the house. The corpses of two of the grandchildren were wrapped in plastic sheets and left in the trunks of abandoned cars near the home.[36] Simmons then nonchalantly visited a local bar and, returning home, sat calmly among the festering bodies and watched television while imbibing beer.[37]

Two days later, Simmons drove to a law office in the city of Russell-ville, where he fatally shot Kathy Kendrick, a twenty-four-year-old woman with whom the forty-seven-year-old killer had reportedly been infatuated. It is interesting to note that Kendrick was the same age as the daughter by whom Simmons had fathered a child. He then went to an oil company office, where, for unclear reasons, he fatally shot a stranger and wounded the owner. He drove on to the convenience store where he had previously worked, and then he opened fire, injuring two more people, before finally visiting the motor freight company that once employed him, shooting and wounding a woman there. It is unknown if she was the former coworker who had reported him for sexual harassment. Simmons then held a woman at gunpoint, telling the hostage that he had "got" everybody who had "hurt" him, before surrendering to police with no resistance, beyond initially giving a false name at the time of his arrest. When the killer refused to speak while in custody and his relatives could not be reached, it was feared that his family might be in danger and police set out to search his home. There, they discovered the gruesome tableau of decomposing bodies, covered with coats and a tablecloth. Some of the corpses had been cleverly doused with kerosene to hide the smell of decomposition. His actual intention may have been to set them or the house on fire to conceal evidence, but this is uncertain. The cars containing the two small grand-children were recovered. Nearby, authorities discovered the remainder of the bodies in the aforementioned mass grave, covered with barbed wire to prevent digging by animals and discovery.[38]

Simmons was found guilty on all counts of murder and, under Arkansas governor Bill Clinton, executed by lethal injection in 1990. At the time, the crime was called "the worst family mass murder in American history,"[39] although the proper term for the pattern of crime displayed by Simmons, which, in fact, went beyond his kin, would be *spree murder*, referring to an individual who kills two or more people at different locations with no cooling-off period between homicides. Among such individuals, there is generally no more than seven days between murders.[40] After Simmons was executed, none of his living distant relatives claimed his body, and he was unceremoniously interred in a pauper's grave.[41] So ended the life of a man who coolly slaughtered sixteen individuals, chiefly family members, and wounded four others. It appears that, in addition to systematically elimi-nating anyone who might have known about his perverse sexual behaviors, both at home and in prior work settings, and who could reveal his location to police while on the lam, he was also punishing them for ruining his reputation and first bringing him to the attention of authorities. Indeed, in a letter written to his daughter when she reported him for sexual abuse six years earlier, he wrote, "You have destroyed me, and you have destroyed my trust in you," adding ominously, "I will see you in Hell."[42]

CATEGORY 11

Killers in this category have a profile very similar to that of murderers assigned to Category 10, with the same underlying motive of eliminating witnesses and other people "in the way." The sole distinction is that, here, a fuller history of traits and behaviors consistent with psychopathy is present. As noted, in Category 10, we might expect a perpetrator to move through life without serious legal problems, although the individual may be prone to argumentativeness, egocentricity, unstable romantic relationships, or other interpersonal difficulties. Despite her stormy dating history and family dynamics, few would have considered Susan Smith capable of murdering anyone, no less her two young children. In the same way, while Ronald Gene Simmons was considered an icy, difficult individual, prior to discovery of the sexual abuse of his daughter when he was forty-one and harassment of a woman at work, he established a respected military career and, to our knowledge, had no other significant problems with the law. By contrast, with Category 11 types, we generally see conduct and possibly legal issues across one's lifetime.

A Category 11 type who, as part of an overall picture of psychopathic traits and behaviors, participates in violent gang activities might kill or order someone killed to prevent an individual from serving as a witness in a legal proceeding. Sometimes, such gang members target someone who has already served as a witness to a crime, constituting a sort of after-the-fact witness elimination. This is more about retaliation for a violation of a code of allegiance and obedience than about prevention of arrest or incarceration, although it is also possible that the gang in such cases fears that the witness might have information about other crimes that have not yet come to light. At any rate, such a retaliatory killing certainly serves as a deterrent against the willingness of other witnesses to inform authorities about the gang's activities. The message is clear: witnesses will be eliminated, before testifying wherever possible, but even afterward, if deemed necessary.

For gang members, violence for practical ends, including homicide, is a daily way of life. There are numerous reasons why individuals might join such a group, including financial gain or a sense of power, respect, or a sense of belonging, which sometimes contrasts with a prior life of poverty, helplessness, or social isolation. The common element tends to be a belief that the gang will protect and provide for them. This comes at a remarkably high price. In exchange, these inductees must reject societal rules and concepts of morality, replacing them with an entirely new code of conduct in which extreme violence constitutes the only acceptable behavior. Obedience to these bylaws is strictly enforced, and the cost of betrayal is almost invariably death by other members of the gang, who renew their own loyalty by killing off those who have turned on them.

On July 13, 2003, a fisherman and his son discovered the badly decomposed body of a teenage girl in some underbrush on the west bank of the Shenandoah River in Virginia. She had been brutally stabbed sixteen times, and her head was nearly severed. She was four months pregnant at the time of her death. In order to help identify this Jane Doe, images of various tattoos on her person were circulated to investigators, one of whom recognized them: the deceased had been a member of Mara Salvatrucha, or MS-13, a large street gang chiefly tied to El Salvador and active in over thirty American states. The gang is known for its long history of violence in Hispanic districts of Los Angeles; New York; and Washington, DC. It has distinguished itself from other street gangs in that, while others generally fight and kill one another for self-protection, MS-13 has engaged in the slaughter of police officers and innocent people, simply to reinforce its fearsome reputation.[43]

The victim was ultimately identified as seventeen-year-old Honduran-born Brenda "Smiley" Paz of Los Angeles, ex-girlfriend of twenty-one-year-old MS-13 leader Denis "Rabbit" Rivera.[44] She had recently been a key witness in several MS-13-related trials for shooting, stabbing, and armed robbery in Virginia and Texas, including one against her ex-boyfriend and several former friends for a murder eerily similar to what would later be her own—that of nineteen-year-old Joaquim Diaz, who was found slashed, stabbed, and nearly decapitated, with his larynx ablated.[45] The gang's reach was so far that, despite the fact that Paz had been tucked away in a Missouri hotel by witness protection program marshals, its members were able to contact her and persuade her to leave of her own accord three weeks prior to her murder.[46]

In 2005, four MS-13 members, including Rivera, were tried for Paz's death. The prosecution argued that the group wanted her to pay for informing on them. Rivera, who was serving a life sentence for the murder of Diaz at the time of the victim's death, was portrayed as the mastermind of the crime, allegedly ordering it, in gang code, from prison. Prosecutors were unable to convince the jury that Rivera had arranged Paz's execution from behind bars, and he was acquitted. Also acquitted was thirty-one-year-old Oscar Alexander Garcia-Orellana, who admitted being present at the murder but claimed he had fled the scene without participating. Prosecutors had argued that he secured Paz's throat while she was butchered.[47] Two other gang members who were accused of taking part, twenty-two-year-old Antonio Grande and twenty-six-year-old Ismael Juarez Cisneros, were found guilty of murder conspiracy and retaliation against an informant.[48]

Between the two men confirmed in the slaying of Paz, let us consider Cisneros, since more is known about his history. He had been one of Paz's closest friends, but, because she had violated his gang's mercilessly maintained moral code, he participated in brutally taking her life and that of her unborn child. His story exemplifies how an individual with an adverse history can be utilized by a gang to ruthlessly kill for the purpose of enforcing its rules. Cisneros and his mother moved from Mexico City to the United States in the 1990s. His father was allegedly a physically abusive alcoholic, reported to have once put a four-month-old daughter into a coma. Cisneros and his siblings often starved and lived on the streets. Upon entering the States, he spoke only Spanish. As a teenager, Cisneros was recruited into MS-13, which offered protection and a feeling of belonging, in the context of a variety of violent activities. He was given the nickname "Araña," which translates to "Spider." Cisneros had a child with a fellow gang member, Maria Gomez, whom he reportedly considered the love of his life. In 1999, he demonstrated loyalty to Grande and the gang by fatally stabbing a fifteen-year-old boy four times in the back at a mall, in retaliation for an argument with Grande. As a result of this crime, he was deported to Mexico and, upon managing to make his way back, learned that Gomez had begun dating someone higher up in the gang's hierarchy. Still, they kept in contact, and it was she who discovered Paz's diary, filled with notations regarding police cooperation, and informed him about it.[49] He, in turn, reported his friend's betrayal to the gang. When someone like Paz threatens a gang by cooperating with authorities, it might feel to some of its members as if the only stable family they have ever known suddenly faces dissolution. This may or may not have been the case with Cisneros.

After being arrested on cocaine and firearm charges, Cisneros confessed to participation in the killing of Paz. He described how, on July 12, 2003, gang members met at a Virginia hotel to determine how to deal with the threat posed by Paz's willingness to testify, as well as how to retaliate for her betrayal. A vote determined that she should be eliminated. Grande, whom Paz trusted the most, agreed to take part in her killing, and Cisneros volunteered to help. The following day, after a night of sleeping curled up in Grande's arms, Paz was lured by Cisneros, Grande, and Garcia-Orellana to the Shenandoah River, under the pretense of a friendly afternoon of fishing. During the outing, she was suddenly attacked and met her gruesome end.[50] Upon his sentencing for the crime, Cisneros evaded the death penalty by agreeing to counsel young people at risk of joining gangs. Later, Gomez, who testified against the gang in the Paz trial, was found dead, and Cisneros was reportedly devastated.[51] He is said to have eventually left gang life behind him.[52]

CATEGORY 12

Category 12 is the appropriate placement in the scale for psychopathic persons whose evildoing takes the form of an extreme need for power and control over others, often in roles such as the dictatorial head of a cult, a corrupt political or religious leader, or the mastermind of a violent gang like the one we just described. Grandiose and paranoid traits are prominent among such individuals, and anyone perceived as an impediment or threat to absolute power is liable to be promptly eradicated. It should be noted that Category 12 types sometimes have other people do their killing for them. Perhaps due to intense pride or a need to retain control right to the very end, people in this category will also, on occasion, refuse to go down easily when they feel they are cornered, taking lives with no compunction or allowing themselves to be killed rather than allow apprehension by the authorities. Note that we would not expect an individual assigned to this ranking to engage in torture but to prefer that killings be as expeditious as possible. As we will see in the coming pages, sadistic torture would require classification in a far higher category of the scale.

To discuss the subject of our next vignette, it is essential to provide some background, beginning with the colorful history of Mormonism. In 1823, Joseph Smith, a young New York farmer, claimed that an angel named Moroni led him to a hillside, where he dug up golden plates, engraved with mysterious, ancient writings. He subsequently translated these scriptures and reproduced them as the Book of Mormon, providing the basis for the Church of Jesus Christ of Latter-day Saints. The plates' mystical message explained that the Jews of ancient times had visited the Americas centuries before Christ's birth and were related to the indigenous peoples discovered there by European settlers. It was further claimed that, following the death and resurrection of Jesus, He visited the New World.[53] Central to Smith's evangel was the idea that God was once a mortal man residing on a distant planet who, by way of obedience to the dictates of the spiritual beliefs of his world, was transformed into a deity who then created Earth. God was said to have married—some Mormons believe numerous times over—and to have sired Jesus through a literal physical union with Mary so that Christ was half human and half god. Smith taught that those who follow God's path of self-perfection can also become deities, capable of creating spiritual children to populate other worlds. A critical component of the creed is that the Prophet—that is, the current head of the Mormon Church, since Smith's authority is passed along a line of successors—can override the word of earlier Prophets. Young men, aged nineteen through twenty-two, are expected to help spread the faith. Any literature critical of Mormonism is deemed to be satanic in origin, distributed by apostates from the faith or the product of ignorance.[54]

Since the Old Testament patriarchs were permitted by God to marry several different wives, Smith came to embrace polygamy. Women, however, were forbidden to engage in polyandry, the practice of taking more than one husband. When mainstream Christians condemned Smith's precept about marriage, he publicly denounced it but appears to have secretly taken as many as thirty-three wives before his death. Polygamy was banned in the United States in 1862 and rejected by the Mormon Church in 1890.[55] Late nineteenth-century debates over this issue led some Mormon purists, who believed the practice to be spiritually sound, to relocate to northern Mexico to found colonies in deserted areas, largely overlooked by local governments. Their establishment only partially sets the stage for the bizarre and fascinating story of the psychopathic, power-hungry cult leader Ervil LeBaron, the subject of our vignette. We must also briefly touch upon his extraordinary family lineage.

Ervil LeBaron's ancestor David Tulley LeBaron was a close ally of Joseph Smith, convinced that God and Christ had personally endowed Smith with the authority of true priesthood. Around 1840, David married Ester Johnson, the sister of Benjamin F. Smith, one of Smith's adopted sons, whom, it was maintained, received the "mantle" of priestly authority from Smith through a special blessing. The LeBaron family would teach over the years that, when Benjamin F. Smith died, he passed this mantle to his nephew, Benjamin LeBaron. In 1886, he fathered a son, Alma Dayer LeBaron, who would prove a driving force in the establishment of one of the previously described Mormon communities in Central America. Considered still spiritually bound to a wife who had died, he controversially remarried in 1904, which led to his being deemed a dissenter from the faith. His wife left him, and he married again, after which he heard what he thought was the voice of God, telling him he would inherit the priestly mantle if he embraced polygamy. Thus feeling justified with regard to his multiple marriages, he took yet another wife and, when subsequently banished by his brethren, fled to Colonia Juarez in Mexico in 1924. There, he fathered nineteen children by two wives.[56]

Mental illness ran rampantly throughout the LeBaron clan. Alma Dayer LeBaron's daughter Lucinda was extremely violent during bouts of psychosis, requiring her to be confined, with a chain around her ankle. One son, Wesley, repeatedly phoned radio talk shows to ramble on about Christ's plan to return to Earth in a spacecraft, while another, Benjamin Teasdale, suffered a "nervous breakdown" in the 1930s, spending years drifting in and out of psychiatric hospitals. Benjamin, who claimed to hear voices and to be the special servant of God, was once found doing calisthenics in the middle of a busy road in Salt Lake City. He committed suicide by leaping from a bridge in 1978. A cousin, Owen, spoke of voices commanding him to engage in acts of bestiality with a pet dog. Nonetheless, it was unquestionably Alma's son Ervil, born in February of 1925, who proved the most dangerously disturbed.[57]

The LeBarons were farmers in Mexico, and Ervil would spend his childhood toiling alongside the same family members he would eventually work to destroy. In early adulthood, he and his brothers proselytized to expand the colony. Alma died in 1951, passing his ministry on to his "saintly" son Joel, who established the Church of the First-Born of the Fullness of Times, with its headquarters in Chihuahua. Worshippers were known as Firstborners. At that time, Ervil was his most trusted assistant, although he was self-absorbed and indolent, scoffing at manual labor. Considered handsome and mesmerizing, he would stare straight into people's eyes as he quoted at length from the Scriptures. Ervil distributed work assignments and schedules, affording him a powerful role in which he could control the actions of others. All the while, he routinely skimmed money, pocketed the portions of worshippers' incomes mandatorily tithed to the church, and attempted a string of get-rich-quick schemes. Once, he offered to sweeten a business deal with a fellow Mormon by offering several young women from his family's congregation.[58]

Ervil developed tastes for flashy clothes and cars, telling the Firstborners that God had commanded him to purchase a shiny new Impala because it would impress and draw in converts. He raised eyebrows by regularly surrounding himself with other men's wives, young girls, older women, and pairs of sisters. He seduced each by claiming God had prompted him to marry her. To earn the trust of female minors, he taught that the Virgin Mary had mothered Christ at age fourteen, so this was an appropriate age at which to take a husband. The colony responded by handing over their daughters to be "brides." For the thirteen who actually married him, he proved a detached and apathetic partner, regarding them as useless beyond bearing children to expand the church. Some would flee with their offspring to the States; others remained loyal, despite his neglect. As we shall see, two would even commit murder at his behest.[59]

Ervil and Joel began to quarrel over these scandalous behaviors around 1965. They also bickered over Los Molinos, a beachfront farming colony in Baja California, founded by Joel in 1964. Ervil envisioned a lucrative tourist destination while Joel wished to further develop it as an agricultural community. Despite Joel's protestations, Ervil sneaked away to meet with would-be investors, dazzling them with talk of resorts, yacht clubs, and guaranteed fortunes.[60]

Around this time, Ervil decided that, like the prophets of the Old Testament, he had the right to slaughter anyone in Los Molinos who disobeyed his will. He established a series of decrees based upon the Ten Commandments, which he called the Civil Law, appointing himself their chief enforcer. Worshippers quaked with fear as he described, with not a hint of feeling, the way insubordinates would be stoned, beheaded, or disemboweled. Ervil revived a controversial 1856 teaching of Brigham Young, the second Prophet of the Mormon Church, known as the *blood atonement*. Young's controversial idea was that certain transgressions are so terrible that the atonement of Christ is inapplicable, such that the perpetrator's own death is needed to make his or her salvation once again possible. Historians note that, from the 1850s through the 1890s, this method allowed Young to eliminate spiritual and financial rivals—and, in reviving it, Ervil could now do the same while pointing to precedent.[61]

Ervil turned his attention to Rulon Allred, a homeopath and chiropractor who oversaw a rival sect of polygamous Mormons, centered in the western United States.[62] They had once been friends and allies. However, in addition to refusing to tithe to the Firstborners, Allred was now openly ridiculing them, prompting Ervil to declare, in a lengthy document, that his actions warranted execution under the Civil Law. From that time onward, Allred was marked for death. Joel, looking on, grew increasingly distressed by Ervil's threats and obsession with financial gain. When, in the summer of 1972, Ervil declared that God wished for them to share the leadership of the Firstborners, Joel refused and stripped him of whatever authority he already had. Shortly thereafter, his brother's name was added alongside Allred's on his rapidly expanding hit list.[63]

The rift between Ervil and Joel led to a schism in the community, with debates over which one was the true prophet. Ervil established the Church of the Lamb of God in California, where he openly proclaimed that Joel's "treason" should cost him his life. In Baja on August 20, 1972, Joel and his fourteen-year-old son Ivan stopped by the home of one of Ervil's disciples.

While the boy slept in their car, a group of Ervil's followers attacked Joel, one of whom pumped two bullets into his head. Joel's assassination left behind seven wives and forty-four children. Ervil was tried and convicted for masterminding the crime, but the conviction was overturned on a technicality, and he was released from jail after serving a single day.[64]

Ervil was dismayed to learn that, instead of joining his faction, Joel's flock turned to their youngest brother, the quiet and reserved Verlan. Terrified that he was next to die at Ervil's hand, he constantly traveled and routinely switched his cars, ultimately settling in Nicaragua. In the meantime, Ervil adopted lofty titles, such as Prophet of God, Lord Anointed, and One Mighty and Strong, and grew increasingly paranoid. He began carrying a firearm, required that his wives and children study marksmanship, and surrounded himself with a group of worshippers who used aliases, operating under sham birth certificates. All were advised that disloyalty could only mean death. Ervil also published a rambling essay, written in the archaic English of the King James Bible, entitled "Hour of Crisis—Day of Vengeance." In addition to demanding that tithes be paid directly to him, it forbade contributions to other factions, punishable by blood atonement. Around this time, Ervil took control of all romantic liaisons in his colony. He would demand first pick of all females, arrange all marriages, and use women as totally objectified rewards for male worshippers' good or loyal behavior. As the group expanded, Ervil relocated it to Utah, where he unsuccessfully tried to extort money from local Mormon factions.[65]

Then, claiming inspiration from God to destroy Los Molinos, where Verlan and his family lived, Ervil called upon Dean Vest, a six-foot-eight, 260-pound Vietnam veteran, to teach a band of loyalists to use weapons and explosives. Vest and five black-clad foot soldiers slipped into Baja by night, firebombing the homes and shooting down its terrified inhabitants as they raced from the flames. The attackers made their way to Verlan's property, where his wife and six of their children watched as their home was ignited and sprayed with bullets. In all, two citizens were killed and thirteen were wounded. Ervil was enraged to learn that his brother had not been home and that he survived the attack, thereafter resorting to using spies to locate him. Moreover, he decided that his usurpation of Los Molinos was inadequate. He wished to take over Mexico and the United States, and ultimately dominate the entire world. To do so, he reasoned, he would have to slaughter his religious rivals, and confiscate their business holdings to finance his mission.[66]

In 1975, Naomi Zarate Chynoweth, a former Firstborner, began vocally opposing Ervil's leadership and threatening to expose his actions to the authorities. Ervil had one of his wives, Vonda White, who long knew the dissenter, drive her to a dark canyon in Mexico's San Pedro Mountains. There, White allegedly shot the woman five times and loaded the body in the trunk of her car, burying her in the middle of nowhere with the assistance of another of Ervil's wives. The body has never been located.[67] Later that year, Ervil turned his attention to Robert Simons, a Utah man who sought to convert the Native Americans to Mormonism. He owned a sixty-five-acre piece of property, coveted by Ervil. Simons refused to cave in to extortion demands. Ervil created an alias and visited Simons at his church, posing as a man seeking theological discourse. The two wound up bickering fiercely and wrestling on the ground. Later, Ervil tried to seduce one of the man's wives. Simons threw him off the property. Reasoning that Simons merited death by refusing to acknowledge him as God's prophet, Ervil had him driven out to the desert by confederates, where he was shot to death and buried, doused in lime to hasten his decomposition. Ervil subsequently ordered that all evidence of the crime be set ablaze by his followers.[68]

Around this time, Dean Vest decided to defect from the Firstborners and seek a new way of life. Considering Vest a traitor who might snitch to the FBI, Ervil again called upon White, who was pregnant at the time. On June 16, 1975, Vest stopped by her home, en route to see his wife and daughter, who had just been in a road accident. After making small talk and feeding the kids, White asked him to have a look at a faulty washing machine, after which he stood cleaning up in her sink. She crept behind him and shot him through the liver and lung with a .38 Colt revolver. After he fell to the floor, she fired a bullet just behind his left ear. She then phoned the police, claiming to have heard mysterious shots in the house while tending to the children. She fled to Denver, Colorado, where Ervil was running a sweatshop.[69]

In 1977, Ervil's clan was split up between Utah and Colorado, and one of his daughters, seventeen-year-old Rebecca, was forced by Ervil to abandon a baby in Denver during the process. She threatened to go to the police about his crimes. In April of that year, Ervil told her he had decided to let her retrieve the infant, and arranged to accompany her during the drive to an airport in Texas, escorted by two young male members of his congregation. She was three months pregnant with her second child at the time. As she happily prattled on about plans to relocate to Mexico and raise her growing family, the boys allegedly pulled off the road in an isolated area near Dallas and slowly garroted her to death with rope in the back seat of the car. Ervil later became furious that the killers let her blood stain the trunk of his vehicle as they were carting away her corpse to dump, like so much rubbish, in Oklahoma State Park. He promptly traded it in for one in pristine condition.[70]

Later that year, Ervil cooked up what he thought to be a foolproof plot, reasoning that, if he successfully assassinated Rulon Allred, his elusive brother Verlan would be compelled to emerge from hiding to attend the victim's funeral. Then, Ervil envisioned, he would have his brother and rival shot dead by faithful followers during the services, in an unforgettable public display of power. On May 10, 1977, at his behest, his wife Rena Chynoweth and an accomplice, Ramona Marston, strolled into Allred's homeopathy clinic, wearing wigs and sunglasses, and mowed him down in an explosion of gunfire. Then, during the funeral, Ervil waited around with bated breath for word that Verlan was dead, but his men had failed to locate him.[71]

Eventually, several members of Ervil's cult broke free of his potent spell and went to the authorities. In 1979, Vonda White was sentenced to life in prison for the murder of Dean Vest. Chynoweth was acquitted of killing Allred but subsequently confessed to the homicide. Ervil was captured, found hiding out in the mountains near Mexico City, and, in 1980, he was sentenced to life in prison. Totally without remorse and refusing to go down easily, Ervil spent his time behind bars in a Utah prison, penning *The Book of the New Covenants*, a lengthy screed laying out the line of succession of his priestly powers, should he happen to die, and a hit list of over fifty people he felt warranted blood atonement. On August 16, 1981, Ervil died of a heart attack—and in a bizarre twist of fate, the elusive Verlan was killed just hours later, in a mysterious car crash in Mexico. Despite Ervil's death, his cruel deeds managed to survive. One by one, those on his hit list began to meet terrible ends, just as he had instructed. As one of many terrible examples, on June 27, 1988, three men identified as traitors in Ervil's missive were simultaneously shot to death by cult members, all around the same hour, hundreds of miles apart, in the infamous "Four O'Clock Murders." Duane Chynoweth, Ed Marston, and Mark Chynoweth, former thugs in Ervil's employ, had all abandoned the church in an effort to pursue happier, normal lives. Duane Chynoweth's ten-year-old daughter was also fatally shot in the mouth and forehead because she was crying for her father and her assassin refused to leave behind a potential witness.[72]

Blaise Pascal, the great French polymath and theologian, famously quipped in his *Pensées*, "Men never do evil so completely and cheerfully as when they do it from religious conviction." Whether Ervil LeBaron actually believed in God or his own theological teachings is open to debate. Whatever the case may be, we observe true "evil" in the power-starved preacher's use of religion to cheat and dominate others, and to justify a long list of wicked deeds, which reportedly included ordering the brutal execution of his own pregnant daughter.

CATEGORY 13

An individual ranked in Category 13 of the scale will have spent a lifetime feeling inadequate and embittered surrounding some personal shortcoming, such as childhood abuse, academic difficulties, unhappiness regarding physical appearance, or low socioeconomic status. The person will present with marked psychopathic traits and seethe with an almost constant anger, sometimes toward some specific demographic group, although this does not, initially, result in serious acts of aggression. While these types are generally detached and isolative in nature, the individual may compensate for feelings of insecurity and inadequacy by way of alliance with some organization that advocates bigotry, misogyny, or anarchistic principles. Ultimately, when built-up hatred and insecurity become paired with some unanticipated, adverse experience or life event, the person is suddenly prompted to plan out some terrible act of violence, which might be sensational in nature and involve murderous rage toward total strangers. We might expect to see some, but not all, spree killers and mass murderers in this category. When such individuals turn to murder, the underlying motive generally appears to be a desire to level life's playing field, which they perceive as having undermined their chances and contributed to their unhappiness. Their attitude is that if they cannot enjoy life, nobody else should. It is not uncommon for individuals in Category 13 to display signs of cognitive impairment or psychiatric illness, although this is not uniformly the case.

We find an example of this type of offender in Benjamin Nathaniel Smith, born in March of 1978 in affluent Wilmette, Illinois, where he was also raised. His mother was an attorney, and his father was a physician, employed at Northwestern Memorial Hospital. Both also sold real estate. As a boy, Smith reportedly played with a crossbow in his family's yard, once firing arrows into a neighbor's fence. A local familiar with him once remarked, "My wife lived in fear of him. She thought he had an evil core, and we both worried about our daughter's safety when he was around. He lived on the fringe and didn't fit in."[73] Another observed, "He seemed to harbor intense anger, but it was never of a physical nature. He never lashed out at anybody. He just had an angry look on his face."[74] At school, one of his teachers sensed that Smith was longing for a meaningful connection and invited him to his home to watch movies with him and his wife.[75]

Although he had no religious background, Smith considered himself a Muslim for a period, but he ultimately came to feel disappointed and frustrated over his attempts at religiosity. By his final year of high school, he was beginning to harbor hostility toward Jews and had tattooed "Sabbath Breaker" on his chest. He also felt himself being drawn to the white supremacy movement.[76] Before graduating, Smith did not pose for a yearbook photograph but provided a quotation attributed to Brutus, the assassin of Julius Caesar: "*Sic semper tyrannis*"—"Thus always to tyrants." The same Latin phrase, which is the state motto of Virginia, was reportedly shouted by John Wilkes Booth as he leaped from the presidential booth at Ford's Theater in Washington, DC, on April 14, 1865, just after firing a bullet into the brain of the Great Emancipator, Abraham Lincoln.[77]

Smith attended the University of Illinois at Urbana-Champaign, where he studied agriculture, and consumer and environmental science. In 1996, it was alleged that he was peeping at women through a window at a dormitory, as well as inappropriately touching female students. When apprehended by police, Smith identified himself as Erwin Rommel, borrowing the name of the field marshal of the Third Reich, dubbed the "Desert Fox." The following year, Smith was accused of possession of marijuana, fighting with other students, and beating his girlfriend. After the latter, he audaciously faxed the young woman a disclaimer to sign, attesting that he had not been abusive to her.[78] Smith dropped out in 1998, transferring to Indiana University's Bloomington campus, where he switched his academic focus to criminal justice.[79] Reportedly uncomfortable in his new culturally diverse environment, he began reading neo-Nazi literature and became a member of the World Church of the Creator, a white supremacist group later known as the Creativity Movement. There, he devotedly—perhaps fanatically—followed the church's leader, Matthew Hale, who may have become something of a father figure to him. Smith soon came to the attention of police for circulating flyers filled with hateful vitriol toward Jews, African Americans, and Asians. He had also taken to driving down residential streets and tossing small plastic bags from the windows into people's yards, containing pamphlets that asserted that whites were being crowded out of their neighborhoods by Jews, blacks, and "mud people," a derogatory term he used to refer to Asians.[80] He signed the missives with the pseudonym August Smith, reportedly abandoning the name Benjamin Nathaniel because it might suggest that he was Jewish. He withdrew about $19,000 from his savings account, dropped out of college for good, and devoted himself to Hale's message.[81] Around 1999, Smith moved out of his parents' home and severed ties with them.[82]

That same year, Hale, who wished to pursue a career as an attorney, passed his law school exams, but the Illinois State Bar Association called for an ethics hearing related to his openly racist views. On April 11, Smith testified before the bar, regarding what he saw as his leader's sterling character. On July 2, Hale was denied a license to practice law on the grounds of "gross deficiency in moral character." Apparently enraged by this, two days later, Smith loaded up his car with guns and ammunition and embarked upon a three-day shooting spree that encompassed two states.[83]

On the evening of July 2, 1999, Smith drove through the West Rogers neighborhood of Chicago, this time firing bullets through the open windows of his car, instead of racist literature. He wounded nine Orthodox Jews before moving on to other victims, who were targeted because of what he perceived to be their racial, ethnic, and religious identities. As African American Northwestern University basketball coach Ricky Byrdsong strolled outside his home in Skokie, Illinois with his young son and daughter, Smith pulled up alongside them and shot the man to death. The following day, Smith traveled to Urbana and Springfield, before reaching Decatur, where he fired at a black clergyman, leaving him wounded. On Independence Day, Smith drove to Bloomington, Indiana, where he fatally shot Won-Joon Yoon, a twenty-six-year-old Korean economics student at Indiana University, who had been en route to a church service. Smith fired at, but missed, nine other individuals. When police caught up with the killer, he engaged them in a high-speed chase on an Illinois highway before the car careened into a metal post. Smith had shot himself twice in the head. Still alive, he pressed his firearm against his heart and pulled the trigger, which finally ended his life.[84]

We will never fully understand Smith's precise state of mind before and during his three-day trail of murder. It appears that, in the white supremacy movement and Hale's organization, a young man with a history of deep-seated rage, existential confusion, and feelings of inadequacy believed that he had, at last, found a sense of personal identity and some-place that felt like a home to him. Moreover, the church's principles might have become a way of inverting the social order, such that Smith would no longer feel invisible and impotent but, rather, superior to those around him. Its teachings may have unwittingly allowed him to feel justified with regard to intense hatred and rage, which initially had nothing to do with his religious or racial beliefs, lending those feelings shape and purpose. He could project blame for his personal failings onto other people, an unseen "them." It is possible that he viewed through this same distorted lens Hale's inability to acquire a law license, reasoning that if it were not for the African Americans, Jews, and Asians, who incurred the group's hatred by simply existing, his leader would have been able to enter into practice. It is intriguing, however, that in his "random" targeting of members of certain racial groups while driving across Illinois and Indiana, Smith does seem to have honed in on people who were walking along, surrounded with family and friends, or at school, or heading into or out of places of worship. One wonders if, beneath his anger and "supremacist" views, he did not feel profoundly inferior and intensely envious of the types of people who love and are loved, who know what it is to belong in a family or a traditional social setting. How symbolic, then, that a man who might have wished to convince himself that he had no longing for any of it—for giving and receiving love within a traditional family or circle of friends—would end his life by destroying his very heart.

The reader might be surprised to learn of our opinion that Ed Gein, mentioned in our introduction, also belongs in Category 13. The crimes we are about to describe, including murder, grave robbing, and the transformation of the skins and body parts of corpses into clothes and various household objects, were certainly gruesome and unfathomably depraved. The case gives us an opportunity, however, to drive home the point that placement in the scale is primarily dependent upon an individual's specific motivation and the degree of amorality associated with that driving factor. Gein cannot be ranked at the scale's lower end, because, as we shall see, there is no evidence that his actions were impulsive in nature, related to situational stressors. There is also no indication that he was killing primarily to eliminate people "in the way" or for personal power. Moreover, his designation cannot be higher. As per the scale, higher rankings involve killing for more overt sexual gratification, to subjugate or terrorize, or following sadistic torture. Instead, it appears that Gein's crimes, like Benjamin Nathaniel Smith's, were driven by anger and resentment surrounding a sense of inadequacy and a disturbed notion that, if he could achieve some end or right some wrong, he could resolve underlying feelings of self-loathing. In both cases, the crimes were part of searching for personal identity and were set in play by a "last straw" event that focused underlying anger and antisocial personality features. This is the essence of Category 13. We should also note that, in addition to possibly psychopathic character traits, it is distinctly plausible that both men were at least sometimes psychotic—that is to say, partially operating under false beliefs, hallucinations, or disorganization of thought processes, a concept we will discuss at some length when we arrive at Category 20. For now, we will say that, if Gein were exclusively acting within the context of psychosis, affecting his ability to distinguish right from wrong, this might reduce his moral culpability and, thus, the "evil" of his actions. As we shall see, however, he displayed a complex blend of both psychotic and psychopathic features.

Edward Theodore Gein was born in August of 1906 in La Crosse, Wisconsin. His parents were farmers who relocated the family to Plainfield when Gein was a boy. His father, an abusive alcoholic who struggled to maintain regular employment, also worked as a tanner, insurance salesman, and carpenter, leaving his mother to look after Gein and a brother and to make the various decisions of the household. Gein's mother despised his father. She was a highly religious Lutheran, speaking sternly against premarital sex and telling the boys that all women, except herself, were whores and instruments of Satan. During daily Bible readings, she concentrated on Old Testament passages concerning death, murder, and divine punishment. Gein's mother chased off any visitors she felt might negatively influence her sons. Gein was shy and peculiar in school, sometimes observed laughing to himself. He was not permitted to befriend his classmates, at the threat of harsh punishment by his mother. Despite these social and family difficulties, he was a generally good student who especially enjoyed reading.[85]

When Gein was thirty-four, his father died of heart failure related to his hard drinking, and he and his brother began taking up odd jobs to make ends meet, typically as handymen. In 1944, the two were burning away marsh vegetation on the property, which, Gein would explain, got out of control. His brother was later found dead, supposedly from smoke inhalation, but the circumstances were suspicious. The brother's head showed signs of blunt force trauma, and no burn marks could be found. Some question exists of whether Gein murdered his sibling and started the fire to mask a jealousy-driven fledgling murder that would have made him the sole object of his mother's attention, following the death of his father.[86] One wonders how many times his mother had read him the story of Cain and Abel from the fourth chapter of the book of Genesis, in which Cain murders his younger brother, who he felt had proved the more beloved in a triangulated relationship with God.

Not long following the tragedy, Gein's mother suffered a stroke, rendering her paralyzed and in need of her remaining son's constant care. She had a second stroke in 1945 and died shortly thereafter. Gein, who had quite literally lost his only friend in the world, took up a hammer and some nails and sealed up his mother's bedroom, the living room, and upstairs and downstairs parlors like sepulchers, leaving everything just as she had left it. These rooms remained immaculately tidy while the remainder of the house fell into utter disarray.[87] Gein passed the time reading about death, cannibalism, South Seas headhunters, and Nazi concentration camp experiments.[88]

From the time of his boyhood, Gein had always been uncertain of his gender identity, with hopes of following in the footsteps of pioneering transsexual Christine Jorgenson and undergoing sex reassignment. However, in addition to the high cost of the procedure, he was terrified by the thought of the castration of his penis. This led Gein to contemplate how he might "turn female" without having to tackle these challenging obstacles.[89] His solution was truly the stuff of nightmares.

Between the ages of forty-one and forty-eight, Gein broke into three local cemeteries by night, disinterring and prying open an estimated forty coffins. Sometimes, he left with entire corpses, which he would, on rare occasions, return to their places of rest. In other instances, he removed various body parts that met his fancy. He claimed to be assisted, for a period, by a developmentally disabled man named Gus, who served as a sort of Igor to his Dr. Frankenstein. When this ally passed away, Gein continued these nocturnal raids on his own. Once back at home, he would set to work embellishing the various rooms, using skullcaps as bowls during meals; upholstering furniture with skins, which were also used to fashion lampshades and wastebaskets; mounting skulls on bedposts and creating objects from bones; decorating a necklace with tongues; crafting mobiles out of lips, noses, and labia; making gloves and leggings from flesh; and concocting a belt bedecked with severed nipples. He claimed to do all this, in part, to provide company for the spirit of his mother. In order to transform himself, at will, into a female, Gein would don the scalp and face peeled from a woman's corpse, and an elaborate vest, to which he had attached breasts and a vagina removed from corpses, the latter resting just above his loins. He found contentment for a while, dancing in this outfit beneath the moon in the privacy of his backyard. He would later admit that he enjoyed pretending to be his mother when dressed in his female suit, a fact that made him the basis for Norman Bates in Robert Bloch's 1959 thriller novel *Psycho*, subsequently adapted by Joseph Stefano for Alfred Hitchcock's classic film version, released the following year. Note that we have no indication that the butchering or wearing of skins provided Gein perverse sexual gratification, at least on a conscious level. He also denied ever engaging in necrophilia, once remarking that corpses "smelled too bad."[90]

By 1954, abusing already deceased bodies was no longer enough for

Gein. In early December of that year, fifty-one-year-old Mary Hogan disappeared from a tavern she managed in the town of Pine Grove. Police found an overturned chair, a pool of blood, and a spent .32-calibre pistol cartridge that, three years later, would be matched to a gun recovered from Gein's home. Then, on November 16, 1957, fifty-eight-year-old Bernice Worden similarly vanished, leaving behind only a trail of blood. Here, it led outside to where the body had evidently been loaded into a vehicle and driven off by the perpetrator. The woman's son recalled that Gein had once expressed romantic interest in his mother. He also recalled Gein speaking to her just the day before, about wishing to purchase some antifreeze. When a sales receipt for the product was found inside the store, investigators paid a visit to Gein's farm. What they encountered there would shake and change them for the remainder of their days.[91]

In a shed near Gein's home, Worden hung upside down from the rafters, decapitated, with her genitals carved away and the innards gutted, much the way one hangs and eviscerates a deer carted home from a hunt. Her heart was found in a plastic bag in front of a stove in the house, and her head, found in a burlap sack, had reportedly been transformed into a macabre decoration, with twine attached to nails driven into her ears. Her organs were stored in a box in a corner. Mary Hogan's flayed face was found in a paper bag, and masks fashioned from other women's faces were found elsewhere in the home. In a cardboard drum, ten heads were discovered. Nine vulvae were found in a shoebox, and a pair of lips was observed dangling from the drawstring of a window shade. Police also recovered four noses, female fingernails, and a corset made from the skinned torso of an unknown woman. Gein confessed to the murders of Hogan and Worden, along with his long history of violating graves. He was able to recall, in vivid detail, which coffins were left empty and which were not. It was never clarified whether he had murdered his brother in the so-called accidental marsh fire.[92] There were additional questions raised about whether Gein was responsible for the disappearance of a man named Travis and his male companion on a hunting trip, or of two missing girls, fifteen-year-old Evelyn Hartley and eight-year-old Georgia Jean Weckler. Although the vulvae of two young women were found in his home, these could not be positively identified. Gein was never conclusively linked to any of these other cases.[93]

In January of 1958, Gein was deemed incompetent to stand trial and sent to Central State Hospital in Waupun, Wisconsin.[94] Proceedings against him were held a decade later. He was found guilty, but insane, and sent back to Waupun. He died of liver and respiratory failure related to cancer at Mendota Mental Health Institute in 1984, aged seventy-seven years.

Gein's aims seem to have been related to dealing with feelings of insecurity, guilt, and self-loathing surrounding his gender identity, generated by his domineering mother's religious zealotry. As to whether Gein's mind was completely aberrant, it should be noted that he was careful to only raid cemeteries and to wear his female costume in the dead of night; to keep his crimes a secret from virtually everyone, except for a developmentally disabled man who posed little threat of blowing his cover; and to never let anyone see the décor or objects he had fashioned out of corpses. If he did, in fact, murder his brother, he also took steps—admittedly, unconvincing ones—to conceal the crime. Additionally, in creating his bizarre objets d'art, Gein demonstrated ingenuity and technical skill, which were not suggestive of disorganization but, rather, frightening detachment from the reality that his materials were the remnants of human beings. One might speculate about whether he had ever observed his father during his days as a tanner, matter-of-factly working with the skins of animals and turning them into eye-catching articles of clothing and other items. Much is made of the killer's desire to impersonate or even transform into his deceased mother, but, in working with skins, it is plausible that he was also incorporating some small aspect of his father's identity. At any rate, various psychiatric evaluations of Gein interpreted him as displaying both psychopathic personality features and schizophrenia,[95] consistent with the way we have understood him here.

Furthermore, Gein exhibited a complex blend of affection, rage, and envy toward women, clearly shaped by his relationship with his mother, who, despite her abuses and manipulations, quite literally meant the world to him. After her death, his mind gave way to his bizarre fantasy of transformation. This may have represented a primitive introjection or incorporation of a key figure in his life, the loss of whom his brittle psyche simply failed to tolerate. In this we see an attempt to deny his mother's death altogether, further manifested by sealing up rooms that reminded him of her. The ultimate in Gein's refusal to accept the reality of death came with displaying corpses, or parts thereof, in various parts of his home, whereby the deceased were suddenly alive again, the lengths of their "new" lives now completely under his control. We trust that this picture of the so-called "Butcher of Plainfield" makes plain, at the possible costs of sleep and appetite, why his various crimes warrant placement in Category 13 of the Gradations of Evil scale.

CONSIDERATIONS WHEN RANKING MUTILATION AND DISMEMBERMENT WITH THE GRADATIONS OF EVIL SCALE

One of the more unusual aspects of the Gein case is the element of dismembering and mutilating disinterred corpses to create household items and articles of clothing, which included the incorporation of various people's skins into his infamous "woman suit." It should be noted that the words *dismemberment* and *mutilation* have hitherto been poorly distinguished, such that they are often used interchangeably in both popular and academic parlance, including in some dictionary definitions. Thus, when writing this book, we worked with forensic researcher Dr. Ann W. Burgess, cocreator of the widely used *Crime Classification Manual*, to attempt to establish proper distinctions between these terms. It was our consensus that *dismemberment* might be best conceptualized as involving the entire removal, by any means, of a large section of the body of a living or dead person, specifically, the head (also termed *decapitation)*, arms, hands, torso, pelvic area, legs, or feet. *Mutilation* might be defined as the removal or irreparable disfigurement, by any means, of some smaller portion of one of those larger sections of a living or dead person. The latter would include *castration* (removal of the penis), *evisceration* (removal of the internal organs), and *flaying* (removal of the skin). It would also include cases in which corrosive acid is thrown in somebody's face—a crime generally committed by males who aim to harm the physical appearances of females who have rejected their romantic advances. Thus, removing a whole hand would constitute dismemberment, while removing or damaging a finger would be mutilation. Decapitation of a full head would be dismemberment, while removing or damaging a part of the face would be mutilation. Removing a whole torso would be dismemberment, while removing or damaging a breast or the organs contained within the torso would be mutilation.

While the reader might envision that dismemberment and mutilation would automatically be associated with some high ranking on the Gradations of Evil scale, the matter is actually a complicated one, since the motives we have found for these decidedly disturbing actions are, in fact, rather varied. For instance, with regard to mutilation involving removal of the skin, it is critical to distinguish between cases in which victims were flayed while dead or still living. Indeed, flaying a victim while alive, an almost unimaginable cruelty, has a long history as an extreme method of torture, especially throughout medieval Europe, and among the ancient Assyrians and Chinese. For instance, three Chinese emperors of the third through sixth centuries—Gao Heng, Sun Hao, and Fu Sheng—were infamous for having criminals' faces removed as a severe punitive action.[96] It is also maintained that St. Bartholomew, one of the twelve disciples of Christ, was flayed alive before being crucified, and he can be seen in Michelangelo's *The Last Judgment*, draping his own sad-eyed skin over the cloud on which he is perched.[97] Death by this means is typically due to blood loss or loss of other fluids, low body temperature, shock, or infection, and can occur hours to days after the removal of the skin.[98] A rare pre-nineteenth-century case involving flaying of living victims for private, psychosexual purposes is Countess Elizabeth Báthory de Ecsed, a Hungarian noblewoman of the sixteenth and seventeenth centuries, believed to have tortured and killed hundreds of female victims. The early female serial killer enjoyed flaying young virgins in cages suspended over razor-sharp spikes and forcing them to eat bits of their own skin, in addition to a variety of other horrendous abuses. Death was followed by the butchering and burning of corpses, and bathing in the women's blood, in an effort to enhance the beauty of her own flesh.[99]

Arguably the most horrendous example of a modern murder involving the flaying of a living victim is that of white supremacist cult leader Michael W. Ryan, who abused and killed Luke Stice, the five-year-old son of one of his followers, reputedly as punishment for the child expressing doubt about the existence of God. After writing "666" on the boy's forehead, he forced the child's father to beat, whip, and sexually assault him and another agnostic cult member, twenty-six-year-old James Thimm. Ryan then shoved the child into a cabinet, causing a fatal blow to the head, and compelled the father and Thimm to dig the boy's grave. Ryan proceeded to torture Thimm for days. The victim was chained up in a hog shed and shot in the face before being forced, while bleeding, to have intercourse with a goat. A shovel handle, marked up like a ruler, was repeatedly forced into his rectum by a group of Ryan's confederates. Reaching a depth of two feet, it ruptured the victim's rectal wall. This was followed by severe whippings. The fingers of one hand were shot off with a pistol, and his left arm was broken. It was only then that Thimm was partially flayed alive with a razor blade and a pair of pliers. As he did not die from the torment, his legs were shattered with wooden boards and Ryan jumped up and down on his chest until Thimm, at last, succumbed. The killer was sentenced to death for these atrocities but, after thirty years in prison, died of natural causes.[100] What is illustrated by this ghastly case is that when flaying is done to a living person, it constitutes unfathomable torture and will almost invariably warrant a ranking of Category 22, the highest level of the Gradations of Evil scale. As we gradually make our way toward areas of the scale in which we begin to encounter the unspeakable horror of torture-based crimes, we must also remember the impact something like flaying would have upon a victim's loved ones, who will have to hear about and envision the slow and brutal death, or, perhaps, even encounter the mutilated body. This all serves to add to the overall "evil" of the act.

In other cases, as with Gein, the flaying is of a corpse, such that there is no pain infliction involved. In the various incidents of this type that we have examined, the perpetrators were suffering from serious psychiatric illness, or else persons who killed and flayed in the context of severe maltreatment and trauma, whose rage toward the abuser burned on long past the person's demise. In a particularly bizarre example of the latter, in 2012, twenty-four-year-old Jeremiah Berry was allegedly raped by his father, who claimed God had commanded that Berry undergo a sex change to become his wife. Berry, in turn, shot his father to death, dismembered him with an axe, and carefully removed the skin with a knife, which was subsequently fed to wild coyote. The body parts were encased in concrete.[101] Despite the gruesomeness of removing a dead victim's skin in this matter, acts of this nature are generally scored lower on the Gradations of Evil scale, perhaps at level 6, where we see impetuous, hotheaded violence from people who lack psychopathic traits, or Category 13, where a rageful, insecure, and possibly disturbed individual with some psychopathic qualities commits violence with a degree of malice aforethought.

Similarly, the dismemberment of victims also seen in the Gein case is yet another terrible action that seems as if it would automatically merit a high ranking on the Gradations of Evil scale, but which, in fact, may not, depending upon a perpetrator's specific motivation, and whether or not victims were alive or dead at the time. As we shall see as we progress along the scale and particularly as we turn to part II of this book, dismemberment of corpses may be for a wide array of purposes, most commonly the "practical" objective of more readily disposing of a corpse to conceal evidence of a homicide. In other cases we have reviewed, some of which we will review in the pages to come, dismemberment of one's deceased victims represented mental disorganization; "overkill" of objects of extreme hatred; a precursor to cannibalism; or part of a psychological thrill, sometimes followed by the retention of heads or other body parts as trophies or for perverse sexual purposes. When we see removal of the limbs of a living victim—a thankfully rare event in peacetime—this is nearly always part of an intentionally prolonged and brutal murder that warrants a high ranking on the scale, involving protracted torture. Decapitation of a living victim is a somewhat more complex matter. In some instances, the beheading is expeditious, involving no sadistic prolongation of suffering. In others, this may be painfully slow, performed with a blunt or small instrument. If the latter is carried out with the intention of inflicting psychological and physical pain, a higher Gradations of Evil scale ranking would be required to capture the element of torture.

CATEGORY 14

Category 14 is the most common ranking for killers on the Gradations of Evil scale, although murder is not required for this designation. It contains a variety of ruthlessly self-centered psychopaths, unlimited in their willingness to cheat and steal to meet their respective personal ends. They are thieves, schemers, and confidence tricksters, sometimes remarkably adept at mimicking sincerity and trustworthiness in order to defraud others.

Their plots are often mind-boggling in their ingenuity, and they experience no compunction about taking days, weeks, months, or even years to build the relationships necessary to bring them to successful completion. Indeed, these skills often allow them to slip seamlessly through life, evading suspicion and apprehension by police, at least for a considerable period. When Category 14 types commit murder, it is purely to achieve some practical, self-serving end. This is the type of offender who unfeelingly shoots a security guard because it is necessary to gain access to a safe or who heads to the altar with a well-heeled victim, who is then quickly eliminated, resulting in a financial windfall. We often encounter this brand of psychopath in cinema and literature, since their diabolical charms and self-absorption make them ideal archetypical villains. Of course, their real-life counterparts are often far more nuanced and complicated.

Of note, it is not uncommon for people ranked in Category 14 to employ the assistance of weaker-willed allies, who recognize their true natures but feel a curious loyalty or even affection for them. Such allies are sometimes manipulated with fear of harm to themselves or loved ones, and are capable of killing if the dynamic is adequately powerful. If lacking psychopathic traits, such accomplices would likely fall into Category 3 of the Gradations of Evil scale.

A fascinating case we would place here is that of Sante Kimes, born Sandra Louise Singhrs in Oklahoma City in 1934. She was the third of four children to an East Indian father and an Irish mother of partial Dutch descent. The family relocated to Southern California in the late 1930s, after which her father abandoned the family and her mother felt compelled to resort to prostitution to help with mounting expenses. The children were placed in orphanages and foster homes. In watching her mother go down this path, Kimes may have come to believe that it is acceptable to resort to immoral or illegal activities to satisfy one's personal needs, amounting to little more than trying to survive unfavorable circumstances.[102]

For a period of time, Kimes wandered the streets of Los Angeles. She was reportedly sexually abused by a number of adults around this period and was once arrested for stealing food. When she was in the seventh grade, Kimes was adopted by a couple who changed her name to Sandra Chambers and who purchased a new home in Carson City, Nevada. There, Kimes earned moderately good grades. Blossoming into a brunette beauty by late adolescence, she was a cheerleader and sang in her high school's glee club, when not flirting with a number of boys.[103] When her birth mother popped up, looking to take her back to California, Kimes flatly refused. It was also during this period that she first took to shoplifting and using her adoptive father's credit card without his knowledge.[104]

Three months after graduating, Kimes married her high school sweetheart, Lee Powers, but divorced him for unclear reasons after several months. At twenty-two, she married another high school boyfriend, Edward Walker, with whom she had a son, Kent Walker.[105] She changed her name to Santee Chambers in 1960. Around this time, it came to her attention that she bore a striking resemblance to actress Elizabeth Taylor, after which she sometimes shamelessly signed autographs as the star.[106] She also began using the attention she garnered from men to her advantage, occasionally taking money in exchange for sex, just as her mother had done decades before.[107] Kimes gradually built up her skills as a con artist and thief and, over two decades, burned down a number of homes she had acquired in order to cash in on insurance claims.[108] In 1965, she managed to charm an automobile dealer into letting her test drive a car alone, and simply never brought it back to the showroom. She then tried to beguile the police officer who arrested her a long while later, audaciously claiming she was still test driving it. She was ultimately charged with seventeen counts of grand theft after racking up $20,000 in debt, using multiple credit card accounts attained by way of a long list of aliases.[109] Arrested for theft again the following year, she pled guilty and received three years' probation but went right on scheming and swindling. She and her second husband divorced in 1968.[110]

In the early 1970s, Kimes met motel tycoon Kenneth Kimes. A decade later, he became her third husband when their son, Kenneth "Kenny" Kimes Jr., was six years of age. It was then that she adopted the last of her many names, Sante Kimes. From his earliest days, Kenny was taught by his mother to lie and steal on her behalf, and, during his college days, there were suspicions, never confirmed, that they were having incestuous relations.[111] In the meantime, the wealthy family owned homes in Las Vegas, California, Hawaii, and the Bahamas. Kimes and her husband began trotting around the globe to address American civil rights groups about patriotism, raking in money by peddling US flags to schools. In order to acquire an official government sanction, they met with First Lady Pat Nixon and inveigled themselves into a 1974 party at Blair House, where they chatted with Vice President Gerald R. Ford about their work. Their success prompted them to continue to crash events at embassies and elsewhere, until the pair's chicanery came to light.[112]

Kimes and her husband were arrested on slavery charges in 1985. She had been making the rounds at various homeless shelters to identify undocumented immigrants, whom she forced to work as servants in her family's home under the threat of deportation. She was incarcerated until 1994 while her husband raised their son and underwent treatment for alcohol abuse.[113] Then, when Kimes lost her husband to a sudden heart attack in 1995, she was more distressed about not being included in his will than she was about his demise. She made up her mind to simply conceal any evidence of his passing, forging the deceased's name to checks and legal documents to blow through the millions of dollars he had left behind.[114] Kimes would thereafter continue her criminal career in tandem with her son, pulling cons and amassing cars and other assets by passing rubber checks, earning them the nickname "Mommy and Clyde" from one journalist. They callously did away with several people who got in the way of plans or posed risks to her freedom, including David Kazdin, a business associate who figured out that she had a notary forge his name on a $280,000 mortgage and threatened to expose her. In 1998, she had her son shoot him in the back of the head and leave his body in a dumpster at Los Angeles Airport.[115]

Then, later that year, Kimes cooked up a plot whereby she would eliminate and assume the identity of a beloved, flamboyant eighty-two-year-old Manhattan socialite, Irene Silverman, thereafter appropriating the victim's $7.7 million mansion. Kimes had her son rent a room in the woman's home and secretly moved in with him. When Silverman was out, the two rifled through her personal papers to cook up the best way to take over her property. Silverman eventually became suspicious of her boarder and his ever-present mother. On July 8, 1998, while Silverman's staff was away for the Fourth of July holiday, Kimes indifferently watched television while her son dragged Silverman into her bedroom. She then zapped the victim in the head with a stun gun and said, "Do it." Her son strangled Silverman, wrapped her body in several trash bags, loaded her into a duffel bag, and dumped her remains in a trash bin at an isolated New Jersey construction site.[116]

Little did Kimes and her son know the FBI was on to them for a number of crimes, including the killing of Kazdin. During a setup with a man they believed to be a friend and ally, the pair were apprehended. In their stolen car, agents recovered handguns, ammunition, blank social security cards, Silverman's passport, the keys to her mansion, and a pad in which Kimes had been practicing how to forge the victim's signature.[117] Kimes was subsequently convicted on fifty-eight counts and sentenced to 120 years in prison. Her son was convicted on sixty charges and sentenced to 125 years. The two were then extradited to California to be charged with Kazdin's murder. Kenneth Kimes entered a plea agreement in 2004 and, to avoid the death penalty, testified against his mother.[118] Beyond describing how and why Kazdin and Silverman were killed, he confessed that they had also fatally drowned Indian investment broker Syed Bilal Ahmed in a bathtub after he had denied Kimes a loan in the Bahamas. His body was reportedly dumped in the ocean. Kimes and her son were never charged for this additional homicide. This time, they were sentenced to life in prison, where the elder Kimes died of natural causes in 2014.[119]

At the time of her sentencing, Kimes raved at length about the unfairness of her legal situation, expressing no remorse whatsoever.[120] Dr. Arthur Weider, a forensic psychologist who observed her throughout the trial, noted that she exhibited a psychopathic personality with "no guilt, conscience, remorse, or empathy." He further described her as socially charming and arrogant. "She feels everyone is stupid and will do her bidding," Weider remarked. He compared her hold over her son to that of master manipulator Svengali in George du Maurier's 1895 novel *Trilby*, explaining that Kimes dominated and controlled her son, having him play out whatever terrible scripts and scenarios she concocted.[121]

Our second Category 14 example is that of Richard Wade Farley, who infamously stalked and shot the object of his longtime obsession, Laura Black. He slaughtered seven of her coworkers, who happened to be standing in the path of his prey. Reflecting upon the case of Mark David Chapman, already discussed in the section on Category 7, it should be evident that stalkers who ultimately commit homicide can fall into a number of rankings on the Gradations of Evil scale, for the reason that this sort of behavior can have an array of underlying motivations, with varying degrees of ruthlessness. As we have noted, individuals ranked here demonstrate egocentric, psychopathic personalities and, by way of cunning and calculation, relentlessly pursue whatever they desire. If this takes the form of stalking, they seek nothing short of the complete possession of some individual upon whom they have become intensely fixated. Stalkers of this type will almost invariably perceive their relentless, obsessive feelings as "love," totally disregarding any pain or difficulty these selfish, one-sided affections entail for their victims. It should also be clear that mass murderers like Farley can fall into a number of categories on the scale, similarly dependent upon their underlying motivations. As we shall see, Farley's murderous attack constituted a deliberate, meticulously planned assault, not an impetuous crime of passion, which would result in a lower ranking on the continuum.

Richard Wade Farley was born in Texas in July of 1948, the oldest of six children. His father, who was allegedly abusive, was a mechanic for the air force, and his work forced the family to move several times around the country until the Farleys finally settled in California.[122] He would later say that he viewed his mother as the only person who ever loved him,[123] which may or may not have figured into his idealization of another female figure later in life. Farley was isolated and self-centered in childhood, as is common among future stalkers, and was domineering with his siblings.[124] After graduating from high school in 1966, he attended Santa Rosa Community College for less than a year before joining the navy.[125] There, it was his mission to gather intelligence by spying on other people, perhaps reflecting or fostering an underlying need to assert dominance over others.[126] He remained there for a decade, after which he found work as a software technician at ESL Incorporated, a Sunnyvale, California, defense contractor. It was there, at age thirty-six, that he first encountered twenty-two-year-old Laura Black, who was employed as an electrical engineer by the firm. They were introduced when Farley visited a colleague in Black's work area, and the three went out for lunch. While she enjoyed a casual outing with colleagues, Farley "fell instantly in love."[127]

Farley took to routinely popping up at Black's desk and incessantly inviting her out on dates. She politely declined, explaining that she was only interested in him as "a work friend," but he plowed on, just the same. He demanded her contact information and began leaving her letters and a variety of gifts. These included homemade baked snacks and, as his behavior grew more peculiar, a heart-shaped mirror and a power shovel. When Black felt compelled to tell him that she would never date him, even if he "were the last man on earth," he harassed her further, reasoning to himself that if she was not going to turn him down in a polite manner, he had every right to continue his campaign of harassment.[128]

Farley proved extremely crafty and resourceful. He joined Black's gym and surreptitiously snapped photographs of her while she was exercising. He conned a coworker into giving him Black's home address by claiming he was a good friend who wanted to drop by to surprise her for her birthday. He rang her home phone on a regular basis, at all hours of the night, and began driving past her house whenever she failed to pick up, making certain he always knew her whereabouts. He broke into Black's work desk and made meticulous tracings of her house keys, which he then used to prepare copies for himself. When she played recreational softball, he attended the games and invited himself to the team's private pizza parties. When Black took a personal leave to visit her parents, Farley rifled through her desk a second time, locating the address where she would be staying. He sent her a letter, eight single-spaced pages long, which was only one of the hundreds he would mail her over the next four years. She repeatedly changed locations and addresses to elude him, but, each time, he managed to find her. Somehow, these obsessive behaviors created a distorted notion in Farley's mind that they were somehow growing closer and, at the very least, forced his victim to constantly acknowledge his existence in a world in which he was otherwise invisible to women.[129]

When several coworkers attempted to reason with Farley, he reacted in a defiant or menacing manner. In the fall of 1985, Black asked their company's Human Resources Department for assistance, which resulted in Farley being mandated to attend psychological counseling. As is nearly always the case when psychotherapy is attempted with stalkers of a paranoid type, the intervention proved utterly ineffective. Not long thereafter, he showed up in front of Black's home, boasting, in an unsettling manner, about his collection of guns and his great skill at firing them. Having assured HR that he would stop trailing her home, tapping into her work computer, and sending her letters and gifts, he returned to stalking her after a respite of just two short months. The company stepped in twice more through early 1986, issuing Farley written warnings to cease and desist at the risk of his position. When these went ignored, the firm finally terminated his employment.[130] Farley wrote to Black about the dismissal, saying he now had "no alternative" but to live with her, as long as he was out of work.[131] Somehow, Black, the victim of his menacing behavior, was being blamed for wreaking havoc on his life by refusing to reciprocate his feelings.

Even after Farley found work with another defense contractor and became engaged to a different woman, his obsession with Black went on, without interruption. She went back and forth in her mind about whether she should pursue a restraining order, fearing, as is often the victim's concern in these situations, that it might stoke her stalker's temper and place her in even greater danger. Things came to a head in early 1988 when he left an envelope on the windshield of her car, containing a note and a reproduction he had made of her latest house key. In February of that year, she was granted a temporary restraining order and Farley was barred from contacting or coming within three hundred feet of her. A court date for a hearing regarding a permanent restraining order was set for a little over two weeks later.[132]

We can only imagine how Farley felt at this point, swimming in debt and now being prohibited from having anything to do with the object of his constant desire. It is likely he felt as if he had lost control over his life—a situation that, for individuals in this category, can constitute the final straw. One week after the temporary restraining order was issued, he used his security clearance from his ESL job to acquire, at a cost of thousands of dollars, a 12-gauge Benelli Riot semiautomatic shotgun and over three thousand rounds of ammunition. He sent Black's attorney falsified "evidence" that he and Black had been romantically involved, in an effort to get the order tossed out, which was promptly dismissed. Then, Farley made his mind up to confront Black at ESL on the eve of the court hearing, giving her the "option" of rescinding the restraining order or watching him shoot himself to death.[133]

On February 16, 1988, Farley approached his former place of employment clad in military fatigues, black gloves, and a scarf, which he had wrapped around his head. He wore a bandolier over his shoulder and was armed with his 12-gauge and a number of other firearms, a knife tucked under his belt, a smoke bomb, and a container of gasoline.[134] Making his way across the parking lot, he unflinchingly raised a shotgun and dispatched forty-six-year-old former colleague Larry Kane. He took aim at other employees and shot his way through the security glass in the building's façade. Firing into one of the offices, he killed twenty-three-year-old Wayne Williams. Five more employees were struck down on a stairwell, three of whom subsequently died from their injuries. Farley then approached Black's office, blasting through the door. Despite his claim that his intention was to force her to witness his suicide, he shot her twice, leaving her with a shattered left shoulder and collapsed lung and knocking her unconscious. The killer then moved from room to room, taking aim at the employees taking cover underneath desks or barricading themselves in their offices. To make certain victims were dead, he shot them in their backs at near point-blank range with his shotgun. There is some question of whether Black's coworkers were massacred for the purpose of emotionally wounding the object of his obsession in a cruel attempt to leave her blaming herself for their tragic deaths. In the meantime, Black, now conscious and heavily bleeding, managed to slip out of the building to safety. Colleagues plugged her wounds with paper towels, selflessly collaborating to save her life.[135]

A SWAT team arrived, and Farley spoke with a hostage negotiator on and off throughout a siege that lasted a grueling five hours. He passed the time by shooting up computers until "it wasn't fun anymore."[136] He expressed no remorse, explaining that none of this would have been necessary if Black had simply agreed to go out with him. The chaos only came to an end when Farley decided he was too hungry to go on without lunch. He agreed to surrender in exchange for a sandwich and a soft drink. Farley had fired ninety-eight shots during his rampage,[137] leaving seven former colleagues dead and four others injured, including his "beloved" Laura Black. The next day, her restraining order against him was rendered permanent.[138] Black spent the next nineteen days in a hospital and would be disabled by her terrible injuries for the rest of her days. Farley, feeling just fine, remarked after the tragedy that if he wound up in the gas chamber, he would "smile for the cameras."[139]

In 1991, Farley stood trial, over three years following the mass shooting, which had been driven by a massive, wounded ego. He confessed to the killings but pled not guilty, claiming that his objective was merely to commit suicide in Black's presence—a statement that was difficult to reconcile with the actual, incontrovertible facts of the case. The defense painted the picture of a previously nonviolent individual with no prior criminal record, whose judgment temporarily lapsed and who would never kill again. Stated another way, he was depicted as having committed a crime of passion, associated with a much lower ranking on the Gradations of Evil scale. The prosecution, in turn, described the painstaking efforts Farley made to make Black's life a living hell, as well as the extensive planning and premeditation that surrounded his deadly attack. Farley was convicted of seven counts of first-degree murder and sentenced to death. He remains on death row as this volume goes to press.[140] In the wake of the massacre, which was followed by the tragic shooting of *My Sister Sam* actress Rebecca Schaeffer by an obsessed fan, Robert John Bardo, in 1989,[141] California passed the United States' first anti-stalking laws in 1990, and other states gradually followed suit.[142]

CHAPTER FIVE

CATEGORIES 15 AND 16

There will be killing 'till the score is paid.

—Homer, *The Odyssey*

T hus far, we have discussed mass and spree killers of the type whose smoldering anger and resentment are ultimately tipped over into acts of explosive, deadly rage. We reviewed cases in which this was impetuous and immediate, and ones in which individuals methodically plotted and then acted, often in horrifying and spectacular ways. The reader may have noted that the killings, while cruel, were generally expeditious, almost invariably carried out with firearms. In such cases, we are left with multiple people robbed of their lives as some egocentric, spiteful point is made by a socially invisible, angry individual who suddenly breaks in upon the public, demanding its undivided attention.

As we move into Categories 15 and 16, we are dealing with spree and mass murderers of an even more vicious and prolific type, who kill multiple people as part of a wider campaign, often with an inhuman degree of cold-bloodedness. While their killings are sometimes slow in nature—for instance, by poison or repeat stabbings—the goal is not to torture victims, which would place a killer at a higher level of the scale. Psychopathy and sheer amorality are typically obvious here, for all to see, and not concealed beneath a superficial layer of charm, as we observed in the case of Sante Kimes.

CATEGORY 15

As we grope for some explanation or motive underlying spree and mass homicides, we sometimes discover that the aim was initially one associated with a lower ranking on the scale, such as jealousy, but, after the object of that more focused rage is dead, the killer's fury burns on in a more generalized way, branching out to affect other people, often including strangers. Some killers ranked here are calculating schemers, simply profiting from their victims, but they murder so frequently and with such indifference to human life that a ranking of Category 14 is insufficient.

In other cases designated to Category 15, the crime is motivated by sheer pleasure or the desire to stir up anarchy, sometimes masquerading as spiritual zealotry. As we discussed in the context of Category 3, this was the case for Charles Manson and several members of his cult. We see, in such types, more than a hint of sour grapes related to their unhappy lots in life. Did Manson want rich and beautiful people killed to stir up Helter Skelter, or was he actually envious of them, having been an abandoned nobody who craved fame, beauty, and power for himself?

Not surprisingly, we almost invariably find that Category 15 killers were maltreated or neglected early in their lives, either from the very start or after some major life event unexpectedly altered their fates. It is not uncommon for these types to have been totally abandoned by parents, sexually exploited, or emotionally or physically abused. Such individuals sometimes feel so cheated by their circumstances that they believe themselves to be entitled to disregard the rights and needs of others, taking whatever they wish from them, without compassion or regard for human life. They display a universalized disdain for humankind and society itself, due to anger at those who hurt them and bitterness toward those to whom life has dealt better hands. In short, as nobody cared about them, they do not care about other people. Since society did not welcome or incorporate them, they do not care about society. They were randomly born into situations in which they were treated cruelly or unfairly, so now, they randomly burst into the lives of those who have been more fortunate, to level the proverbial playing field. Furthermore, rejection by the world makes them feel immune to its rules and moral codes. Manson, for instance, completely redefined right and wrong, the concept of family, the nature of human relationships, and traditional religious beliefs, all in a concerted effort to subvert commonplace society at large.

We see several of these elements in the case of Andrew Cunanan, born in San Diego, California, in August of 1969. He was the youngest of four children born to a Filipino navy man turned stockbroker and his Italian American wife, who suffered from chronic depression. Their marriage was strained, and the young and precociously intelligent Cunanan often took refuge in his bedroom, where he memorized Bible verses and read comic books, romantic adventure novels, and volumes of the encyclopedia. These traits made him an object of pride for his parents, who spoiled him with special privileges, although he alleged that his father sometimes harshly physically disciplined him in childhood, leaving bruises on his body. He attended La Jolla's prestigious Bishop's School, where he earned high grades and demonstrated proficiency in seven languages.[1] His admirable academic performance further contributed to a burgeoning sense of exceptionalism.

Following a sexual encounter with a male at the age of thirteen, Cunanan began identifying as gay. Two years later, he was donning disguises to gain entry to gay bars, posing as a variety of alter egos. He adopted pseudonyms that he felt sounded less ethnic, including Andrew DeSilva, inspired by the name of a prominent art dealer.[2] He proved so adept at the talent of making himself look older or like someone from a wide array of ethnic backgrounds that he could even fool people with whom he had socially interacted the night before. After graduating from high school, ironically voted Most Likely to Be Remembered in his yearbook, Cunanan began studying history at the University of San Diego, where he grew increasingly flamboyant and desperate for attention and validation from others. He acquainted himself with the finer things in life, obsessed with the idea of amassing tremendous material wealth. Cunanan discovered that he could charm wealthy, older men—all, perhaps, surrogates for his father—who brought him to social functions and showered him with gifts, including, on one occasion, a $30,000 car. He also began earning income by way of prostitution and sometimes dabbling in illicit drugs. This lifestyle contrasted sharply with the ailing financial state of his family, since his father was struggling to maintain stable employment. Eventually, his father fled back to the Philippines following embezzlement charges, and his mother was forced to move into a lower-class neighbor-hood. After she and Cunanan had a violent fight, in which he dislocated her shoulder, he dropped out of college and went to live with his father in Manila. Finding himself ashamed of his father's destitution, and longing for the high life he had been living in California, he promptly relocated to San Francisco. There, he worked as a high-end prostitute for older men, which sometimes included diplomats.[3]

From the late 1980s through the mid-1990s, Cunanan became involved with several wealthy men, who sometimes moved him into their homes, under the pretense of his working as a secretary or personal assistant. One of his johns introduced Cunanan to sadomasochistic sex, in which the latter assumed the role of a well-polished slave. He also appeared in several pornographic films with violent themes.

As his social circles expanded, Cunanan began making the rounds at operas, plays, and ritzy soirées. He was supposedly introduced at a restau-rant opening to the extravagant fashion icon Gianni Versace. He would tell the story, which may have been a complete fabrication, for years, boasting that he knew the designer on a personal basis.[4]

In 1996, Cunanan fell in love with Jeffrey Trail, a US Naval Academy graduate, who disappointed him by suggesting that their relationship should be a purely platonic one. Then, when Trail moved to Minnesota with a new significant other, Cunanan was emotionally devastated. He fell into a deep depression, piling on considerable weight and disregarding the polished personal appearance that had previously been his livelihood. Feeling physically run down, he began to wonder if he had contracted HIV, but, after undergoing testing, he never returned to the physician to review the results. They were, in reality, negative. Struggling to make ends meet, Cunanan took to petty theft and dealing prescription painkillers, which he sometimes blended with vodka and consumed himself.[5]

Later that year, when Cunanan learned that Trail had separated from his companion, he traveled to Minneapolis to see him for a week-long visit. There, he met Trail's friend David Madson, a handsome architect, with whom he rapidly became smitten. Upon Cunanan's return to California, he continued to mingle with the rich and famous, meeting a number of celebrities, including Madonna, who allegedly left him feeling slighted by paying him no mind. Around this same time, he developed an erotic preoccupation with actor Tom Cruise, covering his walls with posters of the star. Friends started noticing that he was further neglecting his physique and might be ill. At this point, he was abandoning hopes of securing his next wealthy benefactor.[6]

In April of 1997, Cunanan also became concerned that Trail and Madson might have become romantically involved, prompting a quarrel with Trail over the telephone, during which Cunanan unsettled him with a death threat. For Cunanan, it added insult to injury to consider that Trail and Madson were both professional, successful men while he was financially struggling, perhaps reinforcing the narcissistic notion that only wealthy and attractive people merit love and attention. Seething at the thought of being second best, he made his mind up to visit Minneapolis again, where Madson collected him at the airport. Once they had arrived at Madson's home, Madson and Trail repeatedly tried to explain to Cunanan that his fears were unfounded. During the conversation, a heated argument broke out, culminating in Cunanan fatally smashing Trail's skull with thirty blows from a claw hammer grabbed from a kitchen drawer. Madson helped him to roll up Trail's remains in an Oriental carpet, but it is unknown whether he was forced or did so of his own accord. Over the next two days, the two went about their business, as if nothing had transpired. Madson's unannounced absence from work prompted the superintendent of the building to enter the apartment, where he discovered Trail's blood-soaked body. Cunanan and Madson then took off in Madson's jeep, with Trail's gun in Cunanan's possession. Off Interstate 35, north of Minneapolis, Cunanan suddenly pulled off on a road leading to an abandoned farmhouse. There, he demanded that Madson exit the vehicle and promptly shot his companion of the past few days through the eye, head, and back. It is unclear if Cunanan was inclined to murder Madson because he could serve as a witness in the killing of Trail, or if his death was part of an act of cruel, jealousy-fueled revenge.[7] What is certain is that his rage was not extinguished at that time, instead expanding to include deeds that were even more horrifying.

By May 4, Cunanan, with Minnesota behind him, had grown tired of sleeping in Madson's jeep and decided to stop in Chicago. Entering the city's celebrated Gold Coast area, he managed to gain entry to the home of the beloved seventy-two-year-old real estate developer and philanthropist Lee

Miglin. It is unknown whether the cash-poor Cunanan originally intended merely to rob the victim, but he proceeded to slaughter him—a man who may have been a symbol of all he envied—with unspeakable viciousness. In the garage, he bound Miglin's wrists with electrical cord and wrapped his head in duct tape, leaving only a small space just below the nostrils. With the elderly victim unable to see what was about to happen to him, Cunanan repeatedly stabbed him with a screwdriver and pruning shears before slashing his throat with a gardener's bow saw. Cunanan's frenzy culminated with him getting into the man's Lexus and repeatedly running over his already mutilated body, crushing his bones beneath the wheels. Cunanan then hid the corpse beneath the car and helped himself to the victim's food and bed. The following morning, he gathered up some cash, a pricey wristwatch, and a leather jacket before speeding off in Miglin's Lexus.[8]

Five days later, Cunanan found himself at Finn's Point National Cemetery, an American Civil War burial ground, located in Pennsville, New Jersey. There, he held up the forty-five-year-old caretaker, William Reese, forcing him to hand over the keys to his pickup truck. He then shot the victim point-blank in the head, execution-style, as Reese sat at his office desk. Of note, there was no overkill here, as in the case of Miglin. This time, the apparent motivating factors were the practical ones of wishing to continue his flight in a new vehicle, untraceable to his previous murders, and eliminating a witness. However, Cunanan got sloppy, as is often the case with egocentric killers, leaving copious amounts of incriminating evidence in the now abandoned Lexus. This included his passport, as well as the screwdriver he had used to butcher Miglin. After this fourth murder, Cunanan made his way down to Miami Beach, Florida.[9] He rented a hotel room there under his old DeSilva alias, frequenting gay bars and viewing sadomasochistic pornography for nearly two months before killing for the final time. In the meantime, he was placed on the FBI's ten most wanted list,[10] which may very well have felt to Cunanan like something of an achievement. One can imagine him when he learned of this development, pathetically honing in on the word "wanted" and the fact that he was one of only ten in this criminal elite. To make himself even more "wanted," he would have to find a way to top his already spectacular murder spree, which was making him front-page news throughout the terrified and bewildered country.

On July 12, 1997, Gianni Versace, Cunanan's supposed "friend" and a well-known resident of South Beach, arrived with his entourage for a visit to his mansion, Casa Casuarina. Learning of his appearance, Cunanan decided to stake out in front of the star's home. Three days later, as Versace was unlocking the gate after a morning outing, Cunanan abruptly walked over and fired a bullet into his back. As the beloved designer lay mortally wounded on the sidewalk, Cunanan shot him a second time, at point-blank range through the head, before stealthily slipping away from the scene. Versace died shortly thereafter at a nearby hospital.[11]

Police gradually traced Cunanan's multistate trail of death and were beginning to close in on him. Reese's stolen truck, recovered in a garage, was found to contain a list of other celebrities the killer had wished to target, including Madonna and Julio Iglesias, both subsequently alerted to the threats on their lives.[12] Cunanan took to hiding out on a houseboat parked in Miami Beach's Indian Creek. Eleven days after the murder of Versace, a caretaker went to check on his client's boat, unexpectedly encountering the holed-up killer. As the confused visitor left, he heard what he thought was a single gunshot. A SWAT team surrounded the boat, waiting for hours for some movement from the man they were convinced was Cunanan. Eventually, an assault crew fired tear gas canisters and barged in, only to find the killer faceup in bed, shot through the mouth with the same semiautomatic handgun he had used to kill Madson, Reese, and Versace, in a bloody suicide.[13]

Following Cunanan's death, there was some speculation that he might have been set off by the false belief that he had contracted HIV.[14] This fear, so the story went, prompted him to seek revenge against those he felt might have infected him with the disease, as well as any older, wealthy man who reminded him of those who sought his bedroom services. In reality, we will never know the killer's actual motivations, which he took with him to the grave. Examining the case as a whole, what seems to have begun as a jealousy killing, in the case of Trail, appears to have given way, under the weight of some intense personal crisis involving narcissistic injury, to a reckless murder spree with an assortment of possible motives. These might have included the elimination of witnesses, in the cases of Madson and Reese; displacement of deep-seated rage in the killing of Miglin, perhaps related to envy of his success or resentment of the father who failed him;

and the desire to obtain lasting fame, in the assassination of a beloved fashion guru. As observed with Mark David Chapman, the murder of a celebrated person inextricably binds the killer and celebrated person together in history. Perhaps the core of the case of Andrew Cunanan is best captured by a penetrative line of poetry penned by William Wordsworth, just as true today as it was two centuries ago: "What is glory? In the socket, see how dying tapers flare! What is pride? A whizzing rocket that would emulate a star."

A second case ranked at Category 15—and a particularly macabre one—is that of serial killer Dorothea Puente, dubbed the "Death House Landlady," born in January of 1929 in Redlands, California. There are conflicting details regarding her childhood, due to her proclivity to fabricate elements of her personal history. She was one of anywhere from seven to eighteen children born to alcoholic parents. Her father, who sometimes held a gun to his head and threatened to commit suicide in front of Puente and her siblings, died of tuberculosis when she was eight years old. Her mother, an abusive prostitute, died in a motorcycle accident when Puente was nine or ten. After moving through several homes, she was sent to an orphanage, where she was allegedly sexually assaulted.[15]

At age sixteen, while working in a milkshake parlor by day and as a prostitute by night, she married a soldier named Fred McFaul, who had just returned from military service in World War II. In 1946, they had a daughter, followed by a second in 1948. One was sent to live with relatives, and the other given up for adoption. In late 1948, McFaul left her for unclear reasons, and she was later sentenced to a year in jail when it was discovered that she was forging checks to buy clothing and accessories. When she was released after a mere six months, she immediately violated the terms of her parole by skipping town. She was then impregnated during a casual sexual encounter with a stranger and had another daughter, also put up for adoption. In 1952, she married a Swedish man, Axel Johansson, with whom she lived in Sacramento during a stormy relationship of fourteen years. Flare-ups were typically prompted by Puente's appetites for drinking, gambling, and extramarital affairs.[16] Puente liked to tell improbable tales about meeting an array of celebrities during their time together, including John F. Kennedy and Jackie Onassis, and the glamorous film star Rita Hayworth. Later in life, Puente would claim to have spent time with Clint Eastwood, Ronald Reagan, and Spiro Agnew, among other luminaries. She would even relate that her husband was the brother of heavyweight boxing champion Ingemar Johansson, which, of course, was patently untrue.[17]

In 1960, Puente was arrested for working in a brothel, claiming she had no clue it was a house of ill repute and that she was simply visiting a friend. She was jailed for ninety days. She then spent another ninety days behind bars on a vagrancy charge. Puente, who was able to play the role of a loving, devoted caretaker, found work as a nurse's aide, looking after elderly and disabled persons in private homes, before shifting to managing boarding houses. In 1966, she and Johansson divorced, and, two years later, just shy of age forty, she married twenty-one-year-old Robert Jose Puente in Mexico. They opened a halfway house, which was shut down due to outstanding debts, and the two separated after just two short years. Not long before they divorced, they had acquired a three-story, sixteen-bedroom care home in Sacramento, which Puente took steps to secure for herself prior to the separation. Her fourth marriage, in 1976, was to Pedro Montalvo, a violent alcoholic to whom she had rented a room. It lasted a matter of months.[18]

Around this time, Puente began frequenting bars, seeking out the elderly, alcoholics, and people addicted to drugs who were receiving government benefits, warmly welcoming them to her boarding house. She earned a sterling reputation for her apparent humanitarianism and willingness to work with challenging individuals. It was eventually discovered that she was, in fact, forging boarders' endorsements on benefit checks and pocketing the money. In 1978, Puente was charged with thirty-four counts of treasury fraud and prohibited from operating a boarding establishment. She returned to working as an in-home caregiver, but little changed in her behavior. In the early 1980s, the unfeeling schemer drugged three women with tranquilizers to swipe checks, cash, and valuables from their homes. Once, she slipped a sedative into the drink of a seventy-four-year-old man and, as he swam in and out of consciousness, ransacked his home, removing a diamond ring from his finger as she strolled out the door. She was arrested for these crimes and sentenced to five years in prison. Unfortunately, despite the opinion of a state psychologist that she was dangerous and lacking in remorse, she was released for "good behavior" after just three years.[19]

In 1982, Puente opened another boarding house, unlicensed and in flagrant violation of the terms of her probation. In April of that year, a sixty-one-year-old friend and business partner, Ruth Monroe, began renting a room and, shortly thereafter, died of an overdose of codeine and acetaminophen. It has been alleged that this may have been Puente's first homicide and that she cleverly hornswoggled police into believing Monroe had committed suicide in the context of acute depression.[20]

Several weeks later, seventy-four-year-old Malcolm McKenzie, whom Puente had drugged and robbed, reported her to the authorities, and she was sentenced to five more years in jail. She passed the time corresponding with Everson Gillmouth, a seventy-seven-year-old retiree in Oregon. Released after completing only three years of her sentence, she and Gillmouth met and promptly made plans to marry. Puente convinced him that, beforehand, they should open a joint bank account. In November of 1985, Puente paid a handyman to build a two-by-three-by-six-foot box, supposedly for storage purposes, and, later, after she had filled it with mysterious contents and nailed it shut, he was called back to dump it along a riverbank. It was just some worthless junk, she explained. When the box was discovered by a fisherman months later, it was found to contain Gillmouth's horribly decomposed carcass. In the meantime, Puente continued to collect his pension. She told his concerned family that he was ill and would contact them as soon as he felt up to it. She also handed off the victim's truck to the repairman, saying it had been left behind by an old boyfriend.[21]

Three years later, police visited Puente's boarding house to inquire about a missing tenant, Alberto Montoya, who was developmentally disabled and who suffered from schizophrenia. Investigating some disturbed soil on her property, they discovered the remains of seventy-eight-year-old tenant Leona Carpenter. Seven bodies of victims who were suffocated after being drugged with sleeping pills were eventually disinterred, to which Puente remarked, plausibly feigning shock and bewilderment, "I don't know what to tell you." In reality, the corpses were being used to fertilize Puente's routinely complimented flowers and avocado tree. As police investigated, they initially did not suspect her, and she fled to Los Angeles, where she befriended an elderly pensioner in a bar. Then, when it was announced on television that the authorities had come to believe she might be responsible for multiple homicides, the man turned her in and she was returned to Sacramento. She was charged with nine murders, convicted of three, and sentenced to two life sentences. At the time of her arrest and trial, people could hardly detect any glimmer of a psychopathic multiple murderer in the diminutive, white-haired landlady of a Victorian boarding house, who whipped up large meals for the downtrodden and adopted stray cats. When the death penalty was under consideration, one juror reportedly remarked, "Executing Puente would be like executing mine [*sic*] or your Grandma." The killer displayed no remorse whatsoever, uniformly denying her guilt in the most emphatic of terms. She died in prison of natural causes in 2011, aged eighty-two years.[22]

CATEGORY 16

Category 16 is the ranking for self-centered, psychopathic individuals who commit two or more acts of extreme violence. This may include attempted or completed murder, but someone displaying a pattern of highly vicious acts even without homicide, such as intentionally disfiguring or crippling a victim, can be categorized here. Consequently, this will often be the most appropriate ranking for offenders who repeatedly commit rape or sodomy with adults or children but do not kill their victims, as well as individuals who commit two or more acts of necrophilia, in the absence of murder. Repeat rapists or necrophiles who do commit homicide will be ranked at Category 17 or higher, depending on a number of distinguishing factors we will discuss in the coming chapters. It is critical to note that if any of the individual's monstrous acts are intended for the purpose of any degree of torture of one or more human beings, a designation of no lower than Category 18 is required. However, the torture, killing, mutilation, or sexual maltreatment of animals, in the absence of any torture of human beings, can be assigned here.

Some repeat murderers in this category are so-called "masterminds" of superior intelligence who can evade capture for long stretches of time, possibly even for their entire lives. These types tend to be loners with remarkable technical skills, sometimes adept at communicating in code or building explosives. They also tend to employ clever techniques of concealing finger-prints, footprints, DNA, and other potential evidence. Their attacks are gen-erally so random and vicious that an entire geographic area is set on edge, and they sometimes take extended breaks between killings, leaving the public terrified as it waits for the next terrible crime to transpire. These killers are sometimes motivated by a sheer loathing of society, which they consider a mass of ignorant, unthinking fools, while others are attention seekers with a lust for power over others. Unable to attain celebrity status through socially acceptable means, this type is resolutely willing to do so through homicide.

Other crimes in this category are so gruesome in nature that they will shock and horrify those who hear about them. Consider, for instance, the case of Norman Roderick Harrell, a truck driver and avid hunter about whom little is known, beyond the grisly double homicide of which he was convicted at age forty-five. In May of 1993, fed up with demands for child support payments from forty-three-year-old Diane Magdeline Hawkins, a former girlfriend with whom he had a son, he slashed her throat, cut open her torso, and tore out her heart, intestines, and lungs. He then stabbed her thirteen-year-old daughter, Katrina Denise Harris, twenty-seven times in a bed, mostly in her head, with such ferocity that the knife was broken off in the girl's skull. She was nearly decapitated. Her heart, which was also cut out, was never recovered. Hawkins left behind five other children, one of whom, a twenty-two-month-old named Kiki, was found crying, seated alongside the blood-soaked remains of her older sister. At his trial, jurors were shown a hunting manual belonging to Harrell, in which instructions were given for "gutting" an animal, which closely resembled the manner in which he had butchered Hawkins and Harris.[23] Evidence suggested these murders were not carried out in the heat of some suddenly sparked passion but, unfathomably, plotted in advance. Thinking and scheming in private, the killer did not select some quick and tidy means of eliminating two people he found to be irksome but opted to slaughter them with sickening brutality. Indeed, as we move along the scale, we must steel ourselves for the degree of unspeakable evil we will encounter in its upper limits, to which a story like Harrell's is but a prelude. For now, let us discuss three other Category 16 cases that illustrate the wide variety of crimes desig-nated to this ranking.

Terry Driver was born in rural British Columbia in January of 1965. We do not know much about his parents, save that his father was a decorated Vancouver police officer. His relationships with his parents were reportedly positive ones, which, if true, would make him something of an outlier with regard to both the Gradations of Evil scale and criminology. There is some indication that he may have found himself craving the attention of his constantly busy father. He was reportedly diagnosed with "minimal brain dysfunction" and attention-deficit/hyperactivity disorder in early childhood, although he has denied recollection of any hyperactive behavior in his youth. Due to aggressiveness, he was placed in a special school for troubled youths from ages six to eleven while his younger siblings remained at home. At about twelve, he developed behavioral tics, including flexing his neck and shaking his head. He completed high school as part of a career preparation program in printing, going on to find work as a press operator. He attempted to join law enforcement, following in his father's footsteps, but was rejected. Afterward, he began monitoring the neighborhood in the manner of a cop, listening to one of his father's police radios and making hundreds of calls to a law enforcement tip line to report petty thefts and other crimes. If one imagines all members of law enforcement as stand-ins for Driver's father, it is understandable that he might crave their constant attention—eventually, at any cost whatsoever. At twenty-four, he was diagnosed with Tourette syndrome, and, a year later, he was married, eventually fathering two children.[24]

In Abbottsford, near Vancouver, in October of 1995, two sixteen-year-old friends, Tanya Smith and Misty Cockerill, were accompanying one another to a party at Cockerill's boyfriend's house. It was late at night, and they were chatting about superstitions surrounding the fact that it was Friday the thirteenth. Cockerill would later recall making an "inappropriate joke" to the effect of, "Watch some guy is going to jump out of the bushes and try to rape us." They laughed it off and continued strolling toward their destination. Suddenly, they stopped in their tracks at the sound of a man's voice—Driver's—asking if they wanted to "party," which they ignored. He asked again, and they turned, frozen with fear to notice that he was wielding an aluminum baseball bat. Shoving them into some bushes, he demanded that they remove their clothing, and Cockerill began to beg for their lives. Trying to figure out how to stall or escape him, she feigned an asthma attack, which failed to move or convince Driver, who callously laughed at her. The girls were on the ground, and, as he stood behind them, opening his pants, Cockerill struck him. Driver then bludgeoned her seven times in the head as she slipped into unconsciousness. She woke up hours later with a mixture of blood and cerebrospinal fluid streaming from one ear. Profoundly dazed, she wandered into a nearby hospital, where the sight of her prompted the triage nurse to scream in horror. Catching a glimpse of her own reflection in a window, she passed out a second time. Seven fragments of her skull were later found lodged in the surface of her brain. Four days later, Cockerill was informed by doctors that her friend had not survived the assault. Driver had raped and savagely beaten her, tossing her alive into the Vedder River, where she eventually drowned to death.[25]

Driver attended Smith's funeral with his two young children, playing the role of a baffled, concerned citizen. Over the next seven months, he made repeat calls to police, now not offering tips about local crimes but promising future attacks and taunting that they would never find him. Again, if we interpret all police officers as emblematic of his father, then it was he, symbolically, who would have to come looking for the attention-starved killer. Driver sneaked into the cemetery where his victim was buried, defacing her headstone with a sexual obscenity, a threat to the survivor of his attack, and the promise, "She wasn't the first, she won't be the last." After prying the grave marker from the ground with a crowbar, he first thought to place it near the river, where he had raped and murdered the teenager. Instead, he placed it on the news cruiser of a local radio station and phoned the operator, instructing him to step outside to see what he had left in the parking lot. Driver would later confess that he took pleasure in the ensuing media coverage.[26]

Days later, a local woman phoned the authorities, saying that a letter weighted with a pair of pliers had been hurled through her window, shattering the glass. Written on the envelope was, "From the Abby Killer, call 911." Like many attention-seeking offenders, Driver had adopted a catchy sobriquet that might be utilized in the press. In the enclosed missive, he spoke lewdly about the attacks on Smith and Cockerill and boasted of three prior assaults on Abbotsford women. When he mentioned having bitten Smith's nipple, a fact held back from the public, police knew he was, indeed, the killer. Details of the other referenced crimes also emerged. It was further alleged that Smith's killer had sexually assaulted a twelve-year-old girl after grabbing her from behind as she waited outside a friend's house, but she was able to slip away; that he attacked a second female from behind and struck her in the face; and that he had bludgeoned a third with a blunt instrument, leaving her unconscious and bleeding with a nearly fatal skull fracture.[27]

Two of the victims had been able to provide descriptions to police, which, paired with a voice recording from one of Driver's taunting calls, were released to the public. The killer's mother, Audrey Tighe, recognized his voice and informed the authorities. He was arrested in May of 1996 and ultimately convicted of the first-degree murder of Smith and the attempted slaying of Cockerill. He was sentenced to life in prison without parole for twenty-five years. In 2000, Driver was convicted for attacks on two of his other victims and designated a dangerous offender, allowing for his indefinite incarceration. Cockerill, making the most of a horrible experience, from which she reportedly still physically suffers, heroically took up work as a bereavement counselor, assisting families of the victims of homicides.[28]

In Category 16, we also find the unusual case of Gwendolyn Graham and Cathy Wood, a female couple who committed five serial murders together, as part of a "love bond" between them. Our information about their backgrounds is somewhat limited. Graham was born in California in August of 1963 and raised in Tyler, Texas. She was described as "quiet and respectful" during her school days and as always looking somewhat sad. She would later make the claim, never substantiated, that she was a victim of sexual advances made by her father. At twenty-four, she took a job as a nurse's aide at the Alpine Manor Nursing Home in Grand Rapids, Michigan. Her superior there was Wood, also an aide, who was born in March of 1962. Wood married in adolescence, and, when she and her husband separated seven years later, she was left completely alone. Graham and Wood hit it off right away, and, by 1986, a romance had developed between them.[29]

Wood reportedly fell passionately in love with Graham, who was the more dominant and sexually experimental. For erotic reasons, Graham enjoyed binding her and choking her to the point of near loss of consciousness.[30] By January of 1987, this was no longer enough. The pair began achieving sexual thrills by collaborating to smother elderly female patients at the nursing home, sometimes just before making love. Note that the erotic stimulation did not arise from raping or sexually assaulting the victims, which would have warranted a ranking of Category 17, rather than 16. In their first murder, Graham entered the room of a woman with Alzheimer's disease, selected because of her inability to defend herself, and suffocated her with a washcloth as Wood kept watch. The killers felt that their shared knowledge of the crime prevented either one from leaving the relationship, thereby strengthening the bond between them. Over the next four months, they repeated the ghastly routine four more times. The patients, who ranged from ages sixty-five to ninety-seven, were all suffering from some form of dementia and totally incapacitated. Each was asphyxiated by Graham with a washcloth held to her mouth and nostrils while Wood stood guard. The couple turned the selection of their victims into a macabre game, aiming to choose women whose initials collectively spelled "MURDER." When this proved challenging, they decided to count each killing as a "day," and Wood penned a poem to Graham in which she pledged, "You'll be mine forever and five days." Graham reportedly began collecting souvenirs from the victims in order to relive their deaths, including a handkerchief, an ankle bracelet, a brooch, and a set of dentures, although these mementos have never been recovered.[31]

By April of 1987, the women's relationship was beginning to sour. Wood was uncomfortable with the notion of killing on her own to demonstrate her love to Graham and felt relieved and fortunate when she was transferred to another shift at the facility. In the meantime, Graham began dating another female coworker, traveling with her to Texas and leaving Wood feeling abandoned for the second time in her life. Graham found hospital work back in Tyler. Eventually, Wood confessed her crimes to her estranged husband, and, several months later, she related the killings to the authorities. Both women were arrested in December of 1988.[32]

During the subsequent trial, Wood copped a plea bargain, testifying, in exchange for a reduced sentence, that it was the domineering, hotheaded

Graham who planned and carried out the killings while she merely served as the lookout. Graham protested her innocence, claiming that the murders were part of a "mind game" of Wood's. Despite the absence of physical evidence, the jury was compelled by testimony from Graham's new lover, who reported that Graham had informed her of the five homicides at the Alpine Manor Nursing Home. Graham was found guilty on five counts of murder and one count of conspiracy to commit murder, resulting in five life sentences—that is, forever for five "days." Wood, charged with one count of second-degree murder and one count of conspiracy to commit second-degree murder, was sentenced to twenty years on each count.[33] A book about the case by Lowell Cauffiel alternatively portrays Wood as a psychopathic schemer who may have concocted the entire story to put Graham away for life in retaliation for leaving her for another woman, or else committed the murders herself and then framed Graham for crimes of which she was innocent.[34] However, this is not the version of the facts accepted by the jury that deliberated the case in 1989.

Our final Category 16 case is of the attention-obsessed "mastermind" type, described in the opening of this chapter. Few criminals have entered the public imagination to the degree of the never captured Zodiac Killer of the 1960s and 1970s, with his taunting letters, infernal cryptograms, and techniques for cleverly evading detection. He inspired the fictitious cold-blooded psychopaths in two popular movies, 1971's *Dirty Harry* and 1990's *The Exorcist III*; was the subject of David Fincher's acclaimed 2007 film *Zodiac* and over a dozen books; has been referenced by rock and heavy metal song lyrics; and is believed to have influenced at least two copycats, the New York–based serial killer Heriberto Seda,[35] and Japanese child murderer Seito Sakakibara.[36] We imagine this is all just as the egomaniacal Zodiac would want it. While there have been thousands of suspects in the case since 1968, including a very small handful who were seriously considered,[37] the Zodiac Killer is either still at large or deceased. As a result of his anonymity, we have no pre-offense biographical information to provide. However, we have a wealth of information about his traits and motivations from eyewitness accounts, observations of his various crime scenes, and his own words, culled from the copious letters and cards he mailed to the press and a high-profile lawyer.[38]

Zodiac's first murder may have been that of eighteen-year-old Cheri Jo Bates on October 30, 1966, although this is a matter of some debate. At approximately 9:30 p.m., the eighteen-year-old was beaten and repeatedly stabbed to death with a short-bladed knife in an alley on the campus of California's Riverside City College. There were no indications of robbery or sexual assault, and police could identify no witnesses. After studying in the college library, Bates had walked to her car, which had been intentionally disabled in advance by her methodical and patient killer. A struggle apparently transpired. Police found a Timex watch on the ground, believed to be torn from the killer's wrist, and a footprint from a size 8 to 10 military-style boot in the earth nearby. Almost exactly one month later, an anonymous confession, containing details of the crime held back from the public, was mailed to the Riverside Police Department and a local newspaper, the *Press-Enterprise*. Written in all capital letters, it read, in part,[39]

SHE WAS YOUNG AND BEAUTIFUL
BUT NOW SHE IS BATTERED AND
DEAD. SHE IS NOT THE FIRST AND SHE WILL NOT BE THE LAST
I LAY AWAKE AT NIGHTS THINKING ABOUT MY
NEXT VICTIM. MAYBE SHE WILL BE THE
BEAUTIFUL BLOND THAT BABYSITS NEAR
THE LITTLE STORE AND WALKS DOWN THE
DARK ALLEY EACH EVENING ABOUT SEVEN.
OR MAYBE SHE WILL BE THE SHAPELY BLUE
EYED BRUNETT [*sic*] THAT SAID NO WHEN I
ASKED HER FOR A DATE IN HIGH SCHOOL.
BUT MAYBE IT WILL NOT BE EITHER. BUT I
SHALL CUT OFF HER FEMALE PARTS AND
DEPOSIT THEM FOR THE WHOLE CITY TO SEE
SO DON'T MAKE IT EASY FOR ME. KEEP
YOUR SISTERS, DAUGHTERS, AND WIVES OFF
THE STREETS AND ALLEYS.
MISS BATES WAS STUPID. SHE WENT TO
THE SLAUGHTER LIKE A LAMB. SHE DID
NOT PUT UP A STRUGGLE. BUT I DID.
IT WAS A BALL.

The killer proceeded to describe how he disabled the victim's car by pulling out the middle wire from the distributor. He then waited in the library for her to leave and followed her, watching as she drained the battery with each attempt to start the engine. He offered her a lift in his own vehicle, supposedly down the street, as they chatted amicably. We can envision, at once, that the killer must have seemed trustworthy and innocuous, with no hint of the brutality he had been meticulously plotting all along. As they were strolling along, he suddenly said, "It's about time," to which she asked, "About time for what?" His response was that it was about time for her to die. He explained that, after he pounced on Bates, he did feel her breast, but—and this is critical for our understanding of his motivations—he was more focused upon murdering her as an act of retaliation for rejection:

> ONLY ONE THING WAS ON
> MY MIND. MAKING HER PAY FOR THE BRUSH OFFS [*sic*]
> THAT SHE HAD GIVEN ME DURING THE YEARS PRIOR.
> SHE DIED HARD. SHE SQUIRMED AND SHOOK
> AS I CHOKED HER, AND HER LIPS TWITCHED.
> SHE LET OUT A SCREAM ONCE AND I KICKED
> HER HEAD TO SHUT HER UP. I PLUNGED THE KNIFE
> INTO HER AND IT BROKE. I THEN FINISHED THE
> JOB BY CUTTING HER THROAT. I AM NOT SICK.
> I AM INSANE. BUT THIS WILL NOT STOP
> THE GAME. THIS LETTER SHOULD BE PUBLISHED
> FOR ALL TO READ IT.

If the account was true, Bates may have known her killer. It seems unlikely, however, that she would have willingly accompanied him to his car at 9:30 at night, if she had repeatedly turned him down for dates in the past. It is more probable that they were strangers and that he had known her from afar. She was probably merely a symbol for the killer—an object of focus and displacement for years of rejection by a number of members of the opposite sex, whom he had clearly come to despise. We see evidence of this in the fantasy of mutilating female victims' genitalia. In addition to the scheming, cold-blooded nature and misogyny we can induce from the facts of the Bates case and the detailed confession, the killer's reference to the process of stalking and slaying female victims as "the game" is revealing: it suggests that he drew pleasure from the predatory process, as a means of asserting dominance and control over women. We also see enjoyment in the manipulation of police and the press, and a desire to use the media as a means of provoking fear and attention from the general public. A profound egocentricity is observed in these features of the case, as well as in his demand that his letter be published for "all to read." Indeed, in March of 1971, Zodiac wrote to the *Los Angeles Times*, apparently confessing to the murder of Bates,[40] but, as we shall see, it was not unlike him to take credit for unsolved crimes possibly perpetrated by other people, as a means of building up his victim count and developing his frightening public persona.

In December of 1966, six months after the Bates murder, a poem was discovered in the Riverside City College library, etched into the surface of a desk, in handwriting that would later be attributed to Zodiac. Note the lack of capitalization and poor grammar, almost certainly contrived by an obviously intelligent individual:[41]

Sick of living / unwilling to die
cut.
clean.
if red /
clean.
blood spurting,
dripping,
spilling;
all over her new
dress.
oh well,
it was red
anyway.
life draining into an
uncertain death.
she won't
die this time
someone'll find her.
just wait till
next time.
rh

The significance of the two letters at the close of the poem has never been determined. They may be the author's initials, although they are not those of any seriously considered Zodiac suspect.

Several months later, on April 30, 1967, the police and *Press-Enterprise* received copies of another anonymous letter, this time handwritten. The woman's grieving father received a third copy: "BATES HAD TO DIE THERE WILL BE MORE." Each was signed with an indecipherable letter or number, resembling a "2" or, intriguingly, a "Z."[42] It should be noted that, in 1970, analysis by handwriting expert Sherwood Morrill linked the desktop poem and 1967 letters to the individual who later identified himself as Zodiac,[43] suggesting that, if he did not murder Bates, he was at least in the Riverside area, insinuating himself into the case.

Two years after the murder of Bates, there was a double homicide in Vallejo, California, for which Zodiac would also eventually take credit, demonstrating knowledge of the crime scene that only the perpetrator and police would know. Shortly after 11:00 p.m. on December 20, 1968, seventeen-year-old varsity athlete David Faraday and sixteen-year-old Betty Lou Jensen were sitting in his station wagon on a graveled parking area along remote Lake Herman Road, on the city's outskirts. It was their first date, and the area was commonly used by young people as a lovers' lane. Suddenly, someone approached, firing two bullets into the left side of the car in what appears to have been an effort to herd them out of the vehicle's right door. As Faraday emerged, the stranger pressed the barrel of his gun behind the boy's left ear and pulled the trigger, exploding his skull. He fell into the rear of the car, where he expired. Jensen fled on foot and was pursued by the attacker, who, from ten feet behind under a cloak of almost complete darkness, shot her five times in the back, in a remarkably tight pattern. She died on the road, about thirty-three feet from the car. It would later emerge that he had taped a small flashlight to the scope of his gun, allowing him to see precisely where a bullet would penetrate the victim. There were no signs of robbery or sexual assault, and no witnesses were identified.[44] Many facts of this double homicide are noteworthy, in light of our discussion of the misogyny and the enjoyment related to the manipulation and hunting of people seen in the Bates case. The killer seemed less interested in the male victim, who was promptly eliminated, and the female victim was pursued, probably thrilling the shooter by screaming and displaying unimaginable terror as she fled in the dark. There was also a similar boastful confession, provided to both the police and multiple newspapers. It came following another murder, which occurred nearly seven months later.

Just after midnight, at the close of Fourth of July festivities, on July 5, 1969, Darlene Ferrin, a twenty-two-year-old waitress, was sitting with nineteen-year-old laborer Mike Mageau in the isolated parking lot of Vallejo's Blue Rock Springs Park. As they sat talking, a car abruptly pulled up behind theirs and the driver approached them, holding a powerful flashlight. Imagining him to be a police officer, they readied themselves to show identification. Without warning, the stranger pumped three bullets into Ferrin and two into Mageau with a 9mm semiautomatic pistol. When Mageau howled in pain, the assailant returned to fire two more shots at each victim. This afforded Mageau a look at the attacker. Ferrin expired about a half hour after the shooting, and Mageau recovered and provided authorities his description of the killer. He was a Caucasian male in his late twenties to early thirties, five feet eight or five feet nine in stature, with a stocky build, a round face, and brown hair.[45]

There was, as in the previously described crimes, no robbery or sexual assault. Minutes after Ferrin's death, the police department in Vallejo received a call from a man claiming responsibility for the "double murder." After directing the dispatcher to the scene of the crime, he added, "I also killed those kids last year," and closed with a deep, taunting "Good-bye" before hanging up the phone. The call was later traced to a phone booth directly in front of the sheriff's office, implying that Zodiac was not only brazen but also interested in observing the police activity he had stirred up. Notably, the killer was also able to view Ferrin's home from the booth.[46] Moreover, the victim's husband, along with his parents and brother, began receiving phone calls consisting of only heavy breathing within an hour and a half of her murder, long before the story was circulated in the press.[47] These facts suggest that the killer may have personally known Ferrin or, at the very least, been stalking her. Let us also note that, as in the Faraday-Jensen case, the perpetrator was more focused on the female in this shooting, as indicated by her being shot more times and Mageau receiving less serious injuries, which allowed him to survive the assault.

On the last day of July in 1969, three newspapers, Vallejo's *Times-Herald*, and San Francisco's *Examiner* and *Chronicle*, all received letters from someone who took credit for both the Lake Herman Road double homicide and the attack on Ferrin and Mageau, correctly specifying the ammunition used, the number of shots fired, the positions of the bodies, the location of a wound to Mageau's knee, and the pattern on the dress Ferrin had been wearing. He also sent each paper one-third of a complex cipher, comprised of 408 mysterious-looking symbols, and claimed his identity was contained therein. The author threatened that if the cryptograms were not published, he would go on a spree and murder a dozen people. The ciphers were subsequently printed.[48] While the Office of Naval Intelligence, CIA, FBI, and NSA struggled to decode them, Donald Gene Harden, a history and economics teacher, sat down to give it a go, later assisted by his wife, Bettye. She cleverly surmised that the egocentric type of individual probably behind the killings and the codes would begin with the word "I." She also envisioned that he would use the word "kill" so that the opening phrase might be something like, "I like killing." Her intuitions were on the mark. With that phrase decoded, the remainder of the cryptogram gradually gave up its secrets. The murderer had developed a substitution cipher, in which each letter of the alphabet had been replaced by a letter or symbol. They discovered that the creator had laid a series of clever traps. He used one symbol fifteen times to lead code breakers into incorrectly concluding that it stood for E, the most commonly used letter in the English language. For the actual letter E, he employed seven different symbols. He also appeared to intentionally misspell words. The disturbing message, which lacked punctuation, probably as another ruse to impede deciphering, read, in part,[49]

I LIKE KILLING PEOPLE
BECAUSE IT IS SO MUCH
FUN IT IS MORE FUN THAN
KILLING WILD GAME IN THE FORREST [sic] BECAUSE
MAN IS THE MOST DANGEROUE [sic]
ANAMAL [sic] OF ALL TO KILL
SOMETHING GIVES ME THE
MOST THRILLING EXPERIENCE
IT IS EVEN BETTER THAN GETTING
YOUR ROCKS OFF WITH A GIRL

The author went on to explain that he was killing to collect slaves to serve him in the afterlife. This was probably a red herring to mislead investigators into believing that he was delusional or driven by occult spiritual beliefs, but we do not know this for certain. Even if it were a total fabrication of Zodiac's, the thematic content of his stated motivation was revealing of his grandiosity and hunger for power and domination.

It is interesting to note that his message made a reference to Richard Connell's haunting 1924 short story "The Most Dangerous Game," in which Count Zaroff, a merciless hunter who is weary of shooting beasts, lures people to a secluded island to hunt them instead.[50] It is interesting to note that both *Zaroff* and *Zodiac* begin with the uncommon letter Z. The killer's final point in the excerpt provided here lays bare that he was less interested in sexual thrills than he was in the rush of adrenaline he experienced while pursuing and killing a victim, and the superiority he felt while doing so. Despite his promise to provide his name, the author refused to give it in the actual solution. A week after sending the ciphers, he would again write to the *Examiner*, opening with what would thereafter be his ominous nom de plume: "This is the Zodiac speaking." He proceeded to provide more uncirculated details about the Lake Herman Road and Blue Rock Springs crimes.[51]

Zodiac's most bizarre attack took place on September 27, 1969. Two Pacific Union College students, twenty-year-old Bryan Hartnell and twenty-two-year-old Cecelia Ann Shepard, were relaxing on a blanket on a remote patch of shoreline along glorious Lake Berryessa near Napa. Shepard spied a stocky man watching them, who slipped into a grove of trees, only to reemerge and move closer and closer toward them. He was stalking his quarry. After slipping behind another tree, he popped up again, having donned a midnight black ceremonial hood, with a rectangular shape and a panel that came down over his chest. It was emblazoned with a cross-circle symbol that might evoke the image of a gun snipe. The man's eyes were disguised with clip-on sunglasses, which covered two eyeholes in the mask. On the right side of his belt was a gun holster and, on the left, a ten- to twelve-inch blade in a sheath. On the whole, the costume—not necessary for homicide but probably part of some elaborate psychological fantasy—gave Zodiac the macabre look of a medieval executioner. Several of its features have reminded some of Count Zaroff's hunting attire in RKO's 1932 film adaptation of Connell's story.

The mysterious stranger approached Hartnell and Shepard, holding out a semiautomatic pistol. The couple engaged him in conversation, and he claimed he was a prison escapee who had killed a guard and needed money to flee to Mexico. This was no doubt a fabrication to conceal what were his actual intentions from the start—it makes little sense to wear such an elaborate outfit to a routine robbery. It is also peculiar that the attacker waited only moments before revealing his actual objective. One wonders why he would bother to make pretense of a theft for such a brief period of time, unless catching the victims off guard with a sudden violent assault was part of the thrill for him. The lie may also have served the function of keeping the victims as calm and manageable as possible, until they were incapacitated. To that end, Zodiac demanded that Shepard bind Hartnell with clothesline, which he pulled from his back pocket, before the attacker did the same to her. Then, as Shepard and Hartnell lay on their stomachs, the costumed man abruptly began stabbing them with his lengthy blade. He assaulted Hartnell first, piercing his back six times as Shepard looked on in horror.[52] She was, in turn, stabbed twenty-four times. Following stabs to her back, she rolled over in pain and was pierced in each breast, the groin, and the stomach.[53] The fact that she was stabbed so many more times than Hartnell and in a more vicious manner further supports the notion that Zodiac may have felt more rage toward female victims, but whether there was a sexual element displayed here, in the mutilation of her female parts, is open to speculation. After the brutal attack, Zodiac quietly strolled away, hiking five hundred yards back up to the road, where he drew his cross-circle symbol on Hartnell's car door with a felt-tip pen, and above it notations regarding the locations and dates of his various attacks. He then phoned the Napa County Sheriff's Office from a payphone to report the crime.[54]

Shepard was conscious enough to describe the attacker when deputies arrived. She lapsed into a coma and died two days later. Hartnell, bleeding heavily, survived.[55] At the scene of the crime, investigators discovered size 10 1/2 prints made by Wing Walker boots. As these are special footwear used by military personnel to walk on the wings of planes, it was postulated that Zodiac may have had a military background.[56]

Two weeks later, on the night of October 11, 1969, a passenger boarded a taxi in the Presidio Heights neighborhood of San Francisco.

The driver, twenty-nine-year-old Paul Stine, was driving a cab to make ends meet while earning his doctoral degree in English. After they arrived at the intended destination, the corner of Washington and Maple Streets near the Presidio, the car was either redirected or mistakenly wound up a block away, at Washington and Cherry Streets. This repositioning of the cab, while seemingly insignificant, has, in fact, been a matter of considerable conjecture. Whatever the reason, the passenger proceeded to press a 9mm semiautomatic pistol to Stine's head and pull the trigger, killing him at the scene before taking his wallet and keys, probably to falsely suggest a robbery to police, and a large portion of his striped shirt. Bloody fingerprints, potentially left by the killer, were recovered by investigators. They also interviewed three child witnesses, who saw the horrific episode unfold from a window. Police did encounter a man lumbering along Cherry, but, because their dispatcher had mistakenly told them to be on the lookout for an African American suspect, they never stopped and questioned him. It was, in fact, Zodiac. When the error was caught, they were able to give a physical description that matched what had already been established about the multiple murderer.[57] The Stine killing was originally interpreted as a petty theft that had gone badly, but, two days later, Zodiac sent a letter to the *Chronicle*, taking credit for the shooting and—lest anyone doubt him— enclosing a swatch of the cabbie's blood-soaked shirt. The killer also upped the ante, creating pandemonium by threatening to shoot out the front tire of a school bus, "then pick off the kiddies as they come bouncing out."[58] One envisions the power he might have felt, manipulating the police and the newspapers, and the nameless masses, through which he glided like an unseen serpent. By moving to a new, larger city and murdering a random male, rather than attacking a couple, Zodiac had altered his modus operandi so that now nobody could feel safe from the unknown killer. This may very well have been his purpose in slaying Stine.

On November 8, 1969, Zodiac mailed a greeting card to the *Chronicle*, containing a 340-character cryptogram that has never been solved. The postscript to his note in the card read, "Could you print this new cipher on your front page? I get awfully lonely when I am ignored, so lonely I could do my thing!!!!!!"[59] The following day, he sent a letter to the same paper, claiming that, since the police had told "lies" about him, he would no longer announce his murders, making them look like routine killings and accidents.[60] Indeed, as already noted, the Stine murder was initially understood as a commonplace stickup, gone awry. Celebrated FBI profiler John Douglas, reconsidering this development in the case decades later, wondered whether Zodiac was frightened or had his ego impugned by his close encounter with police on the night of the Stine shooting. He posited that Zodiac might have sought to overcompensate for this with the terrifying school bus threat and by emphasizing that the cops were incapable of catching him because he was too slippery for them. The killer boastfully explained that, on the night of the Stine shooting, officers actually had stopped and spoken to him, and he sent them off on a wild goose chase. Moreover, he might have been scared enough to stop killing—while still craving constant, wide-scale attention and power. In making his statement about no longer announcing his killings and making them appear like garden-variety crimes, Zodiac cleverly made it possible to take credit for any unsolved case he wished. He could now keep everyone wondering, confused, and frightened, without having to commit any risky additional murders.[61] Zodiac also enclosed a hand-drawn, plausible-looking diagram of a bomb, calling it a "death machine" and his "masterpiece," and taunting that it would be a tremendous challenge to try to locate it.[62]

On the one-year anniversary of the Faraday-Jensen murders on December 20, 1969, Zodiac mailed a letter to eminent attorney Melvin Belli, enclosing another portion of Stine's shirt. He claimed that he wanted the lawyer's help, saying that a "thing" in him would not allow him to reach out and he was finding it "extreamly [sic] difficult to hold it in check."[63] It is unclear whether this was a sincere cry for help or, as Douglas has surmised, a ploy for sympathy during a probably lonely holiday season.[64] At any rate, he never actually connected with Belli for assistance.

Consistent with the hypothesis that Zodiac was interested in artificially elevating his victim count while not actually perpetrating additional crimes, he boasted of ten murders in an April 20, 1970, letter to the *Chronicle*, whereas only five could be accounted for, if Bates is included in the sum.[65] Two months later, he wrote to the *Chronicle* again, enclosing a thirty-two-symbol cipher and a map of the San Francisco Bay area with a cross-circle drawn over Mount Diablo, surrounded by mysterious numbers. He claimed the two clues would lead to the location of a bomb, supposedly buried and set to detonate in the autumn—which never transpired.

Zodiac also boasted that he had killed twelve victims, vaguely claiming credit for shooting "a man sitting in a parked car,"[66] a possible reference to the recent, never solved killing of police sergeant Richard Radetich.[67] This execution was supposedly an act of retribution for noncompliance with a request Zodiac made in late April that people wear buttons featuring his cross-circle symbol.[68] He claimed in yet another letter sent to the paper on July 24, 1970, that, as further payback for this slight, he carried out an unsolved crime reported in the press, involving a woman named Kathleen Johns.[69] Elements of the case, which ring true to Zodiac's patterns, have kept debate alive about whether he was, indeed, responsible for her harrowing experience of March 22, 1970.

That night, Johns was driving from San Bernardino to Petaluma, seven months pregnant and sitting alongside her ten-month-old daughter. On a highway near Modesto, a man in a car behind her began honking and flashing his headlights, prompting her to pull off the road. The driver pulled up, explaining, with credible concern, that he had noticed her right rear wheel wobbling. He offered to tighten the lug nuts. After doing so, the apparent Good Samaritan drove off and Johns began to merge back onto the highway. Just then, the purportedly tightened wheel detached itself, and the stranger returned, now offering the stranded woman a lift to the nearest service station. She boarded his car with her young daughter. It struck Johns as odd that they, in fact, sped past several stations without stopping and that he would change the subject whenever she pointed this out. At some point, she asked, "Do you always go around helping people on the road like this?" He reportedly responded, "When I get through with them, they don't need any help." They drove for about thirty minutes, back and forth around the back roads of the town of Tracy, until he abruptly turned to her and remarked, "You know you're going to die. You know I'm going to kill you." To this he added, "I'm going to throw the baby out." When the driver stopped at an intersection, Johns sprung from the car with her daughter and hid in a field, prompting the driver to pursue them with a flashlight while calling out that she had no need to fear him. This calls to mind the false reassurances given to Hartnell and Shepard before they were viciously stabbed at Lake Berryessa. The driver ultimately gave up on finding Johns and her infant and left the scene. Her car was later discovered, torched and gutted out. While speaking with investigators after the ordeal, Johns reportedly recognized the face on a Zodiac wanted poster in the police station as that of the man who had taken her and her child on the terrifying ride.[70] If the Bates murder of 1966 was, indeed, the work of Zodiac, the similar method of posing as a kindhearted stranger who offers a lift to a young woman whose car he has sabotaged does make this case worth considering.

Zodiac sent the *Chronicle* one of his most peculiar letters on July 26, 1970.[71] Returning to his narcissistic wish to see people wearing Zodiac pins and his alleged belief that he would someday be the master of those he has killed in the afterlife, he made a new threat, which revealed a sadistic nature, not readily detected from his expedient murders that involved no intentional prolongation of pain. He also upped his supposed victim count to thirteen. He wrote,

> If you do not wear any type of buttons, I shall (on top of everything else) torture all 13 of my slaves that I have waiting for me in Paradice [*sic*]. Some I shall tie over ant hills and watch them scream + twich [*sic*] and squirm. Others shall have pine splinters driven under their nails + then burned. Others shall be placed in cages + fed salt beef until they are gorged then I shall listen to their pleass [*sic*] for water and I shall laugh at them. Others will hang by their thumbs + burn in the sun then I will rub them down with deep heat to warm them up. Others I shall skin them alive + let them run around screaming.

Then, attempting a theatrical, creative turn, the killer began paraphrasing the song "The Punishment Fit the Crime" from W. S. Gilbert's and Arthur Sullivan's 1885 comic operetta *The Mikado*. He altered part of the "little list" laid out in the lyrics to provide a litany of things he would like to do to slaves and, in a sense, to everyone who had ever irked or slighted him:

> And all billiard players I shall have them play in a darkened dungen [*sic*] cell with crooked cues + Twisted Shoes. Yes I shall have great fun inflicting the most delicious of pain to my slaves.

Zodiac then switched from parodying the titular emperor in the operetta to paraphrasing Ko-Ko, the lord high executioner of Titipu. It is interesting, as we consider Zodiac's identification with this character, to note that, prior to earning this lofty, murderous position, Ko-Ko was a rather insignificant individual who had worked as a tailor. We do not know if Zodiac was a tailor—certainly, his outfit at Lake Berryessa does suggest some skill with sewing—but, at any rate, it is easy to see why the concept of a commonplace person suddenly holding the power of life and death in his hands might have appealed to him. Part of Zodiac's revamped ditty ran,

> As some day it may hapon [*sic*] that a victom [*sic*] must be found. I've got a little list. I've got a little list, of society offenders who might well be underground who would never be missed who would never be missed.

The list ends, "But it really doesn't matter whom you place upon the list, for none of them be missed, none of them be missed." It is interesting to note that, while the tune was intended to communicate the smallness and worthlessness of possible future victims, it could also be interpreted as referring to Zodiac himself—to his own feelings of invisibility. Note that Zodiac followed up his petty tirade with unrelated comments about his Mount Diablo code and the bomb he had allegedly hidden underground. This seems in accord with the aforementioned hypothesis by Douglas, regarding the killer's compensation for feelings of inferiority, with dramatic, violent threats.

On October 27, 1970, Paul Avery, the *Chronicle* reporter covering the Zodiac case, received a disturbing Halloween card featuring a skeleton on the cover, with the words, "From Your Secret Pal: I feel it in my bones, you ache to know my name, and so I'll clue you in." Inside, the printed message read, "But, then, why spoil the game! BOO!" Zodiac had pasted a skeleton alongside the text, suspended in the fashion of a crucified person. He marked the card up with his cross-circle symbol; the words "Paradice" [*sic*] and "Slaves," surrounded by "By Fire," "By Gun," "By Knife," and "By Rope"; images of peering eyes; and the ominous threat, "Pee-a-boo, you are doomed." Soon thereafter, Avery received an anonymous letter, which first brought to light the possible link between the Cheri Jo Bates murder and the Zodiac case.[72]

Four months after Avery unearthed the Riverside case, Zodiac wrote, for the first time, to the *Los Angeles Times*, the paper with the largest circulation in California, which comes as no surprise. Needling the authorities for their failure to apprehend him, he wrote, "I do have to give them credit for stumbling across my riverside [*sic*] activity, but they are only finding the easy ones, there are a hell of a lot more down there. The reason that Im [*sic*] writing to the Times is this, They [*sic*] don't bury me on the back pages like some of the others." After confessing to a crime he may not have committed, he gave his latest probably grossly exaggerated victim tally of "17+."[73] After this, Zodiac fell silent for years—perhaps due to incarceration or a period of treatment in a psychiatric hospital.

The next confirmed letter from Zodiac was sent to the *Chronicle* in late January of 1974. This time, he praised William Friedkin's 1973 film *The Exorcist*, based upon William Peter Blatty's 1971 novel of the same name, as "the best satirical comidy [*sic*] that I have ever seen." In addition to more dark *Mikado* humor, he included a peculiar, never explained symbol and the new murder tally of "37."[74] Six months later, the killer penned an anonymous note to the same paper, in his distinctive penmanship, but lacking the usual probably intentionally misspelled words, which helps to establish that he was feigning poor spelling all along. He expressed "consternation" concerning the paper's "poor taste" and "lack of sympathy" in running ads for Terrence Malick's 1973 film *The Badlands*, loosely based upon the real-life 1958 killing spree of Charles Starkweather and Caril Ann Fugate, and set in the year following their actual crimes. The advertisements read, "In 1959, most people were killing time. Kit and Holly were killing people." Zodiac remarked, "In light of recent events, this kind of murder-glorification can only be deplorable at best (not that glorification of violence was ever justifiable)." Two months later, Zodiac appears to have sent another anonymous note to the *Chronicle*, this time voicing pseudo-concern about anti-feminist columnist Count Marco Spinelli. "Put Marco back in the hell-hole from whence it came—he has a serious psychological disorder—always needs to feel superior—I suggest you refer him to a shrink." This was, of course, the proverbial pot calling the kettle black, and was probably penned in an ironic tone for the killer's own amusement.[75]

With that, the mysterious Zodiac seems to have vanished for good—assuming, of course, that he did not, in reality, go on killing and making his crimes look like routine ones that no one would ever think to link with him. Indeed, on several occasions, there has been speculation that homicides by other serial killers might, in fact, be the work of Zodiac. This has included, for instance, the case of the Unabomber, Ted Kaczynski,[76] a three-time murderer with a similar "mastermind" profile. Zodiac's case in San Francisco was marked "inactive" in 2004 but then reopened in 2007. It remains active in Napa and Riverside.[77] At the time of this writing, investigators are working with a private laboratory that is hoping to create a DNA profile of the killer, using envelopes from two of his letters. Such a profile might allow for the identification of Zodiac through a genealogy website, a technique that, in 2018, led to the establishment of Joseph James DeAngelo as a suspect in another decades-old California cold case, that of the Golden State Killer.[78]

Douglas, reflecting upon the way the killer slipped into silence and the unlikeliness of his reemergence, postulated that Zodiac may have committed suicide, due to a sense that there were no more victims to claim and no reason to perpetuate the dialogue.[79] We may never know. Whether or not the man who called himself Zodiac is ever named, he has long achieved just what he seems to have been hoping for: lots of people "tortured" and fascinated by the grand, Sphinx-like riddle of his words and actions, as he lives on, well past his criminal career, in a sort of folklore afterlife.

CHAPTER SIX

SERIAL MURDER

With the transition to Category 17, we move into the darkest territory of the Gradations of Evil scale—the six designations covering a wide array of serial killers, torturers, and sadists. Such offenders are generally assigned to Categories 17, 18, 20, and 22. Persons designated to Category 19, who terrorize and subjugate others for sexual, financial, or other purposes, and Category 21, who subject victims to extreme torture, are not known to have committed murder. As noted in our first chapter, however, the problematic current definition of *serial killer* employed by the FBI, which omits any reference to underlying motivation, makes it possible for a multiple murderer to technically meet criteria for serial killing and still be ranked below 17 on the continuum. It is known that, almost invariably, this type of offender kills for the purpose of psychological gratification, and, in the majority of cases, this will involve the offender having sexual contact with victims. However, as noted by the FBI, this is by no means the only motivating factor. The notion that serial killing is uniformly about sexual gratification is a myth about this type of crime, perpetuated by depictions in nonacademic literature and films, as well as on television. In reality, there are serial killers who are driven by thrill seeking, financial gain, extreme anger, and the desire to draw personal attention.[1] With that having been said, it is critical to note that consideration of the specific primary motivation of a killer is a sine qua non for ranking on the Gradations of Evil scale. It is the degree of amorality associated with a repeat murderer's intentions, drives, and specific behaviors, as well as the presence or absence of malice aforethought, that establish the offender's most appropriate designation. Thus, serial killers ranked 17 and higher on the scale are not those motivated by attention seeking, greed, or elimination of people who impede their plans, but by strivings for domination and power over others through repeat murder, sadistic torture, or rape or sexual assault.

There are other myths worth dispelling before we proceed with our discussion of the scale. For instance, serial killers are commonly envisioned as dysfunctional loners while, in reality, many live seemingly normal lives and can go about undetected for long periods of time.[2] Many people falsely believe the typical profile of a serial killer is that of a Caucasian male in his middle to late twenties. First, these offenders actually arise from all racial categories.[3] This is made clear by statistical data from the invaluable Serial Killer Database (SKD) developed by Dr. Michael G. Aamodt of Radford University, and Drs. Terry Leary and Larry Southard of Florida Gulf Coast University. As of January of 2018, the SKD contained information about 4,995 serial killers and 13,961 victims of these offenders from the United States and other countries over a period of 118 years.[4] Analyses indicate that only 50.6 percent of US-based serial killers have been Caucasian, while 40.8 percent have been African American, 6.6 percent have been Hispanic, 1 percent have been Asian, and 1 percent have been Native American.[5] Second, only 26.7 percent of 3,204 US-based serial killers included in a 2016 report from the SKD committed their first murders in their middle to late twenties, and just 12.2 percent were both Caucasian and in this age range.[6] Contrary to another popular belief, serial killers do not typically commit their crimes over wide geographic areas but generally adhere to circumscribed areas in which they feel comfortable and in control, unless they are itinerant types or employed in capacities that require regular travel.[7] Serial killers are not all evil geniuses, who masterfully outwit law enforcement. In actuality, they can demonstrate anywhere from borderline to superior intellect.[8] The average IQ among 298 serial killers for whom this information is available is 93.6, which is in the normal range, relative to the general population. The median score is 85.5, which is in the low normal range. The standard deviation for these scores is 25.2–1.7 times the standard deviation of 15 seen in the general population, reflecting a mixture of very low and very high IQs.[9] They are only rarely "insane," by legal standards, and are far more likely to demonstrate disturbances of personality and interpersonal relationships than serious psychiatric impairment.[10] Finally, it is untrue that all serial killers simply cannot stop taking lives or that, on some level, they long to be captured and stopped.[11]

One popular belief about serial killers that holds up to empirical scrutiny is that they are almost always male, which, as the SKD tells us, is the case for an astounding 93 percent of identified worldwide serial killers and 91 percent of those who are US-based.[12] The vast majority of serial killers have been active in the United States, at 67.31 percent of all known offenders. England, the nation that has had the second-highest number of known serial killers, accounts for only 3.4 percent.[13]

Among 11,949 victims of US-based serial killers between 1900 and 2018, the average age has been 33.86, with a median of 30.[14] There have been victims as young as infancy and as old as age one hundred.[15] We see a nearly perfect split between males (49.5 percent) and females (50.5 percent).[16] The vast majority of victims have been Caucasian (67.2 percent), while 25.4 percent have been African American, 7 percent have been Hispanic, 1.8 percent have been Asian, and less than 1 percent have been Native American or Aboriginal.[17] Most were murdered in California (14.18 percent), while the least were killed in South Dakota (0.07 percent).[18] In terms of the most common methods of killing, analysis of 10,495 victims of serial killers in the United States yields that the most have been shot to death (44 percent), while many have been strangled (21 percent), stabbed (14.8 percent), bludgeoned (9.4 percent), or poisoned (6.9 percent). Quite rare have been murders by axe (1.4 percent), drowning (0.9 percent), smothering (0.6 percent), burning (0.6 percent), being run over with a vehicle of some kind (0.2 percent), drug overdose (0.2 percent), and neglect and/or abuse (0.1 percent).[19]

It is well established that most routine murders are committed by individuals who knew their victims during their lifetimes. Thus, it is not uncommon for law enforcement to initiate a homicide investigation by examining those who were closest to the deceased. In serial murder, by contrast, victims are generally unacquainted with their killers. This results in difficulty distinguishing the offender's purpose in committing a given homicide, and thus impedes identification of potential suspects. As a means of narrowing the focus of an investigation, authorities may attempt to discern unusual psychological motivations behind a potentially linked series of killings.[20]

To facilitate this process, since the 1980s, law enforcement, forensic psychiatry and psychology, and other disciplines have aimed to identify the specific drives underlying serial killing, which might be used to construct typologies or systems of classification. These are generally based upon studies of previous offenders, who are thankfully exceedingly rare, constituting no more than 1 percent of all homicides.[21] Some of the models developed to date have been simple and categorical, divvying up serial killers according to specific motivational or demographic factors, or the overall degree of organization displayed in their behaviors and crimes. In broad terms, serial killers generally fall into four categories: those who commit serial sexual homicide, the most commonly encountered variety; "Angels of Death," who are physicians, nurses or other medical professionals who intentionally murder or harm individuals under their care; mothers who smother to death one infant after another, usually at intervals of at least a year between killings; and misanthropic males who murder men, women, and children at intervals, due to a generalized hatred of humankind and with no sexual motivations.[22]

The previously mentioned *Crime Classification Manual*, now in its third edition, categorizes serial killers as *organized*, *disorganized*, or *mixed*.[23] The organized type typically plans his or her crimes and escape tactics methodically, sometimes for weeks, months, or years. After a period of targeting and stalking, a victim is charmed or tricked during some social interaction and then abducted. Control is exerted over the captive, once he or she is brought to some isolated location. This type of offender usually prepares an assortment of weapons and restraints. After the victim is killed, the body is transported elsewhere, typically to a location where it is unlikely to ever be found. These individuals usually own vehicles. They are sometimes well aware of police investigative procedures and are adept at destroying evidence. Such killers are generally in meaningful relationships or married, sometimes raising children; intelligent, educated, and cunning; and competent and gainfully employed as skilled workers. Because of this, they are difficult for authorities to identify. They are avid followers of their own press. With each crime, the organized killer's criminal skills are improved. As a means of evading capture, the offender will sometimes change homes, or places of employment.[24]

The actions of disorganized serial killers are so random and chaotic that behavioral patterns are difficult to identify, making them even more challenging to apprehend than offenders of the organized type. Despite vague, intense fantasies about killing, the individual does not carefully plan crimes, which can transpire at any time, usually when an opportunity presents itself. The victim is typically assaulted with some object found nearby, such as a large rock or heavy tree branch, in a violent "blitz" attack, and then left out in the open, in the place of death. The corpse is often mutilated in an unusual and frenzied way, and body parts or souvenirs are sometimes carried away from the crime scene. Virtually no effort is made to disguise oneself, eliminate evidence, or establish an escape plan. These killers, who are generally of below average intellect or psychotic, typically display poor social skills and tend to live alone, be unemployed and unskilled, not own cars, and kill near their places of residence. Evidence is generally openly displayed in their homes.[25]

Mixed type serial killers exhibit a mélange of organized and disorganized traits and behaviors. When investigators attempting to establish a criminal profile from a crime scene detect both organized and disorganized traits, they sometimes posit that two or more offenders are responsible. It is also key to note that a homicide in this category might begin in an organized way but dilapidate into sheer chaos, due to lack of experience, to interruption while in progress, to drugs or alcohol, or some other factor.[26]

Criminologists Drs. Ronald Holmes, Stephen Holmes, and James De Burger have grouped serial killers' motives into the four categories of *visionary*, *mission oriented*, *power/control*, and *hedonistic*, although multiple motives may overlap in the same individual. Visionary types, who are quite rare, suffer from psychotic illness, believing they are compelled to kill by an unseen entity. This is most commonly God or the devil. Mission-oriented types feel justified in their crimes because they are "ridding the world" of certain individuals they perceive to be undesirable due to race, ethnicity, sex, gender, sexual orientation, religion, or lifestyle, such as promiscuity or prostitution. They are generally not psychotic. Power/control killers wish to gain and exert dominance over victims, sometimes as a means of dealing with long-standing feelings of inadequacy and powerlessness, secondary to childhood abuse or some other factor. When sexual elements are present here, they are part of the process of dominating victims and not motivated by bona fide lust. Hedonistic serial killers seek excitement and draw pleasure from murder, viewing victims as expendable means to an end. This group is subdivided into three subcategories: *lust killers*, *thrill killers*, and *comfort killers*. Lust killers are heavily fantasy oriented and seek sexual gratification from living or dead victims. The perpetrator feels the need to assert absolute control, dominance, and power over others, and pleasure is related to the infliction of pain or mutilation. They tend to select weapons that require closer intimacy with victims, such as knives, and may opt to use their bare hands. Thrill killers are excited by hunting victims and provoking pain and terror of a nonsexual nature as part of relatively brief homicides. Comfort killers seek material gain and easy lifestyles, and their victims are generally family members or close acquaintances.[27]

Other attempts at classification have taken into consideration variants within basic categories. For instance, in addition to distinguishing a sexually motivated serial murderer from one who kills for some other reason, a model might weigh whether a homicide was chiefly driven by rage or sadism. Unfortunately, these typologies tend to be impractical, in terms of actual use by law enforcement. Even if a serial killer's motivation can be established from observable data at a crime scene, the offender may actually have been driven by multiple psychological factors. Moreover, one's motivation may evolve over time. Consequently, the FBI has suggested the use of broader, non-inclusive categories of motivations for serial killing, which are used as general guidelines in serial homicide investigations.[28]

The driving factors noted by the bureau include anger, typically toward a certain subgroup of the population or toward society as a whole; financial gain, as seen in murders during robberies or for insurance money; criminal enterprise, where killing brings one income or status within a gang, drug ring, or organized crime group; and psychosis, which will be discussed at length when we arrive at Category 20. The FBI further notes that, sometimes, ideology is the motivation, as is the case for terrorist groups or those serial killers who target specific racial, gender, or ethnic groups. As indicated in our introduction, those who commit murder in the name of terrorist organizations are omitted from the Gradations of Evil scale. Most relevant to our discussion of Categories 17–22 are the FBI's final two categories—namely, sexually driven serial homicides, which we will discuss in the context of Category 17, and those motivated by power or thrill seeking, such that the offender feels empowered and/or excited when killing,[29] as we have just observed in our discussion of the Zodiac Killer.

Data from the SKD tell us that worldwide offenders from 1900–2018 have chiefly been motivated by sheer enjoyment, related to lust, nonsexual thrill or power (36 percent), followed by financial gain (30.2 percent), anger (16.5 percent), gang activity and/or criminal enterprise (5.1 percent), arrest avoidance (1.15 percent), convenience (1.11 percent), cult activity (0.94 percent), psychosis (0.6 percent), and attention (0.5 percent), as in cases involving Munchausen syndrome by proxy. Multiple motives were noted in 9.1 percent.[30]

The SKD also records the decades in which 4,752 serial killers, during the same 118-year period, are known to have committed their first homicides. We see that 80 appeared between 1900 and 1909, 81 between 1910 and 1919, 103 between 1920 and 1929, 88 between 1930 and 1939, 106 between 1940 and 1949, and 115 between 1950 and 1959. There is a clear intensification in the period from 1960 through 1969, with 305 serial murderers killing for the first time, followed by 798 between 1970 and 1979, 1,017 between 1980 and 1989, and 1,043 between 1990 and 1999. This pattern of increased new serial killer activity between 1960 and 1999 is true for both international and US-based offenders.[31] Interestingly, the pattern still emerges even if we more conservatively define a serial killer as having committed at least three, as opposed to two, homicides in separate events. During this four-decade period, especially from the late 1960s onward, serial murder, which had previously been quite rare, not only significantly increased in frequency but also tended to be, on balance, more heinous, cruel, and depraved than in earlier decades of the twentieth century. We will further expound upon this trend later in this volume, in our discussion of the era of "new evil," associated with overall trends seen in culture and crime in the last five decades. According to the SKB, in the United States, 1981 was the peak year for the most active serial killers, regardless of whether we use the two-victim (191) or three-victim (128) criterion.[32] The period of 2000 through 2009 showed a reduction in the number of new worldwide serial killers, at 714, and the period from 2010 through 2018 has yielded 302 to date—a noteworthy decline, seen both internationally and in the United States, which warrants explanation.[33]

How are we to explain the comparative rarity of serial killers—here, in the sense of men committing serial sexual homicide—prior to the 1960s? Some have suggested that the more sophisticated law enforcement techniques and improved record-keeping in electronic interstate data systems,

relative to the early half of the twentieth century, have facilitated the identification of this type of offender. Thus, some have suggested that serial
killing may have been similarly common in earlier decades but gone less
noticed. We have not, however, found any real support for the notion that
acts of serious violence were underreported in decades and even centuries past. Legal trials involving lethal aggression have routinely been well
reported in the Western world, at least since the advent of newspapers,
although, prior to the nineteenth century, the depth of coverage was related
to whether or not an offender was sentenced to death. In earlier times, even
"ordinary" murders, such as jealousy-related or spousal homicides, were
viewed as warranting execution and were, therefore, duly recorded and
widely circulated by the means of their respective eras.

In part II of our book, Dr. Stone and I will explore an alternative
explanation for the surge of serial killer activity by sexually perverse and
sadistic males, which we observe emerged between the late 1960s and the
late 1990s, overwhelmingly concentrated in the United States. We posit
that this reflected a fierce backlash on the part of some males—especially
working-class men—against women in the wake of the sexual revolution,
since the latter had become active in the workplace, attained access to contraceptives and abortion, and begun leaving abusive husbands. As we will
discuss in some detail, this fury does not appear to have vanished since the
1990s but to have reared its ugly head in other forms, sometimes less overt
than serial sexual homicide.

It is also worth noting that underreporting in earlier decades would
not explain the decline in the overall number of such offenders since the
late 1990s. It has been posited that improved law enforcement methods
may now increase the likelihood that a burgeoning serial killer will be
apprehended and incarcerated following a single homicide and prior to
the establishment of a series. It is also possible that in this era of security
cameras, the internet, and cellular phones, as well as a savvier public, it
may simply be more difficult for serial killers to locate victims and get away
with murdering them. At least in the United States, the drop may also be
reflective of the overall reduction seen in crimes of any type in the present
period, although levels are still nowhere near as low as they were prior
to the 1960s. The true reason, however, for this merciful decline may be
impossible to pinpoint with any degree of precision in the present moment,

until another generation has passed, allowing for retrospective, objective examination.

One intriguing hypothesis suggested by author Christopher Beam is that violent criminals, when aiming to act out in terrifying, shocking ways, may unwittingly draw upon the anxieties of their particular times and places—a hypothesis akin to the notion that horror and science fiction films and literature generally reflect what is most frightening in the cultural contexts in which they are created. Since the horrific terrorist attacks of September 11, 2001, the social narrative in the Western world has seemed to be more about bombs, mass shootings, and the annihilation of the human race, so criminals may not have abandoned serial murder so much as opted for more "current" and less serialized methods of playing out the same motivations we have delineated in the current chapter.[34]

As we discuss the horrifying cases at this end of the scale—and it will not be easy—we will note that some potentially causal elements commonly crop up in serial killers' life histories, generally dating to gestation or childhood.[35] Many of these offenders have significant family histories of psychiatric illness, alcoholism, illicit drug use, and/or behavioral and legal problems. The SKD tells us that 73.8 percent of serial killers were reportedly abused in childhood, in a manner that has generally been psychological (49.8 percent), physical (49.7 percent), or sexual (27.3 percent).[36] Neglect and abuse in childhood are known to increase the likelihood of future violence. Impaired social and emotional coping skills are also commonplace. Some cite the powerful influences of exposure to violent television, films, or pornography. Several of these offenders display no history of violence prior to some head injury or medical condition affecting the central nervous system. Attention deficits, epilepsy, or autism are sometimes seen. Drug and alcohol use, which have disinhibiting effects, can drive violence in serial murderers. In sum, there is probably no single factor that sets one on a trajectory toward serial sexual homicide or any of the less common categories of serial murder we have delineated here. Rather, this likely involves a complex interplay of heredity, biology, upbringing, social and environmental factors, and personal choices made throughout the process of development.[37] Certainly, additional research is required to identify the specific developmental pathways that generate these types of offenders.

Whatever the antecedents, the reader will also note several commonly encountered features among these offenders.[38] Psychopathy is almost universal among serial killers. A small number demonstrate severe mental illness, such as mania or psychosis. It has been proposed that a disproportionate number will demonstrate fire setting, bed-wetting past the age of twelve, and animal torture,[39] but this triad of traits is controversial, as we shall discuss in a later chapter.[40] A sense of powerlessness, sometimes related to abuse, neglect, or loss, often leads to the development of an intense fantasy life, involving themes of dominance, control, sexual conquest, and violence, which eventually spills over into real-life behavior.[41] Serial killers also frequently engage in *paraphilias*—that is, intense, frequent sexually arousing actions, situations, or fantasies of an abnormal nature, which might involve certain objects, children, or nonconsenting adults, or the infliction or enjoyment of pain or humiliation.[42] We will further discuss the latter topic as we progress to Category 17.

CHAPTER SEVEN
CATEGORY 17

Cruelty has a human heart,
And Jealousy a human face;
Terror the human form divine,
And Secrecy the human dress.
The human dress is forged iron,
The human form a fiery forge,
The human face a furnace seal'd,
The human heart its hungry gorge.

—William Blake, "A Divine Image," *Songs of Experience*

Category 17 is the designation for serial killers who are primarily motivated by rape or sexual assault of some other type, and who commit murder, albeit in sometimes extremely brutal ways, generally for the purpose of eliminating witnesses. There is no protracted physical torture, beyond the horrors of the sexual assault itself.

In other cases captured here, a killer repeatedly acts out a sexual fantasy having to do with complete domination over another human being, murdering the victim in order to achieve sexual gratification. Among more disorganized types in this category, such control and power fantasies are sometimes further expressed with postmortem mutilation, or necrophilic actions involving corpses or body parts. On occasion, the inanimate victim is manipulated, like a doll or marionette, according to the will of the murderer.

Understanding this type of offender requires some discussion of the subject of rape, an evil affecting individuals of every age, sex, gender, race, ethnicity, socioeconomic group, and sexuality, and one that is quite challenging to properly define. Its legal definition within the United States varies according to jurisdictions, but it has been broadly defined by the FBI as "the penetration, no matter how slight, of the vagina or anus with any body part or object, or oral penetration by a sex organ of another person, without the consent of the victim."[1] Enfolded within this mechanical, intellectualized description is a human being who has been stripped of personal choice and reduced to a physical object, often with long-term psychological sequelae.

The *Crime Classification Manual* delineates the distinct types of rape and sexual assault.[2] Within each category, there is separate consideration of crimes against adults, defined as individuals eighteen years of age or older, and capable of consent under laws defining sexual activity, with possible exceptions for those with mental impairment or physical damage to the brain; adolescents, who are between the ages of thirteen and seventeen, with the ability to consent varying by jurisdiction; and children, who are twelve years old or younger, and, in all jurisdictions, considered minors incapable of consent.

In *criminal enterprise rape*, sexual coercion, abuse, or assault is committed for material gain. *Felony rape* is committed during the perpetration of a felonious crime. If the offender does not initially intend to commit rape but ultimately does so during the commission of some other criminal act, such as robbery, or breaking and entering, the term is *primary felony rape*. In *secondary felony rape*, this is reversed, such that the sexual assault is the offender's chief objective.

An offender who commits *personal cause sexual assault* is driven by personal and/or psychological internal aggression. The victim can be a stranger or someone known to the attacker. Included among the variations of this type of crime are *adult domestic sexual assault*, in which one attacks a spouse or cohabitating partner, and *child domestic sexual abuse*, in which the victim is a minor living in the perpetrator's home. Also included here are *indirect offenses*, in which there is no physical contact between a victim and perpetrator, as seen in voyeurism; *telephone scatologia* or making obscene telephone calls; exposing oneself; or masturbating in front of an unsuspecting stranger.

In *opportunistic rape*, the assault is impulsive, with little planning or preparation. The motive is chiefly immediate sexual gratification, rather than the enactment of some highly developed psychosexual fantasy or ritual.

In *social acquaintance rape*, the offender and victim have a prior relationship, as seen in "date" rape situations. There are several subtypes: *subordinate rape* involves the abuse of an authority relationship or imbalance of status to take advantage of a child or adult victim. *Exploitative rape* is character-ized by generally a low degree of expressed aggression, not exceeding what is required to force a victim to comply with an attacker. *Power-reassurance rape* typically begins with the sudden, unexpected assault of an unknown individual. Here, the offender uses the rape or sexual assault as a measure of virility and to compensate for sexual inadequacy, sometimes fantasizing, outrageously, that the victim will enjoy the experience.

Anger rape is driven by impulse and intense aggression toward individ-uals of a certain gender, age, race, or the world in general, and *sadistic rape*, in which the offender employs a level of violence that clearly exceeds what is required to gain the victim's compliance, and can result in injuries and/or death. In the latter, it is the victim's pain that arouses the attacker. Note that the definitions of entitlement, anger, and sadistic rape are related to the degree of aggression displayed by the offender. This can be gauged by whether there are injuries beyond minor cuts; whether force exceeded what was needed to attain victim compliance; specific acts during the crime, such as choking, mutilation, or stabbing; and desire or attempts to humiliate the victim, such as using profanity, the use of feces or urine, or forcing someone else to observe the assault.

In *abduction rape*, a stranger transports a victim in a vehicle, within a building or more than twenty feet for the purpose of the assault. *Group cause rape and sexual assault* is committed by three or more offenders, while sexual crimes committed by two offenders would be categorized under personal cause. Here, the motivations are generally varied. Subcategories include *formal gang rape and sexual assault*, in which three or more offenders display a sense of cohesiveness and belong to a group that has some internal orga-nization and a name, and *informal gang rape and sexual assault*, involving three or more loosely organized offenders who possess no internal structure. The latter is typically a spur-of-the-moment crime. Finally, the manual accounts for *rape and/or sexual assault not classified elsewhere*. These crimes exhibit aspects of some of the other specified variants but cannot be readily categorized.

Statistics on rape and sexual assault in the United States are staggering. According to the FBI, 2016 saw a 4.9 percent increase in the number of these crimes, relative to 2015. This rate was 12.4 percent higher than the

2012 estimate and 3.9 percent higher than the 2007 estimate,[3] although, when total reported rapes are considered by decade, we see a decline since the 1990s.[4] It is estimated that every ninety-eight seconds, someone in the United States is sexually assaulted, amounting to over 570 individuals per day. Over the past twenty years, 17.7 million women have been the victims of rape.[5] Individuals are at the highest risk of rape and sexual assault between ages twelve and thirty-four. Young women are especially at risk. Among juvenile victims, 82 percent are female. Females between the ages of sixteen and nineteen are four times more likely than the general population to be the victims of attempted or completed rape, or sexual assault. Ninety percent of adult victims are women, and those between ages eighteen and twenty-four who are also college students are three times more likely than women in the general population to experience sexual violence. One out of ten rape victims is male, and about one in thirty-three American men has experienced an attempted or completed rape during his lifetime, amounting to an estimated 2.78 million assaults. Among TGQN (transgender, genderqueer, nonconforming) college students, 21 percent have been sexually assaulted, compared to 18 percent of non-TGQN females and 4 percent of non-TGQN males.[6] One particularly troubling statistic concerns the number of accused rapists who will go free, which is estimated at 99 percent.[7]

As we progress to a vignette to illustrate various aspects of Category 17, the reader will observe that most of the rapes and sexual assaults ranked therein would fall into the power-reassurance, anger, and sadistic types delineated in the *Crime Classification Manual*. It should be noted that rapes and sexual assaults meeting the manual's criteria for the sadistic type do not necessarily involve physical torture. Thus, we must emphasize that physical torture in the context of rape or sexual assault requires a ranking of at least 18 on the Gradations of Evil scale. If an offender repeatedly commits rape and sexual assault but has not committed at least two homicides, Category 16 is likely the most appropriate designation.

Steeling ourselves, we turn to the story of Richard Ramirez, the Satan-worshipping serial killer, rapist, and house burglar who terrorized Los Angeles and San Francisco between 1984 and 1985. He was born Ricardo Leyva Muñoz Ramirez in El Paso, Texas, in February of 1960, the youngest of five children. His Mexican father worked for both the Santa Fe Railroad and the local police department, and his Colorado-born mother worked at a boot factory, nearly miscarrying due to inhalation of chemical fumes while pregnant with the future killer. It is unclear whether he suffered brain damage from this exposure to toxins while in utero. We also cannot be certain of the possible impacts of concussions he experienced at age two when a dresser fell on him, lacerating his forehead, and at age five when he was knocked unconscious by a park swing. Afterward, he was plagued by frequent seizures, which forced him to give up playing recreational football at school. These lasted until his early teens.[8]

Ramirez was detached and isolative in childhood. Around age ten, he began sniffing glue and smoking marijuana, and his grades at school rapidly declined. To avoid his father, who was allegedly sometimes explosively angry and physically abusive at home, Ramirez began sleeping overnight in local cemeteries. In this and other ways, he was growing increasingly grim and morbid. When he was twelve, his cousin Miguel returned from military service in Vietnam, enthralling him with snapshots of female villagers he had raped, tortured, and killed. They spoke at length about how to conceal oneself and stealthily take another person's life. The following year, Ramirez stood mesmerized as Miguel fatally shot his wife in the face in the heat of a dispute. Even more withdrawn than usual after this event, Ramirez went to live with his sister, Ruth, and her husband, Roberto. His brother-in-law allegedly introduced him to peeping at women through windows, LSD, and Satanism.[9]

Around the same time, Ramirez was routinely abusing cannabis and became truant from school. He was dabbling in burglary, brazenly taking his time to walk aimlessly around strangers' homes and rifle through their belongings, snatching up whatever caught his fancy. His brother Ruben, who had a history of petty theft, allegedly helped him to improve his various methods. During this period, Ramirez enjoyed hunting, both with his family and on his own, relishing the experience of sneaking up behind animals before stabbing and eviscerating them. This is reminiscent of the ambush methods imparted to him by his cousin. He was also an avid fan of horror films, which may have filled his mind with romanticized images of nocturnal predators, misunderstood monsters, and unstoppable slashers. Ramirez began attending Jehovah's Witness meetings, finding himself growingly fascinated by the subject of Satan. One wonders, in light of the career of serial murder and rape he was soon to initiate, if he was somehow inspired by biblical verses such as this one, from 1 Peter 5:8: "Be sober-minded; be watchful. Your adversary the devil prowls around like a roaring lion, seeking someone to devour."[10] These various influences and themes were all aspects of his background when he found work in a Holiday Inn, robbing visitors in their sleep. He was fired when, in the context of growing preoccupation with violent sexual fantasies, he tried to rape a female guest and was badly beaten by her husband. He dropped out of school in the ninth grade.[11]

When Ramirez was seventeen, Miguel, who had been found not guilty by reason of insanity, was discharged after four years at a psychiatric hospital. The following year, Ramirez picked up and moved to Los Angeles, living as a transient. He subsisted by selling marijuana and spending a night or two sleeping in strangers' cars before stealing them. This landed him in jail for several months on a larceny charge. He also developed a cocaine habit. Then, at age eighteen, after smoking PCP with a female companion, he suddenly bound and repeatedly raped her. Around this time, he officially joined the Church of Satan, which further honed his egotistical attitude and his disdain for the common rules of society, which he now felt were totally beneath him.[12]

In 1984, Ramirez embarked upon a long string of horrendous sexual assaults and homicides, all in the state of California. In downtown San Francisco in April of that year, Ramirez beat, stabbed, and raped nine-year-old Mei Leung, dumping her body in the basement of a hotel. Two months later, while high on cocaine, he removed the screen from the window of a home in Glassell Park. After taking what he wished, he raped, brutally stabbed, and slashed the throat of the home's elderly owner, seventy-nine-year-old Jennie Vincow, engaging in necrophilia for the first time with her nearly decapitated corpse.[13] In February of the following year, he entered the San Francisco home of two sisters, Christina and Mary Caldwell, who were fifty-eight and seventy-one, respectively, stabbing each victim dozens of times.[14] In March of 1985, he purchased a .22 revolver and fired at twenty-two-year-old Angela Barrios outside of her condominium before entering her apartment and fatally shooting her thirty-four-year-old room-mate, Dayle Okazaki. Later that day, he pulled Tsai-Lian Yu, a thirty-year-old art student, out of her car and fatally shot her in the chest.

Barrios, who survived, provided police their first description of the man the press was now dubbing "the Night Stalker," "the Walk-In Killer," and "the Valley Intruder." She noted his curly hair, protuberant eyes, and rotten-looking, spaced-out teeth. It was also established that the attacker had extreme halitosis.

Figuratively feeding, like a bloated parasite, on the blood of strangers and probably drawing further sustenance from the subsequent media attention, Ramirez was gradually increasing the frequency and brutality of his crimes. In Whittier on March 27, 1985, he shot sixty-four-year-old pizza parlor owner Vincent Zazzara and repeatedly shot and stabbed his forty-four-year-old wife, Maxine. He carved a "T" in her left breast after she expired and gouged out her eyes, which he carried away from the scene. Ramirez later sat staring into them in a hotel room, reportedly while laughing out loud. From this point onward, it became his modus operandi to rapidly eliminate the male in a household before sexually assaulting and fatally stabbing the victim's wife or significant other. This pattern certainly had an Oedipal ring to it, as did the removal of eyes, although the story goes that Oedipus removed his own with pins taken from the dress of the wife he discovered to also be his mother. As the killer's arrogance—and possibly his drug use—increased, he also grew sloppier, leaving footprints in the flower bed outside the Zazzaras' home.[15]

Six weeks later, Ramirez beat sixty-six-year-old Harold Wu and shot him in the throat before putting thumb cuffs on his sixty-three-year-old wife, Jean Wu, whom he beat and brutally raped.[16] Two weeks later, he entered the Monrovia home of eighty-three-year-old retired school teacher Malvial Keller and her eighty-year-old sister, Blanche Wolfe, who was an invalid. He savagely bludgeoned their heads with a hammer before attempting to rape Keller. Wolfe, whose legs and arms were bound, died when the attacker crushed her ribs with a heavy table. He then used lipstick to draw satanic pentagrams on her corpse and on the wall of the bedroom where her sister lay comatose. Keller miraculously survived the horrific assault.[17]

The following day, Ramirez sneaked into the Burbank home of forty-one-year-old Ruth Wilson, wielding a knife and slapping handcuffs on her and her twelve-year-old son. After ransacking the house and locking the child in a closet, he slashed and repeatedly sodomized the woman, telling her he would cut out her eyes if she looked at him.[18] On June 2, 1985, Ramirez shot twenty-nine-year-old Edgar Wildgans and repeatedly raped the victim's girlfriend, Nancy Brien. Three weeks later, he sodomized and slashed the throat of thirty-two-year-old Patty Elaine Higgins.[19] On July 2, he randomly selected the home of seventy-five-year-old widowed grandmother Mary Louise Cannon, where he found her sleeping in her bedroom. He bludgeoned her into unconsciousness with a lamp and stabbed her to death using a ten-inch butcher knife taken from her kitchen.[20] In Montebello, he kidnapped a six-year-old girl from a bus stop near her school and carried her off in a laundry bag. After sexually assaulting her, he dropped her off alive in Silver Lake. He also kidnapped and raped a nine-year-old girl before stranding her in Elysian Park.[21]

Ramirez went on committing crimes at the same frantic pace, terrorizing Californians with the complete randomness of his violence, which traversed all age groups. On July 5, he savagely beat sixteen-year-old Whitney Bennett with a tire iron as she slept in her bedroom. When he failed to locate a knife with which to stab the girl to death, he instead tried to strangle her with a telephone cord. At the sight of sparks flying from the wire and the unexpected revival of the victim, he fled the house, convinced that Christ had intervened to save Bennett's life in his diabolical attack.[22] The lacerations in her scalp required 478 stitches.[23] Two days later, evidently undeterred by what he had interpreted as divine intervention, Ramirez beat and kicked sixty-one-year-old Los Angeles resident Joyce Lucille Nelson to death while she slept on her couch. Police were able to lift an Avia sneaker print from the woman's face. After scoping out other possible attack sites, he entered the home of sixty-three-year-old Linda Fortuna, handcuffing her at gunpoint and unsuccessfully attempting to rape her. Stealing her jewelry, he made her "swear on Satan" that she was not concealing anything of value elsewhere in the house.[24]

On July 20, 1985, Ramirez burst into the bedroom of a sleeping Glendale couple, sixty-eight-year-old Maxon Kneiding and his sixty-six-year-old wife, Lela. He butchered them with a machete before fatally shooting them both in their heads with a .22-caliber handgun, and continuing the mutilation. He then ransacked the house.[25] That same day, the killer demonstrated that he was becoming even more savage and expansive, now shifting his attention from single people and couples to an entire family. In the dead of night, he broke into the Sun Valley home of thirty-two-year-old Chitat Assawahem, shooting him in the head as he slumbered before repeatedly beating, raping, and sodomizing his twenty-nine-year-old wife, Somkid Khovananth. She was then forced to swear to Satan that she was not concealing valuables. Her terrified eight-year-old son was bound and sexually assaulted.[26]

On August 6, 1985, Ramirez popped up in Northridge, probably feeling rather godlike, with his totally random selection of neighborhoods and houses. After entering the home of thirty-eight-year-old Christopher Peterson and his twenty-seven-year-old wife, Virginia, he shot both in the head, but, following a struggle between Ramirez and Mr. Peterson, the couple survived.[27] Two days later, he again targeted a family, this time in Diamond Bar. After entering their master bedroom, he shot thirty-five-year-old Ahmed Zia while he slept. He handcuffed and beat the victim's twenty-eight-year-old wife, Suu Kyi, forcing her to hand over valuables and pledge an oath to Satan that she would not scream while he sodomized her. The couple's three-year-old son then entered the room, and Ramirez bound him with rope before continuing the sexual assault on the small boy's mother.[28]

Ramirez next emerged in San Francisco on August 18, fatally shooting sixty-six-year-old Peter Pan in the temple as he slept, and beating and sexually assaulting his sixty-two-year-old wife, Barbara, before shooting her in the head. She survived the attack. Before leaving the house, he used lipstick to draw a pentagram on the bedroom wall, alongside the cryptic phrase "Jack the Knife."[29] Police were pleased to discover that ballistic and shoe print evidence from the Pan attack matched those lifted from other Night Stalker crime scenes. Unfortunately, Mayor Dianne Feinstein divulged this fact on television, and the killer, who obsessively followed his own press, tossed his Avia sneakers from the Golden Gate Bridge just hours later.[30]

Six days later, Ramirez was just about to target the home of the Romero family in Mission Viejo, but a thirteen-year-old child heard him lurking outside and, racing to the door, glimpsed Ramirez speeding off. His father contacted the police with a partial license plate number, and the color, make, and model of the killer's car. It was said in the press that the boy essentially brought down the Night Stalker with his chance encounter and keen skills of observation.[31] Ramirez moved on to the home of thirty-year-old Bill Carns and his twenty-nine-year-old fiancée, Inez Erickson, entering through their back door. Finding the couple asleep, he roused Carns by cocking his handgun and shot him three times in the head. The victim survived the attack but was left with memory impairment and his left arm and foot paralyzed.[32] Turning to Erickson, he forced her to swear her love for the devil as he beat her with his fists and bound her with some neckties taken from the closet. After gathering up some valuables, he dragged the terrified woman to another room to rape and sodomize her. Before leaving the house, he instructed, "Tell them the Night Stalker was here."[33] Erickson gave authorities a detailed description of Ramirez, and footprints were attained both in the home and in the car Ramirez had driven that night, which was found abandoned in Los Angeles. On the rearview mirror was a single fingerprint, which led police to the Satan-worshipping twenty-five-year-old drifter with a lengthy rap sheet for drug and traffic violations. An old mug shot was released to the public. To Ramirez's surprise, it was mass-produced in every major newspaper and displayed on television screens across the country.[34]

Ironically, it was Ramirez's egocentricity that would ultimately be his undoing. In the first place, he had grown arrogant and fearless, allowing himself to be seen by several witnesses, intentionally keeping one alive with the directive that she give people the name of his alter ego and leaving traces of himself, including a fingerprint, in a rather obvious area of his car. Second, his case had become major news, and it made sense that some member of the terrified public would ultimately recognize him. Indeed, on August 30, 1985, a group of Mexican women in a store recognized Ramirez as "El Matador"—the killer—and he fled as his own face scowled from the covers of the newspapers on the racks. Panicked, he raced across the Santa Ana Freeway, unsuccessfully attempting to steal a car from a female driver as he was chased down by two bystanders. He hopped fences and tried to swipe two other vehicles, but a group of residents overcame him, one of whom cracked him over the head with a metal bar. He was pinned down and beaten until the authorities took him into custody.[35] Ramirez was ultimately defeated by members of the same public he had assumed to be so powerless against him.

At Ramirez's 1989 trial, which began with him lifting a hand with a pentagram drawn on the palm and yelling, "Hail Satan," the killer was promptly convicted and condemned to die in the gas chamber, but, due to numerous appeals, the execution would never actually be carried out. Unremorseful and callous to the very end, he remarked to reporters, while strutting like a primped-up movie star, "Big deal. Death always went with the territory. See you in Disneyland."[36]

During a bona fide spectacle of a trial, Ramirez somehow garnered a number of female groupies who were utterly devoted to him.[37] The curious paraphilia in which an individual is aroused by the knowledge that one's romantic partner has committed rape, murder, armed robbery, or some other legal and moral outrage is known as *hybristophilia*. One of the Night Stalker's devoted fans, Doreen Lioy, became his wife in 1996. They divorced in 2012. The following year, Ramirez, one of the most monstrous serial killers in American history, died of complications from B-cell lymphoma, twenty-four years after being sentenced to death for his crimes. He was fifty-three years old.[38]

Surely, by now, the reader is convinced that some people do, indeed, prowl like roaring lions, seeking victims to devour. We note, however, that lions and other predatory beasts do so as a result of evolution and instinct, none of which would be termed "evil." It takes a human being to go beyond the expeditious killing observed among such animals to concoct depraved and cruel acts, in service of one's own psychosexual needs and fantasies.

CHAPTER EIGHT

CATEGORY 18

Surely, surely, thou wilt trust me
When I say thou dost disgust me.
O, I hate thee with a hate
That would fain annihilate.

—Henry David Thoreau, "Indeed, Indeed I Cannot Tell"

P sychopathic persons whose crimes are categorized at level 18 of the Gradations of Evil scale are motivated by the desire to kill—put plainly and simply—and, sometimes, in unfathomable numbers. While some torture is perpetrated by these types, it is of secondary importance to the assailant and is never protracted in nature. When rape is present, it is generally not the individual's primary motive and is perpetrated in a manner intended as part of a wider process of murder, which, in and of itself, may provide a psychosexual thrill. We should reemphasize that the murder, torture, and sexual assault described here must involve at least two human victims. Again, torture and/or sexual assault isolated to animals would be considered vicious acts of the type associated with Category 16. Moreover, Category 16 is the highest ranking possible for cases involving a single homicide.

The hatred of humankind exhibited by individuals in this category is so deep-seated and generalized that essentially anybody might fall prey to their savage rage. However, as we shall see in the following vignette, these killers do tend to demonstrate a widespread fury toward a certain type of person—young women, in this instance. In virtually all of the cases we have examined, the killers appeared to be repeatedly playing out powerful fantasies in which they symbolically dominated and destroyed some abusive or rejecting individual in their lives, in a pattern that likely would have gone on indefinitely were it not for incarceration or death. In individuals assigned to this category, this often promptly picks up upon release or escape from prison, should either one transpire. The goal appears to be to bring to life a certain frequently imagined scenario in the most perfect way possible. This often requires that victims be of a certain sex or racial group, or the presence of some distinct feature, such as hair worn in a certain fashion or a particular article of clothing. Thus, the identification of potential victims sometimes requires extensive hunting and prowling. If a psychologically required feature is present to a "perfect" enough degree, the killer may seek to savor it by retaining a corpse, body part, pre- or post-mortem photographs, or some piece of the victim's clothing for paraphilic purposes.

The brutality such individuals inflict—sometimes escalating as the killer's need for stimulation grows over time—is often unspeakably overblown and gruesome, such that one might draw consolation from the fact that their victims are typically eliminated in expeditious ways. Category 18 types are often so enraged and so driven by desires to control and humiliate others that, as with some Category 17 offenders, posthumous mutilation and necrophilic acts might be observed.

We turn now to the case of Jerry Brudos, an insatiable killer who engaged in some degree of torture. He is particularly illustrative of the typical motivations and personality features of individuals associated with this category. Born to a farming couple in South Dakota in 1939, Brudos was the younger of two sons. His father was short-tempered but never abusive. His mother, who had been hoping for a girl, was bitterly disappointed and reportedly spent years belittling and maltreating him, sometimes humiliating him by dressing him in female clothing. He would loathe her across his lifetime. His family relocated to various cities in the Pacific Northwest throughout his early childhood, eventually settling in Salem, Oregon. At age five, he discovered a pair of open-toed high-heeled shoes in a junkyard while wandering around town. When he wore them home, his mother heavily scolded him and set the heels on fire. He would cite this powerful memory—in which women's shoes became forbidden objects—as the origin of his lifelong *podophilia*, or foot fetish, which he would eventually take to a bizarre and macabre new level.[1]

That same year, the Brudos family moved once again, this time to Riverton, California, where the future killer entered grammar school. When he attempted to steal a pair of high heels from his first-grade teacher, she confused him by expressing curiosity about what prompted him to do so, rather than chastising him, as his mother had done. This constituted a mixed message for him.[2] The following year, he failed the second grade. Between the ages of seven and eight, Brudos suffered a series of health issues, including measles, sore throats, swollen glands, laryngitis, and fungal infections of his finger and toenails, requiring several operations. He also experienced vision problems and frequent headaches, which were never explained. Around this time, his family returned to Oregon, where he repeatedly sneaked into the home of a female neighbor to play with her clothes and undergarments.[3]

In adolescence, Brudos began digging a tunnel in a hillside near his family's home, entertaining vivid fantasies of capturing and imprisoning a girl there. During this period, he was not interested in sexually assaulting a female, so much as completely possessing her. For the purposes of masturbation, he was routinely burglarizing local homes to gather up footwear and stealing women's undergarments from clotheslines. At sixteen, after acquiring the underwear of an eighteen-year-old woman, Brudos hatched a scheme to obtain an image of her in the nude. He invited her to his home, claiming he wished to help her to locate her purloined property. Then he disguised himself as a masked intruder, wielded a knife, and forced her to remove her clothes, after which he photographed her. After she fled the house following the incident, Brudos found her and claimed the "attacker" was locked up in his barn.[4] The following year, he abducted a seventeen-year-old female and drove her to a deserted farmhouse, where he severely beat and disrobed her, snapping more photographs for what was now a rapidly growing collection.[5]

Brudos was committed to Oregon State Hospital for psychiatric evaluation and treatment, where he was initially diagnosed with an "adjustment reaction to adolescence with sexual deviation-fetishism." It emerged that his sexual fantasies might be psychologically related to unresolved rage toward his abusive mother, which gave way to a generalized hatred of women.[6] At the time of discharge nearly nine months later, he was deemed to be a "borderline schizophrenic" who posed no further danger to society at large.[7] After high school, he enrolled in two separate technology schools,[8] but his attendance was erratic and he ultimately dropped out to join the US Army at twenty. During his service, he began dreaming about a Korean woman who would creep into his bed at night and seduce him. He was discharged from military service due to "bizarre obsessions" and returned to his family's home, where he lived in their toolshed. At this time, he began preying on local women, knocking them down or strangling them into unconsciousness before running off with their shoes.[9]

At twenty-one, Brudos, who had been working as an electrician, obtained a license from the Federal Communications Commission and took up a job at a local radio station. There, he met seventeen-year-old Darcie Metzler, whom he married after a brief courtship. They went on to have a daughter. He routinely requested that his wife do housework wearing nothing but a pair of high heels while he photographed her.[10] In 1967, his wife gave birth a second time to a son. He was not permitted, for unclear reasons, to be present at the birth, and he went into a psychological tailspin, escalating his thefts of shoes and underwear, which he claimed alleviated chronic migraines and blackouts. He was also electrocuted, almost lethally, after touching a live wire at work. That year, he stalked a woman and followed her home, where he waited for her to fall asleep before raiding her closet. When she unexpectedly awoke, he choked her until she passed out and committed his first rape before racing home with her shoes.[11]

In January of 1968, Brudos received a visit from an attractive nineteen-year-old door-to-door encyclopedia saleswoman named Linda Slawson. Convincing her to follow him into his lower garage, he bludgeoned her with a two-by-four and strangled her to death. After sending his wife and kids out for fast food, he stripped the corpse and dressed it up in various undergarments from his personal hoard, taking photographs to his heart's content. Then, using a hacksaw, he severed the woman's left foot, which he retained in his freezer, taking it out from time to time to slip into various high-heeled shoes while masturbating. Brudos faked a flat tire to pull his car over at the side of a bridge traversing the Willamette River, where he dumped the partially mutilated body over the edge. It was never recovered.[12]

Brudos went on to commit four more murders. After the family moved to Salem, Oregon, he constructed a darkroom in the garage for privately developing photographs, which would also provide him an area to work with victims. He arranged with his wife that she would never enter the space without announcing her arrival on an intercom system.[13] At first, the new workroom went mostly unused, since it was difficult to lure the victims he identified during periods of prowling back to his home. In July of 1968, Brudos strangled sixteen-year-old Stephanie Vikko to death, leaving her corpse in a wooded area.[14] Four months later, he used a strap to strangle twenty-three-year-old Jan Whitney, whom he discovered in a broken-down car along an interstate. He raped her during the murder and repeatedly after death, retaining the body on a hook in his garage for five days before dumping her into the same river where he had disposed of the remains of Slawson.[15]

Brudos then turned to abduction. Stalking a parking garage, he seized nineteen-year-old Karen Sprinker, using a toy pistol, and dragged her to his workshop, where he stripped her and posed her in a variety of outfits while photographing her, like a living mannequin. He then placed a noose, which was attached to the ceiling, around her neck, lifting her slightly above the floor so that she could stand on her toes while he took snapshots. He hoisted her farther up, and, as she slowly asphyxiated to death, he prepared a meal and watched a cartoon. He sexually assaulted the corpse and amputated her breasts, coating them with preservative to use as paperweights. Brudos then dressed the body with a bra, which he stuffed with paper to replace the mammaries he had removed, and hurled the corpse into another river, tied to an engine block to weight it down.[16]

In April of 1969, Brudos attempted to abduct a young woman in a Portland State University parking garage, who attempted to fend him off by biting his thumb.[17] He beat her into unconsciousness but was frightened off by a passing car. Then, brandishing a pistol, he tried to kidnap a twelve-year-old on her way to school, but when a neighbor caught sight of him, he leaped into his car and sped away.[18] Since his method of capture was proving risky, he considered ensnaring a woman by posing as a police officer and flashing a phony badge. At a shopping mall, he spied twenty-two-year-old Linda Salee carrying birthday presents for her boyfriend and, claiming he was a security guard investigating a spate of shoplifting, convinced her to get into his car. He then brought her to his workshop, where he stripped, hanged, strangulated, and photographed her in the manner of Sprinker. After she expired, he put nails in her rib cage and hooked them up to an electrical current to see if the body would twitch or jump. He would later explain that he did not sever her breasts before dumping her weighted body in a river purely because he did not care for the appearance of the nipples.[19]

In May of 1969, a fisherman discovered Salee's body, and divers subsequently discovered the corpse of Sprinker. In the meantime, a tip from an Oregon State student, who had gone on a blind date with Brudos and felt disturbed by his endless talk of the missing women, led authorities to the killer. During a visit by police to his home, he inexplicably gave them a piece of the rope he had used to asphyxiate one of his last two victims, perhaps having grown disorganized or arrogant with regard to attempting to conceal his crimes. While one might wonder whether he had begun to feel regretful or weary of killing, it should be emphasized that Brudos displayed no remorse whatsoever and made concerted efforts to avoid arrest. Whatever the case may be, the rope yielded forensic evidence that linked him to the murders of which he was suspected.[20]

In a last-minute attempt to cover up his crimes, Brudos washed down the inside of his vehicle, claiming water had gotten into the vehicle at a car wash. He was arrested while trying to flee to Canada, hiding under a blanket and wearing silk panties.[21] After an insanity defense was rebutted by seven separate psychiatric evaluations, he ultimately pled guilty and received three life sentences. His wife, who was charged as a possible accomplice but cleared, divorced him in 1970, leaving Oregon with the children and changing her name.[22] Over the years, the so-called "Lust Killer" sometimes laughed while reminiscing about the thrill of murdering and mutilating his victims, and gathered ladies' shoe and clothing catalogs in prison, feeding his psychosexual needs right to the end of his life. He referred to the women he killed as "candy wrappers" that he discarded because they no longer held any use for him. During an interview not long before his death from liver cancer in 2006, he callously remarked, "I'm assuming that I never hurt anybody, because I never got any complaints from anybody."[23]

CHAPTER NINE

CATEGORIES 19, 20, AND 21

*I am sorry for thee. Thou art come to answer a stony adversary,
an inhuman wretch uncapable of pity, void and empty from any
dram of mercy.*

—William Shakespeare, *The Merchant of Venice*,
act 4, scene 1

While serial killers, torturers, and sadists who meet criteria for Categories 17, 18, or 22 of the Gradations of Evil scale are relatively abundant, we find that those who would be ranked at Categories 19, 20, or 21 are all exceedingly rare. As we examine what designates a psychopathic individual to one of these three unusual places on the continuum, we will note that individuals in Categories 19 and 21 are not known—at least for certain—to have committed murder, whereas Category 20 types commit homicide and torture in the context of severe mental illness involving psychotic states—a concept we will explore in this chapter in some detail.

CATEGORY 19

At this ranking, a psychopathic person is chiefly moved by a desire to terrorize, subjugate, intimidate, and/or commit rape. The objective is generally "practical" in the mind of the individual, such as to severely frighten the victim or other people for purposes of extortion, sex, or some other end. These offenders are not driven by the desire to inflict physical harm for sadistic purposes. An offender who commits one or more kidnaps for the purpose of ransom or who retains an abducted individual as a sex slave, without perpetrating torture or murder, might be included in this category. Critically, while these individuals may be accused of murder or claim to have taken lives, there is no confirmed history of homicide.

Consider the case of Gary Steven Krist, born in 1945. Due to stealing boats and automobiles in early adolescence, he was committed to an industrial school in Utah for a year, briefly escaping before being recaptured in Idaho. At eighteen, he was sentenced to a California vocational school following conviction for two more car thefts and released in 1964. Two years later, he was again convicted of the same crime but escaped from police custody.[1]

On December 17, 1968, Krist and a female accomplice, Ruth Eisemann-Schier, entered a motel room near Atlanta, Georgia, where twenty-year-old Barbara Jane Mackle was being nursed by her mother through a case of the flu. Mackle was the daughter of a millionaire land developer who was a personal friend of then president-elect Richard M. Nixon. Krist and his accomplice claimed to be police officers and stated that a friend of Mackle's had been injured in a road accident. Eisemann-Schier was wearing a ski mask. Krist brandished a shotgun, and the two bound and chloroformed Mackle's mother, leaving her in the room. The younger woman was abducted and driven twenty miles away to a pine forest, where Krist and his accomplice had prepared a hole in the ground that resembled a grave. The ordeal to which she was subjected is difficult to imagine. She was placed inside a cramped, coffin-like box with air tubes connected to a pump, stocked with a battery-powered lamp, food and water, sleeping pills, a blanket, a sweater, and sanitary supplies. The box was fastened with screws and buried beneath hundreds of pounds of dirt and branches used as camouflage.[2] Screaming and banging the walls would prove an exercise in futility. Krist's last words to her were, "Don't be such a baby."[3] Mackle could then hear the shoveling, footfalls, and the sounds of the vehicle that transported her leaving the area. Then she found a long note from Krist, boasting of the design of his hostage containment unit. "Do not be alarmed," the note read. "You are safe. . . . You'll be home for Christmas one way or the other." Although the note claimed the battery powering the light would endure for eleven days, it failed after just three hours, leaving Mackle in total darkness.[4]

Krist and his accomplice traveled to the Mackle home in Florida and buried a ransom note in the front yard. They demanded half a million dollars in old twenty-dollar bills, which was paid out by the family as the police searched for the kidnappers.[5] After eighty-three hours underground, Mackle was disinterred. Although she was dehydrated, stiff, and ten pounds lighter, she said afterward that she was treated humanely and felt "absolutely wonderful."[6] Five days after the crime, Krist was taken into custody. Several months later, Eisemann-Schier was apprehended and would serve three years in prison before being deported to her native Honduras.[7]

Once jailed, Krist claimed to have committed a series of unsolved murders. In 1961, he supposedly killed a stranger in a violent fit of anger and dumped his body in Utah. He related that, at age fourteen, he was traversing a ravine bridge in Alaska with a sixty-five-year-old hermit with whom he had a sexual relationship and intentionally tripped him, causing the victim to plummet to his death. At nineteen, he reportedly strangled and beat a girl to death, concealing her corpse under a pile of rocks. Krist made allusions to killing a fourth person but never provided details. Since there was no corroborating evidence for any of these purported murders, they were never prosecuted.[8] As noted, the absence of a confirmed history of homicide allows for Krist's designation to Category 19.

After ten years in prison, Krist was paroled in 1979, attending medical school in the Caribbean. He practiced medicine in Indiana before his license was revoked in 2003, on the grounds that he lied about disciplinary actions during residency.[9] Three years later, it was discovered that he was running a cocaine-processing lab, hidden—naturally—in the ground, beneath the concrete floor of a storage shed in Alabama. The room consisted of a twenty-seven-and-a-half-foot-long tank, reminiscent of the box in which Mackle was entombed. There was also a fifty-foot-long escape tunnel. He was also harboring undocumented immigrants.[10] Krist, who once dubbed himself "the Einstein of Crime," was convicted of these additional offenses.[11]

To our knowledge, no kidnapping of this diabolical sort, involving burial of a living person, occurred in the pre-1960s era. As we shall see later in this volume, it is characteristic of serious offenders of the last half century to expand upon the "practical" methods and motives of more commonplace crimes, such as abduction of a victim for financial gain, in especially inventive and sadistic ways. Thus, these crimes serve a second function, which is psychological in nature, associated with strivings for narcissistic gratification, domination, and gratuitous cruelty. In short, while kidnapping for the purpose of ransom is quite an old crime, Krist's manner of doing so constitutes a "new" and terrifying form of evil.

CATEGORY 20

Individuals assigned to this category have committed both homicide and acts of torture, and have additionally demonstrated delusional beliefs, perceptual abnormalities, or disorganization of thought or behavior, consistent with psychotic illness. It is critical to note that an individual with psychotic illness can also possess a psychopathic character structure, as we saw with Ed Gein when discussing Category 13. The two are not mutually exclusive. The question of whether psychotic illness reduces an offender's culpability—that is, the degree to which the individual fully grasped the difference between what was right and wrong at the time some crime was committed—must be addressed on a case-by-case basis. Psychotic experiences can occur in someone designated to another level of the scale, but where they prompt acts of both homicide *and* torture, the designation must be Category 20. The higher ranking is necessary to capture the extreme nature of such crimes, as well as the bewilderment and breathless horror these terrible acts evoke in others—reactions that are central to our conceptualization of "evil." It is the absence of torture in the case of Ed Gein that excludes him from this level of the scale.

An understanding of the term *psychosis* is necessary for proper use of this ranking. Although an in-depth discussion of psychotic states and disorders is beyond the scope of the present discussion, we will touch, briefly, upon some critical points. First and foremost, psychosis is a symptom of psychiatric illness but not a disorder, in and of itself. Rather, it constitutes an umbrella term, referring to a state in which one loses contact, in some way, with external reality. This might involve *hallucinations*, in which one perceives stimuli, in any of the five sensory modalities, that others do not; disturbances of cognitive organization and fundamental logic, called *thought disorder*; and/or *delusions*, in which one imbues authentic stimuli with inaccurate meaning and holds that misinterpretation in a fixed way, despite evidence to the contrary. Delusions can involve a wide array of contents— some plausible, like being followed, and some patently absurd and scientifi- cally impossible, such as believing that aliens are firing a ray gun at one's head. We will briefly touch upon some delusional ideas more commonly encountered among persons with psychotic illness. Those with *persecutory delusions* believe that they are being mistreated, spied upon, or threatened with harm. A *grandiose delusion*, sometimes called a *delusion of grandeur*, is characterized by a belief that one has more power, talent, influence, or wealth than one actually has, or conviction about a special relationship with God or a prominent individual. A *jealous delusion* is a false belief that one's spouse or romantic partner has been unfaithful. Those with *erotomanic delusions* are convinced that certain people—sometimes celebrities—are in love with them. As we shall discuss in part II, this type of delusion is some- times associated with stalking activity. An individual with a *somatic delusion* is convinced of having a physical defect or medical problem, despite the absence of empirical evidence. *Delusions of guilt* involve unwarranted feel- ings of remorse, fault, or deserving punishment. In a *delusion of reference*, one believes that insignificant occurrences, remarks by other people, or things observed in one's environment have a personal meaning or significance, such that they may constitute "signs" or "messages," alluding, in some way, to the individual. Those with *delusions of control* believe that their thoughts, feelings, or actions are manipulated by an external person, group, or force. *Thought insertion* and *thought withdrawal* are beliefs that thoughts are being placed into or taken out of one's head, respectively. A *delusion of mind reading* is characterized by the belief that some person or group of people can know one's private thoughts. In *thought broadcasting*, one believes that others can hear one's thoughts, playing out loud, like a radio. If no central theme predominates, the term *Mixed Delusion* is applied.

In some individuals, hallucinations and delusional beliefs are intricately interwoven, such that, for instance, hallucinating a buzzing sound coming from one's ear is related to the delusion that one has an electronic tracking device in one's brain. In others, symptoms might be less organized into any sort of quasi-logical narrative. Someone might simultaneously hear what is thought to be the voice of Satan and believe that there is a worm wriggling through his or her innards but struggle to explain how these two experiences might be related to one another. Some psychotic states will also involve disorganization of speech, thought, or behavior.

Several psychiatric categories in current use are associated with discrete periods of psychosis, such as schizophrenia, delusional disorder, brief psychotic disorder, and depression and bipolar disorder with psychotic features.[12] Psychotic conditions typically first emerge during adolescence or young adulthood, often following a period of delusions, hallucinations, and/or thought disorder, which are attenuated in terms of intensity, frequency, behavioral impact, and loss of insight. An attenuated psychosis syndrome, which delineates specific criteria for this "clinical high-risk" (CHR) phase, has been included as a condition warranting further study in the previously referenced *DSM-5*, published in 2013.[13] Approximately 30 percent of adolescents and young adults who meet CHR criteria will go on to develop full-blown illness over the course of two years.[14] Recent research suggests that violent thoughts and mental images, generally experienced as intrusive and ego-dystonic, may be somewhat common in individuals with attenuated psychotic illness. Moreover, the presence of these thoughts in conjunction with subthreshold symptoms of psychosis may strongly predict the later development of a full-blown psychotic disorder, particularly schizophrenia.[15] Further study of violent ideation in the CHR phase of psychotic illness might afford insight into how psychotic ideas associated with violence develop and are experienced by such individuals, and may, with further investigation, serve as a window for early intervention.

It is important to note that psychotic states can occur within the context of traumatic experiences, with the use of certain prescription medications, or due to certain medical conditions. Examples of the latter include Parkinson's disease; Huntington's disease; brain tumors or cysts; dementia, including Alzheimer's disease; stroke; some forms of epilepsy; and HIV and other infections affecting the brain. Psychotic symptoms can also arise while abusing or withdrawing from alcohol or illicit substances, such as amphetamines, hallucinogens, marijuana, cocaine, sedative-hypnotics, and opioids.[16]

Furthermore, transient, short-lived "micro-psychotic" ideas, perceptions, and behaviors can occur in people with certain personality structures, especially under increased duress. Thus, it is also imperative that we at least briefly review the ten personality disorders described in the *DSM*, divided into Clusters A, B, and C. In each, there are inflexible patterns of behavior and internal experiences that cause functional difficulties and personal distress. These patterns are long-term, generally beginning in late adolescence or early adulthood. We should emphasize that some of these traits can occur in individuals in a non-pervasive manner that does not give rise to significant difficulties or internal upset, such that criteria for a *DSM* personality disorder will not be fully met.

Individuals with Cluster A personality disorders exhibit oddness, eccentricities of thought, and social awkwardness and withdrawal like we might see to a greater extent in schizophrenia, never in discrete episodes but across their lifetimes. Three of these conditions have been described. *Paranoid personality disorder* involves a pervasive distrust and suspiciousness of others.[17] *Schizoid personality disorder* is characterized by a general pattern of social detachment and restricted emotionality, with a preference for mechanical or abstract activities involving minimal human contact.[18] Those with *schizotypal personality disorder* demonstrate schizoid traits, alongside perceptual and cognitive distortions, and/or eccentric behaviors.[19] While some of the individuals discussed in our vignettes possess Cluster A traits, this does not imply that they were fully or even partially detached from reality at the times they committed their crimes, or ever in their lifetimes.

There are three Cluster B personality disorders, characterized by emotional, dramatic, and erratic traits, features of which, the reader will note, are reflected at various points along the Gradations of Evil scale. *Histrionic personality disorder* involves a pattern of excessive emotionality and attention seeking, such that one might be perceived as theatrical, flighty, or flamboyant, with hyperbolic, shallow mood states. Persons who meet criteria for this condition are often easily influenced by the suggestions and opinions of other people.[20] Those diagnosed with *narcissistic personality disorder* tend to feel that they possess special talents, powers, or qualities, such that they are entitled to special treatment. They might exploit or manipulate others or demonstrate fundamental disregard for the needs and feelings of those around them. These individuals often feel devastated in situations in which they are made to feel normal, human, or commonplace, cascading into intense anger or shame.[21] As we have seen, narcissism, in some cases, can prove a motivation in acts of extreme violence.

Borderline personality disorder is often characterized by viewing people and experiences in polarized, black-and-white terms, which also involves an unstable sense of one's own identity and life goals. Abrupt vacillations between all-or-nothing perceptions result in impulsive, sometimes self-destructive decisions and intense emotionality, which is difficult to modulate. In some instances, these feelings are dissociated and, paradoxically, experienced as numbness or emptiness. These various difficulties with affective stability pervasively affect one's relationships and psychosocial functioning.[22] It is noteworthy that dissociative states can sometimes be associated with homicide or other serious acts of aggression, typically followed by shock and confusion on the part of the perpetrator, after he or she has reconnected with reality and the self. However, serious violence authentically committed in the context of total dissociation is truly a rare occurrence.

In *antisocial personality disorder*, which we discussed alongside our description of psychopathy, there is the aforementioned general, sometimes reckless disregard for the rights and feelings of other people, manifested as hostility and/or aggression, deceit, and manipulation, followed by little to no genuine remorse.[23] Notably, as per the *DSM*, such a person must display these signs outside of the context of bipolar disorder or schizophrenia. This conceptualization obscures the fact that one can have a psychopathic personality structure in addition to a psychotic mood disturbance or schizophrenia, such that one can be psychopathic at baseline and transiently or fully detached from reality at certain points in his or her lifetime, as we have previously noted. When such individuals commit homicide or other acts of violence, we must carefully delineate, to the extent that is possible, whether the crime was driven by psychosis, aberrant personality features, or some combination thereof.

The *DSM* also delineates three Cluster C personality disorders, which are not typically associated with the brief, fleeting psychotic states sometimes seen in Cluster A and B disturbances. However, in some individuals diagnosed with *avoidant personality disorder*, characterized by a pervasive pattern of social inhibition, feelings of inadequacy, and extreme concern about negative evaluation by others, social withdrawal and hypervigilance may actually represent schizoid detachment or nascent paranoia, which have not yet been identified.[24] *Dependent personality disorder* involves a strong need to be taken care of by others, such that one is intensely afraid of losing supportive relationships.[25] Of note to us here, this disorder is sometimes present in individuals ranked in Category 3 of the Gradations of Evil scale, who blindly follow powerful, psychopathic types who commit heinous acts, sometimes even participating in them. Finally, *obsessive-compulsive personality disorder* involves a preoccupation with orderliness, rules, and regulations, often to the point of rigidity and loss of efficiency. These individuals tend to be viewed by others as controlling and stubborn.[26] Notably, what we do not see here are the magical, psychotic-like ideas that can sometimes be seen in obsessive-compulsive disorder, a condition that should not be confused with this similarly named disturbance of personality.

We should also touch upon the potential relationship between violence and psychotic illness, although an exhaustive review is beyond the scope of this volume. The academic literature indicates that the majority of people with mental illness are not dangerous and that most violence is, in fact, committed by individuals without mental disorders. However, some evidence suggests that psychotic symptoms may be significantly related to risk of violence.[27] It has been reported that 5–10 percent of offenders incarcerated for homicide meet criteria for schizophrenia.[28] A 2009 meta-analysis of 204 studies of psychosis as a risk factor for violent behavior yielded that persons with psychotic illness had a 49–68 percent increase in potential for violence, relative to individuals not meeting criteria for psychiatric illness.[29] Nonadherence to psychotropic medications and poor insight about one's psychotic symptoms have been shown to mediate the relationship between psychosis and violent behaviors.[30]

A review of twenty-two studies found that major psychiatric disorders, particularly schizophrenia, are associated with higher risks for interpersonal aggression, accounting for 5–15 percent of community-based violence.[31] This was true even in the absence of alcohol or substance use. Elsewhere, however, abuse of alcohol or illicit drugs has been implicated as a key mediating factor,[32] and may, in fact, account for more of the risk than the psychotic illness itself.[33] Psychologist Dr. Eric B. Elbogen and psychiatrist Dr. Sally C. Johnson identified a complex interplay between demographic factors, alcohol and substance abuse, adverse life events, and environmental stressors in violent behavior associated with severe mental illness, making violence prediction challenging.[34] The MacArthur Violence Risk Assessment Study (MVRAS), which evaluated 1,136 recently discharged psychiatric patients over the course of a year, attempted to address methodological issues that had previously limited similar research and to disentangle interwoven factors. The prevalence of violent behaviors among those with major mental disorders who did not abuse substances was found to be indistinguishable from a general population comparison group drawn from the same neighborhoods. Violence risk was doubled by concurrent substance abuse. Notably, patients with schizophrenia showed the lowest occurrence of violence throughout the year (14.8 percent), relative to those with bipolar disorder (22 percent) or major depressive disorder (28.5 percent). However, violence associated with these conditions is likely to be most frequent soon after hospital discharge, and community-based samples of individuals with these disorders are not likely to display similarly high rates of violence. Moreover, delusions were not found to be associated with violence in the MVRAS,[35] in contrast to previous evidence linking violence and delusions that threaten to override one's capacity for self-control or make one feel unsafe.[36]

MVRAS data have recently been reanalyzed, with contrasting results, depending upon whether one's objective is to identify statistical predictors of violence or to establish relationships that allow for considerations of causality. Researchers Drs. Simone Ullrich, Robert Kears, and Jeremy Coid found that a prospective model confirms initial findings.[37] However, if the actual timing of psychotic symptoms, relative to violent behaviors, is considered, a relationship emerges between violence and delusions specifically involving thought insertion; possessing unique powers or gifts; and being spied upon, plotted against, followed, or under the control of a person or force. Anger due to these delusional beliefs was found to be a mediating factor, except in the case of grandiose delusions.[38] Elsewhere, command auditory hallucinations—auditory hallucinations that instruct an individual to act in specific ways—with violent content;[39] delusional beliefs, especially of persecution;[40] or both have been linked to higher violence potential.[41]

With all of these concepts and findings in mind, we turn now to a highly unusual case that falls within this sparsely populated category of the Gradations of Evil scale, in which homicide, torture, psychotic illness, and a psychopathic personality structure are all observed. The gruesome story we will describe is all the more interesting, in that it involves a rare pre-1960s serial killer who displayed many of the characteristics we will link, in part II of this book, with the post-1960s era of "new evil." Notably, however, serial murder with a psychotic element appears to have always been uncommon, identified as a clear motivating factor in only 6 percent of serial killers between 1900 and 2018, as we have previously noted.[42]

The case of Albert Fish—the whiskered, seemingly innocuous "Gray Man" who sexually assaulted, mutilated, cooked, and ate children—is truly the stuff of nightmares. He was born in Washington, DC, in 1870, the youngest of four children, to a seventy-five-year-old fertilizer manufacturer, who was said to suffer from "religious mania," and his thirty-two-year-old wife, who experienced auditory hallucinations.[43] There was an extensive history of mental illness in other members of the family: seven relatives were diagnosed with psychoses or psychopathic personalities, two died in institutions, one was an alcoholic, and others were described as "completely crazy." When Fish was five, his father died of a heart attack, and his mother, who found herself struggling to make ends meet, placed him in an orphanage, where he would spend the next four years.[44] His birth name, Hamilton, led the other children to playfully call him "Ham and Eggs," so he rechristened himself Albert, after a brother, who had also passed away. At the orphanage, he was routinely whipped and beaten, already, at this young age, becoming sexually aroused by the experience of physical pain. He also found a peculiar pleasure in being cruel to others, remarking later in life, "I always had a desire to inflict pain on others and to have others inflict pain on me. I always seemed to enjoy everything that hurt." He was a frequent bed-wetter and attempted to run away on numerous occasions.[45]

Around 1879, Fish returned to the care of his mother, who was now gainfully employed. At age twelve, he initiated a sexual relationship with a telegraph boy, who introduced him to *urophagia* and *coprophagia*—clinical terms for the consumption of urine and feces, respectively. The budding killer began passing long hours at public bathhouses, watching the other boys disrobe. In his early twenties, he relocated to New York City, where he worked as a prostitute and began sexually assaulting young males.[46] He also earned money as a freelance decorator and housepainter, which would later raise questions about the possible impact of lead-based paint upon his nervous system. At age twenty-eight, Fish entered into a marriage arranged by his mother, fathering six children, all the while molesting boys without the knowledge of his family.[47] To their surprise, he was arrested for theft in 1903 and incarcerated at Sing Sing.[48]

Following his release, Fish embarked upon a relationship with a male lover who took him to a wax museum, where the two encountered a model of a bisected penis. The image left a powerful impression upon him, and he thereafter found himself morbidly obsessed with the idea of castration.[49] He later tied up nineteen-year-old, intellectually disabled Thomas Kedden in a barn and, after torturing him for two weeks, severed his penis. "I shall never forget his scream, or the look he gave me," Fish would later say. He left the victim a ten-dollar bill and a goodbye kiss before abandoning him to bleed to death. He had considered mutilating the man's entire body and carting it home but was sufficiently clearheaded to recognize how conspicuous he would be, traveling with rapidly decomposing human remains.[50]

In 1917, Fish's wife left him for a male boarder, taking nearly all of their possessions with her and leaving him to raise their children on his own. At that time, he began driving them to a cottage in Westchester, New York, where he would climb to the top of a hill at night and bay at the moon, shouting, with his hands raised, "I am Christ! I am Christ!" He developed a taste for raw meat and served it at family meals.[51] At that time, he began hearing a voice he believed to be that of St. John the Apostle— interestingly, the namesake of the orphanage where sexual pleasure and pain were first coupled in his mind in childhood—and, following the evangelist's instructions, wrapped himself up in a carpet.[52] He experienced intense visions of "Christ and His angels," and quoted God as revealing things to him, such as, "Happy is he that taketh Thy little ones and dasheth their heads against the stones."[53] He came to believe he should purge and atone for his sins with physical suffering and human sacrifices, and that God had commanded him to torture and castrate boys. Fish began subjecting himself to a series of bizarre masochistic acts, including inserting needles into his groin and abdomen, and beneath his fingernails; stuffing lighter fluid-soaked bits of wool into his anus and lighting them on fire; and beating himself, or having his children or other victims do so, with a paddle studded with nails.[54] In 1919, he stabbed an intellectually disabled boy in Washington, DC. It became his preference to assault African

American and/or cognitively impaired children, whom he felt would not be missed. Five years later, he began killing with a meat cleaver, a butcher's knife, and a handsaw, which he called his "Implements of Hell."[55]

In 1928, the nearly sixty-year-old Fish, masquerading as a farmer named Frank Howard, responded to a classified ad placed by an eighteen-year-old New York City man. While his objective was to draw away the intended victim and torture him to death, Fish unexpectedly encountered the man's ten-year-old sister Grace Budd, and his plans were instantly changed. Presenting to the family as pleasant and kind, and charmingly describing his twenty acres of farmland and amiable crew, he readily acquired her parents' permission to accompany her to a birthday party, supposedly being held for his niece. She was never seen again—alive or dead.[56] Seven years later, after another man had served jail time for the murder of Budd, Fish, who was by then a senior citizen, sent an anonymous letter to the child's parents, which callously explained how he had killed, dismembered, and cannibalized her. It read, in part,[57]

> We had lunch. Grace sat in my lap and kissed me. I made up my mind to eat her. On the pretense of taking her to a party. You said yes she could go. I took her to an empty house in Westchester I had already picked out. When we got there, I told her to remain outside. She picked wildflowers. I went upstairs and stripped all my clothes off. I knew if I did not I would get her blood on them. When all was ready I went to the window and called her. Then I hid in a closet until she was in the room. When she saw me all naked she began to cry and tried to run down the stairs. I grabbed her and she said she would tell her mamma. First I stripped her naked. How she did kick—bite and scratch. I choked her to death, then cut her in small pieces so I could take my meat to my rooms. Cook and eat it. How sweet and tender her little ass was roasted in the oven. It took me 9 days to eat her entire body.

It would later emerge that he had placed the girl's head on a paint can, to drain her blood, before packaging up other parts to transport to his home.[58]

In 1930, Fish remarried, but he and his new wife separated after just one week. He was arrested for mailing an obscene letter to a woman who answered a false advertisement he posted for a maid position, and hospitalized at Bellevue for observation through 1931.[59] In deriving pleasure from using obscene language in his message to a relative stranger, the killer was engaging in one of his several paraphilias, known as *scatologia* or *coprolalia*. Three years later, he was arrested for the murder of Grace Budd, threatening the arresting detective with a razor blade.[60]

Fish later confessed to the murder of four-year-old Billy Gaffney, who disappeared from his Brooklyn home in 1927. The child had last been seen playing with a friend, who, when asked about Gaffney's whereabouts, eerily replied, "The boogeyman took him." A witness spied Fish on a trolley, dragging the boy, who was not wearing a coat in the dead of winter and crying for his mother. The killer explained that he brought Gaffney to an abandoned house, where he stripped, bound, and gagged him before burning his clothes. The following day, he beat the boy with tools to "tenderize" him, in the way one prepares meat to render it more palatable. He then whipped the victim to the point of bleeding with a homemade cat-o'-nine-tails, cut off his ears and nose, slit his mouth from ear to ear, and gouged out his eyes. The frenzy culminated with Fish piercing the boy's belly with a knife and drinking his blood as he expired. The killer then bagged up portions of the body in potato sacks and tossed them into a pool of stagnant water. Other parts were brought home. The ears and nose, and pieces of the face and belly were made into a stew, and the buttocks were roasted and prepared with gravy. He remarked in his confession, "I never ate any roast turkey that tasted half as good as his sweet fat little behind did."[61]

During his 1935 trial, Fish was found to be insane by criminal court psychiatrist Dr. Fredric Wertham, who diagnosed "paranoid psychosis," in light of Fish's descriptions of intense hallucinations of the voice of God commanding him to kill. Fish was found guilty and sentenced to death, following imprisonment at Sing Sing.[62] Onlookers struggled to believe that the decrepit, stooped-over Fish was responsible for so much unspeakable evil. Wertham himself would later marvel how meek, benevolent, and gentle the killer seemed. "If you wanted someone to entrust your children to," he wrote, "he would be the one you would choose."[63] He also noted that, when describing the slaughter of Billy Gaffney, "He spoke in a matter-of-fact way, like a housewife describing her favorite methods of cooking. . . . But at times his voice and facial expression indicated a kind of satisfaction and ecstatic thrill. I said to myself: However you define the medical and legal borders of sanity, this certainly is beyond that border."[64]

Fish subsequently confessed to the killing of Frances X. McDonnell, an eight-year-old girl on Staten Island, whom he sexually assaulted, then strangled to death with his suspenders in 1924. He was suspected in the 1932 murder of fifteen-year-old Mary O'Connor, whose mutilated body was found in a wooded area not far from a home Fish had been painting.[65] He was confidently linked to "at least a hundred" sexual assaults across the country, but Fish boasted four hundred victims "in every state."[66]

Prior to Fish's death in the electric chair, he reportedly remarked that the electrocution would be "the supreme thrill of my life."[67] *Daily News* reporter Norma Abrams wrote of the killer's forthcoming execution, "His watery eyes gleamed at the thought of being burned by a heat more intense than the flames with which he often seared his flesh to gratify his lust."[68]

A WORD ABOUT CANNIBALISM AND VAMPIRISM

Albert Fish's acts of cannibalism and vampirism—which refer, respectively, to the eating of flesh and internal organs, and the drinking of blood—may be the aspect of his case that people find most horrifying and unfathomable, particularly because he exclusively feasted upon children. Intriguingly, however, this element of his crimes does not figure heavily into his designation to Category 20 of the Gradations of Evil scale, which is, instead, warranted by his pattern of repeat homicide and protracted torture, in conjunction with both psychopathy and psychotic illness. Indeed, cannibalism poses a unique challenge, on several levels, for the twenty-two-point continuum. First, there is some disagreement about whether or not cannibalism has always been deemed an "evil" act, forbidden on moral grounds across all of time and space. Anthropologists tell us that cannibalism was practiced in past centuries by indigenous peoples in numerous geographic areas, including Sumatra, New Guinea, the Fiji Islands and elsewhere in Melanesia, Australia, New Zealand, areas of West and Central Africa, the Amazon Basin, and parts of the Solomon Islands.[69] Moreover, it appears that Neanderthals, who inhabited the Moula-Guercy cave in modern-day France approximately 100,000 years ago, engaged in some degree of cannibalism.[70] In ancient Egypt and, indeed, at various points in recent centuries, it was employed as a desperate means of survival during periods of famine.[71]

As the reader may have noted, it is possible for such acts to fall into a wide range of categories in the Gradations of Evil scale, depending upon one's context, motive, and psychiatric state, as well as the presence or absence of other elements, such as homicide, sexual assault, and torture. We have reviewed infamous crimes in which cannibalism was the result of severe mental illness, as was the case with Fish, and drug abuse, as when thirty-one-year-old Rudy Eugene, under the influence of marijuana and potentially some other illicit substance, was found naked on the MacArthur Causeway in Miami, Florida, devouring the face of a sixty-five-year-old homeless man in 2012.[72] In a horrendous case from 2009, police visited the home of thirty-four-year-old Angelo Mendoza, who was intoxicated with PCP, and were told by his injured four-year-old son, "My daddy ate my eyes."[73] We have also examined cases in which cannibalism and vampirism were an aspect of cult or alternative spiritual activity, sometimes intended as a perversion of the Christian concept of Holy Communion, or a means of uniting members into a cohesive "family." For instance, blood consumption for the latter purpose was practiced by double murderer Roderick Ferrell as part of a vampire cult, in which he assumed the identity of a five-hundred-year-old vampire named Vesago.[74]

Finally, we have examined crimes in which sport or exhilaration were the chief motivation for cannibalistic acts, occasionally for paraphilic purposes. In 1981, Japan's Issei Sagawa, who had a long history of sexual fantasies involving cannibalizing beautiful women, invited classmate Renée Hartevelt to his apartment to work on a school assignment, shot her in the neck with a rifle, engaged in necrophilic acts, and devoured parts of her body over the course of two days. Arrested while carrying the uneaten remains in two large bags, he went on to gain cult status in his native country following his release from prison, appearing in softcore pornographic films with cannibalistic themes and even working as a sushi critic.[75] More disturbing is the 1985 case of John Brennan Crutchley, dubbed the "Vampire Rapist." After abducting a teenage female hitchhiker, he immobilized her by tying her limbs to a countertop. While taking home videos, he repeatedly raped her, and drank of the 40–45 percent of her blood he had extracted by way of needles inserted into her arm and wrist.[76]

The particularly infamous gay serial killer, necrophile, and cannibal Jeffrey Dahmer murdered seventeen males between 1978 and 1991.

Having solicited prostitutes or lured unsuspecting men from bars, he typically drugged, raped, and strangled victims before dismembering them and engaging in sexual acts with their corpses or body parts. Dahmer eventually became preoccupied with the notion that he could transform his victims into "zombies" to serve as submissive sexual partners, entirely under his control. To that end, he drilled holes into drugged victims' skulls and injected hydrochloric acid or boiling water into their brains. When his crimes came to the attention of authorities in 1991, police raided his Milwaukee, Wisconsin, apartment, which reeked of decaying flesh. To their horror, they found an altar containing candles and human skulls in the closet, two skulls resting on a computer, bodies being dissolved in acid in a large drum, and countless disturbing photographs. They also discovered a severed head and other body parts in the refrigerator, preserved in liquids in jars; a human heart in the freezer; and a decomposing penis and pair of hands. It emerged that Dahmer was eating some of his victims' body parts, including hearts, biceps, and livers, earning him the ghastly nickname "the Milwaukee Cannibal."[77] He would later claim that his primary objective was to keep his victims from ever leaving him by way of his various atrocious acts—a theme that also emerged in the story of another cannibal, Armin Meiwes, whom we have already discussed elsewhere. "The only motive there ever was," Dahmer would say during a 1994 interview with NBC's Stone Phillips, "was to completely control a person—a person I found physically attractive—and keep them with me as long as possible, even if it meant just keeping a part of them."[78]

Cannibalism and vampirism are hardly "new" evils. We shall see, however, upon our transition to part II of this book that, in the post-1960s era, there have been a number of shocking cases involving forcing others to engage in cannibalism against their wills, sometimes consciously, and sometimes not. We observe unconscious forced cannibalism in a 2010 case in which three homeless men in Russia fatally stabbed and beat a man with a hammer, dismembering and cannibalizing his body. They then sold the remnants to a meat kiosk, where they were incorporated into kebabs and pies in a manner reminiscent of the fictional killer Sweeney Todd and his partner in crime, Mrs. Lovett. It is unclear, however, whether the eatery's owners were aware that they had purchased and prepared human flesh. In the end, authorities could locate no trace of the portion of the victim's body sold to the kiosk, since it had been entirely consumed by unwitting patrons.[79] As an example of the conscious form of forced cannibalism, at the time of this writing, it is alleged that five Louisiana residents kept a twenty-two-year-old autistic female relative in a cage, beating her and singeing her with cigarettes, and dousing her with human waste from a septic tank. The horrifying accusation continues that members of the group forced her to open an urn containing the cremated ashes of her late mother, pour them into a cereal bowl, and eat them with a spoon while her captors looked on and laughed.[80]

CATEGORY 21

Like individuals in Category 19, a psychopathic person ranked at level 21 of the scale is not known to have killed, or is suspected in at least one homicide that has not been confirmed. When there is a claim or accusation of murder, it is generally not described as an integral part of the offender's sadistic objectives but, rather, as having occurred in the service of some practical end, such as eliminating a witness. These rankings are distinguished, however, by the fact that persons assigned to Category 21 physically torture human victims. The torture is intentionally prolonged, particularly cruel, and likely to be both psychological and physical in scope. Note that Category 21 torturers differ from those categorized at levels 18, 20, and 22 of the scale, in that the latter three rankings require a history of homicide. Moreover, while the torture seen in Categories 20 and 22 is deliberately drawn out, as it is in Category 21, the torturous acts associated with Category 18 are not protracted in nature. The constellation of traits and behaviors that characterizes Category 21 can be illustrated with the case of Cameron Hooker, born in California in 1953.

Virtually nothing is known of Hooker's background, except that, after graduating high school in 1972, he took up work in a lumber mill. Three years later, at age twenty-two, he married a fifteen-year-old girl named Janice, an alleged victim of abuse by her family. Her husband called her a "whore" and subjected her to sexually sadistic acts, such as repeatedly hanging her, nude, by her wrists and whipping her, or nearly drowning her. Likely terrified of him, she did not resist. After Hooker informed his wife that he intended to abduct a young woman and force her into sexual slavery, Janice reportedly secured a promise that he would whip the slave, in lieu of herself, so that she might more easily become pregnant. She also asked him to forego vaginal sex with the slave.[81]

According to Hooker's wife—and it is critical to note for the reasons just reiterated that this allegation has never been proven—in January of 1976, the couple abducted an eighteen-year-old hitchhiker, Marliz Spannhake, in California. She was reportedly stripped and suspended from the ceiling by her wrists, and tortured for one day before her vocal cords were severed with a knife, possibly to quiet her screams. Janice claimed that her husband fatally shot the woman in the stomach with a pellet gun and buried her in a shallow grave near a state park.[82]

What is known for certain is that, on May 19, 1977, the couple abducted twenty-year-old Colleen Stan as she was hitchhiking from her home in Oregon to visit a friend in the Golden State. Ms. Hooker held a newborn son in the passenger's seat. After driving to an isolated area, Mr. Hooker held a knife to Stan's throat, bound and gagged her, and covered her head with a homemade wooden box—a terrifying contraption, apparently designed to totally disorient her—before transporting her to their home in the Northern California city of Red Bluff.[83] Stripped and removed from the device, Stan was blindfolded, hung from the wrists, and whipped before the Hookers had intercourse beneath the dangling victim. Stan was then stuffed into a coffin-like box, which would have deprived her of virtually any sensory experiences.[84] Chains surrounded her neck and ran the length of her body. A small blower placed inside the box provided air. Anyone who has ever been in a small, tight space, such as a closed MRI scanner, knows how difficult this is to endure for even a single hour. Stan was kept in the box nearly all day for the next three years and not permitted to make a sound. When in need of the toilet, she had to use her feet to slide a bedpan beneath herself. There was virtually no air to breathe, and the temperature inside the box sometimes exceeded one hundred degrees.[85] She would later say of the nightmarish ordeal, "He would keep me in there for, like, 22, 23 hours a day. It was absolutely pitch-black in this box. Totally dark. I had claustrophobia so terribly bad. I would get really anxious and focus on being locked up in the box and listening to that fan next to my head, just going on and on and on, just feeling like I was going to lose my mind."[86]

Fed only cold scraps, Stan lost twenty-two pounds over the first four weeks. It was three months before she was bathed by her captors. Permission was required to speak. She was taken out of the box, like a toy, for daily rounds of whipping and electrical shocks.[87] She was also stretched on a homemade torture rack, which permanently damaged her back and one shoulder.[88] Hooker began raping the victim, using only implements for penetration, lest he breach his vow to his wife.[89]

By November of 1977, Stan was being forced to do chores around the house, always in the nude. In early 1978, Mr. Hooker informed her, falsely, that he was a member of "the Company," supposedly a secret organization that enslaves women for pleasure and profit, and which would retaliate against her and her family should she attempt to escape. She was made to sign a "slave contract," granting full control over her body, soul, and personal possessions to "Michael Powers," which was Mr. Hooker's pseudonym. Her captors also signed. Stan was then placed in a collar and renamed "K," robbing her of the last vestige of her former life and sense of self, which later became "Kay Powers." A new box was constructed and, unimaginably, incorporated into the frame of the Hookers' waterbed. Rack torture and rape were now simultaneous.[90] Stan was referred to as "a piece of furniture." To test her loyalty, she was instructed to put an unloaded gun in her own mouth and pull the trigger.[91]

In 1980, Stan was forced to beg for money, and made no attempt to flee, due to terror of the Company. She was eventually permitted to sleep outside of the box, chained to the toilet on the floor of the Hookers' bathroom. She was allowed to phone her family, claiming that she was employed as a nanny for a "nice couple." In March of 1981, Mr. Hooker drove Stan to see her parents and grandmother, where he was introduced as her boyfriend, Mike. She spent the night with them and was picked up by her captor the following day. Apparently regretting having given Stan so much freedom, Mr. Hooker returned to keeping her in the box upon their return to his home. Her "year out" had come to an abrupt end.[92]

In 1983, Stan's encasement was relocated to a pit, freshly constructed by Mr. Hooker, under a shed. In better spirits, he released her to attend church services with his wife and work as a motel maid under an alias. When Mr. Hooker informed his wife that he intended to acquire new slaves and to add them to the pit, alongside Stan, his wife visited their captive at her place of employment and revealed that the Company was a concoction of her husband's. After an unfathomably horrifying seven years, Stan was able to flee but phoned Mr. Hooker in tears, agreeing not to go to the police, so as to give him an opportunity to "reform." Some believe she may have been experiencing *Stockholm syndrome*, in which a hostage experiences trust, loyalty, sympathy, affection, or, in some cases, even sexual attraction toward a captor, possibly as a strategy for survival.[93]

Ms. Hooker later turned in her husband. In light of her own maltreatment and in exchange for testimony, she was not charged with any crime. She currently works under a new name as an advocate for victims of abuse. During Mr. Hooker's trial, he admitted to kidnapping Stan, who described to a stunned courtroom her seven-year ordeal of being repeatedly tortured and raped, and confined for interminably long periods in a box that resembled a coffin. The judge, who described Mr. Hooker as "the most dangerous psychopath" he had ever encountered, and noted the "cruelty and viciousness" of his crimes, imposed the maximum sentence of 104 years in prison.[94] At the end of the trial, Mr. Hooker remarked to his attorney, "I want you to thank the judge for me. I have a library, a gym, and the time to enjoy them, and it's better than living with those two women."[95] Because there was no homicide in the case, capital punishment was not an option. However, one might be of the opinion that Mr. Hooker's atrocities constituted a crime worse than murder in the first degree.

CHAPTER TEN

CATEGORY 22

People talk sometimes of bestial cruelty, but that's a great injustice and insult to the beasts; a beast can never be so cruel as a man, so artistically cruel. The tiger only tears and gnaws, that's all he can do. He would never think of nailing people by the ears, even if he were able to do it.

—Fyodor Dostoyevsky, *The Brothers Karamazov*, 1879, translated by Constance Garnett in 1912

The reader is forewarned that this will not be an easy chapter to review. The individuals we will discuss herein have all been ranked at the extreme end of the Gradations of Evil scale, and the details of their crimes are the most likely to cause us to avert our eyes, cover our ears, hold our stomachs, and contemplate, in blank bewilderment, the existence of evil in its purest form.

The serial rapist and murderer Tommy Lynn Sells, whose horrifying deeds we will presently explore, once remarked, "Take your worst nightmares, and put my face to them."[1] The people we will describe in the following vignettes might all lay claim to that blood-chilling, dubious distinction. Each one trapped, tortured, and dispatched unsuspecting men, women, and/or children from this life with degrees of automation, detachment, and callousness we simply fail to comprehend in our fellow human beings. In all cases, the infliction of prolonged pain and suffering was the primary objective. For each, this sadism was interwoven with some perverse sexual motivation, which is usually, but not uniformly, the case for individuals designated to Category 22 of the scale. Following their crimes, several of these consummately psychopathic killers used bodies—or parts of bodies—for a variety of unspeakable purposes, sometimes necrophilic, sometimes cannibalistic, and in some cases, these were retained as trophies or mementos of the killer's happier times.

Note that the five individuals we will discuss, all of whom were serial killers by any criteria, were selected for analysis because they are especially illustrative of the typical features and drives associated with this final category of the scale. There are numerous other psychopathic torture-murderers we are unable to cover, due to space limitations. For those wishing to further study this extreme degree of evil, other highly instructive cases are those of Ian Brady and Myra Hindley, the British couple who tortured and killed five young children, recording the screams of one victim for personal enjoyment;[2] Dean Corll, who led a trio who abducted, severely sexually tortured, and killed at least twenty-eight boys;[3] and Charles Ng and Leonard Lake, who imprisoned women in a bunker, raping, torturing, and murdering them, often while taking home videos. Sometimes killing the victims' husbands and young children, Ng and Lake had at least eleven victims but as many as twenty-five.[4]

TOMMY LYNN SELLS

In 2014, Tommy Lynn Sells was executed for a single murder—that of thirteen-year-old Kaylene "Katy" Harris of San Antonio, Texas, on New Year's Eve in 1999. The girl's adoptive father, Terry Harris, reportedly met Sells and his wife at their local church and began counseling them on their marriage in his own home, where Sells first encountered Katy. When her father was out of town one evening, Sells sneaked into the Harris home through a window, where he found the girl sharing a bunk bed with a ten-year-old friend, Krystal Surles.[5] He stripped and sexually assaulted his intended victim and then slashed both of the girls' throats with a butcher's blade so fiercely sharpened that it was whittled down to the width of a boning knife.[6] After stabbing Katy sixteen more times in a frenzy of sadism and sexual pleasure, he coolly gathered up items potentially marked with fingerprints and left the home. Surles, who miraculously survived the severing of her vocal cords, escaped to the home of a neighbor, where she described Sells via handwritten messages. This resulted in the killer's arrest.[7]

Sells would later confess to the rapes and murders of approximately seventy men, women, and children across a wide swath of the United States between 1980 and 1999, although this number has never been confirmed.[8] In light of his vagabond lifestyle, supported by train-hopping, car theft, pan-handling, stealing, working odd jobs, and, occasionally, selling property left behind by victims, he dubbed himself "the Coast-to-Coast Killer."[9]

The transience and seething rage displayed by Sells dated to his earliest days. He and a twin sister, Tammy Jean, were born in Oakland, California, in 1964 to Nina Sells, a single mother with three other children. Following a move to Missouri, both infants contracted spinal meningitis, which only Sells survived.[10] He was thereafter sent to live elsewhere in the state with an aunt, where he remained for two and a half years before returning home. Throughout this period, he was often left to fend for himself, rarely attending school and imbibing alcohol by the age of seven. Perhaps longing for a stable parental figure, he developed a friendship with a man from a nearby town, who showered him with attention and gifts, and took him on frequent outings, only to eventually sexually assault him. By age ten, Sells had graduated to more frequent alcohol use and begun smoking mari-juana.[11] Three years later, when he climbed naked into his grandmother's bed, his mother barred him from their home, and relocated the family to an undisclosed location. Days later, boiling with rage, he reputedly pistol-whipped a young woman. By age fourteen, he was drifting from town to town, stealing and working wherever possible.[12] One day, reflecting on these formative years, he would call himself "the little boy without a dream."[13]

Sells claimed to have committed his first murder the following year. Peering into the window of a home he was intending to burglarize, he sup-posedly spied a man molesting a young boy and found himself reminded of his own childhood sexual abuse. He fatally shot the perpetrator in a fit of intense rage.[14] He would later describe this first homicide as producing a powerful euphoria, resulting in a lifelong passion for killing, which he com-pared to a heroin addiction. In a televised 2006 interview with Dr. Stone, Sells said of the shooting and his subsequent serial murders, "After I did it, it was like a rush, just like a shot of dope. The people don't matter. It's the crime. It's the sensation of the blood. The rush itself is the high."[15] He later shot a man to death who caught him breaking into his home. Sells subse-quently traveled to California, where he stabbed a male victim to death with an icepick, became embroiled in gang activity, and repeatedly stabbed another man, just missing his spinal cord.[16]

In 1981, Sells attempted a reunion with his family in Arkansas, but he was once again evicted by his mother, after he stripped and attempted to initiate sex with her during a shower. Perhaps this retriggered copious anger toward those who had robbed him of his childhood: the mother he felt abandoned him and the sham older "friend" who was, in fact, a pedophile. After seeking help at a mental health clinic, where he stated, "I don't know who I am," Sells spiraled further into alcoholism and senseless violence, reportedly sexually assaulting a stranger for the first time. He claimed to have raped and murdered a woman in 1982, hurling her body into a flooded quarry in central Arkansas. He also shot a man to death.[17]

From this point onward, the killer's fury grew increasingly savage and more generalized so that all of humanity seemed fair game to him. For instance, several weeks after a woman innocently bumped into him on the street of a town through which he was passing, he reputedly returned to the location to stalk her, followed her to her home, and brutally beat her to death with a baseball bat.[18] Space issues prevent a full tally of the unfortunate victims he raped, stabbed, shot, bludgeoned, strangled, slashed, tortured, and, occasionally, mutilated between 1983 and his arrest in 1999, punctuated only by several stints in jail for theft and drug and alcohol charges. However, it is of particular note that, during this period, his depravity expanded to include the sexual assault and murder of children. He also developed a penchant for slaughtering people who were friends or relatives of one another, possibly psychologically rooted in envy of the stable homes and love these people seemed to share. He reportedly beat two young Missouri women and their four-year-old children to death in separate incidents in 1983 and 1985.[19] It is unclear whether, in his mind, these mothers were representations of his own, who had rejected him from the only family he had ever known.

In a controversial confession that is not universally accepted, Sells claimed that, in 1987, he murdered an entire family, the Dardeens.[20] In one account, while hitchhiking through Illinois, he was picked up by Keith Dardeen and invited home for a hot meal;[21] in another, he approached Dardeen when he noticed his trailer was for rent.[22] The man was fatally shot, and his severed penis was placed inside his mouth. The killer then beat Dardeen's three-year-old son to death with a bat and proceeded to attempt to rape his pregnant wife, Elaine, which induced labor. In a violent frenzy, the attacker used the bat to fatally bludgeon her and her newborn daughter, who was reportedly still connected by her umbilical cord, before inserting the weapon into the woman's vagina.[23] Before leaving the Dardeens' home, the perpetrator reportedly positioned the bodies on a waterbed, for reasons that are unclear but may have held some personal psychological significance for him.[24] If Sells did, indeed, commit this atrocity, it might be seen as representing the pinnacle of his rage and resentment. The insertion of a bat into Mrs. Dardeen's vagina emblemizes how inextricably his fury and his perverse sexual desires were intermingled in his mind.

In an interview with serial killer profiler Stéphane Bourgoin, Sells claimed that this savage crime was prompted by a sexual pass by Mr. Dardeen, stating, "I had to kill him . . . and because he decided to make a homosexual advance on me, that cost him his wife's life." If this were true, his rage toward Dardeen may have reflected a merger, in his psyche, of a Good Samaritan and the seemingly kind but actually depraved child molester from his youth. However, it was more likely a blatant fib to disavow personal responsibility. When asked why it was necessary to murder the children, Sells explained that he did not wish for them to grow up hearing about the loss of their parents—that he was preventing their future misery, having experienced parental abandonment himself.[25] In another interview, with Dr. Stone, the killer was asked why, if his objective for sometimes butchering children was to grant them mercy, he opted to do so in such cruel and painful ways. Sells was unable to provide an explanation. Asked further why he opted against using a firearm, he responded, "I don't like guns. They're dangerous."[26]

The callousness and fearless urge to kill without any shred of compassion exhibited by Sells were hallmarks of bona fide psychopathy, as was his complete inability to take responsibility for his actions. As noted, he sometimes attempted to justify his crimes with stories of personal victimization, such as child abuse, a man making a sexual pass at him or someone disrespecting him, which may or may not have been total fabrications. For example, he blamed a Kentucky community for his rape and strangulation of thirteen-year-old Haley McHone, reasoning that in failing to trim a patch of tall weeds alongside a public park, it provided him covering while he took the girl's life.[27] Whatever causality Sells may have attempted to portray, there can be no doubt that the chief motivation for his indiscriminate butchering of men, women, and children was to express intense, wide-reaching rage toward humanity, and to punish other people—especially if they seemed to be part of happy families or friendships, or full of youth and promise—with prolonged and intensely painful psychological and physical torment. Such sadistic behavior provided what he called a "release" of anger, and seems to have occasioned orgasmic sexual pleasure, as well.

Still able to intensely visualize his killings after years behind bars, Sells remarked with a smile in 2006, "There's something about the blade making a slice on you . . . seeing it pierce open . . . seeing the gap and watching the sensation of it all. Maybe I became addicted to that."[28] He may very well have been right: neuroscientist Dr. James Fallon of the University of California, Irvine, who has studied the brains of psychopaths, notes that serial killers behave quite similarly to individuals addicted to illicit drugs. When someone addicted to murder abstains long enough from the rush provided by his or her aggressive and/or sexual acts, an unpleasant tension, which Fallon posits to be related to a buildup of hormones in the amygdala, mounts until it reaches a trigger point, and the offender strikes to obtain a fix.[29]

The developmental pathway to the killer's crimes was likely multi-determined. Possible damage to the brain from meningitis in infancy; an absent father and traumatic home life; a sadistic, psychopathic character structure; and substance and alcohol use were all possible contributors. Whatever the antecedents, his litany of atrocious acts places him firmly in Category 22 of the Gradations of Evil scale. Not long after Sells was executed by lethal injection, one of his biographers, Diane Fanning, poignantly recalled a moment in one of her interviews with the killer in which he abruptly flew into a rage, standing up and pounding his fists upon a table. His face seemed to transform, and she suddenly found herself face-to-face with the true "evil" of Tommy Lynn Sells. "I knew at that moment," she wrote, "I saw the face his victims saw before they died. Because of all of that has happened and all that I know, I feel haunted by his victims, too. Their voices scream in my ears, their horror vibrates in my bones. His presence on this earth created enough poison and pain to rock a continent."[30]

ROBERT BERDELLA

On April 2, 1988, twenty-two-year-old Christopher Bryson leaped from the window of a Missouri home, clad in only a dog collar, and fled to the nearest police station on a broken foot. Drugged and badly bruised, he described four days of unfathomable torture and sodomy at the hand of his captor, thirty-nine-year-old Robert Berdella.[31] Bryson would prove the only surviving victim of the "Butcher of Kansas City." At least six other young men, all minimally educated, and allegedly working as drug dealers or prostitutes, were brutally raped, tortured, and killed before being methodically cut up and stuffed, piecemeal, into dog food bags to toss out with the trash.[32]

Berdella was born on the last day of January in 1949, in Cuyahoga Falls, Ohio.[33] His father, a devout Roman Catholic, would sometimes beat him and his younger brother with a leather strap, or compare the future killer unfavorably with his sibling, who was in better physical condition. Berdella was severely nearsighted, which required him to wear thick eyeglasses from the age of five, and suffered a slight speech impediment. He also had high blood pressure in childhood and had to take several prescription medications. In early adolescence, he was bullied by his peers in school. It was around this time that he began to identify as gay, which remained a secret, especially in his religious household, for several years. He attempted to date a girl, but the relationship was short-lived.[34] Still, he suddenly became more confident—almost overly so—and was experienced by others, especially females, as rude and condescending.[35]

Around age sixteen, Berdella's father died, and, to his great chagrin, his mother remarried. Since he was a rather robotic individual who struggled to adjust to change and tolerate intense emotional experiences, these events prompted a significant change in his behavior. He confined himself to his bedroom, obsessively studying coins and stamps, and writing to numerous foreign pen pals. He also became fixated upon *The Collector*, William Wyler's 1965 film version of the 1963 novel by John Fowles.[36] It tells the tale of Frederick Clegg, an isolated, mentally disturbed man who uses chloroform to abduct Miranda, a beautiful student with whom he has become obsessed, hoping that, with enough time, she will eventually come to care for him.[37]

Berdella was artistically gifted, earning a partial scholarship to the Kansas City Art Institute. He aspired to become a college professor. While completing coursework, he sickened his classmates with bizarre performance art pieces, including ones in which he tranquilized a dog, or decapitated a live chicken or duck, dancing around with the carcasses. He used and sold LSD and marijuana, ultimately leading to a brief stint in jail.[38] He also began abusing alcohol.[39] He left college in 1969, making ends meet as a cook and then as a purveyor of ancient artifacts, primitive art, drug paraphernalia, occult items, and morbid curiosities, such as shrunken human heads, at a booth called Bob's Bazaar Bizarre at the Westport Flea Market.[40] It was there that he met his first victim, nineteen-year-old Jerry Howell, an alleged prostitute who was the son of a fellow merchant. On Independence Day in 1984, the two made plans to attend a dance contest together, after a stop off at Berdella's home, where the fledgling serial killer restrained Howell and tortured him to death over several days. He then made incisions to the victim's inner elbows and jugular vein, and suspended his corpse over a large pot, in order to drain his blood.[41] The following day, he dismembered the body with a chainsaw and kitchen knives, and put the pieces out with his ordinary garbage for routine carting to a landfill.[42] He would go on to meet and lure several other victims with promises of a place to stay, drugs, or a warm meal, typically serving them drinks laced with powerful hypnotic medications to incapacitate them. They were then tortured over time, killed, dismembered, and discarded in the same manner as Howell.[43]

Berdella, whose intellectual curiosity and mechanical detachment had now taken a deeply disturbing turn, retained detailed notes in a torture diary, replete with hundreds of Polaroid snapshots of his victims. He recorded events in cryptic shorthand, in the same clinical, unemotional way a scientist experimenting upon canines or rodents might keep a daily log of his observations, methods, and results. "CP" indicated that the antipsychotic medication chlorpromazine had been administered to sedate and control a victim. Veterinary sedatives were also sometimes used. "EK" denoted electrocution of the shoulders, eyes, or testicles with a 7,700-volt neon sign transformer.[44] He took note of victims' physiques, sleeping habits, sexual positions during rape, and reactions to being sodomized with cucumbers or carrots.[45] To prevent infections that might cut short a victim's life and, thus, his sufferings, Berdella administered antibiotics.[46]

The sadistic killer documented means of punishment, which might include suspending a victim by his ankles from the rafters of his home, sealing his ears shut with window caulk, smashing his hand bones with an iron rod, inserting needles beneath his fingertips, or injecting liquid drain cleaner or bleach into his eyes or trachea. Eye injections caused intense pain and temporary blindness, while vocal cord injections prevented crying out for help. He bound one victim's hands with piano wire with the intention of inflicting permanent nerve damage. On the day he murdered another young man, his only notation was "Stop the project."[47] One victim died of septic shock after Berdella's arm punctured his anal wall during a sexual assault.[48] Some young men died of asphyxiation during torture, others of overdoses.[49] A twenty-year-old Wichita captive, Larry Pearson, was drugged and then beaten with a tree limb in retaliation for nearly severing Berdella's penis during forced oral sex. When he was told by doctors that he required urgent medical care, the killer asked to stop home first to feed his dogs. There, he placed a plastic bag over his captive's head and let him suffocate to death while tending to his beloved pets and making his way back to the hospital.[50]

Locals who knew Berdella described him as a flamboyant loner, eccentric but philanthropically inclined and incapable of committing murder. The young men visiting and leaving his home on a routine basis were believed to be runaways, generously offered shelter by a portly, soft-spoken father figure.[51]

At the time of Berdella's arrest in 1988, investigators searched his property and found heaps of books, papers, gemstones, and unusual artifacts, in addition to his copious records of torture. They also uncovered two human skulls, one in a closet and the other in his garden.[52] They found human vertebrae with scarring from hacksaws and knives,[53] and human teeth gathered in two envelopes.[54] It is uncertain whether the latter were extracted from the mouths of victims before or after death.

Berdella confessed to multiple murders, receiving six consecutive life sentences.[55] While in jail, he orchestrated an auction and sold off his collections of fossils, antiques, and knickknacks in order to cover his legal fees.[56] In an attempt to restore his besmirched reputation, he also opened up a trust fund for victims' families. He was aided by a Christian preacher who noted that the killer never expressed a scintilla of regret for his crimes, instead blaming them on other people.[57] He called the men he tortured to death "play toys" and criticized the police for not stopping him sooner.[58] The Butcher of Kansas City's punishment came to an abrupt end when he died of a heart attack in prison at the age of forty-three.[59]

Berdella displayed a complex personality structure, comprised of a mixture of the schizoid, sadistic, psychopathic, narcissistic, avoidant, and obsessive-compulsive traits we discussed in previous chapters. It appears that the death of his father and his mother's second marriage were simply too psychologically taxing for the emotionally limited young Berdella, who tended to deal with the unpredictability of human relationships by avoiding them altogether, focusing instead on collections and things he might better control. Clearly, he was filled with anger and confusing sexual urges that he denied due to powerful guilt. The death of his rigid, moralistic father, a sort of surrogate conscience, seems to have liberated some of those feelings—and drugs and alcohol removed his inhibitions, further still, until he could act out the darkest of his furious and perverse fantasies.

What is, perhaps, most disturbing is that, when it was necessary for the killer to win the confidence of his victims, or the affections of his associates and neighbors, he could readily mimic an affable, empathic lover of humankind, just as easily returning to emotional deadness and brutality when alone with his victims. It was also his practice to spin profoundly selfish deeds into seemingly selfless acts, due to his utter deficiency of self-awareness. For instance, when he decided that Larry Pearson needed to pay for nearly castrating him, he painted himself as someone so dedicated to the care of his Chow Chows that he left a doctor's office to feed them prior to a surgery. In reality, Berdella found it intolerable that his victim was still at home, living and breathing. The fact that the killer lured young men said to have been prostitutes or addicts under the pretense of helping them restore their lives, only to penalize them for their lifestyles with hellish torments, speaks to a moral grandiosity and perhaps a desire to find anyone he deemed more deserving of punishment and rejection than himself. Given that all of his victims were male, and some or all were homosexual, self-hatred and guilt surrounding his gay sexual identity may very well have played a role in his crimes.

The reason for Berdella's detached style is open to debate. Dr. Helen Morrison, a noted forensic psychiatrist who interviewed the killer, opined that he was more motivated by a desire to experiment than to kill, and that he thought so concretely that he may not have understood the infliction of pain or even sexual gratification the way sexually sadistic types generally do.[60] Noting his ability to win over the trust of his neighbors and those upon whom he wished to experiment, we view him, alternatively, as the very embodiment of psychopathy and sadism, who sought to so dominate his victims as to deprive them of any emotions or sensations that were not dictated by himself. His actions were meticulously designed to inflict prolonged and intense psychological and physical suffering—which, in point of fact, requires some ability to imagine other people's feelings. Berdella's placement at the extreme end of the Gradations of Evil scale is further warranted by the unspeakable gruesomeness of his crimes, which included the dismemberment of corpses and the occasional retention of human skulls, vertebrae, and teeth, blended in among so many macabre souvenirs, trinkets, and gewgaws. Perhaps, in committing torture and reducing human beings to inanimate "collectibles," Berdella had achieved the undoing of the anxieties of his youth, at last feeling dominant and powerful, and establishing relationships that could never end unless he willed them to do so.

GARY M. HEIDNIK

Jame "Buffalo Bill" Gumb, the fictitious serial killer created by Thomas Harris for his 1988 novel *The Silence of the Lambs*,[61] was a composite of three real-life criminals: His technique of feigning an injury to secure the aid of a woman before incapacitating her was drawn from the psychopathic serial killer, rapist, and necrophile Ted Bundy, while his flaying of victims to create a gender-altering suit of flesh was based upon Ed Gein, whom we have already discussed. Gumb's imprisonment of abducted females in a cramped pit in his basement was inspired by Gary Michael Heidnik, the scheming torture-murderer we will discuss in this third vignette.[62]

Heidnik was born in Eastlake, Ohio, near Cleveland, in November of 1943.[63] At the age of two, his mother claimed "gross negligence of duty" on the part of his father and filed for divorce. Two years later, his father and a second wife would gain custody of the child and his brother, due to his mother's heavy drinking.[64] Heidnik alleged that his father both emotionally and physically abused him in childhood, punishing him for bedwetting by dangling him out of a window by his ankles or displaying the soiled bedsheets outside the house for public viewing. His father emphatically denied these claims. Whatever the case may be, mental instability is known to have run in Heidnik's family. His alcoholic mother took her own life in 1970, and his brother had a history of numerous psychiatric hospitalizations and suicide attempts.[65]

While still a boy, Heidnik fell from a tree, smashing his cranium and earning him the hurtful nickname "Football Head" at school.[66] He evaded interacting or even making eye contact with his classmates, once shouting at a well-intentioned female peer who inquired about a homework assignment that she was not "worthy enough" to communicate with him. Despite these social and emotional difficulties, and possible brain damage, he earned high grades and was found to have a nearly genius-level IQ.[67] Increasingly angry, he began torturing the animals he once loved, hanging them from trees.[68]

At age fourteen, Heidnik enrolled in a Virginia military academy, leaving before graduation. After another brief stint in a public school, he dropped out at age seventeen and joined the army, where he was deemed "an excellent student" by his drill sergeant in basic training. Heidnik worked for six months as a medic in West Germany, earning his GED before developing severe headaches, blurred vision, dizziness, and nausea, and being diagnosed with gastroenteritis and possible mental illness. He was prescribed the antipsychotic medication trifluoperazine and transferred to Valley Forge Medical Center, where he was diagnosed with a schizoid personality. He was honorably discharged from the military.

In 1965, Heidnik completed a nursing course and interned at Philadelphia General Hospital. He worked as a psychiatric nurse at Veterans Administration Hospital in Coatesville, Pennsylvania, but was terminated due to a pattern of ill-mannered behavior toward patients and inconsistent attendance.[69] He would spend twenty-five years in and out of psychiatric inpatient units, attempting to take his own life at least thirteen times,[70] the first time following the suicide of his mother.[71]

In the late 1960s, Heidnik began visiting the Elwyn Institute, a home for developmentally disabled women, whom he sometimes took out for picnics, movies, and shopping before bringing them home for nonconsensual sex. By 1967, he had piled up enough disability payments to purchase a three-story house, occupying one floor himself and renting the others to tenants. Four years later, he established the United Church of the Ministries of God, with a congregation consisting of patients from Elwyn, who routinely filled his collection baskets at services. He preached to them about a coming "race war," expressing disdain for African Americans, except as sex objects. Around this time, he began investing in the stock market, earning at least half a million dollars and purchasing an assortment of luxury vehicles, including a Rolls-Royce. All the while, he dodged taxes by claiming himself to be a "bishop."

In 1976, when his tenants complained about property conditions, he barricaded himself in his basement, armed with several firearms, and took aim at a renter, grazing his face with a bullet. This resulted in a charge of aggravated assault.[72] Heidnik fathered a son by a woman named Gail Lincow, to whom he was married for a period, and a daughter by an illiterate, psychiatrically disabled girlfriend named Anjeanette Davidson. Both children were placed into foster care.[73] Shortly after his daughter's birth in 1978, he was arrested for kidnapping Davidson's sister from a psychiatric institution. The woman, who was reported to be severely intellectually disabled, was kept prisoner in a locked storage room in his basement, where he raped and sodomized her, infecting her with gonorrhea.[74] Heidnik spent four years in prison for this crime. He was released in 1983, under the supervision of a mental health program.[75]

At that time, Heidnik was paired by a matrimonial service with Betty Disto of the Philippines, with whom he corresponded for years before they married in 1985. The union rapidly fell apart when he began assaulting and raping his new bride, forcing her to watch him have intercourse with up to three women at the same time. He was arrested and charged for these abusive behaviors. Following their separation, Disto gave birth to a son.[76]

By late 1986, Heidnik had grown tired of his relationships collapsing and having children taken away from him.[77] He concocted a horrifying solution: he would establish a "baby factory" made up of sex slaves, in the basement of his Philadelphia home, whom he would abduct, keep captive, beat, torture, and rape at whim.[78] By gathering a "harem" of young African American women, he hoped to sire a line of children, entirely loyal to him.[79] To that end, he brought home a part-time prostitute, Josefina Rivera, whom he choked into unconsciousness after intercourse and restrained with chains. He then confined the victim to a small, cramped pit he had created in the basement floor, with a board placed across the top, weighted with sandbags. Days later, he kidnapped Elwyn patient Sandra Lindsey from a store, forcing the women to watch one another as he raped them.[80] They were kept underfed, partially clothed, and rarely bathed. To drown out screaming, Heidnik constantly blared loud music through the house. For refusing to keep quiet, one of the women was pulled out of the pit by her hair and badly beaten.[81]

On an icy night in December of 1986, Heidnik offered a lift to nineteen-year-old Lisa Thomas, whom he brought home after a friendly meal at a restaurant. He then strangled her into unconsciousness and, before she came to, raped her and chained her up in the basement. She was sexually assaulted and humiliated in front of the other captives before he made the trio sandwiches.[82] In early January of 1987, he added Deborah Dudley to his growing collection, irked to discover that she was a hostile, uncooperative prisoner.[83] Just under three weeks later, he added eighteen-year-old Jacqueline Askins.[84] The women were forced to consume dog food, as part of a campaign to systematically dehumanize them.[85]

Heidnik employed a variety of techniques designed to minimize insubordination, including punishing one captive in front of the others, bribing prisoners to inform about one another, and sometimes forcing the women to participate in one another's abuses. Disobedience was punished with sadistic torture. Some of the women were rendered deaf by having screwdrivers driven through their eardrums.[86] For some unclear infraction, Lindsey was suspended by her wrists from a pipe for a week, reminiscent of the way his father allegedly dangled him from his window in childhood as a cruel form of "discipline" for enuresis. Lindsey ultimately died of an untreated fever, after which Heidnik dismembered her with a power saw in a tub. He cooked her ribs in his oven and placed her head in a pot, where the flesh was trimmed away. The pieces were broken up in a blender, boiled, and retained in his freezer. These were gradually fed to his two dogs—and, unimaginably, to the other captives, mixed in with other food.[87] When Heidnik's neighbors complained about the terrible smell wafting from Heidnik's home, he was interrogated by the police, whom he bamboozled with a fib about having burned a roast he was preparing for supper.[88]

Rivera privately resolved that she would beat Heidnik at his own psychological game.[89] One day, as a disciplinary technique, he forced the women to stand in the pit and flooded it with water. He then covered it with plywood prepared with a small aperture, through which he snaked a stripped extension cord to electrocute them. Seizing on the opportunity, Rivera assisted him. Then, after Dudley died from the torture, Rivera accompanied Heidnik to discard of the body in a New Jersey state park.[90] When she agreed to sign a document, stating that she participated in the victim's death, she fully secured his trust.[91] "After convincing him I was on his side," she would say years later, "he gradually let me out of the chains and upstairs. He thought I was his partner."[92] She also assisted him in luring an acquaintance, Agnes Adams, to his home, to be added to the pit.[93] She was "rewarded" with being permitted to watch movies outside of the slave area and to be raped in what Heidnik considered a more comfortable environment.[94]

When Heidnik granted Rivera permission to visit her family, she immediately fled to her boyfriend, and the two led authorities to her captor.[95] When police raided his home, they found human remains in a freezer and in the drains, his bedroom walls decorated with currency, and the surviving women in the foul-smelling pit in Heidnik's basement. The killer was arrested,[96] attempting to hang himself while in police custody.[97]

Heidnik's defense team attempted to portray him as not guilty of abducting, raping, and torturing women by reason of insanity, but this was successfully rebutted. His psychopathic traits and behaviors can hardly be denied.[98] While Heidnik sometimes displayed signs of serious mental illness, it is known that he cleverly took advantage of the psychiatric diagnosis he acquired while in the army, as well as the intellectually disabled members of his so-called church, collecting benefits and contributions, which he parlayed into a small fortune by way of shrewd investments. It also emerged during proceedings that, at the time Rivera was forced to sign her "confession," Heidnik assured her that, if he were ever arrested, he would "simply go into court and 'act crazy' by saluting the judge, among other things." He explained that "somewhere in the law it states that if a person acts crazy for a certain amount of years, his case is eventually thrown out."[99]

In a series of self-absorbed letters to psychologist Dr. Jack A. Apsche, Heidnik vehemently denied ever having been a serial killer, describing the deaths of Lindsey and Dudley as "purely accidental." If he had intentionally desired to kill the women, he explained, he would have employed different methods.[100] Then, when it was noted during a televised interview that his abuse and neglect were painful to his victims, he remarked, "I hope so. . . . You know, that's what I was trying to achieve . . . to make them behave."[101] Heidnik, who proved utterly unremorseful, was convicted and sentenced to death, carried out by lethal injection in 1999.[102] When the killer's father was informed of his son's fate in 1988, he reportedly replied, "I'm not interested."[103]

Pertinent to discussion of Heidnik's case is the work of previously referenced researcher Dr. Ann W. Burgess and her colleagues. In a groundbreaking 1986 article, they described patterns of social environments and formative experiences among known serial killers, proposing a Motivational Model of Sexual Homicide. In their youths, these offenders tend to fail to bond with their primary caregivers, and, ultimately, with people in general. They are far more likely than the average child to have experienced parental divorce; abandonment or rejection by one parent or both; emotional, physical, or sexual abuse; the death of a parent; or a severe illness. The negative effects of these experiences are typically compounded by a paucity of friends or other social supports; the lack of positive role models; and few protective factors, such as talents or skills, which might help elevate their self-esteem. This leads to overwhelming feelings of sadness, despair, and helplessness. Such children subsequently begin to engage in destructive behaviors, such as fire setting, cruelty to animals, vandalism, burglary, assault, and sadistic acts. Moreover, they tend to possess negative personality traits, such as anger, hostility, and aggression; entitlement; rebelliousness; cynicism; dishonesty; and a general sense of rejection by society. They are generally socially withdrawn and lack confidence, retreating into a fantasy world, which only intensifies over time. Their fantasies tend to help them to compensate for feelings of inadequacy in the actual world and typically resolve around themes of dominance, control, power, violence, mutilation, torture, death, rape, and revenge. Eventually, these fantasies are not adequate to serve the individuals' psychological needs, and the fantasy—as bizarre or sadistic as it might be—is actually played out in real life.[104]

Considering these typical features, Heidnik's early life seems a virtual recipe for future violent behavior, and his trajectory toward sexual sadism and serial killing is highly consistent with the model described by Dr. Burgess and her colleagues. Some additional points should be made about his formative experiences. First, his mother suffered from alcoholism. Alcohol or drug dependency by one or both parents can be a major contributor to future serial murder.[105] Additionally, his mother's and brother's suicidality, as well as his brother's repeated psychiatric hospitalizations, indicated a strong genetic loading for psychopathology. Heidnik's head injury in childhood may also have affected his future behaviors, either by way of actual cortical damage, or the deepening of feelings of resentment and inferiority, due to the ridicule he experienced surrounding his misshapen cranium.

It is of further note that Heidnik exhibited both bed-wetting and animal torture in childhood. Both of these traits were included in the well-known triad of childhood predictors of future violent offenses, particularly of a serial nature, proposed by Dr. John M. MacDonald in his controversial triad, alongside fire setting.[106] We made brief reference to this construct in our earlier discussion of serial murder. By no means does childhood enuresis universally foretell future aggressive behavior. It has been hypothesized, however, that persistent bed-wetting past age five, especially if associated with humiliation or belittlement by parents or adults, may serve as a sort of gateway to violence, leading to arson or animal cruelty as a means of expressing frustration.[107] This appears to be consistent with Heidnik's case. Consider the symbolism: his father allegedly hanged him from a window; he hanged animals from trees; and later in life, he would hang and kill a woman. Moreover, the transition from abuse to animal torture to torturing a woman resulted in punitive incarceration and public shame. Suddenly, all of the childhood humiliation and abuse he was transferring to his victims returned to himself—culminating in his trying to hang himself in jail, nearly completing the terrible cycle. As a final comment, it is intriguing to note that Rivera was abducted three days after Heidnik's birthday and two days before Thanksgiving Day in 1986; Thomas, two days before Christmas; and Dudley, just after New Year's Day. One wonders if dates and seasons associated with family, friends, and happiness triggered profound feelings of loneliness and resentment of the mother, significant others, and children he had lost. Did he seek to "collect" women and children whom he could literally prevent, by force, from leaving him? Interestingly, Josefina Rivera, who came to know him intimately, attributed her ability to dupe her captor to his longing for human contact. "Heidnik was lonely," she astutely observed. "That's the first thing I realized about him. That's why he wanted all those babies."[108]

JOHN WAYNE GACY

In Stephen King's 1986 novel *It*, an evil, shape-shifting creature feeds on the inhabitants of the town of Derry, Maine. As it finds that its victims taste better when they are maximally frightened—likened, in the book, to the salting of meat—it prefers to consume children, who are easily scared. In the book's opening sequence, the entity, which has assumed the form of a disarming clown named Pennywise, wins the confidence of a young boy and proceeds to mutilate him.[109] It is truly terrifying to realize that, outside the imaginary town of Derry, there once really was a friendly-looking predator who wore a clown suit and secured the trust of young people, luring them to unspeakable deaths. However, the fictional character's real-life counterpart of sorts, John Wayne Gacy, would only kill after he had satisfied himself in a prolonged episode of rape and sadistic torture. That was the particular salt he needed.

Gacy was born in Chicago, Illinois, on St. Patrick's Day in 1942. The future killer had a turbulent relationship with his father, reported to have been an alcoholic who both verbally and physically abused him, his two sisters, and their mother.[110] While he would always resent that his father called him a "sissy" and a "mama's boy" who would "probably grow up queer,"[111] he always denied hating him.[112] His father's homophobic disdain was related to his son's preference for things like cooking and gardening over sports, and, on at least one occasion, stealing women's panties.[113]

Gacy was a Boy Scout in childhood, making some friends in his troupe, and delivered newspapers after school.[114] At the age of seven, he was caught fondling a young girl and, that same year, he was allegedly molested by a family friend.[115] He reportedly engaged in some animal torture as a child, catching mice in a trap and dissecting them alive with scissors as they bled and squealed.[116]

Pertinent to our previous discussion regarding head injuries, Gacy was hit in the cranium with a swing at the age of eleven, resulting in a cerebral blood clot that sometimes caused blackouts. When the condition was resolved six years later, he developed a nonspecific heart ailment. Throughout his life, this vague condition would suddenly flare up whenever convenient to him.[117] One wonders if it was an unconscious justification for him not being as physically active as his father would have liked. Whether he was malingering the condition entirely is open to debate.

Gacy struggled academically, attending four different high schools before finally dropping out. Following a blowup with his father, he abruptly relocated to Las Vegas at the age of seventeen and found work as a mortuary janitor. Because he was short of money, he was permitted to sleep on the premises. It later emerged that, during this period, he would sometimes open the drawers containing corpses, undressing and speaking to the bodies.[118] Once, he embraced and caressed the cadaver of a teenage boy, drawing back in horror at the sudden realization of his own behavior.[119]

Missing his family, Gacy quickly returned to Chicago, where he enrolled in a business school.[120] There, he further developed his knack for fast-talking people in and out of whatever he wished. Following graduation, he worked as a management trainee for a shoe business, quickly being transferred to Springfield, Illinois, to run a men's clothing outlet for the same company.[121] In 1964, he married a woman from a wealthy family, relocating with her to Waterloo, Iowa, two years later and taking over the management of one of her family's fried chicken restaurants.[122] The couple had two children.[123] Those who knew him during this period deemed him gregarious and charming.[124] He at last seemed to have earned his hypercritical father's respect.[125]

This persona masked Gacy's dark and dangerous true character. In 1968, he was arrested for sodomizing a teenage male employee, to the shock of his community.[126] He vehemently denied the accusation, claiming he was being set up by people opposing his candidacy for president of a local chapter of the Jaycees.[127] Privately, however, he hired a teenager to rough up the boy who accused him and to spray him with mace.[128] Despite his indignation and protestations of innocence, Gacy pled guilty and was sentenced to ten years in the State Men's Reformatory in Anamosa, Iowa.[129] His wife subsequently filed for divorce.[130] Then, during Gacy's period of incarceration, his father died and he was not permitted to attend the services. His serious legal issues, the dissolution of his marriage, and his inability to pay his respects at the funeral collectively left him feeling that every hurtful thing his father had said about him had ultimately proved true.[131]

In light of his exemplary behavior, Gacy was paroled after a mere eighteen months. A psychiatric evaluation completed prior to his release noted, "The likelihood of his again being charged with and being convicted of antisocial conduct appears to be small."[132] He returned to Chicago, where he found work as a contractor and married a second time, to a recent divorcée with two daughters.[133] He became active—one might even say overactive—in community affairs, serving as membership chairman of the Chi Rho Club, a board member for the Catholic Inter-Club Council, a captain for the Chicago Civil Defense, a member of the Holy Name Society and the Federal Civil Defense for Illinois, Democratic precinct captain, and vice president for the Jaycees, which once declared him their "Man of the Year."[134] Psychologically, these tireless efforts may have represented an attempt to again merit the approval of his now deceased father, whose harsh critiques had long been internalized. Incarceration for a sexual crime involving a male may have felt to him like a validation of all of the homophobic slurs his father had hurled at him. His frenzied community service might also be viewed as masochistic in intensity, an overcompensation for how much pleasure he drew from cruelty, whereas the sadism, in turn, may have compensated for feelings of powerlessness. Positions of leadership likely further served his desires for domination and control over others, which, as we have seen, are key drives in individuals who commit serial sexual homicide.

In early 1971, Gacy was arrested for molesting a young male he picked up at a bus terminal. The charges were dropped when his accuser failed to appear in court.[135] Around this time, Gacy opened his own contracting business, hiring young teenage boys to work for him, supposedly as a means of keeping labor costs down.[136] Elsewhere, due to growing political aspirations, he threw himself further still into community service, even dressing up as a clown named Pogo or Patches to entertain at children's parties and hospitals.[137] However, these efforts were impeded by growing scuttlebutt surrounding his clandestine gay lifestyle. In 1975, he made a sexual advance on a sixteen-year-old boy in his employ. A month later, he tricked the same youth into slipping into handcuffs before trying to assault him again. The boy was able to free himself, and, after a physical altercation, Gacy vowed to leave him alone. Perhaps surprisingly, the consummate liar kept his word.[138] Sparing the intended victim's life may have provided him a sense of power that served to undo the shame associated with having been outmaneuvered by a teenage boy.

Many other boys and young men would not be so fortunate. The friendly-faced Gacy acquired victims with a variety of methods. In some instances, he suddenly attacked employees, after slowly earning their trust, or enticed strangers to his home with promises of drugs or alcohol. He sometimes convinced hustlers and runaways on the streets of Chicago to enter his car by posing as a police officer, flashing badges and guns at them, and pretending to place them under arrest.[139] At this time, Gacy and his wife began drifting apart as his moods became increasingly volatile, with incidents of violent shouting and hurling furniture. He was also keeping a peculiar schedule, leaving at midnight and returning at dawn,[140] and seemed to his wife to be obsessed with gay men's magazines.[141] They divorced in 1976, and the loss, coupled with his newfound privacy, launched him into a frenzy of unmitigated depravity and serial murder.[142]

It would later emerge that Gacy killed for the first time in 1972, stabbing a young boy abducted from a bus station two times in the chest. Over the following six years, he developed a generally consistent modus operandi in a long string of other homicides. Once he had lured a male victim, he would persuade him to slip on handcuffs under the pretense of playfully performing a magic trick, after which Gacy would say, "There's no key to let you go. That's the trick."[143] He would then chloroform, sodomize, and torture the youth, repeatedly holding his head underwater in a bathtub, urinating on him, singeing him with hot candle wax, whipping him, or placing him in a homemade pillory suspended by chains.[144] Several of Gacy's victims asphyxiated due to having socks or underwear stuffed in their mouths,[145] while most were killed with a makeshift tourniquet in his infamous "rope trick." Here, Gacy would place a rope around a victim's neck, fashioned into a loop into which a stick was placed. By twisting the stick slowly, the victim was gradually choked to death.[146] As victims convulsed and writhed, Gacy sometimes watched or else moved about the house, taking routine calls from friends or clients, or carrying out chores. There is an interesting symbolism here. The tourniquet, which Gacy likely learned to make in the Boy Scouts, is normally associated with healing and lifesaving, but here, it was used for torture and killing. Gacy, too, was, on the surface, a healer and helper, who could suddenly transform into an instrument of death. One might even view the tourniquet as a metaphor for Gacy's own corrupt innocence and transformation into an aggressor. It is also noteworthy that the killer would sometimes read Bible passages while watching his victims suffocate,[147] suggesting that a sense of moral superiority, much like Robert Berdella's, figured into his crimes. Finally, Gacy admitted to sometimes keeping the corpses of some of his victims under his bed or in his attic prior to interring them,[148] although it is unclear whether he engaged in necrophilic acts on these occasions. Gacy is known to have murdered thirty-three males in all,[149] including two boys, ages fourteen and fifteen, who knew one another. The friends were assaulted and killed the same day,[150] one very likely in the presence of the other.

A master schemer, Gacy had his young staff dig trenches in the cramped crawlspace beneath his home or elsewhere on his property, claiming he was intending to install new water pipes. They were actually graves. There, he buried twenty-eight corpses, covering them in limestone to accelerate their decay. He eventually ran out of room and dumped four other bodies into the Des Moines River. When neighbors visiting Gacy pointed out the pungent odor pervading every room, he simply attributed the stench to "sewer problems."[151]

In 1978, the killer came to the attention of authorities in the investigation of a missing fifteen-year-old boy, Rob Piest, who had last been seen at the pharmacy where the boy was employed. Gacy had recently completed a remodeling job there. The smell creeping through the house was recognized by one of the agents who had experience working in a morgue, and ultimately gave rise to a search of the property and the discovery of Gacy's virtual cemetery.[152] By way of a long, arduous process of comparing remains recovered in the cramped, maggot-infested crawlspace with dental records of young men missing from the area, the full extent of the killer's horrifying actions gradually emerged. As of the writing of this book, six of Gacy's young male victims have not been positively identified.[153]

Gacy displayed a complete lack of remorse during legal proceedings. In one revealing moment, during the testimony of one of the victims who had survived the killer's torture, he began laughing out loud.[154] He was ultimately sentenced to death, carried out by lethal injection in 1994, after fourteen years in prison. Still craving notoriety, he passed his time in captivity selling original artworks of clowns, cartoon characters, and skulls, and vehemently denying his guilt. Readers can view an example of his morbid artwork in the illustrations section of this book. Gacy even created a personal telephone hotline, allowing the public to hear his various refutations of his prosecutors' case for $1.99 per minute.[155] The numerous strangers who wrote him letters were asked to fill out a "pen pal questionnaire," as if applying for the privilege of his correspondence. Unrepentant to the last, his final words were, "Kiss my ass."[156]

Mental health experts who testified during the Gacy trial had provided equivocal interpretations of his psychological profile, describing him, in turn, as traumatized by childhood abuse, a sexual sadist, or suffering from paranoid schizophrenia or multiple personality disorder. It was also opined that his personality was organized at a borderline level—that is to say, fragmented, with primitive emotional defense mechanisms—and that he would experience brief psychotic episodes during periods of extreme rage, in which he allegedly believed he was his father and his victims were himself. In this view, his killings would have represented an intense self-loathing of his homosexuality, weakness, or some other aspect of himself. Gacy was depicted as "splitting" off what he felt were "bad" parts of himself, projecting them onto his victims. However, it was also noted that Gacy was never really out of touch with reality. The process of tricking his victims into handcuffs and tying intricate knots for ligatures used for his "rope trick" required some clearness of mind, as did the devious, methodical methods by which he had workers dig graves to conceal evidence of numerous killings, all the while appearing affable and innocuous in social circles.[157]

This ability of Gacy's to pass for a trustworthy, likeable sort speaks to a key distinction between the commonly confused concepts of *compassion* and *empathy*, distinguished by Dr. Stone in *The Anatomy of Evil*.[158] While compassion refers to sympathetic concern and pity for the misfortunes of other people, empathy is the capacity to correctly read the emotions signaled by another person's face or body language. In psychopathic persons, such as Gacy, we would expect an utter lack of compassion but adeptness in terms of empathy. It was the killer's ability to read the feelings of others quite well, in conjunction with superficial charm that allowed him to win the confidence of victims and successfully lure them to their deaths.

In fact, throughout his lifetime, Gacy displayed virtually all of the personality traits associated with psychopathy: a grandiose sense of self-worth, pathological lying, conning and manipulation, callousness, a total lack of remorse for others, and an inability to accept blame for his actions. He also exhibited a number of the classic traits of poor behavioral control, such as impulsivity, irresponsibility, promiscuity, a lack of realistic long-term goals, and numerous short-term marital relationships. While we might be compelled to consider Gacy's head injury in childhood as a contributor to his later aberrant behavior, it is important to note that postmortem examination of his brain by Dr. Helen Morrison revealed no abnormalities—a fact one might find both puzzling and disturbing.[159] Gacy's alleged abuse and humiliation at the hand of his alcoholic father may have resulted in a constant struggle to counter intense feelings of inferiority and internalized homophobia with acts of rage and unfathomable cruelty.

The late Roy Hazelwood, a trailblazer in the profiling of sexual sadists as part of the FBI's Behavioral Sciences Unit in Quantico, Virginia, spent time interviewing Gacy. Hazelwood noted that, for offenders of this type, character pathology is linked with paraphilic arousal so that others must be controlled and degraded for sexual enjoyment. Those he examined were almost uniformly Caucasian and male, and most had occupations involving contact with the public. Forty percent described driving excessively, sometimes with no clear goals, for long distances. Eighty-three percent collected items related to violent and/or sexual themes, most commonly pornography, guns, sexual bondage paraphernalia, and detective magazines. Almost 50 percent were married at the time of their crimes, typically to a "compliant" individual, who was the victim of the sadists' tortures, but which were later carried out to a more extreme degree with strangers. Nearly 75 percent had committed murder. Among their killings are several commonalities, such as careful planning, the use of preselected locations, captivity, a variety of painful sexual acts, sexual domination, the intentional infliction of pain, and death by stabbing or strangulation.[160] With the exception of playing out sadistic sexual fantasies with a spouse, presumably because he had no real sexual interest in women, Gacy displayed all of these classic characteristics.

A manipulative, cold-blooded rapist, torturer, and murderer, Gacy is a quintessential example of the type of offender designated to Category 22 on the Gradation of Evil scale. Enjoyment of these heinous activities had become an integral part of who he was, as an individual, and, had he not been captured, the crimes would almost certainly have gone on indefinitely.

Consider the following: At the time of Gacy's arrest, he had claimed he was on his way to his father's grave to place a Roman Catholic rosary there before heading home to commit suicide—the very picture of guilt, shame, and remorse.[161] Then, while incarcerated, he considered—or, at least, portrayed—himself as having returned to his devout Catholic roots, seeking the sacraments and serving as an acolyte at Masses celebrated by the prison chaplain.[162] During his trial, Assistant State's Attorney Larry Finder described how, during a visit to Gacy in his cell, he asked the killer to demonstrate his infamous rope trick. Evidently, at this particular moment, the captive was not pretending the crimes never happened or that he had no recollection of them. Gacy asked Finder to pass his own hand through the bar and imagine the wrist was a victim's neck. Then Gacy reached into his pocket and fished out his rosary—that potent symbol of his purported repentance. Perverting its innocence, he looped it around Finder's wrist and tied three knots, inserting a pen between the second and third. Turning the improvised handle, he explained that, as the boys and young men writhed and convulsed, the garrote would gradually tighten, such that it was the victims, in his twisted view, who had "killed themselves."[163] An outrageous statement to be sure. Interestingly, however, if we understand that Gacy's fragmented personality was symbolically represented in both the murderer and the young people whose lives he took by force, then, in a curious way, the idea of the victims "killing themselves" takes on a revealing double meaning.

DAVID PARKER RAY

There is little we can say to prepare the reader for the story of David Parker Ray, who represents, incontrovertibly, the upper limits of the highest ranking on the Gradations of Evil scale. As we enter his "Toy Box," the isolated trailer he transformed into a soundproofed chamber of horrors, equipped with countless torture devices of his own devising, we recall the inscription above the gate of hell in the third canto of Dante's *Inferno*: "Abandon All Hope, Ye Who Enter Here." Pioneering criminal profiler Vernon Geberth, who participated in the investigation of Ray, has provided a highly graphic depiction of the killer's consummate degree of evil in the classic book *Sex-Related Homicide and Death Investigation: Practical and Clinical Perspectives*, referring to Ray as "the Devil on Earth."[164]

According to his own disturbingly detailed diaries, Ray abducted, raped, tortured, and killed up to sixty girls and young women in New Mexico, across the breathtaking span of five decades. His criminal career came to an abrupt end on March 22, 1999, when a blood-soaked twenty-two-year-old woman, Cynthia Vigil, entered a stranger's mobile home, after running down a highway wearing only padlocked chains and an iron slave collar. Covered in bruises, burns, and puncture wounds, she informed police that Ray had picked her up in Albuquerque while she was working as a prostitute. He had masqueraded as a police officer, wearing a convincing uniform, flashing a badge and driving an RV equipped with a Kojak light. When she entered his vehicle, he and a female assistant—his girlfriend, Cindy Hendy, who had been hiding in the bathroom—suddenly attacked her. They shocked her with a stun gun and kicked her in the stomach. She was bound, and her mouth, eyes, and head were wrapped in duct tape. Her clothing was removed. The couple then proceeded to make pleasant small talk with one another as they drove her back to the Toy Box, where she was chained to the wall, with a dog collar around her neck.[165]

Vigil was then subjected to Ray's horrifying introduction tape, describing her forthcoming degradation, torture, and retention by her "master" and "mistress" as a long-term sex slave. The recording, which works out to about ten single-spaced pages of transcribed text, had the detached, impersonal tone of a form letter, and cannot be fully reproduced here, in the interest of common decency. It was played for a number of girls and women who found themselves in Ray's trailer following abduction. They were immobilized, nude, and sometimes groggy from having been drugged. Some were hoisted by chains toward the trailer's ceiling, dangling there as the sadist's cool, monotonous voice came over a loudspeaker:[166]

> Hello there, bitch. Are you comfortable right now? I doubt it. Wrists and ankles chained. Gagged. Probably blindfolded. You are disoriented and

scared, too, I would imagine. Perfectly normal, under the circumstances. For a little while, at least, you need to get your shit together and listen to this tape. It is very relevant to your situation. I'm going to tell you, in detail, why you have been kidnapped, what's going to happen to you and how long you'll be here. I don't know the details of your capture, because this tape is being created July twenty-third, 1993 as a general advisory tape for future female captives. The information I'm going to give you is based on my experience dealing with captives over a period of several years. If, at a future date, there are any major changes in our procedures, the tape will be upgraded. Now, you are obviously here against your will, totally helpless, don't know where you're at, don't know what's gonna happen to you. You're very scared or very pissed off. I'm sure that you've already tried to get your wrists and ankles loose, and know you can't. Now you're just waiting to see what's gonna happen next. You probably think you're gonna be raped and you're fuckin' sure right about that. Our primary interest is in what you've got between your legs.

You'll be raped thoroughly and repeatedly, in every hole you've got. Because, basically, you've been snatched and brought here for us to train and use as a sex slave. Sound kind of far out? Well, I suppose it is to the uniniti-ated, but we do it all the time. It's gonna take a lot of adjustment on your part, and you're not gonna like it a fuckin' bit. But I don't give a big rat's ass about that. It's not like you're gonna have any choice about the matter. You've been taken by force, and you're going to be kept and used by force.

The tape was meticulously designed to induce maximum fear and eliminate any last shred of power, hope, or personal identity. At a later point in the recording, Ray explained,[167]

As far as I'm concerned, you're a pretty piece of meat, to be used and exploited. I don't give a flyin' fuck about your mind or how you feel about this situation. You may be married, have a kid or two, boyfriend, girl-friend, a job, car payment. Fuck it. I don't give a rat's ass about any of that, and I don't want to hear about it. It's something you're gonna have to deal with after you're turned loose. I make it a point never to like a slave and I fuckin' sure don't have any respect for you. Here, your status is no more than that of one of the dogs, or of one of the animals out in the barn. Your only value to us is the fact that you have an attractive, usable body. And, like the rest of our animals, you will be fed and watered, kept in good physical condition, kept reasonably clean and allowed to use the toilet when necessary. In return, you're gonna be used hard, especially during your first few days while you're new and fresh.

As the tape droned on, Ray's various rules of the house were imparted, regarding speaking, and punishments for making too much noise or attempting to resist. It was explained, in terrifying detail, that victims would be chained up and kept for months. They would be whipped and electrocuted. They would suffer every conceivable manner of sexual assault, including routine acts of bestiality with Ray's German shepherds, sometimes in front of friends. It was opined that cooperation was easier than the alternative fate:[168]

> It may sound harsh and cold, but if you give us too much trouble, or if you pose any kind of a threat to us, I won't have any qualms at all about slicing your throat. Like I said before, I don't like killin' the girls that we bring here, but occasionally things happen. What can I say? I would really hate to have to dump that pretty little body off in a canyon somewhere to rot. I'm not trying to scare you. That's just the way it is.

Finally, Ray explained that, once he had grown tired of the victim, he would drug her with a cocktail of sedatives and employ hypnotism techniques over the course of several days, in an effort to eradicate any mental trace of the events. She would be thoroughly washed to eliminate DNA evidence, and dropped off "on some country road, bruised, heh, sore all over, but nothing that won't heal up in a week or two." Indeed, one victim who survived Ray's torture chamber was convinced that her vague recollections of severe abuse were simply remnants of nightmares, until she was contacted by the authorities. He closed the monologue with the disturbing platitude, "Have a nice day."[169]

Vigil endured three days of unimaginable torment, including being whipped, sexually assaulted with intricately crafted instruments designed to maximize pain, and shocked with devices that sent waves of electricity into her body. Clamps were placed on her nipples, attached to ropes that were run through pulleys and connected to lead weights, for the purpose of painfully stretching them.[170] One of Ray's dogs was made to lick gravy off of her naked body while he and Hendy looked on.[171] Vigil ultimately managed to break free of her chain, stabbing her female captor in the breast and the back of her head with an ice pick that had been used in her own torture, and fleeing through a window.[172] Later that day, Ray and his accomplice were arrested.[173] The outside world would suddenly become acquainted with the sadist's $100,000 torture dungeon.[174]

Investigators found the trailer equipped from top to bottom with what Ray called his "friends"—sex toys, pulleys, straps, whips, fishhooks, chains, clamps, syringes, surgical blades, pins, saws, a soldering iron, and bars used for spreading victims' limbs. There were detailed diagrams and pornographic drawings, drafted by the killer himself, demonstrating various methods for inflicting unimaginable pain, as well as meticulous instructions for the "handling" of slaves. He had designed devices, such as a contraption to be placed over the head, which would disorient victims during assaults, adding to their torment. In the center of it all was a gynecological chair, to which one might be strapped in a number of sexual positions. Ray's home-made device for electrocuting victims while he looked on in merriment was recovered. There were dolls of women, naked and shackled, with exaggeratedly large breasts, being subjected to extreme torture. Video equipment had allowed for recordings, as well as observations of victims from other rooms. Captives were forced to watch their own abuses in a mirror or on a television monitor. Authorities also discovered a padded coffin, in which victims were sometimes forced to sleep for extended periods of time. On shelves, there were books on sexuality, psychology, and female anatomy—topics with which Ray was acquainted to disturbing degrees—as well as medicine and witchcraft. Investigators also recovered an inhaler and a respirator. It emerged that Ray would intentionally bring captives to the brink of death before reviving them to maximize their suffering.[175] An artist who spent four days in the trailer, making detailed drawings for the FBI, later committed suicide, some thought because of the horrors she had encountered in the Toy Box.[176]

Ray was born in Belen, New Mexico, in November of 1939. He and a younger sister were raised by impoverished parents, Cecil and Nettie Ray, on their maternal grandparents' ranch. His father was allegedly an alcoholic who was abusive toward his wife and children, abandoning the family when Ray was ten years old. The children were sent to live with their grandparents in rural Mountainair, where their grandfather, Ethan Ray, reputedly subjected them to draconian physical discipline. At school, the tall, shy, and socially awkward future murderer was bullied by class-mates, struggling to meet girls and make friends. To make himself seem more interesting to others, he falsely claimed that singer Johnny Ray was his cousin.[177] In early adolescence, he spent the bulk of his time abusing drugs and alcohol in private, and soon developed a fascination with por-nography and periodicals with sadomasochistic themes, supplied to him by his father.[178] A gifted artist, Ray began drawing out his fantasies in perverse images discovered by his sister.[179] Years later, he would claim that, at age thirteen, he tortured and killed a woman after tying her to a tree.[180]

A D-level student, Ray barely graduated from high school. He found work as a car mechanic before joining the army, where he repaired tele-scopes, airplane engines, and other devices. He later received an honor-able discharge and did mechanical work, eventually landing a teaching position at the Spartan College of Aeronautics and Technology in Tulsa, Oklahoma.[181] He went on to find work as a maintenance man for the New Mexico Parks Department. While he was considered a diligent worker, it was noticed that he was something of a pack rat, taking home materials and equipment for personal projects. At the time, no one could have imag-ined that he was using these to construct diabolical instruments of sexual torture. Consistent with the pattern of many short-term marital relation-ships associated with Hare's conceptualization of psychopathy, Ray was married and divorced four times. He fathered two daughters.[182]

Throughout his adult life, Ray presented publicly as a devoted and hardworking family man.[183] In his extensive private journals, however, he described kidnapping and raping over one hundred females between 1955 and the time of his arrest. He recorded ratings of his victims' sexual per-formance. He noted his preferences for prostitutes and hitchhikers, whom he could readily abduct, and schoolgirls and housewives, whom he found easier to humiliate and frighten into submission. He also liked kidnapping women he knew to be gay, considering them less likely to carry sexually transmitted diseases. He described grabbing women who were walking, bicycling, jogging, or in need of help along local roads. Ray also abducted victims from bars, in particular the Blue Waters Saloon near his home, which tended to attract easily targeted drifters. His earliest entries, from the 1950s, detailed sexual abuses with the aid of a female accomplice.[184] By the 1970s, he had become deeply involved in sadomasochistic sex and bondage circles, designing BDSM equipment, which he sold via mail order.[185] He occasionally captured and tortured more than one female victim at the same time, including two young teenage sisters in 1973, and, during this period, set to work creating his infamous torture chamber.[186] Following his arrest, one of his children, Glenda Jean "Jesse" Ray, was arrested and convicted for drugging the drink of a woman at a bar, hitting her on the back of the head, and bringing her home to her father, where the captive was sexually assaulted and tortured for three days.[187]

Ray claimed at the time of his capture that Vigil was a heroin addict he was attempting to detoxify—a statement easily belied by the search of his home and recovery of video evidence.[188] Ray's first trial resulted in a hung jury. A retrial ultimately led to conviction for crimes against three female victims, including Vigil. He was sentenced to 224 years in prison, at which time he agreed to reveal the locations of several buried corpses, but would take his knowledge of the interment sites to his own grave. After having been held for two and a half years while awaiting the first and second trials, he died of a heart attack just eight months after sentencing. During legal proceedings, he was in positive spirits, seeming totally unmoved while his surviving victims described their abuses and subsequent trauma. He regretted only that his arrest resulted in the loss of his home and other assets, and that the stress of his legal woes had adversely affected his physical health.[189] Hendy testified against him, receiving a sentence of thirty-six years for her participation in the crimes. A man named Dennis Roy Yancy, who emerged as another prior accomplice, was later arrested and convicted for using a rope to fatally strangle a former girlfriend after Ray kidnapped and tortured her.[190]

Ray may have inherited sadism, abhorrence of women, sexual preoccupation, and a taste for alcohol from his allegedly abusive father. It is noteworthy that it was the latter who reputedly introduced him to pornography with violent themes. This might have felt like a badly needed bonding moment to the maltreated, overlooked boy, or perhaps a transition point from childhood to manhood. If so, it may have represented the moment at which sharing interests in misogynistic aggression and sexual sadism with another person became confused with affectionate intimacy. Indeed, Ray would involve friends, a romantic partner, his daughter, and even his pet dogs in such activities for the remainder of his life.

It appears that, at some juncture, a split developed in Ray's attitude toward women, whereby they were either viewed as venerable and worthy of proper treatment, or what he called "packages," existing only to be sexually spent and discarded. For instance, one of Ray's surviving victims recalled an incident in which he confided that he found her to be a "good" woman and, consequently, regretted having mistaken her for the type of person he tortured in the Toy Box. Moreover, the women who participated in his crimes were not demeaned. Whereas captives were required to call him "master," Hendy and the other women by his side were referred to as "mistresses."

Certainly, Ray exhibited a textbook psychopathic personality structure and shocking sexual sadism. Yet, what is striking in Ray's history is the absence of so many of the typical childhood antecedents to serial killing we have discussed, including head injury, enuresis, and fire setting. Like Gary Heidnik, Robert Berdella, and several other Category 22 killers not discussed here, Ray was a "collector" of people. For each of these men, victims were mere objects in a series, serving no significant purposes beyond the offender's own. Unfortunately, psychiatry does not presently have a diagnostic term for individuals who feel the need to possess another human being, quite literally, for the purpose of sexual pleasure. All five of the offenders we have described in this section were individuals whose chaotic, unstable upbringings might have predisposed them to want to keep people in their lives by force or, in Berdella's case, retention of body parts. We can also include John Wayne Gacy here, if we take into consideration the way he collected young males in his crawlspace. Interestingly, all but Tommy Lynn Sells were also collectors of inanimate objects, which may have been another manifestation of their desires for control. Heidnik collected coins and paper money, which he affixed to the walls of his home; Berdella was a philatelist and numismatist, and compiled a vast trove of exotic artifacts and occult paraphernalia; Gacy amassed paintings of clowns by various artists; and Ray collected dolls, books, and scrap materials. They seemed to love these inanimate objects, displaying them for all to see. It was certain groups of human beings that they despised. All but Sells, who had an IQ of 80, in the range associated with borderline intellectual functioning, were intelligent men who employed technology in their torments. For Ray, Berdella, and Heidnik, this included novel methods of electrocution, a decidedly "new" form of evil. One can envision these killers sending jolts into their victims and feeling like gods, firing lightning bolts at the petty mortals below. All but Sells were masters of manipulation, posing publicly as benevolent figures—Heidnik as a church founder and bishop; Berdella as a rescuer of young men who had been discarded by society; Gacy as a community-minded friend to all; and Ray, at the time of his arrest, as a redeemer of a heroin-addicted woman. Sells, who went entirely without any family from a young age, may have been left with less of a sense of how to feign socially acceptable behavior.

We trust that there is no question in the mind of the reader about why the actions of the five men we have described warranted placement at level 22 of the Gradations of Evil scale. Their histories of repetitive murder following deliberately drawn-out torment clearly justify this ranking. Equally important for placement in Category 22 is this: we will have experienced a number of key emotional reactions upon reading their histories, including breathless horror, disgust, and bewilderment—reactions that we posit are at the very heart of what we mean by "evil."

The use of this term, which is generally confined to the domains of morality and theology, gives rise to the critical question of whether the individuals we have discussed throughout this book, especially those in the upper limits of the Gradations of Evil scale, were "sick," or simply exercising free will in dark, self-serving, and destructive ways. It is true that there are some offenders—far more often males—who intentionally commit cruel and violent actions, following clearheaded premeditation and followed by no glimmer whatsoever of remorse. As unfathomable as some of their actions might be, such persons are not suffering from any major psychiatric illness, such as psychosis or mania. The serial rapist Ted Bundy was not "crazy" in the least when he methodically conned women into getting into his vehicle, knocked them unconscious, brought them to isolated areas, and brutally murdered them, following—or sometimes during—furious sexual assaults. He knew full well what he was doing when he revisited undiscovered corpses for necrophilic acts, or when he carted home and applied makeup to twelve severed heads for this purpose, supposedly burning victim Donna Manson's in his girlfriend's fireplace to prevent its discovery. In day-to-day life, he was able to blend into the background, playing the role of an upstanding citizen, with an affable personality and a measured, soft manner of speaking. He was routinely called "attractive" and "charming." Bundy understood not to commit his crimes in public or in front of law enforcement officers. He studied psychology before entering law school and even worked for a suicide prevention hotline, speaking to others about the value and importance of their lives.[191]

We have also reviewed a few cases in which psychopathy and bona fide mental illness—generally within the schizophrenia spectrum, or following drug and/or alcohol abuse—did coexist. We saw that Albert Fish, who believed he received commands from St. John the Apostle to castrate young males, was clearly experiencing psychosis, within the context of a wider psychopathic personality structure. Another serial killer, Richard Chase, blended with Coca-Cola the carcasses of animals he had captured and disemboweled so as to create an elixir, which he believed would keep his heart from shrinking. He also injected rabbit's blood into his veins. He progressed to slaughtering six people, engaging in postmortem mutilation and sexual acts, and drinking his victims' blood. On one occasion, he stuffed a corpse's throat with dog feces. Dubbed the "Vampire of Sacramento," the bizarre, disorganized killer was subsequently determined to have a history of schizophrenia, the latter intensified by his use of LSD.[192]

Examination of other cases reveals that psychopathy, sadism, and *malignant narcissism*—psychologist Dr. Erich Fromm's and psychiatrist Dr. Otto Kernberg's term for narcissistic personality disorder accompanied by antisocial features, ego-dystonic aggression, and paranoid traits—exist on a wide spectrum, similar to the way in which only 20 percent of those meeting criteria for antisocial personality disorder would also be termed *psychopathic*. Some offenders exhibit the effects of abuse, neglect, brain damage following head injuries, and other environmental factors. In others, there appear to have been inborn deficiencies, perhaps in the dorsolateral prefrontal cortex, a key area for control of impulses and emotions,[193] and certain areas in the limbic system involved in empathy, chiefly the amygdala.[194] These may lead one to grow up without developing a "moral center." This, in turn, constitutes an "illness" or some form of "mental pathology," often diagnosed as a personality disorder. While such individuals *are* exercising free will, the latter is generally distorted, such that one might deem it acceptable to, on the lower end of the spectrum, lie or shoplift, and on the other to abduct, torture, and kill innocent people. Some of their victims might resemble or call to mind people who once rejected them. There are also killers who were consistently overlooked or abused in their formative years and might demonstrate a sort of secondary psychopathy, with sweeping loathing for all of humanity, as discussed in a previous chapter. Puzzling, however, is the fact that many individuals who are equally maltreated in their youths do not become psychopaths, emerging instead as solidly moral citizens. In short, psychopathy can be conceptualized as representing a psychiatric condition, within the arena of personality disorders, in which the basic moral center is absent or too lax. These may or may not involve abnormalities of the brain, as suggested by some fMRI work and other cutting-edge science. Yet, such individuals rarely see themselves as "suffering" or in need of help.

At the furthest end of the spectrum of nonpsychotic psychopaths are those who go well past the point of merely not understanding why it is wrong to cheat or to walk out of a restaurant without paying the bill. Instead, knowing full well what they are doing, they deem it acceptable to give vent to rage or envy, or to serve egocentric strivings for domination and control, with wholesale sexual assault, homicide, butchery, and even prolonged torture. These are the most psychopathic of psychopaths, the inhabitants of the upper limits of the scale we have been describing. When we encounter such offenders who guiltlessly tear through lives and the world around them, we sometimes feel psychiatric language is inadequate, groping for better descriptors and almost always arriving at the word "evil." Such actions *are* undeniably evil, in their effects and how they make us feel—though whether the people who commit these actions are fundamentally "evil" is a far more complicated question.

It may be, moreover, that adverse biological factors alone are not all that may predispose one to commit the acts we term "evil." There may, in some cases, be the additional elements of injury to the head; a severely adverse environment, such as abuse or neglect during childhood; or the disinhibiting effects of alcohol or illicit drugs. Many of these factors had been present—and been present in abundance—in the vast majority of the extreme offenders we have discussed throughout the first half of this book. We do recognize, however, that there are others, despite some degree of congenitally altered limbic activity, who were raised in better circumstances and subsequently emerged with moral centers that were better developed. Persons of this latter sort may actually seek out professions requiring unusual bravery and fearlessness; they may, at times, willingly engage in aggression for prosocial purposes or tackle disasters head-on in ways that are beneficial to society.

As we shift into the second half of our book, we move on from inquiries about what "evil" means, and how we might quantify and distinguish between its various manifestations. We turn to the new and especially challenging question of whether the culture of the period spanning the 1960s through the current day affected the frequency, scale, and nature of violent crime. We will demonstrate that especially cruel and brutal offenses associated with the higher levels of the Gradations of Evil scale have occurred at greater frequencies during this epoch, as well as that the technological advances of the past sixty years have spawned entirely new categories of criminal offenses.

We hope, by persuasive argument, to convince the reader that just as many persons in this currently more toxic environment have grown coarser, more self-centered, and far less inhibited, and by the same token, the violent offenders have done the same—and, as a result, ended up examples of the most terrible in human behavior. As we bravely advance to this next phase in our discussion, let it be our ardent wish that the expanding inventiveness and sadism of those among us committing such atrocious acts will never require that the Gradations of Evil scale come to include a Category 23.

CHAPTER ELEVEN

AN ALGORITHM TO FACILITATE USE OF THE SCALE

I t is our hope that the descriptions and vignettes provided here have helped to bring the individual categories of the Gradations of Evil scale to life. We trust that our discussion has driven home the point that, when attempting to understand criminal actions, as well as why some such acts might be called "evil," it is imperative to be familiar with and to distinguish carefully between various possible underlying motivations. We have sought to illustrate the fact that isolated or repeat acts of homicide, rape, torture, or other forms of aggression should not simply be collectively examined under wide headings, nor should murderers, rapists, or torturers be considered homogenous groups. We have attempted to explain how even extremely grisly actions, such as dismemberment, flaying, or cannibalism, do not automatically warrant high rankings but must be examined on a case-by-case basis, with consideration of whether victims were living or deceased, and offenders' particular motivations.

In our examination of cases at the lower end of the twenty-two-point continuum, we observed violent acts that were entirely impulsive and unpremeditated; uncharacteristic of their perpetrators; driven by very human feelings of fear, desperation, jealousy, or anger under situational duress; and often followed by genuine remorse. We then transitioned to cases in which certain people lacking psychopathic traits were driven to commit homicide by egocentric yearnings for attention or by smoldering rage that ultimately became ignited by adverse life events. Shifting into the area of the scale associated with persons with more marked psychopathic features, we encountered jealous lovers who committed murder in more premeditated and methodical ways; killers driven by desires to eliminate individuals they felt impeded their various ends; cold-blooded offenders who strove for power over other people at any cost; and a variety of ruthlessly self-centered schemers. We also examined cases in which, in conjunction with certain aberrant personality features, psychotic illness was a motivating factor. Moving into the highest rankings in the scale, we discussed offenders with more severe degrees of psychopathy who, with malice aforethought and no subsequent remorse, engaged in terrorism, subjugation, intimidation, or rape in the absence of murder, or who killed for sport, for perverse sexual pleasure, or out of the sadistic desire to inflict unimaginably protracted pain. As we delineated between these various categories, we observed that the more premeditated a crime and the more suffering it inflicts upon one or more victims, the more people are likely to respond to it with bewilderment and breathless horror—emotional responses we propose are at the very heart of the word *evil* as it is commonly used. The reader will also note that individuals assigned to the lower end of the scale will typically have committed crimes just on one occasion, whereas the tendency to repeat criminal acts in a patterned way becomes more likely with higher degrees of narcissism, psychopathy, and/or sadism.

It is possible that, despite our exhaustive exposition of Dr. Stone's twenty-two categories of persons who commit violent acts, the reader will still find the use of the Gradations of Evil scale somewhat challenging. This may be particularly true when concepts, such as jealousy, rage, psychopathy, egocentricity, psychosis, and torture, constitute criteria in more than one designation.

To that end, we have created the following algorithm to allow for smoother navigation between categories when considering an offender's actions and established motivations. As part of the development process, eight separate raters (four with no training in psychology or psychiatry, two with master's degrees in psychology, one with a PhD in clinical psychology, and one MD specializing in psychiatry) reviewed vignettes about certain offenders and then attempted to identify their most appropriate rankings in the Gradations of Evil scale by way of the algorithm. This helped to identify problematic areas or vagueness in specific inquiries, which allowed for the gradual improvement of the measure until raters were uniformly capable of arriving at the same rankings on the scale. We must emphasize, however, that the measure has not been empirically validated and is not intended for clinical or legal use, but, rather, as a basic decision tree intended to facilitate the use of Dr. Stone's proposed system of classification.

Note that it is virtually impossible to use the algorithm or, indeed, the Gradations of Evil scale itself, unless one is aware of whether an individual displays no, partial, or full personality traits and behaviors of psychopathy. The latter is so essential to the construct that every effort should be made to determine this aspect of the individual's overall picture. If there are even a few psychopathic traits present—for instance, deceptiveness or superficial charm—it is optimal to proceed with "Some traits are present" in the Psychopathy section at the very beginning of the algorithm. Where there is any doubt whatsoever, it is best to proceed from "Definitely no or uncertain," since this will require moving through all questions in the Motivations section.

We are, of course, aware that offenders sometimes have multiple distinct reasons for committing homicide or other violent acts. In our examination of hundreds of infamous, widely publicized cases, however, there is generally one driving force that predominates over the rest. That driving force may have actually served as the impetus for the others—for example, intense rage that was rooted in narcissism. The objective is to gauge, based on all available information, the most prominent of an individual's various motivations, in the rater's best estimation. These designations are, to be sure, open to some debate. Separate users, for example, may have different ideas about which driving factor is first and foremost in a given offender's actions. We have noted, however, that, while rankings sometimes vary, the disparity will rarely amount to more than a one- or two-point difference in the categories selected. As a simple rule, where there is more than one distinct motive present, the motive associated with the higher score on the scale should be used.

For the reader wishing to become adept at the use of Dr. Stone's scale, we strongly recommend revisiting the vignettes provided in the previous chapters and carefully examining them alongside the step-by-step method delineated in this algorithm. This will make clear the numerous categorical decisions that are required when choosing between the instrument's twenty-two levels until their various features have been internalized. Additionally, numerous other vignettes with specific rankings will be presented later in this volume, allowing for further study.

Algorithm for the Gradations of Evil Scale
Developed by Gary Brucato, PhD, and Michael H. Stone, MD

PSYCHOPATHY

Before proceeding:

Does the individual exhibit behavioral and/or personality traits consistent with psychopathy?

Definitely no or uncertain – Continue to MOTIVATIONS question #1.

Definitely yes – Continue to MOTIVATIONS question #7.

If some traits are present, but they are not markedly pronounced – Continue to MOTIVATIONS question #6.

MOTIVATIONS

1. Has the individual committed homicide, and has the killing been established, beyond a reasonable doubt, to have been purely in self-defense?

   Yes – Go to SELF-DEFENSE question #1.
   No – Continue to MOTIVATIONS question #2.

2. Did the person commit homicide, primarily motivated by jealousy?

   Yes – Go to JEALOUSY question #1.
   No – Continue to MOTIVATIONS question #3.

3. Did the individual commit homicide or some other violent crime chiefly due to fear of or loyalty to another person or group that kills or commits other violent acts?

   Yes – Score **CATEGORY 3**.
   No – Continue to **MOTIVATIONS** question #4.

4. Did the individual commit homicide in the context of a traumatic or desperate situation, such as chronic abuse, from which escape seemed nearly impossible, and was this followed by remorse?

   Yes – Score **CATEGORY 5**.
   No – Continue to **MOTIVATIONS** question #5.

5. Did the person commit homicide in the context of a long-standing temperament characterized by hotheadedness, or chronic feelings of anger or resentment?

   Yes – Go to **RAGE** question #1.
   No – Continue to **MOTIVATIONS** question #6.

6. Did the person kill, chiefly motivated by extreme narcissism, attention seeking, or egocentricity?

Note: If the individual has murdered two or more victims in separate incidents and shows some personality or behavioral features of psychopathy, go to **MOTIVATIONS** #7. Answer "Yes" for (a) a parent who lacks psychopathic features and has killed one or more of his or her own children in the interest of drawing attention or sympathy; (b) cases in which the individual's victim, for paraphilic reasons, desired to be abused and/or killed by the perpetrator; or (c) in which murder was in the context of relentless stalking behavior. Otherwise:

   Yes – Score **CATEGORY 7**.
   No – Continue to **MOTIVATIONS** question #7.

NOTE: Individuals from this point onward must exhibit at least some, although not necessarily full, personality and/or behavioral features of psychopathy. If no clear psychopathic features are present, return to MOTIVATIONS question #1 and reexamine.

7. Was the offender a power-hungry type, who committed homicide or arranged that some confederate do so, with the aim of achieving a higher level of status or power in a hierarchical system or group?

Note: Answer "Yes" for power-hungry individuals with psychopathic personality traits and/or behaviors who kill when cornered by authorities or enemies.

    Yes – Score CATEGORY 12.
    No – Continue to MOTIVATIONS question #8.

8. Did the person commit homicide to get one or more individuals "out of the way" because they were impediments to some desired end or to eliminate one or more witnesses?

Note: If the homicide aimed at elimination was related to jealousy or rage, and not merely "practical" purposes, continue to MOTIVATIONS question #9. If the offender (a) eliminated one or more witnesses following sexual assault or (b) committed murder aimed at elimination in the wider context of numerous other vicious acts, go to MULTIPLE MURDERS / VICIOUS ACTS question #1. Otherwise:

    Yes – Go to ELIMINATION question #1.
    No – Continue to MOTIVATIONS question #9.

9. Was there homicide in the context of jealousy, accompanied by marked personality and/or behavioral traits of psychopathy?

    Yes – Go to JEALOUSY question #1.
    No – Continue to MOTIVATIONS question #10.

10. Did the person kill, chiefly motivated by either chronic or sudden anger, accompanied by marked personality and/or behavioral traits of psychopathy?

    Yes – Go to RAGE question #1.
    No – Continue to MOTIVATIONS question #11.

11. Is the offender a ruthless, self-centered, and scheming individual who may or may not have committed homicide, demonstrating marked personality and/or behavioral traits of psychopathy?

Note: Answer "Yes" for repeated serious criminal acts without murder, rape, or torture, such as bank robbery, hijacking, or arson, if aimed at personal gain or profit. For repeated serial criminal acts without murder, rape, or torture, which are driven more by viciousness than by means to personal gain or profit, continue to MULTIPLE MURDERS / VICIOUS ACTS question #1. If the individual has killed two or more victims in separate incidents, continue to MOTIVATIONS question #12. If the individual has never killed, but committed torture, go to TORTURE question #1. If the individual has never killed, but committed acts designed to psychologically terrorize or to subjugate, such as the keeping of an abducted victim as a sexual slave, go to OTHER question #1. Otherwise:

    Yes – Score CATEGORY 14.
    No – Continue to MOTIVATIONS question #12.

12. Does the individual meet current FBI criteria for serial killing (i.e., has the person murdered two or more victims in separate incidents)?

    Yes – Go to MULTIPLE MURDERS / VICIOUS ACTS question #1.
    No – Continue to MOTIVATIONS question #13.

13. Has the individual either (a) killed at least two victims, without meeting current FBI criteria for serial murder because the murders occurred in one incident or during a murderous spree; (b) committed extremely vicious acts, such as child abuse, rape, animal torture, or other violent crimes at least twice without murder; or (c) committed a single murder and one or more other vicious acts?

Note: Answer "Yes" for acts of necrophilia in the absence of murder.

    Yes – Go to MULTIPLE MURDERS / VICIOUS ACTS question #1.
    No – Go to OTHER question #1.

SELF-DEFENSE

1. Did the self-defense occur in the context of aggression that was largely provoked by the killer himself or herself?

    Yes – Score CATEGORY 4.
    No – Continue to SELF-DEFENSE question #2.

2. Did the individual kill not in self-defense in the context of a specific life-threatening incident, but due to an event that was perceived as the "last straw" in a chronically abusive or traumatic relationship?

    Yes – Score CATEGORY 5.
    No – Score CATEGORY 1.

JEALOUSY

1. Was there homicide that, it has been established beyond a reasonable doubt, was entirely impetuous and unplanned?

    Yes – Continue to JEALOUSY question #2.
    No – Continue to JEALOUSY question #3.

2. Was the killing limited to the object of the jealousy and/or the third party in a love triangle, in a "crime of passion?"

Note: If the individual has killed one or more victims to eliminate an obstacle to a romantic connection, such as one's own child, which he or she believes is preventing a partner from initiating or continuing a relationship, go to ELIMINATION question #1. Otherwise:

  Yes – Score CATEGORY 2.
  No – Continue to JEALOUSY question #3.

3. Was the killing extreme in nature, possibly encompassing numerous victims?

  Yes – Continue to JEALOUSY question #4.
  No – Continue to JEALOUSY question #6.

4. Did the killer display some personality and/or behavioral traits of psychopathy?

  Yes – Continue to JEALOUSY question #5.
  No – Score CATEGORY 6.

5. Does the individual meet criteria for mass murder, having killed three or more victims in a single incident? If yes, and the individual exhibits possible signs of psychosis, a developmental disorder, and/or intellectual impairment, score CATEGORY 13. Otherwise:

   Yes – Score CATEGORY 16.
   No – Continue to JEALOUSY question #6.

6. Was narcissism or egocentricity a significant factor in the killing(s)?

   Note: If the killer murdered his or her lover or spouse, continue to JEALOUSY question #7. Also, answer "Yes" for cases in which homicide is committed by a stalker. If murder occurred in a wider context of multiple vicious acts, go to MULTIPLE MURDERS / VICIOUS ACTS question #1. Otherwise:

   Yes – Score CATEGORY 7.
   No – Continue to JEALOUSY question #7.

7. Does the individual display marked or full-blown personality and/or behavioral traits of psychopathy?

   Yes – Score CATEGORY 9.
   No – Score CATEGORY 6.

RAGE

1. Did the individual commit a homicide, related to anger or rage that was established, beyond a reasonable doubt, to have been entirely impetuous, with no major degree of premeditation?

   Yes – Score CATEGORY 6.
   No – Continue to RAGE question #2.

2. Did the individual exhibit marked personality and/or behavioral traits of psychopathy, in addition to some degree of premeditation?

   Yes – Continue to RAGE question #3.
   No – Score CATEGORY 8.

3. Did the individual commit more than one homicide and exhibit personality and/or behavioral traits of psychopathy?

   Yes – Continue to RAGE question #4.
   No – Score CATEGORY 8.

4. Was there murder that was extremely and unusually vicious, above and beyond what would be required for expeditious killing?

Note: Mass murder can sometimes be scored here. If the individual exhibits possible signs of psychosis, a developmental disorder, and/or intellectual impairment, score CATEGORY 8 if there is no accompanying psychopathy, and CATEGORY 13 if some degree of psychopathy is also present. Otherwise:

Yes – Score CATEGORY 16.
No – Score CATEGORY 13.

ELIMINATION

Is there evidence that the killer meets full personality and/or behavioral criteria for psychopathy?

Yes – Score CATEGORY 11.
No – Score CATEGORY 10.

MULTIPLE MURDERS / VICIOUS ACTS

1. Did the murder(s) or vicious act(s) involve the torture of human beings?

Yes – Continue to TORTURE question #1.
No – Continue to MULTIPLE MURDERS/VICIOUS ACTS question #2.

2. Were there at least two homicides in separate events with predominantly sexual motivations?

Note: For acts in which murder or aggression sexually stimulates an individual, couple, or group who do not actually sexually abuse or rape the victim(s), continue to MULTIPLE MURDERS / VICIOUS ACTS question #3. Otherwise:

  Yes – Score CATEGORY 17.
  No – Continue to MULTIPLE MURDERS / VICIOUS ACTS question #3.

3. Does the individual meet criteria for spree murder, having killed two or more people at different locations with no cooling-off period between homicides?

Note: Choose "No" if the individual has committed a murder spree, but elsewhere has committed one or more unrelated homicides. Otherwise:

  Yes – Score CATEGORY 15.
  No – Continue to MULTIPLE MURDERS / VICIOUS ACTS question #4.

4. Was the individual a scheming type who committed murder and/or other violent acts chiefly for personal profit or gain?

  Yes – Continue to MULTIPLE MURDERS / VICIOUS ACTS question #5.
  No – Continue to MULTIPLE MURDERS / VICIOUS ACTS question #6.

5. Does the individual meet current FBI criteria for serial killing, having committed two or more murders in separate incidents?

  Yes – Continue to MULTIPLE MURDERS / VICIOUS ACTS question #6.
  No – Continue to MULTIPLE MURDERS / VICIOUS ACTS question #7.

6. Was there homicide or some other form of violence that was extremely and unusually vicious?

Note: For murders that were expeditious (e.g., by shooting) and chiefly "practical" in nature, select "No." If there has been no murder, continue to MULTIPLE MURDERS / VICIOUS ACTS question #8. If the individual has killed and exhibits possible signs of psychosis, developmental disability, and/or intellectual impairment, score CATEGORY 13. Otherwise:

Yes – Score CATEGORY 16.
No – Continue to MULTIPLE MURDERS / VICIOUS ACTS question #7.

7. Were the killings generally expeditious (e.g., by shooting) and chiefly intended to achieve some financial end or eliminate enemies?

Note: If slow, cruel methods (e.g., slow-acting poison) or a blend of expeditious and slow, cruel methods were employed, select "No." If the latter was used to torture one or more victims, go to TORTURE question #1. Otherwise:

Yes – Score CATEGORY 14.
No – Score CATEGORY 15.

8. Is the individual someone who never committed murder or torture of a human being, but committed (a) sexual assault of a child or adult, (b) animal torture, (c) intentional mutilation or disfigurement of a living person by any means, (d) acts of necrophilia, or (e) highly vicious acts not specified elsewhere in the algorithm?

Yes – Score CATEGORY 16.
No – Go to OTHER question #1.

TORTURE

1. Is there clear evidence of psychotic illness, such as schizophrenia, in which the individual, at least part of the time, committed murder and torture in response to hallucinations, delusions, or thought disorder?

    Yes – Score CATEGORY 20.
    No – Continue to TORTURE question #2.

2. Was there physical torture that was intentionally prolonged?

Note: If torture has been purely psychological and there has been no homicide, go to OTHER question #2. Otherwise:

    Yes – Continue to TORTURE question #3.
    No – Score CATEGORY 18.

3. Is the individual known, for certain, to have killed, in addition to physical torture?

    Yes – Score CATEGORY 22.
    No – Score CATEGORY 21.

OTHER

1. Were there multiple acts of physical or psychological torture of human beings?

    Yes – Go to TORTURE question #1.
    No – Continue to OTHER question #2.

2. Is the offender someone who has not committed murder, who was motivated by a desire to rape, subjugate, intimidate, or instill terror? Note: Answer "Yes" for individuals who have not committed homicide or physical torture, and who have abducted one or more victims for the purpose of sexual slavery.

Yes – Score CATEGORY 19.
No – Continue to OTHER question #3.

3. Were there one or more violent acts other than murder, such as rape, child abuse, or animal torture? Note: Answer "Yes" for acts of necrophilia without homicide.

Yes – Score CATEGORY 16.
No – Return to MOTIVATIONS question #1 and reconsider.

THE ERA OF "NEW" EVIL

Michael H. Stone, MD

Edited by Gary Brucato, PhD

CHAPTER TWELVE

CULTURAL CHANGES THAT AFFECT THE PATTERNS OF VIOLENCE IN PEACETIME

Historians are fond of reminding us that it is usually quite difficult to identify and characterize the era in which we are living, until such time has gone by that the era in question appears to have ended. It then gives way to some new pattern, allowing us, *in retrospect*, to affix a proper label to the preceding time period. We tend also to define an "era" or "period" in accordance with some overarching theme. In the domain of politics, we speak, referring to our own country, of a Colonial period, a Revolutionary period, the Reconstruction period, the Great Depression, the Vietnam era, and so on. We speak, as well, of cultural periods: the Enlightenment, emerging in mid-eighteenth-century Western Europe, and, within that, a Romantic period, from the end of the eighteenth on into the mid-nineteenth century, which witnessed increased emphasis on individual persons and their emotions. The bellwether of the Romantic period was, perhaps, Goethe's 1774 *The Sorrows of Young Werther*, a story of obsession and hopeless love: the hero who commits suicide rather than interfere in the lives of his beloved Lotte and her new husband, Albert.

This period, in turn, overlapped with the "classical" period in music, embracing such figures as Bach, Handel, Haydn, Mozart, Beethoven, Schubert, Chopin, Schumann, and Brahms. On the psychological front, we point to the Victorian period: the latter two-thirds of the nineteenth century, ending with the death of the queen in 1901—occurring a year after the publication of Sigmund Freud's magnum opus on dreams, which, along with his *Three Essays on Sexuality*, ushered in the psychoanalytical period. What is special about the psychoanalytical period is its emphasis on the emotional troubles of ordinary people, in contrast to the usual focus of nineteenth-century psychiatry—namely, the psychoses, as addressed by Wilhelm Griesinger, Emil Kraepelin, and Eugen Bleuler. Freud himself built on a tradition, vis-à-vis interest in ordinary people, that began with Anton Mesmer and his followers, Ambroise-Auguste Liébeault; Amand-Marie-Jacques de Chastenet, the Marquis of Puységur; James Braid; Auguste Forel; and Hippolyte Bernheim, who emphasized hypnosis. It was Freud's discovery that self-revelation and therapeutic benefit could emerge from free association, without the need for putting the patient in a state of altered consciousness. Yet, as we look back, we notice that the red thread running through the "neuroses"—the emotional problems of the ordinary, nonpsychotic men and women of Freud's era, which included the era of the psychoanalytic pioneers of the first third of the twentieth century—was inhibition, as adumbrated in Freud's 1926 essay "Hemmung, Symptom und Angst" ("Inhibition, Symptom and Anxiety"). This inhibition often took the form of problems in the sexual arena: impotence or lack of self-confidence in men; frigidity in women, many of whom Freud saw as experiencing "penis envy" or picturing themselves as "castrated men." Freud emphasized the roles of patients' fathers, as in Little Hans and in his Schreber case, paying less attention to the importance of their mothers. This would be corrected later by Melanie Klein and later still by John Bowlby, in his works on attachment and loss.

Freud was a product of the Victorian era, in which not only inhibition and self-restraint were the prominent psychological attributes, but also the role of women was limited—severely so, as we would now assess it—to the traditional roles of *Kinder, Kirche, Küche*: children, church, and kitchen. To be sure, there were some women in Freud's orbit, such as Lou Andreas Salome and Countess Marie Bonaparte, who were not so reticent of self-expression. Freud still famously posed the question, "What do women want?" Asked but not answered. Yet, there were women who could have given Freud, even in his youth, the answers he was seeking. Most prominent among them was Susan B. Anthony. Born into a Massachusetts Quaker family in 1820, she lived most of her life in upstate New York. A champion for temperance and for the abolition of slavery, she centered her activities around women's rights. Four years before Freud was born, she was prevented from speaking at a temperance society because she was a woman. Within a few years, along with her lifelong coworker Elizabeth Stanton, she helped found the Women's Loyal National League, an abolitionist organization, and the American Equal Rights Association, which campaigned for equal rights and work wages for women and black people. In 1872, Anthony was arrested in Rochester, New York, which was, by then, her hometown, for trying to vote in the presidential election. She was ridiculed for trying to "destroy the institution of marriage." This accusation stemmed from her advocacy, in 1857, of men and women to be educated together at all levels, including college—viewed by men at the time as a "vast social evil" and a "monster of social deformity." So what did and do women want? Well, equality of education, opportunity, pay for comparable work, recognition as independent human beings worthy of respect for their own views and opinions, and suffrage—the ability to vote. There is no indication that Freud ever heard of Anthony's answer to this vital question, though it is of interest that, in 1899, two years before her death, no less a "Victorian" than Queen Victoria herself held a reception in Windsor Castle for the Third International Council of Women— formed by Anthony in 1888. It took Freud and his colleagues in the early twentieth century to free us from the more maladaptive aspects of sexual inhibition, but the beginnings of greater freedom for women had already begun in his early years, stirred by a firebrand revolutionary American woman, and sanctioned by a sympathetic English queen.

SOME REDUCED INHIBITION IN THE FIRST HALF OF THE TWENTIETH CENTURY

The psychoanalytic pioneers were gradually helping to overturn the excessive inhibitions of their patients in the first years of the new century. They received generous, if unanticipated, encouragement from the Great War—a revolutionary period, as it turned out, albeit unnamed. Kingdoms fell, and empires, as with the Austro-Hungarian, were destroyed. Many an aristocrat was suddenly a commoner; many a woman was liberated from her *Kinder-Kirche-Küche* existence, because of the exigencies of the war, and welcomed into the workplace—into the factories now emptied of men, millions of whom were never to return from battle at all.[1] The *named* revolution in Russia also liberated women for work. Yet, divorce remained a rarity. It was still difficult for women to extricate themselves from domineering and abusive husbands. That freedom was still decades away.

In the interbellum period that followed—not yet recognized as "between" wars—until 1939, there did appear to be greater sexual freedom, as manifest in the "flapper era" in the United States and in the Berlin cafés of the Weimar period. After two millennia of Judeo-Christian views of onanism (i.e., masturbation) as sinful, it was being seen more and more as the by-product of an imperious biological urge, rather than as a road to perdition. Psychoanalysis was, in its heyday after World War II, banned in Communist Russia, to be sure, but flourished in the United States and Western Europe, to which many of the German, Austrian, and mainly Jewish analysts fled during the Hitler years. During that period, marriage was still a solid institution; divorce remained rare. Children were born mainly in, rather than out of, wedlock. Educational opportunities were getting better for women throughout the "developed" countries. It was about as common at midcentury for a woman as for a man to earn a great reputation in the psychoanalytic community, as witness Edith Jacobson, Phyllis Greenacre, Annie Reich, Helene Deutsch, Frieda Fromm-Reichmann, Melanie Klein, and her daughter, Melitta Schmideberg.

If we look at crime, including violent crime, up through midcentury, the situation seems very much as it had always been. We are ignoring here the violence committed by armies, despots, revolutionaries, Mafia-type gangs, perpetrators of the Holocaust, and so forth, since groups of men and tyrants have committed unspeakable horrors since the beginnings of human history. In the 1,900 years between the Roman emperor Caligula in 39 CE and Hitler starting World War II in 1939, we see a difference not in the level of sadism, only in the matter of scale. For instance, the Roman emperor Nero (54–68 CE), the last of the "Claudian" emperors, had oil poured over Christians, who were then set afire to create better light for his nighttime reading. Yet, the crimes committed by criminals in *peacetime* appear to have changed by little—until, as we hope to demonstrate, quite recently.

In the notorious American kidnappings before the 1960s, for example, the motive was money, the first instance being the 1874 abduction of two-year-old Charley Ross, in the aftermath of the 1873 depression.[2] The ransom was not paid; the boy was killed, as were the two kidnappers.

Leopold and Loeb, rich adolescents from Chicago, in what was one of several "Crimes of the Century," kidnapped and killed Bobby Frank in 1924, partly for money, partly on a "dare" to see if they could get away with it.[3] Baby Charles Lindbergh was kidnapped and killed eight years later, in yet another "Crime of the Century," even though the ransom was paid.[4] Finally, in 1953, six-year-old Bobby Greenlease was abducted and killed, though a huge ransom was paid; the two kidnappers were executed on the same day a few months later.[5] The murderers dispatched their victims with a minimum of pain. Their families were the ones who suffered—psychologically—the losses of their children. Spousal murders were also done quickly, say, with a gun, garrote, or poison, such as when Ruth Snyder and her lover killed her husband in 1927. Snyder had grown tired of hearing her husband sing the praises of a former fiancée, who had died a decade before.[6] The two garroted him to death and staged a fake burglary. The most gruesome crimes that made the headlines were those of Albert Fish,[7] whom we have already discussed in detail, and Gordon Northcott, a pedophile serial killer who lured Mexican boys to his Los Angeles farm in 1928, whom he would then rape, murder, and dismember, forcing his nephew to bury the body parts in the woods.[8] There was also the murder of aspiring actress Elizabeth Short, the "Black Dahlia," who was posthumously cut in two and left by the side of a road in Los Angeles in 1947.[9] Her killer was thought by some to have been the prominent physician George Hodel, among other suspects.[10] In 1957, the spree killer Charles Starkweather shot to death eleven people as he fled with his fourteen-year-old sweetheart Caril Fugate, after her parents—the first two victims—forbade their marriage.[11] Quick deaths, little suffering, and Starkweather was arguably too quickly executed for the murders—but that was "then."

A SEA CHANGE IN THE 1960s

Apart from the start of a nationwide revolution or a large-scale war, what we come to define later as a "new era" seldom has an easily defined beginning. Yet, if we think of two contiguous eras as perched at either end of a chronological seesaw, the 1960s can lay claim to be quite near to our seesaw's fulcrum, with 1965 serving as the very balance point. From then onward, we note that many aspects of our culture began to move downward. This descent has involved culture, the kinds of personality types and patients who seek the help of mental health professionals, and also the natures and sheer nastiness of both violent and nonviolent crimes. In the following table, I have highlighted some of the important events and trends in this time period, which, collectively, have contributed to such changes as would merit designation as a new era.

A Chronology of Post-1960 Events and Trends
1960: The contraceptive "pill" (Enovid) becomes available
1963: The assassination of President John F. Kennedy Use of marijuana becomes widespread; other drugs are sometimes added to the mix, including LSD, amphetamines, and, to a lesser extent, cocaine
1964: US involvement in Vietnam, following a (largely trumped-up) incident in the Gulf of Tonkin Dr. Timothy Leary's message of "Tune in, turn on, drop out" helps accelerate the burgeoning drug epidemic Protests begin against the Vietnam War, euphemistically called the Vietnam "conflict" The Civil Rights Act is passed
1965: President Lyndon B. Johnson scores a great success in the civil rights movement, but, at the same time, a great failure in his escalation of the Vietnam War, which proves to have neither purpose nor popular support; "hippies" in San Francisco burn draft cards; young men go to Canada to avoid being sent to Vietnam The assassination of social activist Malcom X Soaring divorce rate in the United States; high incarceration-rate of boys born to unwed mothers The Watts-area race riot in Los Angeles

1966: Sudden upsurge of serial sexual homicide and mass murder in the United States, after decades of very low yearly incidence

An upsurge in examples of outré sexual license in forms such as *Plato's Retreat* orgies, wife swapping, and "key" parties

Emergence of militant black groups on the Far Left, notably the Black Panthers, spearheaded by Huey Newton and Bobby Seale, active till circa 1982

Miranda v. Arizona expands the rights of alleged criminal defendants

Richard Speck kills eight nurses in a Chicago nursing school

Charles Whitman shoots to death thirteen from Texas University tower in Austin

1967: In July, a largescale race riot in Detroit in response to police brutality

1968: Richard M. Nixon elected as president

Robert F. Kennedy and Martin Luther King assassinated

Student riots at Columbia University; the feminist revolution is in full swing

In the aftermath of the Tet Offensive in Vietnam, American troops led by Lt. William L. Calley perpetrate the My Lai massacre, killing five hundred defenseless men, women, and children, leading to further public disillusionment with the government and contempt toward the soldiers, many of whom raped and tortured the civilians before killing them

1969: The Stonewall Riots launch the gay liberation movement

The Manson "family" murders in Los Angeles

Notable increase in violent crime, especially robberies and assaults

1970: On May 4, members of the Ohio National Guard kill four students at Kent State, during the anti-war demonstration, prompted by Nixon's April 30 decision to bomb Cambodia; the widespread denunciation of the Kent State killings catalyzes the downfall of the Nixon presidency
1973: United States pulls out of Vietnam *Roe v. Wade*, permitting abortion, becomes law
1974: Nixon steps down to avoid impeachment
Late 1970s: Rapid expansion of the pornographic film industry, due, in part, to the advent of the home video cassette recorder (VCR)
1979: Shah Reza Pahlevi ousted in Iran; militant cleric Khomenei becomes leader Dr. Christopher Lasch publishes *The Culture of Narcissism*, lamenting "me-ism," pathological narcissistic personality types, and the decline of the family
1980: Murder rate in the United States reaches ten per 100,000 people per year, approximately ten times that of Europe or Japan[12]
1981: Beginning of the AIDS epidemic
1983: Two truck bombs strike headquarters of American and French soldiers in Lebanon, killing 299; Islamic jihad group claims responsibility
1984: The crack-cocaine epidemic in full swing in the United States, contributing to the high rate of murder and violence in the "inner cities" across the country
1987: Asymmetric war between Islamic extremists versus the West continues; USS *Stark* attacked by Iraqi Exocet missiles; thirty-seven American seamen killed
1991: Iraq under Saddam Hussein invades Kuwait; the United States counterattacks in the Gulf War
1993: Al-Qaeda's first attempt to destroy the Twin Towers in New York City The dangerous Branch Davidian cult in Waco, Texas, eliminated by the FBI

1995: The internet begins to exert major impact upon culture and commerce, allowing nearly instantaneous communication by email and instant messaging; with the rapid emergence of the World Wide Web comes social networking, online shopping, blogs, and discussion forums

1999: In April, mass shooting at the Columbine High School committed by Eric Harris and Dylan Klebold

2000: In October, the suicide attack off the coast of Yemen by al-Qaeda; USS *Cole* attacked; seventeen sailors killed

2001: On September 11, al-Qaeda suicide bombers in the United States attack the Pentagon, and the Twin Towers in New York City; they also attempt to attack the White House; three thousand killed

2003: The United States and its allies invade Iraq and Afghanistan, attempting to overthrow Saddam Hussein and to crush al-Qaeda

2005: Four jihadist suicide bombers in London attack subways and buses, killing fifty-two; planned by al-Qaeda terrorists

2006: Capture and execution of Saddam Hussein

2008: Collapse of Lehman Brothers in September leads to the most serious economic decline since the Great Depression of 1929; Barack Obama elected first African American president in November

US unemployment rate reaches 10 percent

2010: Murder rate in United States improves, now down to 5.8 per 100,000 people per year;[13] number of serial killers active per year has been dropping gradually over the past decade; mass murders continue at a high frequency and with high casualty rates, associated primarily with semiautomatic guns

Abuse of drugs in the United States is a severe problem, and the menu of illicit drugs is now expanded, including marijuana with higher THC content, methamphetamine, Ecstasy, angel dust (phencyclidine), psilocybin ("mushrooms"), opiates, LSD, and so forth

2012: In December, Adam Lanza commits a mass shooting at Sandy Hook Elementary School in Newtown, Connecticut

2014: Russia takes over Crimea

ISIS group of Islamic jihadists strive to create a caliphate; they murder and behead a number of reporters from the United States and the West

Ebola virus reaches crisis proportions in West Africa; cases crop up in the United States, Spain, and England

Growing concern about income inequality, with fears of the nation dividing into a few "haves" and many "have-nots"

Review of the records of crimes in peacetime reveals instances of atrocities and crimes of unusual gruesomeness and, in some instances, of a type never recorded in the pre-1960s era

2015: The *Charlie Hebdo* massacre in Paris by Islamic jihadists

Greenwings plane crash caused by suicidal German copilot, Andreas Lubitz, killing himself and 149 others

In Charleston, South Carolina, young white supremacist Dylann Roof murders nine black churchgoers

2016: Omar Mateen, a young man of jihadist identification, kills forty-nine people in a Florida gay nightclub

Dakota Access Pipeline protests

Donald J. Trump elected US president in contentious race

Britain votes to exit from the European Union

2017: In October, sixty-four-year-old Stephen Paddock commits large-scale mass murder from his Las Vegas hotel room, killing fifty-eight, plus himself, and wounding hundreds

Start of the Me Too movement

2018: Nineteen-year-old former student Nikolas Cruz allegedly kills seventeen at Parkland, Florida, school on Valentine's Day; large-scale anti-gun protests occur throughout the United States in the weeks that follow

Israel moves its capital to Jerusalem, followed by violent confrontation in Gaza

Abuse of opioid drugs reaches epidemic proportions in the United States, accompanied by many deaths and suicides, especially in young people

Increasing divisiveness and heightened tensions between Sunni- and Shia-dominated countries in the Middle East

Robert Gregory Bowers is accused of killing eleven and injuring seven during prayer services at the Tree of Life synagogue in Pittsburgh, Pennsylvania, the deadliest attack on the Jewish community in US history

What emerges from this list are, for the most part, historical developments of the past fifty to fifty-five years. Many of these events, in turn, set the stage for more subtle, less well-defined, and chronologically less well-pinpointed changes in societal attitude and mood. The easy availability of oral contraceptives, for example, was liberating for many women, who may have felt freed, among other things, from the necessity to bear children whom they worried they could not adequately care for. Sex as a pleasurable activity could, for more and more women, be divorced from sex as a pleasurable prelude to the joys and burdens of motherhood. "Divorced" is the key word here, since, as Henry Allen wrote in his review of Jonathan Eig's book on the pill, here citing journalist Margaret Wente, "The Pill decoupled sex and marriage, and it also decouples marriage and having children."[14] Recreation trumps procreation. The "law" of unintended consequences now came readily into play. Birth control contributed also to less desirable outcomes: a greatly heightened divorce rate, marital infidelity, and single parenthood. Single parenthood often stems from a mother raising a child without a father. Boys from such situations are more prone to getting in trouble with the law. Allen added, "Like all revolutions, this one would devour its children, as an epidemic of venereal diseases ensued, including ones many of us never heard of before: Herpes, chlamydia, genital warts." I do not know if Allen was aware of the hidden play on words in the phrase "devouring its children," in that another side effect of the pill was fewer children, especially among couples, married or not, who were eager to limit their numbers of children to proportions that made more sense, economically and psychologically.

Another unintended consequence to women's greater freedom was male protest—the same sort of angry, not to say vitriolic, denunciation of these new freedoms, as many men expressed in Susan B. Anthony's day one hundred years earlier: women were committing a "vast social evil" and "destroying the institution of marriage." Reading not too far between the lines, the message of these men said, "Women are destroying our hold and control over them!" Of course, not all men are equally susceptible to this threat. It appears that nice-looking men with good personalities and high incomes are more apt to feel secure within a marriage than a cantankerous and impecunious working-class bully. Not surprisingly, in retrospect, the upsurge in serial sexual homicide followed fairly quickly on the heels of this greater liberation on the part of women to ditch unpleasant men, find self-supporting jobs, and take care of their children by themselves, perhaps with some help from relatives and daycare facilities.[15] Examples are legion. The previously mentioned iconic serial killer Ted Bundy, when rejected by his upper-class fiancée, embarked on a career of raping and killing several dozen young women with long, straight, dark brown hair, parted in the middle, who were "lookalikes" of a woman who spurned him.[16] Like the great proportion of serial killers, he came from a working-class background. An even more dramatic example is that of Paul Snider, the low-life con man who "discovered" and then murdered Dorothy Stratten, whom we discussed in detail earlier in this book. In 1979, not long before Snider's murder-suicide, Dr. Christopher Lasch, a professor of history at the University of Rochester, published a book that earned considerable notoriety, entitled *The Culture of Narcissism*.[17] Lasch inveighed against what he regarded as the "organized kindness" of the government and its effects, as he saw it, on the traditional family structure. As writer and critic Lee Siegel points out, Lasch saw such entitlements as the wellspring from which "pathological narcissism" arose, features of which were a weakened sense of self, hedonism, and, with these, a decline in the solidity of family life as it had flourished in the nineteenth century.[18] This was a different brand of narcissism from that of the arrogant, self-satisfied businessman or the haughty woman who, in her privileged life, grew indifferent to the needs of those less well-off. For Lasch, this pathological narcissism, which was new in his day, also underlay the dramatic increase in crime rate and the devaluation of family and social values. Self-indulgence replaced concern for one's fellow man, and self-restraint gave way to impulsivity. Though Lasch placed some of the blame for this social deterioration on the radical political and religious movements of the period of 1960–1970, he did not focus on the pill or on the disillusionment with the government, in the wake of the assassinations of leaders, or of the seemingly useless and despised war in Vietnam. Nor was there mention of the increasing gruesomeness of the violent crimes that began to occur in the 1960s. It appears as though the author was fulminating, lashing out, even, against the transition from the idealistic, socially cohesive Protestant work-ethic-oriented America of our forefathers—the aristocratic Washington and Jefferson, the rough-hewn, but compassionate Lincoln and Garfield—to a more sensate and selfish society in the twentieth century, exemplified by the self-indulgent Warren G. Harding, or the embittered and egotistical Nixon. Widely read historian though he was, Lasch defined narcissism more as a psychiatrist or psychologist might—as a disorder of an individual, as though he had taken a page from the third edition of our *Diagnostic and Statistical Manual of Mental Disorders (DSM-III)*, which was not actually published till a few months after Lasch's book. Perhaps he had hints of how "narcissistic personality" would soon be defined.

SOME QUALITIES OF THE "NEW NARCISSISM"

One attribute of post-1965 "new narcissism" is a heightened tendency to behave in ways that merit terms like *licentious* and *lascivious*. These are old-fashioned words we seldom hear now, though we are seeing more and more of what they describe. *Licentious* covers a wider ground: it connotes sexually unrestrained, wanton—but also unrestrained by law, immoral and, in a more abstract way, going beyond customary or proper bounds or limits, and disregarding rules, including social ones. *Lascivious*, a narrower term, refers only to lustfulness and lack of sexual restraint. Intrinsic to the concept of licentious is *license*, i.e., having the "right" to do as one wishes, akin to one of the key descriptors in the *DSM* definition of narcissistic personality disorder—namely, entitlement.

In a 2012 book by James Patterson, the subtitle of which is *How 1965 Transformed America*, the author, citing an earlier work, Philip Caputo's 1977 Vietnam War memoir *The Rumor of War*, mentioned how American troops began to burn and destroy civilians, livestock, and villages partly as acts of retribution and partly because, in that asymmetric war, Vietnamese women sometimes did toss grenades at US soldiers.[19] Unable to distinguish enemy troops from civilians, and unable to speak their six-tone, monosyllabic, and highly challenging language, US soldiers viewed all the "Vietcong" as the "enemy," to be killed indiscriminately. For Caputo, Vietnam was "an ethical, as well as a geographical wilderness. Out there, lacking restraints, sanctioned to kill, confronted by a hostile country and a relentless enemy, we sank into a brutish state."[20] This brutishness of the military added further fuel to the disillusionment with the government. Patterson observed, "Americans were losing faith in the federal government . . . in early 1965, trust dropping rapidly according to the polls from the post-1965 years to the present."[21] Gallup polls, for instance, showed a drop from 75 percent trust after 1965 to 43 percent in 2014.

Our culture was shifting because of what was happening in political, but also personal, realms, moving away from the earlier "we" culture, in which people were highly concerned for the welfare of others, to a "me" culture, with its emphasis on the self and self-gratification. As noted by Patterson, "Dramatic changes in sexual behavior and family life—more demands for sexual freedom, more premarital sex, more cohabitation, more fatherless children, more divorce—began to shake American society and culture in ways that could scarcely have been imagined before 1965."[22] Fewer children, as a result, grew up in intact families (i.e., with a mother and a father). Children from such backgrounds are more prone to psychological distress and, in the case of fatherless boys, trouble with the law. Here, Patterson is underlining what I have placed under the heading of licentiousness, both in its sexual connotations and in its allusion to abrogation of social rules and conventions.

Aiding and abetting these changes, the media have shown more in the way of violence, both "justified," as in depictions of war or crime fighting, and gratuitous, as in portrayals of sadism serving no other purpose but the titillation of the viewer or reader, than was formerly the case. While most people are not harmed by this, these heavy doses of violence do contribute to a desensitization, in at least some people, to what would otherwise be both horrifying and repugnant. In an individual with an already diminished capacity for self-restraint, this desensitization can, so to speak, grease the wheels toward the acting out of otherwise inadmissible violent fantasies. As an example, Nathaniel White, arrested for serial sexual homicides of six young women in upstate New York, told the authorities that he saw TV shows in which men raped and killed women and then dumped them on the sides of roads—and that this is what "taught" him how to do such things.[23]

What we have, in effect, witnessed over the past fifty years is a coarsening of society: a larger proportion of crimes showing extreme callousness, greater disregard for ordinary human feelings, greater cruelty, and a greater propensity to *relish* in such cruelty—the essence of sadism—in this post-1965 era. This coarsening is not limited to crimes of violence, but it shows up with considerable frequency in the arena of the law courts, where divorce and especially custody issues are too often settled in favor of a moneyed egoist rather than a more deserving, but less affluent, spouse.

By way of illustrating in a more easily grasped way the points we have been making here, we offer a number of examples corresponding to different categories of this new narcissism—and the "new evil" it has spawned. Most of the examples relate to crimes of violence, some to a hitherto seldom witnessed ugliness and unfairness in the courts dealing with interpersonal discord. As we hope to demonstrate, some of the examples concern varieties of evil—by which we mean acts that shock and horrify—that would have been found either rarely or not at all in what one could read or view before the current era. Some examples seem to exceed what authors, playwrights, and scriptwriters before now could even envision in their own minds, thence to be censored by themselves, lest the public be offended. It is pertinent to recall how the playwrights of ancient Greece, as did Aristotle in his comments upon their works, refrained from showing gruesome actions on the stage. Such acts could only be alluded to, in words by the actors or the chorus, as having taken place *offstage*. This is the root of our term "obscene," i.e., not permissible to be shown on the stage or in writing. Now that we can watch Islamic jihadists behead reporters on the internet, view bloody eviscerations in movies, or read pornographic novels about children being raped and dismembered, the territory of the obscene has been shrunk, upon our visual maps, to a very small island indeed. In the categories enumerated below, there will inevitably be some conceptual overlap. Certain cases of bullying prompted by digital devices and ending in death could, for example, fit into our discussions of bullying, the internet, or murder. Violent crime—assault, rape, kidnap, murder— has always been with us, so most of the examples are not new in type but, rather, in the growing grotesqueness of the otherwise very familiar types. A few are quite new and contemporary, even in terms of type. Narcissism is the common denominator running through all of the examples but often a narcissism liberally laced with a component of sadism.

CATEGORIES OF VIOLENCE IN THE ERA OF "NEW EVIL"

Bullying

A common occurrence in schools and the workplace, bullying has often taken on a more aggressive character in recent years, amplified at times as "cyberbullying," through the use of hidden cameras, video streaming, and the internet. Using a webcam and a computer, Dharun Ravi, a student at Rutgers University, was able to record his gay roommate, Tyler Clementi, kissing another man, and make the scene available to others. In the aftermath of this invasion of privacy, Clementi committed suicide in September of 2010.[24] Ravi's behavior was roundly condemned, though at court, he received only a light sentence of thirty days in jail, a fine, and community service. This was not murder in the ordinary sense, although there is a concept in law, sometimes called the "eggshell skull rule," according to which a defendant is held liable for severe damages to a victim owing to the victim's preexisting vulnerability, of which the defendant had no knowledge nor intent to cause grievous injury. Clementi's psychological sensitivity to public embarrassment was presumably much greater than Ravi anticipated and greater than might have been the case with many other gay students. One might claim, however, that *but for* Ravi's act, Clementi would not have died, such that this act of aggravated assault had more serious overtones.

A similar argument can be made on behalf of several adolescent girls—fifteen-year-old Audrie Pott, fourteen-year-old Amanda Todd, fifteen-year-old Phoebe Prince, and seventeen-year-old Rehtaeh Parsons—who, in the past few years, committed suicide after being mocked and shamed repeatedly by their female classmates, envious of the girls' physical appearances. In the case of Pott, she had been gang-raped at a party and photographs of the crime were then distributed via social networking.[25] The cyberbullying in Todd's case consisted of her being sexually exploited into showing her breasts, pictures of which then went "viral" on the web.[26] A common element in these cases is the use of internet-age media to magnify the impact of bullying, such that the embarrassment of the victim, especially in vulnerable young persons, reaches an extreme that may precipitate suicide.

Child Abuse

There have been cases of child abuse in recent years that stand out, in comparison to earlier examples, as being unusually sadistic, prolonged, and—in the sense of being unparalleled in viciousness—diabolical. In Los Angeles, a sixty-one-year-old elementary school teacher, Mark Berndt, was arrested for lewd acts against his pupils.[27] He would put cockroaches on their faces. He held his own semen under the noses of blindfolded young girls, silenced with duct tape, and then take photographs, hundreds of which were later found in his apartment. In Florida, Jessica Schwarz had two children of her own, plus a ten-year-old stepson, Andrew, from her husband's prior relationship.[28] She would make Andrew eat a roach if he did not clean the kitchen to her liking, and make him run down the street naked, pick up dog feces with his hands, or wear a T-shirt that read, "I'm a worthless piece of shit, don't talk to me." She would sometimes push his face in kitty litter. She would call him "fuck-face" and "bastard." Finally, she drowned him in the family pool, for which she was sentenced to seventy years in prison. In yet another example, which I believe is unique, Jeremiah Wright, disgruntled about having a seven-year-old son born with cerebral palsy—wheelchair-bound and unable to talk or feed himself—beheaded the boy with a meat cleaver and left his head in the driveway for his wife to see when she returned home. He was ultimately judged not guilty by reason of insanity in this horrifying case.[29]

Fetus-Snatching

In 1987, Darci Pierce became the first perpetrator of an entirely new type of crime, which for want of an official designation, I have called "fetus-snatching." Obsessed with the worry that having a baby was crucial to preserving her marriage, nineteen-year-old Darci pretended to be pregnant—and finally abducted a woman who was nine months pregnant, forcing her at gunpoint into her car and taking her to an isolated spot. She proceeded to strangle the woman and cut open her abdomen with a car key, stealing the fetus to present to her husband as their "new baby."[30] Since then, there have been seventeen additional cases of this sort, all in the United States.

Gratuitous Cruelty

Two Wisconsin sisters, twenty-four-year-old Valerie Bartkey and seventeen-year-old Amanda Johnson, invited an eighteen-year-old physically disabled man to "hang out." When he refused to have sex with Bartkey, the sisters made him drink a glass of lemonade, which was actually a mixture of their urine. Bartkey then pulled and twisted his penis with a pair of pliers, causing extreme pain, while Johnson called him a "bitch."[31] The crime was all the more shocking and in a sense "new," insofar as it was committed by females. The sentence was much gentler than the crime: Bartkey received a month in prison and three years of probation, and was to write a letter of apology. Johnson was given probation.[32]

Home Invasion

Earlier examples of home invasion were for robbery, as in the celebrated case of Dick Hickock and Perry Smith, who, in 1959, broke into the farm home of the Clutter family on the belief that there was $10,000 in the family safe.[33] The robbery was a flop. There was no safe and no other money. The pair killed the four members of the Clutter family and were later caught and executed. One can point to a measure of restraint in their crime, insofar as Hickock had the idea of raping the sixteen-year-old daughter but was dissuaded from doing so by Smith. Such restraint was notably absent in the 2007 home invasion of Dr. William Petit and his family in Cheshire, Connecticut, by Steven Hayes and Joshua Komisarjefsky. After forcing the man's wife to withdraw $15,000 from the bank, the pair then went into the Petit home, where they proceeded to rape the Petits' eleven-year-old daughter, which was recorded on a cell phone, and Mrs. Petit. The girl and another daughter, age seventeen, were tied to beds, and Mrs. Petit was strangled to death. The men then poured accelerant over all three women, setting the house afire, as if to destroy evidence of the crime. Dr. Petit, whom they had knocked unconscious, survived. Komisarjefsky was an adoptee with a serious drug habit, and his numerous thefts were committed mainly to obtain money for cocaine and methamphetamine.[34]

Infanticide with Unusual Cruelty

Infanticide, whether as a crime or as a desperate means of birth control, has occurred throughout human history and is common to this day in Pakistan, India, and China, helping to account for the exaggerated male-female ratio in those countries. In the West, infanticide is a crime. One such example is that of Dr. Debra Green.[35] Popular and the valedictorian when graduating from high school, she changed into an abusive harridan, becoming abrasive, confrontational, foul-mouthed, and given to tantrums. She became an opiate addict and was considered, in personality, narcissistic, schizoid, and borderline, wearing her husband Michael Farrar's patience thin by calling him a "fuckhole" or "asshole" in front of their three young children. Farrar eventually met another woman and began divorce proceedings. Green started to poison him with ricin, which led to his being hospitalized eleven times before this was discovered. Farrar moved out and sued for custody. At that point, Green spread accelerant all over the house and set it on fire, killing two of their three children. One jumped to safety. Green nonchalantly watched the flames from the ground nearby. She was sentenced to life in prison without parole. There have also been half a dozen cases of women burning children alive in microwaves since 1982. In 2011, a twenty-nine-year-old California woman, Ka Yang, killed her six-week-old infant daughter in this manner. She was given a twenty-six-years-to-life term for the crime.[36]

The Internet

The internet, germinating from ideas by MIT professors in the mid-1960s, was, by 1985, in widespread use, thanks in part to the proliferation of affordable computers. As with scientific and engineering revolutions in general, the internet has been much more a blessing than a curse—but, on the "curse" side, some older types of crime flourished more widely, while a few types have emerged anew. The "blue movies" watched by college men in a previous generation gave way to a much easier and more widespread access to pornography, including the illegal, but not so inaccessible, "kiddie porn." Children have tended to learn about and watch sex in all its forms at earlier ages than heretofore. People can be lured via chat rooms to participate in sexual acts of a more daring sort than were available before, although this has helped undercover police entrap individuals seeking illegal forms of sexual activity, such as those involving minors.

The story of Sharon Lopatka and her wished-for murder represents a unique application of the internet.[37] Rebelling against her Orthodox Jewish family, she married a Catholic. Then, under a pseudonym, she started an internet company, through which she let the world know she was interested in being tortured to death, but also, as a sort of prelude to death, in experiencing stronger orgasms through asphyxiaphilia via strangulation. Given the inordinately wide reach of the internet—one could not place such an ad in the local newspaper—she eventually found a "taker" in Robert Glass, a computer analyst. They met at his trailer in North Carolina, where he indulged her fancy for asphyxiaphilia and torture but, on one occasion, went a bit too far with the nylon cord strangulation, and, in 1996, she died. Even though he could show documents from her attesting to her masochistic wishes, the court concluded that the act nevertheless fell under the rubric of murder, so he was sent to prison, where he died six years later. Cases of this sort create an uncharted territory for the law. Five years after the Lopatka murder—or assisted suicide—came the murder and cannibalism of a willing participant by Armin Meiwes of Germany, discussed in detail earlier in this book.[38]

The ease with which the internet, along with texts, tweets, emails, iPads, Facebook, video clips, and the like, can be used especially by young people has facilitated both enhanced social bonding but also malicious misuse.

Misuse of these devices contributed to the 2012 murder of a sixteen-year-old West Virginia girl by two classmates of the same age.[39] Skylar Neese was at first a close friend of Shelia Eddy, who later distanced herself from Neese, befriending Rachel Shoaf, instead. One night when all three were together, Eddy and Shoaf had sexual relations in front of Neese. Alarmed that Neese might, out of jealousy, expose the two as "lesbians"—all three had boyfriends—as she hinted she might do in her tweets, Eddy and Shoaf decided Neese had to die. They plotted to invite her to a nonexistent party, drove her to a secluded spot equipped with kitchen knives and a shovel, and fatally stabbed her over fifty times. The murder and Neese's body were not discovered for seven months. The readiness with which new devices could spark large-scale public humiliation made the murder seem the only "solution" for the two girls to preserve their proper images in the community.

Jealousy

Since time immemorial, jealousy has been known, when extreme, as a stimulus to murder. Envy, one of the Seven Deadly Sins enumerated by Pope Gregory in the late sixth century, is a close cousin. Both concern a desperate wanting of someone or something that is beyond one's reach. Envy, however, is a two-person situation: "A" wishes he had what "B" has, usually in relation to wealth or social position. Jealousy, by contrast, is a three-person situation: "A" loves "B," but "B" prefers "C." What is "new" about the way in which these emotions may conduce to violent solutions is the hitherto unheard of and often novelistic manner of carrying out a crime inspired by these otherwise ancient motives. An example: James Cahill III, an unemployed layabout from upstate New York, was supported by Jill, his enterprising and successful wife.[40] The marriage deteriorated, and, in 1998, Jill found a more suitable and successful man and planned to divorce her husband. At that point, in a jealousy-fueled rage, James struck Jill over the head with a baseball bat. Grievously wounded, but still alive, Jill was slowly recovering in a hospital. Arrested for the attack, James pretended he only struck her in "self-defense" and was allowed out on bail, generously provided by his mother. James then obtained some cyanide, under the pretext of purchasing "photo lab chemicals," and dressed himself up as a female janitor with an orange wig and a broom. After sneaking into the hospital by night, he entered the wing in which Jill lay recovering, convincing the nursing staff with his disguise, and found his wife's room. He then poured cyanide into her mouth, finishing what he had tried to finish with the bat. It is not the underlying emotion of jealousy that gives this case its "modern" feel; it is the diabolical cleverness and the narcissistic assumption of being much smarter than the police, hence "sure" to get away with the murder. It is not easy to find examples from before 1965 of this kind of complex, fiendishly devious, and—in the eyes of the perpetrator—"surefire" way of committing murder and escaping detection.

Envy, with a tinge of jealousy, was the primary factor in the 2009 murder of a Yale PhD candidate, Annie Le, by lab technician Raymond Clark III.[41] Le, a Vietnamese American woman who had been the valedictorian of her high school in San José, California, was to be married in a week's time. She was strikingly pretty; her fiancé was a doctoral student in physics and math. They were looking forward to what would be a life of great respect and accomplishment. Clark could look forward to no such thing. This disparity in potential was the source of Clark's envy, with, perhaps, a measure of jealousy, in that she preferred her brilliant fiancé to the socially inferior lab tech. On the September morning when Le entered the lab to check on an experiment, she was accosted, raped, and strangled by Clark. Then, as though taking a page from Edgar Allan Poe's famous story "The Black Cat," he immured Le's within a wall cavity in the lab. After burying her—safely, he assumed—upside down behind the wall, Clark sprayed the area with air freshener to hide the odor of the decomposing body. Clark was—like the man in Poe's story—quickly found out, despite his seeming cleverness, and is now serving a forty-four-year sentence.

Kidnapping

Apart from the rare custody battle, in which one parent kidnaps a child so as to deny access by the other parent, kidnap (the shorter name for this crime used in legal circles) has usually been for ransom money. Until now. Here we are focusing on American cases. In many less affluent countries, especially in Central and South America, kidnapping is still most often for ransom. In the last fifty years in the United States and in some European countries, however, the motive has shifted toward kidnap for sex, specifically, for the enslavement of a young woman or, rarely, a young boy by one man for sexual purposes. This shift in motive may reflect, in part, a change in how kidnap is punished. The death penalty is used much more sparingly of late, whereas, before 1960, kidnap-murder was, even in America, a swift ticket to the electric chair, as in the famous cases of Charley Ross (1874), Charles Lindbergh Jr. (1932), and Bobby Greenlease (1953), already referenced earlier. Since the 1960s, a number of men have constructed concrete bunkers beneath their own houses, in which they have then imprisoned their victims—for weeks, months, and, in some cases, decades. A self-proclaimed prophet, Brian Mitchell, kept Elizabeth Smart as his sexual slave for nearly a year until her escape in 2003.[42] The cases of John Esposito and Thomas Hose, who both kept women enslaved, will be discussed in a later chapter. Natasha Kampusch was kept in a bunker in Austria by Wolfgang Priklopil for eight years.[43] The even more famous case of Josef Fritzl, also in Austria, involved keeping his eldest daughter in a bunker beneath his house for twenty-four years, there to sire seven children by incest, in addition to the seven he sired by his wife upstairs.[44] Others have kept their sex slaves locked up in their house for long periods, as was the case with Phillip Garrido, who kept Jaycee Dugard for eighteen years and had two daughters by her before the three were able to escape his grip.[45] The families of these victims assumed their children were dead. They were "legally" dead—i.e., missing beyond seven years. Several years ago, it came to light that, in Cleveland, Ohio, Ariel Castro had kept three women captive, each for approximately a decade, shut up in his house, before their escape in 2013.[46] Though these men have taken narcissism and entitlement to dizzying heights seldom encountered in peacetime prior to the era of "new evil," they were not all identical in personality. Some were ruthless, arrogant psychopaths, such as Fritzl and Mitchell; some were weak, un-self-confident men who could never earn the loyalty and devotion of a sexual partner through socially acceptable means, as in the cases of Priklopil and Esposito; and some, like Castro and Hose, were selfish brutes. What we are witnessing is kidnap with a new and ugly twist.

A related new and ugly twist is seen in a contemporary brand of extortion, in which a wealthy person is abducted, bound, and tortured till credit card or other financial information is revealed, allowing the abductor(s) to steal large sums of money. Unlike kidnap of a child for ransom, this is a type of sophisticated kidnap/robbery. An egregious example is that of Noel

Doorbal and Peter Lugo in Miami in 1995.[47] Lugo was the "brains" of the group; Doorbal was the "muscle." They and their accomplices, dressed as respectable businessmen, would lure rich executives with promises of profitable "deals." During a second encounter, the "mark" would be tied up at gunpoint and tortured by having parts of his body burned till he revealed critical numbers, codes to a safe, and so forth. Once the monies were in the hands of the extortionists, the victims would be killed and dismembered, their body parts dumped in various oil drums around Miami. Later, in 2007, I spoke with Doorbal on Florida's death row to request an interview for a Discovery Channel television program. He proved his con artist credentials once again: he insisted I could not interview him unless the station first gave him a check for $1,000 for his daughter, which we did—only to discover that (a) he did not have a daughter and (b) he declined to be interviewed. What is new in the Lugo and Doorbal case is not the extortion. There has always been extortion. What is new is the brazenness of the robbers, the sophisticated use of modern money-transferring mechanisms, and the barbarous schemes to then murder and "disappear" the victims. Such schemes have long been familiar to us from stories connected with the mafia and other organized crime groups but were, until recently, rarely done by amateurs or men acting alone.

Mass Murder

The FBI does not officially define "mass murder," but, in the 1980s, the bureau established the description as "four or more victims slain, in one event, in one location." This does not include the perpetrator, when suicide follows the killing. As noted earlier, in 2012, Congress defined "mass killings" to mean "three or more killings in a single incident." In my research on the topic, I use the FBI description and also include, marked with asterisks, episodes in which fewer than four persons were murdered, but where the intention to claim many victims was unmistakable—foiled only by the poor marksmanship and/or death of the assailant. From books, magazines, and newspapers, I have collected 328 examples of mass murder between 1900 and May of 2018, the time of this writing: 256 in the United States and seventy-two from other countries. This figure represents about a fourth of the mass murders mentioned in various internet sources from around the world, most of which provide only the barest of details. If we narrow our sights just to America, cases that meet the pre-2012 criterion of four or more casualties (excluding the perpetrators), and those from sources in which information is offered in greater detail, we wind up with 229 cases in my series. These are shown along the upper line, by decade, in the following graph. Clearly, mass murder has been on the rise since 1970. The lower line indicates mass killings that involved the use of semiautomatic weapons, which is also markedly on the rise since 1970.

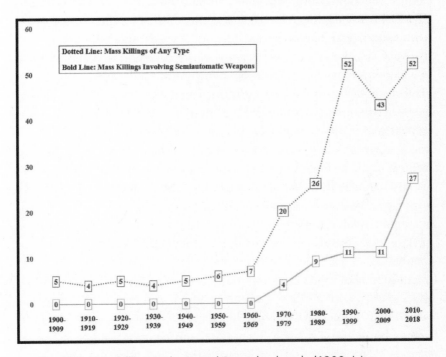

Fig. 12.1. Mass killings in the United States by decade (1900–May 2018), also showing those involving semiautomatic weapons.

Because of the dramatic nature of a mass murder, public attention is drawn to such crimes much more than to random murders of one or two people in a store robbery or violent family dispute. In reality, mass murder is a rare event: the death toll—lately, about 160 per year in the United States—represents only about 1 percent of the gun murders in America per year.

Rarer still are mass murders committed by men with autistic spectrum disorders, such as what used to be called Asperger's syndrome. Three of the worst and most "high-profile" mass murderers, responsible for the combined deaths of sixty-seven people, were said by some to have conditions of this sort: Seung-Hui Cho (2007),[48] Adam Lanza (2012),[49] and Elliot Rodger (2014).[50] This led the public to suspect that autistic persons were at high risk for such violence—which they are not. What is new, vis-à-vis mass murder—and pertinent to our discussion of "new evil"—is the phenomenon of school shootings, to which we have dedicated an entire chapter, later in this volume. Cho, Lanza, and Rodger will all be discussed in detail when we arrive at that topic.

Mass murder is, in general, an explosive reaction to an unbearable humiliation, sometimes spur-of-the-moment but more often planned well in advance. Being fired from a job is one common stimulus; being rejected by a lover or spouse is another. Mass murder is almost the exclusive preserve of males: 97 percent of the perpetrators are men.[51]

The rampant drug abuse from the mid-1960s till today has been a factor in some examples of mass murder, by way of further destabilizing already mentally disturbed individuals, and also diminishing the capacity for self-restraint. A case in point is that of Jared Loughner in Arizona, who attempted to kill US representative Gabrielle Giffords in a mass shooting in 2011.[52] She barely survived while six other bystanders died. Loughner, twenty-two at the time, had been jilted at fourteen by a girlfriend. He became unhinged and began abusing marijuana, alcohol, cocaine, amphetamines, and a host of other psychoactive drugs. He may have had a genetic vulnerability to mental illness to begin with—there were some bipolar relatives—but he rapidly became paranoid and delusional about "big government" and about Giffords, in particular. Loughner has been called "schizophrenic" in the press, but his was a drug-induced schizophreniform psychosis in which he became progressively more unhinged and bizarre in his thinking. In some cases of mass murder, the "accelerant" substance is the more traditional one of alcohol, as in the case of Wade Page,[53] the Wisconsin neo-Nazi who, in 2012 after being fired from his job due to drinking and jilted even by his neo-Nazi girlfriend because of his abusive behavior, entered a Sikh temple and killed six worshippers and then himself.

Murder with Extreme Sadism

Murders with uncommon degrees of brutality and depravity have been common in situations of warfare, or other forms of intergroup conflict, since ancient times. Police are familiar with murders committed in states of rage, since these typically show signs of "overkill," i.e., the use of more than ordinary force or more numerous blows than is required to bring about death. Consider the example of Susan Wright. Her husband had cheated on her repeatedly, had given her a sexually transmitted disease, and was physically abusive. In 2004, when finally pushed too far, she stabbed him 193 times.[54] What appears to be occurring more frequently in the current era are murders accompanied by acts of extreme cruelty, or else devious measures to avoid detection of a kind rarely encountered before the mid-1960s.

The 1974 murders in Utah by Dale Pierre and William Andrews are an example. These men held up two clerks and three customers in a hi-fi record shop in what began as an armed robbery—but they proceeded to tie up the victims and force them to drink Drano, a corrosive lye-containing cleanser, which caused enormous blisters and burned their tongues and throats. Pierre raped an eighteen-year-old woman for a half hour as she choked on the liquid before he shot her in the back of the head. Two other captives were killed. One man, who survived both shooting and strangulation, had a pen shoved through his ear. Pierre stomped on it until it punctured the victim's eardrum and came out of his throat. The three who died were lucky, in a sense. The survivors endured years of agony from mouth and esophagus injuries.[55]

The 1965 murder in Indianapolis of fifteen-year-old Sylvia Likens was, in some ways, more horrific than the Utah murders because of the prolonged torture she endured from Gertrude Baniszewski, the woman entrusted with her care while Likens's parents were away for several months. Likens was considered prettier than Baniszewski's daughters. This aroused considerable envy—dealt with via the systematic brutalization of the young girl. Baniszewski and her daughters would strike Likens with a board, force her to eat feces and drink urine, burn her skin with cigarettes, dump her in a bath of scalding water, and brand her abdomen with hot needles, spelling out the message, "I am a prostitute and proud of it." They then locked Likens in a room, leaving her without food for a week, such that she died the day the parents returned from Florida.[56] The Likens case can be understood as an extreme example of harsh treatment of a child, who is not the biological offspring of a parent. Adoptees are at greater risk for maltreatment. Adoptive fathers are about seven times more likely to molest an adopted daughter sexually than are fathers of their own biological daughters. Likewise, child murder is much more common where (a) there is no blood relationship between parent and child, or (b) even in common law, as opposed to legitimate (i.e., legally sanctioned) marriages.[57] There are exceptions. Theresa Knorr, for example, was morbidly envious of her daughters. In the mid-1980s, she starved to death her daughter Sheila, whom she had earlier forced into prostitution, by chaining her to a pipe in a closet. A second daughter, Suesan, was doused with gasoline and burned alive.[58]

Then there are the aforementioned diabolically clever means employed by killers to escape detection: Phil Skipper in Louisiana, an illiterate and bigoted thug, was befriended by a sympathetic black neighbor, Genore Guillory, who had a good job and was much better off than Skipper and his family. She would give them money for groceries and diapers. In 2000, thinking Guillory's dog had hurt Skipper's pet goat, Skipper and his buddies bludgeoned Guillory to death and raped her necrophilically. To throw the police off the scent, Skipper then went into town and forced a black man at gunpoint to masturbate into a cup. Returning to the corpse, Skipper tossed the sperm over Guillory's body so that the DNA would suggest a black perpetrator rather than a white one—which did delay the detection of the real killers for quite some time.[59] Another example of a "brilliant" but even more repugnant plot to escape detection was that of a famous Brazilian soccer goalie, Bruno Fernandes. Besides his wife, he had a mistress, Eliza Samudio, whom he impregnated. He insisted she have an abortion, but she refused and had the child. Immediately after, Fernandes strangled her and, with the help of his wife and cousin, dismembered the body and fed the pieces to ten Rottweiler dogs so as to eliminate all traces of the body. So far as we know, this is a "first" in the era of new narcissism: feeding one's mistress to dogs. Fernandes would have evaded justice had not his cousin, in a pang of conscience—something quite lacking in Fernandes—confessed to the police.[60]

Paraphilias of an Extreme Nature

The list of paraphilias, a concept we have previously defined, is very long and far exceeds the more innocuous ones, such as voyeurism and foot fetishes. Those on the more dangerous side, such as cannibalism, necrophilia, sexual sadism, and asphyxiaphilia, have long histories, as well. Sexual sadism—arousal and orgasm during a murder—is common among men committing serial sexual homicide. There were even two women who exhibited this paraphilia, neither of them part of the "new evil" era: the sixteenth-century Hungarian countess Erzsébet Báthory used to press her body against the bodies of virgin girls whose bellies she split open with knives, experiencing orgasm before bathing in the blood of the virgins as a kind of elixir to sustain her beauty (with what effectiveness we cannot be certain);[61] nurse Jane Toppan in late nineteenth-century Boston also used to experience orgasm when killing her victims.[62]

In the new era of evil, we encounter several men—the preponderance of paraphilics are male—who showed either unusual twists to well-known perversions, or else sexual aberrations never described before. Graham Coutts in England, for example, was a salesman in his thirties who, in 2003, "disappeared" Jane Longhurst, a teacher of similar age. Coutts had several paraphilias, including violent pornography, drilling holes in bathroom walls so he could peek at women, and an obsession with asphyxiaphilia via strangulation. While he was masturbating to orgasm as he was pulling on the ligature around Longhurst's neck, and perhaps distracted by his own activities, he discovered that she had expired. So far we are not in new territory. What is new is that he then kept her body in a shed and then in a box at a storage depot for five weeks, visiting her remains regularly for necrophilic sex, until they began to decompose. They were then taken to a wooded area and burned.[63] There have not been many cases of prolonged necrophilia until our era, one of the more prominent ones being that of serial killer Dennis Nilsen, also from England, whose sixteen victims between 1978 and 1983 were kept, following strangulation, in his apartment, partly for necrophilic sex, until the bodies grew rank.[64]

A more bizarre, perhaps even unique, case is that of ex–Navy SEAL Ben Sifrit and his wife, Erika. In 1999 they lured another couple to their place in Maryland. Ben forced the couple to strip, killed and decapitated both, and then had sex with the head of the woman.[65] We have as yet no name for such a paraphilia. ("Cephaloepikoinophilia," although accurate, seems cumbersome.) Ben also engaged in bondage and cannibalism. As to the latter, he urged Erika to cook the dead husband's leg in order to eat it. Whether she indulged his cannibalistic fantasy in this way is not clear from the records.[66]

Rape with a Modern Element

Throughout history, women have always been vulnerable to rape. We read in Deuteronomy 22: 25–29, for example, that if a man "seizes and lies with" a young woman who is betrothed, his crime is punishable by death. If the woman were not betrothed, then the man must pay the father fifty shekels of silver and marry her—and never divorce her. Roman emperor Caligula was notorious for sadistic rape. In twelfth-century England, King Henry II, who instituted common law and the twelve-man jury system, was enraged when the Catholic Church forbade him to punish a Worcestershire cleric who had raped a girl and then knifed her father. The church insisted that clergy could be tried only by the much more lenient canon law, which would only defrock such a cleric, not execute him. It was this dispute that led to the falling out between Henry II and Thomas Becket.[67] These are, of course, only a few examples in the long and terrible history of rape and sexual assault.

With the invention and commercialization of the typewriter in the 1860s, many poor women who earlier had little choice but to become prostitutes now earned a livelihood as typists. It was no longer so easy for a man to have his way with a "working girl." In reaction, rape became more common. In the last century, rape in the United States was recorded more often, suggesting a significant increase, beginning in the mid-1960s. The following graph shows the total number of reported forcible rapes in the United States by decade between 1960 and 2017.[68] As noted earlier in this book, these numbers indicate a decline since the 1990s, just as we observed in the number of active serial killers by decade.

It is not clear whether, or to what extent, the period of the 1960s through 1990s saw a true increase in incidence, or it is better accounted for by a greater willingness on the part of women—thanks to the feminist revolution of the late 1960s—to come forward and make the authorities aware that they had been victims of rape. The natures of the sexual violations did not seem to differ from those of rapes committed earlier, except for those perpetrated by men committing serial sexual homicide—"serial killers," discussed at length earlier and in additional detail to come. Serial killers often were extremely violent and degrading toward their victims, in a manner reminiscent of the extreme brutality of rapes perpetrated during wartime, such as those perpetrated by Japanese soldiers against Chinese women in Nanking in 1937, which is but one of all too numerous examples.[69]

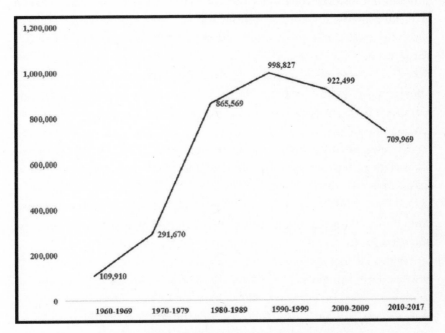

Fig. 12.2. Rapes in the United States by decade (1900–2017).

In the last fifty years, however, there have been a number of rapes by men in peacetime with details so sensationalistic and far-fetched that had they been imagined by a novelist, a reviewer would have rejected them. Surely the most implausible, but nonetheless real, story was that of Canada's Luka Magnotta—which was not his real name. He was born Eric Clinton Newman. Magnotta is to narcissism, which he has carried to unimaginable heights, what the Rolls-Royce is in the world of cars. At twenty-one, he began appearing in pornographic films, also working at times as a male stripper and escort. Impersonating a woman, he ran up large debts on false credit cards. His first brush with fame, albeit local, came with his putting out YouTube videos he had made in 2011 of suffocating and killing kittens, as well as one showing a kitten being eaten by a Burmese python, thereby igniting the wrath of animal rights groups. True fame, this time international, did not come till a year later. After an evening of sex with an acquaintance, Chinese exchange student Lin Jun, Magnotta filmed himself stabbing the man to death with an ice pick, followed by necrophilia. This was a prelude to the real fame Magnotta earned by dismembering the corpse and mailing pieces to various political organizations and schools throughout Canada: the left foot to the Conservative Party, the right foot to a school in Vancouver, the torso to one part of Montréal, the head to another, and so forth. Suspicion by now having fallen on Magnotta, he fled to Germany, where he was finally arrested in an act of narcissism never to be outdone—watching news of his own crimes on the screen in an internet café.[70]

Equally breathtaking in depravity, if less novelistic in detail, are a number of other rape cases in the new era. In 2012, Travis Forbes, who acknowledged, convincingly, "Deep down, I am evil," sexually assaulted Lydia Tillman in Colorado. He then strangled her, shattered her jaw, poured bleach on her body, and set fire to her apartment. Somehow, she managed to survive, though with lasting injuries. The year before, he had raped and killed a woman of nineteen, burying her in a shallow grave.[71] A worse fate awaited eight-year-old Robbie Middleton in Texas who, in 1998, was raped by Donald Collins. After the assault, Collins tied the boy to a tree and poured gasoline over him, setting him afire. The child survived, terribly disfigured, with innumerable hospitalizations and grafts, finally dying of his wounds when he was twenty-one. He was able to name his attacker, who is now in prison for life.[72]

In all of these cases, it is the agony suffered by the victims because of the subsequent acts of depravity—over and above the pain and humiliation of the rape itself—that demarcates rape in the era of "new evil" from the rapes of earlier times. In 2005, the pedophile rapist John Evander Couey sneaked into the home of nine-year-old Jessica Lunsford in Florida and raped her once in the evening and again the following morning. He then put her in a garbage bag and buried her alive in a shallow grave, where she suffocated before she could claw her way out. It is no tribute to our justice system that Couey raped a girl years earlier when he was twenty. He was sentenced to ten years but paroled after only two, following which he raped still another girl and was again released prematurely. After the rape and murder of Lunsford, he was given the death penalty, dying of cancer in prison in 2009.[73] A shocking element of the rape and murder of eight-year-old Victoria Stafford in Ontario is the fact that the killer, Michael Rafferty, was assisted by a female accomplice, Terri McClintic. After the latter lured the girl into their car with the promise of showing her a "nice dog"—an interesting choice, given that McClintic once killed a dog by cooking it in a microwave—Rafferty proceeded to rape the girl repeatedly, after which McClintic bludgeoned her to death with a claw hammer that Rafferty had her purchase beforehand.[74]

Sadism

Aggressive behavior will more often be found in men, thanks, in no small measure, to their higher testosterone titers. This may also relate to the smaller size of the male orbitofrontal cortex, a brain area that subserves inhibition of aggressive impulses. Likewise, men tend on average to be less empathic—in the sense of compassion, rather than the basic ability to understand the emotional states of others—than are women.[75] Similarly, the propensity to inflict pain and suffering on others, and the actual enjoyment of doing so—key ingredients of sadism—is a more male than female phenomenon. I see no difference in the level of *institutional* sadism, committed by kings, dictators, armies, rebel leaders, and so forth at any time in history. Some countries have become more civilized over time, others, less so. England and France no longer subject dissidents to the tortures endured by the Welsh prince Dafydd under Edward I in 1283, or by Jacques de Molay and his Templars when punished for "heresy" by Philip IV in France—who, in reality, simply wanted their money—on Friday, October 13, 1307. The date of the atrocity would give rise to our squeamishness about Friday the thirteenth. We have seen the systematic torture of the leftists in Juan Peron's Argentina; Saddam Hussein ordering that the hands of dissident writers be dissolved in sulfuric acid; and, more recently, the Islamic State torturing and beheading "infidels" with different views. And so on. Sadism has, of course, relevance to the acts of certain criminals during peacetime—and this, too, has a long history. We believe that in the past fifty years, however, we have witnessed a number of sadistic crimes of a sort that were exceedingly rare in earlier times. Some have already been discussed, such as those of Noel Doorbal, Theresa Knorr, Dale Pierre, and Jessica Schwarz. The section that follows deals with serial killers, for whom sexual sadism is a "default position." There are several post-1965 examples of extreme sadism that do not fall easily within the categories outlined here and that strike us as more atrocious and depraved than what we would almost never encounter in the annals of peacetime crime from earlier eras. Here are two examples.

In Kirtland, Ohio, in 1989, Jeff Lundgren, a breakaway Mormon cult leader of a band of some two dozen followers, arranged for the execution of all five members of the Avery family. They had been followers originally but became suspicious when he demanded all of their money, and when they began to realize that, rather than being a prophet who spoke with God, he was a con artist who hid his avarice and lust for power behind the façade of religious specialness. Lundgren had some of his loyal followers lead the Averys, one by one, to a barn, where they were then shot to death by Lundgren. Soon after, the troupe fled the state, where Lundgren, bored with his wife Alice, carried on sexually with the wives of several other adherents. When Alice voiced objections, he punished her by wrapping his own feces around his penis and forcing her to fellate him.[76]

The other case concerns Sedley Alley, whose crime could have been included in our discussion of rape but who demonstrated sadistic elements so extreme as to merit placement in this section. It was alleged that, in 1982, Alley killed his wife by drowning her in the bathtub after she filed for divorce.[77] The evidence was not quite strong enough for a conviction, so he evaded punishment. Three years later, in 1985, he came upon a woman of nineteen, Suzanne Collins, who was about to graduate from the US Marine aviation school in Virginia. As she was jogging through a park near the school on the evening before graduation, Alley abducted her and took her to a nearby park. He then beat her repeatedly, fracturing her skull, before thrusting a yard-long, inch-and-a-half-thick tree limb through her vagina four times. The limb passed through the abdomen, puncturing a lung and killing her, in Alley's macabre imitation of physical rape. Adding insult to this most grievous of injuries, it took the twists and turns of justice twenty-two years before the death penalty could be carried out—three years longer, as authors John Douglas and Mark Olshaker note, than the victim had lived.[78]

Serial Sexual Homicide

We noted earlier in this volume that there is more than one form of serial killing, but we again emphasize that serial *sexual* homicide by men is what people ordinarily reference when using the term "serial killer." This will be the focus here, rather than on hospital personnel who poison a string of patients, mothers who smother one infant after the other, and so on. Serial killers, in the narrower sense used here, and "Angel of Death" murderers, for the most part, share one trait in common—namely, they relish the godlike power they exert over other people, contributing to the narcissistically oriented thrill of elevating themselves, if only transiently, far above the socially inferior status that characterizes their quotidian existences.

Serial killers of the type involved in sexual homicide are all male. The phenomenon was beginning to be recognized and described in the late nineteenth century, around the time rape, in general, appeared to be on the increase. A few such cases were described, under the heading of lust-murder, by Richard von Krafft-Ebing in Germany (1881).[79] The most widely known case in the United States during this period was that of Herman Mudgett, also known as H. H. Holmes, the New Hampshire–born doctor who built a torture establishment disguised as a pharmacy in Chicago.[80] After luring young women there, he raped and tortured them to death, later dissolving their bodies in lye. Whereas many serial killers are "loners"—schizoid psychopaths, with poor capacities for intimacy—Mudgett was a psychopath with enough superficial charm to lead a double life. He maintained three marriages in different cities, each wife regarding him as a devoted husband who had to be away a lot due to his work as a traveling salesman. Finally caught and executed in 1896, Mudgett was one of just a small number of serial killers identified in America—per decade—until we arrived at the 1960s. Earlier in this volume, we reviewed statistical findings from the Radford / Florida Gulf Coast University (FGCU) Serial

Killer Database, which demonstrated that the number of serial killers of all types active in America by decade began to increase significantly in the 1960s, peaking in the 1980s. These data coincide with my own tally of US-based serial killers whose biographies were published in true crime monographs, which is provided here, in figure 12.3. Note that the killers' years of activity are listed according to the decades in which they were first active. Both the Radford/FGCU database and I observe a decline in the number of American serial killers since the 1990s. Note that the low tally for 2010–2018 is likely because true crime biographies have not yet been written about several other serial killers first active during this period.

Serial Killers in the United States Whose Biographies Have Been Published in True Crime Monographs, by Decade (1890–2018)

1890–1899	**3**
1900–1909	**1**
1910–1919	**0**
1920–1929	**3**
1930–1939	**1**
1940–1949	**0**
1950–1959	**1**
1960–1969	**12**
1970–1979	**40**
1980–1989	**42**
1990–1999	**22**
2000–2009	**17**
2010–2018	**4**

Fig. 12.3.

In personality, the majority of serial killers are psychopathic, as defined by the Hare criteria we have delineated elsewhere. The presence of psychopathy as a diagnosis, by itself, has been shown to predict future violence better than any other demographic, clinical, or criminal risk factor.[81] All but a few serial killers also meet criteria for sadistic personality disorder, described in the appendix of the revised edition of the *DSM-III* in 1987—a no longer used diagnostic category that we will discuss in some detail in a later chapter, but one that generally involves deriving pleasure by inflicting discomfort or pain on other people. About half of these murderers are also schizoid.[82] Hence, the description "sadistic schizoid psychopath" would be accurate for a large proportion of serial killers. The peak years of birth for the serial killers in my series were 1930–1959 (65 percent), such that they were reaching adulthood in the 1960s and beyond—during the years, that is, when the changes that characterize this era of "new evil" were occurring.

Granted that sadism is routine among serial killers—if only in the narrowest sense of their feeling sexual arousal during the act of killing, i.e., the *paraphilia* of sexual sadism; what is distinct about many of those active in the current era is their extraordinary degrees of forethought, cunning, and originality, traversing the whole of the sadistic repertoire. Apart from Mudgett's torture palace in Chicago in the late nineteenth century—and we know little of the specific types of torture to which he subjected his victims—most of the serial killers of the pre-1960s era, rare as they were, were men of seemingly limited breadth of sadistic techniques. They would accost, rape, and strangle someone; hide the body someplace, such as a shallow grave or wooded area; and then, after a "decent" interval, move on to the next victim. Among serial killers in the era of "new evil," we observe much more morbid and perverse originality in terms of sadistic methods. In some cases, this seems to have been inspired by sheer hatred—in reaction to extremely abusive or neglectful parents, as in an abused boy who grows up to be the serial killer and vents his rage upon his victims, rather than upon the offending parents. In other cases, in which serial killers have no prior abuse histories, the predisposition appears more related to aberrant cravings for thrill and novelty.

Two examples of the first type were David Parker Ray and Tommy Lynn Sells, whose disturbing cases we have already discussed in detail in the context of Category 22 of the Gradations of Evil scale. As noted, Ray's father was alleged to have been a violent alcoholic who abandoned the family when Ray was ten, and the boy was also reportedly badly treated by other relatives. A loner, he indulged in bondage fantasies and, by early adolescence, would masturbate to orgasm by thinking about murdering women. We saw that he committed his first sadistic murder at the age of thirteen. Sells grew up in even harsher and more pitiable circumstances. The reader will recall how he never knew his father, and his mother abandoned him when he was two. He was, for a time, brought up by an aunt, and, during that time, at about age seven or eight, he became involved with a man who offered him food, clothing, and shelter in exchange for fellatio and other sexual favors. When Sells was fourteen, he ran away, understandably enough, and began the career of violent crime we have thoroughly reviewed. When "rage" came over Sells, nothing would assuage it but going out and killing someone.

When I interviewed Sells on Texas's death row, he remarked, "I would slit their throats, and when I saw the blood gushing out, I would feel relief . . . and I'd be good for two weeks!" Since most of his victims were adolescent girls and young women, I asked him, wearing my psychoanalytic hat, whether he thought maybe he was, in effect, killing his mother over and over again. To that he said, "Anyone touch a hair of her head, I'd kill him in a minute. You only got one mum!" This is a striking example of the mental mechanism of "splitting," whereby one harbors two attitudes that are extreme opposites toward an individual, oscillating between them, in a black-and-white manner, without being able to acknowledge the reality of both at the same time. This splitting showed up in Sells's ability to be charming and warmly caring about a few people in his life—usually older and motherly women—side by side with his utter disregard for the humanity of most others, whom he could carve up with no more feeling than if he were whittling wood. Scott Bonn makes a similar point about serial killers: "Psychopathic serial killers do not value human life, and they are insensitive and brutal while interacting with their victims."[83] Sells was not at that extreme end of the narcissistic spectrum. He could elicit warm concern from others, including his original bail agent, Victoria Zubcic, who visited him often when he was in prison, where I met both of them. Sells was genuinely fond of her and she of him. When I asked him about remorse, Sells told me, "I *do* feel some remorse for those people—but if I let myself feel as much as I should, I'd have to kill myself."

Larry Bittaker, by contrast, is a serial killer much nearer the pole of "absolute" psychopathy, unadulterated, as it were, with the islands of human feeling that made Sells a more sympathetic figure. Bittaker is one of just eleven serial killers in my series (6.5 percent) who were not subjected during their formative years to neglect; verbal, physical, or sexual abuse; or parental separation or divorce—and who were raised in middle-class homes. Two of these men, David Berkowitz, called "Son of Sam," and Joel Rifkin, were adopted by strangers. Bittaker was adopted at about age two. Some records suggest his birth parents were unknown, but, in my correspondence with him, he informed me that his adoptive parents were close relatives of his mother. It would appear that these men, including Bittaker, developed their tendencies toward psychopathy and violent behavior in the context of "prenatal" factors—genetic liability and/or complications during fetal life, which may have affected brain development. A loner throughout his life, Bittaker committed property crimes when he was an adolescent. When arrested for an assault and imprisoned in his early thirties, he was evaluated by a psychiatrist, who diagnosed him as a "schizoid psychopath."[84] While incarcerated, Bittaker met another inmate, Roy Norris. Both were released at about the same time and teamed up with plans to commit the violent crimes for which they became widely known. Their plan was to lure, rape, and kill a girl of each age between thirteen and nineteen—seven in all. Taking each victim to a remote spot, as if for a picnic, they would, after raping the girl, commence to torture her by pinching her breasts with pliers—"Pliers" would become Bittaker's moniker—and, in two cases, Bittaker killed a girl by thrusting an ice pick through one ear, piercing her brain. He would also record their screams and his conversations with them, in which he imparted "master-slave" orders to perform various degrading acts. Unlike Ray and Sells, Bittaker was not, in so doing, symbolically avenging wrongs done to him as he was growing up—though he may have been aware of his mother's promiscuity. It occurs to me that, as with many psychopaths, the impulse behind these horrifying acts was driven by novelty seeking—a morbid thirst for strong and socially repugnant acts that would alleviate the pervasive boredom to which psychopaths are prone. In a letter to Bittaker, I asked what it was that, in the absence of abusive or neglectful parents, could have animated him and Norris to do these things—if it was the thrill and excitement of it. The question went unanswered.

A number of serial killers have boasted of making films of their dying victims, sometimes called "snuff films," but such stories have rarely been authenticated. One who actually did so was a Royal Canadian Air Force colonel, Russell Williams. The son of a prominent physicist and a beautiful British mother, Williams became a highly respected pilot, known, however, for being taciturn and socially aloof. Presumably a transvestite since adolescence, he kept his paraphilia well concealed until his early forties when he began to break into homes in Ontario and steal ladies' bras and panties. He then turned violent, raping several women. He ended up a serial killer who would rape his victims repeatedly, dressed in bra and panties, and film the rape and murder via an elaborate photography setup, presumably capturing these images for his later enjoyment.[85] Not psychopathic like the typical serial killer, in personality Williams was extremely obsessive-compulsive and narcissistic, with an emphasis on godlike domination over others, accentuated by his ability to savor the moments of life-and-death power over others via his recordings. What might account for a man to "come out" as a murderous and open transvestite in his forties, following four decades of conventional, albeit uncommunicative existence, remains unclear.

Serial killers hold a fascination for the public, more so than murderers of other sorts. This is partly because, by definition, each serial killer operates, until caught, over an extended period, unlike a mass murderer, who commits a crime just once. We get to know them. Some, like Ted Bundy or John Wayne Gacy, become iconic figures and, to that extent, represent a new generation of simultaneously feared and celebrated persons, much as cowboys like Billy the Kid and Jesse James became the feared and celebrated killers of a bygone generation. Part of our fascination stems, I believe, from the way such men have taken the law into their own hands and done as they pleased. Many of the rest of us *feel* like doing something awful to others when we are grievously disappointed, fired from a job, jilted by a lover, injured by a mugger, and so on—but we do not. Instead, we often settle for moments of vicarious pleasure when we identify transitorily with someone who can kiss self-restraint to the winds and exact revenge then and there. These "someones" can be an actor in a Hollywood film, like Anthony Hopkins in the previously mentioned role of Hannibal Lecter, who is the antihero / serial killer of a contemporary mystery thriller, or an actual serial killer. Bonn tries to make the point that "society needs serial killers because they are like emotional lightning rods that protect people from their own violent tendencies,"[86] but my impression is different. In my larger survey of serial killers from all around the world, I have identified 465 men who have committed serial sexual homicide: 249 from the United States, 216 from all other countries. If serial killers are so necessary as "lightning rods" that protect us from our darkest impulses, how is it the Scandinavians manage to get along without them? To my knowledge, Norway and Finland have had no such cases; Sweden has had two, and Denmark has had but one. Even countries with large populations and reputations for violence have seen very few serial killers—six in Mexico, five in Brazil, one in Pakistan. I suspect the surfeit of serial killers in America is largely a *cultural* phenomenon and one that may have some relevance in the few other countries that have measurable numbers of serial killers. England has seen twenty-six cases; Germany, twenty; Canada, sixteen; Australia, thirteen. Among the better candidates for cultural factors are those referenced in our chronology table: the feminist revolution and subsequent protest, largely by working-class males threatened with the loss of mates and lessened status; the transition from a more inhibited society to a more pleasure-seeking one, stoked still further by increasing liberties as to what can be shown in the way of sexuality and violence in film and on TV; the high divorce rate and percentage of boys growing up without fathers. All this seemed to create a larger reservoir of men and a small number of women who cleaved to the new philosophy—the new narcissism, as it has been called here—that says, "If I can think of doing it, if I feel like doing it, I can go out there and *do* it."

The motives of each serial and mass killer—also sources of fascination for the public—are not always made clear by the men themselves, but we are occasionally offered edifying glimpses. In Canada, for example, Mark Lépine, whose real name was Gamil Gharbi, fatally shot fourteen young female students at Montréal's École Polytechnique. He claimed he was "fighting feminism," since these women were defying the traditional roles to which women are "supposed" to conform, as per his Muslim father, himself allegedly abusive and contemptuous of women. Lépine also satisfied other criteria that correlate with dangerous behavior: rejection from the army, dropping out of college, having been fired from a menial hospital job because of "poor attitude," admiration of Adolf Hitler, absence of girlfriends.[87] Another clear-cut woman hater was California's Ed Kemper,[88] who was as bright as he was tall, six feet, nine inches (205 cm) in height, with an IQ of 145. His mother was, admittedly, stern, punitive, and domineering, though loyal whenever he was in trouble with the law. His older sister was reportedly abusive, and he cut off the heads of his younger sister's dolls. Still in adolescence, Kemper beheaded cats. Then, in his early twenties, he became a serial killer, murdering six female college students, later beheading his mother and her female friend. Afterward, he was said to have used some piece of his mother's body as a dartboard—some sources claim the head. More disturbingly, as I learned from someone close to the Kemper investigation, it was his mother's genitals—perhaps an even more telling testimony to his misogyny. As to his poor luck developing friendships with women, Kemper remarked following his arrest, "While alive, women were unavailable to me; when dead, they're mine."

Along with the question of motives among serial killers comes amazement at how adeptly some of these offenders are capable of masquerading as "normal," leading "double lives." Perhaps one of the most striking examples is that of Keith Jesperson, who demonstrated an unusually wide disparity between his public and private personas. The son and grandson of allegedly harsh and abusive Danish Canadian men, Jesperson took out his anger on animals, especially cats, many of whom he tortured and killed, by way of relieving his "tension."[89] He became a truck driver and, at age twenty in 1975, married. He and his wife had a son and two daughters before their divorce, seven years later. He was cheerful and pleasant with his children, never abusing them—except that he did kill their pet cats, which they found shocking and seemingly out of character. At thirty-five, he committed the first of eight known rape-murders. When he visited his now teenage children shortly thereafter, he hinted to them about having committed some very bad crimes. He also made his elder daughter, Melissa, uncomfortable by telling her explicit details of his sexual activity with their mother—and with a host of other women. This was Melissa's epiphany about how, inside her doting and sweet dad, lurked a brutal killer of women. After Jesperson was caught and imprisoned for the murders, his father visited him and told Melissa that he had once entertained thoughts of killing his three children. Melissa has written a book about her life as the daughter of a serial killer.[90] Unlike Lépine and Kemper, Jesperson did not hate all women. He instead showed a high degree of compartmentalization or "splitting," as we have described: "good" women and their diametric opposites, "bad" women who deserved death. Moreover, Jesperson grew up in a "broken" home, as did Tommy Lynn Sells, but their cases differed, in that Jesperson had a good mother. It was his father who was the cruel parent.

These vignettes illustrate something about the diversity of background "risk" factors found in serial killers as a group. Some of these are general ones: genetic and constitutional predispositions to psychopathy, hypersexuality, aggressivity, low empathy. Others, to drive our point home, are found in higher percentages among men growing up in the 1960s and 1970s: divorced families, maternal abandonment, absent fathers, resentment of women's lessening dependence on men. About 10 percent of serial killers are gay but growing up during a period in which homophobic sentiments were more common and intense than is the case currently; some struggled with a combination of self-hatred, identifying with the strong cultural prejudice, as well as with rejection by their own fathers, and hatred of other gay men, whom they would kill, as if killing the unacceptable parts of their own self-images. Examples include Randy Kraft, Larry Eyler, John Wayne Gacy, Dean Corll, and Robert Berdella. There is also an overrepresentation of adoptees among serial killers, a reflection most likely of the less favorable genetic background from which adoptees have come, once better birth control in the 1960s allowed young women from economically and educationally advantaged families to avoid unwanted pregnancies. In my series and in that of the FBI, serial killers were six to eight times as likely (12–16 percent) to have been adoptees as would be expected (2 percent) in the general population.

Solicitation

In the United States, the crime of solicitation involves encouraging, bribing, requesting, or commanding that a person commit a substantive crime, with the *intent* that the solicited person be the one who actually commits the criminal act. Before the era of "new evil," many cases were carried out by nonmembers (sometimes called "side arms") of the Mafia, called "Murder Incorporated"—a group of "enforcers" hired for contract killings, usually of persons from one Mafia organization who fell out of favor with the bosses of another. These "hits," however, were not the products of narcissism run wild; they were strictly business—the fee often amounting to $1,000 to $5,000 per killing, non-negligible sum during Murder Inc.'s heyday of 1930–1940.[91]

A more common variety of solicitation to murder concerns the hiring of a "hitman" to eliminate someone whom a person seriously wants "out of the way," in such a manner that the person can feign innocence, often by a convincing alibi, as having been far away from where the murder took place. As noted in our discussion of the Gradations of Evil scale, a fair number of spousal murders are initiated in this fashion. Passions often run high in custody cases, which are, as might be expected, much more frequent in the post-1965 era, thanks to the soaring divorce rate. We will touch upon custody in a separate section, but solicitation of someone to murder a spouse within the context of a contentious custody case is not common. A trial that garnered national attention a few years ago was that of Queens, New York, Dr. Mazoltuv Borukhova—whose first name is Hebrew for "good luck!" She hired her cousin, Mikhail Mallayev, to kill her husband, orthodontist Dr. Daniel Malakov, after the court awarded him custody of their four-year-old daughter.[92]

In some ways more stunning than the preceding example is the solicitation by the mother of convicted serial rapist Fred Coe.[93] Coe was the son of the managing editor of a Spokane, Washington, newspaper. As though in a morbid demonstration of how blood is thicker than water, Coe's mother, a woman of high social standing in the community and a former charm school teacher, not only refused to accept her son's 1981 conviction and sentence of seventy-five years in prison, but also tried to hire a hitman for $4,000 to kill Judge Shields and the prosecutor Donald Brocket. The "hitman" was an undercover policeman. She was found guilty of solicitation and was herself sentenced to prison, though just for a year. This was not family loyalty so much as narcissism, amorality, and arrogance of sorts not unknown before the new era, but encountered more frequently,

I believe, since the mid-1960s. Mrs. Coe discovered the pitfalls of hiring a stranger who can turn out to be a blackmailer or agent in disguise. Others, as in the cases we will now describe, have felt it a wiser choice to "keep it in the family," only to discover it was just as perilous.

Barbara Opel, an irascible, foul-mouthed, twice-divorced virago of forty-eight, worked as the caretaker and companion of an elderly woman.[94] She displayed a mixture of narcissistic and psychopathic traits: entitlement, exploitativeness, envy, arrogance, but also amorality, characterized by a lack of guilt or remorse, and callousness. Her main motive was greed. Jerry Heimann, the son of the eighty-nine-year-old woman, was well-to-do. At first, Opel tried to steal from him by forging checks, but this netted her few additional funds. Next, she tried to poison Mr. Heimann with weed killer, but that, too, proved unsuccessful. So, in 2001, she turned to her thirteen-year-old daughter, Heather, persuading her to seduce her boyfriend, Jerry Grote, as "leverage" to induce him to kill Mr. Heimann. Grote subsequently enlisted the aid of several other teenagers, who hid in Heimann's house until the man returned one day. The boys waylaid him and clubbed him to death with baseball bats. Heather, for good measure, stabbed him in the neck, though, by then, he was already dead. Opel cleaned all the blood off the carpet, seemingly unaware of the impossibility of such a task—given the ease with which crime scene investigators can detect the most exiguous traces—and she and the boys put the body in a car, which was dumped over the edge of a ravine. Heather's younger brother, twelve at the time—the only one in the entourage with a conscience—told the police about the crime a few days later, which put paid to the "cleverness" of his mother's scheme. Opel, Heather, and the boys were all arrested. Opel got life without parole, the others long sentences. What is remarkable about the case and what gives it its overtones of "new evil" is the *chain* of solicitation: Opel solicited Heather who solicited boyfriend Jerry who then solicited his buddies to murder Jerry Heimann, "keeping it all in the family," the way Opel wished, only to be turned in by one of its own members.

This story, lurid as it is, pales by comparison with the murder by solicitation of US Army major David Shannon the following year.[95] David's wife, Joan, had two daughters out of wedlock, fifteen-year-old Elizabeth and sixteen-year-old Daisy. They never knew their father. Joan, married when the girls were about three, had two young sons by the major, who was then stationed in Fort Bragg, North Carolina. Joan was promiscuous and addicted to drugs; David was a basically shy man who had been raised in a stern and morally upright Lutheran family in North Dakota. By the time the family drama unfolded, the elder daughter, Daisy, had already had a child at fourteen; Elizabeth became sexually active and promiscuous at thirteen. Once the family moved to North Carolina a few years before, Joan and David became "swingers," joining chatrooms and clubs dedicated to finding other couples with whom to exchange partners for the purpose of indulging in all manner of sexual activities in various combinations. This is reminiscent of the mid-1960s fad of "key parties," which reflected the aforementioned upsurges in sexual freedom and divorce. It also calls to mind Plato's Retreat, opened in the basement of New York City's posh Ansonia Hotel in 1977, which served as a quasi-legitimate orgy center. The clubs Joan and David joined were not as constrained as was Plato's Retreat, which prohibited alcohol and drugs, and only "straight sex" was permitted. Joan and David frequented clubs in which nothing was verboten. If you could think of it, you could do it. Joan, for example, had a penchant for threesomes in which she submitted to anal sex with one man while simultaneously giving oral sex to another, the scene being videotaped by David, for home viewing later on. David did have one rule: everything was okay, so long as Joan did not begin to have "feelings" for one of the men with whom she "swung." Their life at home was tempestuous: they argued and fought constantly, and, not surprisingly, Joan quickly did develop feelings for another man, a private named Jeffrey Wilson, who was married with four children. Wilson, apart from the swinging pastime, was devoted to his wife and family, and had no romantic interest in Joan. He did spend some alone time with her for lunches and shopping, content to take advantage of the fact that, as a major's wife, she was better off and would pay for everything they did together. He would later candidly admit to this. Joan, in contrast, wanted to get rid of David—quite literally—and live happily ever after with Wilson, sharing the $700,000 she figured she would rake in from David's life insurance. Divorce was out of the question. David would continue to raise his two boys; child support for Joan, whose girls were nearing eighteen, would be too little and too brief to support her in the style to which she had grown accustomed; and a private's salary did not match a major's. Money trumping morals in Joan's internal lexicon, murder was the answer—but not by Joan. If she were caught, the

$700,000 would be forfeited, even if she tried to weasel out of conviction by pretending he had beaten her or had sexually molested his stepdaughter. So, Joan began to pressure Elizabeth to kill her stepfather, reassuring her that even if she—Elizabeth—were caught, she could tell the court he had raped her, and thus they would let her off with no more than a judicial slap on the wrist. Joan badgered her to get hold of a pistol from one of her teenage friends who belonged to the local Crips gang. David, of course, had many guns, but it would not be safe to use one of his own. Joan also urged Elizabeth to offer one of the members of the gang money to "do the job." To their credit, her Crips friends would have no part of either offer. Finally, in desperation, Joan promised her daughter at first a few thousand dollars to do the deed and then later, a fourth of the whole $700,000 windfall. Elizabeth at last promised to kill David, not for the money but because she could not stand the continued pressure from her mother, nor the worry what her mother might do to her if Elizabeth told the police. This was the setting in which Elizabeth, on cue, sneaked at midnight into the bedroom where her mother and stepfather lay and shot David to death in the head and chest with a pistol provided by her mother, as he slumbered. Joan and Elizabeth were quickly apprehended. Joan tried to pretend an intruder had broken in and killed David, and has maintained her innocence even to this day, although now in prison for life with no possibility of parole. Elizabeth has made a moving confession, adding that her stepfather had never laid an improper hand on her. She has been sentenced to twenty-five years in prison. Wilson made an equally eloquent confession—about the "swinging" and about just using Joan for the free lunches and shopping goodies, never having had the slightest intention to leave his wife and family. He was demoted one grade in his army ranking. The Shannon case has earned a great deal of publicity over the years. This is due, I believe, to the radical decoupling of sex and marriage among those swingers, in a much more worrisome and degrading way than anything Christopher Lasch inveighed against decades ago.

Murders of Spouses and Intimate Partners

The original title for this section was "uxoricide"—meaning the killing of one's wife—since wives are much more at risk for being killed by husbands than vice versa. Yet, there are wives who do kill husbands, as was the case in the last example about solicitation. According to a 2017 report from the Centers for Disease Control and Prevention, more than 55 percent of homicides against women in the United States were related to violence on the parts of partners, who were chiefly male. This finding was found to be true across all racial and ethnic groups, although significantly higher rates were observed among women who were black (4.4 per 100,000 people) or indigenous (4.3 per 100,000 people).[96]

US Department of Justice statistics tell us that, between 1980 and 2008, 41.5 percent of female murder victims were killed by intimates, who were chiefly male, while only 7.1 percent of male homicide victims were murdered by intimates. Murdered males during this period were typically the victims of acquaintances (56.4 percent) or strangers (25.5 percent).[97] The risk for intimate partner homicide is increased by a factor of three in homes where there are guns present.[98] Since wife murder is more common than husband murder, we will begin the discussion with "uxoricide." There is no corresponding legal phrase for husband murder. One could coin an analogous term—*mariticide*—from the Latin *maritus* for "husband," but it is awkward.

The typical man who kills a wife or girlfriend does so on impulse, on the spur-of-the-moment, in a moment of rage. This may represent the culmination of long-standing dissatisfaction or disagreement. He usually does so by gunshot, stabbing, or bludgeoning. Even if there has been a bit of malice aforethought, the execution is, in a manner of speaking, unimaginative and not the stuff of a mystery novel. This commonplace picture is as true of the new era as of previous periods. In the earlier two-thirds of the last century, even intimate partner murders among the rich and famous generally followed this mundane pattern. Consider a high-profile murder that took place in 1906. Chester Gillette, the son of wealthy parents, met a woman, Grace Brown, when he was working in his uncle's factory. They had an affair, and Brown became pregnant. She was hoping he would marry her and pressed Gillette for an answer. It came in the form of his inviting her boating on a lake in the Adirondacks. When they had rowed a certain ways out, Gillette struck her on the head with either an oar or a tennis racket and pushed her into the water, where she drowned. The crime became the basis for Theodore Dreiser's famous 1925 novel *An American Tragedy*, but what made it noteworthy was the prominence of the

Gillette family, not the cleverness of the murder, for which Chester Gillette was executed a year and a half later.[99]

Consider also a 1938 murder by Rodney Greig, a young man from Oakland, California, who became enamored of a woman, Leona Vlught, whom he had met in a café and taken on a single date. A half year later, he encountered her again, and without provocation, he plunged a hunting knife into her chest, killing her instantly. Despite an insanity plea, he was executed a year later. Greig was a morose loner but not at all psychotic. The motive seemed to be a kind of abstract jealousy: Vlught was not close to him at all, and he could make no claim she "cheated" on him. It was more a question of his rage that he was infatuated with her but forced to realize she was beyond his reach.[100]

These pre-1960 intimate-partner murders were, for the most part, fairly routine: a drowning and a stabbing, with commonplace motivations. Nothing exotic. As we approach the 1960s, we begin to find stories in which spouses or intimates are murdered in not so unusual ways but in contexts that constitute veritable grade-B novels come to life, sometimes by characters other than the victim's partner. We find an example of this in the case of Frank Duncan, who was one of the many children of the eleven-time—some say twenty-time—married Elizabeth Ann Duncan.[101] Despite her many options, she was pathologically attached, some thought incestuously attached, to Frank, who had lived with his mother all of his thirty years in their Santa Barbara, California, home. Whether the incest was frank (no pun intended) or only psychological remained uncertain. Ironically, when Frank finally began to assert his independence, Elizabeth made a suicide gesture with pills and was then aided in her recovery by a young nurse, Olga Kupczyk. Frank fell in love with Olga and married her secretly in early 1958. By the fall, Olga was pregnant and Elizabeth had learned of her son's "betrayal." In 1958, she and a twenty-five-year-old man, Ralph Winterstein, whom she hired, posed as Olga and Frank in court and had the marriage annulled. Elizabeth then determined to kill Olga. She found some willing hitmen and told them a tall tale about how Olga was "blackmailing" her son, so that the men would feel they were "doing the right thing" in getting rid of a pregnant, seemingly innocent woman. The two hitmen abducted Olga, took her into Mexican territory, and, when their pistol failed to fire, strangled her to death. Four years later, all three—Elizabeth and the hired killers—were executed. So, this was an "uxoricide," too—but a novelistic, if not unique, one in that the wife was murdered not by her husband, who loved his wife, but by his mother. In many of its features, it was a harbinger of the types of homicides to come in the following decade.

The boundless narcissism of Elizabeth Duncan—her selfishness, ruthlessness, arrogance, and contempt for the conventional limits of social behavior—is encountered with a certain regularity in the era of "new evil." The direct means of murder change but little. Murder has only so many direct methods: shooting, stabbing, strangling, burning, bludgeoning, poisoning. What we see more and more of in the current era is a peculiar originality in the planning stage leading up to otherwise not so imaginative *direct* means of killing. The hope behind the planning is to hoodwink law enforcement, elude detection, and thus to get away with murder—thanks to the killer's superiority of mind and cleverness, if not downright genius, in coming up with a method that had *never been thought of before*. If we compare the *high-profile* spousal murders from before the 1960s, such as the Gillette case, with more recent ones, the similarity is that most such murders are done by better educated persons of higher social standings. A key distinction, however, is that modern killers are more apt to resort to hiring a hitman or relying on a close relative to commit the murder, perhaps as clever means of getting around the ever-improving detection methods on the part of law enforcement. In my series of 139 post-1960 uxoricides, for example, there were thirty instances (21.6 percent) of solicitation of a hitman or relative to kill the wife. Even more striking was the reliance on a kind of devilish originality in the planning. Let us review a few examples.

In 1969, Dr. John Hill was eager to get rid of his wife, Joan, freeing himself to be with his mistress. To that end, Dr. Hill fashioned some pastries containing cultures made from different forms of human waste. Joan became mildly sick from these confections and asked her husband for something to cure her illness. As his newly divorced wife Ann Kurth testified at trial, "He told me how he had killed Joan with a needle." She did die of overwhelming sepsis, and Dr. Hill became a suspect. There was a trial, ending in a mistrial, and then a second trial arranged for the fall of 1972. A few weeks before the scheduled hearing, Dr. Hill was shot dead by a masked gunman. It was believed that Joan's father, Ash Robinson, had hired the hitman to kill his daughter's murderer. Robinson became the defendant in a new trial, as the man responsible for killing Dr. Hill, but he was eventually cleared by a jury several years later.[102]

Ed Post, a prominent real estate man from New Orleans, became enamored of his best friend's wife, Kim, and increasingly tired of his wife, Julie, toward whom he had been physically abusive.[103] In 1986, planning to attend a meeting in St. Louis, he drove with Julie to a hotel in that city. During their stay, he drew her bath, making sure the water was just the temperature she liked, and then proceeded to drown her in it. Ed then went for his morning jog, returning to the hotel some time later, pretending that he discovered her dead in the tub. At first, it did seem like an accident—but during an autopsy, a number of head wounds were found. Though he claimed his innocence, credibly at first, detectives were suspicious on a number of counts. The head injuries appeared to have been inflicted by another person and were not consistent with having merely slipped and fallen into a tub. Secondly, Ed declined a polygraph exam, on the grounds that it was "not admissible in court" and he was "innocent," anyway. Finally he had taken out a $700,000 life insurance policy for Julie the month before her untimely demise. Ultimately, Ed was found guilty at trial and sentenced to life in prison.

The common elements in these cases are the *staging* of an "accident" or natural death, often worthy of an Off-Broadway playwright, coupled with the conviction of the murdering spouse—the dramatist—that every conceivable detail has been considered, such that the unfolding plan is ironclad and the crime will never come to justice. Sometimes the dramas are so similar as to suggest that the later versions are "copycat" murders. Robert Marshall, for example, was both in major debt and heavily involved with the wife of his Toms River, New Jersey, neighbor.[104] In 1984, to kill two birds with one stone—that is, to bring in a large sum and eliminate his current spouse—he took out an insurance policy for $1.5 million and arranged for two hitmen to "accost" him and kill his wife, as he and she drove along the highway. When Robert stopped, as if for a "flat tire," the men shot his wife to death, first knocking Robert unconscious, as though their "motive" was to rob him. Arrested three months later, he was convicted and sentenced to life without parole. Five years later, in Boston,

Charles Stuart, perhaps imitating Marshall—or perhaps merely in a "great minds think alike" coincidence—drove with his pregnant wife to an impoverished neighborhood. He then stopped the car, shot his wife to death, and then fired a bullet into his own stomach, telling police that a manufactured assailant he described as black and six feet tall had held them up and shot them in the bellies before fleeing the scene, leading investigators to zero in on an uninvolved man named Willie Bennett.[105] There were several motives at play here, including insurance money, the desire to avoid fatherhood, and the freedom to be with a recently acquired mistress. He gave the gun to a brother, whose conscience later compelled him to inform the police about what Charles had done. The scheming killer then took his own life by leaping into Boston's appropriately named Charles River.

A few years ago, another highly narcissistic and unscrupulous man, Justin Barber, had gotten into heavy debt and was envious of his more successful wife, April. He had also begun an affair. He hatched a plot, consisting of celebrating their third anniversary by night on a Florida beach. After dinner, he shot April to death with a single bullet before shooting himself superficially in four different places unlikely to prove fatal. He then limped to the police and blamed the attack on a manufactured "Mexican" man who robbed them before firing shots, explaining that it was dark on the beach and he was unable to describe the assailant any further. It did not escape the attention of the detectives that he had very recently taken out two $2,000,000 insurance policies on each of them.[106]

It is not clear whether Barber was aware of the Marshall and Stuart cases, or he devised his plot all on his own. Each case involved a kind of "stupid brilliance"—akin to the stupidly brilliant scheme of Joan Shannon, on the part of grandiose and malign egotists, each convinced of having outsmarted the best minds of forensic science. The "brilliance" is, of course, only in the mind of the perpetrator. In reality, these perpetrators are merely cunning—and, in addition, conning, since the personality aberration behind these murders is that of the psychopathic "con artist," with an unshakeable belief in his or her superiority and, vis-à-vis the law, untouchability.

I think it is fair to say that the very assumption one can devise a foolproof plan will ultimately backfire, proving one was . . . a fool. There are too many details to control. Barber failed to consider how unlikely it was that the nonexistent robber could kill April with one shot and fail to kill him with four. Joan Shannon did not grasp that the made-up intruder, had he broken into her home that rainy night, would have left footmarks inside and outside the house. She knew she needed to cry when the police told her about the murder of her husband, and tried hard to think of something to cry about, but she couldn't make a convincing go of it, so she gave herself away. The wife killers were all also blithely unaware of the statistics of uxoricide: the scenario of a murdered wife and live husband points to the male partner as the culprit, wherever he may have been at the time, in over 90 percent of cases before the detectives and crime scene investigation people even get down to work.

Still, my favorite vignette in this area is that of a murder-*manqué*, an uxoricide that *didn't* happen. It concerns a wealthy physician I saw in consultation, who was furious that, in the wake of an acrimonious divorce and custody battle, his ex-wife came away both with the children and the large home they had all once occupied. He wanted to kill her. To that end, he elaborated a plan of unprecedented subtlety, uncomplicated by the usual ulterior motives of a mistress or an insurance policy that might arouse suspicion. He had an elderly friend who was dying of cancer. He could persuade the man to shoot his wife, then quietly succumb to his illness shortly afterward. This was the "clever" part. He was unfazed by the aforementioned dictum *murdered wife, live husband = guilty husband*. What did give him pause was my reminding him that the dying man was indeed a friend of the family. He had no animus toward the wife, hence no motive. The man's Rolodex—his address book— would contain the names of the husband and wife, but this would point to an obvious connection to the husband, no matter where the husband was at the time. That was the "stupid" part. He was finally dissuaded and did not pursue his plan further. The husband did not have psychopathic traits like Ed Post or Justin Barber; he was instead an arrogant and contemptuous narcissist, entitled, in his mind, to the life-and-death powers of a medieval king. He merited his niche in the new narcissism and the new evil: nothing like his plan existed before the 1960s—or perhaps ever.

Spouse and Intimate Partner Murders by Females

We turn now to rarer spousal or intimate partner murders committed by women. The motives behind these crimes differ in their frequencies, though not in their underlying types, from those perpetrated by men. Men are more often prompted by jealousy, wish to be with a mistress, need to preserve social image, or, less often, greed, as in cases involving insurance money. Greed of this type is somewhat more common among women who kill their male partners, seen in 37 percent of sixty-nine cases I reviewed. Among 139 males who committed uxoricide, 29.5 percent were thus motivated. Moreover, women were more often inclined to hire a hitman, or to solicit help from a friend or relative to carry out the murder than were men: 33 percent against 21.5 percent, in my series.

Most women have less in the way of physical strength than their husbands or mates. This predisposes, in cases of murder, to more subtle—and, often, less easily detected—means, such as poisoning. This appears to have been the "weapon" used by the independently wealthy Florence Bravo in killing her abusive husband, Charles Bravo, in 1876—namely, a glass of antimony-containing tartar emetic.[107] Florence displayed some narcissistic traits. She was spoiled and willful and not at all the picture of wifely subservience that prevailed in Victorian England. Charles, a hopeless alcoholic, was, in all fairness, abusive, insensitive, and cruel, and with divorce so unthinkable in that era the case comes close to a justified homicide. Florence's spiritual sisters in the new era, nearly a century later—women who have resorted to poisoning their spouses—are often more narcissistic than she and, in many instances, more imaginative in the poisons they selected. In 1998, for example, Kimberly Hricko, a surgical technician, having embarked upon an affair with another man, killed her husband—on Valentine's Day—with a curariform drug she had taken from the hospital medication cart.[108] She tried to cover up the crime by staging a fire, as if from her husband's cigar while he was asleep, only there was no soot in his lungs at autopsy, as would be expected in a fire death. Another instance of cunning foiled by stupidity. She had also hoped to profit from his insurance policy. A few years later, Michelle Michael, a nurse practitioner, killed her husband with rocuronium she had swiped from the nurse's wagon, another curare-like drug.[109] She, too, decided to cover up the murder by setting fire to the bedroom where she had killed her husband. She left a laundry iron turned on, but it failed to work, so she returned and added an accelerant. The ensuing fire charred the body, but her husband's liver and heart were intact enough to show the presence of the rocuronium.

It would be interesting to know whether these women took their inspiration from a well-known uxoricide in our "fulcrum year" of 1965 when thirty-four-year-old anesthesiologist Carl Coppolino killed his thirty-two-year-old wife, Dr. Carmela Musetto, with succinylcholine.[110] His fortunes waning at the time, he was now free to marry a wealthy divorcée, Mary Gibson. Succinylcholine is a nicotinic acetylcholine receptor agonist, causing muscle relaxation, similar to curare-like drugs, and is difficult to detect postmortem. Yet, science had advanced: Dr. Milton Helpern, New York City's chief medical examiner, and Dr. Joseph Umberger, chief toxicologist, were able to detect the drug in Carmela's brain and liver. This led to Coppolino's conviction and sentencing.

Another husband-murder using an exotic drug was that committed by Kristin Rossum in November of 2000.[111] Kristin came from a distinguished family. A former child model, she had blossomed into a beautiful woman and was also a ballerina, until a foot injury ended her dancing career. She became depressed and addicted to methamphetamine, yet was able to graduate college summa cum laude, with a major in chemistry. Still in her early twenties, she married and found work in a toxicology lab, headed by Michael Robertson. After she and Robertson began an affair, she killed her husband, Greg de Villers, with an injection of fentanyl—a powerful synthetic opioid. Kristin staged the murder scene to look as though Greg had committed suicide and even scattered rose petals on the bed, in imitation of the 1999 movie *American Beauty*. Greg had discovered both the affair and Kristin's ongoing methamphetamine addiction, and threatened to expose her. This appeared to be the precipitant to the murder, for which she was sentenced to life in California's Chowchilla prison.

As for other women who killed with a poison, some resorted to the tried-and-true arsenic, discovered in 1250 by the famous scholar Albertus Magnus and used by many men and women ever since for its lethal potential, perhaps most notably by Cesare Borgia. Chemists learned to detect it in the body in the 1830s, so, in recent times, arsenic, as a now readily detectable agent, is used less often in spousal murders. More "novel" compounds have been relied upon instead, as in the 2007 case of Julia "Lynn" Turner, a Georgia woman married to a policeman, but having an affair with a fireman.[112] She ended up killing both men—her husband in 1995 and her boyfriend in 2001—with ethylene glycol, commonly called antifreeze. It was not detected at first, but, after the murder of the fireman, calcium oxalate crystals were found in his kidneys, which ruled out the supposed "heart attack" and ruled in the actual toxin. A woman of extravagant tastes, she killed both men for insurance policies but had earlier forced her husband to work three jobs to pay for various expensive items, many of which were gifts for the fireman.

In September of 2004 James Keown, a former radio reporter, killed his wife, Julie, also employing antifreeze, in hopes of settling his debts with her $250,000 insurance policy.[113] It is not clear whether Keown was inspired by the Turner case. Called "an evil human being" by a judge who sentenced him to life in prison, Keown had lost his job—the source of his debt problem—when his employer discovered he had lied about having been accepted to Harvard Business School. Then Keown lied again, claiming his wife had "committed suicide" a month after learning she had a "fatal kidney condition." She did actually have a "kidney condition"—but it was induced by the antifreeze he had begun giving her. The clincher came at trial when a computer expert testified that Keown had done an internet search with the terms "ethylene glycol death human."

More recently, Diane Staudte and her daughter Rachel were convicted of killing first Diane's husband, Mark, in April of 2012 and then her twenty-six-year-old son, Shaun, five months later, both with antifreeze.[114] Another daughter, Sarah, twenty-seven years of age, was also poisoned but survived with brain damage. No ulterior motives here; Diane simply hated her sixty-one-year-old husband, as well as her son, because he was "worse than a pest." She was frustrated that Sarah was not working at the time. It does seem odd that Diane had the knowledge that antifreeze had recently joined the ranks of "foolproof" poisons but also the naiveté *not* to know that its presence had, indeed, been detected in a number of cases over the past two decades.

Spousal Dismemberment and Disappearance

In the domain of spousal or intimate partner murder, a feature of the "new evil" seldom encountered earlier is the effort of a husband or a wife to dismember the victim, such that the victim vanishes from the earth. One is reminded of Comrade Stalin's signature phrase, "Nyet chelovyeka, nyet problyema!"—"No body, no problem!" This type of murder is different from the more ordinary attempt to hide the evidence of a murder by burying the body in a shallow grave somewhere in the woods. Cremation followed by the scattering of ashes would be one method of total disappearance, as seen in the large-scale crimes of Hitler and bin Laden, but there are other means of complete eradication of human remains, noteworthy for their gruesome originality.

In the 1986 murder of his wife, airline pilot Richard Crafts reacted to his wife Helle's discovery of his extramarital affairs, as well as to her request for a divorce, by killing her and then dismembering her corpse, chilling the pieces in a deep freezer to render them easier to pulverize with a rented wood chipper.[115] Suspicions arose, despite his claim that Helle was "visiting friends in the Canary Islands," and a search was made of a lake near the Connecticut River. No body was found, of course, but a few ounces of remains were collected: a tooth, a toenail, some hairs, fingernails, and type O blood. A forensic odontologist was able to determine that the tooth had belonged to Crafts's wife. The killer was sentenced to fifty years in prison—the first successful prosecution of a murder in Connecticut in which no body was ever found.

In 2004, Melanie McGuire, a nurse in a New Jersey fertility clinic, began an affair with a doctor colleague.[116] This went on for some three years, and both wanted to divorce their spouses and marry each other. This led to a crisis when Bill, Melanie's husband, wanted to move to Virginia. Solution: Melanie rendered him unconscious with a "mickey"—an alcoholic drink laced with a hypnotic, chloral hydrate, and then shot him with a newly purchased pistol. Next, she trisected his body with a chainsaw and then stuffed the pieces into three suitcases, which she dumped into the Chesapeake Bay, two hundred miles away. Problem: she had placed five-pound weights in each suitcase, not realizing that much greater weights would be necessary to offset the buoyancy of the gases released by the decomposing body parts. The suitcases surfaced, and the contents were identified as the remains of Bill McGuire. Melanie was duly arrested and sentenced to life in prison.

In October of 2009, Dawn Viens, the wife of Lomita, California, chef David Viens, disappeared without a trace.[117] At first, David told the authorities that, after he argued with Dawn over her alcohol use, she walked off, "needing some time away." As time went on and Dawn never returned home, David became a suspect. In response, he tried to commit suicide by jumping off a cliff but survived. The truth then came out: David thought she was stealing money from the cash register and harming his business. As he told an acquaintance, "That bitch is stealing from me. Nobody steals from me. I will kill that bitch." Which he did. The chef then slow cooked his wife's body in a fifty-five-gallon drum for four days, till nothing remained, except the skull and jawbone, which he said he hid "for safekeeping" in his mother's attic. When the police searched the attic, even those parts were not found.

Maricopa County, Arizona, is the site of not one but two cases of dismemberment in which women were implicated. In September of 2004, a many times married forty-three-year-old exotic dancer, Marjorie Orbin, killed and dismembered her seventh husband, Jay Orbin, ostensibly to inherit his money and to free herself for an eighth marriage to Larry Weisberg.[118] Having shot Jay on his forty-fifth birthday, Marjorie proceeded to cut his body into pieces with a jigsaw. She acid-washed the floor of the garage where all of this transpired and coated it with epoxy, making it impossible to search for traces of blood. She was then caught on videotape, buying two large plastic containers at a hardware store, into which she would later pack her husband's dismembered body. Marjorie craved the glamorous life, affiliating with one wealthy man after the other. After the remains were discovered, she was arrested before her "perfect crime" could be consummated. Avaricious and scheming, and lacking remorse, Marjorie is now serving a life sentence.

The other Maricopa County case took place nearly three-quarters of a century earlier. Winnie Ruth Judd, twenty-six at the time, was working at a medical clinic in Phoenix, while her husband was relocating his medical practice to Los Angeles.[119] Ruth became friends with two female coworkers. All three, it seemed, became enamored of John Halloran, a local businessman. Ruth, so it was said, shot the other two women to death and then, with an accomplice, dismembered the bodies, placing the various parts in large shipping trunks, and some of the smaller pieces in a valise and hatbox. She then traveled by train to Los Angeles, the trunks and boxes all aboard. It is not clear how she hoped to dispose of all of this material, but the crime was given away by the foul odor and fluids escaping from the trunks. Convicted initially of first-degree murder, Ruth was sentenced to be hanged, but, at a subsequent hearing, she was declared mentally incompetent and remanded to an asylum. As the years passed, new evidence suggested she may have acted in self-defense, or was perhaps even innocent. The famous attorney Melvin Belli—mentioned in our earlier discussion of the Zodiac Killer—took up her cause in 1969, and, two years later, the governor of Arizona declared her a free and sane woman. She spent many of her years thereafter serving as a maid in a church, where she was welcomed as a sweet and caring woman, even when someone later recognized her as *the* Ruth Judd. She lived on quietly as Sister Ruth, dying at age ninety-three. Whatever her role may have been in the crime, narcissistic traits do not appear to have been a significant part of her personality makeup—noteworthy, in that these were pre-"new evil" crimes.

The vastness of the ocean seems more suited—perhaps ideally—to the disappearance of a body, compared with the more hazardous earthbound alternatives. Still, caution is required. Unless the abdomen is cut open, gases generated postmortem will cause the body to rise, if not *very* heavily weighted down. Also, even if the body is never found, circumstantial evidence may be so compelling as to warrant arrest and even to justify conviction for murder. Illustrative of these points is the notorious case of Scott Peterson.[120] On Christmas Eve in 2002, Scott killed his eight-month pregnant wife, Laci, and transported her to the San Francisco Bay. There, he dumped her body in the Pacific at a time when his prior internet research on tides assured him her body would be washed out into the ocean, far away from the prying eyes of the authorities. One month before the murder, Scott had begun an affair with a young woman, Amber Frey, telling her he was not married and later telling her he had "lost" Laci days before anyone knew she was missing. Considered by some a pathological liar and "white-collar" psychopath—i.e., he had a good job, and no history of prior arrests or juvenile delinquency—he told Amber, after Laci had gone missing, that he was in Paris at a business meeting when he was instead by the bay, checking out the tides. To Amber's question about the water she thought she could hear in the background, he explained adroitly that the business meeting was taking place near the Seine. And so on. By this time, nearly a month after Laci's disappearance, the police had accumulated enough evidence—partly through Amber's cooperation in recording all of her conversations with him—to arrest him, even in the absence of a body. . . .

Actually, two bodies: those of his wife and her unborn baby boy. Then, Scott's tide calculations notwithstanding, both bodies washed ashore and could be identified as Laci and their dead son. Arrested and convicted, Scott is now on San Quentin's "death row," which means life in prison without parole, since California no longer carries out the death penalty.

We alluded to times that a body was dumped in the ocean and never found, yet a murder conviction resulted, based upon equally compelling circumstantial evidence.[121] The Peterson case is, in many ways, a duplicate of Charles Stuart's murder of his pregnant wife. Both were psychopathic men who were romancing mistresses at the time of the murders, but their wishes to marry these new women—unencumbered by divorce and ongoing expenses of childcare—was not the primary motive in either crime. Rather, these murders seemed chiefly motivated by wishes to avoid fatherhood, with all of its responsibilities, financial obligations, and, vis-à-vis extramarital dalliances, limitations. One of the detectives investigating the Peterson case remarked that parenthood was an "anchor" for Scott.[122] Not a stabilizing force, that is, but a heavy, constrictive weight.

Stalking

In its root meaning, "stalking" connotes a stealthy sneaking up, as a preparatory step before finally pouncing on the object of one's desire. This is how members of the cat family operate, in order to secure their dinners. The same basic notion is conveyed in many other languages as well: *auflauern* in German, *traquer* in French, *acechar* in Spanish, *vislyezhivat'* in Russian, and so forth. In our species, stalking has a long history, and can vary, in dangerousness, from harmless to fatal. The objects of stalking, in any of its many forms, are often persons with special advantages: beauty, wealth, power, exalted social status, fame, and celebrity. In the early days of Queen Victoria's reign, for example, an adolescent known as Boy Jones sneaked several times into the palace to steal some of the queen's underwear and to sit for a moment on the throne. He meant her no harm, but some remonstrance was in order, so he was sent to Australia.[123]

There are several taxonomies in the realm of stalking. Paul Mullen and colleagues distinguish between the rejected stalker, the resentful stalker, the paraphilic stalker (as in cases of voyeurism, pedophilia, fetishism, and telephone scatologia), the predatory stalker, the intimacy-seeker, and the incompetent suitor.[124] The *rejected* type is generally narcissistic, overly dependent, low in self-esteem, and markedly possessive and jealous, as though the love object were the "only one in the world" who could make the individual happy. The *resentful* stalker is one who feels persecuted or otherwise unfairly treated, usually by a boss or by someone else in a superior position, against whom the stalker must "fight back," often with insulting phone calls, poison-pen letters, or worse. The *predatory* stalker, almost always male, lies in wait for an assault, usually sexual, meantime gathering information about a victim and rehearsing a plan of attack. An example is the serial killer Dennis Rader.[125] The *intimacy-seeker* aspires to achieve a relationship via unwanted attention, calls, and following a victim. Stalkers in this category are usually lonely and friendless, impervious to the indifference on the part of their love objects, and near delusional in the belief that their pursuits will one day be crowned with success.

A variant of the intimacy-seeker brand of stalker was described centuries ago, under a number of headings: *Melancholie Érotique* (by Jacques Ferrand, 1623), *monomanie érotique* (by Jean-Étienne Dominique Esquirol, 1838), and *erotischer Wahnsinn* (by Richard von Krafft-Ebing, 1881). Persons of this type are often said to manifest "obsessive love." Persons described by Gaetan Gatian de Clérambeault, however, are almost all women, often quite disturbed, psychologically, and of lower social status. They are convinced that men of superior status are communicating their "love" for them through hidden signs and signals. A patient I once worked with, for example, thought that if the professor she admired assigned the class a reading that began with the letter "L," it meant he secretly "loved" her.

While many stalkers, apart from the predatory, are harmless, though at times extremely irritating and frustrating, stalking with fatal consequences has become a recurring phenomenon in the era of "new evil." Some of the victims have been celebrities, others, persons in ordinary walks of life who, for one reason or another, had taken on special significance in the eyes of their stalkers. Some of these offenders have been grossly psychotic. They tend to be among the most persistent and untreatable. A nonfatal case was that of the schizophrenic woman whom psychiatrist Dr. Doreen Orion once saw in her consulting room.[126] Dr. Orion's "mistake" was to be her usual kind and sympathetic self when speaking with a patient. Lonely and friendless, the woman took this display of common kindness as a token of the doctor's "genuine" affection. The patient would silently hover around the doctor's house, peeking in the windows and so forth, with such frequency as to impel the doctor and her husband to move from Arizona to Colorado—where the situation repeated itself, once their new address was discovered. Dr. Orion finally took legal action and eventually managed to get some satisfaction from laws related to stalking that had recently been enacted, capable of imposing incarceration for certain periods of time. At the time, the latter was new territory for the courts, since the type of stalking Dr. Orion suffered had not previously led to extended jail sentences. Her patient was *erotomanic*, a psychotic woman who had been in a psychiatric hospital prior to the consultation with Dr. Orion. Because of the psychotic component, individuals of this type are incapable of grasping how unwanted their attentions are—hence, the irremediable persistence. Dr. Orion commented on the more common type of stalker: "One who has been in a relationship with the victim and can't let go. These people are extremely narcissistic—They want what they want and they do not care if the victim does not want the same."[127]

In a high-profile case that partook of both *erotomania* ("obsessive love" combined with the irrational belief that the love is "returned") and the rejected stalker subtype described by Mullen and colleagues, Robert Bardo of Arizona became fixated on the twenty-one-year-old model and television actress Rebecca Schaeffer, the star of the sitcom *My Sister Sam*, which aired from 1986 to 1988.[128] The nineteen-year-old Bardo sent her innumerable letters and also made several attempts to visit her when she was onset. He had even built a personal shrine to Schaeffer in his home. At one point, she—or her secretary—sent him a signed photo of herself, as stars often do for their fans. The word "fan" has ominous overtones here: it is a shorthand for *fanatic*, meaning nothing more than someone *enthusiastic* about some celebrity. It does not mean "crazy," but Bardo *was* chronically psychotic and took the photo to mean that Schaeffer "returned" his love. So far so good, but when Bardo happened to see a movie in which Schaeffer acted in a sex scene, he felt betrayed and then determined to kill her. He managed to learn her Los Angeles address via the Department of Motor Vehicles, traveled to LA, knocked on her door, and shot her to death. Arrested soon after, Bardo is now serving a life sentence. His pattern of celebrity stalking was established well before his fixation on Schaeffer. He had previous obsessional "loves" toward Madonna, Tiffany, and other stars. In prison, he has been a prolific artist, creating meticulously drawn close-up portraits of beautiful movie actresses. The killer's behavior satisfied the legal definition of stalking: *someone who willfully, maliciously, and repeatedly follows or harasses someone, making a credible threat to that person's safety.* California and other states put stronger anti-stalking laws into effect after the Bardo case; among other improvements, it is no longer possible to obtain someone's address through the DMV.

Had it not been for the high-profile nature of the murder, Bardo—who had been hospitalized psychiatrically twice before—would probably have been remanded to a forensic hospital. When I corresponded and spoke with him several years ago, his responses from prison, fifteen years after the 1989 murder, were clearly irrational and bizarre, well in keeping with a schizophrenic psychosis.

The 1969 case of Prosenjit Poddar had also become "high profile," not because a celebrity had been killed but because of a failure on the part of the psychiatric profession to warn a person of imminent danger.[129] Poddar, born in India, was a student at the University of California, Berkeley. He had attended folk dancing classes at International House, where he met Tatiana Tarasoff. At a New Year's Eve party held there in 1968, she kissed him. Poddar interpreted this innocent gesture in a much more serious way, along the lines of the culture of his Dalit ("untouchable") social caste, in which such a kiss would betoken a serious relationship or even an engagement. She did not return such feelings and made this known to Poddar, who then felt intense resentment and began stalking her. While she visited Brazil the next summer, Poddar, in a state of depression and rage, saw a campus psychologist and spoke of wanting to kill Tarasoff. The psychologist, diagnosing paranoid schizophrenia, recommended civil commitment, but a psychiatrist who interviewed Poddar later decided the man was rational. Several months after Tarasoff's return, in October of 1969, Poddar shot and stabbed her to death. This led to the decision by the California Supreme Court that a mental health professional has a duty to warn individuals who are specifically threatened by a patient. The issue is still debated: most states have adopted this opinion, but not all.

In comparison to spousal murderers, kidnappers, serial killers, and the like, stalkers are much more likely to show signs of mental illness, if not frank psychosis. The reader is reminded of our vignette about stalker and murderer Mark David Chapman earlier in this volume, in which we discussed his killing of John Lennon in 1980. Before his trial, over a dozen psychiatrists evaluated Chapman, at least six concluding that he was psychotic, with most favoring a diagnosis of paranoid schizophrenia. Some argued, in an odd twist of language, that his delusion "fell short of psychosis." He was sentenced to prison, where he remains to this day, though, as with Bardo, absent the publicity from killing so famous a person, Chapman might have been sent indefinitely to a forensic hospital.

A more florid example of mental illness in a stalker is that of Arthur Jackson, a schizophrenic man from Aberdeen, Scotland.[130] In one of the earliest of the violent incidents of celebrity stalking, Jackson had become obsessed with the actress Theresa Saldana, whom he had seen in the 1980 movie *Defiance*. This was not erotomania, since he did not harbor the delusion that she loved him. Instead, he had the delusion that, if he killed her and was then executed for the murder—he considered suicide a sin—he could join her eternally in heaven. One can only stand in awe at the powers of madness that Jackson found no trouble in imagining that, as Saldana's murderer, he, too, would go to heaven, rather than the "other place," and that she would welcome his eternal companionship. To fulfill his ambition, at all events, he sneaked into the United States illegally and made his way to Los Angeles. There, he tracked her down, obtaining her address, and encountered her on the morning of March 15, 1982. He stabbed her numerous times, but she was rescued when a passerby heard her screams and pulled Jackson away. After his arrest, Jackson was placed in the Atascadero forensic hospital and was later sent to a psychiatric hospital in England, where he died in 2004 at the age of sixty-eight. One might speculate that his efforts to find out where Saldana lived inspired Robert Bardo to track down Rebecca Schaeffer's whereabouts seven years later, but this is not known for certain.

We have dwelled thus far mainly on stalkers who targeted well-known people. Stalking is hardly confined to the famous. Estimates in the United States point to how one woman in twelve reports having been stalked at some point in her life, as opposed to only one man in forty-five. As to the risk of having been victimized in the previous year, stalking, at 1 percent, occupies an intermediate position between rape (0.3 percent) and physical assault (1.9 percent). Erotomanic forms of stalking are common in the larger group, though there are, as hinted at above, important differences in how the disorders manifest themselves. As Dr. J. Reid Meloy points out, the classic de Clérambeault type—those with the conviction of being secretly loved by the object of their affections, who may be quite unaware of the erotomanic person's existence—is the less common form.[131] Meloy designates these as exhibiting *erotomanic delusional disorder*. More common are disorders of "obsessive love" in which the person in question does recognize the lack of reciprocity on the part of the love object. Consider the case of John Hinckley Jr., who tried to kill President Reagan in 1981. He knew very well that his inamorata, the actress Jodie Foster, far from returning his love, had no interest in him whatsoever and, when they were both at Yale, regarded him as quite rude—for slipping love letters and poems under her door. Hinckley imagined that in killing the president, he would "elevate" himself to her level of fame, becoming somehow worthy of her affection. Just before the shooting, Hinckley tried to convey his sense of urgency in a letter to the star, never mailed, in which he said, "I will admit to you that the reason I'm going ahead with this attempt now is because I cannot wait any longer to impress you. I've got to do something now to make you understand in no uncertain terms that I am doing all of this for your sake."[132] Meloy calls this type of fixation *borderline erotomania*. This is also where one might categorize Richard Farley, whose fixation upon Laura Black and murderous rampage at her place of employment we have already reviewed.

Farley, by the way, is not the only stalker who also committed a mass murder. In 1983, Michael Perry, a schizophrenic man who stalked actress Olivia Newton-John in California, failed in his plan to find and harm her. He returned to his home in Louisiana and killed his entire family. At the time of his arrest, he was also planning to kill Supreme Court justice Sandra Day O'Connor.[133] Darnell Collins, an ex-con who had been stalking his ex-girlfriend April Gates, shot and killed her, her mother, and five others after Gates attained an order of protection against him.[134] The Collins case differed from the more typical erotomanic types in that she had actually been his girlfriend, whereas Newton-John knew nothing of Perry's existence, Rebecca Schaeffer was likely not aware her staff had ever sent Bardo her picture, and Jodie Foster knew of Hinckley only as a terrible pest from her past. The Collins case was less newsworthy but more ordinary: the majority of stalkers have had at least some acquaintance with their victims.

Persons in the grip of this kind of obsessive love need not be psychotic, although Arthur Jackson was. Bardo occupies an intermediate position, to my way of thinking, insofar as he felt that the photo of Schaeffer that she sent him, on which she scribbled "Love you," perhaps signified that she did love him a little. That is to say, he completely misread a meaningless thing, but he did *not start out* with the conviction that she was secretly in love with him. He was not thoroughly delusional in relation to her, although he was unmistakably schizophrenic in general, as was Jackson, who, again, was aware Saldana did *not* love him. As to the personality attributes seen with frequency in erotomanic persons, especially borderline erotomanics, uppermost are the narcissistic, with an emphasis on entitlement; the paranoid; and often the antisocial and schizoid, in the sense of socially aloof and awkward traits.

The ability to engage in these sorts of behaviors has been amplified by the internet, which has facilitated stalking at a distance and also given a kind of false encouragement to would-be stalkers via the ease with which one can create fictitious names for oneself when contacting potential victims. This "cyberstalking" has currently become a priority for the FBI and represents a new variety of crime, another "new evil" of the present era. The narcissistic element is fortified, in great measure, via the anonymity behind which the stalker can hide when reaching out to other people, even in locales far removed from the stalker—geographic proximity no longer being a necessity. Cyberstalking is ordinarily a nonlethal form of stalking, except in the cases mentioned above under "Bullying," though nonetheless potentially highly disturbing and threatening.

Some recent examples: Joseph Ostrowski, a twenty-nine-year-old head football coach in a Pennsylvania high school, used social networking sites in order to harass, threaten, and intimidate a number of female students at the University of Michigan.[135] He had been exploiting personal information his victims had posted online. In addition, he was found to have child pornography stored in his computer. In 2013, Ostrowski was sentenced to thirty years in prison for the two offenses. A Detroit man, James Allen, was arrested on charges of cyberstalking at least ten women in the Buffalo area, threatening them with the comment, "Communicate with me, or I'll send nude pictures of you to your friends and family."[136] He was arrested on felony charges of cyberstalking, trafficking in computer passwords, and making harassing telephone calls. Allen went so far as to create fake Facebook profiles and to pose as a site administrator, asking the women to contact him via their webcams. In a final example, in 2014, a twenty-two-year-old New York political activist, Adam Savader, was sentenced to thirty months in prison for extortion and stalking.[137] He hacked into the online accounts of fifteen women and found nude photos of them. The intimidating aspect was in his warning his victims: "Let's make this simple. . . . You have until noon. I am not bluffing. Don't be stupid. Once I send pics of you they cannot be unsent." He apparently suffered from "mental health problems" of some sort, as even the court agreed, but as Judge Marianne Battani wisely added, "You can't use mental illness as an excuse, as long as you know right from wrong." As for these three cases of cyberstalking, I would not have been able to learn of them were it not for the internet—so it has its upside, as well.

No discussion of stalking, particularly of the *borderline erotomanic* sort, can be considered complete without reference to the phenomenal case of Diane Schaefer and her deliberate intrusion into the life of Dr. Murray Brennan, a world-renowned cancer specialist in New York City.[138] People who have suffered through a particularly dreadful marriage or an ego-crunching work situation are often wont to describe their plights as having lived through a "bad movie." In the case of Schaefer and Dr. Brennan, a movie actually was fashioned after his eight-year ordeal with Schaefer. The 2002 film called *Obsession* was quite good, the story behind it anything but.

There are, to be sure, obsessive elements in any case of stalking. There are the repetitive, driven behaviors, which a victim is powerless to control and stop; alongside these are preoccupations and fixations that gobble up one's mental activities throughout the waking day. One's dreams may carry these concerns on into the night. Yet, by "obsessive love," we are usually referring to one of two main situations. In the first scenario, one has a serious "crush" on a man or a woman whom one knows but has not dated, merely admiring the person from a distance. In Goethe's story *Werther*, mentioned earlier (and perhaps based on Goethe's own youthful and temporary obsession with Charlotte Buff), Werther knew and loved his friend Lotte, though there was no intimacy. He remained obsessed with her after she married her fiancé, Albert—even committing suicide so as not to interfere with her life with her husband. A man of scruples, in other words, who would never harm the person he loved, albeit obsessively.

In the other situation, one has had a *real, and often intimate* relationship with someone—and then, after a breakup, becomes obsessed with this former lover. Everyone knows such a person, and many a play and opera has such a story as its theme. In *La Bohème*, the hero, Rodolfo, falls in love with the beautiful Mimi in act 1, and then, in act 3, becomes obsessed and morbidly jealous to the point of forcing her to leave him. Of this type, there are those with scruples, and then there are those obsessed not only with the former lover but also with revenge and the desire to harm the individual.

Diane Schaefer, in contrast, does not fit easily into these schemata. She was engulfed in an obsessive love for a man with whom she had no connection, unlike Werther and Lotte, and knew only by reputation. Hers was not a classic de Clérambeault–type erotomania, either, because she did not harbor the delusion that Dr. Brennan loved her secretly from afar, though he did occupy a higher social station, as in the classic description. Schaefer was a medical writer, the same age as the doctor she was pursuing. What was noteworthy was the manner in which she invaded the doctor's life, following him—insofar as she was able—wherever he went. Robert Bardo and Arthur Jackson, though both were grossly psychotic schizophrenics, did not insert themselves in the everyday lives of the women whom they obsessively loved. Diane Schaefer's mental state is not as clear-cut as theirs, and harder to assess. Her overriding wish was to be near the object of her fixation. To that end, she took pains to learn Dr. Brennan's travel schedule, the names of his wife and family members, and the times and places of his professional meetings; she left him numerous gifts and love letters, and called him repeatedly, disguising her voice at times, so as to get past his secretaries. On one occasion, she showed up at his apartment, dressed in nothing but a gossamer négligée.[139] She tried to disrupt his marriage by also stalking his wife and eventually made threats of violence. One of her more inventive ruses was to phone the airline carrier on which Dr. Brennan was about to fly to a meeting, telling the receptionist she was "Mrs. Brennan" and had changed her mind and now wanted to accompany her "husband" so that a seat next to him would be appreciated. Having no reason to doubt the woman, the receptionist would accommodate "Mrs. Brennan," with the result that Schaefer could now sit beside her beloved the whole length of the flight. With equal adroitness, Schaefer could end up in the same taxi in which Dr. Brennan was riding. Because Schaefer could speak in a rational and coherent way, I would have to ascribe such behavior to cunning and unscrupulousness, rather than to the sheer delusory thinking of a Bardo or an Arthur Jackson. Yet, she was a "madwoman," in the sense of a kind of willed craziness in her behavior. It was engineered, as it were, in the service of her erotomanic fixation and superimposed upon an underlying mental illness that was primarily of the mood disorder type—specifically, depressive. Added to this, Schaefer had, besides her depressive mood and narcissistic feelings of entitlement, clear-cut antisocial traits. She falsely reported Dr. Brennan as a "child molester," for example, and, on another occasion, threatened to kill him, telling him, "I can't live while you are alive on this earth. . . . I am going to kill you or kill myself. . . . I am degraded by your being alive."[140] Needless to say, Dr. Brennan consistently rejected her advances, which he endured from 1982 through 1990, before finally documenting her deceptions and recording her phone calls. Armed with this information, Dr. Brennan was able to have her arrested for "aggravated harassment"—the usual legal designation for stalking—and convicted to serve two years in prison. Schaefer's stalking days were not over. Later, upon her release, she even pursued a judge, as well as her own attorney.[141] It must have required considerable ingenuity to keep abreast of Dr. Brennan's whereabouts, since Schaefer was operating in the pre–internet age when privacy was still easier to safeguard and she could not conduct a simple search for details of his private and professional life.

I have had occasion to work with a woman who was obsessively in love with a man during a brief affair and, after he broke off the relationship, obsessively preoccupied with getting back at him. Her stalking consisted of deluging her former lover with phone calls, letters, and emails. She took to sending some emails from the computers of friends, so that the internet protocol addresses would be different from that of her home computer. She would also pretend to be these other people whose computers she was using, and write scurrilous letters, chiding the ex-boyfriend for treating the girl he rejected so shabbily. The woman did not tell me the truth about how often she contacted her "ex." I contacted him via my computer and had him document by email each day how often she had tried to contact him by whatever means. I made a chart of all of this information, which I could then use to remind the woman how often she was actually communicating with him. I was able in this way to persuade her to stop the harassment and, as they say, *move on* with her life.

As I think some of the vignettes about stalking demonstrate, the law has not been well equipped to deal with such cases, using measures of appropriate severity—that is, measures of the impact upon victims, which might warrant more severe sentences. Some small steps were taken, it is true, after each high-profile incident. Anti-stalking laws were put in place after the harassment endured by Dr. Orion, and, as we mentioned, access to people's addresses through the DMV was curtailed after the Rebecca Schaeffer murder. Yet, the brief sentences given to offenders who stalk, but do not kill, their victims are often far too lenient, not taking into consideration how resistant to treatment stalkers of such severity typically are. In the case of Diane Schaefer, she was, after all, trying by ever more aggressive steps to ruin Dr. Brennan's life and, perhaps, ultimately kill either him or his wife. The situation is analogous to certain cases of "attempted murder." Because the victim has survived, the law often hands down a sentence that is considerably less severe than might have been given in the case of the victim's death. Often, the individual's survival in an attempted murder is merely the result of some "miracle of modern medicine," not available twenty years before, or a bullet fired by the perpetrator that shifts a few millimeters to the left or the right of the femoral artery or the aorta or the heart, so that the victim does not bleed out or die. Yet, if it is demonstrably clear that the intention of the perpetrator was to kill, then the difference, with respect to the severity of the crime, between murder and attempted murder is academic. The length of the sentence should not vary by much, since the level of the criminal's dangerousness was the same. A stalker who disrupts the daily life and the tranquility of a victim as severely as some of the people we have discussed here should, I believe, be considered highly dangerous and given a sentence in accordance with that level of dangerousness—with forensic experts' best estimates of the likelihood for a repetition of the stalking behavior. In England, there are some felons, for example, whose sentences consist of being released "at the Queen's pleasure"—that is, when competent authorities in the penal system have, upon reexamination, concluded that the felon in question can be trusted not to reoffend. That could vary from a short time to a long stretch, or even forever—depending upon the stalker's capacity or lack thereof for genuine remorse and rehabilitation. Some stalkers, when defending their actions in the courtroom, invoke "external" forces, saying things like, "I don't know what possessed me to do the things I did." Yet, such words may come more from the tongue than the heart. Even such phraseology is worrisome: "What possessed me" suggests the wish to convey that such behavior was influenced by some force—the devil or an evil spirit?—that took over their brains from the outside, and thus they were not responsible. After release, such persons generally go on stalking, as we have already noted. Nothing changes. The queen would not have been pleased. As the preceding vignettes have shown, the term "obsessive love" is used in a variety of clinically different situations. The categories depicted here do not quite do justice to the "fifty shades of gray" that populate the region between the extremities—that is, stalking versus no stalking, psychosis versus no psychosis. Diane Schaefer is a good example of the complexity in any discussion of obsessive love. The seriousness of her depression was great enough to suggest a "depressive psychosis," but the outward manifestations of this condition consisted of outrageous behaviors, more than the primarily cognitive distortions and delusions of the more commonly encountered depressive psychosis. An example of the latter would be a woman, recently divorced, who was admitted to a psychiatric hospital some years ago, suffering from the delusion that her husband was causing "rays" to pass from his house to the house where she was now living—rays that were exerting an injurious effect on her brain. Her delusion, we can understand, was the concretization of her sadness and sense of despair and bewilderment over being rejected by her husband. Schaefer was in her early forties and alone. Perhaps that was the crisis that mobilized her "mad" behavior. Yet, her cruel and persistent stalking meant that her depression was overshadowed by the severity of her personality disorder, which contained narcissistic, paranoid, borderline, and also psychopathic features. As with many "white-collar" psychopaths, Schaefer showed mostly the *narcissistic* traits, such as pathological lying, manipulativeness, callousness, failure to accept responsibility for one's behavior, and lack of genuine remorse, rather than the *criminological* ones—arrests for many different types of crime and so forth. Furthermore, her cognitive impairment was not as severe as that of the divorced woman disturbed by the "rays." I hope the vignettes on obsessive love included here, especially that of Schaefer, demonstrate how such persons are resistant to the interventions of psychiatry, often to the point of being altogether untreatable.

The persons we have discussed here, exemplifying obsessive love combined with stalking, represent a comparatively new form of psycho-pathology. The famous cases came mostly from the 1980s, well into the era of "new evil." These individuals exhibited a narcissism of unbridled entitlement, in which relentless pursuit, injurious always and at times fatal, was carried out without the merest scintilla of compunction or restraint. Diane Schaefer and Richard Farley represent the extreme end of this spectrum, thanks to the sheer inventiveness of their maneuvers and their years-long dedication to their morbid art. Farley was a few months shy of forty when he killed the seven workers at his old firm and fired bullets into Laura Black; Schaefer was in her forties in the early period of her stalking Dr. Brennan. The prior lives of both were devoid of successful intimate relationships; socially, they were loners, unsuccessful at love. Perhaps the approach of middle age, with no history of romantic successes, contributed to the "now-or-never" desperation that drove these two to their stalking. That cannot be the whole story, since there are many people in similar circumstances who never engage in such intrusive, let alone dangerous, behaviors. We can barely diagnose them. We cannot explain them fully. The French have a better word for their behavior: *monomanie*, implying a delusional preoccupation that is strictly limited to a small territory on the psychic map—in essence, a monomania, with the rest of one's mental function remaining free of psychotic distortions.

We end this discussion of stalking with a description of the only other patient I have ever encountered who displayed the de Clérambeault type of stalking behavior—a fifty-year-old divorced physician with one adult child. The latter lived in a different country. For reasons of confidentiality, I have changed relevant names and places. Ingrid, as I shall call her, came from Austria, and in her post-divorce loneliness, she developed a delusional preoccupation with a famous opera baritone. Unlike the classic de Cléram-beault patient, she was well-to-do and of the same social class as the object of her erotomanic love, though his fame still put him a notch above her socially. She would buy a ticket to whatever opera the famous baritone appeared in, traveling to whatever country he would sing in: Germany,

France, Italy, England, the United States, and so on. It was her conviction that her great *Bewunderung* (admiration) for him, coupled with the spirit in her brain, would leap out of her head and instill itself in the baritone's head, enabling him to sing more wonderfully than he could without this invisible transmission from Ingrid, who was somewhere in the audience. She was also convinced that he appreciated her "gift" and loved her as keenly as she loved him. In her imagination, however, he was not at liberty to show this affection, because of his wife's jealousy. Worse yet, Ingrid believed she was being followed by German-speaking people hired by the wife to protect her "turf" and make sure Ingrid "made no trouble for their marriage." Ingrid never approached the baritone, so that, although she followed him—the first half of stalking—she never invaded his privacy. Her delusion had another key feature. If, perchance, while at home, she saw a man standing a hundred yards away from her kitchen window, she assumed it was the baritone, trying as best he could to signal his love to her, which he dared not do any more openly, because of his wife's consuming jealousy. In a way, her erotomanic delusion was quite satisfying: she was not exactly *with* the great baritone, but she was not entirely alone either. In her mind, they were ill-fated lovers, destined to share an intimacy only of the spirit, rather than of the body. I wondered what prompted her to seek treatment. The reason had to do with the more paranoid part of her delusion: those German "hirelings" who made sure she never got all that close to her beloved. If I could do something to shoo them away, perhaps she could get close to the baritone, after all. She pictured his marriage as shaky. She was not far off the mark. A year after I began working with her, the baritone did divorce. Yet, she still never approached him. I had occasion to approach him years later when he sang at the Metropolitan. After the performance, I told him about this woman who felt her spirit leaped into his head, enabling him to do his best. He smiled and said that, as he had no way of knowing how he sang when she was *not* in the audience, since she always was, he hoped she continued. What if having such a loyal fan was a help after all? Ingrid was, of course, different from the types of stalkers we have delineated here. There was none of the "new narcissism" or "new evil." She was a sweet, sad, and lonely woman, whose only possibly narcissistic trait was a grandiose assumption that her secret love of the baritone was the key to his enormous success.

CHAPTER THIRTEEN

SCHOOL SHOOTERS

With depressing regularity, but at intervals that are, of course, not equally spaced, we are electrified by the news of yet another school shooting. Because these shootings occur every so often, but not on schedule, we are taken by surprise each time. This intensifies our shock and horror over yet another atrocity—another evil. School shootings are a particular species within the genus of mass murder. To our discomfiture—and our discredit—America outpaces other countries, not by metaphorical yards or furlongs but by leagues. We are in a different "league," chalking up these atrocities over other countries by a factor of approximately fifty.

I maintain a spreadsheet of mass murderers who have garnered high degrees of attention in the press, ranging from 1857 through the time of this writing, in May of 2018. Currently, these number 333. Among mass murders of all types, the school shooters number twenty-two, or 6.6 percent of the total. These are about evenly distributed, with twelve in the United States and ten in seven other countries. Among mass murderers of whatever type, my file contains only one example from some thirteen nations. I note larger numbers from a few countries: twelve in Canada; six each in Germany, China, and New Zealand; five in France; and four each in England and Sweden. By no means does this give an accurate picture of worldwide mass murder going back to the beginning of the twentieth century, since some cases have occurred, albeit rarely, in more obscure countries. Moreover, large numbers of mass murders occur in the United States that receive little attention in the press, or involve fewer than the three cases the FBI has required since 2013 or the four previously needed before an attack meets an arbitrary standard. Sometimes the victim count is less because of (fortunately) poor marksmanship or some other "failure" on the part of the killer. The latter was the case with one of the few females among the school shooters, Laurie Wasserman-Dann, who, in a Chicago suburb, shot at a group of kindergarten children, wounding five but killing only one, before committing suicide.[1] As previously noted, mass murderers, who include school shooters within their ranks, are overwhelmingly male, accounting for about 97 percent.[2]

Throughout 2018, a number of articles about school shooters sprung up rapidly in the aftermath of the high school rampage in Parkland, Florida, in which nineteen-year-old Nikolas Cruz, expelled from the school the year before because of aggressive behavior, was accused of carrying out a massacre on Valentine's Day in 2018. It is alleged that, using a recently purchased—and easily accessible—semiautomatic rifle, an AR-15, added to his already large collection of at least ten rifles and shotguns, he killed seventeen students before he was finally captured by the police. The "captured-by-the-police" part of the story is the most unusual feature, since the majority of mass murderers, including school shooters, commit suicide as the police close in, or are killed by the police, in what is sometimes called "suicide by cop." Few survive to tell their stories. If these accusations were confirmed, it would appear Cruz chose Valentine's Day as a kind of jealousy-prompted revenge for having been rejected by a girlfriend at the school some months before, when she switched her affections—understandably enough, as it turns out—to another boy. According to published reports, Cruz had earlier been treated for depression, and had cut himself and attempted suicide by drinking gasoline.[3] He was thought to have been affected with the fetal alcohol syndrome (FAS) by a presumably alcoholic mother who had given him up for adoption.[4] If this allegation proves accurate, it may be that FAS was a contributing factor to the unleashing of violence Cruz reportedly committed that day. The disorder has been in the background of a number of other prominent murder cases as predisposing to poor impulse control and to outbursts of violence.[5] If, indeed, present, FAS may also have contributed to Cruz's suicidal ideation and attempts, given the high proportion of persons with the syndrome who (a) die at an average of only thirty-four and (b) whose deaths are caused by suicide in 15 percent of cases, according to recent research by Dr. Carl Bell.[6]

The focus in this chapter is on school shooters whose acts took place in elementary school through high school. Many compilations in the literature include shootings in colleges, as well. Granted that massacres are trag-edies, irrespective of locale or of the victims targeted, there is something particularly heart-wrenching about the slaughter en masse of younger children. This is why the 2012 murder of twenty kindergarteners in Newtown, Connecticut,[7] had, perhaps, an even more devastating impact on the public than the murder five years earlier of thirty-two students and teachers at Virginia Polytechnic Institute and State University,[8] commonly called Virginia Tech. Both of these massacres were carried out by severely autistic men in their early twenties—Adam Lanza in Newtown and Seung-Hui Cho in Virginia—which, as noted earlier, subsequently surrounded autistic persons with undeserved stigma, since they are less prone to violence than are groups of individuals with certain psychiatric disorders. As it turns out, school shootings of either type deserve a place in a book concentrating on forms of "evil" that have manifested themselves with special force in the last half century. School shootings, for example, have been scrupulously recorded and documented since the beginning of the nineteenth century. The same is true for mass murders in general. We have created three relevant graphs: one, showing the growth, by decade, of the population in the United States between 1840 and May of 2018 (again, the time of this writing); another, showing the number of school shootings involving any number of casualties during the same period; and a third, showing the number of deaths inflicted by these shootings. The graphs show the smooth, gradual increase in the American population over the last 188 years, in contrast to the number of school shootings and the number of victims, both of which show a dramatic increase since the 1960s.

For the most part, the school shootings in America throughout the nineteenth and into the first half of the twentieth centuries were highly personal affairs. Deaths and injuries were limited to one, or perhaps two or three persons. The participants knew one another. What precipitated the violence was usually an argument, a sense of outrage over an injustice, or a triangle of jealousy in which one boy killed another over a girl. Of the Seven Deadly Sins enunciated in the year 590 by Pope Gregory I—namely, Pride, Envy, Greed, Sloth, Lust, Anger, and Gluttony—our ancestors who perpetrated school shootings were motivated largely by Anger, Pride, and Envy. The examples seem almost quaint, compared with what we are witnessing in the current era. One can often sympathize with the actors in these small-scale dramas.

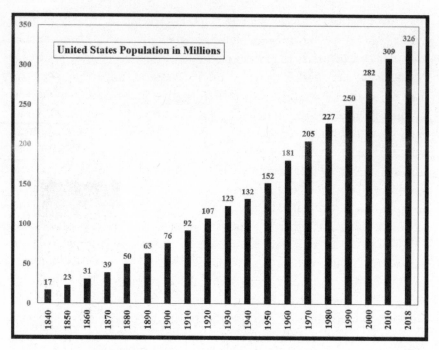

Fig. 13.1. US population (1840-May of 2018).

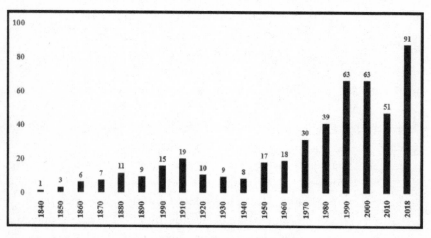

Fig. 13.2. US school shootings (1840-May of 2018).

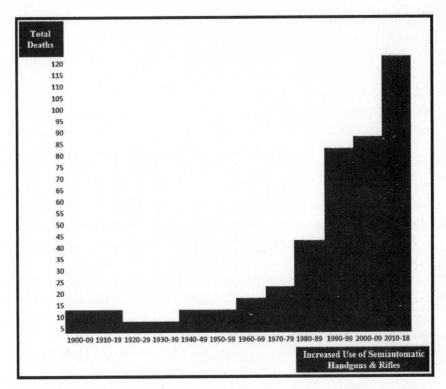

Fig. 13.3. Deaths from US school shootings (1840–May of 2018).

In one early example dating to 1856, a schoolmaster in Florence, Alabama, had a pet sparrow and warned his pupils not to harm it, or else he would murder whoever did it. One of the boys stepped on the bird and killed it. The schoolmaster shortly thereafter strangled the boy to death as he had promised. The boy's father then went to the school and shot the schoolmaster to death.[9]

In a similar example, also prompted by the urge to avenge an injustice, a Mr. McGinnis was the father of a girl who had been expelled from school by her teacher. This was in Knight's Ferry, a small "gold rush" town in central California founded in 1848 by a Dr. William Knight, who had been murdered the very next year. When, in 1867, the father went to his daughter's school to complain, the teacher shot him to death. Once the victim's son learned of this, he went to the school and shot the teacher to death, avenging the murder of his father via what, in the laws of that time, might have been viewed in the gray zone of homicide as a kind of vigilante justice.[10]

A few years later, another school shooting took place, this time, with a more contemporary quality, centered on anger in a disobedient and perhaps antisocial pupil who "got even" when punished by his teacher. A twenty-year-old, Thomas Squires, from the small town of Agency, Montana, near the Crow Indian Reservation, fatally shot his teacher, Mr. Hayes, following ejection from the school. Shades of the rampage allegedly committed by Nikolas Cruz, except that Cruz, having been expelled the year before, might have intended to kill everybody there, not only a teacher.[11]

Jealousy was behind the 1904 Chicago murder of one teenage student by another. Two sixteen-year-olds had been fighting for months over a girl. The rivalry ended when Henry Shaze pushed Paul Jelick to the ground and then shot him to death with a revolver.[12]

Even throughout the first two-thirds of the twentieth century, school shootings involved only a very small number of deaths and were generally confined to situations in which the participants knew one another, and in which the perpetrator had been nurturing a grudge of some sort against the victim. The first large-scale incident of a shooter killing many, as opposed to one or two persons, and at random, not knowing any of the victims personally, was that of Charles Whitman, an engineering student at the University of Texas, in August of 1966. Yet, that was a college shooting, not a primary school affair. Besides having first stabbed to death his mother and wife, Whitman fatally shot three people in a tower on the university's campus. Then, for approximately ninety-six minutes, he randomly fired at students on the ground from an observation deck on the tower's twenty-eighth floor. There were eleven additional deaths, which included an unborn child, and thirty-one others were wounded before Whitman was killed by police.[13] Looking back, we can see this incident as the inauguration, so to speak, of the massacres of random persons by a shooter—more often a college, rather than a high school, student—using a semiautomatic weapon.

Although primary school shootings greatly outnumber those associated with colleges, as is noted in the larger compilations of such data,[14] statistics on both are remarkably similar, showing dramatic and abrupt increases beginning in the late 1970s and surging upward since 1980.

In either setting, the readily available and easily acquired semiautomatic pistols and rifles that became available increasingly in the late 1960s and early 1970s have played a major role in these shootings, especially in the large-scale massacres. This is by now a commonly held view, as echoed in the remark of a journalist: "not surprisingly, given the ready availability of firearms in the United States, the phenomenon [of school shootings] is overwhelmingly American."[15] Furthermore, it is not just any American students perpetrating school shootings. The great majority are American white male teenagers, most of whom, as author Justin Peters pointed out, had studied the Columbine massacre of April 1999, deriving inspiration, if that is an acceptable term, or, at least, a morbid kind of justification from the comments of the two perpetrators, Eric Harris and Dylan Klebold.[16]

Among primary school and high school, as well as college, shooters, there are some discernible differences between those who have killed just one person—or one person and then themselves in a "murder-suicide" situation—and those who have killed larger numbers of victims. Those who killed only one victim often did so for reasons we find more understandable, on a basic, human level: arguments, jealousy, anger at a teacher's seeming unfairness, or being bullied by other students. In some such killings, there was little more than youthful bravado, coupled with an accidental shooting. These were the same sorts of motives behind the school shootings in the nineteenth century and earlier years of the last century. Anger that culminated in murderous rage was the main underlying emotion, in young persons who were not otherwise known to be mentally ill. Those who killed larger numbers of victims, in contrast, were usually severely disturbed emotionally—and were often recognized as mentally ill by relatives, acquaintances, or school authorities well before their murderous outbursts. These school shooters, understandably, get more attention from the media and contribute inadvertently to the public's impression that mental illness is *the* primary antecedent factor behind these tragic events. There is more to be said about this further on, but, at the moment, it will be instructive to look more closely at several examples of *small-scale* (fewer than four deaths) versus *large-scale* shootings in recent years, specifically, the years following the Texas Tower massacre in 1966.

SCHOOL SHOOTINGS INVOLVING FEW DEATHS

In Northlake, Illinois, some nine months after the Texas Tower massacre, eighteen-year-old Michael Pisarski killed seventeen-year-old Christine Mitchell in her high school in May of 1967. The summer before, they had considered themselves engaged. Pisarski had given Mitchell a diamond ring, which she ordinarily wore on the ring finger of her left hand—but, in April of the following year, when Pisarski went to his fiancée's home, her brother handed him back the ring, along with other gifts he had given her. Her mother then told Pisarski he was not permitted to speak with her or see her at all. This was apparently not Mitchell's idea, since she phoned him a week later, told him she still loved him, and arranged to meet with him in a week's time. Pisarski and she went for a ride on that day. Three days later, however, when Pisarski returned to her home, her mother once more told him he was not to see her daughter again. A week later, on May 3, Pisarski went to Mitchell's school—from which he had dropped out—and confronted her. There is some uncertainty about what followed. She told him she still wanted to marry him, or so he testified, whereupon he raised the pistol he had brought with him and pointed it toward his head, as if to commit suicide. He claimed he had told her there would just be more trouble because of her family's opposition. If his commentary in court is true, she then grabbed the gun, and it discharged, killing her. Pisarski had no previous criminal record. He had been depressed before the shooting, but that seemed related more to the strong opposition on the part of his fiancée's family. The court viewed the event as one of murder, and he was sentenced to thirty to sixty-five years in prison.[17]

In Littleton, Colorado, seventeen years before the Columbine massacre for which Littleton became instantly well-known, fourteen-year-old Jason Rocha, carrying a .38-caliber revolver, had gone gopher hunting with his friend Andy near their junior high school. Later, as they entered the school, two other boys, John and Scott, were coming out. Rocha pointed his revolver at John and said, perhaps imitating a police officer, "Freeze!" When John said the gun was loaded, Rocha pointed it toward Scott. The gun discharged, killing Scott. Andy and Rocha then ran away, not before urging the other two to say it was an accident. Rocha later phoned the sheriff's office and was taken into custody. Though Jason Rocha had no prior history of violent behavior, he did suffer from depression, which was considered due in part to family neglect and abusiveness. Though several expert witnesses argued that the boy should be remanded to a secure adolescent treatment center, the court sentenced him to twelve years in prison.[18]

In Lewistown, a town of barely six thousand people in the center of Montana, a fourteen-year-old schoolboy, Kristofer Hans, angry that he had received a failing grade from his French teacher, Ms. LaVonne Simonfy, barged into the school armed with a .44 Magnum and knocked on the door of her classroom one morning in December of 1986, asking her to come out. He had spoken to a classmate the day before, telling him, "I'm going to blow Simonfy's head off!" The teacher did come to the door, and he did shoot her to death—but it wasn't Ms. Simonfy. It was a substitute teacher, Henrietta Smith, who had been asked at the last moment to replace the regular teacher. Hans also fired at the vice principal, Mr. John Moffatt. Moffatt, who survived, was wounded so severely and lost so much blood that when the priest came shortly afterward to give him last rites at the hospital, he told his wife, Maggie, to go home and pay their life insurance policy, assuming he would not live out the day. Hans, as it turned out, was a reasonably bright student but was doing poorly at school at a time when his parents had divorced. It emerged later that he hated his father, who, albeit a school psychologist, was as stern and unsympathetic as his mother was relaxed and permissive. Hans had been warned that, unless his grades improved, he would be sent to live in Wyoming with his father. This seemed to fuel his rage at the French teacher, as though it were her "fault" he might have to go and live with the hated parent. There is an unusual twist to this story. Six years later, Diane Sawyer from ABC's *Primetime Live* asked Moffatt if he would like to meet Hans, who was now serving two life sentences in prison. Moffatt agreed, and when they met, the young man cried uncontrollably, expressing remorse for what he had done. Having been for so many years, in the eyes of Moffatt and his wife and children, a monster of evil, he now became a human being.[19]

In West Palm Beach, Florida, two middle-school boys argued outside their school in late January of 1997 over a wristwatch, worth about forty dollars, that fourteen-year-old Tronneal Mangum had borrowed from his friend John Pierre Kamel, also fourteen. For unclear reasons, Mangum refused to return the watch to Kamel. During the dispute, Mangum took a

.38-caliber pistol from his pocket and shot Kamel in the chest, killing him. Neither youngster had any history of violent behavior before. At the trial, which concluded about a year later, there had been testimony from another pupil at the school to the effect that on the school bus the day before the murder, Mangum had told another boy he was going to use his gun to shoot Kamel. The idea of possible "premeditation" may have led the court to impose a life sentence—which made Mangum the youngest person in Palm Beach ever to be ordered to spend the rest of his life in prison. His sentence was later reduced to forty years, of which he had already served almost half. At the time of the trial, though the original sentence was draconian in its severity, the judge decried the scourge of guns and violence, noting that violent felonies by juveniles had increased markedly in Palm Beach during the prior year. He also lamented the glorification of violence in general among young males—worsened by the easy acquisition of guns.[20]

Not long after, in the fall of 1997, another teenage school shooter made headlines—this time in Pearl, Mississippi, a suburb of Jackson. The shooter was Luke Woodham, armed with a lever-action Marlin model 336/.30-30 hunting rifle, concealed under his trench coat. He entered Pearl High School and shot to death his former girlfriend Christina Menefee and her friend Lydia Kaye Dew before he himself was subdued by the assistant principal, who had then retrieved a .45 pistol from his truck and shouted at him to stop. The school deaths were thus two. There had been, however, an earlier death. That morning, Woodham had bludgeoned and stabbed his mother to death before driving her car to the school. Shortly before, Woodham had written a note to a friend, stating, "I am not insane, I am angry. I killed because people like me are mistreated every day. I did this to show society: Push us, and we will push back. . . . All throughout my life, I was ridiculed, always beaten, always hated." He was made fun of mostly for being overweight, but also at home—especially after his parents' divorce when he was seven. His mother, Mary Ann, had allegedly been overbearing, abusive, and humiliating, telling him he would never amount to anything. Woodham had become part of what was described as a satanic cult, headed by Grant Boyette, who, along with five other boys, were arrested for possibly conspiring with Woodham to commit the murders. Sentenced at his trial, Woodham converted back to Christianity and wrote a confession to a minister, David Wilkerson, hoping he could give testimony

and somehow help with Wilkerson's ministry. There had been other manifestations of Woodham's festering rage. He and Boyette had once beaten
Woodham's dog, set it on fire, and thrown it in a pond. Woodham had
written, "I'll never forget the sound of her breaking under my might. I hit
her so hard I knocked the fur off her neck . . . it was true beauty." After his
conviction, he spoke to the courtroom, saying that his crime was "sick and
evil." He added, "If they could have given the death penalty in this case,
I deserve it." What the judge handed down was not the death penalty but
two life sentences and seven twenty-year sentences for those Woodham had
wounded at the school.[21] Though defense attorneys argued that Woodham
was suffering from borderline personality disorder, it was clear that he was
not legally insane and was perfectly able to stand trial.

SCHOOL SHOOTINGS INVOLVING MANY DEATHS

A gifted but otherwise highly disturbed graduate student in physics, Gang
Lu, originally from mainland China, was enraged and embittered that he
had not received a prestigious dissertation prize after he was awarded his
PhD at the University of Iowa. He sought revenge. As a young man of
twenty-eight, with no criminal record of any kind, it was easy for him to
obtain pistol permits. He purchased two, including a .38-caliber revolver,
shortly after earning his doctorate. In preparation for the execution-style
murders he now sought to carry out, he wrote four letters to various news
organizations and another in Chinese. None has ever been published. On
November 1, 1991, Lu quickly shot to death the chairman of the physics
department, a physics professor, an associate professor of physics, and
then his rival—a fellow graduate student and former roommate, also from
China. The latter, Linhua Shan, was the one who did win the coveted
prize and the monetary award that went with it. Shan was as well-liked
and outgoing as was Lu the opposite. Lu was described by those who knew
him via a long catalog of pejorative descriptors: combative, argumentative, envious, bitter, ill to live with, shy, a loner, quiet, brooding, resentful,
slovenly, a know-it-all, self-centered, nitpicking, abrasive, rigid, aloof,
hypercritical, hotheaded, a spoilsport, arrogant, haughty, paranoid, and
schizoid. He spent much time watching pornographic and violent films.

Though nothing of substance is known about his upbringing, he apparently had three normal siblings back in China.[22]

Of college age when he committed his murders, Patrick Purdy had not been a student. His victims were pupils in the same Cleveland Elementary School in Stockton, California, that he had attended some fifteen years before when he was ten. Though the Vietnam War had just started when he was born in 1964, he developed a withering hatred of Asians, particularly the Vietnamese, specifically those who had managed to get to the United States after the war. He hated them ostensibly because he believed they were robbing native-born Americans of jobs. Thus, when, in January of 1989, he went in the school playground, he used his semiautomatic rifle—itself, the Chinese Type-56 of Asian origin but actually modeled after the AK-47—and opened fire randomly, killing five children between the ages of six and nine. Only one was Vietnamese; the others had come from Cambodia. He then shot himself to death with a pistol. Before the rampage, he had burned his car with a Molotov cocktail in a beer bottle, which strongly suggests he intended to commit suicide once he had killed as many children as he could. Purdy had been a loner and a drifter, working briefly as a welder but often getting fired. His antecedents were not promising. When Purdy was two, his mother divorced his US Army veteran father after he tried to kill her with a gun. Having remarried when Purdy was five, she divorced again four years later. She moved to the Sacramento area, where she was investigated by Child Protective Services for abusiveness. Purdy gave as good as he got, punching his mother in the face when he was thirteen, after which he lived as a drifter and prostitute. On one occasion, he was arrested for soliciting sex from a police officer. A childhood alcoholic who was addicted to drugs, he spent only a little time in high school and was considered mildly intellectually disabled. He was arrested many times for drug possession and dealing, armed robbery, and firing a semiautomatic pistol at trees. He identified with white supremacists but now and again made suicide attempts, which led to a psychiatric examination in which he was viewed as a danger to himself and to others. Bigotry, a mechanism favored by the weak to feel strong and by the socially lowly to feel superior, was not confined in Purdy just to Asians. He was said to have developed a deep hatred for everybody. After the massacre, *Time* magazine asked the prescient question, "Why could Purdy . . . who had

Often misrepresented as mad, Roman emperor Gaius Caesar (24–41 CE), known as Caligula, was an egomaniacal psychopath with predilections for rape, torture, and murder. Sexual sadists have always existed, but, prior to the late 1960s, it was uncommon for them to kill. *From J. Eugene Reed, ed.,* The Lives of the Roman Emperors and Their Associates from Julius Caesar (B.C. 100) to Agustulus (A.D. 476), *vol. 1 (Philadelphia, PA: Gebbie, 1883).*

While serial killers before the "new evil" era were few and far between, female serial murderers have always been exceptionally rare, especially the sexually sadistic type. Countess Erzsébet Báthory de Ecsed (1560–1614) of Hungary abducted, tortured, and killed hundreds of young women for paraphilic purposes, sometimes bathing in their blood, hoping thereby to preserve her beauty.

An early female serial killer of the Munchausen syndrome by proxy variety, Germany's Gesche Gottfried (1785–1831) used rat poison to murder fifteen people—spouses, children, and friends—when she was between the ages of twenty-eight and forty-two, motivated by the sympathy these losses brought her. *Illustration by Rudolf Friedrich Suhrlandt (1830).*

Intimate partner murders prior to the 1960s were expedient and uninventive, generally motivated by jealousy, desperation, or desire to eliminate an impediment to a new romance. In 1906, Chester Gillette (1883–1908), a philanderer who dreaded settling down, pushed his pregnant lover from a canoe, clubbed her with a tennis racket or an oar, and left her to drown. *Portrait by Daniel Zintmaster (1906).*

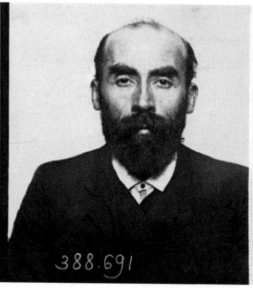

France's real-life Bluebeard, Henri Désiré Landru (1869–1922), lured ten well-heeled widows, via newspaper ads, and gained access to their wealth before killing them and dismembering and burning their bodies. The "practical" motivations for his crimes are typical of serial killing prior to the era of "new evil." *Mugshot from the Paris Préfecture de Police (1909).*

Albert Fish (1870–1936), a psychopath who was also influenced by religious delusions and hallucinations, savagely raped, murdered, and cannibalized children. While he shared many characteristics with sexually sadistic serial killers of the post-1960s era, serial murder in the latter epoch has rarely been associated with psychosis. *Police mugshot (1903).*

A bona fide psychopathic, sexually sadistic serial killer predating the "new evil" era was Gordon Northcott (1906–1930), who raped, tortured, shot, and axed as many as twenty young males he dragged to a chicken coop on his family's farm, dissolving the corpses in quicklime. *Police mugshot (1928).*

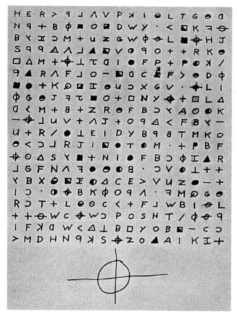

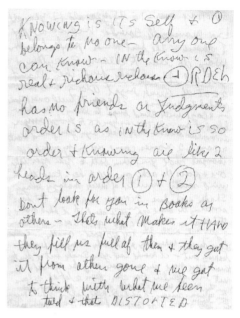

This 340-symbol cipher created by the Zodiac Killer in 1969 has gone unsolved for nearly fifty years. The "mastermind" brand of killer, willing to kill in pursuit of attention and a sense of superiority, is a post-1960s phenomenon.

This rambling letter from cult leader Charles Manson (1934–2017) reflects his years of mind-altering drug use and poor education. With its pseudophilosophical egotism masquerading as deep truth, it is emblematic of the era of "new evil."

In this original painting, John Wayne Gacy (1942–1994), who dressed up as a clown named Pogo or Patches to entertain at children's parties, reveals his actual nature. He brutally raped, tortured, and killed at least thirty-three boys and young men. *Courtesy of a private collection.*

The terrifying contents of the "murder kit" carried by Ted Bundy, who ferociously raped and murdered at least thirty young females in seven states between 1974 and 1978. *Courtesy of Kevin M. Sullivan.*

In this poem by Arthur Shawcross (1945–2008), the Genesee River Killer, he describes an idyllic, unspoiled nature scene that must give way to "winter's sleep." The symbolism is unsettling, in that the serial murderer's criminal career began with him luring a ten-year-old boy into a wooded area, like the one he describes, before sexually assaulting him and beating him to death.

WITHIN THE WOODLANDS THERE IS A MEADOW
ALIVE WITH COLOR'S OF CRUSHED VELVET GREEN
OBJECT'S DRIFTING THROUGH THE CENTER OF SHADOWS
IN MOVEMENT OVER A SLOWLY WANDERING STREAM.

THE MANY COLORFUL BUTTERFLIES
ARE DARTING AMONG THE WILD FLOWERS
AND GRASSES UNDER A SAPPHIRE SKY
FLIRTING IN NATURES BOWER'S.

ALL THE TREE'S OF THESE WOODS ARE IN RUBY REDS,
GOLDEN YELLOWS, PUMPKIN ORANGE AND SEA GREEN
SHOWING THE BRILLIANCE OF GOD'S FLOWER BEDS,
PLUS A BREEZE BLOWING SLOWLY OVER ALL THAT IS SEEN.

WHAT WITH THE ABUNDANT LIFE THAT ABOUNDS,
YOU MAY SEE CREATURES ONLY TRYING TO SURVIVE
IN AN AREA UNTOUCHED BY MAN AND HIS HOUNDS,
FOR ONLY THEY HAVE A CHANCE TO STAY ALIVE.

KEEP THE POLYCHROMATIC OF BRIGHNESS OF DEEP
INTENSE RICHNESS FOR IT TO BE SEEN EVERMORE
IN GETTING READY FOR WINTER'S SLEEP
JUST AS IT'S DONE MANY EON'S BEFORE,....

BY ARTHUR JOHN SHAWCROSS

Ottis Elwood Toole
Barbecue Sauce

2 cups tomato sauce ¼ cup Vinegar
¼ cup Vegetable Oil ½ brown
Sugar, 1 large onion chopped, 3
cloves of garlic minced,
½ tsp chili powder, 1 tbsp
Worcestershire sauce 2 tsp. dry
mustard, 1 tsp dried oregano,
½ tsp salt, pepper 3 cup
Vodka.

Combine all ingredients in
medium sauce pan, simmer
over low heat stir Occasionally
25 to 30 minutes.

Here, drifter and serial killer Ottis Toole (1947–1996), the criminal partner of Henry Lee Lucas (1936–2001), records his barbecue recipe for use in acts of cannibalism. *Courtesy of a private collection.*

Here, rapist and serial murderer Danny Rolling (1954–2006) depicts his eight victims beneath the shadow of the Grim Reaper. The provocative offender dismembered victims, posing them in positions designed to shock others. This gave his homicides a decidedly "new" quality. *Courtesy of a private collection.*

Part of a letter by serial killer Tommy Lynn Sells (1964–2014), in which he writes, "I really hate society. I don't hate everyone in society. . . . I don't believe I was born this way. I believe I was made this way." He speaks to the question of whether the inclination to commit serial murder is inborn, the result of adverse experiences, or some mixture thereof.

The first of two disturbing drawings by the serial rapist and murderer Richard Ramirez (1960–2013), who was dubbed the "Night Stalker." Here, he morbidly plays with popular song titles, pairing them with an image of a dismembered victim. With his wanton depravity, misogyny, Satan worship, and egocentricity, Ramirez embodied the era of "new evil." *Courtesy of a private collection.*

Ramirez depicts a "trophy collection" containing the upper half of a female corpse, its arms and eyes removed, and throat apparently slit. The crumpled paper that reads, "Love you mom," lends the sketch a vaguely Oedipal feel, which was also seen in many of his crimes. *Courtesy of a private collection.*

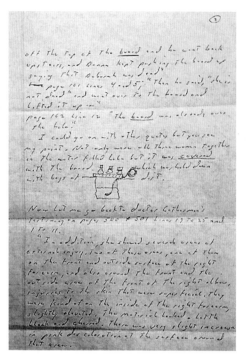

Gary M. Heidnik (1943–1999) illustrates the pit in which he kept six sex slaves, hoping to sire a line of loyal children. He callously describes how one captive died from "electro-thermal injury" after he filled the pit with water and applied live currents from a stripped extension cord. *Courtesy of a private collection.*

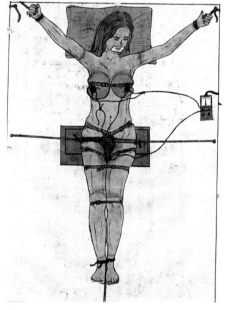

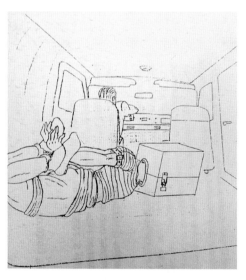

A sketch by sexually sadistic serial killer David Parker Ray (1939–2002), who filled notebooks with depictions of his methods for abduction and torture. Here, he is shown driving toward his "Toy Box" with an abductee wearing the head box he constructed to disorient victims.

This second piece by Ray depicts a woman in a mock crucifixion pose being subjected to torture by electrocution. The image emblematizes the era of "new evil," in which numerous male offenders displayed desires to dominate, objectify, and brutalize women in the wake of the sexual revolution. *Courtesy of the Geberth files.*

been arrested for such offenses as selling weapons and attempted robbery, walk into a gun shop in Sandy, Ore., and leave with an AK-47 under his arm? . . . Weapons . . . which have no purpose other than killing human beings."[23]

In 1998, just after spring break in Westside Middle School, near Jonesboro, Arkansas—a city of about seventy-five thousand—an eleven-year-old boy, Andrew Golden, sounded the school's fire alarm, with the result that some eighty-seven students and nine teachers evacuated the schoolhouse. That left them prey to Golden and his thirteen-year-old friend, Mitchell Johnson, who, armed with nine weapons, shot to death a teacher and four students. Their weapons included semiautomatic, as well as bolt-action, rifles and a variety of pistols. Golden had taken the weapons from his own home and also from his grandfather's—along with two thousand rounds of ammunition. The boys fled the school toward a van they had parked a half mile away, in which they hoped to make their escape. Johnson was the more troubled of the two boys. His parents divorced when he was seven, and, not long after, his mother, a prison guard, married an inmate of the prison. It was said that Johnson had been sexually abused when, around the time of the divorce, he had been in daycare. Later, he had been charged with molesting a girl of three, though the case was dropped because of his age. Golden also came from a working-class family. Both his parents were postal workers. Having been given a gun by his father when he was merely six, he had become quite familiar with firearms. Golden had once killed a classmate's cat. Both boys were known as bullies at school and aspired, though white, to join the Bloods, a black gang. They also abused marijuana. Johnson had a fascination with guns and at one point threatened to kill his former girlfriend, a sixth grader who had broken up with him. Because of their young age, the court was limited as to what was permissible in the way of punishment, though, had they been adults, the prosecutor might have sought the death penalty. As it was, they were both sentenced to confinement till they reached twenty-one. It outraged the public that so light a sentence could be given for so egregious a crime. Exactly a decade after the massacre, Golden, now a free man of twenty-four, then applied, true to his nature, for a concealed weapon. He had in the meantime changed his name, but the police were able to identify him via fingerprints and deny the request. Johnson's subsequent trouble with the law was more serious:

two years after gaining his freedom, he was arrested for carrying a weapon and marijuana possession. A year later, he was arrested again, this time for theft, marijuana possession, and identity fraud. Although sentenced to eighteen years, he was released in 2015 after serving about seven years, and remanded to a drug rehabilitation program.[24]

The story of Kipland Kinkel, usually called just "Kip," is one of the most poignant in this dreadful catalog of school shooters. His history touches on all of the important elements: mental illness, parental irresponsibility, adolescent impulsivity, semiautomatic weapons, animal killing, and the inadequacy of the legal system. Kinkel was the younger of two children in Springfield, Oregon, a middle-class, medium-sized town—population sixty thousand—midway between Washington and California. Both his parents were schoolteachers. Born in 1982, he was hyperactive early on, and treated for a time with Ritalin. Dyslexic and considered immature, he was made to repeat the first grade. He was given to tantrums and violent behavior, once tossing a rock at a passing car. Kinkel showed an interest at an early age in firearms and explosives. His father discouraged this at first but later gave in and bought him a .22 rifle and a 9mm Glock pistol when Kinkel was fifteen. He developed morbid fascinations with violence and hurting or killing animals. He shot squirrels, for example, and liked to see the blood spurt out from the dying creatures. He built bombs, which he kept hidden in his footlocker at home. In his early teens, he was seen by a psychiatrist, who viewed him as depressed and prescribed Prozac. Kinkel began to abuse alcohol and marijuana. At fifteen, he was threatened with expulsion from school after having brought in a loaded handgun—a Beretta Model 90 .32-caliber pistol, which another pupil had stolen from his father and sold to Kinkel for $110. The boy's father reported the missing weapon to the police, after which the school offered a list of students who might have been responsible for taking it. Kinkel was confronted, and confessed. He was arrested but then released from custody and taken home by his father. Hours later, at home in the kitchen, his father warned him that if he did not change his behavior, he would be sent to military school. Those were his father's last words because Kinkel then went to his bedroom, where he fetched his Ruger .22 semiautomatic rifle and then the bullets from his parents' bedroom. Returning to the kitchen, he then fatally shot his father in the back of his head, covering the body with a sheet. When his mother returned from school at suppertime, he told her he loved her—and then shot her to death with six bullets, also covering her body with a sheet. In a perverse twist to the already morbid scene, when the police arrived later that night, they found that Kinkel had been listening to the "Liebestod" from Wagner's *Tristan und Isolde*—from the scene in which Isolde sings the erotic "Love-Death" aria over her lover's dead body. Kinkel left a note explaining why he had killed his parents, stating, "I just got two felonies on my record. My parents can't take that! It would destroy them." He added that he had been hearing voices in his head and said, "I have to kill people. . . . I have no other choice." These were what forensic specialists call "command hallucinations." As it turned out, however, Kinkel had already been experiencing hallucinations on and off for a number of years, though he never acknowledged this. The next morning, May 21, 1998, Kinkel drove his mother's car to the school, armed with four concealed weapons, including the semiautomatic rifle, killing two students and wounding two dozen more. Arrested and convicted, he was sentenced at the trial the following year to 111 years in prison, without parole. He apologized at trial, and the defense tried to mount an insanity defense, but this could go nowhere, since Kinkel had clearly understood what he had done was wrong, and had included in his note at the time that "I'm so sorry. I am a horrible son. I wish I had been aborted. It's not their fault. My head doesn't work right. Goddamn these VOICES inside my head. But I have to kill people. I don't know why." Kinkel's sister testified that in middle school, he had become more withdrawn and dressed all in black. Whereas the psychologist who had interviewed him the year before the murders felt he was depressed and preoccupied with guns and explosives, with instances of violently "acting out," he did not see Kinkel as psychotic. Later, Dr. Orin Bolstad, the psychologist who interviewed the shooter extensively during the trial, concluded that Kinkel was distinctly psychotic, suffering from a paranoid condition that seemed a prelude to schizophrenia. Some of Kinkel's delusions were bizarre, and thus a stronger indicator of incipient schizophrenia, such as his fear that the Chinese were poised to invade America—hence Kinkel's storing of explosives under his house so as to be "prepared"—or thoughts that there were "chips" implanted in his head by the government. Kinkel reported auditory hallucinations that commented, "You are a stupid piece of shit . . . not worth anything." A psychiatrist, Dr. William Sack, similarly diagnosed Kinkel as psychotic: probably "schizoaffective" or "paranoid schizophrenic." Yet another expert witness revealed that, in Kinkel's extended family, there were multiple cases of mental illness, including schizophrenia. The judge at the trial concluded that the protection of society was of greater importance than the possible reformation or rehabilitation of any individual defendant.[25] Not much was said at trial about the effects of marijuana abuse, though it is known that marijuana, especially in adolescents, can either produce a schizophrenia-like psychosis, with prominent paranoid features, or else effect the earlier emergence of a hereditary schizophrenia that might not have surfaced till the early twenties.[26]

The mass murder of thirteen persons carried out by Eric Harris and Dylan Klebold at Colorado's Columbine High School in 1999 served as a benchmark against which other school shootings were to be compared—until, that is, the even more deadly school shooting in Parkland, Florida, in 2018.[27] As a newspaper reported recently, the especial dreadfulness of the Columbine shooting served as an "improbable inspiration for future mass murders"—given that a dozen-and-a-half subsequent school attacks were considered linked to the Columbine massacre. These included the attacks at Virginia Tech and Sandy Hook Elementary School, the perpetrators of which were obsessed with Columbine and which both involved higher numbers of deaths.[28] In the immediate aftermath of the Columbine massacre, it was widely thought that the perpetrators were motivated primarily by having been bullied by the other students and that they had styled themselves as "outsiders"—goths or part of some Trench Coat Mafia—determined to get back at their tormentors. Dave Cullen, in his book published a decade later, while acknowledging that bullying did occur, provides us with a more accurate and compelling explanation.[29] Harris and Klebold had been planning for a whole year to stage a much more deadly massacre, which they hoped to carry out on the anniversary of the April 19, 1995, massacre at the Alfred P. Murrah Federal Building in Oklahoma City, for which Timothy McVeigh was executed six years later. Unable to complete their dream of far outdoing the 168 deaths at the Murrah building, on the nineteenth, they settled for what they considered to be an equally satisfying date, April 20, the 110th anniversary of Hitler's birthday. As Cullen reminds us, shooting was not even their preferred method. They had planted propane bombs in the school cafeteria, in hopes of killing perhaps six hundred people, using their semiautomatic guns merely to kill those who managed to survive the bomb blast. More bombs were placed in their cars, presumably to finish off those who somehow even endured the shooting—but the bombs failed to detonate. The two killers were alike in their desire to murder on a historical scale, yet, they differed markedly in their psychological makeups. Harris, the mastermind and initiator of the massacre, could be outwardly "nice" but was cold, calculating, and filled with hatred. He met Dr. Robert Hare's criteria for psychopathy, described earlier in this volume, with his grandiosity, exploitativeness, callousness, pathological lying, and lack of remorse—that is, extreme narcissistic personality traits, along with an utter contempt for the feelings of others.[30] In Cullen's words, Harris was a "killer without a conscience." He was also sadistic. Harris appeared to revere the Nazis and often gave Nazi salutes, which irritated the other students—and probably fueled their bullying. Psychopathy and sadism, however, are personality abnormalities, not symptom disorders, like depression, nor psychotic illnesses, like schizophrenia. Klebold, in contrast, though also filled with rage and hatred, was depressed. The other students *had* bullied the two. One threw a cup of fecal matter at the two; some tossed ketchup packets at them. Others called them "faggots." This led Klebold to write, "You've been giving us shit for years. You're fucking gonna pay for all this shit!" He was of quite a different disposition than his compassionate parents, who were both pacifists. The bullying may have led Klebold to ally himself with Harris, as a way of "getting even" with bullies; Harris seemed more indifferent to it. His hatred and desire for revenge were more related to his underlying "malignant" narcissism. After the massacre, Harris and Klebold returned to the school library, where they killed most of their victims, and both then shot themselves to death, Klebold using his semiautomatic pistol, and Harris, his shotgun.[31]

In October of 2002, at the University of Arizona nursing school in Tucson, forty-one-year-old US Army veteran Robert Flores shot to death three of his teachers and then himself, using one of the five guns he had brought with him. He had been a licensed practical nurse but was studying to achieve the higher rank of registered nurse. A divorced man with two children, he was also in debt and having trouble making child support payments. He had been in a state of depression over these failures but was now facing a third: dropping out of school because of his flunking grades. Flores was more than depressed. As everyone who knew him could attest, he was angry, belligerent, intimidating, rude, and boastful about his car-rying a concealed weapon. Two of his victims expressed their fear about him to their husbands, and one of them, Robin Rogers, had even asked the members of her church to pray for her protection from Flores. The murders were premeditated. Flores had written a twenty-two-page suicide note, which he had mailed to the local paper, headed with the phrase "Greetings from the dead." He mentioned in the note that he was well aware of being depressed, but "even with treatment, it will not change my future." His anger was directed specifically at his teachers, not at his fellow students, some of whom he chased away, reassuring them he was not going to harm them. Ironically, his third victim, nurse Cheryl McGaffic, had been scheduled to teach a course that afternoon entitled "Death and Dying." One of her students commented that, had she not been killed just before the lecture, "she would be counseling us right now how to cope with this whole situation."[32]

Though dead for the past three-quarters of a century, Hitler seems not to have lost his allure for the sadistic class. As witness, the sad but intriguing case of Jeffrey Weise, who killed nine people and then himself, five of his victims students at Minnesota's Red Lake High School, in the spring of 2005. A Native American of the Ojibwe tribe, raised on the Red Lake Indian Reservation, not far from the Canadian border, Weise styled himself as "Native Nazi"—in reaction, it would seem, to the outrage he felt toward the schoolmates who had picked on him for his odd behavior and, perhaps, also to the unfairness he felt he had had to endure as a Native American in a predominantly white country. In addition, his personal life throughout his sixteen years had been little more than a succession of trag-edies. Weise's parents had not been married, and, before he was born, the two separated. When he was three months old, for reasons not clear, his mother, Joanne Weise, was forced by her parents to give the baby into the care of the father. Three years later, however, she reclaimed her son, though she was allegedly alcoholic, and both emotionally and physically abusive toward him. The next year, she began living with a man who also reportedly subjected the child to abuse. When Jeff was eight, his father shot himself to death. Then, two years later, Joanne was in a car accident and suffered serious brain damage. Jeff then moved from Minneapolis to the Red Lake Reservation, where he was under the care of his paternal grandmother. School was a struggle. He had failing grades, was truant, and was taunted and bullied. Partly, this was due to him being withdrawn. He was also quite tall and overweight, always dressing in black. He disliked the reservation, complained about the rampant alcoholism there, and became depressed, suicidal, and prone to self-cutting. A year before the shooting, he was hospitalized for depression and treated with Prozac. He drew pictures of skeletons and talked all the time about death. His anger was not confined to himself. He told others, "It'd be cool if I shot up a school." He wrote blogs on a site frequented by neo-Nazis and called himself *Todesengel*—"Angel of Death." His admiration for Hitler was based partly on what he supposed had been the "courage" to take on larger nations, perhaps unware that Hitler's fatal move was to attack Russia. He was also attracted to Hitler's obsession with "racial purity" and objected to those who, on the reservation, disagreed with his idea that the Ojibwe should not mix with other races. In a prelude to the school massacre, Jeff first shot to death his grandfather, who was a policeman on the reservation, and the grandfather's female companion. Jeff stole his grandfather's police-issued firearms, then drove to the school, where he fatally shot an unarmed security guard and a teacher before killing five students, all aged fourteen or fifteen years. He then took his own life. Though persons investigating the incident could not determine the precise motive or immediate precipitant for the rampage, it was discovered that Jeff had very recently watched a film about a Columbine-style school massacre. That may have had something to do with the timing of the incident, but, after all, Jeff had been brooding about a school massacre and about suicide long before.[33]

As we have already seen from the foregoing vignettes of school shooters, singular and multiple, adolescent or young adult, they are a psychologically strange lot: a few grossly psychotic, the others with marked disturbances in personality, usually with paranoid and narcissistic features. Few are as strange, with motivations less recognizable, than Charles C. Roberts IV. A Pennsylvania truck driver who served a number of Amish farms in the Nickel Mines hamlet of Lancaster County, Roberts was one of the few school shooters who was married. There was no prior history of psychiatric illness or of criminal offenses. He and his wife, Marie, had three children, and a fourth, a daughter, died shortly after birth. The latter event loomed large in the tragedy that followed. Roberts, at thirty-two, had made elaborate preparations for the torture and sexual molestation of young girls and for the school shooting he was about to commit. He brought with him several guns, along with a tube of lubricant—for use on his penis, not the guns. He claimed he had molested two young relatives twenty years earlier and now dreamed of sexually abusing young girls again. Or so he said, for, in the aftermath of the murders, no corroboration of his molestation as a twelve-year-old could be made. At all events, on the morning of October 2, 2006, he approached the West Nickel Mines School, an Amish institution, and ordered all the girls to line up against the chalkboard but allowed the boys, a pregnant woman, and three parents with their children to leave. He then shot to death five of the girls, who ranged in age from six to thirteen, wounding five others before finally shooting himself to death as the police were approaching. Among his guns was a Springfield XD semiautomatic pistol, advertised by its manufacturer as a "premiere concealed-carry firearm," with a four-and-a-half-inch barrel, affordably priced at $599.99. He did not sexually molest any of his victims, as he had seemingly been planning to do. Roberts left four suicide notes: one for his wife and one for each of his children. Before the massacre, he phoned his wife, telling her he had been dreaming lately of abusing young girls again, as he had when he was twelve, and that his life had been warped by anger and grief over the loss of their newborn daughter nine years earlier. In his suicide note to her, he added that he was "filled so much with hate, hate toward myself, hate toward God, and unimaginable emptiness. . . . Every time we do something fun, I think about how Elise [the dead newborn] wasn't here to share it with us and I get right back to anger."[34] With their remarkable stoicism and capacity for forgiveness, the Amish, though acknowledging their "terrible hurt," urged mercy for what Roberts had done, adding, "We must not think evil of this man." Hours after the shooting, an Amish neighbor extended forgiveness to the Roberts family. The community even set up a charitable fund for Marie and the children. Their merciful attitude was by no means shared by the wider, non-Amish population. Several commentators, for example, argued that forgiveness was not appropriate when no remorse had been expressed—granted that Roberts committed suicide before he could comment one way or the other about his act. Forgiveness in such circumstances may also be seen as denying the existence of evil.[35] I saw no comments at all on what, for me, was one of the most remarkable aspects of the "psychology" of Charles Roberts—namely, that he continued to harbor, despite having three alive and healthy children, intense grief and a soul-consuming anger over the loss of a neonate, nine years before. I speak not without some familiarity with this topic, given that I am the "middle child" of three: a brother who died hours after birth four years before me, and a sister who died a few hours after birth when I was four. My parents were, of course, saddened for a time after their deaths but then surmounted their grief and continued to lead contented and productive lives as parents of an "only child." I recall being a bit cross when my father told me, resorting to euphemism, that my mother had "lost" the baby, asking him, not yet understanding such subtleties of language, "How could Mama lose *baby*? I haven't even lost my mittens." Tens of millions of people have suffered the death of a child at or shortly after birth; the vast majority handle the loss with the customary sequence of grief, sadness, emotional recovery, and recuperation. We live in better times now. Neonatal death is uncommon. Not many must cope with the kinds of neonatal death that the mothers of Mozart and Beethoven suffered—who lost more children than the ones who survived. So I cannot escape the conclusion that Roberts *did* show a psychiatric illness, one within the spectrum of depression that was fairly severe, and certainly untreated. As for whether or not he had ever molested a girl when he was a boy of twelve, the fact that he had been planning to molest the Amish schoolgirls before killing them—even though he ultimately did not—bespeaks another and more serious warp of personality: a pedophilic perversion.

The mass murder at Virginia Tech in April of 2007 remains the school shooting, in either a primary school or a college, with the greatest number of fatalities in US or world history to date: thirty-two, plus the suicide of the shooter, Seung-Hui Cho. At age eight, Cho and his family had immigrated to America from South Korea. By the time he was in middle school in Virginia, mental health professionals had diagnosed Cho with severe anxiety and, because of his seeming refusal to speak, selective mutism. His greataunt back in South Korea had spoken—correctly—of his having autism, but this was somehow not at first appreciated here. Similarly, during childhood, his grandfather remarked that Cho never made eye contact, never called him Grandfather, never touched him—all signs compatible with a severe autistic spectrum disorder. When in grade school, he cried and threw tantrums every time he came home. As an adolescent of fifteen, he was mesmerized by the Columbine massacre, in response to which he had written on a school binder, "Fuck you all, I hope you burn in hell." He went so far as to write in a school assignment about wanting to "repeat Columbine." The school then told Cho's sister about this. She let her parents know about it, and they sent him to a psychiatrist. While at school, Cho looked down at the floor and refused to speak when teachers called on him. The other students mocked and picked on him for his shyness and unsocial behavior. When his parents took him to church, the pastor noted that he had never heard Cho say a complete sentence. He considered the boy autistic and urged his mother to have him hospitalized, but she declined. When Cho graduated high school and entered Virginia Tech, his situation deteriorated markedly. Unable to connect socially with his classmates or to "chat up" a girl in hopes of making a date, he became angry and intimidating. Without their permission, he took photos of girls' legs under their desks and wrote obscene or violent poetry. One of his teachers asked the head of her department to have him taken out of her class.[36] He was ultimately removed from the course, but, otherwise, it seems little was done. The department head met with him for a time but found him obnoxious and menacing, and feared for her safety. She, too, recommended he seek help, but Cho refused. During the first day of a new class, when the students introduced themselves to one another, Cho refused to speak, and when asked to sign their names, he wrote only a question mark—such that he was thereafter known simply as Mr. Question Mark. He later began to stalk girls from his class and made harassing phone calls as though from "Cho's brother, Question Mark." On other occasions, he would enter a girl's room unbidden and claim he "saw promiscuity in her eyes." One young woman complained to campus police, saying she thought he was "schizophrenic" and managed to persuade them to bar him from further contact. His troubling behavior intensified to the point that Cho was found, near the end of 2005, "mentally ill and in need of hospitalization." Yet, even though a judge ruled that Cho was a danger to himself and to others, he recommended only that Cho be treated as an outpatient. That became important, since in Virginia, unless Cho had been either involuntarily committed or else ruled "mentally incompetent," he was still permitted to purchase guns. There was some controversy. Some officials argued that the judge's order meant, in effect, Cho had been declared "mentally defective" and therefore ineligible for gun purchase, but the state did not enforce that rule. Cho duly purchased a Walther P22 semiautomatic pistol and a Glock 19 semiautomatic pistol, the first by mail order from Wisconsin in February of 2007, the other from a gun dealer in Virginia in March—the month before the planned massacre. To make sure the ensuing carnage would be maximal, Cho also purchased hollow-point bullets, which expand upon entering tissue and cause more damage than their conventional full metal jacket counterparts. Cho prepared a "manifesto" of the massacre he was planning, in which he stated, "All the shit you've given me, right back at you with hollow points." A chilling act 1 to the drama that was about to unfold, his writing showed the extent of his paranoia and hatred and, with it, the incapacity of certain severely autistic persons to grasp that they are themselves the authors of their social rejection. Not able to understand that other people avoid someone like Cho because of the social handicap, Cho, and others like him, will sometimes cast blame onto ordinary people, as if their avoidance is born of intrinsic cruelty, meanness, and hatred. Cho had at one point become obsessed with a female student, Emily Hilscher, and became outraged when she rejected his romantic overtures. She would become one of the first victims of his rampage.[37] To cite some items from Cho's manifesto, which contained written material but also the now famous videos of him holding two guns in a defiant stance:

> Only if you could be the victim of your reprehensible and wicked crimes, you Christian Nazis, you would have brute-restrained your animal urges to fuck me. . . . You could be at home right now eating your fucking caviar and your fucking cognac, had you not ravenously raped my soul. . . . To you sadistic snobs, I may be nothing but a piece of dog shit. You have vandalized my heart, raped my soul, and torched my conscious again and again. You thought it was one pathetic, void life that you were extinguishing. Thanks to you, I die, like Jesus Christ, to inspire generations of the Weak and Defenseless people—my Brothers, Sisters, and Children— that you fuck. . . . By the power greater than God, we will hunt you down, you Lovers of Terrorism, and we will kill you.[38]

The manifesto ended with, "Let the revolution begin! Die you Descendants of Satan! Fuck you and die now! I am Ax Ishmael. I am the Anti-Terrorist of America." Cho's morbid envy of ordinary people shines through many passages in the manifesto:

> Do you know what it feels like to be humiliated and impaled upon a cross? And left to bleed to death for your amusement? You have never felt a single ounce of pain in your whole life. . . . You had everything you wanted. Your Mercedes wasn't enough, you brats. Your golden necklaces weren't enough, you snobs. Your trust fund wasn't enough. . . . Your debaucheries weren't enough. . . . You loved inducing cancer in my head, terrorizing my heart, raping my soul. . . . When the time came, I did it.

By the latter, he meant the massacre of April 16, 2007. He made references to Eric Harris and Dylan Klebold of the Columbine massacre, which Cho hoped to emulate and to outdo—and did. He actually chose the same week in April as that in which the Columbine shooting occurred eight years before. His first victims were the female student Emily Hilscher, and a male student, Ryan Clark, both in her dorm room. He then went to the engineering building, having locked the doors with a chain, so as to prevent escape, and killed another thirty people before shooting himself in the head.[39]

People often use the phrase "copycat killer" when a murderer bursts into action shortly after some headline-making episode, where a killer carried out his act with a particular method and in a particular arena. Many of the school shooters, especially the notorious ones, have indeed admired, and then imitated, their predecessors, even if their attacks were separated by a few years, rather than days or weeks. Such was the case with Steve Kazmierczak, a graduate student at Northern Illinois University, who staged his rampage to coincide with Valentine's Day in 2007—the same date of the mass shooting allegedly committed a decade later by Nikolas Cruz. One of Kazmierczak's models was Seung-Hui Cho, whose model was Columbine's Eric Harris, whose model was Hitler and the Nazis. And so it goes. Unlike Harris or Cho, Kazmierczak could appear more "normal," had girlfriends, and was a dean's list student. Yet, he was profoundly mentally ill. He suffered from bipolar disorder, with a pronounced paranoid twist, which led some psychiatrists to diagnose him, reasonably accurately, as schizoaffective. Because of his quasi-normal interludes, he had extended friendships. His friends' reminiscences, coupled with his writings, give a much richer biography than available for many of the other school shooters—in effect, a mostly downhill roller-coaster ride from his childhood days to the denouement in 2007 when he killed five students at the university and wounded twenty-one others before shooting himself to death. His venue was a large auditorium-size lecture hall at the university where he mounted the stage, sporting a black T-shirt with the word "terrorist" placed over the image of an assault rifle. He had brought with him a guitar case loaded with half a dozen guns, including several semi-automatic pistols and many rounds of ammunition. The fatalities were, beside himself, at age twenty-seven, four students of nineteen or twenty, and another of thirty-two. There was a layering of motives. Topmost in his mind was that of "punishing" the university for cutting half the faculty from the sociology department where he was studying for his doctorate in, of all things, criminology.[40] Other stresses: his mother, with whom he had mostly a negative relationship, had died a year and a half before of amyotrophic lateral sclerosis, known as Lou Gehrig's disease; the relationship with his main girlfriend, Jessica Baty, was unraveling; and he did poorly on the LSAT exam, dashing his hope of going to law school. Furthermore, he had by then been off his psychotropic medications for five years, and his psychosis was reemerging. Having been treatment-free for so long, he was then eligible, under Illinois law, to buy guns. This permitted him to purchase several additional semiautomatic pistols. What this says about the inadequacy of the state's control over such purchases is another—and very discouraging—story. Kazmierczak now spent his time at the shooting range, rather than at school. His bipolar disorder had shown itself in different forms from his earliest days. As a child, for example, he and his mother, who was also mentally ill, would continuously watch horror movies about torture and plagues. There was depression and alcoholism on his father's side. Kazmierczak was cruel to his dog; made bombs out of Drano, which a childhood friend taught him how to make; became a goth in high school, wearing black trench coats and boots with chains and spikes; and started wearing swastikas. In the tenth grade, he had sex with girls but, occasionally, also with men. He became suicidal and, at sixteen, took a serious overdose of Tylenol. This led to the first of a total of nine hospitalizations, mostly for suicidality via overdoses with a variety of drugs, including sleeping pills and mood stabilizers, or for cutting his wrists. Along the way, he developed obsessive-compulsive disorder, with compulsive handwashing, key checking, and repetitive acts of all sorts. At school, the others called him "Suicide Steve" or "faggot." He had violent mood swings and abused marijuana with some of his classmates. Doctors prescribed one drug after the other, hoping to control his condition: antidepressants like Prozac and Paxil, mood stabilizers like lithium and Depakote, and antipsychotic medications like Seroquel or Zyprexa, which made him gain weight so that he wound up weighing three hundred pounds. Finally, someone had the wisdom to prescribe Clozaril, the antipsychotic that often works when the others do not, but he did not remain on the drug.[41]

At eighteen, Kazmierczak decided to go off all of his meds and be "normal." He got a tattoo saying, "FTW" for "fuck the world," but then always had to wear long sleeves to cover it. He enlisted in the US Army, lying about his history of mental illness and illegal drug use. He felt self-confident at last; the army trained him to shoot and how to kill, and his habit of checking everything several times fit in well with the ordered cleanliness of barracks life. All was well. Until the army did a background check and realized that he had been lying about the mental illness and drugs, and sent him to a military psychiatric unit. The army then discharged him. Kazmierczak returned to college and regaled his fellow students with his fascination with Hitler and serial killers Ted Bundy and Jeffrey Dahmer, concentrating on how they committed their murders. During his senior year, he did especially well academically. One of his professors wrote a glowing recommendation letter for graduate school: "He is extremely patient and calm . . . He has the highest ethical and academic standards, he thinks abstractly and analytically, and relates at an emotional and empathic level with others."[42] College is where he had met Baty, his special girlfriend, and they enrolled together at Northern Illinois University—but this is where the aforementioned unraveling began. Kazmierczak stopped going to classes and, ironically, took a job as a safety officer at an Indiana prison. He was soon dismissed from that job. Now rootless, he became part of the "hookup" culture of ever-changing "one-night stands" with different partners, in which so many college students or others in their twenties are currently immersed.[43] Despite all the brief encounters with others, he remained attached to Baty and even showed her his mental health records. For Christmas in 2007, he bought himself a new shotgun and semiautomatic pistol. He isolated himself and got a new tattoo, which symbolized the devil. In the first months of 2008, he bought more guns and ammunition. He called Baty, apologizing that things did not work out better between them, and told her he loved her. As he had not said that to her before, she worried he was getting depressed again. Two days before the Valentine's Day shooting, Kazmierczak bought her some presents— including a wedding ring. The evening before the fourteenth, he called her to say goodbye. On Valentine's Day in the lecture hall, Kazmierczak shot forty-eight rounds with his pistols, six with his shotgun, killing the five students and himself.[44]

Valentine's Day was coincidentally the "anniversary" of Kazmierczak taking the correction officer's exam in 2007.[45] He had told Baty not long before, "If anything happens to me, don't tell anyone about me."[46] She could not bring herself to unite the two sides of Kazmierczak's nature, commenting, "The person I know was not the one who went into Cole Hall and did that. . . . He was anything but a monster. He was probably the . . . nicest, [most] caring person ever."[47]

In April of 2012, Oakland, California, was witness to a mass shooting at Oikos University by a former student. Oikos, Greek for "home," is a Korean Christian college, founded a few years earlier in 2004, that offers a graduate degree in nursing, besides courses in theology, music, and Asian medicine. The forty-three-year-old shooter, though his birth name was Go (or "Ko") Su-Nam, had changed it to One L. Goh because he felt his original name sounded "like a girl's name."[48] He had been expelled from the college, where he had been enrolled in the nursing school, seven months before the attack, due to poor behavior and "anger management issues."[49] An administrator had been the one to expel him, and he sought revenge by killing her—except she was absent from the college on April 2 when he went back, armed with a .45-caliber semiautomatic pistol, looking for her. Instead, he entered a nursing classroom and ordered the students to line up against a wall. Goh then shot at them, killing seven and wounding three. He then phoned his father and revealed what he had just done. The police arrested him. Six of his seven victims were women. There had been several antecedent stresses in his life. In 2011, his brother was killed in a car accident in Virginia, and his mother died later that year in Korea. He had also been chronically in serious debt. Goh also complained that the students had disrespected and mistreated him. At the trial several months later, two psychiatrists, expert witnesses for the defense, diagnosed Goh as "paranoid schizophrenic," and thus not mentally competent to stand trial. The judge acknowledged that Goh was an angry and socially isolated loner, and mentally ill, as well, but not "insane" by legal standards. Goh actually asked for the death penalty, but, even if given as a sentence in California, it is no longer carried out. Instead, the judge handed down seven consecutive life sentences. Of his seven victims, all were from different countries—Korea, Nigeria, Tibet, and the Philippines—apart from a college secretary.[50]

With respect to horror and to the impact upon the public, Adam Lanza's school shooting at Sandy Hook Elementary School in Newtown, Connecticut, represents the outermost example. Lanza murdered first his mother, then, at the school, twenty small children and six of their teachers before finally killing himself. These twenty-eight deaths were a bit fewer than the thirty-three for which Seung-Hui Cho was responsible, but, of the twenty children, four were seven years old, the others only six. Like Cho, Lanza also suffered from a severe form of autistic disorder: he was highly intelligent but even more socially incapacitated and, ultimately, even more bizarre. Because of the enormity of the crime and the understandably great outpouring of journalistic reports on the case, the literature devoted to it is vast—of encyclopedic, and not merely book, length. Where to begin? Perhaps with the victims. The first victim during the December 14, 2012, rampage was Adam's mother, Nancy Lanza. He shot her in the morning at least four, some said five, times in the head with an (appropriately named) Savage MK-II bolt-action rifle. He then drove to Sandy Hook, armed, among other firearms, with his mother's Bushmaster XM15 semiautomatic rifle, one of the five such weapons and a half dozen other firearms his mother owned, since she was a gun enthusiast in her own right. He then shot to death the twenty first-grade children and six teachers. It was not yet ten in the morning when the twenty-year-old Lanza committed suicide with a Glock 20SF semiautomatic pistol. Lanza had brought three semiautomatic firearms into the school, along with considerable unused ammunition. Another rifle was found in his car. Not everyone reading this chapter would necessarily know what the assault rifle Lanza used to kill the children and teachers even looks like, let alone know of its power. I didn't either—but when I was lecturing on mass murder a few years ago in Juarez, Mexico, which had once been that nation's "murder capital" because of all of the kidnappings and drug gang-related murders, the forensic team there invited me to see what it was like to shoot an assault rifle. In a fifty-foot-long room, at the end of which was a "wall" of water behind a plastic sheet, I was handed such a rifle to shoot at the wall. When I did so, the water splashed back at me from the fifty feet between me and that target. Very powerful. Now imagine a little girl or boy being shot with such a weapon from just a few feet away. Perhaps it is best to avoid this mental exercise and to turn, instead, to the next important question: what motivated Lanza? In part, his motivation was an outgrowth of his progressive alienation, related to his severe form of autism, from ordinary social life—apparent already from his earliest days. His abnormalities showed themselves even before he was three: he showed communication and sensory difficulties. Later, in grade school, he was manifestly anxious when in the midst of other pupils. At thirteen, a psychiatrist diagnosed him with the autistic spectrum disorder called Asperger's syndrome, a condition described in 1944 by an Austrian pediatrician, Hans Asperger. The main features are a lack of nonverbal communication, limited understanding of others' feelings, and physical clumsiness.[51] Another characteristic is restricted and repetitive interests, accompanied by inflexible routines and pursuit of narrow areas of interest, to the exclusion of most ordinary interests. Lanza was also diagnosed in adolescence with obsessive-compulsive disorder because of his repetitive handwashing and his insistence on changing his socks twenty times a day.[52] Also, he had what used to be called "germ-phobia"—a compulsive avoidance of germs that, in Lanza's case, led him to avoid touching doorknobs, except with tissues. It is not clear to what extent his peculiarities of behavior could have been ameliorated via therapy, appropriate to his condition during his adolescent years, but such measures were not taken. There was no contact with potential therapists after he was fourteen. His parents separated when Lanza was nine. Afterward, he lived exclusively with his mother, and his older brother with their father. He was homeschooled from fourteen on because of his inability to adjust to conventional school. He spoke rarely and barely to others. If he went for a haircut, his mother had to tell the barber what to do, since Adam would say not a word. He had an intense, fixed stare, as is quite noticeable from the photographs in the newspapers and magazines after the massacre, which would signal to others that he was a most strange and unsocial person. When he was in school, the other pupils would be sure to make fun of him as "weird," both because of his peculiar appearance and his uncommunicativeness. One could not expect him to have the sagacity of an older and more self-confident person—who could say to himself, "Ah well, I am an odd one, so I can understand their mockery, but I'm not a bad person." Instead, Lanza would feel an ever-increasing hatred toward "normal" people—and ultimately, toward the world. Because he received no real treatment for his condition, his anger and hatred intensified as time went on. The nature of his social and emotional handicaps appeared so severe, unfortunately, it remains unclear what treatment could have accomplished anyway, even had he been willing to partake of it—but we cannot be certain about this. It is generally true that as a young child gets older, the social tasks become more challenging. It is one thing to play checkers or Ping-Pong, or go out with a friend for a bite to eat; it is another to have the social skills to get a job or to get a date or to have the charm to maintain a sexual relationship. Lanza, as he neared twenty, was becoming less and less capable of "fitting in" in those ways. His hopes for ever becoming an accepted member of the human community were becoming ever dimmer, his fury over the hopelessness of his life ever more intense. Not surprisingly, he became obsessed with fantasies of revenge; he immersed himself in reading about other mass shootings, such as those of Harris and Klebold at Columbine, and the one by Kazmierczak in Illinois. Toward the end, he had become so reclusive as to live in the house with his mother yet completely apart from her. He kept to his own room, communicating with her only via email. He placed black garbage bags over his windows to shut out the light. In the last two years of his life, he cut off contact with his father and brother. Yet, Lanza's becoming ever more incapable of participating in the things that make one human does not account fully for why he chose to do *what* he did *when* he did. Concerning the issue of motivation, there is more to the story. Already four years before the murder-suicide rampage, a man had told the Newtown Police Department in 2008 about a conversation he had with Lanza, who told him that he had an assault weapon and was planning to kill children at Sandy Hook, as well as his mother. The man was told that "Lanza's mother, Nancy Lanza, owned the guns and there was nothing NPD could do about it."[53] Another woman who had connected with Lanza online two and a half years before the massacre said that he was working on a spreadsheet, meticulously documenting the details of hundreds of spree killings and mass murders. Other contributing factors concerned the deteriorating relationship between Lanza and his mother. Nancy was herself a mentally disturbed woman with decidedly paranoid ideation. She was a "doomsday prepper" who believed foreign powers or perhaps other cataclysmic events were threatening our country, such that she and the other members of that group felt it an urgent matter that they stock up on all manner of survival items—dry foods, flashlights, shovels, medical equipment, medications, and guns—so that they would be the ones prepared for doomsday, and thus the ones most likely to survive. She went with Adam during his adolescent years to the shooting range, where they practiced with her collection of rifles. Shortly before the massacre, she had told Adam that the world was coming to an end on December 21, 2012, according to what the Mayan calendar predicted. Whether her bizarre belief played a role in Adam's choosing to end *his* world a week before that, we can never know. He was falsely suspected of being the person who conveyed to someone in a computer chatroom, "I'm going to kill myself on Friday and it will make the news; be watching at 9 a.m."[54] If this had been true, it would have been reminiscent of the comment an earlier and also mentally ill mass murderer, nineteen-year-old Robert Hawkins, once said to a friend shortly before he went out to kill eight people at a Nebraska shopping mall: "Watch the news! I'm gonna be fuckin' famous."[55] A number of mass murderers, that is, have craved celebrity, even as an infamous person—which plays a role in their final acts. Journalist David Kopel wrote a week after the shooting that "the media, cable TV . . . and the Internet today greatly magnify the instant celebrity that a mass killer can achieve."[56] Joshua Flashman, a marine and son of a pastor in Newtown, familiar with the Lanza family, suggested yet another element in Adam's motive. Flashman had been told that Nancy, finally at her wit's end and realizing that Adam was too ill to be taken care of at home, was at last preparing to commit Adam, if need be involuntarily, to a psychiatric facility—perhaps one in Seattle—a plan Flashman thought might have been what set Adam off. In addition, Nancy had years before been a volunteer at the Sandy Hook school, which led Adam to suppose, some thought, that she loved those children more than she loved him.[57] We have reviewed here a number of facts, speculations, and impressions, in hopes they have some explanatory value to make sense out of the "senseless" murders in Newtown, Connecticut—murders that inspired Connecticut's governor, Dannel P. Malloy, to remark that "evil visited this community today."[58] The impressions vary between the factual and fanciful. The severity of Adam's autistic disorder is factual—as were Nancy's own paranoid tendencies. His mother's desperation and plan to place him in an institution, not far from where she lived, seems highly likely. That she spoke about the world coming to an end on a date presaged by the Mayan calendar? Possible, though perhaps fanciful. Because of the deaths of both Adam and his mother, there is much to this tragic story that must remain in the realm of the unknowable. A year and a half after the massacre, Peter Lanza, Adam's father, accepted an interview with the prominent author and journalist Andrew Solomon, who then wrote an article about the meeting in the *New Yorker* magazine.[59] Mr. Lanza spoke of observations made by himself and by Adam's teachers. Already in fifth grade, for example, Adam and another boy wrote a disturbing story in which an old woman with a gun in her cane kills wantonly. Later, a teacher noted "disturbing violence" in Adam's writing, referring to him as "intelligent but not normal, with antisocial tendencies." Adam avoided eye contact and said he hated birthdays and holidays. Peter and Nancy separated in 2001 when Adam was nine. Adam was "not open to therapy." Peter confirmed the impression that Nancy was, indeed, planning to move to Seattle, though he believed she did not tell this to Adam. As for his reaction to his son's multiple murders, Peter said, "You can't get any more evil."[60]

About a year and a half after the Sandy Hook massacre, another high-profile school shooting took place on the other side of the country, at the Santa Barbara branch of the University of California. The shooter, Elliot Rodger, was the son of a British filmmaker, Peter Rodger, and a Malaysian mother, Li Chin. The parents divorced, and Elliot was raised partly with a stepmother—an actress from Morocco. More ordinary in appearance than Cho or Lanza, and from a prestigious family, he was nevertheless socially handicapped from his earliest years, though less so than those two. Various psychiatrists and therapists saw and worked with him from the time he was eight. Though Rodger showed many signs of a high-functioning autistic spectrum disorder, compatible with Asperger's syndrome, the latter term was usually avoided, in favor, during his early adolescence, of the vaguer "pervasive developmental disorder not otherwise specified." He alienated other age-mates in school and was ultimately abandoned by the one friend he had. In middle school, many of his classmates bullied him because of his social oddness, to the point that he cried by himself every day. What therapy he got was of little efficacy; psychiatrists prescribed medications as might be indicated for psychotic conditions like bipolar disorder or schizophrenia, but he refused to take them. As it turns out, they would have been of little use in alleviating his underlying autistic condition. His life situation became much more serious as he reached puberty. While other male classmates were beginning to learn how to talk to girls and go out on dates, his social deficit became more apparent. His awkwardness around girls led to their rejecting him. He began to hate them and became morbidly jealous of the boys who were more at ease with them, so he hated them as well. When he was twenty, there was an incident in which two girls did not smile back at him, so he splashed them with coffee. A few months later, he spotted what he saw as a group of happy college kids—"typical fraternity jocks, tall and muscular, with their beautiful blonde girls," he would say. He quickly went to a grocery store to buy orange juice and sprayed them with it.[61] The next year, he complained angrily to his parents about his loneliness and virginity. Their solution was to insist he see yet another psychiatrist; his solution was to buy a gun. No problem, since he was of age and had no criminal or mental hospital record. Over the next year, he bought three semiautomatic pistols and began practicing at a shooting range. He soon began to plan his day of retribution. Meantime, he went to a party, hoping against hope finally to lose his virginity, but became violent and enraged, and tried to push people off a ten-foot ledge. The intended victims fought back, pushing Rodger off the ledge, causing him to break his ankle. Rodger, as his day of retribution neared, became violently misogynistic, in the true etymological sense of the term—*hating* women, not merely desiring, while not respecting them, as in the current crop of notorious male predators. He also composed a book-length manifesto shortly before the murders, which he called *My Twisted World: The Story of Elliot Rodger*.[62] It is a strange biography, written by an obviously highly intelligent person. Apart from the brief and venomous introduction, the writing progresses, as did its author, from a fairly contented period during early childhood, through increasingly difficult and unhappy middle years, and on to the final post-puberty years—filled with poisonous hatred, grandiosity, denunciation, and sadism, ending up with even less humanity and more verbal savagery than one finds in *Mein Kampf*. In the introduction, he stated, "All of my suffering on this world has been at the hands of humanity, particularly women. . . . I was cast out and rejected, forced to endure an existence of loneliness and insignificance, all because the females of the human species were incapable of seeing the value in me. . . . It is a magnificent story . . . pulled together from my superior memory." In the first dozen pages of the 141-page document, Rodger describes happy memories of his Malaysian mother, his early years in London, a pleasant birthday party, trips to six different countries, and moving to America at five, but then the first dark-ening—his parents' divorce when he was seven, a "life-changing event," compensated for partly by "my mother's kind and loving nature." Rodger comes across more and more as entitled and "superior" and is given to tantrums to get his own way. At age ten, he shows neither interest in, nor animosity toward, girls.

In puberty, girls become objects of desire for Rodger, mostly as crea-tures, such as "hot blondes," whose possession would heighten his self-image. Since he is most unsuccessful in this pursuit, he begins to demonize both the girls and the boys who succeed in winning their favor, including their sexual favors, from which he is excluded. In one passage he writes, "How could an inferior, ugly Black boy be able to get a White girl and not me? I am beautiful, and I am half White myself. I am descended from British aristocracy. He is descended from slaves. . . . If this ugly Black filth was able to have sex with a blonde White girl of 13 while I've had to suffer virginity all my life, this proves how ridiculous the female gender is: They would give themselves to this filthy scum but they reject ME!" Toward the end of high school and beginning of college, his attitude hardens: he begins to feel such hatred for those who have sex as to wish to make sexual relations "illegal." He will quit a college class if he sees a happy-looking couple in it. Obsessive longings to become rich and to drive in a luxury car fill his mind, as though if he were equipped with such outward signs of wealth and desirability, these hated but desirable creatures will flock to him. Finally, toward the time of his "retribution," he sees sex as something to be outlawed and done away with: "If I can't have it, I will destroy it." As his mental collapse falls to the bottom, shortly before the murders, he adds, "I would use my car and guns to kill as many people as possible, until the police catch up with me—and then I will kill myself." He added that "there is no creature more evil and depraved than the human woman," all but a few of whom should be destroyed, with the rest remaining incarcerated and tolerated for breeding purposes.[63]

Though he had planned originally to begin his Day of Retribution on Halloween of 2013, when many people (himself excepted) are happy and dancing in the streets, he put the date off, fearing that there would be too many police monitoring the activities. Instead, it was May 23, 2014, that he embarked on his mission to kill as many people as possible. One would imagine that he would mostly target women, but he loathed men almost as much. His first three murders were of three Asian men in an apartment, all roommates of his, whom he stabbed to death. It was only three hours later that he began to use his semiautomatic pistols. He shot to death two young women near their Delta Delta Delta sorority house, then, a male student in a delicatessen. All of his victims were between the ages of nineteen and twenty-two. He then took to his car, wounding seven others by gunshot and another seven by striking them with his vehicle. By this time the police were giving chase. Firing at Rodger's car, one managed to shoot him in the hip; soon after, he committed suicide by a gunshot to the head.[64] Many in the public were outraged that more attention was devoted to the shooter and his family than to the victims. The families of the stabbing victims filed a federal lawsuit against the police and other local authorities, alleging that there had been a failure to recognize the earlier warning signs and to have taken preventative action, as though the rights of the mentally ill took precedence over the rights of the public. Though the Santa Barbara rampage served as the finale to the troubled life of Elliot Rodger, it serves as a prelude to the life of another school shooter with Asperger's syndrome—Christopher Harper-Mercer, who carried out his rampage 496 days later.

If you were told that, in Oregon, on the other side of the country from Lanza's Connecticut, there was another divorced paranoid woman who regularly took her autistic son for shooting sessions with their large assortment of semiautomatic rifles and whose son then became the deadliest school shooter in his state, it might strike you as yet another R-rated, made-to-shock

Hollywood film. But happen it did! At age five, Christopher Harper-Mercer was diagnosed with Asperger's syndrome. He was often rageful. His mother, Laurel Harper, who was herself diagnosed with both paranoia and Asperger's syndrome, did her best to defuse him. In childhood, he once pointed a shotgun at her. Not wanting him to end up in jail, where she worked as a part-time night nurse, she withheld that information from the police.[65] By late adolescence, he owned nine guns, including an assault rifle. He and his mother, using her own AR-15, would go to the shooting range, as though it were a healthy mother-son activity. She would later profess to have no clue as to why, on October 15, 2015, Christopher used his six guns to shoot to death nine students at the Umpqua Community College near Roseburg, Oregon, before then shooting himself to death. With the studied exaggeration of many a paranoid, grudge-holding killer, as we saw with Elliot Rodger, Harper-Mercer regarded himself as "the most hated person in the world . . . under attack from morons and idiots . . . one loss after the other. . . . And here I am at 26, with no friends, no job, no girlfriend, a virgin. I long ago realized that society likes to deny people like me these things . . . people who stand with the gods."[66] A militant atheist, he would ask the students in the classroom, into which he herded them for execution, if they believed in God. One student said he was Catholic. "Thank you for standing up for your beliefs," Harper-Mercer told him—and then shot him to death. His motive for the shootings was revenge against those he felt had wronged him. His heroes, whom he was now emulating, were Seung-Hui Cho, Adam Lanza, and Elliot Rodger. His admiration for these "mass shooters," whom he studied extensively, was tempered somewhat by his criticism that they were "not working fast enough," such that "their death toll is not anywhere near where it should be. . . . They also didn't take out the cops. Why take out other people, but you won't take out the cops?" He stated this in a manifesto, in which he also wrote, "For all those who never took me seriously, this is for you. For all those who haven't made their stand, I do this. I am the martyr for all those like me. To quote Seung-Hui Cho: 'Today, I die like Jesus Christ.'" Habitually silent and withdrawn, Harper-Mercer would not answer a neighbor's question about how he was doing. He spent most of his time indoors with his mother, clad always in combat boots and green US Army pants. He was also hypersensitive and would sometimes yell at neighbors if their dogs barked or if their children made noise while playing. If he were to talk at all, it would only be about guns. He would write on the internet that he had "zero" girl-friends, adding that he had never really been with anyone—no woman, no man, not even a dog, he lamented.[67] As another example of his quest for notoriety or of fame, however perverse, he commented, after he learned that a TV reporter, Vester Flanagan, had been fired and then fired—literally—on two former colleagues, killing them, "I've noticed that when people like him are all alone and unknown, but then when they spill a little blood, the whole world knows who they are." Claiming he was "spiritual," but not religious, he joined an organization called, paradoxically, "Doesn't-Like-Organized-Religion."[68] After the shooting, an Oregon law, passed in 2017, would allow a law enforcement officer or a family member to petition the court to block someone from purchasing a deadly weapon. It is hard to imagine Lauren Harper invoking that law so as to prevent her son from doing so. The victims of the Umpqua shooting consisted of five young students, between the ages of eighteen and twenty, and two older persons, including a woman who was trying to climb back into her wheelchair, and a sixty-seven-year-old professor. Seven years before the shooting, Harper-Mercer had gone from wearing his US Army clothing to actually joining that branch of the military, but this was short-lived. He was discharged soon after for failing to meet "minimum administrative standards," though some officials said he was let go because of a suicide attempt. He then went to a special school for those with learning disabilities and emotional problems. Later, after the shooting, people spoke of him as harboring anti-religious and white supremacist attitudes. Precisely a month before the October shooting, Christopher was placed on academic probation because of his failing grades and was told he would be suspended if he did not improve. He also owed the college $2,000 for back tuition. Factors such as these may have contributed to the *timing* of the massacre, though not to the desire to carry it out. The notion had been festering in his mind for a long time. Because he had never been involuntarily committed to a mental institution and had no criminal record, he could always, of course, have passed a background check for buying guns, including the .380-caliber semiautomatic handguns he used to commit several of the murders.

Whereas almost all of the school shooters we have been discussing have been socially awkward, isolated, and sometimes autistic, there have been a few who were much more self-confident and at ease in social situa-tions, even to the point of being gregarious. Jaylen Fryberg, a boy of fifteen from Washington State was an example. Fryberg grew up on a large reservation for members of the Native American Tulalip tribe. He attended Pilchuck High School, where he was a freshmen student, in Marysville, a medium-sized town some thirty-five miles north of Seattle. Only a portion of the students were from the Tulalip tribe while the rest came from other races and backgrounds. Described as "generally happy" and a "nice kid," Fryberg was good at wresting, football, and hunting. He was even honored with the title of "homecoming prince" of a certain football game, a week before he used his expertise with guns for a different purpose. He came from a large family that lived on the reservation. Several events occurred in the weeks before the shooting of October 24, 2014. He had gotten suspended from school, for example, after getting into a fight with another student who had made a racial slur, saying, "Natives are a bunch of good-for-nothing slaves. . . . Natives don't deserve to live."[69] During that same week, he had apparently gotten into a verbal tussle with his girlfriend, who told him, "You had a really short fuse with me lately." She had gotten mad at him, at a party, for flirting with another girl. Some thought he may have then gotten physical with her. At all events, they then broke up, after which Fryberg went hunting, saying, "I'm going to the woods to shoot something." That, in itself, was not surprising, since he had always been an avid hunter. He often went hunting with his father, Ray Fryberg, who bought him guns for his birthdays. Jaylen would pose for pictures with his father and brother, after downing an elk or other big game. There was uncertainty about the immediate precipitant to the murderous event at the school, but he was distraught over the breakup with his girlfriend. There was yet another girl who had turned him down for a date around the time of the shooting. She had apparently been dating one of Jaylen's cousins, fifteen-year-old Andrew Fryberg.[70] Jaylen chose for his life's finale the school cafeteria at lunchtime. He approached a table where his friends were sitting, got into an argument, and then reached for his .40-caliber Beretta Px4 Storm semi-automatic handgun, calmly and with precise movements firing eight shots, killing four students with single shots to their heads and wounding three others. What was singular about this school shooting, differentiating it from the others we have described here, is that all of the victims were his friends and relatives. One was a girl of fifteen, Zoë Galasso—the girl who had turned him down—and another was the cousin it seems she was dating. A teacher, hearing the shots, tried to intervene, but at that moment, Jaylen killed himself with a shot to the neck. The murders were not spur-of-the-moment, having been planned at least a number of days in advance. He had sent his father a text, for example, stating, "Read the paper on my bed. Dad I love you." Earlier that morning, Jaylen had sent several texts: "I needed to do this"; followed by another about his forthcoming funeral, "I want to be fully dressed in camo in my casket"; and "make sure all of my trust money or whatever goes to my brother."[71] The year after the massacre, Jaylen's father was arrested and convicted for illegally purchasing and owning the gun—one among eight other guns—his son had used to kill his friends. He was sentenced to two years in prison.[72]

As of the time of this writing, it is alleged that, on Valentine's Day of 2018, nineteen-year-old Nikolas Cruz, a former high school student who had recently been expelled from the Marjory Stoneman Douglas High School in Parkland, Florida, returned to the school and, using a legally purchased AR-15 semiautomatic assault rifle, killed fourteen students, a teacher, a football coach, and an athletic director. It was only one of about ten other legally purchased firearms in his possession. Cruz then reportedly tossed his gun away and blended in with the other students who were fleeing the scene, but was later apprehended and jailed. What is known is that, though he had not been doing well academically, he had been expelled for getting into fights with the other students. Parkland, a town of about thirty thousand in the Miami metropolitan area, was where Cruz grew up. Roger and Lynda Cruz adopted Nikolas when he was three days old and, a year later, adopted his half brother, Zachary. The seeds of the trouble and subsequent tragedy seem to have been planted early on. Lynda, childless at fifty, paid $50,000 to adopt Nikolas from his birth mother, reportedly a drug-addicted, alcoholic woman with a criminal record who became pregnant after "one-night stands" with men she did not know well. She was in prison when she gave birth to Zachary.[73] Nikolas was "trouble" from as soon as he could walk. He had a cold stare and got into numerous fights with other kids. When he was only two, he threw a neighbor's four-month-old baby into a pool.[74] He shot at squirrels or other small animals with his pellet gun, bit another boy's ear, and, at school, was disciplined frequently for unruly behavior or using profanity. A neighbor spoke of how Nikolas, an "evil" kid, was always getting into trouble or how the police were summoned to the house almost every other week. When he was a little older and his mother, after he had misbehaved, took away his Xbox, he called her a "useless bitch" and threw a dog bowl and a chair at her. On that occasion, the police came but declined to take him into custody as a "mentally ill person" because he seemed not so much a "crazy" individual as a mean one.[75] Another neighbor complained about his shooting chickens with a BB gun. While in high school at seventeen, he began talking about shooting up a school. The next year, just after his eighteenth birthday, a girlfriend broke up with him, at which point he cut both his arms but also started to buy guns. He wrote racist slurs and drew Nazi symbols on his schoolbags, identifying with white supremacists and casting aspersions at blacks, Jews, and gays. He boasted of his ambition to be a professional school shooter on a video blog. His father having passed away when Nikolas was five, he was orphaned when, in November of 2017, his mother also died. Afterward, he briefly lived with a foster family, then, with another, by which time he was, at nineteen, known to participate in white nationalist paramilitary drills. He had purchased an AR-15—the rifle he used in the school shooting. The timing of the attack, on Valentine's Day, came shortly after Cruz was rejected by a girlfriend, which was allegedly felt "not to be a coincidence."[76] A less immediate factor that may have played a role in the massacre reportedly committed by Cruz was, as we have seen with many school shooters, a quest for fame, or at least notoriety: to become, finally, a "somebody," rather than remain a nobody. This issue was poignantly addressed by Anderson Cooper in a television broadcast a week after the shooting. Cooper showed photos of all seventeen victims, along with vignettes about their all-too-brief lives. At the end of each, he intoned, "You will be remembered." At the end, he showed a picture of the alleged killer, followed by, "You will not be remembered."[77] Unfortunately, the young students who were murdered, the football coach who thrust himself in front of others to protect them from the bullets, and the two other men will not become household names, though they will long be remembered by their loved ones. Also unfortunate is that, if found guilty of mass killing, Nikolas Cruz will be long remembered—famous, albeit in infamy—for the same reason as Adam Lanza, Seung-Hui Cho, Eric Harris, Dylan Klebold, and the other school shooters, who took many victims, as embodiments of evil. Though the Cruz trial is still a ways off as of the time of this writing, he has confessed to the shootings, claiming that he had long been prompted to injure others by a voice or demons.[78] His defense team has consistently said that Cruz is willing to plead guilty and spend the rest of his life in prison, with no chance of parole, to avoid the death penalty.[79] It is presently unclear whether the defense will attempt an insanity defense.[80]

COMMENTARY

We have focused in this chapter on persons who killed pupils in an elementary school or a high school, also discussing a smaller number who killed college students. Though school shootings have occurred in other countries, as mentioned earlier, the vast majority have occurred here in the United States. The main reason for the great disparity is the remarkable ease with which our citizenry—even teenagers—can gain access to guns, compared with those in most other countries. Of the vignettes offered here, those involving school shooters who killed only one or two others were teens between the ages of fourteen and seventeen. Those who had killed four or more were about evenly divided between those twenty and under, and those above that age. Those described here were all male, as is true of the vast majority of school shooters.

Among the eight female school shooters identified over the past thirty years, only one killed two students at a college; the others killed just one other person.[81] Three committed suicide afterward. They usually knew their victims. For example, fourteen-year-old Elizabeth Bush wounded thirteen-year-old Kimberly Marchese in 2001, ostensibly "to show everybody how much teasing hurts," though Marchese was not one of the guilty parties. The teasing, which consisted of being called "homosexual" and "vicious names," had occurred elsewhere, while Bush attended a Williamsport, Pennsylvania, public school.[82] Another girl who shot at others randomly was Brenda Spencer, a sixteen-year-old girl who had grown up in poverty in San Diego, living, after her parents divorced, with her father. Brenda had suffered a head injury from a bicycle accident and was epileptic. She was a truant from school and, at times, felt suicidal. For Christmas in 1978, her father gave her a Ruger .22 semiautomatic rifle and five hundred rounds of ammunition, though she had asked for a radio. A month later, she fired shots from her house into an elementary school across the street, killing both the principal and a custodian, both of whom were trying to protect the children. None of the children was injured.[83]

The predominance of males among the school shooters parallels the male predominance in violent crimes in general. From an evolutionary standpoint, the strategies for reproductive success in our species vary between the sexes. Females must devote considerable time and devotion to the (comparatively) few children to whom they can ever give birth. Males, as Netherlands psychologist Dr. Mark van Vugt postulated, evolved more aggressive and group-oriented behaviors by way of acquiring territories, higher status, and, if possible, a multiplicity of mates—by whom they can sire, potentially, a large number of offspring, devoting comparatively less involvement with each.[84] Testosterone figures importantly in male aggression—at the extreme end of the spectrum, violent, including criminal behavior in males tends to correlate with higher testosterone titers, especially in the decades following puberty until the middle to late thirties.[85] A related correlation is that of sex ratios for violent crimes. In the United States, for example, men account for 90 percent of homicides and 80 percent of violent crimes in general, including murder, assault, rape, robbery, arson, and kidnap.[86] With respect to school shooters in particular, these two correlations create an inter-correlation, insofar as almost all of the shooters are male and the majority are adolescents, spanning the years between puberty and the early to middle twenties, when testosterone levels are at their peak. From a neuroanatomical standpoint, there is another important correlate, emphasized recently by Dr. Jay Giedd of the National Institute of Mental Health—namely, that areas in the prefrontal cortex that subserve impulse control, judgment, and long-range planning are still developing and undergoing the myelination allowing for enhanced connectivity of neural circuitry in different parts of the brain. The latter process is scarcely complete until about age twenty-five. These differences underlie what Giedd has spoken of as the disparity between impulsivity, which peaks in adolescence, and impulse control, which will enhance the brain's "braking system" a decade later.[87]

Beside these biological factors related to the morphology of the developing brain, there are important social factors that have had a bearing on adolescent behavior—on the tendency to violence in general and to the phenomenon of school shootings, in particular. Of special significance is the sharp spike in the divorce rate in the late 1960s. For many decades in our country, the divorce rate was comparatively low and stable, affecting about 22 percent of marriages.[88] The rate rose rapidly between 1968 and 1974, reaching 50 percent, remaining close to that number since then. Associated with the high divorce rate has been the marked increase in boys growing up without fathers or with little paternal contact. In the years after World War II, 80 percent of babies born were, as Lykken pointed out, reared by both biological parents, who were married to one another.[89] By 1990, in contrast, 19 percent of white, 62 percent of black, and 30 percent of Hispanic children under eighteen lived with only one parent, usually their mothers. Children, especially boys, in these circumstances are, by a factor of about seven, more likely to get in trouble with the law.[90] During this same time period, the percent of young persons, ages fifteen to twenty-five, who were arrested for violent crimes also rose precipitously from approximately twenty-seven per 100,000 individuals per year in the years before 1965 to eighty or ninety per 100,000 in the 1975–1985 period, moving still higher to one hundred or more in the recent years. About half the children born in the United States during the past thirty years will have spent part or all of their formative years either in a mother-only home or in a family setting where there is little contact with their biological fathers, and have an increased risk of suffering physical abuse or emotional neglect, when compared with those reared in intact families.[91] Of the school shooters sketched in this chapter, half came from divorced families. Most came from working-class or middle-class backgrounds; a few were born into poverty (e.g., Purdy) or else into wealth (e.g., Lanza and Rodger). Yet the high divorce rate and diminished paternal contact among school shooters are connected, it would appear, to yet another factor. Substantial improvements were made in the lives of women following World War II, though many areas of rampant unfairness persist. Women were at least more able to enter the workforce, in respectable and better-paying jobs—but as often accompanies the "good," there were "unintended consequences" of a negative sort. Women were more able to support themselves and, thus, leave husbands who were physically abusive or cruel. Thanks to the "pill" and to abortion rights, many women now had better control over their bodies and their overall fates. Better, though fuller and ideal control is still a far-off dream for too many. The unintended consequence was a male backlash, especially among working-class men, some of whom resented no longer having absolute power over their wives or live-in sexual partners. Some women who, to escape abusive husbands, have packed their bags and walked out of their houses—and into divorce—have sadly paid for their freedom with their lives. I have examined 127 "true crime" biographies of husbands who have killed their wives. The murder was, in a quarter of the cases, in response to imminent desertion by the perpetrator's wife.[92] Another manifestation of men reacting with violence to rejection by women is the sudden and sharp increase in serial sexual homicide. From the late years of the nineteenth century until the mid-1960s, serial killers were a rarity: only three or four in a decade. The graph of such men shows a marked and abrupt increase starting in the latter years of the 1960s, another aspect of the era of "new evil" we have been discussing.

Since the majority of school shooters, especially those who kill in primary school, are still in their adolescent years—when aggressive tendencies, especially in males, are on the increase—many have asked whether certain societal factors may contribute to the upsurge in the sheer number of school shootings, over and above the hormonal and neurobiological factors to which Giedd has drawn attention. Can the sensation seeking, impulsivity, preoccupation with sex, and the allure of violent—as opposed to coolly reasoned—solutions to problems be intensified or aggravated by the scenes and sounds of violence in the movies and TV shows; the readily accessible views of sexual scenes, pornographic and otherwise; the all-too-realistic views of violence and wartime battle scenes; the rapes, murders, and tortures inflicted by terrorists on the innocent? Can all of these "normalize" a still-impressionable adolescent to violent "solutions" when confronted with some interpersonal stressor? Are we desensitizing our young people to the horrors of what human beings can do to one another—and do the new video games and deafening pop music, and the misogynistic lyrics of rap music,[93] grease the skids for troubled adolescents to opt for violent solutions, murder included, as a way of getting back at those who bully them in school or steal their girlfriends? Are these the reasons we are seeing so many more incidents of adolescents shooting their schoolmates over the past fifty years, since the internet era and all of the new machinery of amplified sensation? In agreement with Giedd, Dr. Laurence Steinberg, a psychology professor at Temple University, likens the teenage brain to a car with a good accelerator, but a weak brake, adding that with powerful impulses under poor control, the likely result is a crash—and, perhaps, a crime.[94] Still, it would be premature to assign a major role in a specific phenomenon of violent aggression, such as school shootings, to the media displays of violence and sex. As Dr. Gaetano Di Chiara has reminded us, in our brain's reward system vis-à-vis basic drives, such as sex and hunger, dopamine plays a key role.[95] The hormonal changes that usher in puberty, which defines the beginning of adolescence, affect the dopaminergic system, and thoughts and desires related to sex and aggression increase. These changes are necessary to our survival. Only in excess or in adverse circumstances are they associated with adverse consequences.[96] Subtle differences in brain chemistry and personal experience predispose one adolescent to fight off an intruder and protect family members, while another uses aggression in another way—and becomes a school shooter. Different research groups studying the impact of violent video games on actual outbreaks of violence have come to quite different conclusions: some, seeing a strong correlation; other groups failing to find such a connection.[97] There is, after all, a bewildering array of variables among adolescents—social, socioeconomic, scholastic, family environment-related, constitutional, hereditary, physiognomic (concerning attractiveness or lack thereof), drug-abuse related, and so forth, the complexities of which make for a daunting task to predict which adolescent—which boy, in particular—will go on to be a valued and productive citizen, or a pariah who ends up a school shooter. It is true that, over the past quarter century, the menu of illicit drugs is far greater than it had been before. Some agents, such as phencyclidine or angel dust,[98] methamphetamine,[99] and methylene-dioxy-pyrovalerone, known as bath salts,[100] abused currently by many adolescents, can all lower inhibitions and lead to violent behaviors. These drugs do not seem to have played much role in school shooters, from what I can gather from the literature, although marijuana, given its disinhibitory effects on the adolescent brain, has been a factor in several of the school shooters mentioned earlier, including Mitchell Johnson, Kip Kinkel, and Steve Kazmierczak.

Unfavorable genetic factors can predispose to violent tendencies, more in male than in female children and adolescents. Among the factors at issue are those associated with schizophrenia, bipolar disorder, attention-deficit/hyperactivity disorder (ADHD), and autism. These conditions are traditionally viewed as clinically separate, but, from the standpoint of brain physiology, we now understand them to spring from similar sources, including those parts of the limbic system that predispose one to hyper-activity.[101] Intervening life circumstances in childhood and beyond may nudge the outward clinical appearance in one or another direction during the life course.[102] In cases of adoption, it is often difficult or impossible to obtain adequate information about any possible genetic disadvantages. As we saw with accused school shooter Nikolas Cruz, information regarding his biological father is lacking and the mother's psychological picture was unfavorable. Recently, it came to light that Lynda and Roger Cruz had arranged for a private adoption through an attorney.[103] It is clear that Nikolas was genetically disadvantaged on both sides. Beside the already mentioned conditions present in his earliest years, his adoptive mother had told some persons close to her that he also suffered from autism and obses-sive-compulsive disorder. He was "peculiar," unable to make friends, and disobedient and disruptive in school, which he was never able to complete. The issues surrounding adoption in the last fifty years make for a topic that is controversial, highly sensitive, and even taboo. It is similar to the "third rail" that politicians and researchers fear touching when talking about dif-ferences among ethnic groups. One aspect concerns another "unintended consequence" of women's enhanced rights to control their own bodies and destinies. Women in more favorable circumstances are less likely to have unwanted pregnancies and less likely to give children up for adop-tion. Babies given up for adoption are more likely than was the case before the 1960s to harbor either genetic or "constitutional" disadvantages—that is, adverse factors during the months of pregnancy, such as the mother's abuse of alcohol or illicit drugs—or, in the case of adoption from Eastern European orphanages, disadvantages of being left in an orphanage for many months, or even two or three years.[104] While we do not know the percentage of school shooters who come from genetically disadvantaged backgrounds, it is of interest that among serial killers—largely a post-1965 phenomenon, as we have stated—the percentage of adoptees among them is approximately 16 percent, roughly eight times the national average within the American population.[105]

Besides these potential adverse pre-birth factors, which may play a role in those who later become school shooters—and we can even include being male as a "hereditary" factor (i.e., being born with a Y chromosome)—there are important postnatal factors we need to consider. We also need to examine factors that relate to the physical appearance with which one is born, a "constitutional"/partly hereditary factor that has a strong impact upon how one is regarded and treated by others. In his biography of the Columbine pair Eric Harris and Dylan Klebold, Cullen described both as rather normal-looking, yet dissatisfied with their appearances: Eric had a "long pointy nose, a sloping forehead, and a weak chin. The spiky hair worked against him aesthetically." Dylan was "considerably less handsome than Eric. . . . He hated his oversize features on his slightly lopsided face. His nose: he saw it as a giant blob."[106] Since both aspired to be popular with the "hotties," they felt disadvantaged, as though they could not get the dates they wanted, and would be vulnerable to humiliation. Yet, their self-regard was nowhere nearly as diminished as that of the truly odd-looking Adam Lanza. Matters of this sort feed into the heightened aggressiveness and preoccupation with sexual desirability that accompany puberty; the lower the self-regard, the more shattered the self-esteem and the greater the actual humiliation by peers combine to play a prominent role in the lives of many school shooters. The feelings of despair about ever succeeding in the dating game, ever finding a significant other about whom one feels proud, has nudged some of these adolescents and young men not only to murder in school settings, but also to commit suicide as the final act in their respective dramas. Just as with mass murderers in general, half or more of the school shooters make themselves the last victims of their murderous impulses. These suicides have even been categorized as "deaths of despair," a phenomenon that recently has been on the rise, in such events as drug- and opiate-related deaths and suicides among school shooters. Also, the reverse side of the coin of shattered self-esteem is *envy*. Among the most notorious school shooters, envy was clearly a dominant feeling in the autistic killers (e.g., Cho, Lanza, Rodger, Harper-Mercer, possibly the accused Cruz), since their social skills in knowing how to start and carry on conversations or ask for dates with girls varied between abysmally low and nonexistent. Unable to accept their social awkwardness, these men turned to murderous rage, as though the reason they kept getting rejected was not that there was something wrong with them but that women were just horrible "bitches"—as Rodger called them[107]—who would not give a "nice" guy the time of day. For these, and similarly socially handicapped men, murder—multiple murder—proved so much more gratifying a solution than self-acceptance and the search for pleasures in other areas of life. For evidence of self-acceptance of a diagnosis of Asperger's syndrome, for example, there is the story of Greg Krueger, a Minnesota man who lives contentedly with his cats in a "cat palace" he created out of his home, filling it with catwalks, spiral staircases, and all manner of architectural marvels. Saying, "I'm probably not the best at socializing," Krueger has made an alternate life for himself, which seems to make him and his cat family feel happy and fulfilled.[108]

Humiliation is another strong emotion that can readily awaken desires for revenge against those who have, through verbal or physical bullying, made one feel inferior. Bullying of one sort or another has spurred many a school shooter to take up arms and seek revenge through murder. Luke Woodham, mentioned earlier, had been ceaselessly humiliated by his mother, who, even when Luke finally had a girlfriend when he was fifteen, insisted on accompanying the two when they were on a date. It was his mother's humiliating behavior that made her Luke's first victim. Unfortunately, he then went to the school, where his girlfriend became his second victim, and her friend the third, even though the girls had not mistreated him.[109] Barry Loukaitis had been another victim of severe bullying. A fourteen-year-old student at a Washington State high school, he had been bullied by classmates, one of whom, Manuel Vela, had called him "faggot" and had spit on him. In 1996, Loukaitis brought a rifle and a semiautomatic pistol to school, killed his algebra teacher and then two students, including Vela. Rivalry may have been one of the motives: Loukaitis had a crush on Vela's girlfriend.[110]

The connection between being bullied in school and then becoming a school shooter appears to be a "guy" thing—specifically, a vengeful act by heterosexual boys. Schoolgirls, and also gay or lesbian students who have been mercilessly bullied, rather than "getting back" at their victimizers, are more apt to take their own lives, often by hanging, in what has been called "bullycide," many examples of which Dr. Laura Finley mentions in her essay on the subject.[111] Among the male school shooters, I know of none who identified as gay when they were actually in school as students. There are rare examples of middle-aged gay men who killed school students. One concerns a school teacher, Albert Fentress, to whom reference was made in the previous chapter. In 1979, at the age of thirty-seven, he lured a high school student to his house, whom he then immobilized, forced to say he was "gay"—though he was not—and castrated, cannibalized, and shot to death.[112] Before the murder, Fentress had molested at least half a dozen boys, whom he was supposedly tutoring in his home. In 1996, Thomas Watt Hamilton, a forty-four-year-old man who ran a boys' camp in Scotland, took out his grievances at being labeled—albeit correctly—a pedophile by entering a primary school, armed with two revolvers, at which point he shot to death sixteen students, their teacher, and then himself.[113] This was the largest mass murder in England, eclipsing Michael Ryan's massacre of sixteen persons plus himself nine years earlier in Britain's town of Hungerford.

As for the rates of suicide by school shooters versus other men (and the rare women) who commit massacres, they are approximately equal, at about 50 percent.[114] Because mass murderers of whatever sort—including school shooters with many victims—tend with such regularity to commit suicide, we know less about many of them than we know about killers who have been captured. We count mass murderers who end up killed by the police or who kill themselves just as the police are closing in on them—like Charles Whitman and Joseph T. Wesbecker—as suicides also, since their intention from the beginning was to die either by their own hands or by the police. There are no court trials, no snitching by cellmates, no psychiatrists for the defense or prosecution—no journalists to gather information about the childhood backgrounds of the killers or how their lives unfolded, what spurred them into murderous action, and so on that would help us understand these killers or what led to their final acts. Another point relevant to school shooters, and to mass murderers in general, is that they are unlike those who take hostages as bargaining chips to force acquiescence, at the price of killing the hostages if need be. Mass murderers intend to kill coworkers, family members, persons at random, and, half the time, themselves.[115] Negotiation is not an issue—retribution is. Hope has already been extinguished for them.[116]

SCHOOL SHOOTING AS A PART OF THE "NEW EVIL"

We have already touched briefly on some of the societal changes over the past half century that appear to have played a role in the substantial increase in certain forms of violence—forms, that is, that evoke the word "evil." Mass murder, serial sexual homicide, and school shootings are some of the varieties. Others, dealt with elsewhere in this book, involve murders of particular gruesomeness—atrocities of a sort seldom or never encountered in peacetime before the 1960s. If we restrict the phrase "mental illness" to those with demonstrable psychosis, as manifest by delusions, hallucinations, or cognitive aberrations short of outright delusions, as opposed to personality disorders—even if the latter is severe, such as antisocial, psychopathic, paranoid, borderline, or schizotypal—it turns out that only about a quarter of mass murderers are "mentally ill." Fewer still among the serial killers, as noted earlier in this volume. By contrast, a greater proportion of the more widely known school shooters have been mentally ill—especially those with the greatest victim counts. Dr. E. Fuller Torrey, a notable psychiatrist from Washington, DC, has rightfully criticized the all-too-common practice of "deinstitutionalization" for sending thousands of hospitalized mentally ill patients out into shelters or even the streets, starting back in the 1960s.[117] He has stated that the mentally ill account for about 5 percent of all homicides in the United States. Many of these unadvised discharges of patients ended up in worse situations than if patients had been allowed to remain in hospitals. Another example of the "law of unintended consequences," this supposedly humanitarian impulse was a disaster. Within the domain of mass murder, perhaps some 22 percent have been mentally ill. Only a few had been in the hospital before their (premature or unjustified) releases, prior to committing mass murders. Among the younger school shooters, few had ever even been in a hospital, so one cannot ascribe the murders they committed to inappropriate discharge from a mental hospital. Several, of course, *should* have been institutionalized, even for life, in some humane facility, such as Seung-Hui Cho and Adam Lanza, but were not. Some of the other school shooters would *not* have met criteria for hospitalization, let alone chronic institutionalization. Eric Harris, for example—the "leader" in the Columbine massacre—was not mentally ill; he was a psychopath, for whom human beings were seen as "chemical compounds with an inflated sense of their own worth."[118] At one point, a psychiatrist had prescribed an antidepressant when Eric, urged by his father to get help, said he had "anger issues" and spoke of "suicidal feelings," as though depressed. The real problem, however, was that Eric had contempt for others and lacked a moral center, which could not be supplied by an antidepressant. Yet, he could appear sociable and better behaved. He was likely unreachable by psychotherapy. Dylan Klebold was depressed and troubled by self-hatred and feelings of inadequacy. Once he allied himself with Eric Harris, he redirected his hatred and anger toward the outside world, becoming a carbon copy of Eric. Hatred is a key word when discussing murder. To *dislike* someone conveys a sense of wanting to distance oneself from that person, excluding that person from one's social circle. To *hate* someone often implies the wish to destroy or kill that person. The FBI psychologist Dr. Dwayne Fuselier, who studied the journal Eric had begun making during the last year of his life, read and was aghast, at the opening line, "I hate the fucking world"—as he was to demonstrate all too vividly with his TEC-9 semiautomatic pistol on the day of the massacre.[119]

In discussing the Columbine killers at a church service after the massacre, a minister, Reverend Don Marxhausen, spoke of the two boys as having "hatred in their hearts and assault weapons in their hands."[120] In that brief remark, the minister summed up succinctly the situation with school shooters—as with many murderers of any sort: *hatred plus a weapon*. Yet, the damage one can do with an assault weapon is considerably greater than what one can inflict with conventional firearms—and, when we combine hatred and assault weapons with the negative societal changes in the last half century, we end up with a very potent and very fatal brew, indeed. Mark Steyn has remarked on this in his essay on the Parkland massacre. "Some of us," he wrote, "have changed, and for the worse." He cites several factors: "The decline of organized religion, the collapse of the family . . . the metastasization of narcissism, and the worship of the self . . . and somewhere in the void, a particular combination of these factors incubate the depressingly similar young men who gun down their fellow pupils."[121]

This brings us to the controversial subject of assault weapons. Fuller Torrey and Steyn have made what I believe to be valid remarks about the cultural changes in the last two generations. If we then add Reverend Marxhausen's comment about hatred and assault weapons, we come closer to the essence of the current situation with school shooters. By this I mean the close correspondence between the rise since the mid-1960s of school shootings with many deaths, as opposed to just one or two, and the increasing availability of semiautomatic assault weapons. What is to be done?

After the Parkland massacre, an editorial in the *New York Post* offered some solutions—ones that do not require the brilliance of an Einstein or a Stephen Hawking, which, in essence, require only five words: *Get rid of the guns*.[122] Hunters do not need an assault weapon to bring down a deer. The AK-47, developed in 1947 by the Russian tank commander Mikhail Kalashnikov, and the Uzi, developed the next year by the Israeli major Uziel Gal, were designed to win wars, not to kill rabbits or people one does not like. Other than for soldiers in battle or for police in SWAT teams, there is no need for them in peacetime. Two former US senators have made noteworthy comments on this topic. Howard Metzenbaum said, "No, we're not looking how to control criminals. . . . We're talking about banning the AK-47 and semiautomatic guns." John Chafee remarked, "I will shortly introduce legislation banning the sale, manufacture or possession of handguns—with exceptions for law enforcement."[123] In an article in Canada's *National Post*, a student, seventeen-year-old David Hogg from Parkland, was quoted during an interview, saying, "I should not have to witness what I saw and my sister should not have two dead best friends. She's 14. How do you unsee that? The politicians are supposed to be the adults, and the fact that we have to stand up as students is a testament to the broken and decrepit state America is in." Another Parkland student, fourteen-year-old Isaah Jean, said, when asked what he wanted to say to President Trump, "I want to tell him we need to get rid of the guns."[124]

In Australia, the government did actually get rid of the guns, after the 1996 massacre committed by the intellectually disabled Martin Bryant, who, after finishing his lunch at a Tasmanian café, killed thirty-five people with his AR-15 semiautomatic rifle—the same gun used in the Parkland massacre allegedly committed by Cruz. Within a few weeks, the Australian government banned such rifles and other military-style weapons across the country, also prohibiting their import and even offering to buy back such firearms as were already owned. In the two decades since that incident, there have been no mass killings in their country.[125] In the United States, estimates point to about three hundred million guns among its citizenry,

40–50 percent of which are semiautomatic. This is a bit less than the 320 million people in the nation. Yet, it would not be easy to persuade the politicians and American citizens to go the route of the Australians. Since one does not hunt with such weapons, they are only made for killing people. A ban would be theoretically feasible, Second Amendment notwithstanding, though the ban would be politically fraught. There are many men, after all, whose desire for owning such weapons seems based, since there are no valid practical reasons, on certain psychological reasons. There are men, that is, for whom ownership of armaments like an assault rifle reinforces a sense of masculinity, as if the typically six-inch penis is not quite as reassuring as the thirty-six-inch arms they can carry, visibly, in their arms.

SCHOOL SHOOTERS AND THE GRADATIONS OF EVIL SCALE

Few would argue against applying the term "evil" to the *actions* of students in a primary school or college who have killed three or more of their fellow students. Of the sixteen such school shooters reviewed here, the numbers of deaths also included the suicide of the killer in twelve cases. Probably because background information about the killers is so scant—few ever went to trial, having died at the scene of the shooting, as we have discussed—few "true crime" biographies have been devoted to them, with exceptions like Gang Lu, Kip Kinkel, and Eric Harris. No others had become the subjects of books in my collection of eight hundred criminal biographies. As we have noted elsewhere, evil *actions* must be distinguished from evil *persons*. One would not call a person "evil," unless that person's history revealed an inveterate propensity, an ineradicable habit of repugnant, destructive, or violent acts throughout adolescent and adult life, without ever a hint of genuine remorse. Persons of this sort will usually meet diagnostic criteria for psychopathy.[126] The term would not be applicable to the young school shooters discussed here. Among the older school shooters, true psychopaths would include Purdy, Harper-Mercer, and, most definitely, Eric Harris. Harris kept extensive diaries, starting even two years before the Columbine massacre, about plans to kill as many people as possible. He showed pathological lying, a variety of crimes during adolescence, including vandalism and fire setting—in short, almost all of the criteria for psychopathy, while growing up in a family that did not subject him to the kinds of neglect or cruelty that sometimes sets in motion an environment-based "secondary" psychopathy, rather than the more common condition, which is possibly genetically determined.

School shooters, despite having a particular action in common, display a variety of motives and a complex array of psychological peculiarities. Many of the younger ones somehow obtained a gun, illegally, or else pilfered from family members, while still in mid-adolescence. The motives behind the shootings were usually intense anger or rage, and the murders were mostly spur-of-the-moment affairs. There was typically little in the way of methodical planning in the days or weeks before these outbursts. This was particularly true of the shooters mentioned in the vignettes we have discussed, who killed only one, or two or three others, and who themselves usually survived. Three of them, for example, fit criteria for Category 6 in the Gradations of Evil scale, the ranking for those who commit hotheaded murder(s), anger-driven, and impulsively carried out. This would be true of eighteen-year-old Michael Pisarski, and Kristofer Hans and Tronneal Mangum, both fourteen. Gradation 8 would be more appropriate for Luke Woodham, the sixteen-year-old who killed first his mother, then his girlfriend and her friend, in murders that stemmed from ignited rage but with a measure of ahead-of-time planning. Category 8 would also be appropriate for one of the adult school shooters, Gang Lu, whose rage was stirred up when he was bested by a rival in graduate school, and who then carefully planned the murder of his rival and the "offending" professors. Harder to rank are the severely autistic killers Seung-Hui Cho and Adam Lanza. Neither was clearly psychopathic; instead, they were profoundly mentally ill, socially handicapped young men, filled with hatred for ordinary people to whom they were completely unable to relate. For them, Gradation 13 might be appropriate: murderers with inadequate, rageful personalities, though they did not have the "marked psychopathic features" shown by others in that category.

For the alleged Parkland shooter, Nikolas Cruz, questions have been raised about whether his features may represent a mixture of inherited and, owing to his biological mother's drug and alcohol abuse during pregnancy, constitutional abnormalities. In his upper middle-class adoptive home, the parents, though reportedly sorely tried by his violence, were long-suffering and loving. Nothing changed in Cruz's behavior after the death of his mother in November of 2017. Afterward, he was placed in the care of Rocxanne Deschamps. She had found it necessary to call 911 three times within a month—twice after finding guns and bullets in his room, and then, after he punched holes in the wall, following which she had to force him out of her house. Ms. Deschamps told the authorities that Nikolas had once put a gun to his mother's head and to his half brother Zachary's head but that "law enforcement said nothing could be done."[127] If Cruz is found guilty of the allegations against him, the facts reported thus far and the number of victims might make Category 13 the most appropriate ranking. For Eric Harris, Category 16, the ranking for "Psychopaths committing multiple vicious acts, including murder," seems applicable. It is a common ranking for many nonschool-related mass murderers and for some serial nonsexual murderers.

The school shooters with a large number of victims, though not all psychopaths, often had an unusual characteristic in common: they wrote manifestos shortly before their final acts of multiple murder and suicide. As noted earlier, this was true of Cho, Harper-Mercer, Rodger, and Harris. What shines through in their writings is an intense narcissism—a marked feature of which is a grandiosity that assumes godlike proportions. Harris, writing, "It's humans I hate!" spoke of how he and Dylan were "going to kick-start a revolution," adding, "I declared war on the human race."[128] How better to deal with the ineptitude—the powerlessness—of not having a girlfriend or even having sexual relations than to assert the supreme pow-erfulness of a sadistic and vengeful God who *murders* the girl, or whole bunches of girls, who refuse some man their friendship and sex. In Harris's manifesto, which was written a year or so before the Columbine massacre, he mirrors the credo of the serial killer Mike DeBardeleben, written some two decades earlier. DeBardeleben wrote, "The wish to inflict pain is not the essence of sadism. The central impulse is to have complete mastery over another person . . . to become the absolute ruler over her, to become her god . . . to force her to undergo suffering without her being able to defend herself. The pleasure in the complete domination over another person is the very essence of sadism."[129]

For many of the older school shooters, sadistic murder was the antidote to rejection and impotence. If Cruz committed the seventeen murders of which he is accused, they may have served the same purpose and been built on the same foundation: social fecklessness and, in Cruz's case, recent rejection by a girl. Large-scale murder was also the antidote to the hopelessness based on the assumption that one's life would remain forever unfulfilled: no success in work, no sexual partner, no firm friendships, no respect, not even the satisfaction of having made one's mark—one's small page in the book of humanity. That is a path to oblivion and suicide. Here, even the suicide is a flop: a recognition that one will never be recognized. As a valued member of society? No. As a saint? Surely not. As the embodiment of evil? Probably. For such a person, fame trumps ignominy. As journalists are all too aware, "If it bleeds, it leads." So, if a desperate and angry student brings a gun to school and is quickly apprehended, or else is arrested after wounding or even killing one or two others? Page 7 and then oblivion. Given the large number of gun murders in the United States, even killing three or four victims means the bottom of the newspaper's fold and Warhol's "fifteen minutes of fame." But real carnage? Headlines! Here, semiautomatic weaponry gives the fame-hungry murder-suicide type at least a fighting chance. This helps account for the infatuation of the fame-hungry class with this category of firearm. School shootings remain an evil that will not be put to rest until the anti-gun people begin to outnumber the gun enthusiasts, and until, among the citizenry, semiautomatic firearms are outlawed, instituting reforms like those passed in Australia.

CHAPTER FOURTEEN

MAY JUSTICE TRIUMPH OVER LAW

Contemporary Forms of Evil
Not Involving Violence,
Including a Commentary on
Child Custody Cases and the Courts
That Preside Over Them

W hen we think of evil, our minds turn usually to acts of violence—kidnap, rape, murder, and torture—especially when preceded by planning, deliberation, or what is called in law *mens rea*: literally, "guilty mind" or *malice aforethought*.[1] There are, however, other acts of a nonviolent nature that so seriously violate social norms or have such severely adverse psychological effects on others that they rise to the level that society would regard as evil. Incest is an example, even in the rare instance where the victim has been coaxed into giving a kind of consent. In many recent child custody cases, one parent will have been recognized as acting out of spite against the other parent in such a way as to deviate markedly from what would be in the best interests of the child. Many of the examples in this chapter will focus on situations that have gone dreadfully wrong in legal matters surrounding custody, foster care, divorce, and sexual predation, where not just the level of injustice, but also the level of pain inflicted on the injured party, have risen to "evil" levels. The cases all revolve around intimacy gone awry: the worst things that can happen among intimate partners before marriage, during marriage, after a marriage dissolves, or in cases in which the parents are unmarried but involving acrimonious disputes between the parents or the child's close relatives. Custody disputes occur most often in the aftermath of divorce—except in the less common cases precipitated by the death of one parent—and are now encountered more frequently than in earlier times, in this era of "new evil."

DISORDER IN THE CUSTODY COURT

Nature, having put a premium on preservation of the species, has rigged it so that procreation can often be achieved in twenty minutes or less, and is often enjoyable, whereas, in our species anyway, parenting takes some twenty years. Enjoyment is not guaranteed. Child custody disputes are a testimony to this disparity. Many a couple comes to the custody courts having enjoyed the procreation part but having rued the promise they once made at the altar to remain together, for companionship if possible, but primarily for the proper nurturing and raising of whatever children they might bring into the world. Paradoxically, both parents in these disputes often have considerable and, at times, approximately equal affection for their children, even as they have developed over the years a cordial dislike or even a withering hatred for one another. The same is true in the less common situation in which a nonmarital partnership has broken up, and a child becomes a pawn in an ugly game of "ownership."

Many years ago—though still within my lifetime—when divorce was a rarity, custody courts were probably not very busy, if they existed at all. Divorce rates in the United States began to increase in the middle of the last century, peaking in the 1960s, to almost 50 percent of marriages, and tapering off a bit lately. In the early twentieth century, many more people took their religious beliefs more seriously than they do now. Divorce was discouraged by several religions, and forbidden by others. As we noted earlier, the feminist movement, which became a major social force in the 1960s, had the great advantage that women who were bullied, abused, and otherwise mistreated by their husbands now had freer access to the divorce courts. They also had freer access to the pill and to other means of contraception. Women could not as easily be impregnated into marriages for which they had no enthusiasm, nor as easily forced to have more children than they could handle. That was the good news. The bad news was that not all men took these freedoms lying down. Some protested vociferously, at times pugnaciously, at the notion of losing the women they "possessed." Yet, if wives were no longer "possessions" for some of these men, surely the children were their "possessions"—after the manner of families in certain Islamic countries, where children "belong" to their fathers and revert to their care in cases of divorce. Male pride and male strength manage, in these instances, to trump the uncertainty of paternity—a dicey thing, at best, since, in the days before DNA testing, the only men in the world who could be absolutely sure that their children were really *their* children were the Ottoman sultans, whose harems—gilded cages, basically—consisted of girls captured before puberty and guarded by eunuchs of a different race.[2] Male pride enters into the equation of custody disputes in a proportion of cases. Fathers are not very well equipped, in the main, for the total care of infants. Still, some fathers, in divorce cases involving very young children, are reluctant to give up their "proprietary rights" to the mothers, even where the mother would have been the far better choice to retain custody and the father had little talent or free time for the job. But I am getting a bit ahead of my story.

Given the fairly large number of divorces, including those in which there are children, one might expect the custody courts to be inundated with disputes way beyond their capacity for resolution. The situation is not quite so desperate. Fortunately, most divorcing couples with children consist of two reasonably mature persons who are capable of harmonious decisions regarding visitation schedules, and nutritional, medical, educational, and legal issues, and who demonstrate mutual respect for each other's style of parenthood, and rights and privileges. Above all, they show flexibility in dealing with whatever stipulations their attorneys draw up in separation agreements. Parents of this sort are not seen in custody courts, instead handling matters quite well by themselves.

The parents who are seen in custody courts are of a different nature. Each such couple has had at least one major problem regarding their children that could not be resolved without the intervention of the court. Although Tolstoy reminds us in the opening page of his *Anna Karenina* that "happy families are all alike; every unhappy family is unhappy in its own way," in reality, custody disputes constitute a genus with only three main species. There are couples in which the father deserves custody because the mother is ill-fitted to the task; there are those in which the mother deserves custody because the father is ill-fitted to the task; and there are the rarer cases in which both parents are dreadful and no adequate solution can be found short of foster care or, if the children are old enough and the parents can afford it, boarding school. My own impressions on this subject stem from my serving as an expert witness in many custody disputes, helping to decide on the worthiness of one or another parent. Occasionally, I was appointed by the court to evaluate both parties. Depending upon the financial means of the participants, each of whom has attorneys and an expert witness, plus a court-appointed psychiatrist or psychologist, legal guardians, and sometimes persons from child protective services, the bills can add up quickly to high amounts. Lady Justice is traditionally depicted as wearing a blindfold to ensure fairness, but it has been my experience that, sometimes, she is blinded not by a black cloth but by a blank check made out by one of the parents. What does sometimes happen is that a wealthy parent can hire the best and most vigorous attorneys, the most prestigious experts, and so on—in such a way as to present a picture that, sometimes beyond its actual merits, can impress a judge or sway a jury toward a decision favored by, as the saying goes, the "more monied party." Sometimes, the attorneys for the more affluent parent can create one after another motion and counter motion, ultimately exhausting the resources of the other parent, who then relinquishes custody.

In the past quarter century, I have been involved in over fifty custody cases, mostly concerning parents from states in the Northeast, less often, from the Southern states or the West Coast. I have looked at the outcomes in these cases, with a view to determining how often the more worthy parent prevailed or the less worthy parent was awarded custody. There is admittedly a measure of subjectivity in such an exercise. Not all would agree with my opinions, just as the court sometimes did not. I will offer here a number of vignettes about some of the problematical cases as fairly as I can, in hopes the reader can at least understand how I arrived at my conclusions. As for the distribution of the custody cases, this can be summarized as follows:

The mother was the better parent and was given custody: 11 cases
The mother was not the better parent, but was given custody: 5 cases
The father was the better parent and was given custody: 6 cases
The father was not the better parent, but was given custody: 23 cases
Neither parent was adequate, and custody was divided: 1 case
Custody was divided 50/50, or else undecided: 7 cases

These figures suggest that, within my patient sample, the less worthy parent prevailed in about two-thirds of cases. If one omits the eight equivocal cases, then the less deserving father won custody in half of these custody battles. This is quite discouraging because, as we shall see, for a few of these men, the phrase "less deserving" would be euphemistic: some were pedophiles whose wealth and power allowed them access to their children that should clearly have been denied.

One of the thornier problems relates to a kind of "old boy network" of professionals upon whom the judges rely: psychiatrists, psychologists, social workers within the forensic system, familiar with the workings of the court, competent up to a point, rarely of any academic standing, and not much known outside their own circles. There will be disputes now and then in which a parent is denied custody based on arguments put forward by a court-appointed consultant. Those arguments may strike the parent as unfair, or based on insufficient knowledge of the family and its patterns of interaction. As a remedy, the parent may ask for a new evaluation, to be carried out by a new expert, often enough a psychiatrist of wide experience and high academic standing, and with a well-established reputation for objectivity and fairness. So far so good. Yet, if the parent on the opposing side happens to have "legal custody" vis-à-vis decisions about who may be hired to serve in such capacities, that parent can deny permission for the other parent to use the services of the outside expert. The presumption is that this new person could marshal evidence that would reverse the original decision, to the benefit of the other parent. Honoring the rules as they are laid down, the judge may support the wishes of the first parent, creating a *fait accompli*, in which, contrary to the spirit of this chapter, the law will have triumphed over justice. This is arid casuistry, I grant; I will give examples further on to bring alive the point I am trying to make.

REGARDING THE DIFFERENT SPECIES

The outcomes in custody disputes referenced above allow for a little more variety than I had earlier indicated. There were several custody disputes, for example, in which the better parent did eventually prevail but only after a lengthy period of heated dispute. In pyrrhic victories of this sort, sometimes the child was restored to the better parent only after so many years went by that adulthood was now only a few months away, and the courts no longer had jurisdiction.

The situations were a little more complicated than the list above would suggest. In three of the custody disputes, a father who would have been the wiser choice lost initially, but he was eventually awarded custody after a protracted court battle. In another two disputes, a more deserving mother initially had to forfeit custody, only to regain it after a similarly protracted process in the court. The disappointing aspect of the distribution is that the less worthy parent, far from prevailing only *rarely*, actually succeeded in gaining custody more often than the desirable outcome of the better parent gaining custody. This lopsidedness was more apparent in the cases in which the father ended up with custody but was not the more appropriate parent. In the following vignettes, I offer examples built around these main outcome differences. In order to preserve confidentiality, I have omitted all names and altered certain details, while preserving the flavor and essence of each story. I also include some notable examples that were reported in the press.

CASES INVOLVING A MORE DESERVING FATHER

The More Deserving Father Was Granted Custody

The parents, both now in their early forties, were already divorced; the issue to be decided in family court was one of custody and visitation schedules concerning their teenage son and daughter. Both parents came from working-class families, but the father had succeeded in expanding what started out as his own father's grocery store into a large chain of wholesale grocery outlets in two New England states. The marriage had been tumultuous, especially after the birth of the children. The father, a man of unflappable temperament, in hopes of retaining fairly free access to the children after the divorce, had bought a large house across the street from the original marital home. The mother was emotionally volatile, alternating between rageful outbursts over minor matters and moments of self-destructive, at times frankly suicidal behaviors. On one occasion, for example, she purposely drove her car into a tree, totaling the vehicle, and fracturing an arm and a shoulder. During the year-long court battle over custody, she kept the children shuttered in her house and blocked access to their father. He would from time to time leave gifts at the doorstep, along with loving notes expressing an eagerness to get back together with them, but these were all thrown away by the mother. The children were left with the impression that their father did not much care about them. Meanwhile, the court appointed a psychiatrist to evaluate the parents as to their relative merits vis-à-vis custody. A man of meager competence, he seemed to have regarded his mission, in the interest of "fairness," as one of finding both parents psychologically handicapped—one no better than the other—so that the original court decision to give custody to the mother could remain valid. In his report, he characterized the mother's personality as "border-line" because of her extreme moodiness, self-destructive behaviors, and rage outbursts, and the father's personality as "obsessive-compulsive." The father had none of the negative traits of that style, such as stubbornness, parsimony, or emotional remoteness, though he was scrupulously honest, perfectionistic, and detail oriented. These are not character flaws, let alone pathological traits that would adversely affect his role as a father. Being the "more monied" parent was not an issue either, since he was just as generous in hiring attorneys and expert witnesses for his ex-wife as he was for himself. I was able, as the father's expert witness, to make it clear to the court that the parents were in no way "equal" in their level of psycholog-ical illness. He was not ill at all. The court did finally grant him full custody. He was also able eventually to overcome the children's guardedness, such that they too came to recognize his excellence both as a parent and as a philanthropic man in the community.

The More Deserving Father, Suspected of Incest, Was Granted Custody

I received a letter some years ago from a man in Illinois, asking if I could help him in a difficult marital situation. He and his wife had a son of eleven and a daughter of thirteen. The wife had become inordinately sus-picious that he was "carrying on" in a sexually inappropriate way with their daughter. She was unable to demonstrate anything that would, in a court of law, have "evidentiary value"—but not for want of trying. He discovered that she had secreted tape recorders throughout the house, under beds, in cupboards, and behind glassware in the kitchen cabinets so that any sexual noises, footsteps in and out of different rooms, and so forth could be captured on tape, by way of corroborating her suspicions. Several weeks of negative results did not allay her anxieties. Still at a fever pitch of worry and suspicion, she then took her daughter to a motel some distance away, under an assumed name. They became missing persons, their whereabouts unknown. Eventually the two returned, the mother now suing for divorce. The father, having somehow gotten hold of my book *The Borderline Syndromes*, got in touch with me. He asked if I could meet with the family, determine whether his wife were "borderline," and in any case help calm her fears and, if possible, heal the rift in their marriage. I spent several days interviewing both parents and both children. What I learned from my conversations with each of them was that the father, who owned and ran a modest pharmacy in the town, had never laid an improper hand on his daughter, and that the daughter was very comfortable with her father and had no idea why her mother had hurried her off to some hideaway. Both children were doing very well socially and academically; neither showed any signs of emotional distress. The mother's story was quite different. As a teenager, she had been raped by her three older brothers. She tried to tell her father what had happened, but he mocked her for daring to accuse them of any such thing and took the side of her brothers. The experience was not confined to a one-time event, and it became the wellspring of her continual distrust of men. Her suspiciousness grew stronger during her married life with each passing year, culminating in the delusion-strength conviction that, as her daughter reached the same age as when her brothers first raped her, history would repeat itself, never mind that her husband was psychologically and in his everyday behavior a very different person from any of her three brothers. There is a quaint German metaphor to describe a person who manages to overcome past traumata: *über seinen eigenen Schatten zu springen*—to jump over one's own shadows. She was unable to do this. Instead, she went through with the divorce, despite conceding that her fears were probably exaggerated. The children lived afterward with their father, who kept in touch with me over the years and let me know how both had continued to do well in their lives. Yet, even this example of a false accusation of a father molesting a daughter, the only one known to me personally, was not driven by an ulterior motive like greed. Instead, it arose out of the mother's fear that her terrible history would repeat itself.

The More Deserving Father Loses Custody

In an example taken from news reports from 1997, Daryl Kelly, a father of five and US Navy veteran who ran an electronic repair shop in upstate New York, was convicted of raping one of his daughters on a number of occasions. He was sentenced to twenty to forty years in prison.[3] Both parents were struggling with drug habits back at the time of the conviction, though the mother's was more severe, to the point that she was trying to supplement her income through prostitution to defray the cost of the drugs. For reasons unclear, the mother, Charade Kelly, asked the oldest girl, Chaneya, nine at the time, whether her father ever touched her in what her mother euphemistically called her "no-no spot." The girl said no, whereupon her mother threatened to beat her, unless she gave her the answer she wanted. The daughter capitulated—and the father was hauled in for questioning. Despite the lack of any definitive evidence, the case went forward and the father was put in prison. He saw no reason to accept a plea in order to get a reduced sentence of six years, since he knew and asserted he was innocent. Hence the lengthy sentence. After sixteen years, the daughter confessed that she lied about the rape for fear of being beaten by her mother. Around that time, the mother, now having overcome her addiction, also acknowledged that she had coerced her daughter's false accusation. Initially, both the governor and the court had, to their discredit, declined to exonerate and release the father, though the prosecutors were gradually "looking into the matter." The father, African American, was a middle-class man with no prior arrest record for anything, let alone pedophilia. (Notably, not many fathers who have committed incest also offend sexually against girls outside the family.) He was not poor, but he was not rich. It is not clear how good his defense attorneys were in trying to clear his name. Granted that polygraph testimony is not admissible in court, it can nevertheless be helpful as a step in the process of exoneration if one repeatedly passes a polygraph test of the kind that O. J. Simpson failed. The records available to me do not show whether steps of this sort were initially taken, but let us say for the sake of argument that he *had* molested that daughter. The sentence of twenty to forty years would carry way past the time that Kelly could ever have reoffended—the daughters are now all adults—so that he would, at worst, be a no-risk offender at this time, even though everything pointed to his being innocent from the beginning. In 2012, Chaneya wrote a letter to the authorities in New York, recanting her former testimony about the supposed incest, asking the court, in so many words, "Free my innocent father."[4] Her petition garnered nearly 200,000 signatures. Yet, the prosecutors refused to accept her recantation. As of this writing, Daryl Kelly is awaiting a retrial but remains in prison.

CASES INVOLVING A LESS DESERVING FATHER

Introductory Remarks

The "less deserving father" relates to the largest portion of the abovementioned distribution. The fathers I have placed in this category are of two main types. In one group are those who are remarkably self-centered and who entertained remarkable dislike—contempt would be more accurate—for their former wives. Their insistence on gaining custody arose more out of vengefulness than out of any profound affection for their children, the pawns in the perverted chessboards of their parents' acrimonious battles. By "capturing" the mothers' most cherished possessions, their children, these fathers hoped to inflict the greatest possible hurt upon their ex-wives—pain quite possibly lasting forever. As a rather morbid analogy, I remind the reader of the 1996 school shooting carried out by Thomas Hamilton of Scotland, described earlier in this book. After he was accurately accused of pedophilia by the parents of a number of schoolboys, he did not vent his anger by shooting the parents, whose suffering would then have been very short-lived indeed. Instead, making himself the personification of evil, he shot to death sixteen of their children, knowing that, in so doing, he would prolong their parents' suffering to the end of their days.[5] The other important feature of these spiteful fathers is that they did not molest their daughters, nor were they accused of doing so by the mothers. The fathers were operating on a different plane—namely, spite. The other and larger group of less deserving fathers had molested their daughters sexually—in one case, a son—sometimes in not too prolonged or severe a fashion but enough to prompt the mother to sue for divorce and custody. In other cases, there was molestation to the point of incest. In the cases known to me, the fathers were well-to-do and spared no expense to insure that they did not face public humiliation. They tried to blacken the mothers' names, gaining custody by "proving" they, the fathers, were the "better" parents, meantime escaping social stigma. Even in the numerous cases of frank father-daughter incest with intercourse, as I encountered in the histories of hospitalized young women with "borderline" personality throughout my clinical work, I have never seen a wealthy father jailed for the offense, which was the fate of several fathers of low income. Daughters who have been incest victims, especially by a father, have a higher than expected risk for depression, borderline personality disorder, and suicide.[6] The 1971 suicide of Andy Warhol's muse, Edie Sedgwick, born in 1943, is an example. I find it ironical that in the Old Testament, incest was not only considered a grievous sin but was also punishable by death (Leviticus 20: 11–20); it's more ironical, still, that, among the many varieties of incest, father-daughter and father-son were not included.

In recent years, there have been some father-oriented organizations that have argued that fathers have become an endangered species in the custody courts, by virtue of having been accused of sexual molestation unfairly and without any wrongdoing on their parts. They claim this as an example of "parental alienation" by certain mothers who show their spitefulness via these false accusations. Dr. Richard Gardner, a child psychiatrist, popularized this notion, as though parental alienation syndrome deserved a place in psychiatry's official nomenclature.[7] It has never been accepted as a valid diagnosis. In my experience, it is not common for a mother to point the finger at an ex-husband as having molested their daughter when the father was innocent. Most often, the mothers have been able to document the inappropriate sexual behavior, sometimes by taking the child to a pediatrician right after such an incident, or by recording noises or cries that strongly suggest such behavior.

A Less Deserving Father, Motivated by Spite

I had occasion to work some years ago with a mother who had been divorced for about a year. She was seeking custody of her ten-year-old son, the only offspring of the marriage. By day, her ex-husband was a highly successful real estate entrepreneur, widely admired for his savvy in purchasing properties with great promise before they began to escalate in value. By night, he was a confirmed aficionado—an addict, really—of pornography (adult pornography, let it be said), which he would watch in a separate room, to the near exclusion of contact with his wife and son. The wife, herself a former model, might be considered at least as attractive as the women he ogled on the screen, and had the added advantage, so she initially assumed, of being real. It was her inability to persuade him of the desirability of switching back from two-dimensional women to the three-dimensional woman he had married that led her to divorce him. For a time, she had gained primary custody, the father's visitations being limited to Wednesday evenings and alternate weekends. It did not sit well with him that she now had the upper hand in parenting their son. The father then launched a campaign to gain custody and to limit sharply the mother's time with the boy. He went on the offensive, submitting affidavits to the court and accusing the mother of being "paranoid" and "delusional" for characterizing him as a pornography addict. She then sought my help in showing, via an evaluation of her personality and general mental state, that she was in no way either of these things. An easy task, or so it seemed, since she was a remarkably calm, candid, and sweet woman who, even on objective psychological testing, showed no signs of any abnormality. The court appointed a psychiatrist to interview both parties, by way of helping the court make the wisest decision. The psychiatrist eventually issued a report of Dickensian length, an interesting feature of which was a detailed description of my impressions about the mother: impressions gained during his phone call to me, with which he disagreed item by item, proving to his satisfaction that I was wrong on all counts. The *interesting feature* was that he had never had a phone conversation with me at all, nor any other interchange, and had given as the date of this pretend conversation one on which I was lecturing in Japan, where he had no way of reaching me. I had hopes that her attorneys, in drawing attention to this fraudulent material, could help the mother in her quest to retain custody. This was not to be. Her attorneys were intimidated by the array of legal talent the father was able to engage, by way of bolstering his cause. In addition, a court-appointed psychiatrist enjoys immunity from prosecution in almost every state, including the state in which this trial was taking place. To challenge one becomes a task like that of the male mating salmon: an uphill battle with a fatal ending. The court came down in favor of the father. The mother henceforth saw very little of her son throughout his adolescent years. Sometimes, spite trumps right. Justice does not always triumph over Law.

The father in this case bore a strong resemblance to the "dominant males," sometimes called "alpha males," who make up about 5 percent of the men in any culture: men with leadership abilities, usually with strong sexual drives, some also blessed with charisma that proves highly attractive to women—especially younger women, some of whom are drawn like proverbial moths to a perilous flame. Colin Wilson, in his monograph on rogue messiahs,[8] alludes to the evolutionary value of the dominant male and his superior capacity to produce dominant and healthy offspring. "Dominant men often have a harem," he adds—shades of the Ottoman sultans—akin to a dominant male lion who take over a pride, and kills both its previous "lord" and his cubs before siring a new batch of supposedly evolutionarily better-equipped cubs with the lioness. At the further end of the spectrum of male dominance, one often confronts a paradoxical situation: men who excel at *fathering* large numbers of offspring but at the price of failing, sometimes abysmally, as *fathers*. These men, that is, have little capacity to relate to women except as vehicles for sexual pleasure—and for making babies—and little capacity for relating to the children as individuals in their own right. Over time, the women in their lives, who, like females in general, have greater empathy and capacities to relate to others as individuals,[9] often tire of finding themselves prized only as sexual objects and seek divorce. Another oddity of men, dominant or otherwise, who are psychologically wired for sex *qua* sex, rather than for sex as the strawberry atop the cake of marital relationship, is the propensity to activities *related* to sex but shorn of intimacy. By this I refer to the sexual paraphilias, referred to often in the public as perversions, such as exhibitionism, fetishism, voyeurism, transvestism, and the like. The father in the example just above, beside his addiction to pornography, also indulged in voyeurism, in which looking at attractive and *nameless* females is accompanied by sexual arousal and becomes an end in itself.

A fair proportion of male movie stars are of the one-in-twenty "dominant male" type, some of whom are well-known, beyond their acting skills, for their numerous marriages and affairs, their lives an odyssey from one alluring female to the next. One thinks of the sailors in the ship steered by Odysseus. Traveling home from Troy, they disobediently refused to stopper their ears and were lured to the enchantress Circe and the fellow sirens she led. These "dominant males" are the ones depicted on the covers of movie magazines at supermarket checkout counters: the envy of many a more ordinary man but whose lives, on closer inspection, are often unfulfilling and shallow—gold-plated rather than solid gold.

Most of the fathers in my cases, who obtained custody despite being the less worthy parent, could be classified as dominant males. Many had molested a young daughter, ranging in age from five to eleven, by touching their vaginal areas but, notably, never with penetration or the male experiencing an orgasm. In one instance, a father had encouraged his teenage son to carry on an incestuous relationship with his teenage daughter, but the father himself did not touch the girl inappropriately.

As we might expect, dominant males are typically of a narcissistic bent from the standpoint of personality classification. The opposite is not true. By no means are all narcissistic men "dominant"—but one of the attributes of narcissism is to care considerably more about oneself than about others. Not surprisingly, a dominant/narcissistic (and heterosexual) man may be highly attracted to women, especially those who are young and attractive, and will be sexually active and competent with them—but not with a great deal of regard for who they are as unique, individual persons. As females, they are necessary. As women, they are "expendable."

The following vignette concerns sexual molestation by a father who nonetheless succeeded in gaining custody. The father was a man who treated women as "necessary"—as objects of sexual gratification—but expendable as persons in their own right. To that extent, he could be considered narcissistic, but, unlike the father in the preceding vignette, he was not a "dominant" male.

A Less Deserving Father, Anxious to Avoid Scandal

The setting of this case was in Texas, on a large ranch owned by an elderly widower and run—nominally—by his son, who was in his fifties. The son bore the title of "administrator" but did no actual work. That was done by a large coterie of farmhands, drivers, bookkeepers, and managers, who made the ranch the prosperous enterprise it was, permitting the son to enjoy his sinecure position with its handsome salary. He had been married before and had a son who was now in the army. By his second marriage, he had fraternal twins—a son and a daughter, both six years old when I became involved in the case as an expert witness on behalf of the mother. A woman of twenty-eight, she had divorced the father a year before when she found evidence that her daughter had been sexually molested by him. The girl had come crying to her mother, saying, "Daddy put his finger in my pee-pee," and there was also soreness, redness, and a few drops of blood in the area, corroborated by a pediatrician right after the event. Meantime, she sued for full custody of the children and visitation by the father only under supervision. Child Protective Services (CPS) for the county was brought into the case. A CPS worker confirmed that the incident in question had taken place, further, that the molestation was continuing, since the father, who vigorously denied the allegations, had the usual unrestricted visitation, awaiting adjudication by the court. The CPS worker reported the situation to her own supervisor, but the latter allegedly warned her that, no matter what the girl said or showed, the worker was to come back with "unsubstantiated" or "inconclusive" findings. If there was any dominant male in this scenario, it was the paternal grandfather, whom the surrounding community looked up to as the real "boss" of the ranch, and who was eager to protect his son from public humiliation as a child molester. The father, of course, wished to avoid obloquy of this sort and enjoyed the support of the community—specifically, of its police, its investigators, and court personnel—in shielding the powerful family. As for the mother, she was accused of creating stress for her daughter by reporting molestation to the authorities, as though this constituted "parental alienation." On the strength of that accusation, the court ordered that the mother see the children only under supervision in the presence of a social worker. Besides the emotional hardship for the mother and the children—especially the daughter—there was financial hardship, since she and her family had nowhere near the means to sustain a long legal battle compared with the wealth of her ex-husband's family.

A Less Deserving Father with Hebephilic Tendencies

When sexual arousal is dependent primarily upon attraction to adolescents of either sex, the condition is called, technically, *hebephilia*. The condition, one of the paraphilias, takes its name from Hébé, the Greek goddess of youth, who was the daughter of Zeus and Hera. As a divinity, Hébé had it in her power, so it was said, to make aged persons young again. In common parlance, *pedophilia* is used as a general term for those who seek sexual gratification with younger-than-adult persons, but the term "pedophile" more correctly refers to those who seek prepubescent children, while "hebephile" is applicable to those who seek adolescents who are not yet adults. The participants in this custody issue consisted of a recently divorced couple: a woman in her midtwenties and her considerably wealthy ex-husband, who was twice her age. He had never had a sustained relationship with a woman until he met his wife. His sex life had previously consisted of brief episodes in massage parlors or similar institutions, in which the girls were really fifteen or sixteen but claimed they were "adults" of eighteen or twenty, by way of sidestepping any imputation of statutory rape. Once married, he insisted his wife undergo depilatory treatments, rendering her quite hairless apart from the top of her head, taking on the appearance more of an adolescent than that of the young adult she was. He was heavily involved in pornography, with a strong preference for scenes of ménage à trois with three adolescent females. The couple had a daughter during the second year of their marriage. He continued to indulge in what were now extramarital escapades, in the course of which his wife acquired several sexually transmitted diseases. Those and her husband's outbursts of anger led to their divorce when the daughter was five. On a few occasions, he became physical with his wife during arguments and once broke one of her ribs. For a few weeks after, she took medications for pain and anxiety. This became an issue during the ensuing custody dispute. The wife, who was warm, competent, and devoted as a mother, asked for residential custody, since the father had already relocated to a locale quite far from where they had been living. The court-appointed examiners saw fit to construe the mother, by virtue of her brief use of those medications, as an "addict" in whose care it would be "dangerous" to entrust the daughter. The father was able to prevail, gain custody, and take the daughter to his new locale— far enough away that the mother rarely had any opportunity to visit with the girl. There was the aroma of prejudice surrounding the case: the court, including the judge and the court-appointed evaluators, acquiesced too readily to the less deserving parent who had greater power and wealth, meantime denying custody of a five-year-old daughter to her mother, who would have been the more empathic, caring, and ever-available parent. All the more so, the needs of a girl of five would, in this contentious custody situation, have been better served by the mother.

SOME SYSTEMIC ISSUES IN CUSTODY CASES

In communities or in countries in which children are, for the most part, born to married people (or, as in modern Scandinavia, couples who generally remain together, albeit without a state-sanctioned certificate) of good degrees of emotional maturity, divorce or separation would be uncommon, and custody disputes even more uncommon. Mature couples, even when they split up, cooperate in ways ensuring what is in the best interests of their children. Arrangements are worked out harmoniously. Court intervention is seldom necessary. Since the courts, in such blessed environments, are not swamped with cases, judges, court personnel, and the panel of advisers, they have adequate time to look carefully, and leisurely, into the details, affording the courts the best chance of reaching a conclusion that indeed is in the best interests of the involved children. From my experience in Scandinavia over the past thirty-five years, I believe this is pretty much true of Denmark, Norway, and Sweden. Perhaps less populated parts of the United States enjoy this kind of unhurried custody negotiation, but in the densely populated urban centers, case overload is the norm; family courts are swamped. To hire the best-trained people in adequate numbers would cripple the budget of any municipality, which could never cut corners on public safety, such as the police and fire departments, in any case. The wisest decisions would come, ideally, from well-qualified child psychiatrists—preferably those who are parents themselves, interacting with judges and other key court personnel, who also know about parenthood from the inside and could make decisions from the heart, not just from the book.

In New York City, cultural heterogeneity is a special problem—actually, a double problem. The borough of Queens, for example, is the most cosmopolitan place on Earth, populated as it is by substantial groups of people from 120 or more countries, speaking as many languages and representing as many different cultures. The city's CPS hires, at modest wages, workers from many different countries, where levels of training may have also been modest. In questioning young girls about possible sexual abuse, ample time and considerable finesse are needed. This finesse may include skill in the use of play therapy with stuffed animals or dolls, through which the child may reveal what she—it will usually be a she—would not or could not reveal in words. It has been my sense that CPS workers seldom have the skill sets or the luxury of time to form a firm impression whether abuse occurred or not. If a girl denies that her father touched her in a sexual area, there are several possibilities: (1) he never did any such thing, and her words should be taken at face value; (2) she senses he would get in trouble if she tells the truth that he, in fact, did so, and she wishes to protect him; or (3) he did so and warned her to say otherwise so that her denial is in the service of self-protection. It is better for a seasoned child psychiatrist or psychologist to sort this out.

Sometimes, in the most egregious cases, custody does not even come into the issue. I had some years ago worked with a girl of seventeen whose father—a high executive in a major company—had impregnated her after nine years of sexual molestation, which later progressed to intercourse. He then drove her, with her mother in the car, to an abortion clinic some miles away, the mother making no protest. In all fairness, I have also treated women whose mothers divorced their fathers immediately, upon learning of father-daughter incest, but sometimes, just having some money, as opposed to none, makes the difference. I once supervised a psychiatric trainee whose patient was a sixteen-year-old girl. Her father had forced her to submit to incestuous relations with him, in the aftermath of which she had become depressed and suicidal. When she told her mother, the mother said, "Just put up with it, dear. In two years, you'll be on your own; meantime, daddy puts bread on our table." These were not even contests between Justice and Law, because they never got as far as the law. These were contests between Justice and Money. The girl who underwent the abortion was warned by her father that, if she ever told of what happened, he would kill her. Her parents abandoned her after the procedure. She had to hitchhike the one hundred miles back to where she lived. Understandably enough, she suffered a mental breakdown and had to be hospitalized. She became "selectively mute" and told none of us about the incident for over a year. After learning about it, we noted that it was wiser, in the interest of her safety, to not make a formal legal accusation. If the father had been put to trial for the incest, he would never have been sentenced to life in prison without parole. This was not a murder case. It was not even an easily verifiable case of incest. Even had the aborted fetus been preserved, the event occurred three years before DNA testing became available, which could have confirmed the father's guilt. At most, he would have received a brief sentence and then become free to carry out his warning. There is a saying in Russian: *lucheh zhivaya sobaka chem smyertnii lyev*—better a live dog than a dead lion. So to ensure that no harm befell the victim, we felt it necessary to back away from seeking legal action.

In custody disputes in which a mother has raised allegations of sexual misconduct by a father—unlike the preceding examples, in which the mothers themselves kept silent—the mother is, in the great majority of cases, correct in her suspicions and expresses them out of protective feelings toward the child in question—almost always a daughter, rarely a son. Even when the mother's suspicions turn out to have been not fully substantiated or even groundless, she will generally have been motivated by protectiveness and not by vengefulness or greed, as attorneys for the father will sometimes insinuate. In the following case, a mother served as a whistle-blower for an incest case that had a particularly modern ring to it, since a young girl's privacy was further violated by concomitant use of the internet.

A Less Deserving Father Who Was Awarded Custody

A Pennsylvania family consisted of parents in their late thirties and two daughters: one nine, the other five. The parents had recently separated, largely because comments from both girls were strongly suggestive of their having been molested sexually by their father. The mother had made numerous cell phone recordings and videos of her conversations with her daughters. The five-year-old would say, "There's a monster under my bed. . . . Daddy is my monster." The older girl told her mother that "Daddy dances naked in front of me and waves his penis [she knew the word] up and down and side to side." She had told her teacher in school that she was "scared to see Daddy." The older girl also complained to her mother: "My vagina [she knew that word as well] and bum have been hurting me." She has been afraid to wipe herself after using the toilet. She told her mother that, when she would be in bed at night, "Daddy pulls me tight into him and makes me feel uncomfortable," adding that "Daddy has a sick brain . . . he touched me on my private parts." She often had night terrors, thrashing about in bed, and yelling, "Stop it, Daddy!" The younger girl complained to her mother that "Daddy stuck a pencil in my privates [e.g., her vagina]." Perhaps more disturbingly, the father exposed the girls to pornographic videos in which the dialogue consisted of an older man "turning on" a young girl with all manner of highly explicit sexual "come-ons" of the "master-slave" type. In one video, the two participants used the fictional names "Dolfus" and "Accalia." In one part of the dialogue, Dolfus tells Accalia to take off her clothes and put on the bathrobe he provides, adding, "You'll need to be ready to be photographed. Do you think you can handle that?" To this, she replies, "Oooh, I love the robe. You got it in pink. . . . Oh, Uncle—the robe feels so silky." Dolfus leans forward to kiss her cheek, his hand grazing her private areas. He says, "Maybe we can go for a swim in the lake. . . . I'll go get my camera." Accalia replies, "Wow, that would be fun." The behavior of the father in this case was seductive and reprehensible. Yet, he was able to get custody away from the mother, claiming that she could not prove her allegations—despite the recorded conversations and videos—and that one could not put children at the age of five or even nine on the stand to be examined and cross-examined. It is puzzling that the court and its examiners were reluctant to give credence to a mother complaining that her husband had been sexually molesting their children. Fathers are far more likely, statistically speaking, to offend in this way than are mothers. Within my fifty-four years of psychiatric practice, much of it devoted to working with "borderline" (BPD) patients, I have encountered one case of mother-daughter incest, two hospital-based cases of mother-son incest (both sons committed suicide), two outpatient cases of mother-son incest, two hospital-based instances of father-son incest, and one outpatient victim of father-son incest—but I have seen many dozens of hospitalized and ambulatory female patients who had been molested by a father, stepfather, uncle, or grandfather. On the other side of the equation would be innocent fathers falsely accused by their wives of molesting one or more of their children. This is uncommon. An example is the case of Daryl Kelly mentioned above. There are a few others in the legal literature. It is common knowledge that men vastly outnumber women as persons committing crimes of violence—murder, rape, assault, and kidnap—and crimes of sexual impropriety, including incest and creating or trafficking in child pornography. The mother in the present case should have been heard, her fears and accusations respected and carefully investigated.

THE PERILS OF FOSTER CARE: AN UNJUSTLY ACCUSED COUPLE

As we have seen, custody disputes that require court intervention decide which of two parents would, in the best interest of the child, be better suited to have primary custody and greater time with the child. Foster care becomes the solution for children whose home environments are so destructive as to warrant their removal from a home and placement instead in the care of individuals other than the parents. Depending on circumstances and availability, foster homes may contain a new father and mother, or at times just one parent figure—usually a foster mother. Again, depending on circumstances, the court mandating fosterage may anticipate that the placement need only be for a short time, followed by the child's return to the original home, or for a long time, or even permanently. Permanent abrogation of parental rights and subsequent placement until a child reaches legal adult age—usually eighteen—is a rare event, precipitated by *well-documented* horrific physical and/or sexual abuse by one or, in cohabiting or married couples, both parents. The more usual situation is that foster care is temporary; the adverse conditions that prompt the need for foster care, worrisome as they may be, fall short of "horrific." Things can go wrong in either of two main ways, if not both. First, if the home environment was not truly bad enough to justify foster care, the children may be moved from a perhaps less than ideal situation to a worse one, being deprived of parents who were not at all as bad as the authorities, such as teachers, school psychologists, and workers from child protective services, have declared. Second, if the original home environment truly warranted transfer to foster care, the environment provided by the foster family may actually be worse than the parental home.

Before discussing one of the more complex foster care cases in which I have been involved, it is worth mentioning that there are many more poor families than bad ones. Sometimes, an otherwise very decent family overwhelmed by financial straits asks the authorities in their community to arrange foster care for some of their children. If all goes well, there is nothing more to be said—but I recall, during a visit to New Hampshire when I was giving a workshop on "borderline" patients, I was asked to interview a man of about thirty who had a rather explosive temper. He had been in a group therapy session the day before, and another man had insulted him. The man I was to interview right away "decked" the fellow, punching him and knocking him down. He was apologetic for having lost control and proceeded to tell me his life story. He was one of five children from a poor family. His parents tearfully gave the youngest two to foster parents, in hopes they would be better fed and better looked after. Each child went to a different foster family. When my interviewee was in elementary school, he was not allowed to enter the new home if the foster parents had not returned from work. Given no key, he had to wait outside, sometimes for hours. If he had to use the toilet, he had no option but to relieve himself on the lawn. The neighbors—who would not let him use their own bathrooms—then informed the foster parents about his urination and defecation on their lawn, which prompted the foster parents to beat the child mercilessly and make him kneel for an hour upon small pebbles with his hands tied behind his back. He was then sent to bed without his supper. The full account of what he endured at the foster home puts one in mind of Dickens's *Oliver Twist* or, for a contemporary account, of Janet Fitch's heartbreaking story of Astrid in her novel *White Oleander*. Sometimes, the man I interviewed would get angry at his own two small children, but he was so afraid of hurting them as he had once been hurt that he would run out into the woods outside his house, cut his wrists, and sit there till his temper cooled down. He never struck his wife or his children—but with the stranger in the group who had insulted him, he did not curb his rage. This was my first experience with foster care; over the years that followed, I have heard many a similar tale from other patients who had been mistreated by foster parents. Admittedly, as an expert in personality disorders, I do not get to hear about the good cases, so my impressions are skewed and cannot be taken as "representative." Yet, the absence of a blood tie does appear, in some cases, to heighten the risk of maltreatment in foster families. One must also distinguish between foster families who take in one child from those to whom large numbers of children are sent simultaneously for foster care, in what amounts to a cottage industry by persons whose only job is to accept such children at the behest of the local authorities. The man I interviewed in New Hampshire was a victim of cruelty. Children who find themselves in homes where fosterage is done "wholesale" are probably less likely to be treated with cruelty but may be at risk for comparative neglect, since it is not easy to give much individual attention to a dozen or more foster children.

The following case concerns two children who ended up in a "wholesale" foster home, where they had to share the foster parents with three other sets of foster children, plus three natural children of the foster parents, amounting to eleven children in all. Foster care for the two children—a boy and his sister—was problematical, but first came a miscarriage of justice. The boy in question was four and in pre-kindergarten. He was of average intelligence, according to psychological testing, but his behavior at school earned him the label "unmanageable." Though purportedly toilet-trained, he would sometimes relieve himself next to the toilets rather than in them. He would knock over the building blocks of the other children and scatter their drawings all over the classroom. Most troubling, at least for the teachers, was his tendency to tell stories of terrible things happening to him at home: being fed "garbage" while his sister and their parents ate the good food, having his hair pulled if he said bad words, and being beaten with a belt when he misbehaved, among other excessive and outmoded punishments. His five-years-older sister, a well-behaved and unusually bright pupil at school, suffered no such indignities and was known to have a much higher IQ. One day, during snack time at school, the boy tossed the other children's food off the table and told the teacher that his mother had struck him with a stick. There were no marks, scars, or scratches anywhere on his skin, but the teacher was alarmed and called

CPS. A worker from that agency came to the school posthaste, talked to the boy briefly, and summoned the police to take both the boy and his sister to a hospital for evaluation and to arrest the parents. Since the boy was as widely known in the school for lying, as well as for misbehaving, it did not speak well for the CPS agent to have arranged no meeting with the parents to hear their side of the story. Granted that polygraph results are not admissible in court, it might have been helpful to test the parents anyway. If the "lie detector" detected no lies, it might have helped persuade CPS that the parents had not really abused the boy. During the parents' brief stint in jail, CPS sent the children from the hospital—where no signs of bruising or other evidence of parental mistreatment were discovered—straightway to a foster home in a dangerous neighborhood. After two years of neglect and bare-minimum care by the foster parents, who were in no way similar to the parents either in background or financial resources, CPS realized the inadequacy of the foster parents. During those two years, the birth parents saw their children on rare, brief occasions and only under supervision. The children were then assigned to a different foster home, run by a single woman, albeit more sympathetic than the first foster parents, who lived nevertheless in an even more dangerous neighborhood. The children could never play outside after returning from school. Three more years went by—again, with only the sparsest of contact with the birth parents. The children now called the replacement foster guardian "Mom," reacting to the birth parents as though they were strangers. This was especially so of the boy, whose memory of the birth parents was less vivid than that of his now thirteen-year-old sister. As for the CPS personnel—mainly social workers and psychologists—they are often modestly paid persons with no academic credentials. Yet, the court paid no attention to the contrary opinions of experts brought into the case, who uniformly regarded the parents as innocent of any wrongdoing. Judges in cases of this sort are often reluctant to change their opinions, no matter the strength of exculpatory evidence. There is the fear that, if the children were returned to the parents, and there were truth in the "1 percent chance" they had, in fact, abused a child, the parents might do so again. This would leave the judges with "blood on their hands." So fosterage remains in place, which, in this case, has gone on for more than half a decade.

PREDATORS

From all that we can gather about the history of our species, including material from ancient relics even before we developed picture writing (6,600 BCE) and word writing (3,500 BCE), men used their greater physical strength to dominate the so-called weaker sex and to ensure sexual access to women. The earliest marriages appear to have been in the Mesopotamian area of Sumer (in what is now southern Iraq), where monogamy had become the rule. Sumer was the birthplace of Abraham, who developed the new religion of Judaism and who became the spiritual father of the three major "Abrahamic" religions. Philosophies that emphasized wisdom, fairness, and the virtues we subsume under the heading of humanity were developing in the West, and also in China, India, and Japan. This new spirit was beginning to supplant the less social, more dog-eat-dog atmosphere that characterized our species in pre-agrarian times. Power and violence came before wisdom.

In our own time, before the cultural changes that occurred in the mid-1960s, when women in increasing numbers were able to work and to fill half the rosters of medical and law schools, the typical family consisted of the man, as "breadwinner," and the woman, as "homemaker." As the economic provider for the family, the man, whatever his background and level of training, tended to rule the roost. The "Me Tarzan, You Jane" mentality that was so pervasive in bygone times did not disappear during the new era. There remain a great many men who continue to use their power, physical and otherwise, to control the women in their lives—men who habitually use their power to control women and, in tomcat fashion, to move from one to the next, grabbing or extorting sexual favors along the way. We call them "predators." The word comes from the Latin *praeda*, meaning "booty" or "plunder," like the things victors in wartime seize from the conquered. So predatory males are not a new species, nor a "new" form of evil. They represent an old evil in new contexts. Examples are legion. One that has seemed almost endemic among men in privileged positions concerns men at higher levels in the hierarchy of the movie industry who are entrusted with hiring attractive young women to be actresses. Some of the women were dismissively said to have "slept their way to the top," prompted by ambition or economic necessity, or both, but in any case having to endure the advances or rough handling by men they would never have chosen of their own accord. In earlier times, it was known that certain titled men living in luxurious estates would take advantage of one or another of their female servants. As mentioned in the chapter on cultural changes, the invention of the typewriter led to many women in the 1860s becoming able to support themselves and to no longer feel at the mercy of men who could have their ways with them for two shillings. What happened was a male backlash and an increase in the occurrence of rape. In the 1960s, we saw an abrupt increase in serial sexual homicide—especially in the United States—in part as a backlash against the greater freedom women were enjoying in work, control of their sexuality, and the ability to divorce abusive husbands.

Beginning in the fall of 2017, what began to happen was an outpouring of complaints by many women, from all social strata, but with many celebrities among them, against predatory men who had taken advantage of them sexually, over a whole spectrum of bad behaviors: verbal pressuring for sexual favors, inappropriate touching, pedophilia and pederasty, and actual rape. Nor was the victimization limited to women. One in seven of the victims in a catalog I prepared of these predatory men was another male: a young boy, an adolescent, or an adult, usually much younger than the perpetrator. As of this writing, I have collected ninety-eight names—all men, except for one woman in the political arena who harassed a male coworker. Not many of the men could bring themselves to own up to the indignities or crimes they had committed. There were nine such men who did, five of whom were sports figures—one each in soccer, basketball, football, hockey, and tennis. Three of the men were either gay or bisexual, and had molested young men they had coached: Jerry Sandusky, a football coach;[10] Lynn Seibel, who was not a coach but was connected with a group of hockey players;[11] and Barry Bennell, a British soccer coach.[12] Three of the men committed suicide: Dr. Robert Browne, a Hawaiian psychiatrist who had masturbated and fondled hundreds of male students who had been sent to him for counseling;[13] Gary Wilensky, a tennis coach who stalked girls;[14] and Garrison Keillor, a state representative.[15] Four of the men were convicted and sent to prison, though Seibel served only a short time. Another eighteen of the men I considered had either apologized, or at least acknowledged that the women and men whom they had molested were correct in their accusations. These twenty-seven men accounted for

28 percent of the entire group. The large remainder denied, trivialized, or minimized the acts of which they had been accused. Of the sixteen men who had committed the most serious sexual offense—namely, rape—their most common response, seen in ten instances, was denial.

The bravery of the first women who pointed fingers at the men who had misused them sexually emboldened other women and a number of men to come forward with their disturbing stories. These revelations combined to paint a picture of what appears to be a coarsening of our society in recent times. The accusations were leveled almost entirely against men in high places: actors, directors, politicians, movie moguls, media hosts, opera and orchestra conductors, business executives, publishers, physicians, financiers, celebrities in movies and sports, and fashion photographers. We know that in the first half of the last century, men in these privileged positions were sometimes misusing and taking advantage of women, and sometimes of men. Yet, the women and also the victimized men were less willing to come forward. So it is hard to be certain whether what we are now witnessing is a true increase in these types of sordid behavior—a truly "new" evil—or primarily a heightened public awareness of sexual misdeeds and crimes that had been occurring to approximately the same extent as before. I suspect that what is occurring now is not dissimilar to the earlier, more hushed-up offenses but is happening more often.

Some of the earlier incidents have been documented. We find this example of a mogul taking advantage of a young woman. Blanca Errázuriz Vergara, born in 1894, was considered the most beautiful woman in her native Chile. She was also an heiress of the richest family of that country. As if proof that advantages of that sort do not guarantee a good life, she ended up, when she was seventeen, marrying an American real estate mogul twice her age. Not as well-off as people thought, John De Saulles was, in reality, a rakish and philandering gold digger who hoped to sponge off her family's millions. Known usually as "Jack," he and Blanca had a son, Jack Jr., born the next year, in 1912. Besides cheating on her in liaisons with actresses and Broadway stars, he also took to living apart from her and, at one point, tried to prevent her from seeing her son. Shortly afterward, she shot De Saulles to death in 1917 and was later acquitted at trial in what was seen as akin to justified homicide.[16] Unlike De Saulles, Blanca was a proper young woman, who had a platonic friendship with a dancer, Rodolfo Guglielmi, famous later as the silent film star Rudolph Valentino. All of this was a decade later than the infamous murder of Evelyn Nesbit's former lover, Stanton White, by her husband, Harry Thaw. White, who cared deeply for Nesbit, was a bit of a philanderer, but by no means a scoundrel. White, the great architect, was a gentleman in an era in which it was a virtue held high for a man to be gentlemanly.[17] The word itself comes from the Latin *gens*, meaning "stock," connoting "coming from a noble family." We now think of the "gentle" part of gentleman as a man who is thoughtful and kind to others, who opens the door for a woman and helps her with her chair. I got a rude awakening about such customs several years ago at a group therapy conference for mental health professionals. The participants were divided into groups of eight, supervised by group leaders. Among those in my group were an elderly Episcopal minister and a young woman in her eighth month of pregnancy. When the minister tried to help her with her chair, the woman—who viewed it as a form of sexism—yanked it back and yelled at him: "Fuck you! I can do my own chair!" *O tempora, o mores!* We are in a different era. This brings me to one of the best commentators on the new wave of predators in which we have become inundated. Peggy Noonan, one of the premier editorial writers for the *Wall Street Journal*, had this to say in her January 2018 commentary on the topic: "All the stories we've read the past few months about predators—not those accused of rape and sexual assault, which are crimes, but of general piggishness, grabbiness, manipulation and power games—have a common thread. The men involved were not gentlemen."[18] She goes on to say, regarding gentlemanliness, "We have lost track of it. In the past 40 years, in the movement for full equality, we threw it over the side. But we should rescue that old and helpful way of being. The whole culture, especially women, needs The Gentleman back." Amen.

In a similar vein to the sentiments of Ms. Noonan, the recent remarks of Kate Upton are particularly appropriate. She writes from the vantage point of a woman who has endured harassment. The photographer's model commented, "Harassment has plagued the fashion industry for decades, but allegations have often been ignored." After giving examples of the experiences she endured when she was eighteen at the hands—literally, at the *hands*— of an executive for whom she worked for a time, she added, "He used his power to make me feel insecure and powerless, but I'm not going to let him intimidate me anymore. These men think they're untouchable, but times are changing." Her word "untouchable" is more apt than she perhaps realized: the women in these situations were viewed as too "touchable." That's been the crux of the problem. Some of the women Upton had spoken with and who had been harassed told her, "It's not all that bad . . . at least it wasn't rape." To which she replied, "That's our only line?—At least it wasn't rape?" Upton did offer a hope for the future: "Good men do exist . . . but we need to make sure we're hiring men with respect for women, not their bodies, but their minds and professionalism."[19]

Among the men in my catalog of predators, many of whom the public regarded as "gentlemen" before the sordid details of their behind-the-curtains behaviors became exposed, were those ten who committed rape—defined correctly by Ms. Noonan as a crime, not just mere nastiness[20]. What will happen to the others? Some have already had to resign from prestigious positions, a few have paid fines to those they mistreated, and a few others were quickly abandoned by their wives or partners. Others suffered moments of public obloquy in the media. Justice did not triumph much over the Law in many of these cases.

Even in the more serious cases of stranger-rape accompanied by violence, committed by men at the opposite end of the social spectrum to that of the privileged predators we have been discussing, Justice often does not triumph over Law. We saw this in the case of Phillip Garrido, who was sentenced to fifty years in prison for raping a young woman but prematurely released after eleven, free then to kidnap and rape Jaycee Dugard, keeping her a sex slave for eighteen years.[21] Much of our current legal system developed over the centuries from British, and later American, jurists, now as a bulwark of stability in a democratic society. Societies have a way of changing at a more rapid pace than the laws that safeguard them.

The safeguards against unjust punishment that are among the glories of Anglo-American law, such as not letting a jury know all of a defendant's previous offenses, lest the jury be prejudiced, allow for early release for inmates whose behavior in prison had been good, and, in the case of those below age eighteen, refraining from giving life sentences without parole. These safeguards do not always serve the public well in recent times, however, given the increase in recent decades of crimes of an unusual and heinous nature of a sort seldom seen before—as thoroughly sketched in other chapters in this book. These changes have occurred even as the murder rate, focusing on the United States, has decreased substantially since the late 1990s.

The crime of rape is notably problematical, from forensic and statistical standpoints. Many cases go unreported. Some jurisdictions count only stranger rape; others include rape when committed by a marital or other sexual partner. If participants are intoxicated, it is not always clear whether this is an aggravating or a minimizing factor, unless a mind-altering drug, such as Rohypnol, is given purposely and surreptitiously to a woman, who is then raped. This would make the man as culpable, in effect, as though it were a "stranger rape." The latter is the least common, but most serious type of rape, often accompanied by violence that may include mutilation or death.[22] Some men who have raped did so only once or twice in their lives, but there is a major problem that involves *repetitive* rapists. A man convicted and imprisoned for raping a woman has little opportunity to repeat such an offense while incarcerated in the all or predominantly male atmosphere of the prison. If sentenced to, say, ten or fifteen years, he may have his sentence be reduced by a third or more for "good behavior." If he is still in the high-risk years for rape—seventeen through forty—he may reoffend. In the more serious domain of men committing serial sexual homicide, many of the "serial killers" had been imprisoned before being later identified as such, for one or two rapes without murder, and then released, whereupon they embarked on their career as serial killers. In my previously mentioned private study of true crime biographies of serial killers who were men committing serial sexual homicide, premature release was a feature in about a third of cases—fifty-four of 169, or 32 percent. Among them were some of the "iconic" and otherwise fairly well-known offenders, several of whom we have discussed in earlier chapters: Rodney Alcala, Ted Bundy, John Wayne Gacy, Nathan Bar-Jonah, Edmund Kemper, Jeffrey Dahmer, and the Sacramento, California, "Vampire Killer," Richard Chase. The miscarriage of justice seems more egregious in these cases because of the great number of rape-murders these men committed once they were released for less serious rapes. They usually already showed abundant signs of psychopathic personalities during the earlier incarcerations. The presence of psychopathy should, ideally, have been a warning sign, alerting the prison authorities that the men in question were not good candidates for release, irrespective of their "good behavior" while in prison.

Recidivism—reoffending after release from prison or, in the case of mentally ill offenders, after release from a forensic hospital—is a challenging problem. The rate will be greater where psychopathy is present and tends to be greater also in certain types of crime, such as rape, especially stranger-rape, and crimes set in motion by some of the paraphilias: voyeurism, exhibitionism, sexual sadism, and the kinds of sexual harassment committed by the predators we have discussed in this chapter. The relevant force here is the repetitive nature of the sexual impulse, fueled in men partly by testosterone, whose titer does not descend appreciably till middle to late middle age—although this is, of course, no excuse. There is no shortage of "career criminals" who commit many varieties of crimes, some violent, others not, with almost clocklike regularity. The legal system does not often deal adequately with criminals of this sort, tending to give many of them quick releases, as though their previous criminal histories—their extensive record of arrests and prosecutions or "rap sheets"—should not be invoked too vigorously against them. Sometimes, in other words, judges or forensic hospital administrators do not heed the warnings inherent in criminal histories of multiple offenses, in which the times between successive incarcerations have been shockingly brief before the next offense.

Here is an example from a forensic patient who ended up committing a rape of unusual brutality in 1990. A man of forty-three had been admitted involuntarily to the psychiatric unit of a municipal hospital because of a psychotic episode following abuse of phencyclidine or "angel dust." That had been the man's eighty-fourth incarceration, whether in jails, prisons, or hospitals. Released after a brief stay, he then, two weeks later, accosted a woman as she was getting into the elevator of her Bronx apartment and attempted to rape her. After erectile failure rendered his attempt unsuccessful, he instead thrust a metal pipe into her vagina, causing severe lacerations and profuse bleeding. He fled the scene but was quickly apprehended. The woman recovered after a lengthy hospitalization, sustaining some permanent injuries. Perhaps because of his mental illness history—though mostly drug related—he was remanded to a forensic hospital, rather than to jail. Meticulous review of his checkered past showed that two weeks was about the maximum time he had ever been "out" before reoffending and being placed back "in" a secure setting. Dr. Robert Hare and his colleagues developed a scale: the Criminal Career Profile (CCP), which shows graphically the differences between "time in" various institutions versus the "time out" when an offender had been living free in the community.[23] With "Time In" plotted on the y-axis and "Time Out" on the x-axis, the CCP, in this case, would show a jagged line almost parallel to the y-axis, meaning that the offender was hardly ever "out." In contrast, a person jailed for a few weeks on two or three occasions would show a CCP that hugged the x-axis, meaning that the person was living free in society almost all of the time. Although the rule in forensic hospitals is for biannual review to assess whether the patient is ready for transfer to a less secure facility, the recommendation was that he never be released; otherwise, the likelihood for re-offense was almost a certainty.

The legal system has not fully caught up with the problem of what one might call high-frequency multiple offenders, who are seen more often in the past two generations. Juries are seldom privy to the whole menu of "priors" so that individuals with numerous previous arrests may wind up with light sentences, while the CCP might suggest that a lengthier incarceration should be considered.

Law triumphed over Justice in an earlier case the week after the 2016 presidential election. Trump supporter Maurice Braswell, furious that the rest of his family had voted for Hillary Clinton, took a meat cleaver and severed his sister's thumb, almost severed his mother's thumb, and slashed at his brother and nephew. Braswell, forty-nine at the time, had seventeen prior arrests and had been in and out of prison for robbery for which he had shortly before completed a twenty-year parole.[24] Since all of the victims survived, the court will not "throw away the key" on the man, though one would like to think that this eighteenth crime would keep him away from the public for a long time. In a more serious case, Clifford Olson, a Vancouver serial killer born in 1940, was first arrested at thirteen for theft but afterward racked up dozens of convictions and spent much of his time in prison for offenses like armed robbery, animal torture, firearms misuse, fraud, and escape before, at age forty, switching to serial sexual homicide of eleven children. When finally arrested and convicted, he faced only twenty-five years in prison, at which point lax Canadian laws would have permitted him to apply for parole. In fairness to Canada, Olson's crimes were so heinous that Canada then eliminated the "faint hope" clause and placed restrictions on early parole for murderers. Olson died of cancer while in prison, at the age of seventy-one.[25]

CHAPTER FIFTEEN

A NEW CHALLENGE TO JUSTICE: KIDS WHO COMMIT EVIL

C hildren who commit murders or other violent acts that rise to the level of barbarity or atrocity were not entirely unknown before the last two generations of the "new evil." They were just rare. Jess Pomeroy, for example, born in 1860—the birth year of America's first prominent serial killer, Herman Mudgett—tortured other children and also cats when he was only six years old. Later, at age eleven, he would experience sexual arousal while beating the penises or testicles of young boys. At twelve, he tried to castrate a boy, for which he was sent to a reformatory. Released after a year and a half for "good behavior," he promptly castrated and killed a boy of four. For this, he was given the death penalty at sixteen, but that was changed to life in prison, where, fifty-six years later, he died in 1932.[1] In Argentina in 1896, Cayetano Godino—also known, because of his ears that stuck out, as El Petiso Orejudo ("Flappy-Eared Fatso")—was born to alcoholic and abusive parents. In childhood, he killed cats and birds, brutally assaulted other children when he was seven, and later killed four children. At sixteen, he lured a boy to a country house, where he hammered him to death before driving a nail through his skull. Arrested and imprisoned for the murder, he spent the next thirty-two years in prison, until, in 1944, he was murdered by other inmates for killing their pet cats.[2]

In the infamous murder of Chicago's fourteen-year-old Robert Franks, the two killers were just at the cusp of adulthood: Nathan Leopold was nineteen, Richard Loeb eighteen. Highly intelligent young men from wealthy families, they aspired to commit the "perfect crime" as a kind of proof of their superiority. They identified with Nietzsche's notion of the Übermensch who was "above" society's rules and norms. Loeb was the psychopath, who talked his friend into joining him in the scheme. They were quickly apprehended and sentenced to death. The famous defense attorney Clarence Darrow argued eloquently against the death penalty; the two were sent to life in prison. Loeb met death in prison, where he was killed by other inmates. Leopold was rehabilitated and released in 1958, whereupon he became a social worker in Puerto Rico, dying in 1971.[3]

In the foregoing cases, Justice and the Law were in equilibrium. Given the culture of the times, the sentences were appropriate for the crimes committed. When we move into the new period we have been discussing, this equilibrium is not always so evident. When Michael Hernandez slit the throat of a classmate, Jaime Gough, killing him, in Florida's Dade County in 2004, both boys were fourteen. Hernandez had at first been sentenced to life in prison, but he was given a chance at release under a new Florida law granting "judicial review" after twenty-five years in prison. This followed the US Supreme Court ruling in 2012, banning life terms without the possibility of parole for minors (i.e., those under age eighteen) convicted of murder. The idea was that a life sentence for a minor constituted "cruel and unusual punishment." Law came close to trumping Justice by not allowing for the possibility that there are murder cases of a cruel and unusual nature that cry out for condign—that is, righteous and equitable—punishment. The judge at the ensuing trial noted that Hernandez's was, indeed, an "uncommon case," given that the boy was preoccupied with becoming a serial killer and had stabbed Jaime forty times and cut his throat. The judge further noted that, during a jail call with a girlfriend, Hernandez had played a song by the death metal band Cannibal Corpse with grisly lyrics about someone dying from a torn trachea. Remarking, "Basic human decency should make it unbearable for anyone who took an innocent life by this means to enthusiastically listen to such lyrics," he decided to reinstate the life sentence.[4]

In 2008, a week before his sixteenth birthday, Boy Scout Nicholas Browning of Cockeysville, Maryland, waited until the rest of his family were asleep and—taking one of his father's guns—shot to death his parents and two younger brothers. He then went out and spent two days with friends before returning home to stage the "discovery" of the family's deaths. He had tossed the gun into the bushes near his house, but the weapon was quickly found and readily shown to be the murder instrument used by Browning. His father had been a scoutmaster and a church leader. Browning was aspiring to become an Eagle Scout, the highest rank for a Boy Scout, supposedly living by the oath to be trustworthy, loyal, helpful, friendly, courteous, kind, obedient, cheerful, thrifty, brave, clean, and reverent. Perhaps we need to add *merciful* and *nonviolent*. He had begun to talk to his schoolmates about killing his parents, but no one took him seriously. He disliked his father and called his mother a dumb, ditzy blonde. He also mentioned how rich his father was and how he wanted some of that money. Perhaps this is why he killed even his brothers, since he would now be the sole legatee of his father's will. If he got away with the murder. Again, however, because of his youth, he may be exempt from serving the four life terms of his original sentence; he could be eligible for parole in twenty-three years "for good behavior."[5]

Contributing to the greater incidence lately of murder by children are factors mentioned elsewhere in the book: the high frequency of post-1960s divorce; many boys growing up without fathers; the violent video games to which many young persons—boys, especially—are, without exaggeration, addicted; and, in America more than elsewhere, the easy access to guns, even to semiautomatic rifles. There is also the internet. The internet played a role in the courtship of fourteen-year-old Nonie Drummond and Spencer Lee King, seventeen, who carried on hundreds of internet and telephone conversations over a nine-month period back in 2001 and 2002. Drummond boasted to her friends how she and King would be married one day on her grandfather's farm in upstate New York. In talking with King, Drummond had upped her age a bit to seventeen. Finally, King arranged for them to meet at a house Drummond shared with her grandfather in Fabius, a rural village near Syracuse. King became angry that she had lied to him about her age. Telling her he had a "surprise" for her, he guided her to a stool. He then stabbed her repeatedly in the throat with a kitchen knife he had brought along. After killing her, he set the house on fire. After King's arrest and conviction, the judge lowered the sentence from thirty years to twenty-four when King confessed to the murder—with more years off for "good behavior."[6] Some might find it hard to grasp fully the dreadfulness of the crime. How might another Romeo have dealt with his telephonic Juliet who was untruthful about her age? He might have said, "Nonie, it really bothers me you didn't tell me you were only fourteen. I think we have to go our separate ways." Or, "Sweetie, it bothers me a little you weren't up front about your age . . . but you're so lovely, I'm going to wait till you're eighteen, and then we'll marry." But slash her throat and burn the house down? A murder of this level of brutality paints a different picture from the kind of impulsive adolescent who commits one spur-of-the-moment act of violence for whom the law—and the community—can afford greater leniency, as in the case of Billy Sinclair. Sinclair was a man who, when he was twenty, fired a pistol over his shoulder as he fled an armed robbery and inadvertently killed the store owner.[7] Not at all psychopathic, he became the editor of the prison newspaper, was eventually released, got married, and now works in a law firm dedicated to helping other prisoners.

Quite a different person is Craig Price, known as the Warwick Slasher. Even as a child in Rhode Island, Price showed criminal versatility, the psychopathic trait described by Dr. Robert Hare that, as we discussed earlier, is characterized by indulging in a wide variety of criminal activities. His repertoire included robbery, breaking and entering, drug use, stalking, assault, and burglary. At thirteen, he invaded a neighbor's house and murdered twenty-eight-year-old Rebecca Spencer, stabbing her fifty-eight times. Then, at fifteen in 1989, he broke into another house and killed a thirty-nine-year-old mother and her two daughters, crushing the head of one girl with a kitchen stool. Interrogated by the police, he failed a polygraph, then confessed, with no sign of remorse—another psychopathic trait. According to Rhode Island law, he could only be remanded to a Youth Correction Center till he turned twenty-one. He was then released, which enraged the community and the surviving members of the victims' families. While at the center, he refused treatment. The outrage led to passage of a bill allowing the attorney general to commit a mentally ill offender to a forensic hospital, if still deemed a threat to the public. While there, he threatened the life of an employee and was then sentenced to fifteen years in prison. In jail, he got into a fight with another inmate and a guard, for which an extra year was added to his sentence. Several more years were added when, on several occasions, he attacked prison guards in the years between 1998 and 2009. He got one thing right when he claimed, "I'm going to make history."[8] In 2017, now in his midforties, Price tried to stab to death another inmate. His prison sentence was, *mirabile dictu*, about to expire—but he was then given another two and a half years for the attack on the cellmate. Because Rhode

Island, like many states, does not take into consideration the personality configuration of young defendants as a factor relevant to decisions about release or continued retention, Price's confession while still fifteen, after the murder of the mother and her daughters, meant that the state could not hold him past age twenty-one. Even now, he could be released within the next few years, in 2022—unless he does what he has always done: periodically attack prison guards or other inmates.[9] Justice has had a rough time triumphing over Law and has mostly the Rhode Island citizenry to thank.[10] The citizens may not have known the details of Hare's psychopathy checklist, but they know incurable evil when they see it.

Some of the school shooters we described in an earlier chapter were, of course, minors who committed mass murder. As I am writing these lines, there has been another large-scale school shooting: this time in Santa Fe, Texas, not far from Houston. The alleged shooter was Dimitrios Pagourtzis, a seventeen-year-old high school student who, on May 18, 2018, reportedly took his father's Remington 870 shotgun and .38-caliber revolver and shot to death eight students and two teachers. One of the victims was sixteen-year-old Shana Fisher, who had recently rejected his advances, making it clear she would not date him. Fisher was "afraid the creep would kill her" and had told her mother that he was going to do so. He is suspected of making good on his promise, allegedly killing Shana plus nine others and wounding another thirteen. Described as a "weird loner"—as many school shooters have been regarded by schoolmates—a reported quick confession by Pagourtzis obviated the death penalty. Yet, even in Texas, a seventeen-year-old would not likely be given a death sentence or even a life without parole sentence. Perhaps in an imitation of what the Columbine shooters had done, explosive devices, Molotov cocktails, were left around and in the school, supposedly to create further destruction—but they failed to explode, just as those in the Columbine massacre did not detonate.[11]

The Pagourtzis case raises the same serious questions about the law, as did the Craig Price and other similar cases involving perpetrators under eighteen. The laws were fashioned for the most part in "kinder and gentler" times when children and adolescents rarely committed the kinds of crimes we would call heinous. Unfortunately, in the past two generations, we have seen a disturbing number of such crimes by young boys. (It will rarely be girls.) There are, to be sure, many children and adolescents who, out of impulsivity or desperation, commit a crime but who do not have callous-unemotional or psychopathic traits. Capable of redemption, these are the ones deserving of briefer sentences and the possibility, if upon release, to lead exemplary lives for some number of years, of their records being sealed.

One of the men I interviewed for the Discovery Channel's program *Most Evil* struck me as deserving of a benevolent treatment of this sort. The devout Mormon Ron Luff, who fell under the spell of the charismatic, psychopathic cult leader Jeff Lundgren we discussed earlier in this book, walked the five members of the Avery family—who had begun to see Lundgren for whom he was—to the barn, where the leader then shot the family to death, one by one. A good person, but brainwashed, as he soon realized, he was sentenced to life in prison. Now in his late fifties, Luff told one of his prison guards, "Shedding that [brainwashed] mindset has afforded me a great sense of freedom, even in the captivity of incarceration. . . . My hope is that we can grow from this type of tragedy, and learn not only what cultivates such bizarre and self-destructive behavior, but ultimately how best to defuse it."[12] How different from Kirby Anthony. Born out of his mother's "one-night stand" with an unknown man, Kirby was adopted into the Anthony family in Alaska. Besides his potential genetic disadvantages, he was allegedly physically abused by his tyrannical adoptive father. Cruel to cats and dogs, and regularly using cocaine, at fifteen, Kirby committed burglary; at sixteen, he set off a bomb in his school, for which he spent a month in juvenile detention; at seventeen, he committed breaking and entering, for which he was remanded to a reformatory for four months; at age nineteen, he committed armed robbery; and at twenty-two, he raped a twelve-year-old girl and left her for dead. His girlfriend left him because of his abusiveness. He later choked another girlfriend and threatened to kill her if she left him. This soured the relationship, so she fled to the other side of the country. At twenty-three, he murdered an Inuit man, for which he was not arrested; set fire to a shop from which he was fired; and broke into his aunt's house, strangling her and then raping and strangling two female cousins. When he was finally apprehended, examiners noted that he had the one-thousand-yard stare of the cold psychopath. Convicted and sentenced to life in prison, Kirby Anthony continually denied having committed the familicide, according to Burl Barer, author of a book about the case.[13] Barer also alluded to Hare's observation that, for a normally socialized person, it is next to impossible to picture the world as the psychopath sees it. Family members, juries, and the people who hear about the psychopath's behavior and crimes all tend to have trouble realizing that the person is all that different from how they see and deal with the world. Juries and sometimes judges get flummoxed and cannot imagine how a human being could have perpetrated such crimes—and sometimes give acquittals, or else, as in the case of Phillip Garrido's first rape conviction, a reduced sentence with "time off for good behavior." Barer underlined another important fact: having a vicious and abusive father does not, in and of itself, destine one to end up as a psychopath. Genetic underpinnings are too often overlooked. Anthony's stepbrother, the biological son of their father, was beaten as severely as was Anthony but remained a law-abiding citizen. Even a group of brothers by the same father can show remarkable differences. The sadistic murderer Gary Gilmore, whose life Norman Mailer chronicled in his *Executioner's Song*,[14] was brutalized by his violent father, but so were the other three brothers, including the author Mikal Gilmore, who became a highly responsible and productive man and a commentator on the family tragedy. It seems safe to assume that Gary Gilmore, who began committing robberies and assaults when he was fourteen, had been dealt a poorer genetic hand.

Returning to the custody issue—and the "new" evil—I can find no parallel in the pre-1960s era of a crime so evil that it sits in one's brain, inescapably, like a hot coal, leaving one with no words to match its horror. It happened in mid-May of 2018. When she was seventeen, Virginia-born Amanda Simpson was in frequent internet correspondence with twenty-seven-year-old Justin Painter, finally meeting him after a few years in Dallas, Texas. They were married and had three children. After Painter proved angry, violent, and overly controlling, Simpson decided to divorce him. He had made a suicide threat with a gun at the time, and it wound up in her possession. Later, he demanded she return the firearm, threatening that, if she refused, he would claim she "stole" it. She reluctantly gave it back. Even so, the court, paying no attention to his mental instability, gave *him* full custody of the children,[15] although both parents would spend time with them.[16]

Not long after, Simpson makes another acquaintance through the same internet source—World of Warcraft—named Seth Richardson, whom she

had also known in her teens, just as she knew Painter. Simpson and Richardson
fall in love in this internet-inspired way, and Richardson travels to Texas to
be with her. They spend their first night together. Painter, having gotten wind
of the new alliance, comes to the house the next morning and, with the now
returned gun, shoots Richardson to death. The bullet also wounds Simpson.
He also fatally shoots his three children, who are visiting their mother that
day, before taking his own life—but not before telling Simpson that he has
killed them all, making sure that *she* remains alive so that she will suffer all
of the rest of her life. Their children were four, six, and eight years old at
the time of their deaths.[17] What words are there for this new evil? Diabolic
cruelty? Malice aforethought? Sadism with extended mental torture? They
all fall short. I have recently been called "the Einstein of Evil"—as though I
know all about this sort of thing—and take it in stride.[18] Yet, I cannot get the
Amanda Painter story out of my mind.

CHAPTER SIXTEEN
AN ALPHABET OF "NEW" EVIL

I n this chapter, the focus is on the varieties of violent acts, chiefly involving murder, of a sort that were uncommon before the critical "turning point" in the mid- to late 1960s, which we have described in previous chapters. Here we provide vignettes that describe an assortment of other character-istically "new" or contemporary evil acts, which would generally rank high on the Gradations of Evil scale. They derive from a variety of sources, pri-marily true crime biographies, but also briefer descriptions in magazines and newspaper articles. There are many such stories from this nearly fifty-five-year epoch—enough to constitute a kind of Alphabet of Evil, covering the field, literally, from A to Z.

-A-

Born in England in 1968, Beverley Allitt began to show signs of peculiar behavior during adolescence, especially in matters pertaining to her health. In addition to becoming quite overweight, she engaged in strange attention-seeking behaviors. She would, for example, wear bandages that supposedly covered various cuts or wounds, but would not allow anyone to probe what may lie beneath them. On numerous occasions, she would end up in hos-pitals, complaining of one or another physical ailment, but, often enough, the doctors could find no physical abnormalities to substantiate her claims. She even hoodwinked the medical staff to perform an appendectomy on what turned out to be a normal appendix. Even so, she interfered with the healing of the surgical scar by picking at it. On other occasions she engaged in deliberate self-injurious acts, as is often the case in patients with border-line personality disorder, which we have previously described. She would go from one doctor to another, with the result that many knew her superficially, but she gave no one particular doctor the opportunity to know all of her ailments, many of which were fictitious, or else grossly exaggerated. Collectively, the doctors gave her a fair amount of the attention she craved, in what then amounted to a case of Munchausen syndrome, as factitious illness is sometimes called—specifically, a feigned illness designed to elicit sympathetic attention from others. Beverley graduated, however, to a condition much more serious—and much more malicious—than pretending to have appendicitis. She went on to nursing school but failed to complete the program because of a new series of feigned illnesses, including a false pregnancy, and weird behaviors, such as smearing feces on the wall of a nursing home. Even so, she was hired in 1991 on a temporary contract by a hospital in Lincolnshire County, north of London, to work the night shift. It was not long after that a series of babies and young children became alarmingly sick—more than expected from the illnesses for which they had been admitted. Four of the young patients died shortly after admission, from what seemed like respiratory crises or cardiac arrests. All of these crises and deaths occurred within a few months of Beverley's time on the night shift. There were other children who also suffered medical emergencies during her months on the unit but who managed to survive. As all of these cases occurred just when Beverley was the "on-duty" nurse, she was eventually suspected of foul play. Chemical assessments of the children, including the four who had died, revealed high levels of insulin in some cases, or else of lidocaine, which is used to treat severe cardiac arrhythmias. Beverley was finally arrested and convicted of four murders and nine other instances of deliberate, life-threatening acts. For these, she was given thirteen life sentences.[1] Because her actions were meant to draw attention, and perhaps sympathy, by inflicting illnesses on others—rather than on herself—she emerged as a case of Munchausen syndrome by proxy, mentioned earlier in our discussion of Marybeth Tinning. First described in the mid-1970s, the syndrome, in over 90 percent of the cases, is set in motion by mothers or nurses.[2] Interestingly, the syndrome itself is named improperly after a real German nobleman, Hieronymus Karl Friedrich, Baron von Munchausen of Bodenwerder (1720–1797). A book of fantastical tales of adventure, entitled *Baron Munchausen's Narrative of His Marvellous [sic] Travels and Campaigns in Russia*, was published in England in 1785, allegedly written by the baron, but actually composed by a former student at Göttingen University, Rudolf Erich Raspe (1737–1794). Raspe had been introduced to the baron and assumed, correctly as it turned out, that his little pamphlet of Gulliver-like tall tales would be more widely read and more profitable if ascribed to the famous baron, rather than to a nonentity—like Raspe. The book was, indeed, widely read, and translated into many languages. It caused great embarrassment to the baron, since people assumed he was, in fact, the author, rather than Raspe, the clever con artist who impersonated him. All of this was well before the institution of copyright laws—of which, had they existed, Raspe would have been in serious violation. I own an edition of 1792.[3] So, the Munchausen syndrome and the proxy variant represent faked illnesses—named, perhaps fittingly, after a faked author.

Because Beverley was considered, besides someone whose murders might be called evil and appalling, a mentally ill person under Britain's Mental Health Act, she was, and remains, incarcerated at a forensic hospital, the Rampton Secure Hospital in Nottingham, from which she will never be released. Even there, she has resorted to the original type of Munchausen syndrome: she has eaten ground glass and poured boiling water on her hand. In light of her multiple murders of children, she would be ranked in Category 16 of the Gradations of Evil scale.

Another murderer among the As is China Arnold. When she was twenty-five in 2005, she had been living with Terrell Talley, by whom she had the last of her several children, a girl named Paris. Although he had been cheating on her, he worried that he may not have been the child's real father. China worried that Terrell would leave her if he found out that he was not the father. DNA later confirmed that he was, indeed, the father—but when he confessed to having had sex with a female neighbor, China became furious. She then placed one-month-old Paris in a microwave and literally cooked the baby to death. China was arrested, tried, and convicted. The judge at her trial described her act as a "heinous atrocity." She was sentenced to life in prison without parole.[4] Since her egocentric motivation appears to have been to eliminate a child who posed a threat or impediment to her relationship with Terrell, China would be ranked at level 10 of the Gradations of Evil scale.

-B-

Mark O. Barton, born in 1955, was a spree killer from Georgia who, in July of 1999, while in the process of losing considerable money as a day trader in an Atlanta brokerage firm, shot and killed nine people in two adjacent trading companies. These murders came in the aftermath of his having hammered to death his second wife and his two children, as they lay in bed. Barton had already been the only suspect in the fatal bludgeoning of his first wife, Deborah Spivey Barton, and her mother, Eloise Spivey—though he might have been clever enough to eliminate evidence that may have led to his conviction. Shortly before those (presumed) murders, Mark had tried to take out a million-dollar insurance policy on Deborah, with himself as beneficiary. The insurance company was suspicious and limited him to $600,000. After his wife's death, the company was all the more suspicious and gave him only $250,000, placing the remainder in trust for the children. People said Mark was never the same after he took psychedelic drugs during his adolescence. The drugs gave him strange visions and "demons," and he was hospitalized following a psychotic break. While at college, he learned to synthesize methamphetamine—some for sale, some for himself. In personality, he was noted to be paranoid, devious, quick-tempered, and malicious. The murders of his wife and mother-in-law, for which we might assume his guilt, were committed so he could be free to marry his mistress, Leigh-Ann Lang, whom he married soon after. Mark proved to be as abusive and controlling toward her as he had been with Deborah. Obsessed with get-rich-quick schemes, he got involved with the risky business of "day trading" in stocks. At one point, he shot to death his daughter's kitten. A year later, Leigh-Ann had had enough, and sued for divorce in July of 1999. This was only a matter of hours before he embarked on the murder spree, the first victims being Leigh-Ann herself and his two children from his first marriage, Matthew and Mychelle. As the police closed in after the spree, Mark shot himself to death. Psychiatrists had earlier viewed Barton as a "sadistic borderline" or else an "explosive psychopath." There were also intimations that he had sexually molested his daughter.[5] Barton's numerous acts of extreme ruthlessness, in the context of a psychopathic personality, would place him at level 16 of the Gradations of Evil scale.

Spousal murder is, of course, not a "new" form of evil. In the past, there have been a few men who have killed two wives, such as Richard Bennett, Carroll Cole, Dr. Patrick Henry, Harold Henthorn, Eric Napoletano, Sgt. Drew Peterson, and Randolf Roth. All of these men committed their wife-murders within the past fifty years. There have been women who killed two or more husbands, including Betty Lou Beets, Judith Buenoano, Stacey Cantor, Jill Coit, Belle Gunness, Sharon Harrelson, and Virginia McGinnis. Prompted primarily by greed, these women killed their husbands for insurance money, and, with the exception of Gunness, their crimes all took place within the past fifty years. Gunness achieved fame in the criminological domain for killing possibly dozens of husbands in the nineteenth century.[6]

Of note, Mark Barton's antisocial tendencies may have been intensified following his abuse of hallucinogenic and aggression-promoting drugs, which were scarcely available in the pre-1960 period. LSD came into use in the United States, for example, in 1962. A few cases of methamphetamine abuse were recorded in the early 1960s; by 1964, however, its abuse had become quite common.

In a case that exhausts the vocabulary of adjectives we use for acts of evil—heinous, depraved, atrocious, monstrous, unspeakable—a forty-one-year-old Utah man, Jerrod Baum, allegedly murdered two teenagers and dumped their bodies a hundred feet below the ground, down an abandoned mine shaft. The families of eighteen-year-old Riley Powell and his seventeen-year-old girlfriend, Brelynne Otteson, reported them missing for some three months before their bodies were finally found in the mine shaft near the Utah town with the inadvertently appropriate name of Eureka—Greek for "I found it." On the morning of December 30, 2017, Jerrod reportedly came home and saw his thirty-four-year-old girlfriend, Morgan Henderson, chatting with the young couple. A morbidly jealous man, he had forbidden Morgan from inviting any male friends to their house. Apparently, the prohibition was in force even when the "male friend" was half Morgan's age and accompanied by his girlfriend. The allegation continues that Baum proceeded to immobilize the young pair, silence them with duct tape over their mouths, and place them in the trunk of the boy's own Jeep. He then reportedly drove them, with Morgan by his side in the passenger seat, to the mine site. Once there, Jerrod allegedly forced the girl to witness him beating her boyfriend and then stabbing him to death—before killing her, as well, and tossing their bodies down the shaft. When their remains were later discovered, it was noted that their killer had tied their hands behind their backs. Jerrod and Morgan soon became suspects because the police found messages on the boy's Facebook account that he had exchanged with Morgan. Questioned by the police, she reportedly told various lies, until she eventually told the true story two months later and led the police to the murder and burial site. She then reportedly tried to hide the Jeep, driving it to a remote spot in hopes it would not be found. Jerrod is now being held awaiting trial in this capital case. The families of the murdered teenagers do not oppose the death penalty. Morgan is being held for possible obstruction of justice. The crime of which Jerrod Baum, who was arrested for attempted murder at age fifteen, is accused was one of the most sickening in recent times, adding psychological torment to physical torture[7]—of which it can only be said that the torture was briefer and less methodical than that of David Parker Ray, whose case we previously discussed. If allegations are proved true, the Gradations of Evil ranking for this double murder would be 18.

-C-

Natasha Wallen Cornett, born in 1979, was a participant in the multiple murder of a young couple and their six-year-old daughter just two months after her eighteenth birthday. Natasha was born into harsh circumstances and with many disadvantages. Natasha's mother, Madonna, had been briefly married to Ed Wallen, from whom she was soon divorced. The biological father was a policeman, Roger Burgess, with whom Madonna had been having an affair. Natasha grew up in poverty, raised by her mother, living in a trailer in the eastern edge of Kentucky near the town of Pikesville, in what has been called "hillbilly country," as described by another citizen of that blighted region, J. D. Vance, whose moving and compassionate memoir *Hillbilly Elegy* was published in 2016.[8] On her seventeenth birthday, Natasha married Stephen Cornett but was devastated when he ended the marriage only a few months later. So, despite her full name, her mother's divorce and her own divorce meant that she was hardly ever a "Wallen" and hardly ever a "Cornett." In mid-adolescence, Natasha suffered from anorexia nervosa and was also diagnosed with bipolar disorder. Her behavior had been unconventional in a way that left her all but friendless when in school. She became part of the goth subculture, wearing black, listening to lugubrious music, abusing drugs and alcohol, and indulging in self-harm—all sometimes associated with borderline personality disorder, though this is not mentioned in the various accounts of her history. Natasha became the leader of some half dozen similarly inclined adolescents whom she encouraged to join her, by way of trying to escape their unhappy lives, in a journey to the "promised land" of New Orleans. Along the way, at a rest stop in Tennessee, they encountered a Jehovah's Witness family: a Norwegian immigrant, Vidar Lillelid; his wife, Delfina; and their two small children, six-year-old Tabitha and two-year-old Peter. Natasha and her troupe stole Vidar's car and fatally shot the couple and their daughter. Peter, who was also shot and seriously wounded, survived. There is some dispute as to who carried out the shooting, but all were quickly apprehended in Arizona before a planned escape to Mexico. Natasha and the five other Kentucky-born coconspirators are serving life sentences. In her early twenties, she had become a Satan worshipper, presumably as an extension of her enthusiasm for the goth life during her late teens. It is not lost on me that her name, spelled backward, is "Ah Satan." She has tried to be useful in prison, working for a time as a teacher's aide.[9] A lead detective in the case, John Huffine, has expressed dismay that the case has garnered so much attention, since, as he put it, the troupe represents the opposite of all of the values mainstream America holds valuable—including adherence to conventional religion. Huffine added that some people wanted to view the case in the larger terms of good and evil, God and the devil. People often blame poverty as a root cause of future violent crimes. Certainly, crime, including violent crime, occurs more often among the very poor than among the very rich—but there are many among the poor who maintain stable marriages, are steady and diligent at work, and espouse the best values of the religion in which they were raised. This enables a good many to escape their original poverty and to enable their children to become prosperous, to live, in effect, what we are fond of calling the American Dream. Natasha grew up in a poverty that was impoverished monetarily but also spiritually. There was no emotional stability, no parents staying together and helping their children, no anchoring in religion or in any similar set of socially constructive values, and no medical help for conditions that are generally quite treatable, even in low-cost clinics, none of which did anything of any real help to Natasha. She was not a full-blown psychopath, destined to commit evil acts. Instead, she was pushed in the direction of evil action by neglect, chaotic circumstance, rejection at school, and the same factor that conduces so many boys (though not so many girls) to end up with a criminal record—fatherlessness. As the murders in which she participated were carried out expeditiously, for the purpose of eliminating witnesses following the theft of a car, Category 10 would be the appropriate ranking.

James Carson and his second wife, Suzan Barnes, known as the Witch Killers, achieved notoriety in the 1980s. Drug abuse seemed to have played an even more prominent role than in the Cornett case, since both his and Suzan's personalities appear to have undergone transformations—for the worse—once their drug habits were firmly in place. James had a young daughter, Jenn, by his first wife. She became frightened of his changed, aggressive behavior. Taking her daughter with her, the two left James and moved from one place to another, fearing he might find and harm them. But he showed no interest in doing so, instead teaming up with Suzan Barnes, whom he then married. The two settled eventually in the Haight-Ashbury area of San Francisco, epicenter of the "hippie" culture—or rather, counterculture, as it embodied mind-altering drugs, in opposition to the attitudes and traditions of the predominant culture, and adoption of mystical beliefs and "alternative" religions that most others found bizarre, or even abhorrent. James changed his name to Michael Bear, but I include him here within the Cs in deference to his birth name. Suzan fancied herself a "yogi" with knowledge of past, present, and future. Both, adopting a different religion, styled themselves as vegetarian Muslim warriors who believed that witchcraft, abortion, and homosexuality were mortal sins, and that a "higher power" authorized them to kill persons guilty of those transgressions. Their first victim was a young aspiring actress, Keryn Barnes, who had shared a room with them. Suzan felt she had received orders from On High to kill the woman, as though she were really a witch bent on stealing Suzan's "yogic powers." They stabbed her to death, smashing her skull with a frying pan for good measure, before fleeing the area. This was in 1981. Their next known victim was a farmhand on a Northern California marijuana farm, Clark Stephens. James and Suzan got it into their heads that Clark was a "demon" who had "sexually abused" Suzan. They shot him twice in the head and burned his body, meantime leaving behind, as they fled, a manifesto, in which they designated several famous people whom they regarded as "deserving of assassination," such as Johnny Carson and President Reagan. Come 1983, the couple was hitchhiking in Southern California. A Jon Hellyar picked them up. After a while, they got into an argument, and Suzan decided Jon was a "witch" and should die. All three got out of the car, whereupon Suzan began stabbing Jon, and James— well, "Michael"—shot the man to death in full view of the many passing cars. Someone called the police, and the two were finally arrested. Each ultimately received sentences of seventy-five years to life: twenty-five years for each of the three known murders, though they are suspected of committing about a dozen other murders in the United States and in Europe. Neither has shown a scintilla of remorse over the thirty-two years thus far that they have been in prison.[10] The sister of Keryn Barnes, the first victim, said, after hearing about their long sentences, "They are pure evil." And James's now grown daughter, Jenn, spoke of the couple as heavy drug users who made their own moral and religious code, which she likened to a "match meeting dynamite." We know nothing of their early backgrounds or whether they already showed paranoid, all-consuming hatreds even before their heavy drug abuse. So, it remains uncertain whether their murderously antisocial mind-sets preexisted the abuse and was simply intensified by it, or else somehow transformed them from potentially peaceful citizens to deluded, bigoted murderers. As for Suzan's conviction about the Qur'an forbidding abortion, witchcraft, and homosexuality, only the latter is mentioned. I see nothing in any of my four copies of the Qur'an about witchcraft, nor anything about abortion per se, only an injunction against killing one's children (Suras 6:151, 17:31, and 60:12). The couple would be ranked in Category 16 on the Gradations of Evil scale, in light of their multiple vicious homicides.

An Indiana woman, thirty-five-year-old Kelly Cochran, having already been convicted in Michigan and sentenced to forty-eight years in prison for the murder of her lover, Christopher Regan, was sentenced to an additional sixty-five years for the murder of her husband, Jason, in Indiana, two years later.[11] The earlier conviction stemmed from the murder of her fifty-three-year-old lover, whose body was dismembered. A documentary concerning the case alleges that, in addition, Cochran had fed Regan's remains to neighbors at a barbecue in Michigan's Upper Peninsula.[12] What makes crimes of this sort repugnant is not what one might call "conventional" cannibalism, which involves killing and eating the flesh of another person, but a still greater evil—namely, the crime of making other people into the unwitting and inadvertent cannibals of someone's flesh, provided for what appears as the generosity of the murderer. A murderer, that is, who has killed and butchered another person into pieces—then cooked and served the victim as though that victim were beef or pork. Or, as in the case of Daniel Rakowitz, a soup he made from the brain of a dancer, Monica Beerle, whom he murdered in 1989—the soup then offered to the homeless of New York City's Tompkins Square Park.[13] In a similar fashion, in 1993, David Paul Brown, who later restyled himself as Benjamin Nathaniel Bar-Jonah, fed parts of a child victim to his Montana neighbors under the pretense that it was deer meat.[14] There were, to be sure, isolated cases of cannibalism, including the feeding of human flesh to neighbors or the poor, in the first part of the last century. Cases of cannibalism included those of Albert Fish in the United States,[15] whom we have discussed in detail earlier in this book, and Fritz Haarmann in Germany,[16] both in the 1920s. Based upon what we presently know for certain about Cochran, the most appropriate placement on the Gradations of Evil scale is Category 10, taking into account the elimination of people "in the way." If the allegation were confirmed—about Kelly Cochran's having fed human body parts to neighbors—the ranking would increase. The case would also constitute an unusual "new evil," inasmuch as Cochran is a woman. All of the other perpetrators of this sort have been men. Nor had a barbecue been used in so barbaric a way.

-D-

Westley Allan Dodd was born in 1961 in Washington State, near the Oregon border. The eldest of three boys, he grew up in a blue-collar family that was in turmoil all during Westley's early days. His father was domineering and harsh, arguing constantly with his wife over trivia. They divorced when Westley was fifteen, by which time he had already shown signs of serious sexual abnormalities for several years. He began sexually abusing boys when he was thirteen, would expose himself to neighbors when he was fourteen, and, by fifteen, would walk in the park naked and masturbate in public. He would search for boys of around ten and expose himself, occasionally flashing girls as well, but he felt safer with boys because he felt they were less likely to report him to the authorities. He had been arrested, nevertheless, for exhibitionism at age fifteen, but nothing was done except for the judge to recommend "counseling." By seventeen, he would molest boys sexually, including anal rape and cruel bondage. He impregnated a girl, having a son, whom he never saw. Abuse of illicit drugs was common in the era of Dodd's early years, but he himself never did drugs and never smoked or drank alcohol. At nineteen, he joined the US Navy but was kicked out two years later for committing pedophilic acts with boys. When he was twenty-eight, he moved to Vancouver, where he cornered ten-year-old Billy Neer and his eleven-year-old brother, Cole Neer, in David Douglas Park—a convenient area, he figured, to kidnap, rape, and kill young boys. Dodd bound them and tied their wrists together, then stabbed both to death. The younger boy, Billy, was discovered by police, bleeding severely, but died before he could tell them what happened. Dodd meantime concluded that he got more thrill out of killing his victims than out of raping them. Some months later, Dodd attacked again, this time a boy of four, Lee Iseli, whom he raped and then murdered, dumping the "garbage," as he called it, in a wooded spot near Vancouver Lake. This time, Dodd was caught and arrested. As he revealed in letters he wrote while awaiting trial, he had become interested in eating a boy's genitals, and keeping the castrated boy alive long enough to see Dodd cook and eat them. Though he never carried out such an act, he felt this was a more supreme act of torture than anything else he might devise. In this respect, his sadistic ambitions resembled those of Albert Fish, as well as Albert Fentress, in his rape, castration, murder, and cannibalism of Paul Masters in 1979. The actions of Fentress seemed so "crazy" at the time that he was diagnosed (incorrectly as it turned out) as "schizophrenic," and remanded to a forensic hospital, rather than being sent to prison. Fentress never acknowledged that he had committed the crime.[17] To Dodd's credit, he insisted not only on being punished but also on being executed for the sexual murders of the three boys. He demanded to be hanged, rather than executed by some other means. Dodd wanted his execution to be carried out with no delays, warning the court that if he were ever given the opportunity to escape, or to assault someone within the prison, he would rape and kill, and enjoy every minute of it. This put paid to the protests of the anti–death penalty crowd, and Dodd was duly hanged on January 5, 1993.[18] The only other instance known to me of such candor and acceptance of blame by a serial killer was that of another gay serial killer, Carl Panzram, who snarled at the hangman for dillydallying with the rope. But that was in 1930; Panzram's punishment was not for pedophilic crimes but for raping and killing some two dozen or more men.[19] With respect to the postulate of cultural change and what we might call a "new evil," the crimes of Westley Dodd are not "new," as if unheard of before the 1960s. There were men, of either sexual orientation, committing serial sexual homicide in the earlier years: Gordon Northcott, Albert Fish, Panzram, and Herman Webster Mudgett (aka H. H. Holmes), Earl Nelson, and Harvey Carignan—but their numbers pale by comparison with the much more numerous group of the post-1960s killers. Dodd, who killed during the 1980s, belongs to the recent group, where broken families and drug abuse were the rule, rather than the exception. The sexually perverse torture-murderer would be ranked at the extreme end of the Gradations of Evil scale, in Category 22.

Joanna Dennehy, born in England in 1982, grew up in a working-class home in Hertfordshire, southeast of London. She was raised in an intact family, in which neither she, nor her sister, suffered any verbal, physical, or sexual abuse, and no neglect. She played with dolls when she was young, was a bright and athletic student, and did well on the flute. Her life began to spin out of control in her teens when she began to spend time with older students, and to drink alcohol and smoke marijuana. She would skip school and became sexually involved with a young man of twenty, five years older than she. Her parents disapproved. At sixteen she ran away from home for good, having reached an age when she could stay away legally. Pregnant the following year, she gave birth to a daughter in 1999. She found motherhood an inconvenience and an imposition on her "freedom"—shades of the accusation in the case of our Casey Marie Anthony in Florida. Under the influence of drugs, which now included cocaine, Joanna became temperamental and violent, as well as promiscuous. The estranged father of her daughter would take her back, and, when she was twenty-four, she had a second daughter. By now, she had become abusive toward the father, punching him, giving him a black eye, and hitting him with a racket. She also began mutilating herself with knives and razor blades, and put a metal stud in the middle of her tongue. She was now emerging as a woman with "borderline personality disorder," with the emphasis on "inordinate anger." When she then threatened the boyfriend/father with a knife, he finally left her, married another woman, and took care of the two daughters he had with Joanna. She now turned to prostitution, by way of paying for her drug and alcohol habits, consuming as much as two quarts of vodka a day. Joanna began living with another man, Kevin Lee, but had begun to lose her attractiveness and developed a new addiction to violent pornography. She was hospitalized psychiatrically, where she was considered "antisocial" or else "psychopathic." A diagnosis of "sadomasochism" was added, since she seemed as fond of hurting others as hurting herself. After her release, her life took a turn for the worse. When she was thirty-one, she stabbed three men to death, ostensibly just for the fun of it. Though she spoke of hating men, she took up with yet another—a seven-foot-three man named Gary Richards. With help from Gary and a third man, they dumped the bodies of her victims along ditches in remote areas. Meantime, she tried to stab two other men to death. This time she was caught and arrested, no longer protected by her vicious dog, whom she named Hitler. Given a stiff sentence for the three murders, she was put in prison, but there, she conceived a plan so clever and so devious as to elevate her to a unique spot among the ranks of the "new evil," insofar as no similar attempt has been recorded in the past. Her plot was to escape from prison by killing a guard and then cutting off his finger, which she could then use to deactivate the security devices on the prison doors. The novelty and brilliance of this idea won her a certain grudging admiration from the authorities, but the judge scotched the plan, putting her in solitary confinement with no possibility of parole. Joanna felt the kind of sexual excitement from her acts of violence and murder that mirror the sexual sadism of men who experience sexual arousal when committing acts of serial sexual homicide.[20] There are few such women. England's Rose West, wife of serial killer Fred West, comes to mind,[21] and perhaps Florida's Aileen Wuornos.[22] Joanna would be ranked at Category 16 of the Gradations of Evil scale.

-E-

As previously noted, raping a woman or a man occupies a high number on the Gradations of Evil scale: 16 at a minimum, and higher, if followed by murder or torture preceding murder. Raping a child, especially in a series of such acts, strikes us as even more vile, as though a kind of "evil squared." The case of Richard Mark Evonitz, which would be assigned to level 18, due to the elements of murder and non-protracted torture, is illustrative. Born in 1963, he was the eldest of three. There were two sisters, Kristen and Jennifer. Richard grew up in a working-class South Carolina family. His father, Joe, was reportedly alcoholic, had a violent temper, and was abusive to the rest of the family. Joe would upbraid his son mercilessly if he got a bad grade, warning him, "You'll get an A, or you'll get a beating!" Jennifer likened family life to living in a prison. Richard graduated high school at sixteen and showed no disciplinary issues. Right afterward, however, he got into drugs and alcohol, did "B and Es" (breaking and entering), and consorted with criminals. One of his offenses was to write a bad check, at which point his father made him choose either living on the streets or joining the armed forces. He chose the navy. His parents divorced at this point, his mother then marrying a man who had raped and killed a woman—but that crime was not uncovered until later, and was not an influence on Richard. While briefly on leave from the navy, he exposed himself to Kelli Ballard, a girl of fifteen, who then saw him masturbate. She complained to the police, and he was arrested. He admitted that he had a problem masturbating in front of girls, and was drunk at the time.

The navy demoted him one grade and put him on probation for three years. Even so, five years later, at twenty-eight, he was given an honorable discharge, a Good Conduct Medal, and a Navy Achievement Medal for leadership. During the middle of his navy duty, he married a girl of sixteen, Bonnie Lou Gower. She later said their sex life was "normal," even though his custom was to bind and blindfold her, and rape her for three hours at a time. After leaving the navy, he worked as a salesperson, earning a bad reputation for anger and for insulting women. In 1995, he broke into the house of two sisters, aged eleven and thirteen, raping the older girl while he kept the younger one locked up. In the following year, his wife left him, troubled by his inability to perform sexually unless via bondage. Soon after, he raped and murdered a girl of sixteen, Sofia Silvia, whose body was later found floating in a creek. His next victims were two young sisters, Kristin and Katie Lisk, ages fifteen and twelve, respectively. He abducted them at gunpoint, bound and gagged them, shaved their pubic hair, and raped and fatally strangled them, dumping their bodies afterward over a bridge. The murders were unsolved until, in 2002, he abducted another adolescent girl, fifteen-year-old Kara, whom he bound to the four bedposts in his house, raped, and forced to call him "Daddy" while watching some of his many pornographic films. They fell asleep, but Kara awakened first, wriggled out of her handcuffs, ran away, and hailed a passing car, urging the driver to take her to the cops. The police were then able to link him to the unsolved murders in another state. Evonitz tried to escape, but the police gave chase. As they closed in, he committed suicide, shooting himself in the head.[23]

What is unusual about Evonitz, among the ranks of men committing serial sexual homicide, is his mixed predilection for either prepubescent children (pedophilia proper) or adolescents (hebephilia). For some of these men, "practical" considerations may weigh heavily in the balance: children are easier to capture and subdue, and easier to dispose of. For others, pedophilia/hebephilia may stem from abnormalities in brain regions that play a prominent role in sexual-object choice. Head injuries affecting these regions may contribute to the preference for children, rather than for adults. This seemed to have been a factor in the histories of Fred West, John Wayne Gacy, and Arthur Shawcross—and also in the pedophilia of Phillip Garrido, who kept Jaycee Dugard as a sex slave, starting when she was eleven. His rape fantasies involving child victims began right after the severe head injury he suffered at age fourteen.[24] In any event, the public's reaction to child killers, in naming them as evil, tends to be stronger and swifter than when the victims have grown past the innocence and helplessness of childhood.

The victims of serial sexual homicide by the Category 22 torture-murderer Larry Eyler, born in 1952, were young gay males, at least three of whom were in mid-adolescence, aged fourteen or fifteen years, the others from late adolescence to about twenty-five. Eyler may have killed about two dozen victims from 1982 to 1984, some never identified. His early circumstances were even harsher than those of Richard Evonitz. His parents divorced when he was two and a half, and, because he was unmanageable, he was later placed either in foster homes, where the stepfathers often beat him, or in homes for unruly boys. He struggled with his homosexual tendencies, which he experienced as repellent, at a time when the surrounding culture held homosexuality in opprobrium to a greater extent than is currently the case. In his late twenties, he became a "highway killer," waylaying adolescent boys—three of his known victims were fourteen—and men in their twenties. Some were gay "hustlers," easy prey for Eyler, who tied up and then tortured his victims for an hour or more before killing them. Quarrelsome, pathologically jealous, and deceitful, he was described by the few who knew him as a "Jekyll and Hyde" personality. He had no real friends. Eyler began his secret life as a serial killer in 1982, the year the AIDS epidemic was first recognized in the United States. His first known victim, Steven Crockett, was stabbed to death near Chicago in March, his body left in a cornfield. Seven months later, the body of fourteen-year-old Delvoyd Baker was found strangled near Indianapolis. A few months after that, the body of fifteen-year-old Danny Bridges was found dismembered. By then, the police were able to connect the Bridges case to other recent victims. After his arrest and trial, he offered information about other murders he committed, in hopes of avoiding the death penalty. He did manage to avoid death by court order, only to die of AIDS while in prison in 1986.[25]

-F-

In a case of bewildering complexity, Franklin Delano Floyd was born in Georgia in 1943, the youngest of five in a troubled family. His abusive and alcoholic father, Thomas, died when Franklin was one. He was then placed in a Georgia Baptist Children's Home. A troublesome boy, he constantly got into fights and stole. He was raped by the bigger boys and would have his hand thrust into boiling water if caught masturbating. At sixteen, he was expelled from that institution for bad behavior and placed into the care of his married sister, Dorothy. But her husband kicked him out after a few weeks—again, for bad behavior—placing him now in the care of his mother, Della, who was living in Indiana and working as a prostitute. Della got rid of him a different way: she lied about his age and enrolled him in the US Army, when he was only sixteen. When the lie was discovered six months later, he was thrown out. He then led a criminal life, stealing guns and getting put into and escaping from various prisons. At nineteen, he abducted and raped a girl of four, got caught and imprisoned, but escaped—this time to commit armed robbery—which led to another round of imprisonment, escape, re-confinement as a child molester, parole at age twenty-nine, and rearrest at thirty for kidnapping a woman. He now disappeared for sixteen years until finally caught and arrested again, as a fugitive from justice. He had been using many aliases, taking names from gravestones, meantime kidnapping a girl of four or five, raising her himself, and pretending that her mother had died. He gave her the name Sharon Marshall, though later changing it to Tonya Tadlock, using a name taken from another grave. He forced her, when she was older, to partake in nude dancing and prostitution, living off the money she earned. Sharon was quite bright and earned a scholarship to Georgia Tech. She dared not reveal her true situation, lest she provoke a homicidal rage in her "father." Franklin did not allow her to go to the college, instead moving with her to Florida, where she again danced nude, and supported him with her earnings. In the meantime, Franklin had made a cache of pornographic photos of Sharon—and also of Sharon's friend, Cheryl, another nude dancer. Cheryl suspected Franklin was guilty of incest, not knowing Sharon was not his real daughter, although it was legally incest, since he had raised her as though she were. At any rate, when Franklin found out about Cheryl's intention to alert social services, he shot her to death. He then fled with Sharon to New Orleans—this time marrying her so as to prevent her from testifying against him. She was no longer "Sharon" at this time, since he changed her name now to "Tonya." Moving once more, this time to Oklahoma, he again lived off her earnings as a nude dancer and prostitute—but she now met a man who urged her to escape with him. When Franklin found out about that plan, he bludgeoned her in the head and left her by the side of the road, to suggest she had been run over by a car. Taken to the hospital, Sharon/Tonya was slowly recovering when Franklin slipped into the hospital and killed her. Back in 1988, Sharon had a son, Michael, by a man, Gregg Higgs. Murder could not as yet be proved, but Franklin insisted on his right to care for his "grandson." The authorities doubted his paternity, but he twice refused DNA testing. After he was forced a third time to give a blood sample, it emerged that, to the surprise of no one, he was not Sharon's father, nor Michael's grandfather. A bit later, Franklin, still demanding custody, went to Michael's school and, at gunpoint, forced the principal to yield up Michael. In 1993, he then killed the five-year-old child, telling others that the boy had "drowned." The FBI finally figured out who and where Franklin was—he had adopted numerous aliases along the way—and arrested him. He was given the death penalty and placed in Florida's Raiford prison. The girl he kidnapped, raised as his daughter, married, and murdered now lies in a grave labeled "Tonya," though her real name and origin remain unknown. Franklin Delano Floyd, born two years before Franklin Delano Roosevelt died—he may or may not have been named after the president—remains in the Raiford prison.[26] Called a "violent sexual predator and a career criminal" by the judge at the time of his conviction,[27] he is rivaled by few in his malignancy, except perhaps by England's Ian Brady and our David Paul Brown, alias "Bar Jonah." I note that he displayed virtually every feature of psychopathy described by Dr. Robert Hare. His numerous cold-blooded, murderous acts place him in Category 16 of the Gradations of Evil scale.

Taylor Behl was a seventeen-year-old freshman at Virginia Commonwealth College. The only child of Janet Pelasara, Taylor had just started classes in September of 2005 but had disappeared on the September 5. She had met a few men in her new setting, most of whom were young like herself, but there was also a man of thirty-eight, Ben Fawley, who had two daughters of his own. The police began questioning anyone who knew Taylor, including Ben, who claimed he was by himself at the time. It turned out, however, that he had a long criminal record and was even discovered to have child pornography in his computer. He was arrested and jailed for that offense. Continuing their investigation, the police then searched his house, where they discovered various sex toys, a machete, a hatchet, and a gun cartridge, along with a set of whips and chains. Ben was noted to have been preoccupied with very young women and had created a website that he called *deviantart*. Other images found in his computer were photos of his twelve-year-old daughter dressed in a provocatively sexy way. A week and a half later, Taylor's body was found several miles from the campus. Her car had Ohio plates, newly added to replace her Virginia plates. The police questioned Ben again and asked that he also take a polygraph test. He made up a story, as though he had been robbed the night of Taylor's disappearance, but that did not ring true. It also came out that Ben's rap sheet contained information about previous arrests for car theft, assaults against women, and reckless endangerment. Exactly a month after Taylor's disappearance, her body was discovered some seventy-five miles from where she had been abducted, in a shallow grave, decomposed and identifiable only through dental records. Ben now made up a story, as though Taylor had died accidentally during some rough sex, of asphyxiation, and that he then "panicked" and dumped her body in a shallow ravine. Ben was arrested following this dubious account. Actually, Ben had killed her while trying to abduct and rape her. In court, Ben pled guilty—actually, to second-degree murder—and was sentenced to thirty years in prison.[28] The police were aided in their search for the perpetrator through the use of Ben's internet "footprint," including his activity on the site MySpace, which helped lead them to Taylor's body. This was considered one of the earliest cases where social networking sites on the web proved instrumental in solving a puzzling murder case.

The problem of child pornography had become a serious social issue well before Ben Fawley's arrest in 2005, for viewing it, and then for murdering Taylor Behl. Serious questions accompany the issue itself. Accessibility to internet child-porn viewing is one of the great problems—and great new evils—that accompany the many virtues of the internet. The creation of child pornography came shortly after the invention of the camera in the mid-nineteenth century.[29] As Drs. Richard Wortley and Stephen Smallbone point out, relaxation of censorship standards in the United States in the 1960s made child pornography more readily available,[30] such that, by the mid-1970s, about 250 child pornography magazines were in circulation, often imported from Europe.[31] The internet coming into common use in the 1980s made the problem more acute. In effect, child pornography, though available for over a century, has become a much greater problem in the "new evil" period of the 1960s and beyond. A related problem is the thorny issue of the correlation between watching child pornography and going on to commit sexual offenses against children. Some studies have reported a worrisome correlation between child molestation and watching child porn, especially among men who already had prior records of offenses against children. That is to say, child pornography offenders who had prior criminal records were more likely to reoffend during a follow-up period. But in a Swiss study of over two hundred men charged with viewing child pornography, those who had no prior convictions for offenses against children were unlikely to offend against children during a follow-up period. These men tended to be better educated and often held good, well-remunerative positions, in contrast to poorly educated and less well-off men, who were more likely to offend against children.[32] As for Ben Fawley, he would fall into the poorly educated, less affluent group. He subsisted only on checks from Social Security. He would be ranked at level 16 of the Gradations of Evil scale.

-G-

Kristin Gilbert (née Strickland) was the elder of two daughters from a middle-class family in Fall River, Massachusetts—a town famous for being the hometown of Lizzie Borden, who in 1892, was—or wasn't—guilty of the axe murders of her father and stepmother. Kristin was a habitual liar and also stole things from her sister, then denying she had taken them. She was also known for being manipulative, abusive, and vindictive, all behind a pleasing façade. She was highly intelligent, graduating with honors and finishing high school young, at age sixteen. She became a nurse and married Glenn Gilbert, by whom she had two sons. Working after graduation in a Northampton, Massachusetts, Veteran's Administration hospital, she began to inject patients with very strong solutions of epinephrine, the cardiac drug digoxin, or even ketamine—used at the time as anesthesia during surgeries for horses. The patients usually died. The first murders began around 1994, a couple of years after the "centenary" of the Lizzie Borden murders. But Kristen kept at it for another six or seven years, killing more patients and creating hundreds of medical "Code Blue" emergencies. The other nurses took little or no action, or, if they did, the nursing supervisor would upbraid them for denigrating such a "fine, upstanding nurse as Ms. Gilbert."[33] Having grown bored with her husband, she began an affair with James Perrault, a hospital security guard. Once, she killed a patient so she could quit work two hours early to meet her lover. On a few occasions, she staged bomb threats at the hospital, or else painted swastikas on tissue boxes to make it appear that there were vandals in the hospital. Once she was finally arrested, a psychiatrist speculated that she may have created these emergencies by way of displaying her proficiency as a nurse.[34] When confronted, she denied all charges but was convicted in 2001 and sentenced to four life sentences, now being served at a changed venue in a Texas prison. Though psychopathic personality is more common in men, perhaps by a factor of eight, Gilbert displayed psychopathic traits, with extreme narcissism, buttressed by amorality. This, coupled with her multiple murders, places her in Category 16 of the Gradations of Evil scale. The true number of fatalities for which she is responsible will probably never be known, though some estimated there may have been as many as eighty. If that figure is even approximately correct, Gilbert would join the ranks of Angels of Death who have hastened to heaven the greatest number of patients. The prize, if that is the proper word, goes to the Norwegian nurse Arnfinn Nesset, who, in the years 1981–1983, poisoned to death perhaps as many as 138 patients with suxamethonium chloride, the compound we know in the United States as succinylcholine, used for short-term paralysis in general anesthesia.[35] Remarkably, though sentenced to Norway's maximum term of twenty-one years, he was released after just twelve years "for good behavior"—there being no way, after all, to pursue his bad behavior while in a prison! He is now living as a free man under an assumed name at an undisclosed location somewhere in Norway.

Born in 1970 near Detroit in a middle-class family where his alcoholic father ran a small tool-and-die shop, Stephen Grant became a risk-taker with grandiose and psychopathic traits, a daredevil who ended up with many arrests for reckless driving, speeding, and driving without a license. In school, he was an arrogant braggart who affected to know everything but was actually an indifferent student who later never finished college, though he would boast that he had. Fearless as an adolescent, he did a lot of shoplifting and felt he could talk his way out of any challenge to his willfulness. Considered basically amoral, he came up with rationalizations for doing whatever he wished, no matter how indiscreet or illegal. He had the psychopath's "superficial charm" and partook of a number of affairs before marrying a girl he met while in college. She was Tara Destrampe, from Michigan's Upper Peninsula. She majored in business and was dynamic and ambitious, attracted to Stephen because he came from the big city, in contrast to her rural background. Hers was a healthy, hardworking family, whereas Stephen came from a dysfunctional family in which the parents kept separating and getting together in an unpredictable way. Stephen tried his luck at various jobs, got fired from one because he stole from the cash register, and earned very little. Tara was quite different. She showed great administrative abilities and traveled around the world for her large corporation, earning a handsome salary. They had two children in 2002 and 2004, but Tara was seldom home, with the result that Stephen ended up a stay-at-home dad, increasingly resentful of her absences. He began an affair with their au pair, Verena Dierkes. Tara returned from San Juan one evening in 2007, mentioning that she had to return there a bit earlier than she expected. That was the "last straw" for Stephen. They argued, and, in a fit of rage, he strangled her. He then pretended she had simply abandoned the family, as if to be with a lover. Then, using his dad's tool-and-die equipment, he sawed and dismembered her body into fourteen pieces, which he discarded in a wooded area not far from their suburban home. Meanwhile, a woman found one of the garbage bags containing a body part, around the time that Stephen went back home to retrieve the largest piece—Tara's torso—which he hoped to bury someplace where it would not be found. The police did find it and confronted him. Stephen now confessed and even had a twinge of remorse. Found guilty of murder and dismemberment, he was sentenced to fifty years in prison.[36] At Stephen's trial, the judge called him "demonic," as well as "manipulative, barbaric, dishonest, and a coward"; the prosecutor called him "evil personified."[37] He would be ranked in Category 11 of the Gradations of Evil scale.

With respect to the "behind-the scenes" neuroanatomical aspect of violent acts, some of which evoke from us the reaction of "evil," functional magnetic resonance imaging (fMRI) studies over the past two decades have pointed to important differences in the brains of what has been called "reactive" aggression versus "proactive" aggression. In a recent book by Dr. Adrian Raine, entitled *The Anatomy of Violence: The Biological Roots of Crime*, there is an illuminating chapter that explains and demonstrates these distinctions. Reactive aggression concerns hot-blooded persons who "lash out emotionally in the face of a provocative stimulus. Someone has insulted them. . . . They've been verbally threatened. So they hit back in anger."[38] This contrasts with predatory people, the "proactives," who carefully plan their actions, and act in a methodical, logical, calculating way—and who are "regulated, controlled, and driven by rewards . . . cold-blooded and dispassionate."[39] Robert Rowe, the attorney who bludgeoned his family to death in a fit of despondency and rage, exemplifies the "reactive" type.[40] Rowe, after spending several years in a forensic hospital, where he was eventually able to overcome his depression, then remarried, returned to work and led an exemplary life. He had committed one violent act in his life but would not be considered an "evil" man. Stephen Grant was a quite different person: a killer of the "proactive" type. In his methodical, cold-blooded way, he carved up his wife, the mother of his children, as though she were nothing more than a side of beef. Psychopathic wife killers, who carefully conjure up clever, "fool-proof" ways to "disappear" their wives, are clearly of the proactive type, as are most men who commit serial sexual homicide. The word "evil" is regularly used in describing them, as well as the repugnant crimes they commit. Raine highlights such men as Randy Kraft and Leonard Lake. There is no shortage of others. Among them are Charles Albright, Ian Brady, Mike DeBarde-leben (the most articulate of these men), Ed Kemper, David Parker Ray (who devised the most cunning tortures), and the aforementioned Fred and Rose West. Citing the research of several neuroscientists, including Sweden's Dr. Henrik Söderström and Dr. Ken Kiehl in the United States, Raine draws attention to abnormal function of certain key areas of the brain in psycho-paths,[41] including the hippocampus, the parahippocampal gyrus, and the posterior cingulate gyrus. Pictorial plates depicting these brain regions are provided in Raine's book.[42] These findings should be understood, thus far, as correlational, rather than causative factors in psychopathy. We do not as yet know, for example, whether abnormalities in these areas—if detected, say, in the childhoods of sons born to persons like Stephen Grant, or some of the persons displaying psychopathic traits and behaviors just mentioned, or to Ted Bundy, who sired a child after he was foolishly allowed "conjugal visits" while in prison—would "predestine" these boys to become psychopaths, even if raised in more harmonious families. This is a task for future research.

-H-

Thomas Hose was an untrained school security guard in a high school in McKeesport, Pennsylvania, a small town of about twenty thousand people, not far south of Pittsburgh. One of the students there was Tanya Kach, a thirteen-year-old girl from a disturbed family. Her father was reportedly completely indifferent toward her; her mother was allegedly an alcoholic and psychotic woman who divorced the father but had earlier, and on many occasions, either severely scolded or struck Tanya. Because of all of the mistreatment, Tanya had run away from home on many occasions. The school guard sensed that she was a troubled girl and, by steps and stages, befriended, lured, and, ultimately, seduced her. A man three times Tanya's age—he was thirty-nine, born in 1957—he invited her to stay in his house, where he lived with his parents. Tanya became a missing person, albeit holed up in a house only a few blocks from her father's home. Hose proceeded to keep her imprisoned in a small room, where she was warned to be silent so that his parents, living downstairs, would not guess he was holding her captive just upstairs. She could no longer go to school and had to void her wastes in a bucket. She was given nothing to do, except watch television, though he eventually let her have a cat. Hose threatened to kill her if she dared try to leave. Tanya developed a kind of Stockholm syndrome, growing attached to her captor, though hating him at the same time. When she turned eighteen, he had her change her name so that, on the rare occasions he now permitted her to go to a grocery store, people would not recognize her as the by now well-publicized missing girl. Tanya's name was even put on milk cartons, after the manner of other missing children such as Etan Patz, kidnapped and killed in 1979, and Adam Walsh, kidnapped, whose severed head was found by fishermen two weeks later. Both boys had been six when abducted. At thirteen, Tanya was a much more formidable victim for a child snatcher to control, so it is a testimony of sorts to Hose's ingenuity that he managed to keep her for ten years. He made her his sex slave, making her perform only anal and oral sex. It is not clear whether these were his preferences, or if he were avoiding impregnating her. He also forbade her to go to a doctor, with the result that she developed psoriasis and blurry vision from untreated conjunctivitis. Tanya finally managed to escape in 2006 when she was twenty-three. It is a large blot on the escutcheon of the local police that they seemed to put little effort into finding her, though, once kidnapped, she lived within walking distance from her home. A similar blot on the judge who, when Hose was then arrested, claimed that the police were protected from malfeasance and guilt, since the "statute of limitations" had run out. It was a travesty of the law that in cases where a child had been unlawfully imprisoned as a sex slave, the timing began from the child's disappearance, rather than from the time the child managed to escape. Tanya did not delay three or four years before suing the police: she did so immediately. It was pure foxiness to attend only to the letter, rather than to the spirit, of the Law in maintaining that, in the decade-long sequestration of an innocent young woman, she had "waited too long" to sue. There was more evil in this case than just in the actions of Thomas Hose, which included rape and subjugation, in the absence of murder. For these crimes, he would be ranked at level 19 of the Gradations of Evil scale—a sparsely populated category. His sentence after trial—a mere fifteen years—was also absurdly brief, considering that he forced Tanya to be a missing person for more than seven years; she had become *legally dead*.[43] In this respect, Tanya joins the ranks of other children who, in the post-1960s "new evil," have been held as sex slaves for protracted periods. Some, such as Jaycee Dugard in California and Elizabeth Fritzl in Austria, have born children to their kidnappers. Fortunately, Tanya was able to make a good recovery: she finished high school, went to college, married, and wrote a book about her capture and eventual escape.[44]

Steven Ray Harper was born in 1953 in a middle-class family in Nebraska. When he was nine, he was severely burned over two-thirds of his body when he and some other boys were playing with fire. Afterward, he had numerous grafts and operations, though he felt repulsed by his image in the mirror because of the scars. His self-confidence plummeted, and he became a loner, withdrawing from others. He loved animals, though, and hoped one day to become a veterinarian. By the time he finished high school, his facial scars were less prominent. Shy and inexperienced with women, he had been acquainted with a girl from high school, Sandra "Sandy" Betten, who was the same age as he. A difficult young woman, she had already married at seventeen. She was tempestuous and quarrelsome, throwing away her wedding rings, one after the other, which her husband, James Murphy, kept buying for her. She smashed dishes, cut furniture, and once hit James with a table leg. The marriage did not last, and she then seduced Steven—who was happy to be initiated into sex with an attractive woman. They were both twenty at the time. He refused to marry her until he finished veterinary school some four years later. She would then threaten to leave him for another man. Provoked by her jealous taunts, he once choked her in a violent rage. She then made good on her threat, leaving him for Duane Johnson. Steven began stalking her and Duane, whom she then married, and would send threatening letters, or else shoot buckshot at members of Sandy's family. Escaping to an uncle in Oklahoma, Steven was caught when he was twenty-three and sentenced to one to five years of hard labor. He was soon paroled, however, and was now free to plan a more serious revenge. Having played with literal fire at nine, he now began playing with metaphorical fire—via a plot to kill Sandy and her family. Rejected by veterinary school because of his felony, he got a job instead working in a laboratory. He also joined a cult involved in Satanism. At the lab, he got hold of a poison that was said to cause cancer in chickens: methyl nitrosamine, a methylating compound that attaches to and alters one's DNA. He tested the drug on a cat and a dog, who duly expired as expected, though from bleeding, not from cancer. The drug attacks the liver and damages the clotting system, causing massive bleeding, and predisposes one to cancer over the course of time. In 1978, Steven sneaked into the Johnson home and laced some milk and lemonade with the poison. Later that day, Sandy's husband and daughter, Sherrie, had some of the milk. Sandy's sister and her husband, and their eleven-month-old baby, Chad, also had some of the milk and lemonade. All five quickly became ill. Sandy's husband, Duane, and their nephew, Chad, died within a few days from extensive liver damage and profound bleeding from everywhere because the drug reduces the platelet count to near zero.[45] Steven prided himself on having created the "perfect murder"—using an agent that would cause cancer some time later, a cancer that would not be suspected of having been set in motion by some carcinogenic compound years before. When the police recognized that five people became seriously ill from the Johnson household, two dying within days, they suspected foul play. Knowing of Steven Harper's record, and his animosity toward Sandy and Duane, and learning from the two autopsies that a chemical toxin had caused the deaths, they checked his home. There, they discovered vials of dimethylnitrosamine, as well as the fact that he had worked at a lab where that compound was made. The police now arrested Steven and charged him with two counts of murder and three counts of poisoning with intent to kill. This was a death penalty case. Steven spent twelve years awaiting execution and submitting one appeal after another. Considered mentally unstable after a while, he was given the antipsychotic medication chlorpromazine (Thorazine), which he did not swallow, saving the pills up instead, with which he then committed suicide.[46] What makes the case of Steven Harper special is not the jealousy aspect. Jealousy murders are common. His murders had unusual features. He was not trying to kill an unfaithful spouse or significant other; his main intended victim was his former lover. Also, he was not relying on one of the more often used poisons, such as cyanide—as in the case of James Cahill, who killed his wife as she was about to divorce him and marry another man. Harper had hoped to induce a cancer of some sort, a disease that could develop in anyone—and years later, so that it could not, therefore, be linked to him. He aimed at a "perfect," albeit not immediate, murder. Also, he was using a poison never before used as a murder weapon. That was the "new" part of the otherwise old evil of jealousy murder. Harper, a cold-blooded multiple murderer, would be ranked in Category 15 of the scale.

Another novel poison, rare outside of Asia, is aconite from the Aconitum plant, a cardiac and nerve poison. A jealous woman from the Sikh community in England, Lakhvir Singh, forty-five, had been lovers for many years with Lakhvinder Cheema, but, as he wanted to "settle down" and have children, he was about to marry a woman of twenty-one, Gurjeet Choong. As their wedding day approached, Lakhvir sneaked some curry into their fridge, laced with aconite. Later that day, her former lover and his fiancée ate some of the curry and soon fell ill. Lakhvinder became suspicious Lakhvir was trying to poison them and called for an ambulance. He died within hours; Gurjeet survived. Aconite was found in Lakhvir's purse. She was arrested and sentenced to twenty-three years in prison.[47]

-I-

The Long Island cab driver Sal Inghilleri was thirty-one when he was charged in 1994 with sexually abusing the then eleven-year-old Katie Beers, years before, when she was a toddler. He was not charged at the time for that offense. He compounded his mistreatment of Katie further by taking Katie's cat and bashing its head against a wall, killing the animal as Katie watched.[48] Inghilleri, who never committed murder, would probably best be ranked in Category 16 of the scale. He served twelve years for the sexual molestation of Katie, who later, at age nine, was kidnapped again, by another Long Island man, John Esposito, a family friend of the Inghilleri family. Esposito had created a dungeon right below his house, where he kept Katie as a sex slave for two and a half weeks in 1991, until he was finally caught and arrested. Though paroled in 2006, Inghilleri was arrested again, for failing to notify the authorities that he had moved to a different location, in North Carolina. Esposito was sentenced to fifteen years to life. His was one of the earliest cases of kidnap for sex slavery before the more prolonged cases of Ariel Castro, the aforementioned

Thomas Hose and Phillip Garrido, and, in Austria, Wolfgang Priklopil and Josef Fritzl. Inghilleri died in prison in 2018.[49]

Fortunately, Katie Beers was made of strong stuff. Now in her mid-thirties, she is married with two children and has become an inspirational speaker. She has told her story in her book *Buried Memories: Katie Beers' Story*.[50] By the time she was imprisoned by Esposito, she had already endured physical and sexual abuse at the hands of her godmother's husband, Inghilleri, and, as she put it, was "physically, emotionally, and verbally abused by all the adults who were supposed to take care of me." Despite the depravity she experienced, she tried to keep a shred of hope, saying, "I knew from an early age that not all people were bad." Katie had the good fortune, after her release from Esposito, to be placed with a supportive foster family and, after that, to receive treatment from an excellent therapist in East Hampton, Mary Bromley.[51] Katie has expressed the hope that "one day, after enough survivors have the courage to speak out about their abuse, that there will no longer be a 'stigma' associated with surviving."[52] We know a few things that helped Katie Beers surmount the evil influences that bore down on her so hard during her younger days: the good foster parents, the good therapist—but we know little about the basic makeup of persons who have endured such a past and been able to rise above it. All too many girls who have gone through what Katie Beers went through do not do as well. Some become promiscuous, some become morbidly jealous, some avoid sex altogether, some develop borderline personality disorder, and some become seriously depressed and even commit suicide. Others may have been dealt from birth a certain resiliency to extreme duress, possibly even by genetics—the nature of which we scarcely understand. Katie Beers is an example of what has been called in child psychiatry an "invulnerable child."[53]

Another in the annals of imperfect "perfect murders" is the story of the Category 14 schemer Mel Ignatow and his killing of his girlfriend, Brenda Sue Schaefer, in 1988. She had complained of his abusiveness and had planned to break off their relationship. He did not take the rejection lightly and then planned with the help of a former girlfriend, Mary Ann Shore, to lure Brenda to Mary Ann's house. They all lived in Louisville, Kentucky. When Brenda showed up, returning some jewelry he had given her, Mel, at gunpoint, locked her in the house, having blindfolded and gagged her, and bound her hand and foot. After stripping her naked and photographing her in suggestive positions, he then raped and sodomized her, beating her, and killing her with chloroform. He and Mary Ann then buried her behind the house. Though Mel was a suspect, there were no witnesses or other evidence—just Brenda's mysterious disappearance. The police did interview Mel, anyway, and he mentioned Mary Ann's name. This gave them reason to talk with her, as well, and she confessed not only to the murder they had so meticulously planned, but also to the photographs Mel had taken during the crime. Promising Mary Ann that she would be charged with no more than evidence tampering, they got her to wear a wire and talk with Mel. He reassured her authorities would never find Brenda's body, because it was "buried too deeply." It was not interred "too deeply" for the police to exhume and find it, by now decomposed. There was a trial, but it did not go well for the prosecution, because the star witness, Mary Ann, dressed in a vampish manner and laughed during her testimony. The jury thought perhaps she was the killer, and at all events acquitted Ignatow. Half a year later, however, workmen at Ignatow's house discovered a plastic bag under a floor vent. The bag contained rolls of film, which showed, when developed, photos of Mel abusing and raping Brenda Schaefer. Because of the laws concerning double jeopardy, Mel could not be tried for the murder, to which he now confessed. He was instead sentenced to prison on two separate occasions, on charges of perjury. Released in 2006, he died at home two years later from an accident—in what might seem to some like God's belated punishment, Mel fell and struck his head against a glass coffee table, bleeding to death.[54] What give Ignatow's murder of Brenda Schaefer the overtone of a "new evil" is the grotesque and totally unnecessary preliminaries to the eventual taking of someone's life. The killing was also not a response to any cruelty she inflicted on him. All she did was to say she did not want to see him anymore. The murder was a far cry—far in the direction of heartless egoism—from the murder of Ruth Snyder's husband by Ruth and her new lover, for which both were executed in 1928. They only throttled the husband so they could then be together. No prolongation of pain, no naked pictures. People throughout the ages, when cruelly wronged by someone, have been prone to elaborate fantasies of cruel retribution. Fantasies rarely acted out. We are seeing a greater number of persons in the last half century in whom the moral barriers and restraints against actually carrying out torturous acts of revenge are no longer in place. If you can think it, you can do it—as in Ben Sifrit's having sex with the head of a woman he beheaded after inviting her to his home, described earlier in this book.

-J-

Sadism is encountered much more often in men than in women, but there are some notable exceptions. Lois Jurgens (née Zerwas) was one of an evenly divided sixteen children—eight boys, eight girls—born to a shiftless, usually unemployed, impoverished alcoholic father known for being brutally abusive toward his wife and children, including Lois. She had been enuretic till thirteen, and was a compulsive "neat freak," preoccupied with fears of cancer and death, and subject to frequent nightmares. She married Harold Jurgens and lived in White Bear Lake, a suburb of Saint Paul, Minnesota. Unable to have children because of Harold's sterility, the couple tried to adopt a child but were at first turned down because of Lois's history of two previous psychiatric hospitalizations for depression and psychosis, treated with electroconvulsive therapy (ECT). She and her husband then went by the informal route and adopted first a boy, Robert, in 1960, and then another boy, Dennis, in 1962, after he had spent a year in a foster home. Robert, more obedient and placid, gave Lois little trouble. Dennis was a more typical boy, active and high-spirited. This stressed Lois, an angry woman with a short temper, far beyond her capacities. Toward Dennis, she became extremely punitive, battering him for trivial things. She indulged in a kind of sexual sadism, rare in a woman, doing such things as pouring boiling water on his penis if he were to wet his diaper too often, putting a clothespin with a pinch clamp on the penis's end, or biting him on the penis or scrotum, leaving scars all over his genital area. She would tie his limbs to the bedpost to make sure he stayed in bed or tie him to the toilet until he finally had a bowel movement. All of these cruelties she justified as part of being a staunch Catholic, doing God's work by making Dennis "perfect." She made Dennis pray and recite the rosary while kneeling on a broomstick. On other occasions, she would feed him bitter foods and then cover his mouth and nose, till he sickened and vomited; she would then force him to eat the vomit. When Dennis had been with the Jurgens family for two and a half years, Lois smashed him in the abdomen with a blunt object. That blow caused a traumatic rupture of the bowel, which then led to a fecal peritonitis, causing his death in 1965. Lois pretended the child had just "fallen down the stairs"—even though he had bruises all over his body, some new, some old. In the mid-1960s, child abuse cases of this sort were not always recognized and diagnosed as such. A diagnosis at autopsy was not one of homicide; the only word given was "deferred." Absent a homicide designation, Lois and Harold were free to adopt four more boys, who also suffered repugnant forms of abuse, such as slamming a child's head into a nail sticking out of a wall, or shoving used sanitary napkins into a child's face. Years later, when the biological mother, Jerry Sherwood, learned that Dennis had been abused, she was able to persuade the police to look into the case—twenty-one years after his death. After his body was exhumed, pathologists were able to discern that the boy had suffered multiple bruises and could see the perforated bowel that had led to the fatal peritonitis. There being no statute of limitations for murder, Lois was finally tried for murder and sentenced to twenty-five years in 1987. She served only eight and died in 2013.[55] Lois, a torture-murderer, would be designated to level 18 of the Gradations of Evil scale.

This case drew national attention and helped pave the way to broader recognition of child abuse, specifically of what came to be known as the battered child syndrome.[56] A large literature, both scholarly and governmental, on child abuse in general and on sexual abuse of children, began to emerge in the 1960s and 1970s. Among them, the Childhood Abuse Prevention and Treatment Act,[57] and articles on deciding the truthfulness of sexual abuse allegations in custody disputes.[58]

Jerry Jenkins and Ron Kennedy were two men in their early twenties from working-class families in Caspar, Wyoming. Both were juvenile delinquents. Ron's father was alcoholic and died in 1969. Jerry's father was a truck driver who beat Jerry and his other three children mercilessly. Jerry and Ron teamed up and slashed the tires of a young woman whom they would then "help" to get her tire fixed. They would then abduct and rape her. In 1973, they pulled this trick with Rebecca "Becky" Thompson and her younger half sister, Amy Burridge. They drove them, as if to help Becky with her car, to a remote area near the Freemont Canyon Bridge. After torturing and raping Becky, they threw both girls over the bridge—a 110-foot drop. Amy, age eleven, died instantly. Becky, eighteen, survived, with severe injuries.[59]

Jerry had the more serious record of juvenile delinquency. He had been in and out of jail numerous times. When he was twenty-eight, he married a girl of sixteen. They had two children, but he mistreated her and she planned to divorce—on the same day, as it happened, that the murder on the bridge occurred. Both Jerry and Ron were tried for the murder and given the death penalty, which later became life in prison without parole, since around that time, the death penalty was ruled unconstitutional. Jerry, whose crimes would place him in Category 18 of the scale, died in prison when he was fifty-four.[60]

As for Becky, one could hardly imagine her life going more down-hill, literally or figuratively, but it did. She was reportedly later raped by her psychiatrist. She married and then divorced after becoming seriously depressed. Two decades after the incident on the bridge, she went with another boyfriend and her young daughter to the site of the assault. This time, she threw herself over the bridge, committing suicide.[61] The well-known true crime writer Vincent Bugliosi, when reviewing a book about the murder, said that this was a "type of evil not too often succeeded." Perhaps prophetically, Becky, the week before her return to the bridge, had bought a movie called *Ode to Billy Joe*, watching it over and over. It was about a boy who could not cope with the memory of having been sexually abused by an older man and then committed suicide by jumping off the Tallahatchie Bridge in Mississippi.[62]

-K-

A teenager from a broken family in Moline, Illinois, Sarah Kolb was uncertain of her sexual orientation: She had sex at times with boys but considered herself a lesbian. She was part of a group of seriously disordered, drug-abusing high school dropouts, among whom she was the most domineering, cruel, and sadistic. When a new girl, Adrianne, came to town, Sarah at first felt sexual attraction toward her, and the feeling was reciprocated. Both girls were sixteen. Adrianne did not do drugs and had sex with many different boys, including Cory Gregory, who saw himself as bisexual and who was a close companion of Sarah's. Her gang was involved with metal piercings and abused marijuana, Ecstasy (3,4-methylenedioxymethamphetamine), regular methamphetamine, cocaine, and Xanax. At one point, Sarah became enraged that Adrianne had sex with a boy. Sarah lured Adrianne into a car, as if to restore their friendship. Instead, Sarah fought with Adrianne and, with Cory's help, strangled her to death. Realizing the girl was now dead, Sarah figured the best thing to do would be to pour accelerant over the body and burn it to ashes. But this was midwinter in 2005, and the proper degree of heat, 1500 degrees, could not be generated. Sarah and Cory then decided to use a friend's hacksaw and cut up Adrianne's somewhat bulky body into more manageable pieces, which could then be buried in the woods or deposited in sewer drains. Cory broke down and told his father and the authorities what had happened. The participants were convicted: Sarah was sentenced to life in prison, Cory to forty years. Looking back, it might be said that Sarah's whole group consisted of truants, school dropouts, and drug addicts from broken, working-class families—social rejects who tried to make up for their inadequacies by acting "tough." Sarah, more than the others, had distinct psychopathic traits: callousness, manipulativeness, lack of remorse, and pathological lying. Before the murder, she had been medicated for aggressiveness. Several years before the killing, she had fantasies of killing someone, dismembering the body and getting away with murder. The case was described as "replete with evil."[63] Sarah's crime, aimed at eliminating someone "in the way," would place her in Category 11 of the Gradations of Evil scale.

Until he was fifteen, Alec Kreider lived under the radar of the authorities as the second of three children in a divorced family near Lancaster, Pennsylvania. He would divide his time between the two parents, spending a week with one, then a week with the other. He was outwardly normal and had a close friend, Kevin Haines. Underneath this façade, he was what has in recent years been called a "callous unemotional youth," or else "life-persistent," as opposed to "adolescent-onset" antisocial type. Alec and Kevin were, at all events, A-level students and seemed to have a good connection. In May of 2007, however, Alec sneaked into the Haines home and, armed with a knife, stabbed Kevin's parents to death, and brutally slashed and stabbed his friend, mutilating Kevin's body with multiple wounds. The viciousness of the attack seemed compatible with someone who was in a state of rage, yet there seemed to be no discernible motive, apart from the desire to kill people, as had been smoldering in Alec for a long time. Shortly after the murders, which, at first, defied solution, Alec became infatuated with a girl named Caroline. He threatened suicide if she did not become his girlfriend. As a result of his suicidality, he was admitted to a psychiatric hospital. As much as he detested the hospital, toward the end of his two-week stay, he surprised everyone by confessing to the murders. Alec showed no remorse. He was then arrested, pled guilty, and sentenced to life in prison without parole. Alec had kept a diary, which was now open to the public. There were comments that showed his arrogance and egoism, his contempt for social convention, and his consuming desire to kill people indiscriminately. There were comments that suggested he identified with the Nazis. His diary was described as a "portrait of evil." While in prison, he told his cellmates he would kill again if he were ever released. No clear motive ever came to light. There was no answer to the "why" of his actions, which seemed to be a reflection of a pure hatred of humankind and an overwhelming desire to murder people, even his erstwhile best friend and his family, in a way that is reminiscent of Raskolnikov in Dostoesvsky's *Crime and Punishment*. Alec, who would be ranked in Category 14 of the Gradations of Evil scale, had never been abused physically or verbally by either parent. He may instead be an example of a "bad seed"—someone with a genetic predisposition to "callous-unemotionality," itself a prelude to psychopathic traits.[64]

-L-

Sabrina Limon lived with her husband, Robert, and their two young children, Robbie and Leanna, in the Tehachapi/Silver Lakes region in southeast California, near Bakersfield. Not long after the children were born, they began to engage in sex with other couples and to drink heavily. Bored with her husband, Sabrina then met a man eleven years younger than she, Jonathan Hearn, who was a medic and a fireman. Their affair began in 2012, and, by the next year, they were eager to marry. Both were given to a kind of treacly religiosity and to a Hallmark card–like sentimentality about how God had "willed" their being together, and how eager He was to see them united—all enunciated in their innumerable calls made on "burner" phones to avoid detection. They would arrange clandestine meetings for sex while Robert was still alive, but many of the calls were spent planning how best to do away with Robert so they could finally marry and live happily ever after. At first, they thought about poison but, that route being fraught with uncertainty, opted for shooting, what with that being the surer method and Jonathan having so many pistols (including semiautomatics) and rifles. Sabrina persuaded Jonathan to kill Robert while he was at work at his job, which was fixing trains with mechanical problems. Jonathan carried out his assignment in 2014, for which Sabrina was, of course, a coconspirator and accomplice. Detectives soon began to suspect that Jonathan was responsible for the murder—and that Sabrina knew of it. One particularly dogged investigator, Detective Meyer, managed to get permission to have their phones tapped. He listened to the many conversations between Sabrina and Jonathan. The police also had a camcorder image of a man near the scene of the crime on a motorcycle that looked like Jonathan's. Gradually, detectives amassed enough material to have them both arrested. They also learned that one of the "swinging" couples, the Bernatenes, knew about the crime. The wife, Kelly Bernatene, who had been Sabrina's best friend, told the police about the murder plan. As the evidence became more convincing, the two members of the love triangle who had carried out the murder were tried in court for the crime. The judge gave Jonathan a twenty-five-year sentence, and Sabrina a sentence of life without parole. Not much is known about the early years of either conspirator, though Sabrina had several psychopathic traits: superficial charm, pathological lying, and manipulativeness. On the Gradations of Evil scale, Category 10 appears to be the most appropriate ranking. Jonathan did not display psychopathic traits; rather, he was a young man smitten with his sexy lover.[65] Both were devout Protestants who knew their Bible thoroughly, with all of its passages about love and morality. Perhaps in the current era, when the institution of marriage, while still regarded widely as sacred, is honored more often in the breach than was the case in the pre-1960s, acts that strike us as evil occur within the marital domain more often than was formerly seen.

The word "evil" has been used often, even routinely, to describe the acts of many of the murderers, rapists, and other villains who figure prominently in these pages. But, in many instances, the parents of these people match, or even outdo, them in the barbarity of their behavior toward their children: mothers and fathers who are more "aren't" than "p-arent." Such was the case in the family of Melinda and her two sisters, who shared an ominous surname—Loveless. Born in 1975, Melinda was the youngest daughter in this Indiana family. Along with three of her girlfriends, Melinda brutally stabbed, pummeled, and burned twelve-year-old Shanda Sharer in 1992 because Shanda had made love with Amanda, Melinda's lesbian lover. Shanda was burned alive when one of the girls went to a gas station and filled a two-liter Pepsi bottle with gasoline, which was poured over Shanda before she was set on fire. Shanda's wrists and ankles had been bound. She had been beaten repeatedly on the head with a blunt object and sodomized with a foreign object, before being burned beyond recognition.

Melinda's ranking on the Gradations of Evil scale would probably be level 7. The real villain in this story of jealousy and murder may have been her father, Larry—allegedly a bisexual Pentecostal zealot and psychopathic transvestite, who would wear his wife's and his daughters' underwear and makeup. He was himself reported to be pathologically jealous, and a phi-landering, hypersexual gun nut and wifebeater who had years-long inces-tuous relations with his nieces and all three of his daughters. It is further alleged that he thrust guns into the vaginas of his daughters and once choked the middle daughter, Michelle, into unconsciousness when she tried to rescue her mother while he was beating her. He denied that Melinda was truly his daughter, accusing the mother of "whoring," though subsequent blood tests proved that she was his, after all. Marjorie, the mother, was reportedly an intensely masochistic woman who outrageously neglected her daughters, carrying on innumerable affairs as a way of getting back at Larry—yet, she could never bring herself to divorce him for twenty-five years, until, one day, she actually witnessed him having sex with her niece. Even then, the two rapidly remarried. This enraged Melinda who, just fifteen and still enuretic, became depressed and developed post-traumatic stress disorder and borderline personality disorder. All three daughters were gay. Melinda remained extremely attached to her father, despite the abuse and his killing her pets. It was in this setting that Melinda, along with her three friends—Laurine, Hope, and Toni—killed Shanda. In the trial for Shanda's murder, Melinda and Laurine both got sixty-year sentences; the other two received briefer ones.[66]

There was evil upon evil in this case, some of it consisting of the injustices done by the justice system. The girls were punished with stiff sentences for the depraved manner in which they tortured and murdered twelve-year-old Shanda Sharer. Larry Loveless, who had earlier been highly regarded as a Vietnam hero and then, back home, as a lay preacher in the Baptist church and even a marriage counselor, was finally arrested for incest, rape, sodomy, and sexual battery in 1993—crimes committed mostly between 1968 and 1977. Larry spent two years in prison awaiting trial, until spared by one of the peculiar injustices of the justice system: the statute of limitations for such crimes was only five years in Indiana, so he was released. Even worse, Larry was, given the impact of his countless acts of depravity against all of the women in his family, the true author of the even more depraved crimes connected with Shanda's torture and murder at the hands of his daughter, Melinda, and her friends. Larry was the teacher, Melinda but the pupil. The statute of limitations is, of course, not inherently "unjust." It is quite reasonable in many cases. But, in the case of serious sexual crimes committed years before, the nature of which only comes to light many years later and which may profoundly affect the victims, the statute may need to be modified, so as not to excuse perpetrators whose acts, seemingly so rare or so unimaginable, were not recognized at the time they took place.

In a crime that had all of the ingredients of a mass murder, except that no one was killed, Edward Leary, a fifty-year-old computer analyst recently fired from Merrill Lynch, brought two firebombs, made from Hellmann's mayonnaise jars, kitchen timers, batteries, and flashbulbs, onto two Manhattan subway trains. One of the bombs went off unexpectedly in Leary's hands, burning him over 40 percent of his body and injuring four dozen people. The mind-set behind the bombings was typical of mass murderers in general: a disgruntled and angry man, reacting to loss of a job or loss of a love relationship. When Leary was arrested and tried, the judge called him a "vengeful and self-aggrandizing man," adding that "evil exists in the world: No reason for it. It's just there."[67] The judge sentenced Leary, who would be designated to Category 13 of the Gradations of Evil scale, to ninety-four years in prison. The defense attorneys in the case tried to argue that Leary was "driven mad by an incompatible mixture of drugs to treat depression"— Prozac, Effexor, and a mild antianxiety drug, Buspar. This form of absurd defense has a modern ring to it, reminiscent of the now infamous "Twinkie defense" used in the 1979 trial of policeman Dan White, who assassinated San Francisco mayor George Moscone and supervisor Harvey Milk. The notion was that eating those sugary snacks had worsened White's existing mood swings and somehow rendered him incapable of the premeditation required for rational thought. The jurors were apparently hoodwinked by that silly argument, such that White was convicted of involuntary manslaughter, rather than first-degree murder. "Twinkie defense" has become a catchword for improbable legal defenses cooked up by defense attorneys perhaps more committed to winning than to justice.

-M-

Martin MacNeill came from a chaotic, wildly dysfunctional, and impoverished family in Camden, New Jersey. His parents were divorced. His father, who had abandoned the family, was reportedly an alcoholic. His mother supported the six children via prostitution, the children listening to the grunts of her clients. Of Martin's five siblings, two committed suicide, one died of a heroin overdose, and another died of alcoholism. Martin, handsome and bright, was diagnosed with bipolar disorder. He was briefly in the US Army but was let out because of mental illness, which he managed to parlay into veteran's benefits, conning the system into continuing them for the rest of his life. When he was nineteen, he switched from Catholicism to the Church of Jesus Christ of Latter-day Saints (LDS) and moved to Utah as a member of the Mormon community. Two years later, he committed a large check fraud of some $35,000 but was caught and spent six months in jail. He then went to Mexico and somehow managed to get into medical school in Guadalajara. From there, he went to California and got into a school of osteopathy, conning his way into a degree. Right after, he conned his way yet again—this time into law school, managing to end up with a degree in law besides the one in osteopathy, allowing him to affix an LLD to his MD degree. People who knew him considered him a cold, rude, arrogant, dishonest, narcissistic, intimidating braggart, who was also lacking in medical skills. So much for the good side. The bad side was that, while in Utah, he met a woman from a well-respected Mormon family. A former model, she was quite beautiful and was swept off her feet by Martin, not listening to those who did not trust him. He threatened to commit suicide if she left him—a time-honored trick that often works with naïve individuals of her personality type, who are sweet, trusting, and easily cowed into submission. So they did marry. Michele, née Somers, was one of seven children. Her parents had divorced when she was twenty. Martin and Michele lived luxuriously in a huge house, and he set himself up as a "medical" doctor. At home, he was argumentative and offended Michele by watching pornography, which is forbidden among LDS adherents. He was an inveterate philanderer who also had sex with one of his female patients, besides having raped other women. He and Michele had four children in rapid succession: Rachel, who had bipolar disorder, like her father; Vanessa, a heroin addict; Alexis, who became a medical doctor; and Damian, who also had bipolar disorder and later committed suicide. Vanessa had gotten pregnant by a man she met in her late teens. Her daughter Ada then also lived with the MacNeills. In addition, Martin and Michele adopted four girls from Ukraine: Noel, Elle, Giselle, and Sabrina. Martin continued to work various scams to enrich himself, but these were not detected for many years. In the meantime, the whole family of eleven lived in luxury. There were times when Michele sensed that Martin was cheating on her and, because of his hypercritical, bullying nature, suspected that, as the marriage began to deteriorate, she might end up dead. She told some friends that were she to be killed, Martin would be the one responsible. After they had been married thirty years, Martin grew tired of her and became enamored of a rebellious "hot number," Gypsy Jill Willis, a woman twenty years younger than Michele. Willis had shamed her Mormon family by having a child out of wedlock, raised by her parents, who then had nothing more to do with her. Martin now hatched a plot to kill Michele, so as to avoid the nuisances of divorce and child support, meantime taking advantage of acquiring an "accidental death" insurance policy—one that pays double in cases of death by accident.[68]

At this time, Martin begins to complain of minor facial imperfections in Michele, such as crow's-feet lines near the eyes, and insists she undergo cosmetic surgery of five different sorts on her face, all at the same time. Managing to find a plastic surgeon to do all of that, Martin then persuades him to prescribe antianxiety pills and opiate painkillers. Once back home, Michele is groggy from all of the surgery, and Martin crushes all of the pills together and gives the whole mixture, via enema, assuming that the opiates will kill her. They don't quite kill her, so he then drowns her in the bathtub. Pretending she is still alive, he dials 911 for emergency help, meantime faking resuscitation maneuvers and pretending also that he cannot get her out of the tub, due to a fake foot injury that rendered him too weak to lift her by himself. The emergency team arrives, realizes she is probably dead, but, pro forma, takes her to the hospital, anyway, in case she is still revivable. At this point, Martin "hires" his mistress, Gypsy, as the nanny for the smaller children. He gives her the name Jillian Giselle MacNeill, taken from one of his adopted daughters who has returned to Ukraine. Their shared surname makes it seem as if they are married.[69] Gypsy is further depicted as a nurse he had gotten to know through the hospital. Michele's sister, Linda, is convinced Martin had killed her, and spends the next several years gathering bits of evidence that will ultimately lead to his arrest and conviction.[70]

Martin now begins to molest two of his daughters. The whole truth does not come out for six years. Martin is finally jailed in 2012, awaiting trial. While in jail, he acknowledges to his bunkmate that he had held

Michele's head underwater—but the bunkmate "snitches" and testifies against him at the trial.[71]

The jury convicted Martin of murder, as well as molestation of two of his daughters. The court gave him two fifteen-year sentences, adding that "evil had prevailed."[72] Alexis, the daughter who became a physician, said, "My father's evil did not begin or end with the murder of my mother. Shortly after my mother's death, my father sexually assaulted me on two different occasions. He destroyed my world and created a living nightmare in its place." In 2017, three years after his incarceration, Martin, then sixty, was found dead in the Utah State Prison, perhaps by suicide.[73]

What is special about Martin, who would be ranked at level 14 of the Gradations of Evil scale, is the sheer and malevolent artistry he brings to the domain of crime. There have always been fraudsters and mountebanks, and men who fleece the public by selling fake nostrums. There are few who have successfully impersonated a variety of other highly successful men, tricked wealthy women into marriage, and committed murder along the way. Another example was the equally clever German-born Gerhard Gerhartsreiter, who moved to the United States and began to use such aliases as Chris Crowe, Chip Smith, and Clark Rockefeller. Mostly, he fooled well-to-do women into marrying him, but along the way, he murdered Jonathan and Linda Sohus, for which, after much trouble in identifying whom he really was, he is now serving a twenty-seven-year sentence in a California prison.[74] MacNeill was an imposter of perhaps even greater skill, at least initially. During a forty-year career, he fooled others as a fake Mormon, fake lawyer, and fake doctor, doing fake CPR on the wife he just murdered, and was a cheating husband and incestuous father. MacNeill was never true to anyone. By committing murder, MacNeill and Gerhartsreiter also differ from many of the previous "con artists"—named, I believe, after Herman Melville's book *The Confidence Man*, published on April Fools' Day in 1857[75]—in that con men usually trick people out of their money, rarely committing murder. There are other con men in the current post-1960s era who kill not for money but to escape humiliation for their lying, as in the case of Mark Hacking, who killed his wife in 2004 when she discovered that he had lied to her about being a physician.[76]

Anthony Morley, born in 1972 in Leeds, a large city in the West York-shire area of England, became a model and dancer, winning the "Mr. Gay" contest when he was twenty-one. He later took classes in cooking and became a sous chef in a fish restaurant. This latter career has impor-tance for the way in which his life later unfolded. He was, more accu-rately, a bisexual man. About two-thirds of his affairs were with men, and a third were with women. His first homosexual relationship having taken place when he was a teenager, Anthony was himself confused about his orientation, but he tended to call the intimacies with men "adventures," as though they were not indices of his true nature. He developed a serious alcohol problem around the time he became a sous chef. At one point, he got into a serious dispute over money with a man, Shaun Wood, after a five-year relationship. He went after Wood with a meat cleaver but tripped and fell before he could injure his former lover. Sometime after, he invited another male lover, Damian Oldfield, to his place, where he used his culi-nary skills in preparing a fish dinner for the two of them. They then went to bed. Anthony soon fell asleep, only to be awakened by his friend, who was pushing moves before Anthony felt ready for such advances. Becoming enraged, Anthony stabbed Oldfield to death with multiple knife wounds. Anthony, resuming his main occupation, then cut pieces from Oldfield's leg and chest, which he then seasoned, oiled, and cooked. He tried to eat some of this preparation but then discarded it. Anthony then stumbled into a nearby restaurant, with bloodstains all over him, and asked someone to call the police. He was then arrested, convicted, and sentenced to a minimum of thirty years in prison.[77] Anthony differs from the more notorious gay cannibal, Armin Meiwes, discussed at length elsewhere in this book. Whereas Meiwes was cool, deliberate, and unhurried in his months-long ingestion of his victim's body parts, Anthony's attempt at cannibalism took place during an impulse spurred by inebriation and rage, quite without premeditation. He would thus be placed in Category 6 of the Gradations of Evil scale. It is of interest that, in our review of fifty-three cases of canni-balism, all but two were male. Among the males, twenty-four were hetero-sexual, twenty-three were homosexual (including three who were bisexual but identified as gay), two transvestites, and two of uncertain sexualities. This suggests a strong preponderance of males among cannibals and of homosexuality among the men—to a level nearly ten times what would be expected in the general population. If this distribution were corroborated in a larger survey, it would point to something strange and not yet fully understood about pathological cannibalism. Clearly, his is entirely separate from the understandable and well-accepted cannibalism by the few survivors of the 1972 crash of an Uruguayan plane in the Andes, who made the agonizing decision to subsist on the flesh of those passengers who had died, until they were finally rescued.[78]

-N-

Stella Strong Nickell, née Stephenson in 1943, was one of eight children. She was raised in a chaotic and neglectful family, reportedly abused both physically and sexually by her alcoholic father. Her mother, Alva, was from a Cherokee family and had been married three times before, also to alcoholic men. Chaos continued in Stella's adult life. She often ran away from her home, where she badly burned herself on two occasions, after pouring kerosene into the fireplace, thinking it was water. During an affair with a soldier when she was eighteen, she had a child who was given up for adoption; she had earlier had a daughter, Cindy, by another man when she was sixteen, and later, a second daughter by her first husband, Bob Strong. She had briefly been in jail for stealing a cousin's welfare checks and had tried, unsuccessfully, to hire someone to kill Strong. When she remarried a man named Bruce Nickell, with whom she moved to Washington State, her dreams of a life of ease reasserted themselves, and she now planned to kill him, shortly after she bought $175,000 in life insurance policies on her husband's life, with herself as the beneficiary. Money was not even the primary motive. Bruce had been an alcoholic but became sober, preferring to stay home and watch television, rather than go to the bars where Stella could live it up. Bruce wasn't fun anymore. Her idea was to give him an Excedrin capsule for his headaches, which she had laced with cyanide and placed in a pharmacy. In her too-clever-by-half "perfect-murder" plan, she also figured to poison some other Excedrin users with cyanide, so that the relatives of the dead victims and the police would think the deaths had been caused by a criminal with no knowledge of, and no ill will toward, any particular person, such as her husband. Meantime, she had been physically abusive toward her daughter Cindy, both of whom supplemented their incomes by prostitution. In June of 1986, Bruce died from the cyanide-laced capsule, as did a woman who bought another Excedrin bottle from that same pharmacy. Catching Stella as the killer proved difficult. Once she became a suspect, she was asked to take a polygraph examination. At first, she refused to comply but later took the test—and failed. The police learned that she had taken out books from the local library about poisons. One was found to be overdue, since she had never returned it. Her fingerprints were found on other books on poisoning still in the library—on pages that dealt with cyanide. Stella was finally arrested in 1987, found guilty of the two murders, and sentenced to two ninety-year terms.[79]

We observe an unusual degree of evil in Nickell's plan to kill one or two others with the same poison she used to kill her husband, so as to portray herself as one of the "random" widows or other survivors of some would-be mass murderer, who had no animosity against any particular victim. She would be ranked in Category 14 of the Gradations of Evil scale. Had she been a bit more vicious, she might have put cyanide in Excedrin capsules in different towns so as to kill a dozen people and make herself seem an all the more tragic figure who had lost a loved one, yet who all the while *was* the perpetrator.

What makes Stella not just a figure of uncommon evil but also of a *new* evil is that she is the first person *caught* for a multiple poisoning used to divert suspicion away from the actual perpetrator. She can be considered a "copycat" killer, in the sense that she was probably inspired by the September 1982 poisonings in Chicago, where cyanide was put in Tylenol capsules. Seven people were murdered in that episode. The killer in that case has never been caught, but new methods were then developed by Johnson & Johnson and other drug manufacturers to protect against product tampering, and are now used for all over-the-counter medications.[80] Fortunately, these killings by cyanide-laced capsules, albeit new, are rare. However, one 1991 episode, also in Washington State, appears as a copycat killing based on the Nickell case. Joseph Meling had laced Sudafed (pseudoephedrine) capsules with cyanide in an effort to kill his wife and collect an even bigger life insurance payout of $700,000. The thirty-one-year-old insurance salesman had placed the poisoned Sudafed bottles on the shelves of several local stores, so as to mislead the authorities about both the intended victim and an actual perpetrator. Meling kept losing one job after the other, and often disparaged his wife in public. The wife survived, but two others, a man and a woman in their forties, both died. Meling was identified and arrested. During his trial, he was described as an "abusive man devoid of moral and social values." He was sentenced to life in prison.[81]

The mother of Narcisa Novack (née Veliz) doubtless had no idea the name she gave her daughter would one day help define her as an outrageously narcissistic psychopath. In her early adult years, Ecuadorian-born Narcisa was a prostitute and pole dancer who had immigrated to Miami, and who would seduce and then marry Ben Novack Jr., the son of the owner of the Fontainebleau Hotel. She had been married or else cohabiting with several men before and had a daughter, May. Narcisa was a jealous, greedy woman, said to be totally devoid of scruples. Ben was a strange piece of work himself—a stammerer who could barely make himself understood, until a speech therapist corrected his impediment. He was intensely narcissistic himself: arrogant, abrasive, rude, demeaning—but successful as an organizer and caterer for large conventions. He also had some strange sexual habits, including looking at amputee porn or having sex with amputated women (as well as with women with no amputations), maintaining several affairs throughout his nineteen-year marriage to Narcisa. He had insisted on a prenuptial agreement, in which Narcisa would not collect anything, except a small payment, if they divorced in less than ten years. Yet, he tried to divorce her within that period, at which time she hired hitmen to bludgeon him. They were never caught. In 2002, when she was forty-seven, she conspired to kill her eighty-five-year-old mother-in-law, Bernice Novack, so the older woman would not inherit any money. The murder, carried out by two thugs Narcisa had hired, was improperly ruled an accident. Seven years later, Ben again threatened divorce and Narcisa hired the same two thugs to bludgeon Ben to death, which they did, also gouging his eyes out, at her suggestion. Narcisa made sure this happened in New York, which does not have a death penalty the way Florida does. At first, she was not implicated and was thus free to inherit many millions, but, a year later, new evidence became available and she was arrested, despite her crocodile tears at the funerals. She failed a number of polygraph exams. Narcisa would be ranked at level 16 of the Gradations of Evil scale, for her multiple vicious acts. She and her brother, Cristobal, both got life sentences without parole. Admittedly, virtue was in short supply on both sides of the marriage. Ironically, Letitia, Narcisa's sister, was as religious and morally upright as her sister and Ben were not. Letitia even wrote a letter condemning Narcisa for Ben's murder, but the letter—unfortunately unsigned—was not taken seriously until the time of the New York trial. Ben, on his side, cheated on Narcisa as often as she did on him; he maintained a stable of prostitutes with whom to have kinky sex, besides his huge collection of porn featuring amputees that she would use to blackmail him. He dared not try to divorce her, until he finally tried to, anyway, in 2009, regardless of consequences. Narcisa, on her side, managed to carry hypocrisy to new heights, as when she declared, after arranging for Ben to be murdered, "Only a monster could do such an evil thing!"[82]

-O-

Most people are aware that the body needs certain amounts of naturally occurring elements, like sodium, potassium, chlorine, zinc, magnesium, lithium, and manganese. Fewer know that we also need, in small quantities, selenium, and that there are symptoms both of deficiency and of excess. Richard Overton knew. In 1988, the psychologist in Orange County, California, fatally poisoned his third wife, Janet, with cyanide. Unlike Joseph Meling and Stella Nickell, Overton confined his use of the drug only to his spouse. Earlier, he had tried to poison his first wife, Dorothy, with selenium, after she found out that he was a bigamist, having been married at the same time to Caroline Hutcheson. Selenium is used in the body to convert the thyroid hormone thyroxine to the active compound tri-iodo-thyronine, and has other uses, such as in DNA synthesis. Excess amounts can be fatal. Overton eventually admitted the attempt, but Dorothy did not press charges, so he was not arrested and tried in court. Overton had a deep distrust of women and was prone to jealousy. He was convinced, for example, that Janet was cheating on him. After he antagonized her past a certain point, she did have an affair. He would pretend to be hired by some secret government organization that required his "travel" to out-of-the-way places like Costa Rica but would, in fact, be having affairs in Los Angeles with other women. He showed the full panoply of narcissistic traits, including arrogance, grandiosity, and contemptuousness, along with deceitfulness and other psychopathic traits. He even married a fourth time, after being arrested for killing Janet, presumably on the assumption he could get away with this crime, as well. He was convicted in 1995 and sentenced to life in prison, dying at eighty-one, some fourteen years later.[83] At the time of his trial, then deputy attorney Christopher Evans called Overton the "single most blatant, arrogant, yet curiously effective liar and manipulator of the truth" he had ever seen, and a "comprehensively dangerous sociopath of the lowest order."[84] A killer who sought to eliminate spouses "in the way," he would be assigned to Category 11 of the Gradations of Evil scale.

In a case described as "one of the city's most heinous crimes in recent memory," a nanny hired by Kevin and Marina Krim from Manhattan's Upper West Side stabbed and then drowned their two-year-old son and six-year-old daughter in a bathtub. The mother happened to be out with the third child at the time, discovering the murders when returning home. The nanny, Yoselyn Ortega, was forty-nine at the time of the 2012 incident.[85] At the trial, the father called Ortega an "evil and utterly dangerous narcissist."[86] Ortega was convicted of both first- and second-degree murder, and she and her family were criticized in addition of deceiving the Krim family, as though Ortega had been an "experienced nanny" when, in fact, she was not.[87] As far as could be determined, Ortega's premeditated murders were prompted by her to spite Mrs. Krim, out of envy for her being able to provide her children with what Ortega could not give her own son, whom she had left to be raised by her sister in the Dominican Republic.[88] In the absence of additional information about Ortega's background, it appears that this crime would be best ranked in Category 8 of the Gradations of Evil scale, for individuals with few or no psychopathic traits who kill when underlying, slow-burning rage is ignited.

Nanny murders are fortunately rare. Those publicized in the media have occurred within the past twenty years. In 2016, for example, a sixty-six-year-old nanny, Oluremi Oyindasola, was arrested in Maryland for the death of a baby girl whose crying she allegedly drowned out, literally, by pouring two bottles of milk down the girl's throat. The nanny is charged with second-degree murder and is held in the local Department of Corrections, awaiting trial.[89] In North London, a thirty-four-year-old Hungarian nanny, Viktoria Tautz, allegedly caused the death of a ten-month-old infant, Joshua Paul, in 2014 by excessive shaking that caused brain injuries and spinal cord bruising.[90] Considerable publicity surrounded the case of a nineteen-year-old nanny, Louise Woodward, who, in 1997, was convicted of involuntary manslaughter of eight-month-old Matthew Eappen in Newton, Massachusetts. This also was considered a death via the "shaken baby" syndrome. The judge in the case reduced the charge from murder to involuntary manslaughter, commenting that the British au pair had acted out of "confusion, inexperience, frustration, immaturity, and some anger, but not malice in the legal sense."[91] Perhaps the nanny murders in recent years, rare as they are, are related to some degree of women being more emancipated from the old German shibboleth of *Kinder, Kirche, Küche* (Children, Church, Kitchen) we discussed earlier. Wealthy and titled women always had governesses and nannies—but the women were often still in the home (or the castle). The greater number of women in the workforce since the 1960s has meant that there has been greater reliance on nannies and au pairs. Not all are as well trained; a tiny fraction resort to violence.

-P-

We know little about the origins of vicious Category 16 killer Victor Paleologus, except that he was born in 1962 to a Greek immigrant father who was a chef in a Philadelphia restaurant. He claimed to have gotten a bachelor's degree from one institution and a master's in business from another, but neither could be verified. He seems to have had a brief marriage in his late twenties that ended in divorce. Victor was an inveterate liar and con artist whose modus operandi was to dress in spiffy clothes and to lure pretty young girls with promises that, because they had "just the right look," they could be right for parts in the next James Bond movie with Sean Connery—and maybe earn $100,000. Oh, but first, a girl had to show up at a certain very remote house at a certain time, wearing a black miniskirt, a white shirt, and black stiletto heels. Some fell for the scam; others were shrewder and took along some muscular bouncer-type man, which scared Victor off. One girl, Kristi Johnson, took the bait and met him at the designated place in February of 2003—and disappeared. Victor raped and then killed her, dumping her body from a hilltop, where it was discovered some time later by two boys. Victor had many arrests for various scams, using all manner of lies to weasel out of jail time. To a certain woman, he pretended, as did the wife killer Donnie Rudd, that he was dying of cancer and just needed to see her one last time. Or he would fool real estate agents into thinking he could afford certain posh houses in Los Angeles and, while inspecting the properties, pilfer checks and identification cards from the owners, then passing himself off as "Mr. Morton Robert" or whoever else's name was on the IDs. Later, when he was arrested for murder, Detective Obenchain described Victor's actions as a chronicle of evil behavior by one of the most diabolical con men she had ever encountered. Another detective said Victor was the most outrageous liar anyone could imagine. Within days of Kristi's disappearance, for example, another young woman came forward and spoke of having been approached with the same scam about the James Bond film, the need to wear stiletto heels and a black miniskirt—so it was clear to the court that this was the same con man who had lured Kristi. At his trial, the prosecution tried for the death penalty, but Victor was sentenced to only twenty-five years. Paleologus was one of the most malignant of the Hollywood scam artists who trick wannabe actresses, and then rape or kill them.[92] Another example is that of Charles Rathbun who, in 1995, lured twenty-seven-year-old blond model and rising actress Linda Sobek, sexually assaulting and killing her. Rathbun was given a life sentence for the crime.[93] Hollywood has been fertile ground for a long time for male predators, often posing as photographers making promises to attractive young women that their pictures will give them entrée to fabulous lives in the movies. One such case from the mid-1950s was that of Harvey Glatman, who would troll around modeling agencies and persuade girls to come to his apartment, where he would tie them up, violently rape, and finally strangle them, later burying them in remote spots in desert plots near Los Angeles. Glatman was caught and executed at San Quentin in 1959, at the age of thirty-two.[94]

Recently, a most unusual case came to light, involving incest with a new twist—that of Steven Pladl and his daughter, Katie Rose. In 1998, Steven and his wife, Alyssa, gave birth to a daughter they felt unable to care for by themselves, so the baby was given up for adoption. Anthony and Kelly Fusco were the adopting parents and named the girl Katie. She had originally been named Denise when Steven, then twenty, and Alyssa, then fifteen, became parents of the baby. When Katie became eighteen, she began the process of finding her birth parents, as many adoptees in recent decades have done, now that the laws changed in a way to make it both possible and practicable to do so. This led to her discovery of the Pladls, with whom she reconnected. Oddly enough, she and her birth father, Steven, became more than drawn to one another: they fell in love. Steven and Alyssa divorced, and he and Katie married. Katie became pregnant, delivering a son, Bennett, in September of 2017. Four months later, however, Steven, now forty-two, and the new Mrs. Pladl, now twenty-year-old Katie, were arrested in Virginia on charges of incest and adultery. The story seemed destined to have a tragic ending, much as that of Sophocles's *Oedipus* saga. The analogy is not perfect: Oedipus unwittingly ends up marrying Jocasta, his mother, not his daughter. Then, when they find out the truth, Jocasta hangs herself and Oedipus blinds himself with two pins from her dress. Steven Pladl's story ends differently. After a while, Katie told her father/husband that she was severing the relationship. Steven then killed their son Bennett and drove to New York, where he killed Katie and her adoptive father, Tony Fusco, before committing suicide.[95] Incest is no less a taboo today than it was in Sophocles's time, 2,500 years ago, so it is hard to imagine how the new couple could have had a happy life. Steven Pladl would be ranked in Category 7 of the Gradations of Evil scale.

One of two children from a Texas town near Houston, Christine Paolilla lost her father, apparently because of alcohol and drug addiction, when she was two. She was born with alopecia totalis and always had to wear wigs. Because of her baldness, she was bullied constantly by classmates. Two girls did nevertheless befriend her in high school: Rachel Koloroutis and Tiffany Rowell, both pretty girls from better-off families. The two girls were very kind to Christine and helped her with her appearance, but Christine was wild and heavily into drugs and, when she had a boy in her life, clingy, rageful, and morbidly jealous. One boyfriend, Chris Snider, was antisocial and already had a rap sheet for petty crimes. When Christine was seventeen, she and Chris, using guns Chris had stolen from his father, invaded the home of Tiffany, where she and Rachel, and their friends Marcus Precella and Adelbert Sanchez, were partying. Christine and Chris promptly shot all four to death and then fled. The girls had been shot in the groin repeatedly, an act suggestive of intense sexual envy and personal hatred. They were not caught till 2006, three years after the massacre. They had fired forty shots in the kind of overkill that signifies a murder animated by extreme hatred. In the meantime, Christine had married a man of twenty-seven, Justin Rott. The two lived off a $400,000 inheritance Christine acquired, going through enormous quantities of heroin and cocaine. For half a year, they were holed up in a hotel, where, at one point, Christine intimated that she and her then boyfriend, Chris, had killed the four young people. The police finally caught up with the shooters, at which point Chris committed suicide. Christine was convicted and sentenced to forty years in prison, though had she been eighteen instead of seventeen at the time, she would have been given the death penalty.[96] Some who knew of the details of the crime expressed the feeling that they were "staring in the face of pure evil."[97] She would be assigned to level 6 of the Gradations of Evil scale, the ranking for impetuous, hotheaded murderers without marked psychopathic traits.

One reason for the long delay in suspecting and apprehending Christine stems from the fact that women are much less prone than are men to commit murder, all the more so for teenage girls. Mass murder by females is especially uncommon.[98] In my compilation of 330 mass murderers from around the world since 1900, for example, I could identify ten females, the earliest being Priscilla Joyce Ford, a paranoid schizophrenic teacher who, in 1980, mowed down six persons as she drove her car into a crowd. All ten of the female killers suffered from a psychotic disorder such as schizophrenia, bipolar disorder, or, in the most well-known case, psychotic depression. The latter was that of Andrea Yates, who, in 2001, drowned her five children when forced by her husband, a religious zealot, to live in a converted Greyhound bus, within which she was to homeschool and teach religion to their children.[99]

-Q-

In the spring of 2011, when Matthew Quesada was sitting in a London café with his three-year-old daughter, seated nearby with family was a sixty-three-year-old retired bus driver, Alan Smith. The little girl was crying, and Smith chanced to ask, solicitously, if she was "all right." Quesada retorted angrily with, "What's it got to fucking do with you?" Quesada then went back to his house, grabbed a knife, returned to the café, and proceeded to stab Smith five times in the chest, puncturing his heart and lungs, and killing him. Quesada had for some time been obsessed with Robert Ludlum's fictional character Jason Bourne, studying the various combat moves the spy would make when dealing with adversaries. He then acted as though he were a heroic spy, himself. Running from the café, he began looking up the flight schedule for planes to Sao Paulo, Brazil, where there are no extradition rules that would have forced him to return to England to face the authorities. He was, however, quickly apprehended and then tried to feign mental illness, by way of avoiding responsibility for the murder. The judge at his trial told Quesada that he had committed a totally unprovoked attack in front of the victim's relatives and all of the other persons in the café. It emerged that, in the brief time he had gone home to get the knife, he had burned the clothes he had been wearing and had his mother shave off his hair, so as to look different from the killer. Quesada had a record of previous arrests for assaults and threatening behavior. A psychiatrist at the court expressed the opinion that Quesada was either schizophrenic or had some other sort of paranoid illness, one sign of which was that, when Smith had innocently inquired after the welfare of the daughter, Quesada concluded he must be a "pedophile." Although he made some clever efforts to conceal himself after his crime, the Quesada case represents the action of an impulsive "hot-blooded" killer of the Category 6 type, rather than that of a controlled, psychopathic killer who carries out his lethal acts with considerable aforethought and planning. His evil act was stabbing a harmless man to death in full view of the café patrons and the victim's own family members. He then tried to feign insanity and, if that failed, to catch the next plane to Brazil. A truly insane man would likely have stood next to the corpse and proudly told the police how he ridded the world of a dangerous pedophile.[100]

-R-

The rates of divorce have increased markedly in the United States and England since the late 1960s and early 1970s.[101] As we have seen in these pages, many of the men and women who have committed the kinds of violent acts that strike us as "evil" came from fractured families. In many of these cases, one cannot draw up the traditional kind of family tree, with grandparents and parents who stayed together, in which the children grew up knowing who their parents were and who felt, for the most part, genuinely loved and cared for by their parents and grandparents, and uncles and aunts and cousins as well. Instead, the family tree diagram becomes an impossible mishmash of lines crossing every which way, and sometimes, as in the case of the Pladls discussed above, with marriage lines looping back to show how a daughter ended up later as yet another of her father's wives. Boys growing up without fathers show increased propensities for trouble with the law.[102] Many persons, both male and female, who grow up in fractured families tend to have greater burdens of emotional problems, including difficulties establishing solid relationships with others when it is their turn to do so.

Jack Wayne Reeves is an example of these disadvantages, having grown up in a family where the parents divorced when he was seven, and then going on to live a life even more fractured and violent than the one in which he was raised. He was fifty-six when his wife at the time, Emelita, a woman of only twenty-six—a "mail-order" bride from the Philippines, by whom he had a three-year-old son, Jeff—had apparently disappeared. She turned out to be more of a "male-order" bride, in the sense that Jack ordered her about in all manner of demeaning ways, subjecting her to a succession of sexual perversions, besides maltreatment and physical cruelty. Preoccupied with the total subjugation of women, he also took photos of Emelita in obscene poses, though, by that time he had become mostly impotent sexually, though still sadistically controlling. He walked around the house with a pistol, also sleeping with one. As for Emelita's disappearance, this was because she finally tried to obtain a divorce—and Jack killed her. Some eight years earlier, he had a Korean wife, Myong Hui Chong, who drowned as mysteriously as Emelita had disappeared. It later became clear that Jack had drowned her and made it look like an accident. He told police who inquired about her death that she had fallen from a rubber raft and drowned while he was busy catching insects for fishing bait, which raised suspicions among Myong's family, who remembered her as a woman who could not swim, was afraid of the water, and would never get in a boat. He insisted her body be cremated. Eight years before that incident, Jack's second wife, Sharon, née Vaughan, died in what was considered a suicide by shotgun. When suspicions were raised, however, and she was later disinterred, the pathologist declared that her death was by a murder staged to look like a suicide. Before that marriage ended, Jack would never eat with his in-laws, the Vaughans, until they tasted the food first—to make sure they had not tried to poison him. When interrogated later by detectives, Jack would boast of his exploits in Vietnam, killing many Vietcong, sometimes by shooting into covered-over holes the enemy had dug while awaiting American troops. He seems to have adopted their skills, since he had later dug such a hole in a wooded area, in which he buried Emelita. In his early years, Jack seldom saw his father even before his parents' divorce. His father was an army man, often away. Though his mother was a kindly woman, his maternal grandmother would punish him by bullwhipping him. Indeed, she had killed one of her own sons by bullwhipping. When he was seventeen, Jack married a girl of fifteen, but the marriage was then annulled at the insistence of her mother. He was already possessive, sexually perverse, and domineering toward that first wife—a pattern he continued with all of the other wives and liaisons. After killing his third wife, Myong, for example, he raped her sister at the funeral. Following the murder of Emelita, he tried to acquire another mail-order bride from the Philippines. When questioned by detectives after the disappearance of Emelita, Jack showed no emotion, even when informed that they suspected she had been killed. Yet, he talked to them about his obsession with pornographic videos, anal sex, forced fellatio, and so forth, to

the point that they became convinced he had killed her. He refused a polygraph exam but then hired a lawyer and did take the polygraph, which he
failed. Ultimately, Jack was arrested and sentenced to fifty years in prison,
which amounted to a probable life sentence, given that he was already fifty-
six.[103] For his multiple vicious acts, he would be ranked at level 16 of the
Gradations of Evil scale.

Born in 1938, the same year as Jack Reeves discussed in the previous
vignette, Father Gerald Robinson was a Roman Catholic priest, born
in Toledo, Ohio, of Polish extraction on his mother's side. He was an
unfriendly and uncommunicative man whom some suspected was part of
a satanic cult of other priests who allegedly kidnapped girls they would
later torture and rape. When he gave sermons in Polish, he was considered
charismatic, but otherwise he was seen as timorous and unsuccessful. He
ended up as a chaplain in Toledo's Mercy Hospital. While there, he got in
trouble with a sacristan thirty years his senior, Sister Annunciata, née Margaret Ann Pahl. A meticulous woman, she criticized him for his poor work
habits. This made him furious, and around Easter time in 1980, when he
was forty-two, he sneaked up to her in the sacristy, strangled her, stabbed
her thirty-one times with a letter opener, and inserted a small crucifix into
her vagina, also cutting an upside-down cross on her abdomen. Another
priest immediately figured he was the killer, but the church and the police
allegedly covered up the murder, which remained a cold case for twenty-
four years. Enough evidence was finally accumulated to merit an arrest.
He was convicted and given a twenty-year sentence for a crime he still
continues to deny. He had failed a polygraph exam when first interrogated,
but nothing was done at the time.[104] He would be assigned to Category 22
of the Gradations of Evil scale, due to the brutal and perverse manner in
which he tortured Sister Annunciata to death.

This was only the second time in US history that a priest had been
convicted of homicide. The first concerned a German-born priest, Hans
Schmidt, who immigrated to America in 1909. There was mental illness
on both sides of his family. He himself had odd preoccupations with blood
and dismemberment. Identifying as bisexual, he had molested altar boys

but also had affairs with several women. In 1912, he had taken a position in a New York City church where he met the housekeeper of the rectory, Anna Aumüller. Schmidt claimed to have heard God's voice ordering him to "love" Anna. They embarked on a secret sexual relationship, at the same time that he was in a homosexual relationship with a dentist. He and Anna were then "married" in a secret ceremony, during which he wrote their names on the wedding certificate. Not long after, he heard God's voice again, this time telling him to "sacrifice" Anna. Accordingly, he slashed her throat, drank her blood, dismembered her body, and threw the pieces into the East River. Through meticulous search of Schmidt's belongings, the police were able to tie him to the 1913 murder. They also discovered that Anna was pregnant, which may have played a role in his decision to abort Anna rather than just the baby. This makes the case reminiscent of the Chester Gillette murder of his pregnant girlfriend, Grace Brown, which we described earlier in this book. That was in 1906, just seven years before Schmidt's murder of Anna. Schmidt feigned insanity during his first trial, which ended in a hung jury. At the second trial, he was declared guilty of first-degree murder and was executed at Sing Sing in 1916. When initially confronted by the police, he said, "I killed her because I loved her!"[105]

The Father Robinson case has a more modern ring to it than that of his lone predecessor, Father Schmidt. Robinson's murder of the nun smacked of extreme narcissism and sadism, as we have seen more often in a proportion of the post-1960s murders: he was bent on degrading and humiliating Sister Annunciata, mocking her faith with that crucifix in her vagina. At least Schmidt said, "I killed her because I loved her"—an excuse that is incomprehensible but at least gracious.

-S-

Clara Schwartz, born in 1982, was the youngest of three daughters born to a celebrated biometrics and DNA scientist, Robert Schwartz, and a mother who suffered from bipolar disorder, for which she had often been hospitalized. The family lived in Leesburg, Virginia, not far from Washington, DC. Clara's maternal grandmother had also suffered from manic-depressive illness. Her father and his relatives all appeared psychiatrically normal.

When Clara was about eighteen, her mother died of cancer, after which her college grades dropped and she lost interest in school. In the meantime, she became deeply involved in the goth subculture and developed a dark fantasy world. She became obsessed with vampires, assassins, black magic, and role-playing games. The distinction between reality and delusion became blurred. She began to hate her father, claiming he had tried to poison her by putting something in her pork chop or a lemon, and complained to others that he would punch her or pull her hair. Clara would try to get other acquaintances to sympathize with her plight. Her most avid supporter was a boy her age, eighteen-year-old Kyle Hulbert. Kyle had come from an extremely troubled background. He had been an "incorrigible" child, in and out of foster homes, prisons, and psychiatric wards, where, depending upon his display of symptoms at any given time, he was diagnosed as either bipolar or schizophrenic. When he turned eighteen, a judge, unwisely it would seem, granted him emancipation, whereupon—as is frequently the case with such persons—he stopped taking his antipsychotic medications and again descended into psychosis, in which fantasy and reality traded places. He accepted Clara's story and succumbed to her manipulations, to the point of making it known to her that he would gladly kill her father for his allegedly malicious treatment of Clara. In December of 2001, Kyle went to the home of Dr. Schwartz, who was now living by himself. It should be understood that Clara had been nurturing the idea of killing her father for some time already, and had initially studied up on herbal poisons, so that his death might appear more "natural." She also spoke to her friends about how much money she would inherit upon his death, though she did worry that he might disinherit her. In any case, Kyle used a sword, a more certain instrument of death, with which he stabbed the doctor to death. Clara and Kyle had also been abusing various drugs along the way: LSD, "shrooms" (i.e., mushrooms containing the hallucinogenic substance psilocybin), angel dust (phencyclidine, which often leads to both hallucinations and violent behavior), and marijuana. These drugs would, in effect, add a chemically induced psychosis on top of the hereditary psychosis from which both Clara and Kyle suffered—a bad combination. Clara figured on inheriting a third of $1.2 million, what with her having to share the amount with her two sisters. She assumed she could get away with the murder, by getting someone else to do it for her. In a way, she wasn't far off the mark. The two were soon arrested, and at trial, Clara, who would be ranked at level 14 of the Gradations of Evil scale, was given a sentence of only forty-eight years, whereas Kyle got life without parole.[106]

Given the diabolical manner in which Clara manipulated Kyle, who was more emotionally disturbed and more vulnerable to psychosis than she, one might think her the more culpable in the murder of her father than was Kyle. Certainly, he would never have thought to kill the man, absent her influence and control over him. The law is not well equipped to make distinctions of this sort. He did the stabbing, after all. Kyle has now been in prison fifteen years and has begun to realize that if, as Clara told him, her father had wanted to poison her, a man of his scientific acumen would have known how to do it. At the time, Kyle was in thrall to her malignant influence. Clara herself was influenced by the goth subculture that, having drawn inspiration in part from early nineteenth-century romanticism—think of Mary Shelley's *Frankenstein* of 1818—got its start in the late 1970s and early 1980s, making it, to some extent, part of the "new evil" of the post-1960s. The movement embraced punk rock music, dark dress, horror movies, a fascination with death, and deviation from mainstream culture. The new use of the term "gothic" was coined, or at least popularized, by the young lead singer of the British band Siouxsie and the Banshees. Born in 1957, her name was originally Susan Janet Ballion but, using a play on her name, became Siouxsie Sioux (i.e., Suzie Sue).[107]

Samantha Scott was the more enduring name Andrea Claire used as she began to work in her early twenties as a model, exotic dancer, pinup girl, bit player in TV shows and movies—including *M*A*S*H* and *Beyond the Valley of the Dolls*—and roles in "nudie cuties," like *Horny Hobo* and *Nude Django*. She worked under many pseudonyms, such as Donna Duzzit and Sarah Stunning, but Samantha Scott was the main one used. Born in 1941, she had grown up in New Jersey, where her mother forced her, at age fifteen, to marry a twenty-two-year-old friend of her sister's, who allegedly raped her. They stayed together for two years, though he beat her violently during the marriage, and had a second child, besides the one conceived following the alleged assault. She got only as far as ninth grade in school. She married for a second time to a man who did not like the idea of being stuck with two kids that were not his and insisted she give them up. That marriage lasted all of three days. Her third marriage was to a Jordanian student, who needed an American wife in order to stay in the States, but he left her after a few years to marry his childhood sweetheart. Her acting career made no real progress, so she turned to working as a high-dollar call girl—a calling that was facilitated by her beauty. She once fell off a horse during that time, suffering a painful back injury, and began to use morphine, as well as barbiturates, marijuana, and cocaine. In 1980, now nearing forty, she married for the fourth time, after a ten-day courtship, but the marriage lasted only a few days longer than the courtship because of the man's jealous rage. Realizing her beauty would not last forever, she now sought a "sugar daddy" and became involved with a man thirty years her senior, Robert Sand—a wealthy lumber magnate who was now confined to a wheelchair because of multiple sclerosis. He had engaged prostitutes frequently, and at first Samantha was his $800-per-week "habit." She provided sex and massages, but the expense moved his accountant to suggest he simply marry her. So, in this odd union, Samantha married him to have money; Sand married her to save money. This seemed to be the answer to her dreams—but Robert was a voyeur who forced her to pose nude for photo sessions and to walk around their posh Rancho Mirage condo naked. He also made her remain in the house as his beautiful sex slave, which is pretty much all she had ever been since the age of fifteen. When, in May of 1981, he demanded she come into his room to perform her sexual "duties," she finally rebelled. Seizing a knife, she stabbed him twenty-seven times, piercing his heart and aorta. This was understood as a murder prompted by pent-up hatred and rage. She tried to pretend there had been an intruder who killed Robert, but the police quickly discredited her story. She was charged with first-degree murder and sentenced to twenty-six years in prison. For a while she was out on bail and met yet another older man, Joe Mims, who found her irresistible and became her sixth husband in March of 1982. Mims had the marriage annulled but, still in love with her, came to the prison four years later to remarry her. He then, however, suffered a fatal heart attack.[108]

While in prison, Samantha—now back to being Andrea—had converted to Buddhism and won awards for her artwork. She married for a seventh time while incarcerated, to Rick Jackson, who befriended her and was briefly allowed conjugal visits. The union lasted about seven years. Jackson wrote a letter to the California Board of Prison Terms, urging Andrea's parole. She was seventy-one at the time. He spoke of Andrea's two sons, one in Los Angeles, one in Hawaii, to whom she was still close, and by whom she had several grandchildren. Thanks in part to Jackson's letter, Andrea was paroled in 2012. She died later of ovarian cancer in a convalescent hospital.[109] Andrea, aka Samantha Sand is an example not of a person given habitually to commit acts of an evil nature, rather, of how someone who had the capacity and attributes to lead a normal, socially acceptable life can be damaged through the cruelty of others to, one day, in a fit of desperation and rage, resort on impulse, without malice afore-thought, to murderous violence. More evil was done to her by her first and by her fifth husbands than any evil done by her. As such, she would be assigned to Category 6 of the Gradations of Evil scale.

Born in 1941, the same year as Andrea/Samantha Sand, Joel Steinberg became, in connection with the killing of his illegally adopted six-year-old daughter, Lisa, the "ultimate face of evil."[110] A single mother, Michele Launders, had sought to have her baby daughter adopted by a suitable family and hired attorney Joel Steinberg to make the arrangements. Instead, he took the child to his home to be raised by Steinberg and his live-in partner, Hedda Nussbaum. Steinberg had, for a long time, abused Hedda physically, bruising her about the face to such an extent that former acquaintances could barely recognize her. There were scars, and scabs and welts all over her body from Steinberg's beatings. Steinberg was heavily under the influence of crack cocaine at the time when he struck Lisa, age six, on the head, then leaving the apartment for a party with friends. She lay dying in the bathroom from her brain injuries while Hedda sat for hours in the apartment, doing nothing. Brain-dead when finally taken to the hospital, she was soon taken off life support and declared deceased. Hedda had been the victim of domestic violence, raised to the level of what soon came to be called the battered woman syndrome. After Stein-berg was arrested and tried, his sentence was merely eight and a half to twenty-five years in state prison, since the jury was unable to convict him for second-degree murder.[111] He has expressed no remorse at the time for what he had done to Lisa or to Hedda—or to Michele Launders, whose baby he improperly took and then destroyed. What could a six-year-old girl have done, we must wonder, to draw such wrath as to have her head smashed by the fist of a 180-pound man? There are acts we recognize at once as evil, but the roots, the sources of the personality aberration that predispose individuals to such acts, often remain, as in the Steinberg case, inscrutable. We cannot expect that a man in his late seventies will finally come forward and "open up" about motives that have remained hidden for so long. For killing someone who posed an impediment to a personal aim, Steinberg would be ranked in Category 10 of the Gradations of Evil scale. On the night of the murder, little Lisa had reportedly been "staring" at her adoptive father and had inadvertently—by innocently asking if she could eat dinner with him—gotten in the way of his plans.

-T-

Category 22 torture-murderer Gary Taylor, even in the usual photographs of him in articles or books, has a look of insolence and contempt. He managed to be even scarier than he appeared. Born into a blue-collar Detroit family in 1936, he was a bully from his earliest days in school. At eleven, he was violent with schoolmates. When he was thirteen or fourteen, he would assault women verbally or by hurling objects at them. Some, he would shoot with pellets from his BB gun as they were waiting for buses. He claimed his mother behaved seductively toward him and that his father was physically punitive. He allegedly almost murdered a woman when he was eighteen, but, at a trial, the jury excused him because of an alibi, which was, as it turned out, false. He also attacked prostitutes. He also had both homosexual and heterosexual contacts, and seemed ambivalent about his own sexuality. At twenty-one, he was declared "insane" in Michigan because of what in that state was oddly considered "irresistible impulse"—namely, the impulse to shoot and rape female victims. He was sent to Ionia State Hospital for the criminally insane and, two years later, transferred to Lafayette Clinic. Given the freedom there to attend a welding class as part of his "occupational therapy," he impersonated an FBI agent and raped a woman, for which he was remanded back to Ionia. He abused alcohol heavily, which seemed to heighten his murderous impulses. At thirty-four, however, he was reevaluated and declared "sane." Three years later, after more assaultive behavior, Taylor was sent to the Center for Forensic Psychiatry in Ypsilanti. Two years later, the hospital director felt Taylor was "sociopathic" but an acceptable risk for release, so long as he took his disulfiram, a drug given to discourage one from drinking alcohol, and checked in periodically with the hospital. He, of course, did neither, and in fact then married the secretary of his defense attorney, Helen Mueller. Taylor then set up a soundproof torture chamber in his house, unbeknownst to his wife. In that secret space, he set about raping, mutilating, and killing women he knew or believed to be prostitutes. He buried some of the women in his backyard. He was a con artist without a trace of compassion or remorse. He was eventually sentenced to life in prison in Wyoming. His wife left him in 1974.[112] The creation of a torture room or chamber in one's own home is a relatively new phenomenon. There was Dr. Herman Mudgett's "pharmacy" in Chicago in the 1890s, but most examples have emerged within the past fifty years, especially among serial killers, including Wesley Dodd, Robert Berdella, Leonard Lake, and David Parker Ray. We have speculated elsewhere about serial sexual homicide, in many instances, representing a backlash against the "daring" of women in the post-1960s years, who now enjoy greater opportunities to work, and have abortion rights and contraceptive measures available to them. This often serves to diminish the power of certain controlling and abusive, mostly working-class, men over their mates.[113] Gary Taylor would fit into this category.

Fred Tokars was born in 1957 into a privileged Hungarian American family. His father was a physician, and Fred went on to become an attorney. His degree came from an undistinguished law school, and he then obtained a PhD from a diploma mill on the West Coast, after which he began calling himself Dr. Tokars. He married Sara, née Ambrusko, the daughter of a Buffalo surgeon, in 1985. They had two sons, Rick and Mike. A totally controlling man, he refused his wife credit cards or a checking account and paid for everything in cash, by way of sidestepping the IRS. He abused

Sara physically, had a secret vasectomy after the birth of the second child, and took out a $250,000 life insurance policy on Sara's life, with himself as beneficiary. Fred became a "crooked" lawyer, defending drug dealers—he himself was abusing cocaine—and criminals in shady dealings that earned him huge amounts of money. He had unpredictable outbursts, screaming at Sara, who, at this point, hired a private investigator and ascertained that Fred was cheating on her. Discovering the combination to Fred's safe, Sara learned of his illicit money-laundering activities and of his having taken out yet another life insurance policy for $1,750,000, with himself, again, as beneficiary. Two forces now converged: Sara tried to divorce and to expose him for all of his illegal dealings, and Fred hired a hitman in 1992, who, when she opened the door, shot Sara to death in front of her children. Earlier, as it turned out, she had sent copies of the incriminating documents to the authorities. These were made available at the trial for murder after Fred was arrested, and helped convict him. The verdict, rendered five years later in 1997, was life in prison without parole. Perhaps he still radiated a bit of charm: ten members of the jury voted for the death penalty, but two women declined.[114] He would be ranked at level 14 of the Gradations of Evil scale—at least, when actively engaged in crime. In retrospect, the two women may have been on to something—for the story ends better than it began. Currently, twenty years after going to prison, he has used his legal skills, for good this time, rather than for evil ventures. Tokars has helped solve six murders, providing testimony that sent one man to death row, another to prison for life. He is in the federal government's witness protection program, his name expunged from prison records. He lives by himself in a cell, keeping up with current events and communicating occasionally with friends. He has become religious and hopes, via helping the government prosecute killers who have been hard to convict, to leave a favorable legacy to his sons, compensating, to some degree, for taking their mother from them.[115]

-U-

Jack Unterweger was born in Austria in 1950, shortly after World War II, to an American soldier—perhaps Jack Becker, or else Donald van Blarcom;

his paternity has never been firmly established—and a Viennese barmaid. She was arrested for fraud and theft, following which he was sent to live with his maternal grandfather, Ferdinand Wieser. Wieser had lived for twenty years with Maria Springer; she helped raise Jack till he was about seven. During his adolescence, Jack committed theft, fraud, burglary, and robbery; at twenty, he tried to coerce a girl into prostitution. When he was twenty-four, he committed his first murder, that of Margaret Schäfer, for which he was sentenced initially to life in prison. That sentence, however, was downgraded to fifteen years, after he achieved a certain notoriety for a book he had written while in prison, entitled *Fegefeuer oder die Reise ins Zuchthaus* (*Purgatory, or the Journey in the Prison*). The book was filled with lies and omissions. There was no reference to murder, only to robbery, as if that was why he had been imprisoned. Unterweger was lionized by the leftist and counterculture press, and by socialist-leaning people from the journalistic world. A movie was made based upon his book, and various people championed his cause, as though he were now a reformed man with no more murderous inclinations. They argued persuasively for his release, which he was granted in May of 1990. He immediately used his charisma to acquire young girlfriends and supporters, in the meantime embarking on a career of serial sexual homicide. He abducted, sodomized, bound with ligatures, strangled, and murdered six more prostitutes in the Vienna Woods. Then, ostensibly on a tour to study the red-light districts of America, as though he were a social psychologist with a "scientific interest" in fallen women, he murdered three more prostitutes in Los Angeles. Thanks to his charm and facility at lying, two of his many psychopathic traits, he was able to con many people in high places in Austria, including psychiatrists, who assured the public that Unterweger had developed genuine remorse during his fifteen years in prison. They went on to say that now, at thirty-nine— when he was released, thanks in part to their persuasive arguments—he had "overcome" his hostility toward women, which had supposedly been engendered by his hatred of his mother. Therefore, they continued, Unterweger could certainly be counted on never to kill again. Several journalists, some of whom were females, championed his cause, as well, and stuck up for him to the bitter end. Unterweger was now able to lead a double life, garnering young girlfriends, one after the other, with whom he had sex—often enough, kinky sex involving bondage. He is reputed to have had intercourse with literally dozens of women, perhaps fifty, during the first year after his 1990 release. Meantime, he would be trolling for prostitutes in the red-light districts of Vienna, Graz, and elsewhere. He murdered six, until he was finally arrested, not counting the additional three in Los Angeles, during the one month he spent there. He had really fled to Los Angeles because he grew concerned that the Vienna police were beginning to suspect that he was the "Vienna Woods Killer." This was because he had strangled each prostitute with her own bra, tied in an intricate and unusual way that amounted to a "signature" killing method, a concept described earlier in this volume. There were literary types who gave Unterweger hefty sums for his books, stories, and magazine articles. This permitted him to live a lavish life—though, even so, he spent way more than he was given. He dressed in a flashy way, like a cowboy or a dandy, and drove a sports car. In his main book, he described his grandfather as having been extremely abusive. His stepmother Charlotte accused him in public of lying; he affected not to recognize her and scared her off. He began to coerce his new girlfriends into prostitution, claiming he had run out of money—which was probably true—and therefore needed them to become "escorts" or do "go-go" dancing, in order to make ends meet. One of the girls did reluctantly do some dancing when they both took off for Miami. This was when the "heat" was on about an imminent arrest. The girl was Blanca Mrak, a Slavic girl of seventeen whom he had seduced. He had isolated her from her family, invited her to engage in bondage, and asked her to marry him. Although she agreed, they never married, but the arrangement had probably been intended as a ploy, since, as his wife, she could not testify against him. Unterweger had a daughter, Claudia, when, at twenty, he had gotten a sixteen-year-old girl pregnant. Unterweger was finally arrested, and by that time, Claudia had two children of her own. In 1990, there was one aborted murder—of a prostitute whom he bound and sodomized in the Graz woods. When she screamed, he uncharacteristically let her go. She later told her story to investigators in 1992, which heightened their suspicions that he was, indeed, the Vienna Woods Killer. When the Vienna police finally obtained search warrants, they found all manner of murder paraphernalia in his apartment, along with an address book listing forty women with whom he had had sex after his release—not counting the girlfriends and journalists he had seduced but not harmed—supplemented with descriptions of the relations with each. When Unterweger was finally brought to justice, the people who had stood by him were flabbergasted at how they had been betrayed and conned, though there were still a few who refused to believe he was guilty. While incarcerated, he made a noose from strings in his prison clothing and hanged himself the very first day of his sentence. Unterweger was a classic psychopath of the charmer / con man type, who was also a sexual sadist, experiencing orgasmic release upon strangling and killing his victims. Some he would apparently strangle and release a little and then strangle again—in effect, torturing them with breathlessness for a while before finally dispatching them.[116] As Unterweger was a serial killer who practiced non-prolonged torture, the most appropriate ranking on the Gradations of Evil scale would be Category 18.

-V-

Born in 1955 in Eugene, Oregon, Allen William Van Houte legally changed his name thirty years later, while living in Hawaii, to get around things he was doing illegally. He became Allen Blackthorne, moving afterward to San Antonio and leaving behind $300,000 in debts.[117] A decade later, he was arrested for the hired-gun murder of his ex-wife, Sheila Bellush. Allen and Sheila had two daughters, Stevie and Daryl, who had been adopted by Sheila's second husband, Jamie Bellush, whom she married after divorcing Allen. By that time, Allen had given up custody of the two girls. Acting under his new name, Allen spent $54,000 to hire killers to murder Sheila, who, by then, had given birth to quadruplets. She was killed in 1997, leaving behind a total of six children. At the trial after Allen was apprehended for the murder, his daughter Stevie, thirteen at the time, testified that she had discovered her mother dead on the kitchen floor in a pool of blood.[118] She had been shot in the cheek, and her throat was slit. As is sometimes the case when a hitman is hired to "do a job," there is a lengthy chain of command. Allen asked his golf buddy, Daniel Rocha, to help find the right person. Rocha then reportedly asked Sammy Gonzales to see what he could do. Sammy sought out his cousin, Jose Luis Del Toro, to be the actual hitman. Del Toro confessed and also begged for mercy, though he still received a mandatory life sentence. Allen also faced a life sentence and was imprisoned in Terre Haute, Indiana, where he died in 2014 at the age of fifty-nine. The cause of death was not made public. The seventeen years he spent in the prison had been the only ones in his life that were free of turbulence. His early years were so appalling that one would not have been surprised if he had gone on to lead a life of continual violent crime, committing many more acts that rose to the level of "evil" than the one murder of his wife by a hired hitman. We must also take into account certain mitigating factors that acted as counterweights to the otherwise "expected" outcome. His parents, Guy and Karen, had been high school sweethearts who married after graduation but who divorced while Karen was still pregnant. Allen's father disappeared for sixteen years. Karen allegedly once held Allen's arm over a stove burner and, on another occasion, reportedly poured gasoline on him, threatening to set him on fire. After reportedly suffering many beatings from his mother, Allen came to live with his grandparents on their farm in Oregon, who found him disruptive and manipulative. Occasionally, he spent some time at his mother's, but she beat him to the point of his having to be hospitalized several times, as when she struck him on the head with a board after he had left his tricycle behind her car. When Allen was twenty-one, his mother tried to commit suicide with a shotgun. She survived but lost an arm—awakening from anesthesia to tell him he was to blame for all of her problems. He hardly ever saw her again. He later moved back to his father's place, but they became rivals, rather than developing a better father-son relationship. At eighteen, Allen joined the US Army, having just married for the first time. He was discharged a few months later. Allen divorced in 1982 when he was twenty-seven and, the following year, married Sheila, the woman he would later have killed. In between all of this, Allen had started several businesses, some of them highly successful, but he faced challenges on several occasions because of illegal transactions. He was at times rich, then broke, then rich again, and was a millionaire when tried for the murder. It was when he was thirty-one that he changed his last name to Blackthorne, partly to avoid creditors.[119] There were times that he beat Sheila and he was convicted of assaulting her in 1987, for which he was put on probation for a year, around the time of their divorce. Allen married again in 1994, to Mary Weingeist, by whom he had two more children, before ending up in prison three and a half years later. That marriage was more harmonious.[120]

For his murder of someone "in the way," Allen would be ranked in Category 10 of the Gradations of Evil scale.

Looking back, it may be some combination of high intelligence *and* genetic endowment—part of which may simply be a smaller predisposition to low empathy and to other psychopathic traits—that allowed Van Houte/Blackthorne to have had a better "bad life" than, say, serial killer Lawrence Bittaker. Bittaker was also intelligent, with a reported very high IQ of 138,[121] and both men reportedly had biological parents with distinctly antisocial lives and psychopathic personalities, so perhaps Allen possessed some unclear genetic trait that accounts for the difference.

-W-

Rachelle Waterman hailed from the small Alaskan town of Craig. Born in 1989, she was the daughter of a real estate broker, Carl, and his wife, Lauri, a teacher's aide. Her mother went missing in November of 2004, when Rachelle was fifteen, and was later found dead inside a car by state troopers, burned beyond all recognition. She could only be identified later by forensic odontologists at autopsy, who had access to her dental charts. Suspicion eventually fell on two men: Jason Arrantt, a janitor at Rachelle's school, and Brian Radel. Both were in their midtwenties and had slept with Rachelle on several occasions. Jason was passionately in love with Rachelle, which inspired the title of a book about the case, Michael Fleeman's *Love You Madly*.[122] Jason was considered unattractive and overweight, which probably made him especially vulnerable to the blandishments of a young and fairly pretty girl who showed him a lot of attention. She complained to him that her mother was too strict—but she went further and made up stories about her mother being abusive to her. At her high school spring prom, Rachelle had wanted to wear a black velvet Japanese dress, but her mother supposedly said she was "too fat and ugly" to pull off such an outfit and forbade her to wear it. She also claimed that her mother had "bitten" her and had pestered her to go to a "fat camp" to lose weight. Generally, she was an honor student, but if she got a C in some subject, her mother would criticize her sharply. We are, of course, at the mercy of Rachelle's allegations. Her mother is dead, and there is no one else to confirm or refute her diatribe. Just for the record, photographs of Rachelle and her mother standing next to one another make it clear that Rachelle was a wholesome young woman, certainly not "fat" or "ugly." In mid-June of 2004, her mother scolded Rachelle over something not specified in Fleeman's book. She called her mother a "psycho bitch" and fled to a friend's house for the night. Her mother grounded her for three days, which prompted Rachelle to hate her mother even more. She also told people her mother had once pushed her down a flight of stairs. After her mother's body was identified, the police took Rachelle's computer to look for any evidence of possible complicity. No incriminating messages were found. The year before, people noted that she had begun to wear black clothes and paint her fingernails black; she showed an interest in Wicca, a form of modern paganism, often encountered in the aforementioned goth subculture, which encourages proponents to put "spells" on people they do not like. Jason believed whatever Rachelle told him—lies, exaggerations, truths, whatever. He said he saw bruises on her body, as if from her mother pushing her down the stairs. It is likely that Rachelle fabricated this story by way of whipping up Jason's fury at her mother's "wickedness," making the case that she deserved to die. He even believed her claim that her parents were getting ready to sell her into slavery. Brian, also duped by Rachelle's stories, agreed to kill her mother but felt he had to be the main mover in the plot because, in his opinion, Jason didn't have the "stones" (i.e., the "balls") to commit murder on his own. So, one evening, when Mr. Waterman was away on business, Brian managed to enter the house, pick the lock to Lauri's bedroom, and immobilize her with duct tape. He then carried her down to her car, put her in the back seat, and had Jason drive to a remote spot. They then poured gasoline over her and set her afire. Brian tried to make the murder look like a car accident by a drunk driver, forcing her to swallow a whole bottle of wine before carrying her to the car. He failed to take into consideration that, if her body were destroyed to the point that only bones remained, there would be no evidence of alcohol intoxication. Eventually, the police caught on to the likelihood that Jason and Brian were involved. At first, Jason denied playing any role in the murder, but he eventually came clean and admitted that, yes, he did feel the mother needed to be killed. Then, Brian finally acknowledged his having played a major role in the murder. At trial, Jason was sentenced to fifty years in prison; Brian, as the main instrument in the murder, received ninety-nine years. Rachelle had been in jail during the interim of her arrest and the conclusion of the trial two and a half years later. The judge did not declare murder in her case but only what he called "criminally negligent homicide." Rachelle was let go for time served. Subsequently, she disappeared—some think, perhaps, to Florida. This represents a serious miscarriage of justice. The law seems not to have caught up with the temper of the times: murders, for example, that have been engineered, induced, or maliciously set in motion by influencing another person to kill on the "originator's" own behalf, to get some victim out of the way. This was the case with Clara Schwartz, whom we have already discussed, who persuaded a young man to kill her father. Crimes of this sort are rather new and often depend on the internet, texting on cell phones, where it is easy to preserve anonymity, or to concoct malicious rumors, so as to induce belief that the intended victim truly deserved to be killed, as though one were doing a valuable service in ridding the community of a "terrible" and "evil" person. Women are more apt to induce such sentiments in a gullible man, sometimes portraying themselves as members of a "weaker, gentler" sex, more "vulnerable" to the malefic influences of some cruel individual, such as Rachelle's mother or Clara's father, and "unable" to deal with their abusers on their own. On rare occasions, a man manages to get a woman to do the dirty work, as in the 1992 case of Joey Buttafuoco, who allegedly manipulated sixteen-year-old Amy Fisher to acquire a gun and shoot his wife, Mary-Jo, who managed to survive.[123] The point is that the Waterman case involved a young woman influencing a man—actually, two men—to do something few women could bring themselves to do on their own: subdue her mother, bind her, and carry her down to the car, thrusting her into the back seat. This might be seen as a "guy thing," which calls for considerable strength and heavy lifting. Think of ballet. How many times have you seen a male dancer carry a ballerina over his head for a bit? How many times have you seen a ballerina twirl a male partner over her head? As for Rachelle, how could she manage to murder her mother and get away with it? At fifteen, where could she buy a gun, even in Alaska? Or buy a jug of gasoline, or drive a car and carry her mother's body into it? Instead, and not surprisingly, she relied on the influence she could exert via sexual favors—on an unattractive, socially awkward man several rungs lower down on the social ladder than hers—to get the job done. Rachelle would probably best be ranked at level 10 of the Gradations of Evil scale. She didn't show unmistakable signs of psychopathy, but she did urgently want someone "out of the way." Ranking 10, the reader will recall, is the same spot Susan Smith was placed. She is the woman who pushed her car with her children in it into a lake to drown, so she could be free to marry the son of the boss who ran the factory where she worked. One could argue, however, that killing one's children for an ulterior motive is more repugnant than killing one's mother. Had it not been for Rachelle's manipulation of Jason and Brian, needless to say, the mother would not have been murdered, so it seems pure sophistry to argue she is "less guilty" than the men simply because it was not she who set her mother on fire.

There are some men—it will usually be males—belonging to the category of Murder with Extreme Sadism, whose early years seemed ordinary and unremarkable. This was the case with Eric Williams, who completed law school and became a justice of the peace (JP) in Kaufman County, near Dallas, Texas. He had hoped to become a judge and grew embittered at having to settle for the less prestigious post. Even as a JP and attorney, however, his income was substantial; he and his wife, Kim, lived in luxurious circumstances. Eric was proud, to the point of arrogance, about belonging to Mensa, a society for individuals with high IQs of at least 138, representing the upper 2 percent of the general population. Kim developed rheumatoid arthritis, treated (improperly) with opiates, to which she became addicted. Eric made it clear he did not want children, warning Kim he would divorce her if she became pregnant. Kim was aware of one disagreeable habit: Eric's delight in killing cats. She also had some concern about her husband's obsession with guns. He had forty-seven pistols and rifles at home—more an arsenal than a collection. Eric's ambitions came to a screeching halt when, at age forty-four in 2011, he was caught stealing three computer monitors from his JP office. This was a felony, for which he was arrested. He could no longer practice law and had to relinquish his title. Mark Hasse and Mike McLelland, who were prosecutors in the case, now became Eric's sworn enemies. At his trial, Hasse spoke of him as narcissistic and entitled, depicting him as a man who held public office and who then committed a felony—as "evil."[124] Eric now hatched a plot to kill Mark Hasse, convinced he could do so without ever being caught. He needed Kim's help, but, at first, she refused, to which he warned her, "You're my wife. You're going to help me. . . . If you don't, I'm going to kill your mother, your father, and then I'll come back and shoot you."[125] Eric also planned to kill Mike McLelland and his wife in the same never-to-be-detected way. He rented a huge compartment for storing his forty-seven firearms, as well as the getaway car he bought for the occasion, which could afterward be stored and thus never found. Using camouflage, Eric first shot Mark to death as he walked to work. People were aware of Eric's hatred for both prosecutors, so he was questioned at his home. Mike had, after all, called Eric a "narcissistic psychopath." Cleverly, Eric came to the door with his right arm in a sling he had fashioned for the occasion, to portray himself as someone who could not possibly have fired a gun. No record was found of his ever sustaining an arm injury or of his having gone to an orthopedist, but he was given the benefit of the doubt. Eric then went to McLelland's house early one morning, with his wife at the wheel. Mike had prepared himself for Eric's murderous wrath, arming himself with guns all over his house and on his person, but, because Eric had taken him by surprise, Mike was easily outgunned.[126] Eric also shot the wife, Cynthia, with multiple shots to the torso and then, when she lay on the floor bleeding, shot her in the head, as a coup de grace. As is usually the case with "perfect murders," there were flaws. The storage facility was discovered, and bullet fragments at the scene pointed to guns discovered to be Eric's. Eric and Kim were both arrested. At their trial, Eric, who would be ranked in Category 15 of the Gradations of Evil scale for his cold-blooded multiple murders, was convicted and given the death penalty. Kim, who had been his accomplice, no matter how unwillingly so, had finally begun divorce proceedings and could now testify against Eric. She had never dared to tell the authorities about Eric's murderous plans before, because he never let her out of his sight in their home, and monitored all of her calls and computer activity. Kim was sentenced to forty years in prison.

It is useful at this point to review the diagnostic criteria for sadistic personality disorder (SPD). While the condition is not included in later editions of the American Psychiatric Association's *Diagnostic Manual of Mental*

Disorders, the revised third edition of 1987 (*DSM-III-R*) delineated the following features:[127] (a) Uses physical cruelty to establish dominance in relationships; (b) humiliates or demeans people in the presence of others; (c)
has treated or disciplined someone under his control with unusual harsh-
ness; (d) takes pleasure in the psychological or physical suffering of others,
including animals; (e) lies for the purpose of harming or inflicting pain
on others; (f) is fascinated by violence, weapons, martial arts, injury, or
torture; (g) gets people to do what he wants via intimidation or terror, and
(h) restricts the autonomy of people with whom he has a close relationship,
e.g., will not let spouse leave the house unaccompanied. Showing at least
four of these traits sufficed for the diagnosis. The reason for the removal of
sadism from the *DSM* was political. Battered women were understandably
afraid that a defense attorney would argue, "Your Honor, my client suffers
from sadistic personality disorder!" as if that were somehow exculpatory.
Lamentably, sadism has not disappeared from society. SPD remains relevant and useful in academic works on sadism.[128] At all events, Eric Williams
showed all eight criteria—as well as the characteristics, mentioned earlier,
seen so often in men committing mass murder: bitterness, grudge holding,
disgruntlement over having been "wronged," and a paranoid mind-set.

George Woldt carried out one of the most horrific crimes of the current
era. He was the elder of two children born to an American veteran, William
Woldt, and his Korean wife, Song Hui. The family was troubled from the
beginning. William was reportedly an alcoholic and tended to be abusive
to George. Song Hui was a paranoid schizophrenic who expected him to
be "perfect," and became rageful toward him when he strayed from her
impossible demands. He was highly intelligent and had many friends but
was boastful and grandiose, telling others that he was a "contract killer" or
claiming to have had sex with dozens of women. When he graduated high
school, he had already gotten his girlfriend pregnant but left her before the
birth of the child. George became an aficionado of pornographic films that
focused on torture and killing. In general, the women he dated found him
to be abusive. He had a dominating fantasy: one in which he would corner
a girl, or else find a couple parked in some lover's lane in a remote part of

Colorado where he lived, and kidnap and rape the woman, or if it were a couple in a car, rape the woman in front of her boyfriend and then kill both of them with rocks. George was also using a menu of drugs at this time, including marijuana, alcohol, and LSD. When his regular friends invited to become involved demurred, he turned to a fellow who was inordinately shy and totally inexperienced with women. This was Lucas Salmon, who knew George from high school—a fellow from a strict evangelical family whose life centered around the church. Lucas was ashamed at still being a virgin at twenty-two and became slavishly attached to George, hoping George would provide him with a girl to have sex with, preferably by rape, since he had no confidence that he could charm a girl enough to make her willing to start a sexual relationship. One night in 1997, when George had turned twenty-one, he and Lucas drove on purpose into a female biker, intent on kidnapping and raping her, but she sensed danger and ran to safety. A few months later, they found a young woman, twenty-three-year-old Jacine Gielinski, who was just about to enter her home. They forcibly kidnapped her and shoved her into George's car, where they proceeded to rape and torture her. George raped her first. When it was Lucas's turn, he failed to achieve an erection. George persuaded him to masturbate first until becoming erect and then insert quickly, thus ending his virginity. They then clumsily tried to murder the victim with knives, cutting her throat, then stabbing her in the area of the heart. Even so, she did not die, so they stomped her on her stomach until she bled out and died. They then stuffed mud into her vagina, as if to hide their semen, so the police—they imagined—could not find DNA evidence with which to arrest them. Their "perfect murder" was foiled when not one but several witnesses took down their license plate numbers and phoned the police. George and Lucas were quickly caught and arrested, Lucas's IQ of 134 not adequate to outsmart the authorities. Lucas, as it was learned, often had pedophilic fantasies and, oddly, his Bible-thumping father was reportedly a pedophile himself, divorced from Lucas's mother. In Steve Jackson's book about the pair,[129] the word "evil" is used numerous times, especially in relation to George. The heinous nature of the murder was felt to warrant the death penalty. Jacine's parents were firmly in favor, as were almost all of the townspeople of Colorado Springs, where the trial was held. The malice aforethought of the perpetrators argued for the death penalty. George was viewed as a sexual predator and psychopath. During the crime, for example, George had asked Lucas, "Do you want to cut her pussy out?" That was before their "bright idea" of the mud. The prosecution contended George had "free will." The defense argued George had "mental illness" because of his "obsessive rape fantasies"—plus, a scan of his brain demonstrated a small calcium deposit. The jury voted for the death penalty, but for death penalty cases in Colorado, there is a second trial, involving three judges who must all be in agreement. One judge held out for only a life sentence. Unlike greed or revenge, the motives that lie behind so many murder cases, this rape-murder was purely for the momentary gratification of causing intense pain and suffering to a helpless person. These crimes warrant placement in Category 22 of the Gradations of Evil scale. The violation of Jacine Gielinski's body and personhood by George and Lucas is among the worst examples of sexual sadism in the literature—a literature that was scant before the 1960s. One of the most complete—and both pictorially and verbally graphic—expositions concerning sadism and sexually sadistic murder is that of previously mentioned homicide consultant Vernon Geberth, a retired lieutenant commander of the New York City Police Department.[130] The crime also fits philosopher Roger Scruton's definition of "evil," as equating with the dehumanization of one's victim.[131]

-X-

Among the Hmong people who fled Laos after the 1975 Communist takeover was Kao Xiong, who settled in Sacramento with his wife, Mai Thao. They lived in straitened circumstances in a one-bedroom apartment with their five young children, ages one to seven, and two older stepchildren, ages nine and fourteen. Xiong was mostly unemployed and had great difficulty earning enough to support the large family. On one night in December of 1999, Xiong told his wife he was going to get a new hunting jacket that would cost $400. His wife had wanted to use the money to buy jackets for the children. They argued, apparently vehemently, over this, and the wife left the house afterward. When she returned, she discovered that he had shot to death all five of their children. The two stepchildren had managed to escape by jumping out the bathroom window. Xiong had no record of previous violent offenses and no criminal record—though he was known to have a short temper. As far as one could tell, this was an impulsive, rather than a planned, murder.[132] Xiong would be ranked at level 6 of the Gradations of Evil scale, the designation for impetuous hotheaded murderers without psychopathic features.

-Y-

Graham Young was born to a middle-class family in London in 1947. His mother died shortly after his birth, and three years later, his father remarried. He grew up hating his stepmother, Molly. At age nine, he began reading up on Nazism, black magic, and poisons. Young was a schizoid loner, as well as being—although it only became clear later on—a psychopath.[133] Though the term was not as yet in psychiatric parlance during his earlier years, he would probably be considered a "callous unemotional youth."[134] He became fascinated with poisons and began to kill cats with one or another toxin to see how they worked. He graduated, so to say, to poisoning acquaintances—he had no friends—with poisons he purchased, under assumed names, from various drugstores. These included antimony, atropine, and thallium. He used the atropine on his elder sister, Winifred, in 1961, when he was fourteen. Their father suspected Graham but took no action. A year later, he poisoned his hated stepmother with thallium, after trying slower-acting agents. She was found writhing in the garden of their home, with Graham looking on. Molly was taken to the hospital, where she died some hours later. Poisoning was not suspected. Her death was ascribed to a vertebral collapse, and she was cremated, such that no further investigation was possible. Graham experimented with his father as well, and he, too, was admitted to the hospital, where the doctors were able to ascertain that he had been poisoned with antimony. Again, his father took no action. In fact, it was Graham's chemistry teacher who became the whistleblower, calling the police when he discovered various poisons and articles on the subject in Graham's school desk. The police arrested him in May of 1962, whereupon he admitted to poisoning his sister and father, but not his stepmother. Graham was considered a "mentally ill criminal" and, at age fifteen, was sent to Broadmoor Forensic Hospital, supposedly for a period of fifteen years. While there, he decorated his cell with photos of the Nazi leaders. Soon after, another inmate died of cyanide poisoning. Graham spoke to the hospital personnel about how one could extract cyanide from laurel bush leaves. No action was taken, and the inmate's death was called a "suicide." Graham was eventually considered "cured" and was released at age twenty-three in 1971—even though he had told a nurse that he intended to kill one person for each of the eight years he had been in Broadmoor. He was, indeed, charged with eight counts of poisoning within the next year. In 1971, he got a job and killed two coworkers, poisoning others, as well. Graham viewed people as potential guinea pigs for his experiments. One of the victims had been cremated, but, when Graham was finally suspected, the man's ashes were tested and proved positive for thallium. This was a "first" in the history of forensic pathology. Ultimately, he was done in by his narcissism, boastfulness, and arrogance, bragging to a number of police officers about his knowledge of poisons and their remedies. This time, he was arrested but sent to a regular high-security prison, Parkhurst, on the Isle of Wight, reserved for the most serious criminals. While there, Graham made friends, probably for the first time in his life. One was Ian Brady, England's "Moors Murderer," who, as briefly mentioned in our discussion of Category 22 on the Gradations of Evil scale, kidnapped and strangled several children with the help of his sidekick, Myra Hindley. The men became fast friends, playing chess and sharing their infatuations with the Nazi higher-ups. Graham now wore a Hitler moustache. He died in his cell at Parkhurst in 1990, aged fifty-two years, perhaps by suicide via poisoning himself—or perhaps poisoned by some of the other inmates.[135] Ian Brady, who had uttermost contempt for most human beings, especially those he considered second-rate serial killers, such as Arthur Shawcross and Richard Ramirez, truly admired Graham Young.[136] Dr. Jeremy Coid, a prominent forensic psychiatrist in London who interviewed Brady, called him "the most narcissistic person I have ever encountered."[137] Perhaps Graham Young can be considered Brady's "identical twin"—both were quintessentially ruthless narcissists, although Young would be ranked lower on the Gradations of Evil scale, at level 16, the placement for psychopathic persons who commit multiple vicious acts, including homicide.

Charles W. Yukl was born to Czech American parents in 1935. His father, also Charles W., was a trumpeter, his mother, Dorothea, a pianist. Charles had a brother, Tex, who was three years younger. His parents divorced when he was seven, he and his brother then moving to California with their father, who remarried when Charles was thirteen. Charles was musically gifted like his parents. He could play piano and sight-read when he was four and later became a ragtime pianist in New York City.[138] He came, it appeared at first sight, from favorable beginnings—talented parents, good financial resources—but, two years after his parents' divorce, he began setting fires, and suffered beatings and other cruelties from his "perfectionist, demanding" parents.[139] At twenty-six, he married a Danish photography student named Enken. One evening five years later, when he was living in the Greenwich Village section of Manhattan, he called the police and told them he had "found" the nude body of his pupil, the twenty-five-year-old Suzanne Reynolds, in a vacant apartment in his building, after he had returned from walking his dog. Charles was questioned at the local police station, where one of the detectives noticed stains on Charles's shoes and trousers. After hours of interrogation, Charles admitted having argued with the woman and later added that he had sodomized her body after he discovered it. Eventually, he confessed to having strangled her with a necktie and mutilated her body with a knife. Because he had not been notified of his rights before the interrogation, Charles was convicted only of manslaughter and sentenced to seven and a half to fifteen years. Having been a "model inmate" in prison, he ended up serving only five years and four months, after which he was released in 1973, returning to his wife's apartment in the Village. The prosecutor felt the sentence was too lenient; a psychiatrist opined that Charles was now "rehabilitated." He apparently remained "rehabilitated"—the quotation marks now becoming more ironic than genuine—given that, fourteen months later, another young woman was found dead on the roof of his apartment building. The body, which had been strangled, stripped, and mutilated, was that of twenty-three-year-old Karin Schlegel. This was after Charles had advertised for an actress or photographer's model to work on a movie for which he was, despite no prior experience, the "director." Charles was quickly arrested and, after pleading guilty, received a less than maximal sentence of fifteen years to life. On August 21, 1982, the eighth anniversary of Schlegel's murder, Charles hanged himself in his prison cell.[140] He would be ranked at level 17 of the Gradations of Evil scale, alongside other sexually perverse serial murderers who do not torture those they kill.

What makes his case puzzling is that he came from what seemed like a better background than that of the vast majority of serial killers. He was musically talented, from a family of the musically talented; well educated; married and living in good circumstances—and he was a serial killer. Even though he had raped, killed, and mutilated only two victims, Yukl's modus operandi was consistent with serial sexual homicide. He just happened to have been arrested and imprisoned after murdering the second woman before he could kill again. So, the question arose: what impelled Charles to swerve from conventional civilian life onto this sadistic and murderous path? The psychiatrist who had evaluated him suggested that, underneath his exterior, Charles hated women, who reminded him of his severely critical and demanding mother.[141] As an example, his weakly restrained fury suddenly unleashed itself when his first victim, Suzanne Reynolds, had mistakenly left some songs at home she was supposed to bring to her lesson. He became enraged, telling her, "You're a slob! You're a goddam slob!" He then pushed her against the piano and tried to rip off her blouse. That is when he grabbed the necktie and choked her to death, dragging her down to the empty apartment below his, where he now felt exhilarated and sexually aroused. He sodomized the corpse and, using a knife, mutilated her body. All of this before his wife returned home. It was at his wife's urging that Charles, after being interrogated by the detectives at the precinct, finally stopped pretending he was innocent and made a full confession. So, in a sense, Charles had committed a sexual homicide, experiencing orgasm during the violation of the body, in an hour of psychotic rage. This differed from the behavior of a more typical, organized serial killer. As we discussed earlier in this book, an organized serial murderer would calmly, and with planning beforehand, go out and *hunt* for a potential victim, usually a stranger, as was the case with murderers like Jack Unterweger, Ted Bundy, Ed Kemper, Derrick Todd Lee, and David Parker Ray and end up violating victims in much the same way. The psychiatrist may have been correct in his opinion that Charles was acting out his hatred of his mother during the "brief psychotic rage," as one might call it, when triggered by a pupil doing something that irked him, the way his shortcomings annoyed his mother. Yet, Charles was not chronically mentally ill and certainly not legally "insane." Chronic psychosis, such as schizophrenia or bipolar disorder with psychotic features, is quite rare in men guilty of serial sexual homicide. Richard Chase, the "vampire" killer in Sacramento, and cross-dressing cannibal Hadden Clark were probably schizophrenic, and Chase's symptoms may have been worsened in part by his abuse of LSD.

-Z-

The family histories of almost all of the persons in this "alphabet" are characterized by divorce, abandonment, adoption, disharmony, and instability. I suspect that persons raised in such uncertain and insecure environments come to doubt the steadfastness of human relationships altogether. The idea of marriage vows taken "till death do us part" must seem like a fairy tale from medieval times, hardly something one could count on in this day and age. The murder of Jeff Zack by John Zaffino in 2001 involves a cast of characters whose lives were commingled in a bewildering olio of marriages, divorces, adulteries, affairs, children born outside of wedlock, and finally, the murder in one corner of a love triangle. The story is told in a number of books and articles.[142] Put simply, Cynthia George, née Rohr in 1954, was married to a millionaire restaurateur in Akron, Ohio, named Ed George. They had six children by one another, and Cynthia had a daughter, Ruby, via a decade-long affair with an Israeli businessman and former paratrooper, Jeff Zack, who was married to Bonnie Cook after he moved to the United States. The Georges and the Zacks became friends, and Jeff would often come to the Georges' home and take Cynthia on bike rides or walks. Cynthia eventually broke up with Jeff. Still in love with Cynthia, he tried to reestablish their relationship, though still connected to Bonnie and their son. In the meantime, Cynthia was carrying on an extramarital affair with a truck driver, John Zaffino, who, like Jeff, was also twelve years younger than she was. Zaffino was twice divorced: the first time, from Nancy Bonadio; the second time, from Christine Todaro. He had a child by each wife. But Jeff's attempt to reconnect with Cynthia was rudely cut short in mid-June of 2001 when, as he was stopping at a gas station, he was shot to death by a man dressed in black, driving a ninja-style motorcycle with a green trim. The case went unsolved for fifteen months, until Zaffino was arrested and charged with the murder. In 2003, Zaffino, who would be ranked in Category 10 of the scale for this killing of someone "in the way," was sentenced to life in prison. Two years later, Cynthia was charged with conspiracy and complicity to commit murder. The judge acquitted her of conspiracy but found her guilty of complicity, sentencing her to twenty-three years. Cynthia was freed on appeal in 2007 when the court decided that there was insufficient evidence to convict. She remains free.

Elizabeth Zehnder was born in 1966 and adopted into her family in Virginia, the family later moving to Kentucky. From her earliest days, she was noted by her family to be rebellious, incorrigible, and given to constant lying. She was considered an example of a "bad seed," as though genetically predisposed to amoral behavior. She often got her way by upbraiding her mother and father by taunts that "you don't really love me, you're not my real parents!" She would manipulate others by lies created to elicit sympathy, or else to shock other people. When she was nineteen, she seduced a twenty-year-old college boy, Mike Turpin, and married him, apparently at his insistence, despite her contemptuous treatment of him and his mother's dislike of her. Elizabeth became more and more promiscuous at the University of Kentucky campus, cheating on Mike, and abusing marijuana, alcohol, and cocaine. At one point, she took up with a gay woman, Karen Brown, who imitated drag queens at sleazy bars and sold cocaine. She manipulated Karen and also a young mechanic, Keith Bouchard, via lies, about Mike's supposed abuse of her. Elizabeth convinced them, eventually, into killing Mike, carried out by Keith and Karen, who stabbed him to death in February of 1986. Earlier, during their whirlwind courtship, Elizabeth had manipulated Mike into staying with her (after a brief breakup prompted by her outrageous behavior). She took an overdose of the mild analgesic Fiorinal in a contrived suicide gesture. Mike took her back out of guilt, despite his mother's pleading. Prosecutors had suggested that the motive was the $60,000 life insurance policy on Mike's life that Elizabeth was eager to collect. After the murder, Mike's body was pulled out of a pond near a golf course. The case was a statewide sensational murder. The Zehnders emerged as good parents, and not at all abusive—to which their other adopted child, Mel Jr., was testimony. At trial, Elizabeth got a twenty-five-year sentence without parole in a Kentucky prison, though later emended to "life, with the possibility of parole after 25 years." Characterologically, she was brash, flippant, amoral, and sensation seeking, and also met criteria for borderline personality disorder.[143] Attorney Ray Larson called her "probably the most evil, manipulative woman that I've ever prosecuted."[144] After serving twenty-five years, Elizabeth, who would be ranked in Category 13 of the Gradations of Evil scale, was scheduled for a hearing about parole. Meantime, almost five thousand people had signed a petition against parole for both Elizabeth and Karen Brown. Both remain incarcerated.[145]

FINAL THOUGHTS

Gary Brucato, PhD, and Michael Stone, MD

We have arrived at the end of our brave pilgrimage into the belly of the modern-day *Inferno*—an extensive survey of twentieth- and twenty-first-century crimes in peacetime that might be called "evil." From start to finish, we have had to face a number of highly uncomfortable truths: first and foremost, while we would prefer to tell ourselves these acts were merely dark and terrible dreams, they really did transpire—and, we can say with confidence, will continue long after this volume goes to press. As much as we would like to believe that the people who commit such crimes are random, monstrous abominations of nature, the fact is, they share our DNA, and behave and look like the rest of us much of the time. As we have seen, the majority of serial killers, torturers, rapists, mass killers, and other serious offenders are not "sick," in the psychiatric and legal sense, as much as psychopathic and morally depraved.

We have also been faced with incontrovertible statistics that reveal sharp increases in mass killings, school shootings, serial homicide, and rape since the 1960s, which, as we have noted, cannot be dismissed as mere reflections of improved reporting and recordkeeping over the past six decades. While we observe declines in recent years in some forms of violent crime, including rape and serial killing, these are nowhere near the levels seen in the decades preceding that threshold era. Moreover, while not limited to our country, these atrocious acts have been committed, in shocking disproportion, in the United States. Thus, the cause must be at least a partially cultural one, which demands some explanation—and possibly some distressing introspection. The fact that nearly all of violent crimes are committed by males has a longer precedent and may represent either some biological difference between the sexes, a sociological phenomenon, or some combination of the two.

We are not alone in this observation. The point about our culture was made most eloquently by Peggy Noonan, whom we have quoted elsewhere, writing in the *Wall Street Journal* a week after Steven Paddock used semi-automatic weapons to perpetrate the largest mass shooting in American history, leaving fifty-eight dead and 581 injured. After reviewing snippets of typical contemporary news headlines related to crimes of all sorts—"was found strangled and believed to have been sexually molested," "which they said has gone beyond violence to sadism," "showed no remorse"—Noonan summed it up: "This is the ocean in which our children swim. This is the sound of our culture. It comes from all parts of our culture and reaches all parts of our culture, and all the people in it. . . . We were bringing up our children in an unwell atmosphere. It would enter and distort them."[1]

The justification for the undeniable intensification and diversification of "evil" acts in the 1960s is open to debate. The crux of the second portion of this book has been the hypothesis that, sometime in the middle of that decade, Western—particularly American—society unwittingly traversed a critical threshold. Thereafter, profound philosophical, cultural, and psychological changes within individuals and in the wider population were increasingly reflected in particularly heinous and spectacular crimes. These had previously been virtually nonexistent across the long history of humankind, outside of wartime. Additionally, new technologies in communication, such as the internet and cellular phones, and wide-scale civilian access to weaponry designed for cutting-edge military use, such as the AK-47, have given rise to several new forms of aggression, which we have cataloged throughout our discussion.

An exhaustive exposition regarding all of the various factors that contributed, in some way, to the era of "new evil" we have described would be voluminous and beyond the scope of this book. Perfunctorily, we will note that, in the first half of the twentieth century, Fascism and Communism in several nations contributed to a reduction of the individual to a meaningless entity within the larger mass or "party," casting aside, in many ways, personal responsibility, as well as morality rooted in long-established religious principles. It is also noteworthy that psychoanalysis, which, by the 1960s, had spent half a century emphasizing sexual liberation and the elimination of old taboos for the purposes of reducing neurotic stress in the common person, had the unanticipated consequence of implying that very little should be inhibited and that all feelings are worthy of expression. It is easy to forget that, when psychoanalysis was in its heyday from about 1900 through the 1960s, it was widely decried by some Western religious authorities as a perilous school of thought for this very reason. It was, after all, fathered by Sigmund Freud, an ardent atheist. While liberating for many, psychoanalysis had a potentially problematic impact upon the way people deal with issues of guilt, sexual impulses, aggression, and morality, which it may not have initially intended.

There is a plethora of literature demonstrating that, in the wake of these schools of thought, as well as the Second World War, Western culture gradually abandoned norms rooted in ancient traditions and religious teachings and replaced them with an ever-evolving "moral relativism," in which one's sense of what is right and wrong is viewed as a personal decision, or as a social and historical construction, rather than depending upon long-standing customs or objective truths.

One might make a solid argument that the new freedoms people experienced in the wake of these social changes were thoroughly abused, giving rise to a period of narcissism, reduced responsibility to one's neighbor, wanton hedonism, and escapism. Some academics have proposed that the current tensions between Islamic and Western nations, for instance, stem from the desire of fundamentalist Muslim peoples to reestablish absolute values that are at serious odds with relativist thinking.

With the gradual collapse of clear modes of philosophical thought, the 1960s became something of a farrago of oftentimes conflicting principles, which, in turn, profoundly corroded basic elements of personal identity and existential purpose. Moreover, upheaval of the societal roles previously forced upon women—certainly a positive development—had some unfortunate, unintended side effects, including a "counterattack" from certain brittle, enraged men, in the form of serious crimes against women, whom they now saw as capable of rejecting them as romantic options. It has been our contention throughout this book that serial sexual homicide—the most common form of serial murder, uniformly committed by males—became markedly more common from the 1960s through 1990s as a direct result of the sexual revolution. We also view this as the root of the current spate of celebrated males whose pasts as sexual predators are suddenly coming to the fore. We feel this proposal is worthy of further research and discussion.

There was a metaphor, sometimes employed by philosophers and social commentators in the nineteenth century, regarding a frog placed in a pot of boiling water: if you drop a frog in a pot of water that is already boiling, it will instantaneously try to escape to safety. However, if you place the frog in cool water, which is gradually heated up, the animal will feel comfortable in its new environment, even as it subtly grows warmer, remaining complacent until it meets its end. Although scientists who actually attempted to confirm this found it to be untrue, it still provides an excellent insight into the danger of a culture that is gradually becoming more coarse, uninhibited, amoral, and selfish. We posit that the water has been bubbling and simmering since the 1960s and is rapidly coming to a boil.

In addition to trying to explain the post-1960s era of "new evil" in terms of sociocultural developments, we have proposed that the "evil" of homicide and other serious acts of violence might, somehow, be quantified along a continuum of degrees of depravity, related to the specific motivations that drive homicide and other heinous acts. To that end, we have carefully delineated and illustrated, in more detail than ever before, the twenty-two categories of Dr. Stone's Gradations of Evil scale, and have additionally provided an algorithm to facilitate proper ranking, which, with validation and further development, may prove useful in future forensic research.

As we saw, there are homicides and other violent crimes perpetrated by individuals with non-psychopathic personalities, impetuously, under immense duress; there are some carried out by egotistical and brittle persons with long-standing resentments that finally explode into spectacular displays of rage; there are individuals who commit crimes because they are operating within the context of psychotic illness; and there are power-hungry psychopaths and entirely self-absorbed schemers, who murder anyone who impedes their plans. At the extreme end of the spectrum, there are persons who are even more amoral and sadistic, not robbing or killing for "practical" purposes, in expeditious ways, but instead deriving pleasure from protracted torture, subjugation, sexual violence, repeat murder, and the perverse abuse of human remains. We believe that the separate consideration of violent crimes in terms of specific motivations, and degrees of narcissism, psychopathy and sadism, constitutes a significant contribution to the forensic literature.

Above all else, we trust that we have compellingly argued that Evil—

with a capital E—is not only an authentic phenomenon, universally grasped on some difficult to articulate level, but also constitutes a topic worthy of serious academic discussion. In the meantime, the world's peoples will carry on, as always, making choices to kill, maim, steal, kidnap, rape, abuse, and hate, or else heal, give, share, respect, and love. Although, as we have seen, various demographic, psychological, situational, and genetic factors might incline some individuals more than others to criminal behaviors, it appears that the bulk of "evil" actions are the results of selfish choices made by fully cognizant individuals. In the era of "new evil," we have seen the rise of a sort of "false compassion," in which the most relentless, psychopathic persons are sometimes viewed as "victims," "driven" to crime by terrible circumstances that have "overridden" their minds' braking systems. There is minimal emphasis on the role of personal will and the consequences of one's actions. This growing tendency to blame outside forces is, in fact, a hallmark of narcissism, now encountered on a sweeping, societal scale.

For many of the offenders in our terrible catalog, the issue at hand has been one of power and control, as a sad substitute for basic, stable love, never known or understood. It is our ardent hope that, after a period of terrible growing pains, our culture will eventually learn that true power and control come only after a lifelong process of mastering and inhibiting the self, and coming to understand oneself as a small, yet integral droplet in a vast ocean of other people, never more valuable than others, and never capable of standing alone. In doing so, we may elevate ourselves above the animal and ugly aspects of the post-1960s era of "new evil," entering a period of "new goodness." Perhaps, as a first step, we should admit that the water in our collective pot is growing disquietingly warmer, day by day.

AFTERWORD BY
ANN W. BURGESS, DNSc., APRN

*T*he *New Evil* is a groundbreaking, timely book written as America is
struggling with mass shootings, bomb threats, and murders. Violence
and its counterpoint of evil is a constant headline in the news and media. As
serial murderer Sean Vincent Gillis, who stalked, raped, killed, and mutilated eight women, said of one of his crimes, "I was in a real bad place. I
was pure evil. No love, no compassion, no faith, no mercy, no hope."[1]

Philosophers have spent centuries presenting a broad concept of evil
and trying to explain the various horrors that occur in a society. More
recently, the psychiatric community has been studying the type of person
who commits evil acts. A landmark book was written in 1941 when psychiatrist Dr. Hervey Cleckley published his *Mask of Sanity* on the psychopathic
personality. Then there was Dr. Robert Hare's *Without Conscience* in 1993.
A third landmark book was Dr. Michael H. Stone's book *The Anatomy of
Evil* in 2009. And now a decade later there is a fourth landmark book by
psychiatrist Dr. Stone and psychologist Dr. Gary Brucato: *The New Evil.*

This comprehensive and thoroughly engaging book on murder and
violent crime provides an organized way to learn and apply a gradation
scale to various serious offenses, with a particular emphasis on homicide.
Not only is there practical content on the psychodynamics of murder, but
most importantly, the framework is grounded in the cultural changes of
the second half of the twentieth century. In their book, Drs. Stone and
Brucato identify the emerging social trends that bear responsibility for the
major increases in certain forms of violence that trigger the word "evil."
The authors make a powerful case for tackling this serious and increasingly
repetitive topic of modern violent crime.

But first, behind every important book is a story of its beginning. The
idea for the *New Evil* began over a decade ago with Dr. Michael Stone's
interest in researching and writing a book on evil.

Earlier, between 2003 and 2004, Dr. Stone had written some papers in forensic journals and books about "evil" and sadism. His motivation to develop a gradation scale of evil crystalized after he was asked by crime writer Joe McGinniss and his attorneys to be an expert witness on Joe's behalf when Joe was sued for breach of contract by Jeffrey MacDonald. MacDonald at the time was in prison after having been convicted of killing his pregnant wife, Colette, and their two young daughters, when they were living in North Carolina (after MacDonald came back from Vietnam in the 1970s). MacDonald had been found not guilty after the first government trial. Later, Colette's stepfather found previously overlooked evidence, and there was a second trial where MacDonald was found guilty and sentenced to prison.[2]

McGinniss and MacDonald had started writing a book together after the first trial, but with the second trial's conviction, McGinniss rewrote the book, declaring MacDonald was a psychopathic killer. Dr. Stone testified on behalf of McGinniss at a California trial where MacDonald sued for the royalty money. A settlement came three months after a bitterly divided jury failed to reach a verdict in the seven-week trial, which featured testimony from a variety of publishing executives about the need to preserve a writer's independence in determining the outcome of a book.[3]

Dr. Stone wanted the jury to understand where MacDonald's crime fit into a hypothetical scale of evil. He began reading true crime books, by way of situating MacDonald's crime in the system he was developing. Clearly MacDonald's crime was worse than Jean Harris's murder of the Scarsdale diet doctor (Tarnower) when she discovered he was cheating on her (a "crime of passion"), but not as bad as Ian Brady's crime: serial murder following torture of children in the English moors area. Eventually, Dr. Stone read hundreds of true crime books (since then he has read over eight hundred) and made a scale, which at MacDonald's trial only had a few different gradations.[4]

Dr. Stone continued working on his scale that eventually turned into twenty-two gradations. Then, Ben Carey, journalist of the *New York Times* read his work and wrote a piece for the science section of the paper—about his work on evil. Psychiatrists rarely wrote about evil, so Dr. Stone was opening up a new subject. Then the Discovery Channel was interested in the topic. They invited Dr. Stone to travel around the country to interview prisoners whose crimes he felt illustrated the concept of evil, and Dr.

Stone hosted that show in 2006–2007. That experience fired up his energy to write a book about evil and about the men and women he had interviewed and had read about in those true crime books.

Dr. Stone's *Anatomy of Evil* book came out in 2009. In some ways this book—*The New Evil*—is a sequel to the first book and zeroes in on the downward slope, and coarsening, of our culture since the 1960s—when certain extremely repugnant crimes have become more common than was the case earlier. These crimes were serial sexual homicide, mass murder, school shootings, dismembering spouses, people killing and barbecuing their neighbors, cannibalism, and many examples of which are in this new book.

Parallel with Dr. Stone's momentum for writing a book on evil, Dr. Gary Brucato also had a long-standing interest in violent crime. In both authors' work in clinical, prison, and legal settings, they have evaluated and treated killers, rapists, and other violent offenders. Dr. Brucato's research and clinical work over the past decade has focused on early psychosis and, for two years now, on how this might relate to violence. With his team in the Columbia University Department of Psychiatry, at the New York State Psychiatric Institute, he is studying aggression in the context of psychosis and developing novel methods of predicting it, which might someday, with further study, affect how clinicians screen for violence risk.

As Dr. Brucato considered how to best get at the roots of violence for this purpose, he began contemplating his interactions with serious offenders over the years. More precisely, he became interested in what distinguishes aggression among individuals with commonplace motives that are "human" in quality, or among people with psychiatric conditions, such as schizophrenia or mania, from the actions of psychopathic offenders, who go beyond committing violence for "practical" or delusional purposes, to instead play out disturbing psychological needs and fantasies with torture and other brutality.

Thinking this might, perhaps, make for an interesting book, Dr. Brucato began heavily researching what is known about the relationship between psychopathy and violence. This work led him to two individuals, desiring anonymity, who provided large caches of writings and artwork of serial murderers and other violent offenders, which they had acquired mostly by corresponding with incarcerated people. Dr. Brucato realized it might be helpful to consider these pieces in a manuscript, as a way of demonstrating the themes and fantasies that seemed common in these people—and which do not commonly emerge in more mentally ill individuals.

A psychoanalyst colleague at Columbia, Dr. Clarice Kestenbaum, suggested that Dr. Brucato show the art and writings to Dr. Stone, who might be interested in working together on Dr. Brucato's proposed project. As it turned out, Dr. Stone had been approached by the publisher of his seminal *The Anatomy of Evil* to do another book—and the idea was born that they should collaborate on the current manuscript.

They began reviewing numerous cases, especially Dr. Stone's records about violent offenders dating back centuries in some cases, as well as the artworks and writings, and they noted that there was something decidedly "new" about these killers. First, some of the crimes simply did not happen or rarely happened before the 1960s, and second, the crimes, as well as the themes observed in the artwork and writing, were "new" in that they were especially heinous, narcissistic, and sadistic, reflecting more perverse psychological motivations, relative to the more "practical" motivations of the offenders of earlier decades. Drs. Brucato and Stone also discussed the existent literature on serial murder and other violence and realized they had independently come to similar conclusions: society, especially American society, was changing and getting coarser since the 1960s—and, with it, so was violent crime.

It soon became clear that Dr. Stone's twenty-two-point scale offered an ideal framework to discuss the growing frequency and heinousness of "evil." Thus, they decided to provide an exposition on the scale in part I and the thoughts on cultural changes in part II, with a few illustrations and writings from various sources in a separate section. The authors considered some of the artwork they examined, vividly depicting scenes of rape and murder, which were either actually committed or dreamed up by convicted offenders, simply too disturbing for publication.

And so, Drs. Stone and Brucato weave the two components of the Gradation of Evil and the cultural shifts since 1960 with precision. Their case descriptions of types of murderers in each of the twenty-two levels of evil show great insight and depth in understanding the emergence of modern violent crime. Many debatable issues include the following: Are some acts more evil than others? Can the acts be classified into meaningful categories and ranked by severity? What accounts for offenders being classified in different categories by different murders they commit? Is it a cultural phenomenon that America has so many serial killers compared to other countries? Have we become normalized to violence?

There is something for everyone in this well-written, compelling book. Those who appreciate current data will find that the statistics of the various violent crimes inform us of the changes over the decades. The rich literature reviews inform us of advances in knowledge as to the nature of the research on a specific crime. Those who are focused on the psychodynamics of a crime will find that the detailed cases illustrate childhood abuse and developmental red flags that were missed.

For those who want to learn how to categorize murderers, the end of part I includes the algorithm developed to determine an offender's ranking in the Gradations of Evil scale. The authors describe numerous other systems of categorizing violent offenses, including the subtypes of rape and murder I delineated, alongside John Douglas, Allen Burgess, and Robert Ressler, in *Sexual Homicide: Patterns and Motives* and the *Crime Classification Manual*.

The part I chapters move us through the twenty-two categories from justifiable homicide to impulsive murders in persons without psychopathic features to murders with murderers of a more severe type to spree or multiple murders where psychopathy is apparent and, finally, to serial killers, torturers, and sadists. The teaching points in Categories 9–22 distinguish between psychological concepts of psychopathy, psychosis, and sadism and include the diagnostic criteria from the fifth edition of the *Diagnostic and Statistical Manual of Mental Disorders* (*DSM-5*) for antisocial personality disorder, explaining how the latter does not capture some of the features of psychopathy described by Dr. Hare.

A major contribution to the book is an alphabet of "new" evil where a wide range of cases are analyzed, organized by the last name of the offender, and include the gradation of evil. The meticulously studied case histories are gripping in their detail. Illustrations corresponding to both parts I and II of the book emphasize the reality of the cases.

Part II analyzes some cultural trends (birth control, increase in divorce rates, marital infidelity, single parenthood) in the period of new evil from the 1960s into the twenty-first century to include bullying; child abuse; mass shootings; fetus-snatching; internet-related crimes; stalking murders;

cyberstalking; school shooters; gratuitous cruelty; home invasion; spousal murders, including dismemberment; and gang murders, such as by members of MS-13. Contemporary forms of evil not involving violence are also described in the book, including child custody cases and how the courts preside over them, foster care, divorce, kids who commit evil acts, the unjustly accused, and sexual predation.

While all of the chapters are compelling, there are specific topics and points that are especially enlightening:

- The chapter on **school shooters** contains fresh insights on the dynamic elements of envy and misogyny, adolescent brain development, cases involving autism, details on premeditation, and murder-suicide (twelve of the sixteen cases suicided).
- While mass murder by a female is uncommon (the book cites ten who suffered from a psychotic disorder), the crime of **fetus abduction** involves primarily female offenders and includes sadism, e.g., a North Dakota woman admitted cutting out the female fetus from her neighbor while the neighbor was still alive.
- There is a growing literature on the **neurobiology of violence and childhood trauma** with a focus on the HPA axis stress response.
- The postmortem act of **dismemberment** has a long history in medieval as well as contemporary times, but not among private citizens. In the era of "new evil," we see more dismemberment of victims by killers, often serving the purpose of "disappearing" bodies so that they are never found but sometimes for other purposes, including cannibalism and necrophilic sexual acts. Drs. Stone and Brucato and I have collaborated to systematically define *dismemberment* and to distinguish it from the act of *mutilation*, since these terms are sometimes used interchangeably. Our definitions are noted in the discussion of Category 13 of the Gradations of Evil scale.

This landmark book is immensely illuminating whereby Drs. Stone and Brucato explain the post-1960s era of "new evil" in terms of sociocultural developments along a continuum of degrees of evil/depravity related to motives that drive the violent acts of homicide. Their analysis and categorizing of twenty-two levels of evil is provocative as well as profound. Drs. Stone and Brucato point to more crimes in the last fifty years showing extreme callousness, greater cruelty, and plain disregard for ordinary human feelings, and a propensity to relish in such cruelty—the essence of sadism—in this post-1960s era. Not only was this noted in crimes of violence but witnessed in court where divorce and custody of the children were settled by financial evaluation rather than by a fair process of assessment of the more deserving spouse.

In conclusion, Drs. Stone and Brucato propose that an offender's "need for power and control with a victim is a sad substitute for basic, stable love never known or understood." The goal, they argue, is to elevate the culture above this new evil to a period of "new goodness." This cutting-edge book should be in every mental health and legal professional's bookshelf and required reading for students, nurses, educators, law enforcement, researchers, clergy, and social service staff whose work brings them into contact with crime victims and criminal offenders.

ACKNOWLEDGMENTS

Dr. Michael Stone:

The acknowledgments section is the one happy area of a book otherwise devoted to mankind's darkest side—the topic of evil. Here, I have the opportunity to thank those who dwell on mankind's brightest side: the many good—the many especially good—people who served as inspiration for my work in this area. To the prestigious journalist of the *New York Times*, Ben Carey, I am most indebted for his having featured my writing on evil in the paper's science section in 2005. It was his article that caught the attention of the Discovery Channel, whose staff then sent me around the country to interview prisoners who had committed serial killing, mass murder, torture, cannibalism, and other forms of violent crimes that the public and the legal community label unequivocally and unhesitatingly as "evil." Getting to know those prisoners firsthand helped launch my earlier book on the subject, *The Anatomy of Evil*. Many of the persons featured in the book merited the diagnosis "psychopath"—which, along with sadism, is at the far end of the spectrum of abnormal personality. I learned about the nature of psychopathy from the foremost author on the subject, Dr. Robert Hare, whom I had gotten to know during my years in forensic psychiatry. As to my knowledge about personality disorders in general, I have benefited greatly from my colleagues in the United States, especially from Drs. Otto Kernberg, John Gunderson, Thomas McGlashan, Theodore Millon, Adrian Raine, and Bessel Van der Kolk. When I began to concentrate on forensic psychiatry, I had many teachers, from many countries. Among them: Drs. Reid Meloy, Katherine Ramsland, Paul Ciolino in the United States; from Canada, Drs. John Livesley, Marnie Rice, Christopher Perry; from England, Drs. Jeremy Coid, Sheila Hodgins, Conor Duggan; and from Scotland, Dr. David Cooke, who, with his colleagues in Glasgow, has developed another important measure of psychopathy. I owe debts of gratitude to many on the European continent, including Drs. Wolfgang Berner, Norbert Nedopil, Maya Krischer, Friedemann Pfäffelin, Horst Kächele, and Thomas Bronisch from Germany; from the Netherlands, Drs. Henk-Jan Dalewijk, Thomas Rinne, and Hjalmar van Marle; from Switzerland, Drs. Jules Angst, Gerhard Dammann, and Luc Ciompi; from Sweden, Drs. Maria Åstberg and Kristina Hillgren; from Norway, Drs. Bjørn Østberg and Alv Dahl; from Denmark, Drs. Tove Aarkrog, Eric Simonsen, and Fini Schulsinger; Dr. Mikhail Reshetnikov in Russia, who enlightened me about serial killer Andrei Chikatilo; Drs. Mario Iannucci and Sergio Dazzi in Italy; Dr. José Carrasco-Perez in Spain; Drs. Winfred Huber and Charles Hershkowitz in Belbium; and Dr. Jean Bergeret in France. Fruitful exchanges on personality disorders, including those relevant to forensics and the topic of evil, came also from colleagues in more far-flung places: Drs. Paul Mullen and Alan Unwin in Australia; Drs. Tsuyoshi Ishii and Yutaka Ono in Japan; Drs. Chantima Ongkosit and Sritham Thanaphum in Thailand; Dr. Xiao Ze-Ping in China; Drs. Michael Bond and Patrick Leung in Hong Kong; and Dr. Vedat Şar in Turkey; Dr. Francisco Vallejo in Ecuador; Dr. Hilda Morana, with whom I visited imprisoned serial killers, in Brazil; Drs. Nestor Koldobsky, Jorge Folino, and Javier Didia-Attas in Argentina; Dr. Andres Heerlein in Chile; and in Mexico, Dr. Manuel Esparza, who introduced me to the advanced forensic laboratory in Ciudad Juarez.

People often ask me whether my thirty-five years as a combined psychoanalyst and forensic psychiatrist, part of which has been devoted to the study of violent crime and cases we tend to regard as evil, have not left me soured on the human race and a bit depressed. No. Because I have had the good fortune to be surrounded by family, friends, and colleagues who embody the *good* in our species—who, fortunately, vastly outnumber the persons we regard as evil. And most of all, my wife Beth, whose beauty, both spiritual and physical, serve as a constant—and close to home—reminder of not just the good, but the best, our species has to offer. Thanks to my friends and colleagues, and most of all to her, I have been able to view evil as something fascinating and dramatic, yet distant—something "out there" and far away, as though viewed from a different planet. Dr. Brucato and I of course hope that our book about what we regard as the "new evil"— and the coarsening of our culture in the past half century—can stimulate those in positions of power to effect salutary changes in our culture so that evil, while perhaps not eradicated, becomes a rarity—a topic more for historians, rather than for the majority of good persons who must otherwise remain on guard against those who would do evil.

It would take more words than our space permits to express my gratitude to my coauthor, Dr. Gary Brucato. Among his many contributions: a sharpening of the definitions of the Gradations of Evil scale, enabling others to better understand the various distinctions, and more readily to agree with the appropriate spot on the scale where any given offender would belong. Dr. Brucato dug more deeply into the lives of many of the arch criminals, especially the men who committed serial sexual homicide, than I was able to do. The result: we know more chilling details about many of these men, making the reader more certain than ever that the rape, torture, and murders of which these men were guilty would indeed evoke the reaction of "evil!" Dr. Brucato was also able to gain access to a large collection of letters and artwork (much of the latter very disturbing) by dozens of notorious killers. The resulting illustrations in the book make vivid how they bear out what we mean when we use the word "evil." The book brings alive the old adage "two heads are better than one"—the more so when one of the "heads" is that of Dr. Brucato.

Dr. Gary Brucato:

The New Evil represents, for me, the culmination of two decades of studying, evaluating, treating, and contemplating severe psychopathology and violence in my training, clinical work, and research at six New York City–based hospitals, as well as my professional and volunteer work with forensic psychiatric patients and incarcerated individuals. Throughout the course of my career, I have had many brilliant and selfless teachers. I am grateful for my years at Cathedral Preparatory Seminary, where I learned the joy of helping others, including prisoners and the mentally ill. It was also there that I was first introduced to the writings of Sir Arthur Conan Doyle, which taught me to pay attention to motive and "small" details when considering cases of violent crime, as well as the work of Soren Kierkegaard and Venerable Fulton J. Sheen, who strongly influenced my thinking regarding morality and "evil." I am grateful to my mentors, Dr. John D. Hogan at St.

John's University, and, at the New School for Social Research, Drs. David Shapiro, Herbert Schlesinger, Marcel Kinsbourne, McWelling Todman, Jeremy Safran, and especially forensic psychologist Dr. Ali Khadivi, with whom I worked for nearly two years at Bronx Lebanon Hospital Center, training in the assessment and treatment of serious psychiatric illness and violent behaviors. I am indebted to Dr. Albert Dreisinger, who taught me to conduct psychological evaluations for legal purposes; Dr. Thomas M. Pabon, who, on the Women's Forensic Unit at Mount Sinai Services / Elmhurst Hospital Center, oversaw my assessments and treatment of numerous persons who had committed unspeakable crimes; Dr. Barbara Cornblatt of the Zucker Hillside Hospital, who introduced me to the field of early psychotic illness, in which I have now worked for over a decade; and to those who helped me to become involved in conducting psychological and risk evaluations for the various colleges in the City University of New York (CUNY) system, especially Ryan Camire.

Many thanks to my gifted colleagues in the Columbia University Department of Psychiatry and the New York State Psychiatric Institute, particularly Dr. Ragy Girgis and the team at our Center of Prevention and Evaluation, where I have served as assistant director since 2013. The work I have done there, treating, studying, and teaching and writing about psychosis and violence, has been one of the great blessings of my life. Special thanks to Dr. Jeffrey Lieberman, chairman of psychiatry at the Columbia University College of Physicians and Surgeons, as well as Drs. Paul Appelbaum and Michael B. First, for their invaluable guidance on several projects related to violence and psychotic illness. Much appreciation to Dr. Clarice Kestenbaum, who introduced me to Dr. Stone for the purpose of a writing collaboration, and, of course, to my friend and coauthor for his endless knowledge, insight, humor, and kindness. Reading and rereading his groundbreaking *The Anatomy of Evil* over the years, I could never have imagined that he would someday invite me to cowrite this, its follow-up volume.

Heartfelt thanks to Prometheus Books for inviting us to write about the difficult, timely subject of evil, and to its expert team, which has made every aspect of writing this, my first of hopefully many books, both smooth and endlessly enjoyable. I am indebted to Steven L. Mitchell, Bruce Carle, Jeffrey Curry, Hanna Etu, Mark Hall, Jill Maxick, Lisa Michalski, Cate Roberts-Abel, and Nicole Sommer-Lecht. Each was endlessly patient, generous, and indispensable as *The New Evil* came into being. Much appreciation to those who helped with historical information and images, including Vernon J. Geberth, retired lieutenant commander of the New York City Police Department; author Kevin M. Sullivan; and two private parties who wish to remain anonymous. Thanks, in particular, to Aboud Mounayerdji, not only for providing artwork and writings but also for many fruitful discussions about their contents, and to Justin Segovia, who reviewed the rough first drafts of my chapters of the book.

Much appreciation to Drs. Terry Leary and Larry Southard of Florida Gulf Coast University, and Dr. Michael G. Aamodt of Radford University for invaluable statistical data from their outstanding Serial Killer Database. I am endlessly grateful to Dr. Otto Kernberg, John Douglas, Vernon J. Geberth, Dr. Katherine Ramsland, Diane Fanning, Kevin M. Sullivan, Dr. Michael B. First, and Dr. Ali Khadivi for providing blurbs for the book, and to Dr. Ann W. Burgess, who authored our wonderful afterword. Dr. Burgess also collaborated with us to systematically define the words *mutilation* and *dismemberment* for use in our manuscript. These terms have typically been used interchangeably in both popular and academic parlance. It has been a distinct honor to have my writing weighed and so well received by masters who have contributed, for decades, to my thoughts on personality disorders, psychotic illness, serial killing, sex crimes, criminal classification, and motivations for violent offenses.

Finally, my deepest thanks to those I hold dearest to my heart: my family and friends, especially my parents, Gary and Patricia; my brother, Mark, his wife Janice, and my nephew, Marco; my grandparents, Elena, Michael, Julia, and Andolpho; my dear friend Attila; and Kathleen, whose unfailing support and affection have meant the world to me throughout this profoundly challenging project. Their unlimited generosity and kindness represent the very best in humanity—the inversion of the evils described in this book. My cup runneth over. Truly, such good people constitute a brilliant flame of hope, which cannot be extinguished by any degree of darkness—no matter how terrible.

NOTES

CHAPTER ONE: INTRODUCTION TO THE
GRADATIONS OF EVIL SCALE

1. Steve Myall, "I Wish I'd Killed the Monster Who Murdered Our Daughter the First Time I Saw Him," *Manchester Evening News*, February 22, 2005, https://www.manchestereveningnews.co.uk/news/greater-manchester-news/wish-id-killed-monster-who-8694736; "Teen Girl 'Horrifically Tortured before Her Murder,'" *Irish Independent*, November 12, 1997, https://www.independent.ie/world-news/teen-girl-horrifically-tortured-before-her-murder-26202114.html.

2. David Ward and Jamie Wilson, "Man Who Tortured Girl to Death Jailed for Life," *Guardian*, November 20, 1997.

3. Ibid.; "Teen Girl 'Horrifically Tortured.'"

4. Ward and Wilson, "Man Who Tortured Girl."

5. "Torture Killer Jailed for 20 Years," *Irish Independent*, November 20, 1997, https://www.independent.ie/world-news/torture-killer-jailed-for-20-years-26202465.html.

6. Heather Sutfin, "The Murder and Torture of Kelly Anne Bates," Sword and Scale, June 16, 2015, http://swordandscale.com/the-murder-and-torture-of-kelly-anne-bates/.

7. "Parents' 'Bad Feeling' about Teenage Daughter's Lover Comes Too Late to Prevent Tragedy," LifeDaily, http://www.lifedaily.com/story/parents-bad-feeling-about-teenage-daughters-lover-comes-too-late-to-prevent-tragedy/9/.

8. Michael H. Stone, *The Anatomy of Evil* (Amherst, NY: Prometheus Books, 2009).

9. Robert J. Morton, ed., *Serial Murder: Multi-Disciplinary Perspectives for Investigators* (Washington, DC: Federal Bureau of Investigation, 2008), p. 8.

10. Ronald M. Holmes and Stephen T. Holmes, *Contemporary Perspectives on Serial Murder* (Thousand Oaks, CA: SAGE Publications, 1998), p. 1.

11. Terry Sullivan and Peter T. Maiken, *Killer Clown: The John Wayne Gacy Murders* (New York: Pinnacle, 1983).

12. Carla Norton, *Disturbed Ground: The True Story of a Diabolical Female Serial Killer* (New York: W. Morrow, 1994).

CHAPTER TWO: CATEGORIES 1–6

1. Arthur Conan Doyle, "The Adventure of the Devil's Root," in Doyle, *The Complete Sherlock Holmes* (New York, NY: Barnes & Noble Books), p. 970.

2. "Hopkins Student with Samurai Sword Kills Burglary Suspect," *Washington Post*, September 16, 2009, http://www.washingtonpost.com/wp-dyn/content/article/2009/09/15/AR2009091503930.html; "Md. Samurai Sword Death Not Homicide," *Washington Times*, September 18, 2009, https://www.washingtontimes.com/news/2009/sep/18/samurai-sword-death-not-homicide/.

3. Clifford Ward, "Aurora Woman Acquitted of Murder in Boyfriend's Stabbing Death," *Chicago Tribune*, June 26, 2012, http://articles.chicagotribune.com/2012-06-26/news/ct-met-martin-trial-0626-20120626_1_aurora-woman-willie-arrington-kitchen-knife.

4. *Most Evil*, season 2, episode 1, "Jealousy," featuring Dr. Michael H. Stone and Neil Dudgeon, aired on August 12, 2007, on Investigation Discovery, https://www.investigationdiscovery.com/tv-shows/most-evil/full-episodes/jealousy; "Collins Guilty in Stabbing," *Lewiston Sun Journal* (Lewiston, ME), July 24, 1998.

5. Philip Caulfield, "Belgian Woman Skydiver Gets 30 Years for Murder after Sabotaging Rival's Parachute," *Daily News* (New York), October 21, 2010, http://www.nydailynews.com/news/world/belgian-woman-skydiver-30-years-murder-sabotaging-rival-parachute-article-1.190947; "Belgian Skydiver 'Murdered Love Rival'" During Jump," BBC News, September 24, 2010, http://www.bbc.com/news/world-europe-11404581.

6. Steven V. Roberts, "Charlie Manson: One Man's Family," *New York Times*, January 4, 1970.

7. Sherryl Connelly, "'Manson: The Life and Times of Charles Manson' Draws Portrait of Psychopath as a Young Man," *Daily News*, July 28, 2013, http://www.nydailynews.com/entertainment/music-arts/hedline-article-1.1410785.

8. Jeff Guinn, *Manson: The Life and Times of Charles Manson* (New York: Simon & Schuster, 2014), p. 86.

9. Vincent Bugliosi and Curt Gentry, *Helter Skelter* (New York: W. W. Norton, 1974), p. 15.

10. Alice B. Lloyd, "Charles Manson's Infectious Evil," *Weekly Standard*, November 20, 2017, http://www.weeklystandard.com/charles-mansons-infectious-evil/article/2010557.

11. Michael Newton, *The Encyclopedia of Serial Killers*, 2nd ed. (New York: Checkmark, 2006), p. 173; Charles Manson and Nuel Emmons, *Charles Manson in His Own Words: The Shocking Confessions of the Most Dangerous Man Alive* (New York: Grove, 1986), pp. 5–6.

12. Bugliosi and Gentry, *Helter Skelter*, pp. 320–21.

13. Guinn, *Manson*, pp. 66–67.

14. Jon Blistein, "Charles Manson, Cult Leader behind Tate-LaBianca Murders, Dead at 83," *Rolling Stone*, November 20, 2017, https://www.rollingstone.com/culture/news/charles-manson-dead-at-83-w458873.

15. Bugliosi and Gentry, *Helter Skelter*, pp. 240–44.

16. Christopher Sandford, *Polanski: A Biography* (New York: St. Martin's, 2008), p. 156.

17. Ibid., p. 141.

18. Bugliosi and Gentry, *Helter Skelter*, p. 244.

19. Jay Robert Nash, *The Encyclopedia of 20th Century Murder* (Lanham, MD: Rowman & Littlefield, 2004), p. 388.

20. George C. Cohn, ed., *The New Encyclopedia of American Scandal* (New York: Facts on File, 2000), p. 371.

21. Vickie Jensen, ed., *Women Criminals: An Encyclopedia of People and Issues*, vol. 1 (Santa Barbara, CA: ABC-CLIO, LLC, 2012), p. 625; "Leslie Van Houten, Ex-Manson Follower, Approved for Parole," *NBC News*, September 17, 2017, https://www.nbcnews .com/news/us-news/leslie-van-houten-ex-manson-follower-approved-parole-n799431.

22. Cohn, New Encyclopedia of American Scandal, p. 388.

23. Bugliosi and Gentry, *Helter Skelter*, p. 432; Jensen, *Women Criminals*, p. 625.

24. Ibid., p. 626.

25. Linda Deutsch, "Release Leslie Van Houten. If She Hadn't Been a Manson Follower, She Would Have Left Prison Long Ago," *Los Angeles Times*, September 17, 2017, http://www.latimes.com/opinion/op-ed/la-oe-deutsch-van-houten-release-20170917 -story.html.

26. Lorenzo Zazueta-Castro, "Former CBP Officer Convicted of Murder to Get New Trial," *Monitor* (McAllen, TX), April 9, 2016, http://www.themonitor.com/news/ local/article_dcf992ce-fea0-11e5-8564-8b476b46edbb.html; Greg Pickett, "Former CBP Officer Jose Rodriguez-Elizondo Pleads Guilty to Murder," *Mimesis Law*, January 31, 2017, http://mimesislaw.com/fault-lines/former-cbp-officer -jose-rodriguez-elizondo-pleads-guilty-to-murder/15809.

27. Tim Weiner, "Samuel Cummings, 71, Trader in Weapons on a Grand Scale," *New York Times*, May 5, 1998; Ian Shapira, "Fauquier Heiress Selling Ashland Farm Estate," *Washington Post*, September 7, 2003.

28. Ian Shapira, "Slain Polo Player's Son Sues Heiress," *Washington Post*, January 14, 2003.

29. Michael H. Stone, *The Anatomy of Evil* (Amherst, NY: Prometheus Books, 2009), p. 66.

30. Lisa Pulitzer, A Woman Scorned: The Shocking Real-Life Case of Billionairess Killer Susan Cummings (New York: St. Martin's, 1999), p. 119.

31. Gini Graham Scott, Homicide by the Rich and Famous: A Century of Prominent Killers (Westport, CT: Praeger, 2005), p. 88.

32. Stone, *Anatomy of Evil*, p. 66.

33. Vicky Moon, The Middleburg Mystique: A Peel Inside the Gates of Middleburg, Virginia (Sterling, VA: Capital Books, 2001), p. 121.

34. Jennifer Ordonez, "Va. Heiress to Claim Self-Defense," *Washington Post*, May 5, 1998.

35. Andrew Marshall, "Wealthy Daughter of Arms Dealer Shot Her 'Violent' Lover," *Independent*, May 8, 1998, https://www.independent.co.uk/news/wealthy -daughter-of-arms-dealer-shot-her-violent-lover-1160720.html.

36. Associated Press, "Arms Heiress Convicted of Killing Boyfriend," *New York Times*, May 14, 1998, https://www.nytimes.com/1998/05/14/us/arms-heiress-convicted-of -killing-boyfriend.html.

37. Cathy Comerford, "Woman 'Driven' to Kill Husband," *Independent*, August 10, 1998, https://www.independent.co.uk/news/woman-driven-to-kill-husband-1170893 .html.

38. "Judge Frees Wife Who Was Driven to Kill Husband," *Herald*, August 10, 1998, http://www.heraldscotland.com/news/12252325.Judge_frees_wife_who _was_driven_to_kill_husband/.

39. "'Severe Conduct' Led Man to Stab Partner of 30 Years to Death, Judge Rules," *Guardian*, October 7, 2010, https://www.theguardian.com/uk/2010/oct/07/severe -conduct-stab-partner; "'Nagged' Man Jailed for Stab Death," *Powys County Times*, October 7, 2010, http://www.countytimes.co.uk/news/8439705._Nagged__man_jailed_for_stab _death/; "Hen-Pecked Man Who Killed Partner after 30 Years of Abuse Is Cleared of Murder," *Daily Mail*, October 8, 2010, http://www.dailymail.co.uk/news/article-1318754/ Hen-pecked-man-killed-partner-30-years-abuse-jailed-years-months.html.

40. Scott A. Bonn, "How Mass Murder and Serial Murder Differ: Mass Murder Is a Catastrophic, One-Time Event," *Psychology Today*, February 23, 2015, https://www .psychologytoday.com/us/blog/wicked-deeds/201502/how-mass-murder-and-serial -murder-differ.

41. David Carson, "Execution Report: Coy Wesbrook," Texas Execution Information Center, March 9, 2016, http://www.txexecutions.org/reports/535-Coy-Wesbrook.htm; Allan Turner, "Schedule to Die, Killer Says He's Better than Most on Death Row," *Houston Chronicle*, March 7, 2016, https://www.houstonchronicle.com/news/houston-texas/ houston/article/Scheduled-to-die-killer-says-he-s-better-than-6875968.php.

42. Jolie McCullough, "Man Who Killed 5 Executed Wednesday," *Texas Tribune*, March 9, 2016, https://www.texastribune.org/2016/03/09/man-who-killed-5-faces -execution-wednesday/.

43. Carson, "Execution Report."

44. Ibid.

CHAPTER THREE: CATEGORIES 7 AND 8

1. Bryan Ethier, *True Crime: New York City—The City's Most Notorious Criminal Cases* (Machanicsburg, PA: Stackpole, 2010), p. 65.

2. J. D. Salinger, *The Catcher in the Rye* (New York: Little Brown, 1951).

3. Ethier, *True Crime*, p. 66.

4. Paul Alexander, *Salinger: A Biography* (New York: St. Martin's, 1999), p. 270.

5. Ethier, *True Crime*, p. 66.

6. Alexander, *Salinger*, p. 270.

7. Ethier, *True Crime*, p. 66.

8. Alexander, *Salinger*, p. 270.

9. *Wikipedia*, s.v. "Mark David Chapman," last edited October 22, 2018, https:// en.wikipedia.org/wiki/Mark_David_Chapman; James R. Gaines, "Mark David Chapman: The Man Who Shot John Lennon," *People*, February 23, 1987.

10. Gaines, "Mark David Chapman."

11. Ibid.; *Wikipedia*, c.v. "Mark David Chapman."

12. Ibid.

13. Ibid.

14. Ibid.

15. Ibid.

16. Jeremy Meyer, "Lennon Assassin Mark David Chapman Says He Did It to Get Attention," The Know, August 29, 2012, https://theknow.denverpost.com/2012/08/29/mark-david-chapman-parole-interview/54812/.

17. Peter Vronsky, *Female Serial Killers: How and Why Women Become Monsters* (London: Penguin, 2007), p. 281.

18. Ibid., p. 282.

19. Michael Newton, *The Encyclopedia of Serial Killers*, 2nd ed. (New York: Checkmark, 2006), p. 255.

20. Ibid.

21. Steven Cook and Bill Buell, "Convicted Child Killer Marybeth Tinning Released," *Daily Gazette*, August 21, 2018, https://dailygazette.com/article/2018/08/21/marybeth-tinning-released.

22. Keith Dovkants, "The Boy Who Became a Cannibal," *Evening Standard*, January 5, 2004, https://www.standard.co.uk/news/the-boy-who-became-a-cannibal-6976790 .html; *Most Evil*, season 2, episode 14, "Vampires/Cannibals," featuring Dr. Michael H. Stone and Tim Hopper, aired February 21, 2008, on Investigation Discovery, https:// www.investigationdiscovery.com/tv-shows/most-evil/full-episodes/vampire -cannibal; "The German Cannibal Files," Crime & Investigation, http://www .crimeandinvestigation.co.uk/crime-files/armin-meiwes-german-cannibal.

23. Ibid.

24. Roisin O'Connor, "Armin Meiwes: Interview with a Cannibal Documentary Sheds New Light on One of Germany's Most Infamous Murders," *Independent*, February 6, 2016, https://www.independent.co.uk/news/world/europe/armin-meiwes -interview-with-a-cannibal-documentary-sheds-new-light-on-one-of-germany-s-most -infamous-a6863201.html; ""

25. *Most Evil*, "Vampires/Cannibals"; *Wikipedia*, s.v. "Armin Meiwes," last edited October 28, 2018, https://en.wikipedia.org/wiki/Armin_Meiwes.

26. *Wikipedia*, s.v. "Armin Meiwes"; O'Connor, "Armin Meiwes"; "The German Cannibal Files," Crime & Investigation; "Cannibal's Video of 'Victim's' Final Hours Played to Court," *Scotsman*, December 9, 2003, https://www.scotsman.com/news/world/cannibal-s-video-of-victim-s-final-hours-played-to-court-1-497095.

27. "Cannibal's Video of 'Victim's' Final Hours"; O'Connor, "Armin Meiwes"; *Most Evil*, "Vampires/Cannibals"; Wikipedia, s.v. "Armin Meiwes."

28. *Criminal Minds Wiki*, s.v. "George Hennard," http://criminalminds.wikia.com/wiki/George_Hennard.

29. Don Terry, "Portrait of Texas Killer: Impatient and Troubled," *New York Times*, October 18, 1991.

30. Mara Bovsun, "Luby's Massacre in Texas Has Eerie Link to Robin Williams' Movie 'The Fisher King,'" *Daily News* (New York), September 20, 2014.

31. H. Thomas Milhorn, *Crime: Computer Viruses to Twin Towers* (Boca Raton, FL: Universal, 2005), p. 179.

32. Bovsun, "Luby's Massacre"; Ron Franscell, *Delivered from Evil: True Stories of Ordinary People Who Faced Monstrous Mass Killers and Survived* (Beverly, MA: Fair Winds, 2011), p. 102.

33. William Booth, "Texas Killer Said to Have 'Problem with Women,'" *Washington*

Post, October 18, 1991, https://www.washingtonpost.com/archive/politics/1991/10/18/texas-killer-said-to-have-problem-with-women/0af79d27-5ed2-4a1a-afb2-f6a38e9c32c2/?utm_term=.cf56a0399e80.

34. Paula Chin, "A Texas Massacre," *People*, November 4, 1991, http://people.com/archive/a-texas-massacre-vol-36-no-17/.

35. J. Michael Kennedy and Richard A. Serrano, "Police May Never Learn What Motivated Gunman Massacre: Hennard Was Seen as Reclusive, Belligerent. Officials Are Looking into Possibility He Hated Women," *Los Angeles Times*, October 18, 1991.

36. Franscell, *Delivered from Evil*, pp. 102–103.

37. Bovsun, "Luby's Massacre."

38. Bovsun, "Luby's Massacre"; *Criminal Minds Wiki*, s.v. "George Hennard."

39. Chin, "Texas Massacre."

40. Milhorn, *Crime*, p. 179.

41. *Criminal Minds Wiki*, s.v. "George Hennard."

42. Lawrence Wright, "Taking Cover in Texas," *New Yorker*, May 14, 2013, https://www.newyorker.com/news/daily-comment/taking-cover-in-texas.

CHAPTER FOUR: CATEGORIES 9–14

1. Hervey M. Cleckley, *The Mask of Sanity* (Maryland Heights, MO: C.V. Mosby, 1941).

2. *Encyclopedia.com*, c.v. "Hare Psychopathy Checklist," last updated November 2, 2018, https://www.encyclopedia.com/psychology/encyclopedias-almanacs-transcripts-and-maps/hare-psychopathy-checklist; Robert D. Hare, *Without Conscience: The Disturbing World of the Psychopaths among Us* (New York: Guilford, 1993).

3. Robert Siciliano, "Psychopath vs. Sociopath: What's the Difference?" *Huffington Post*, last updated November 24, 2014, https://www.huffingtonpost.com/robert-siciliano/what-is-a-sociopath_b_5877160.html.

4. American Psychiatric Association, *Diagnostic and Statistical Manual of Mental Disorders: DSM-5* (Arlington, VA: American Psychiatric Press, 2013), pp. 659–63.

5. Ibid.; pp. 469-471.

6. *Wikipedia*, s.v. "Psychopathy Checklist," last updated October 16, 2018, https://en.wikipedia.org/wiki/Psychopathy_Checklist.

7. M. J. Rutherford, J. S. Cacciola, and A. I. Alterman, "Antisocial Personality Disorder and Psychopathy in Cocaine-Dependent Women," *American Journal of Psychiatry* 156, no. 6 (1999): 849–56.

8. *Wikipedia*, s.v. "Psychopathy Checklist."

9. Danielle Egan, "Into the Mind of a Psychopath," *Discover*, May 4, 2016, http://discovermagazine.com/2016/june/12-psychopath-and-the-hare.

10. Julian C. Motzkin, Joseph P. Newman, Kent A. Kiehl, and Michael Koenigs, "Reduced Prefrontal Connectivity in Psychopathy," *Journal of Neuroscience* 31, no. 48 (2011): 17348–57.

11. Jay G. Hosking, Erik K. Kastman, Hayley M. Dorfman, et al., "Disrupted Prefrontal Regulation of Striatal Subjective Value Signals in Psychopathy," *Neuron* 95, no. 1 (2017): 221–31.

12. Cleckley, *The Mask of Sanity*; B. Karpman, "The Myth of the Psychopathic Personality," *American Journal of Psychiatry* 104 (1948): 523–34.

13. Hare, *Without Conscience*, pp. 192–206.

14. George C. Cohn, ed., *The New Encyclopedia of American Scandal* (New York: Facts on File, 2000), p. 364; Teresa Carpenter, "Death of a Playmate," *Village Voice* 25, no. 45 (November 5–11, 1980): 1, 12–17.

15. Carpenter, "Death of a Playmate."

16. Ibid.; Cohn, *New Encyclopedia of American Scandal*, p. 364.

17. Cohn, *New Encyclopedia of American Scandal*.

18. Ibid.; Carpenter, "Death of Playmate."

19. Carpenter, "Death of a Playmate."

20. Ibid.

21. Jane Caputi, *The Age of Sex Crime* (Bowling Green, OH: Bowling Green University Popular Press, 1987), p. 175.

22. Dariel Figueroa, "The Pimp, the Playmate, and Peter: How a Famed Hollywood Director Lost the Love of His Life to Jealousy," UPROXX, https://uproxx.com/movies/story-behind-dorothy-stratten-tragic-murder/.

23. John Gardner, "'I Am Not the Monster Society Thinks I Am': Child Killer Susan Smith Who Murdered Her Young Sons and Feigned Their Kidnap by a Black Man Tries to Explain Herself on 20th Anniversary of Her Life Sentence," *Daily Mail*, July 22, 2015, http://www.dailymail.co.uk/news/article-3171009/I-not-monster-society-thinks-Child-killer-Susan-Smith-murdered-young-sons-feigned-kidnap-black-man-tries-explain-20th-anniversary-life-sentence.html; Charles Montaldo, "Profile of Child Killer Susan Smith: The Tragic South Carolina Case of the Murders and Michael and Alexander Smith," Thought Co., April 1, 2018, https://www.thoughtco.com/susan-smith-profile-of-child-killer-972686.

24. Montaldo, "Profile of Child Killer."

25. Ibid.; Rick Bragg, "Mother in South Carolina Guilty of Murder in Drowning 2 Sons," *New York Times*, July 23, 1995; Gardner, "'I Am Not the Monster Society Thinks I Am.'"

26. Rick Bragg, "Arguments Begin in Susan Smith Trial," *New York Times*, July 19, 1995. Hannah Parry, "Child Killer Susan Smith's Secret Life of Sex and Drugs Behind Bars While She Serves Life for Drowning Her Two Sons," *Daily Mail*, September 26, 2017, http://www.dailymail.co.uk/news/article-4923748/Susan-Smith-s-secret-life-sex-drugs-bars.html.

27. Elizabeth Gleick, "Sex, Betrayal and Murder," *Time*, June 24, 2001, http://content.time.com/time/magazine/article/0,9171,134423,00.html; Montaldo, "Profile of Child Killer."

28. Montaldo, "Profile of Child Killer."

29. Gleick, "Sex, Betrayal and Murder."

30. Parry, "Child Killer Susan Smith's Secret Life"; Montaldo, "Profile of Child Killer."

31. *The Encyclopedia of Arkansas History & Culture*, s.v. "Ronald Gene Simmons," last updated December 21, 2017, http://www.encyclopediaofarkansas.net/encyclopedia/entry-detail.aspx?entryID=3731 (accessed April 2, 2018).

32. Ibid.

33. "Incest, Abuse Dark Background of Killings," *Bangor Daily News*, December 31, 1987; "The Father from Hell," *New York Daily News*, December 13, 2008, https://www.nydailynews.com/news/crime/father-hell-article-1.354501.

34. Ibid.

35. "Twenty-Seven Years Later: The Horrific Story of 16 Murders," *Red River Leader*, December 29, 2014, http://www.rivervalleyleader.com/life_in_the_river_valley/article_3fab88f0-8fda-11e4-9c08-b3bd14fc427a.html.

36. Ibid.

37. *Wikipedia*, s.v. "Ronald Gene Simmons," last updated October 18, 2018, https://en.wikipedia.org/wiki/Ronald_Gene_Simmons; Michael Buchanan, "December 28, 1987, Ronald Simmons Kills 2, Later 14 Bodies of Relatives Discovered, Today in Crime History," December 27, 2011, https://reasonabledoubt.org/criminallawblog/entry/december-28-1987-ronald-gene-simmons-kills-2-later-14-bodies-of-relatives-discovered-today-in-crime-history.

38. "Twenty-Seven Years Later," *Red River Leader*.

39. *Encyclopedia of Arkansas History*, s.v. "Ronald Gene Simmons."

40. Scott A. Bonn, "Why Spree Killers Are Not Serial Killers," *Psychology Today*, July 21, 2014, https://www.psychologytoday.com/us/blog/wicked-deeds/201407/why-spree-killers-are-not-serial-killers.

41. "Twenty-Seven Years Later," *Red River Leader*.

42. Clark County Prosecutor, "Ronald Gene Simmons: Executed June 25, 1990 by Lethal Injection in Arkansas," http://www.clarkprosecutor.org/html/death/US/simmons131.htm.

43. Terry Frieden, "Two Convicted, Two Acquitted in Suburban Virginia Street Gang Trial," CNN, May 17, 2005, http://www.cnn.com/2005/LAW/05/17/ms13.trial.verdicts/index.html?_s=PM:LAW; Matthew Brzezinski, "Hillbangers," *New York Times Magazine*, August 15, 2004.

44. Brzezinski, "Hillbangers."

45. Maria Glod, "Prosecutors Describe Gang-Style Execution," *Washington Post*, November 6, 2003.

46. Brzezinski, "Hillbangers."

47. Associated Press, "2 MS-13 Gang Members Guilty of Murder," NBC News, May 17, 2005, http://www.nbcnews.com/id/7889812/ns/us_news-crime_and_courts/t/ms--gang-members-guilty-murder/#.WssR4ojwb7k.

48. "MS-13 Jurors Told Not to Seek Advice," *Washington Times*, June 9, 2005, https://www.washingtontimes.com/news/2005/jun/9/20050609-105044-1525r/.

49. *Most Evil*, season 2, episode 17, "Gangs," featuring Dr. Michael H. Stone and Neal Dudgeon, aired on March 13, 2008, on Investigation Discovery, https://www.investigationdiscovery.com/tv-shows/most-evil/full-episodes/gangs; "Background for Ismael Cisneros (26 Years Old)," (Austin, TX: Briscoe Center for American History), https://danratherjournalist.org/investigative-journalist/60-minutes/ms-13/document-ms-13-ismael-cisneros-background (accessed April 2, 2018).

50. Jamie Stockwell, "In MS-13, a Culture of Brutality and Begging," *Washington Post*, May 2, 2005; Jerry Markon, "Gang Trial Witness Flees But Is Caught," *Washington Post*, March 29, 2005; "Background on Ismael Cisneros."

51. "Background on Ismael Cisneros."

52. Jamie Stockwell, "Convicted Gang Members Urged to Help Teens," *Washington Post*, September 10, 2005.

53. Dan Harris, "What Do Mormons Believe?" ABC News, August 22, 2012, http://abcnews.go.com/US/mormons-/story?id=17057679 (accessed April 3, 2018).

54. "The Fourteen Fundamental Articles or Beliefs of Mormons," Index Page of Mormonism, http://main.nc.us/spchurchofchrist/fourteenfund.htm.

55. Laurie Goodstein, "It's Official: Mormon Founder Had Up to 40 Wives," *New York Times*, November 10, 2014.

56. Janet Bennion, *Desert Patriarchy: Mormon and Mennonite Communities in the Chihuahua Valley* (Tucson: University of Arizona Press, 2004), pp. 55–57.

57. Ibid.; Julia Scheeres, "Killing for God: Ervil LeBaron Story," Cult Education Institute, August 15, 2006, https://www.culteducation.com/group/1099-polygamist -groups/16860-killing-for-god.html.

58. Sheeres, "Killing for God."

59. Ibid.

60. Ibid.

61. Ibid.

62. *Wikipedia*, s.v. "Rulon C. Allred," last edited October 11, 2018, https://en .wikipedia.org/wiki/Rulon_C._Allred.

63. Scheeres, "Killing for God."

64. Ibid.

65. Ibid.

66. Scott Anderson, *The Four O'Clock Murders: A True Story of a Mormon Family's Vengeance* (New York: Doubleday, 1993), p. 129.

67. Scheeres, "Killing for God"; Lee Davidson, "Ervil's Followers Murder Routinely in 20 Years, 18 Ex-Associates Have Been Slain or Reported Missing," *Deseret News* (Salt Lake City, UT), June 28, 1988.

68. "Grisley Tale of Polygamist Cults and Killers," *Washington Post*, January 12, 1982, https://www.washingtonpost.com/archive/lifestyle/1982/01/12/grisley-tale-of -polygamist-cults-and-killers/1278869d-425c-4ce3-8cf2-a37ddc6d78a8/; Scheeres, "Killing for God."

69. Scheeres, "Killing for God"; Brooke Adams, "Polygamous Murderer Denied Parole," *Salt Lake Tribune*, February 3, 2007.

70. Scheeres, "Killing for God"; "The Nation: A Deadly Messenger of God," *Time* 110, no. 9 (August 29, 1977), http://content.time.com/time/magazine/0,9263 ,7601770829,00.html; Davidson, "Ervil's Followers Murdered Routinely"; James Coates, "Polygamy, Slayings Link Mormon Cults," *Chicago Tribune*, December 6, 1987.

71. Scheeres, "Killing for God"; *Wikipedia*, s.v. "Rulon C. Allred."

72. Joel Campbell and Lee Davidson, "4 Murders in Texas Linked to LeBarons," *Deseret News* (Salt Lake City, UT), June 28, 1988.

73. Kirsten Scharnberg, Evan Osnos, and David Mendell, "The Making of a Racist," *Chicago Tribune*, July 25, 1999.

74. "Suspected Shooter Said His Hate-Filled Leaflets Spoke 'The Truth'," CNN, July 6, 1999, http://www.cnn.com/US/9907/06/smith.profile.01/.

75. Scharnberg, Osnos and Mendell, "Making of a Racist," *Chicago Tribune*.

76. Ibid.

77. "Suspected Shooter."

78. Bill Dedman, "Midwest Gunman Had Engaged in Racist Acts at 2 Universities," *New York Times*, July 6, 1999; Jeff Elliott, "Benjamin 'August' Smith: Poised to Kill," *Albion Monitor*, July 26, 1999, http://www.albionmonitor.com/9907a/wcotc.html.

79. *Wikipedia*, s.v. "Benjamin Nathaniel Smith," last edited May 24, 2018, https://en.wikipedia.org/wiki/Benjamin_Nathaniel_Smith.

80. Dedman, "Midwest Gunman."

81. Elliott, "Benjamin 'August' Smith."

82. Kirsten Scharnberg and Ray Long, "Killer's Parents: We Didn't Teach Hate," *Chicago Tribune*, August 27, 1999.

83. Elliott, "Benjamin 'August' Smith."

84. Scharnberg, Osnos, and Mendell, "Making of a Racist."

85. Michael Newton, *The Encyclopedia of Serial Killers*, 2nd ed. (New York: Checkmark, 2006), p. 93; *Criminal Minds Wiki*, s.v. "Ed Gein," http://criminalminds.wikia.com/wiki/Ed_Gein.

86. *Criminal Minds Wiki*, s.v. "Ed Gein"; Newton, *Encyclopedia of Serial Killers*; Anil Aggrawal, *Necrophilia: Forensic and Medico-Legal Aspects* (Boca Raton, FL: CRC Press, 2011), p. 133.

87. Newton, *Encyclopedia of Serial Killers*.

88. Devan Sagliani, "The Mad Butcher Who Inspired *Silence of the Lambs* & *Psycho*," *Escapist*, November 6, 2015, http://www.escapistmagazine.com/articles/view/comics andcosplay/columns/darkdreams/14936-Who-Was-Ed-Gein-The-Mad-Butcher-of -Plainfield.

89. Newton, *Encyclopedia of Serial Killers*; Aggrawal, *Necrophilia*, p. 134.

90. Newton, *Encyclopedia of Serial Killers*, p. 94; Aggrawal, *Necrophilia*.

91. Ibid.

92. Ibid.; *Criminal Minds Wiki*, s.v. "Ed Gein."

93. Newton, *Encyclopedia of Serial Killers*, p. 94–95.

94. Ibid., p. 94.

95. *Criminal Minds Wiki*, s.v. "Ed Gein."

96. *Wikipedia*, s.v. "flaying," last edited November 20, 2018, https://en.wikipedia .org/wiki/Flaying.

97. *New World Encyclopedia*, s.v. "Saint Bartholomew," last edited August 5, 2015, http://www.newworldencyclopedia.org/entry/Saint_Bartholomew.

98. Ernst G. Jung, ed., *Kleine Kulturgeschichte der Haut* (Darmstadt, Germany: Steinkopff-Verlag Darmstadt, 2007), p. 69.

99. Martin Gilman Wolcott, *The Evil 100* (New York: Citadel Press, 2002), pp. 61-63.

100. State v. Ryan, 444 N.W.2d 610 (1989); "State vs. Ryan," *Justia*, https://law .justia.com/cases/nebraska/supreme-court/1989/946-0.html.

101. "Report: Son Dismembered Dad after Being Raped," *Denver 7 & The Denver Channel*, May 16, 2008, https://www.thedenverchannel.com/news/report-son -dismembered-dad-after-being-raped.

102. *Criminal Minds Wiki*, s.v. "Sante Kimes," http://criminalminds.wikia.com/wiki/Sante_Kimes.

103. Michael H. Stone, *The Anatomy of Evil* (Amherst, NY: Prometheus Books, 2009), p. 136.

104. *Criminal Minds Wiki*, s.v. "Sante Kimes."

105. Ibid.

106. Kent Walker and Mark Schone, *Son of a Grifter: The Twisted Tale of Sante and Kenny Kimes, the Most Notorious Con Artists in America* (New York: Avon, 2001), p. 14.

107. Stone, *Anatomy of Evil*, p. 136.

108. *Criminal Minds Wiki*, s.v. "Sante Kimes."

109. Adrian Havill, *The Mother, the Son, and the Socialite: The True Story of a Mother-Son Crime Spree* (New York: St. Martin's, 1999), p. 98; *Mysteries of the Criminal Mind: The Secrets Behind the World's Most Notorious Crimes* (New York: Time Life Books, 2015), pp. 98–99.

110. Jeanne King, *Dead End: The Crime Story of the Decade; Murder, Incest and High-Tech Thievery* (New York: M. Evans, 2002), p. 324.

111. Leanne Phillips, "Modern Day Grifters: The Sante and Kenneth Kimes Story," LegalZoom, https://www.legalzoom.com/articles/modern-day-grifters-the-sante-and-kenneth-kimes-story.

112. *Criminal Minds Wiki*, s.v. "Sante Kimes"; Annie Groer and Ann Gerhart, "The Reliable Source," *Washington Post*, July 21, 1998, https://www.washingtonpost.com/archive/lifestyle/1998/07/21/the-reliable-source/585b64c6-dd63-4b5e-8993-f6cbeed84432/?utm_term=.3cded33d9bd0.

113. *Wikipedia*, s.v. "Sante Kimes," last edited November 10, 2018, https://en.wikipedia.org/wiki/Sante_Kimes; *Criminal Minds Wiki*, s.v. "Sante Kimes."

114. Phillips, "Modern Day Grifters."

115. Ibid.; *Wikipedia*, s.v. "Santa Kimes"; "Son against Mother in Murder Trial," *Los Angeles Times*, June 15, 2004, http://articles.latimes.com/2004/jun/15/local/me-kimes15.

116. Larry McShane, "Murder, Grifting Mastermind Sante Kimes Dead in Prison at 79," *Daily News* (New York), May 20, 2014; Thomas J. Lueck, "Murderer Reveals New Details in Slaying of Socialite in 1998," *New York Times*, June 24, 2004.

117. *Criminal Minds Wiki*, s.v. "Sante Kimes"; Phillips, "Modern Day Grifters."

118. Phillips, "Modern Day Grifters."

119. *Criminal Minds Wiki*, s.v. "Sante Kimes."

120. Phillips, "Modern Day Grifters."

121. King, *Dead End*, pp. 250–51.

122. *Criminal Minds Wiki*, s.v. "Richard Farley," http://criminalminds.wikia.com/wiki/Richard_Farley; *Most Evil*, season 2, episode 2, "Stalker," featuring Dr. Michael H. Stone and Neil Dudgeon, aired on August 19, 2007, on Investigation Discovery, https://www.investigationdiscovery.com/tv-shows/most-evil/full-episodes/stalker.

123. John Douglas and Mark Olshaker, *Obsession: The FBI's Legendary Profiler Probes the Psyches of Killers, Rapists, and Stalkers and Their Victims and Tells How to Fight Back* (New York: Pocket, 1998), p. 309.

124. *Most Evil*, "Stalker."

125. *Criminal Minds Wiki*, s.v. "Richard Farley."

126. *Most Evil*, "Stalker."

127. Douglas and Olshaker, *Obsession*, pp. 295–96; *Criminal Minds Wiki*, s.v. "Richard Farley."

128. *Criminal Minds Wiki*, s.v. "Richard Farley"; Douglas and Olshaker, *Obsession*, p. 296.

129. Douglas and Olshaker, *Obsession*, p. 299 and 301; *Criminal Minds Wiki*, s.v. "Richard Farley"; Charles Montaldo, "Mass Murderer Richard Wade Farley: Stalking

and Workplace Violence," Thought Co., April 1, 2017, https://www.thoughtco.com/mass-murderer-richard-wade-farley-973100.

130. *Criminal Minds Wiki*, s.v. "Richard Farley"; Douglas and Olshaker, *Obsession*, pp. 301–304.

131. Douglas and Olshaker, *Obsession*, p. 305.

132. Ibid., pp. 305–306.

133. Ibid., pp. 306–308; *Criminal Minds Wiki*, s.v. "Richard Farley."

134. Montaldo, "Mass Murderer Richard Wade Farley."

135. Ibid.; Douglas and Olshaker, *Obsession*, pp. 308–309; Michael D. Kelleher, *Profiling the Lethal Employee: Case Studies of Violence in the Workplace* (Westport, CT: Praeger, 1997), p. 46.

136. Michael Molinski, "Witnesses Describe Shooting Rampage," United Press International, July 21, 1988, https://www.upi.com/Archives/1988/07/21/Witnesses-describe-shooting-rampage/8450585460800/.

137. *Criminal Minds Wiki*, s.v. "Richard Farley."

138. Kelleher, *Profiling the Lethal Employee*, p. 46.

139. *Criminal Minds Wiki*, s.v. "Richard Farley."

140. Ibid.

141. *Wikipedia*, s.v. "Robert John Bardo," last edited October 30, 2018, https://en.wikipedia.org/wiki/Robert_John_Bardo.

142. *Criminal Minds Wiki*, s.v. "Richard Farley."

CHAPTER FIVE: CATEGORIES 15 AND 16

1. *Criminal Minds Wiki*, s.v. "Andrew Cunanan," http://criminalminds.wikia.com/wiki/Andrew_Cunanan; *Most Evil*, season 2, episode 1, "Jealousy," featuring Dr. Michael H. Stone and Tim Hopper, aired on August 12, 2007, on Investigation Discovery, https://www.investigationdiscovery.com/tv-shows/most-evil/full-episodes/jealousy; John Douglas and Mark Olshaker, *Anatomy of Motive: The FBI's Legendary Mindhunter Explores the Key to Understanding and Catching Violent Criminals* (New York: Pocket, 1999), p. 241.

2. Douglas and Olshaker, *Anatomy of Motive*, p. 242; *Criminal Minds Wiki*, s.v. "Andrew Cunanan."

3. *Criminal Minds Wiki*, s.v. "Andrew Cunanan"; *Most Evil*, "Jealousy"; Douglas and Olshaker, *Anatomy of Motive*, pp. 243–44.

4. Douglas and Olshaker, *Anatomy of Motive*, p. 245; *Criminal Minds Wiki*, s.v. "Andrew Cunanan."

5. Douglas and Olshaker, *Anatomy of Motive*, pp. 246–47; *Criminal Minds Wiki*, s.v. "Andrew Cunanan."

6. Douglas and Olshaker, *Anatomy of Motive*, pp. 247–52.

7. Ibid., p. 250; *Criminal Minds Wiki*, s.v. "Andrew Cunanan."

8. Ibid.; Douglas and Olshaker, *Anatomy of Motive*, pp. 252–53; Maureen Orth, "The Killer's Trail," *Vanity Fair*, September 1997.

9. Dave Saltonstall, "A Nice Guy Caught in a Torturous Tale," *Daily News*, July 20, 1997, http://www.nydailynews.com/archives/news/nice-guy-caught-tortuous-tale

-article-1.774258; "Cunanan Left a Trail of Lies and Deception," *Journal Times*, July 19, 1997, http://journaltimes.com/news/national/cunanan-left-a-trail-of-lies-and -deception/article_5223b7a6-76eb-5f57-b46b-048fa3aa5a24.html; Douglas and Olshaker, *Anatomy of Motive*, pp. 256–57.

10. *Criminal Minds Wiki*, s.v. "Andrew Cunanan."

11. Ibid.; Douglas and Olshaker, *Anatomy of Motive*, pp. 260–61.

12. Douglas and Olshaker, *Anatomy of Motive*, p. 261.

13. Ibid., p. 264.

14. Associated Press, "Cunanan Was HIV Negative, Paper Says," *Los Angeles Times*, August 1, 1997, http://articles.latimes.com/1997/aug/01/news/mn-18398.

15. Rich Connell, "Dorothea Puente Dies at 82; Boarding House Operator Who Killed Tenants," *Los Angeles Times*, March 28, 2011; *Wikipedia*, s.v. "Dorothea Puente," last edited November 7, 2018, https://en.wikipedia.org/wiki/Dorothea_Puente.

16. *Wikipedia*, s.v. "Dorothea Puente"; "Background of Serial Killer Dorothea Puente," *World History*, July 24, 2017, https://worldhistory.us/american-history/ background-of-serial-killer-dorothea-puente.php.

17. Martin Kuz, "The Life and Deaths of Dorothea Puente," *Sactown Magazine*, http://www.sactownmag.com/August-September-2009/The-Life-and -Deaths-of-Dorothea-Puente/.

18. Ibid.; "Background of Serial Killer Dorothea Puente."

19. Kuz, "Life and Deaths of Dorothea Puente."

20. *Wikipedia*, s.v. "Dorothea Puente."

21. Ibid.

22. Ibid.; Sheree R. Curry, "Serial Killer's California Home Is to Die For," AOL News, March 1, 2010, https://www.aol.com/2010/03/01/serial-killers-california -home-is-to-die-for/.

23. Paul Duggan, "Ex-Boyfriend Convicted in Slaying-Mutilation of Mother, Daughter," *Washington Post*, August 16, 1994; Henri E. Cauvin, "Aftermath of a Savage Scene," *Washington Post*, March 6, 2007.

24. Stanley Semrau and Judy Gale, *Murderous Minds on Trial: Terrible Tales from a Forensic Psychiatrist's Case Book* (Toronto: Dundurn, 2002), p. 59; *Most Evil*, season 3, episode 9, "Attention Seekers," featuring Dr. Michael H. Stone and Neil Dudgeon, aired on January 30, 2015, on Investigation Discovery, https://www.investigationdiscovery.com/ tv-shows/most-evil/full-episodes/attention-seekers.

25. *Most Evil*, "Attention Seekers"; "One Woman's Journey from Horror to Helping," *Oliver Chronicle* (Oliver, British Columbia), April 16, 2014.

26. Semrau and Gale, *Murderous Minds on Trial*, pp. 56–57; *Most Evil*, "Attention Seekers."

27. Semrau and Gale, *Murderous Minds on Trial*, p. 58.

28. Ibid., p. 58; "One Woman's Journey."

29. Michael Newton, *The Encyclopedia of Serial Killers*, 2nd ed. (New York: Checkmark, 2006), p. 99.

30. Ibid.

31. Ibid., p. 100; *Wikipedia*, s.v. "Gwendolyn Graham and Cathy Wood," last edited October 27, 2018, https://en.wikipedia.org/wiki/Gwendolyn_Graham _and_Cathy_Wood.

32. *Wikipedia*, s.v. "Gwendolyn Graham"; Newton, *Encyclopedia of Serial Killers*, p. 100.

33. Newton, *Encyclopedia of Serial Killers*, pp. 100–101; *Wikipedia*, s.v. "Gwendolyn Graham."

34. Lowell Cauffiel, *Forever and Five Days* (New York: Pinnacle, 1992).

35. *Criminal Minds Wiki*, s.v. "Heriberto Seda," http://criminalminds.wikia.com/wiki/Heriberto_Seda.

36. *Wikipedia*, s.v. "Kobe Child Murders," last edited July 17, 2018, https://en.wikipedia.org/wiki/Kobe_child_murders.

37. Tom Voight, "Zodiac Suspects," ZodiacKiller.com, http://zodiackiller.com/Suspects.html; Robert Graysmith, *Zodiac: The Shocking True Story of the Hunt for the Nation's Most Elusive Serial Killer* (New York: St. Martin's, 1976).

38. Graysmith, *Zodiac*; Tom Voight, "Zodiac Letters and Ciphers," ZodiacKiller.com, http://zodiackiller.com/Letters.html.

39. Graysmith, *Zodiac*, pp. 168–69.

40. Ibid., pp. 175–76.

41. Ibid., pp. 170–71.

42. Ibid., p. 170.

43. Ibid., pp. 171–72.

44. Ibid., pp. 1–12.

45. Ibid., pp. 22–33.

46. Ibid.

47. Ibid., p. 34.

48. Ibid., pp. 47–49.

49. Ibid., pp. 51–55.

50. Ibid., pp. 60–61.

51. Ibid., pp. 56–57.

52. Ibid., pp. 62–73.

53. "Zodiac the Killer," *Tuscaloosa News*, October 27, 1969.

54. Graysmith, *Zodiac*, pp. 76–77.

55. "Girl Dies of Stabbing at Berryessa," *San Francisco Chronicle*, September 30, 1969.

56. Graysmith, *Zodiac*, pp. 77–78.

57. Ibid., pp. 82–92.

58. Ibid., p. 102.

59. Ibid., p. 121.

60. Ibid., pp. 122–26.

61. John Douglas and Mark Olshaker, *The Cases That Haunt Us* (New York: Lisa Drew/Scribner, 2000), pp. 219–21.

62. Graysmith, *Zodiac*, p. 126.

63. Ibid., pp. 127–28.

64. Douglas and Olshaker, *Cases That Haunt Us*, p. 224.

65. Graysmith, *Zodiac*, pp. 144–45.

66. Ibid., p. 150.

67. Jim Herron Zamora, "1967–1971—A Bloody Period for S.F. Police," *SF Gate*, January 27, 2007, https://www.sfgate.com/news/article/1967-71-a-bloody-period-for-S-F-police-2654263.php.

68. Graysmith, *Zodiac*, pp. 147–48.

69. Ibid., p. 152.

70. Ibid., pp. 134–40.

71. Ibid., pp. 152–53.

72. Ibid., pp. 158–62.

73. Ibid., p. 176.

74. Ibid., p. 183.

75. Ibid., p. 196.

76. "Theodore Kaczynski 'The Unabomber,'" Zodiac Ciphers, https://www
.zodiacciphers.com/theodore-kaczynski.html.

77. *Wikipedia*, s.v. "Zodiac Killer," last edited November 2, 2018, https://en
.wikipedia.org/wiki/Zodiac_Killer.

78. Kiki Intarasuwan and Jodi Hernandez, "Investigators Renew Hope in Finding
Zodiac Killer with DNA: Report," NBC Bay Area, May 3, 2018, https://www
.nbcbayarea.com/news/local/Investigators-Renew-Hope-in-Finding-Zodiac-Killer-With
-DNA-Report-481639931.html.

79. Douglas and Olshaker, *Cases That Haunt Us*, p. 232.

CHAPTER SIX: SERIAL MURDER

1. R. J. Morton, *Serial Murder: Multi-Disciplinary Perspectives for Investigators*
(Washington, DC: Federal Bureau of Investigation, 2005), pp. 4–5.

2. Ibid., p. 3.

3. Ibid., p. 4.

4. Michael G. Aamodt, Terry Leary, and Larry Southard, *Radford/FGCU Annual
Report on Serial Killer Statistics: 2018* (Radford, VA: Radford University, 2018), p. 5.

5. Ibid., p. 36.

6. Michael G. Aamodt, "Serial Killer Statistics" (Radford, VA: Radford University/
FGCU Serial Killer Database, September 4, 2016), p. 10, http://maamodt.asp.radford
.edu/serial killer information center/project.

7. Morton, *Serial Murder*," p. 5.

8. Ibid., pp. 5–6; Scott Bonn, "5 Myths about Serial Killers and Why They
Persist [Excerpt]: A Criminologist Contrasts the Stories Surrounding Serial
Homicide with Real Data to Help Explain Society's Macabre Fascination with These
Tales," *Scientific American*, October 24, 2014, https://www.scientificamerican.com/
article/5-myths-about-serial-killers-and-why-they-persist-excerpt/.

9. Aamodt, Leary, and Southard, *Radford/FGCU Annual Report*, p. 48.

10. Morton, *Serial Murder*," pp. 5–6.

11. Ibid., p. 6; Stephanie Slifer, "Serial Killers: Rare in Real Life, Prominent in
Pop Culture," CBS News, October 22, 2014, https://www.cbsnews.com/news/serial
-killers-rare-in-real-life-prominent-in-pop-culture/.

12. Aamodt, Leary, and Southard, *Radford/FGCU Annual Report*, pp. 28–29.

13. Ibid., p. 24.

14. Ibid., p. 67.

15. Ibid., pp. 68–69.

16. Ibid., p. 66.

17. Ibid.

18. Ibid., pp. 73–74.

19. Ibid., p. 70.

20. Morton, *Serial Murder*," p. 17.

21. Ibid., pp. 17–18.

22. Michael H. Stone, *The Anatomy of Evil* (Amherst, NY: Prometheus Books, 2009), p. 143.

23. John E. Douglas, Ann W. Burgess, Allen G. Burgess, and Robert K. Ressler, *Crime Classification Model: A Standard System for Investigating and Classifying Violent Crimes*, 3rd ed. (Hoboken, NJ: John Wiley & Sons, 2013).

24. Peter Vronsky, *Serial Killers: The Method and Madness of Monsters* (New York: Berkley, 2004), pp. 100–101.

25. Ibid., p. 101.

26. Ibid., p. 102.

27. Vronsky, *Serial Killers*, pp. 147–201.

28. Morton, *Serial Murder*," p. 18.

29. Ibid.

30. Aamodt, Leary and Southard, *Radford/FGCU Annual Report*, p. 77.

31. Ibid., p. 15.

32. Ibid., p. 18.

33. Ibid., p. 15.

34. Christopher Beam, "Blood Loss: The Decline of the Serial Killer," *Slate*, January 5, 2011, http://www.slate.com/articles/news_and_politics/crime/2011/01/blood_loss.html.

35. Vronsky, *Serial Killers*, pp. 269-85; Stone, *Anatomy of Evil*, pp. 200–18.

36. Aamodt, Leary and Southard, *Radford/FGCU Annual Report*, p. 54.

37. Morton, *Serial Murder*," pp. 10–11.

38. Vronsky, *Serial Killers*, pp. 269–85.

39. John M. MacDonald, "The Threat to Kill," *American Journal of Psychiatry* 120, no. 2 (August 1963): 125–30.

40. Katherine Ramsland, "Triad of Evil: Do Three Simple Behaviors Predict the Murder-Prone Child?" *Psychology Today*, May 16, 2012, https://www.psychologytoday.com/us/blog/shadow-boxing/201203/triad-evil.

41. Jennifer L. Murray, "The Role of Sexual, Sadistic, and Misogynistic Fantasy in Mass and Serial Killing," *Deviant Behavior* 38, no. 7 (2017): 735–43; Scott A. Bonn, "Serial Killers and the Essential Role of Fantasy: Obsessive Fantasies Drive Serial Killers to Murder Repeatedly," *Psychology Today*, October 13, 2014, https://www.psychologytoday.com/us/blog/wicked-deeds/201410/serial-killers-and-the-essential-role-fantasy.

42. Catherine E. Purcell and Bruce A. Arrigo, *The Psychology of Lust Murder* (Burlington, MA; San Diego, CA; London, UK: Academic Press, 2006), pp. 3–7.

CHAPTER SEVEN: CATEGORY 17

1. The Federal Bureau of Investigation, Criminal Justice Information Services Division, "2016 Crime in the United States: Rape," https://ucr.fbi.gov/crime-in-the-u.s/2016/crime-in-the-u.s.-2016/topic-pages/rape.

2. John E. Douglas, Ann W. Burgess, Allen G. Burgess, and Robert K. Ressler, *Crime Classification Model: A Standard System for Investigating and Classifying Violent Crimes*, 3rd ed. (Hoboken, NJ: John Wiley & Sons, 2013); Ann Wolbert Burgess and Robert R. Hazelwood, "The Victim's Perspective," in *Practical Aspects of Rape Investigation: A Multidisciplinary Approach*, 3rd ed. (Boca Raton, FL: CRC Press, 2001); Ann Wolbert Burgess and Carrie M. Carretta, "Rape and Its Impact on the Victim," in R.R. Hazelwood and A. W. Burgess, *Practical Aspects of Rape Investigation: A Multidisciplinary Approach*, 5th ed. (Boca Raton, FL: CRC Press, 2001), pp. 3–18.

3. Federal Bureau of Investigation, "2016 Crime in the United States: Rape."

4. United States Crime Rates 1960–2016," Disaster Center, 2018, http://www.disastercenter.com/crime/uscrime.htm.

5. Alanna Vagianos, "30 Alarming Statistics That Show the Reality of Sexual Violence in America," *Huffington Post*, April 5, 2017, https://www.huffingtonpost.com/entry/sexual-assault-statistics_us_58e24c14e4b0c777f788d24f; Rape, Abuse, and Incest National Network, "Victims of Sexual Violence: Statistics," 2018, https://www.rainn.org/statistics/victims-sexual-violence.

6. Rape, Abuse, and Incest National Network, "Victims of Sexual Violence."

7. Vagianos, "30 Alarming Statistics."

8. *Criminal Minds Wiki*, s.v. "Richard Ramirez," http://criminalminds.wikia.com/wiki/Richard_Ramirez; Stav Dimitropoulos, "Was a Bad Childhood to Blame for 'Night Stalker' Richard Ramirez Becoming a Serial Killer?" *A&E Real Crime*, November 1, 2017, https://www.aetv.com/real-crime/was-a-bad-childhood-to-blame-for-night-stalker-richard-ramirez-becoming-a-serial-killer.

9. Ibid; *Criminal Minds Wiki*, s.v. "Richard Ramirez."

10. English Standard Version.

11. *Criminal Minds Wiki*, s.v. "Richard Ramirez"; Dimitropoulos, "Bad Childhood."

12. Ibid.

13. Michael Newton, *The Encyclopedia of Serial Killers*, 2nd ed. (New York: Checkmark, 2006), p. 218; *Criminal Minds Wiki*, s.v. "Richard Ramirez."

14. David Freed, "Night Stalker Suspect Tied to '84 Killing: Fingerprint on Screen Where Glassell Park Woman, 79, Was Slain," *Los Angeles Times*, September 5, 1985.

15. Newton, *Encyclopedia of Serial Killers*; "Alleged Night Stalker Victim: L.A. Deputy Describes Mutilation of Woman," *Los Angeles Times*, March 20, 1986; Philip Carlo, *The Night Stalker: The Life and Crimes of Richard Ramirez* (New York: Citadel, 2016), pp. 49–52.

16. Carlo, *Night Stalker*, p. 64.

17. Ibid., pp. 69–79; Newton, *Encyclopedia of Serial Killers*; *Criminal Minds Wiki*, s.v. "Richard Ramirez."

18. Carlo, *Night Stalker*, pp. 72–76.

19. *Wikipedia*, s.v. "Richard Ramirez," last edited November 2, 2018, https://en.wikipedia.org/wiki/Richard_Ramirez.

20. Carlo, *Night Stalker*, pp. 90–91.

21. Newton, *Encyclopedia of Serial Killers*; *Wikipedia*, s.v. "Richard Ramirez."

22. Carlo, *Night Stalker*, pp. 95–98.

23. Ibid., p. 101.

24. Ibid., pp. 105–108.

25. Ibid., pp. 120–21.

26. *Wikipedia*, s.v. "Richard Ramirez."

27. Carlo, *Night Stalker*, pp. 135–37.

28. Ibid., pp. 139–47.

29. Ibid., pp. 154–55.

30. Ibid., pp. 157–58.

31. Paul Buchanan, "How a 13-Year-Old Boy Brought Down L.A.'s Most Notorious Serial Killer," *Los Angeles*, May 15, 2017, http://www.lamag.com/citythinkblog/13-year-old-boy-brought-down-notorious-serial-killer-richard-ramirez-night-stalker/.

32. . Keith Sharon, "After 3 Bullets in the Head, He Still Can't Escape the 'Night Stalker,'" *Orange County Register*, September 30, 2012, https://www.ocregister.com/2012/09/30/after-3-bullets-in-the-head-he-still-cant-escape-the-night-stalker/.

33. Carlo, *Night Stalker*, pp. 160–64.

34. *Wikipedia*, s.v. "Richard Ramirez."

35. Carlo, *Night Stalker*, pp. 245–52.

36. *Wikipedia*, s.v. "Richard Ramirez"; "U.S. Killer Richard Ramirez Dies in Prison," *Guardian*, June 7, 2013, https://www.theguardian.com/world/2013/jun/07/richard-ramirez-night-stalker-dies.

37. Newton, *Encyclopedia of Serial Killers*, p. 219.

38. "U.S. Killer Richard Ramirez Dies in Prison"; *Wikipedia*, s.v. "Richard Ramirez."

CHAPTER EIGHT: CATEGORY 18

1. Peter Vronsky, *Serial Killers: The Method and Madness of Monsters* (New York: Berkley, 2004), p. 169.

2. John Douglas, *Mindhunter* (New York: Pocket, 1995), p. 132.

3. Vronsky, *Serial Killers*, p. 170.

4. Ibid., pp. 173–74.

5. Anil Aggrawal, *Necrophilia: Forensic and Medico-Legal Aspects* (Boca Raton, FL: CRC Press, 2011), p. 113.

6. Ronald M. Holmes and Stephen T. Holmes, *Serial Murder*, 3rd ed. (Thousand Oaks, CA: SAGE Publications, 2010), p. 109.

7. Brian A. Sharpless, ed., *Unusual and Rare Psychological Disorders: A Handbook for Clinical Practice and Research* (New York: Oxford University Press, 2017), p. 127.

8. R. J. Parker, *Serial Killers Unabridged* (Toronto: R. J. Parker Publishing, 2014), p. 143.

9. Michael Newton, *The Encyclopedia of Serial Killers*, 2nd ed. (New York: Checkmark, 2006), p. 27.

10. Ibid.; Sharpless, *Unusual and Rare Psychological Disorders*, p. 127.

11. Vronsky, *Serial Killers*, p. 177.

12. *Criminal Minds Wiki*, s.v. "Jerry Brudos," http://criminalminds.wikia.com/

wiki/Jerry_Brudos; Mara Bovsun, "Sicko Shoe Fetishist Goes on a Killing Spree," *New York Daily News*, June 14, 2014, http://www.nydailynews.com/news/crime/ sicko-shoe-fetishist-killing-spree-article-1.1829333.

13. *Criminal Minds Wiki*, s.v. "Jerry Brudos."

14. Newton, *Encyclopedia of Serial Killers*, p. 27.

15. Vronsky, *Serial Killers*, p. 180.

16. Ibid., p. 182; *Biography*, "Jerome Brudos," directed by Jeff Woods, aired 2008, on A&E Network, https://www.biography.com/video/jerome-brudos-full-biography -15259715875 (accessed April 6, 2018).

17. Gini Graham Scott, *American Murder* (Westport, CT: Praeger, 2007), p. 34.

18. *Biography*, "Jerome Brudos."

19. Ibid.; Aggrawal, *Necrophilia*, p. 115.

20. *Biography*, "Jerome Brudos."

21. Ibid.

22. Ibid.; Bovsun, "Sicko Shoe Fetishist," *New York Daily News*.

23. *Biography*, "Jerome Brudos"; Michael H. Stone, *The Anatomy of Evil* (Amherst, NY: Prometheus Books, 2009), pp. 228–29.

CHAPTER NINE: CATEGORIES 19, 20, AND 21

1. Michael Newton, *The Encyclopedia of Kidnapping* (New York: Checkmark, 2002), p. 179.

2. Michael Thomas Barry, "Buried Alive: The Kidnapping of Barbara Jane Mackle; 1968," *Crime Magazine*, December 17, 2012, http://www.crimemagazine .com/buried-alive-kidnapping-barbara-jane-mackle-1968; Jay Robert Nash, *The Great Pictorial History of World Crime*, vol. 2 (Lanham, MD: Rowman & Littlefield, 2004), p. 708; "The Daring Kidnapping of Barbara Mackle: Part 1 of 3," *Coastal Breeze News* (Marco Island, FL), January 13, 2010, https://www.coastalbreezenews.com/articles/ the-daring-kidnapping-of-barbara-mackle-part-1-of-3/.

3. Barbara Stepko, "Barbara Jane Mackle: The Kidnap Victim Who Spent More Than Three Days in a Box Buried Underground," *Vintage News*, May 9, 2018, https:// www.thevintagenews.com/2018/05/09/barbara-jane-mackle/.

4. "Daring Kidnapping of Barbara Mackle."

5. Michael Newton, *The FBI Encyclopedia* (Jefferson, NC: McFarland, 2003), p. 105.

6. "The Nerve-Wracking Rescue of Kidnapped Heiress Barbara Mackle: Part 2 of 3," *Coastal Breeze News* (Marco Island, FL), January 28, 2010, https://www .coastalbreezenews.com/articles/the-nerve-wracking-rescue-of-kidnapped-heiress -barbara-mackle-part-2-of-3/.

7. Newton, *FBI Encyclopedia*, p. 105.

8. Newton, *Encyclopedia of Kidnapping*, pp. 179–80.

9. "Man Who Buried Girl Alive Becomes Doctor," ABC News, November 15, 2002, http://abcnews.go.com/US/story?id=91055&page=1; Barry, "Buried Alive."

10. "Cocaine Lab Found Under Auburn Home," *Gwinnett Daily Post* (Gwinnet County, GA), March 16, 2006, http://www.gwinnettdailypost.com/archive/cocaine-lab -found-under-auburn-home/article_d0962728-8ecb-5d6c-9602-d3eb3e50c889.html.

11. Frank Schmalleger, *Criminology Today: An Integrative Introduction*, 5th ed. (Columbus, OH: Pearson/Prentice Hall, 2008), p. 158.

12. American Psychiatric Association, *Diagnostic and Statistical Manual of Mental Disorders: DSM-5* (Arlington, VA: American Psychiatric Press, 2013), pp. 87–122.

13. Ibid., pp. 783–86.

14. P. Fusar-Poli, I. Bonoldi, A.R. Yung, et al., "Predicting Psychosis: Meta-analysis of Transition Outcomes in Individuals at High Clinical Risk," *Archives of General Psychiatry* 69, no. 3 (2012): 220–229; Gary Brucato, Michael D. Masucci, Leigh Y. Arndt, et al., "Baseline Demographics, Clinical Features and Predictors of Conversion Among 200 Individuals in a Longitudinal Prospective Psychosis-Risk Cohort," *Psychological Medicine* 47, no. 11 (2017): 1923–1935.

15. Gary Brucato, Paul S. Appelbaum, Jeffrey A. Lieberman, et al., "A Longitudinal Study of Violent Behavior in a Psychosis-Risk Cohort," *Neuropsychopharmacology* 45, no. 2 (2018): 264–71.

16. APA, *DSM-5*, pp. 110–18.

17. Ibid., pp. 649–52.

18. Ibid., pp. 652–55.

19. Ibid., pp. 655–59.

20. Ibid., pp. 667–69.

21. Ibid., pp. 669–72.

22. Ibid., pp. 663–66.

23. Ibid., pp. 659–63.

24. Ibid., pp. 672–75.

25. Ibid., pp. 675–78.

26. Ibid., pp. 678–82.

27. P. Lindqvist and P. Allebeck, "A Longitudinal Follow-Up of 644 Schizophrenics in Stockholm," *British Journal of Psychiatry* 157 (1990): 345–50; S. Hodgins, S. A. Mednick, P. A. Brennan, F. Schulsinger, and M. Engberg, "Mental Disorder and Crime: Evidence from a Danish Birth Cohort," *Archives of General Psychiatry* 53, no. 6 (1996): 489–96; J. W. Swanson, M. S. Swartz, S. M. Essock, et al., "The Social-Environmental Context of Violent Behavior in Persons Treated for Severe Mental Illness," *American Journal of Public Health* 92 (2002): 1523–31; P. J. Taylor, "Psychosis and Violence: Stories, Fears, Reality," *Canadian Journal of Psychiatry* 53, no. 10 (2009): 647–59; P. Gottlieb, G. Gabrielson, and P. Kramp, "Psychotic Homicides in Copenhagen from 1959 to 1983," *Acta Psychiatrica Scandinavica* 76 (1987): 285–92; Swanson et al., "The Social-Environmental Context of Violent Behavior," *American Journal of Public Health*; S. Fazel, P. Buxrud, V. Ruchkin, and M. Grann, "Homicide in Discharged Patients with Schizophrenia and Other Psychoses: A National Case-Control Study," *Schizophrenia Research* 123 (2010): 263–69; K. S. Douglas, L. S. Guy and S. D. Hart, "Psychosis as a Risk Factor for Violence to Others: A Meta-Analysis," *Psychological Bulletin* 135, no. 5 (2009): 679–706.

28. J. Shaw, I. M. Hunt, S. Flynn, et al., "Rates of Mental Disorder in People Convicted of Homicide: National Clinical Survey," *British Journal of Psychiatry* 188 (2006): 143–47; M. Large, G. Smith, and O. Nielssen, "The Relationship between the Rate of Homicide by Those with Schizophrenia and the Overall Homicide Rate: A Systematic Review and Meta-Analysis," *Schizophrenia Research* 112 (2009): 123–29.

29. Douglas, Guy, and Hart, "Psychosis as a Risk Factor."

30. J. A. Yesavage, "Inpatient Violence and the Schizophrenic Patient: An Inverse Correlation between Danger-Related Events and Neuroleptic Levels," *Biological Psychiatry* 17 (1982): 1331–37; E. B. Elbogen, R. A. Van Dorn, J. W. Swanson, et al., "Treatment Engagement and Violence Risk in Mental Disorders," *British Journal of Psychiatry* 189 (2006): 354–60; E. B. Elgogen, S. Mustillo, R. Van Dorn, et al., "The Impact of Perceived Need for Treatment on Risk of Arrest and Violence among People with Severe Mental Illness," *Criminal Justice and Behavior* 34 (2007): 197–210.

31. C. C. Joyal, J. L. Dubreucq, C. Gendron, and F. Millaud, "Major Mental Disorders and Violence: A Critical Update," *Current Psychiatry Reviews* 3 (2007): 33–50.

32. M. Eronen, J. Tiihonen, and P. Hakola, "Schizophrenia and Homicidal Behavior," *Schizophrenia Bulletin* 22 (1996): 83–89; P. Rasanen, J. Tiihonen, M. Isohanni, et al., "Schizophrenia, Alcohol Abuse, and Violent Behavior: A 26-Year Follow-Up Study of an Unselected Birth Cohort," *Schizophrenia Bulletin* 24 (1998): 437–41; M. S. Swartz, J. W. Swanson, V. A. Hiday, et al., "Violence and Severe Mental Illness: The Effects of Substance Abuse and Nonadherence to Medication," *American Journal of Psychiatry* 155 (1998): 226–31; L. Arseneault, T. E. Moffitt, A. Caspi, et al., "Mental Disorders and Violence in a Total Birth Cohort," *Archives of General Psychiatry* 57, no. 10 (2000): 979–86; E. B. Elbogen and S. C. Johnson, "The Intricate Link between Violence and Mental Disorder," *Archives of General Psychiatry* 66, no. 2 (2009): 152–61.

33. S. Fazel, N. Langstrom, A. Hjern, et al., "Schizophrenia, Substance Abuse, and Violent Crime," *Journal of the American Medical Association* 301, no. 19 (2009): 2016–23; H. J. Steadman, E. P. Mulvey, J. Monahan, et al. "Violence by People Discharged from Acute Psychiatric Inpatient Facilities and by Others in the Same Neighborhoods," *Archives of General Psychiatry* 55, no. 5 (1999): 393–401; P. Appelbaum, P. Robbins, and J. Monahan, "Violence and Delusions: Data from the MacArthur Violence Risk Assessment Study," *American Journal of Psychiatry* 157 (2000): 566–72.

34. Elbogen and Johnson, "Intricate Link."

35. Appelbaum, Robbins and Monahan, "Violence and Delusions."

36. Bruce J. Link and Ann Stueve, "Psychotic Symptoms and the Violent/Illegal Behavior of Mental Patients Compared to Community Controls," *Violence and Mental Disorder*, ed. John Monahan and Henry J. Steadman (Chicago: University of Chicago Press, 1994), pp. 137–59.

37. S. Ullrich, R. Keers and J. W. Coid, "Delusions, Anger, and Serious Violence: New Findings from the MacArthur Violence Risk Assessment Study," *Schizophrenia Bulletin* 40, no. 5 (2014): 1174–81.

38. J. W. Coid, S. Ulrich, C. Kallis, et al., "The Relationship between Delusions and Violence: Findings from the East London First Episode Psychosis Study," *Journal of the American Medical Association Psychiatry* 71, no. 5 (2013): 465–71.

39. D. E. McNeil, J. P. Eisner, and R. L. Binder, "The Relationship between Command Hallucinations and Violence," *Psychiatric Services* 51, no. 10 (2000): 1288–92.

40. P. J. Taylor, M. Leese, D. Williams, et al., "Mental Disorder and Violence," *British Journal of Psychiatry* 172 (1998): 218–26; R. Keers, S. Ullrich, B. L. DeStavola, and J. Coid, "Association of Violence with Emergence of Persecutory Delusions in Untreated Schizophrenia," *American Journal of Psychiatry* 171, no. 3 (2013): 332–39.

41. J. Bartels, R. E. Drake, M. A. Wallach, and D. H. Freeman, "Characteristic Hostility in Schizophrenic Outpatients," *Schizophrenia Bulletin* 17 (1991): 163–71.

42. . Michael G. Aamodt, Terry Leary, and Larry Southard, *Radford/FGCU Annual Report on Serial Killer Statistics: 2018* (Radford, VA: Radford University, 2018), p. 77.

43. "Randall Fish," Find a Grave, added July 28, 2011, https://www.findagrave.com/memorial/74073798/randall-fish; *Criminal Minds Wiki*, s.v. "Albert Fish," http://criminalminds.wikia.com/wiki/Albert_Fish; Moira Mortingale, *Cannibal Killers* (New York: St. Martin's, 1993), p. 44.

44. Mortingale, *Cannibal Killers*.

45. *Criminal Minds Wiki*, s.v. "Albert Fish."

46. Ibid.

47. Michael Newton, *The Encyclopedia of Serial Killers*, 2nd ed. (New York: Checkmark, 2006), p. 77.

48. Christopher Berry-Dee and Victoria Redstall, *Cannibal Serial Killers: Profiles of Depraved Flesh-Eating Murderers* (Berkeley, CA: Ulysses, 2011), p. 158.

49. Ibid.

50. John Borowski, *Albert Fish in His Own Words: The Shocking Confessions of the Child Killing Cannibal* (Chicago: Waterfront Productions, 2014), p. 314.

51. Nash, *Great Pictorial History of World Crime*, p. 303.

52. Berry-Dee and Redstall, *Cannibal Serial Killers*, p. 158.

53. Harold Schechter, *The Serial Killer Files: The Who, What, Where, How, and Why of the World's Most Terrifying Murderers* (New York: Ballantine, 2003), p. 185.

54. Newton, *Encyclopedia of Serial Killers*, p. 77.

55. *Criminal Minds Wiki*, "Albert Fish."

56. John E. Douglas, Ann W. Burgess, Allen G. Burgess, and Robert K. Ressler, *The Crime Classification Manual: A Standard System for Investigating and Classifying Violent Crimes*, 2nd ed. (San Francisco, CA: John Wiley & Sons, 2006), p. 462.

57. Tim Unkenholz, "Read This Twisted Letter from an Infamous Cannibal to the Mother of His Victim," Viralnova, January 15, 2016, http://www.viralnova.com/fish-letter/.

58. Douglas, Burgess, Burgess, and Ressler, *Crime Classification Manual*, p. 462.

59. Berry-Dee and Redstall, *Cannibal Serial Killers*, p. 163.

60. Michael L. Birzer and Cliff Roberson, eds., *Introduction to Criminal Investigation* (Boca Raton, FL: CRC Press, 2012), p. 5.

61. Douglas, Burgess, Burgess, and Ressler, *Crime Classification Manual*, p. 463; *Criminal Minds Wiki*, "Albert Fish"; Berry-Dee and Redstall, *Cannibal Serial Killers*, pp. 161–63.

62. Bart Beatty, *Fredric Wertham and the Critique of Mass Culture* (Jackson: University Press of Mississippi, 2005), p. 30.

63. Katherine Ramsland, *The Mind of a Murderer: Privileged Access to the Demons That Drive Extreme Violence* (Santa Barbara, CA: Praeger, 2011), p. 45.

64. Colin Wilson and Donald Seaman, *The Serial Killers: A Study in the Psychology of Violence* (London: Virgin, 2007), p. 172.

65. *Criminal Minds Wiki*, "Albert Fish."

66. Newton, *Encyclopedia of Serial Killers*, p. 77.

67. Berry-Dee and Redstall, *Cannibal Serial Killers*, p. 174.

68. Mark Pulham, "The Werewolf of Wisteria," *Crime Magazine*, August 1, 2011, http://www.crimemagazine.com/werewolf-wisteria.

69. Bruce M. Krauft, *From Primitive to Post-Colonial in Melanesia and Anthropology* (Ann Arbor: University of Michigan Press, 1999), p. 104; W. D. Rubinstein, *Genocide: A History* (London: Pearson Education), pp. 17–18; *Encyclopaedia Britannica*, s.v. "cannibalism," last edited 2018, https://www.britannica.com/topic/cannibalism-human-behaviour.

70. . Elizabeth Culotta, "Neanderthals Were Cannibals, Bones Show," *Science* 286, no. 5437 (1999): 18–19.

71. . Jason Thompson, *A History of Egypt: From Earliest Times to the Present* (Cairo, Egypt; New York: American University in Cairo Press, 2008).

72. Richard Luscombe, "Miami Face-Chewing Victim: Attacker Rudy Eugene 'Ripped Me to Ribbons,'" *Guardian*, August 9, 2012, https://www.theguardian.com/world/2012/aug/09/miami-face-chewing-victim-attack.

73. "Dad Ate My Eyes, Boy Tells Cops," CBS News, May 19, 2009, https://www.cbsnews.com/news/dad-ate-my-eyes-boy-tells-cops/.

74. *Wikipedia*, s.v. "Rod Ferrell," last edited October 29, 2018, https://en.wikipedia.org/wiki/Rod_Ferrell.

75. Michael Kaplan, "Meet the Cannibal Who Became a Folk Hero in Japan," *New York Post*, October 20, 2018, https://nypost.com/2018/10/20/issei-sagawa-the-cannibal-who-became-a-folk-hero-in-japan/.

76. *Wikipedia*, s.v. "John Brennan Crutchley," last edited September 16, 2018, https://en.wikipedia.org/wiki/John_Brennan_Crutchley.

77. Don Davis, *The Jeffrey Dahmer Story: An American Nightmare* (New York: St. Martin's, 1991); Brian Masters, *The Shrine of Jeffrey Dahmer* (London: Hodder & Stoughton, 1993).

78. *Jeffrey Dahmer: Confessions of a Serial Killer*, documentary, featuring Stone Phillips (New York: MSNBC Network, 2012).

79. NewsCore, "3 Sentenced in Russian Case of Human Meat Sold at a Kebab Stall," Fox News, June 23, 2010, https://www.foxnews.com/world/3-sentenced-in-russian-case-of-human-meat-sold-to-kebab-stall.

80. Crystal Bonvillian, "Five Charged with Keeping Autistic Relative in Cage, Forcing Her to Eat Dead Mom's Ashes," *Atlanta Journal-Constitution*, July 27, 2018, https://www.ajc.com/news/national/charged-with-keeping-autistic-relative-cage-forcing-her-eat-dead-mom-ashes/9w86O1kXtCnF8oKK2N4zTI/.

81. *Criminal Minds Wiki*, s.v. "Cameron and Janice Hooker," http://criminalminds.wikia.com/wiki/Cameron_and_Janice_Hooker.

82. Ibid.; Wilson and Seaman, *Serial Killers*, pp. 144–45.

83. Nicole Weisensee Egan, "The 'Girl in the Box' Speaks: How I Survived Being Held Captive for 7 Years," *People*, September 7, 2016, http://people.com/crime/girl-in-the-box-speaks-how-i-survived-my-seven-year-ordeal/.

84. *Criminal Minds Wiki*, s.v. "Cameron and Janice Hooker."

85. *Wikipedia*, s.v. "Kidnapping of Colleen Stan," last edited November 3, 2018, https://en.wikipedia.org/wiki/Kidnapping_of_Colleen_Stan.

86. Catherine Townsend, "Raped, Tortured, and Locked in a Coffin for Seven Years: The True Story of Colleen Stan," Investigation Discovery Crime Feed, September 9, 2016, http://crimefeed.com/2016/09/bound-in-a-box-the-true-story-of-colleen-stan/.

87. Newton, *Encyclopedia of Kidnapping*, p. 294.

88. Hannah Parry, "'Girl in the Box' Psycho Cameron Hooker Who Kept Kidnapped Hitchhiker in a Tiny Box 23 Hours a Day for Seven Years Is Denied Parole

and Told: 'You'll Spend At Least 15 More Years in Jail,'" *Daily Mail*, http://www
.dailymail.co.uk/news/article-3043291/Cameron-Hooker-kidnapped-young-hitchhiker
-held-SEVEN-years-denied-parole.html.

89. *Wikipedia*, s.v. "Kidnapping of Colleen Stan."

90. Newton, *Encyclopedia of Kidnapping*, pp. 294–95.

91. Townsend, "Raped, Tortured, and Locked in a Coffin."

92. Newton, *Encyclopedia of Kidnapping*, p. 295.

93. Lucia Binding, "Shocking Story of a Woman Held Hostage in Coffin for Seven
Years Made into Documentary," *International Business Times*, September 9, 2016, https://
www.ibtimes.co.uk/shocking-true-account-woman-held-hostage-coffin-seven-years-made
-into-documentary-1580568.

94. "104-Year Sentence Given Man in Sex-Slavery Case," *Los Angeles Times*,
November 24, 1985.

95. Newton, *Encyclopedia of Kidnapping*, p. 295; *Criminal Minds Wiki*, s.v. "Cameron
and Janice Hooker."

CHAPTER TEN: CATEGORY 22

1. Joseph Sguigna and Sharon Sguigna, *Of Pathics and Evil* (Bloomington, IN:
iUniverse, 2009), p. 104.

2. Emlyn Williams, *Beyond Belief: A Chronicle of Murder and Its Detection* (New York:
Random House, 1968).

3. Jack Olsen, *The Man with the Candy: The Story of the Houston Mass Murders* (New
York: Simon & Schuster, 1974).

4. Don Lasseter, *Die for Me: The Terrifying True Story of Charles Ng & Leonard Lake
Torture Murders* (New York: Pinnacle, 2000).

5. John MacCormack, "Killer Smile," *Dallas Observer*, September 28, 2000.

6. Barbara Nacek and Laurent Abellard, *Dans la Tête d'un Tueur en Série avec Stéphane
Bourgoin* (Boulogne-Billancourt, France: Patrick Spica Productions, 2010).

7. Ken Paxton, Attorney General of Texas, "Media Advisory: Tommy Lynn Sells
Scheduled for Execution," press release, April 3, 2014, https://www.texasattorneygeneral
.gov/oagnews/release.php?print=1&id=4700.

8. Michael Newton, *The Encyclopedia of Serial Killers*, 2nd ed. (New York: Checkmark,
2006), p. 237.

9. Michael Graczyk, "April Execution for Inmate Tied to Multiple Deaths,"
Statesman, January 3, 2014, https://www.statesman.com/news/april-execution
-for-inmate-tied-multiple-deaths/MQlCjyu8ylLkHTfTjFPfiI/.

10. Newton, *Encyclopedia of Serial Killers*, p. 234.

11. Diane Fanning, *Through the Window: The Terrifying True Story or Tommy Lynn Sells*
(New York: St. Martin's True Crime Library, 2007), pp. 21–23.

12. Newton, *Encyclopedia of Serial Killers*, p. 235.

13. Nacek and Abellard, *Dans la Tête d'un Tueur en Série avec Stéphane Bourgoin*.

14. Katherine Ramsland, *The Mind of a Murderer: Privileged Access to the Demons That
Drive Extreme Violence* (Santa Barbara, CA: Praeger, 2011), p. 172.

15. *Most Evil*, season 1, episode 2, "Cold-Blooded Killers," featuring Dr. Michael H. Stone and Tim Hopper, aired on July 20, 2006, on Investigation Discovery, https://www.investigationdiscovery.com/tv-shows/most-evil/full-episodes/cold-blooded-killers.

16. Newton, *Encyclopedia of Serial Killers*, p. 235.

17. Ibid.

18. Nacek and Abellard, *Dans la Tête d'un Tueur en Série avec Stéphane Bourgoin*.

19. Newton, *Encyclopedia of Serial Killers*, p. 235.

20. Becky Malkovich, "Interview with a Murderer," *Southern Illinoisan* (Carbondale), May 16, 2010.

21. Newton, *Encyclopedia of Serial Killers*, p. 235.

22. Kevin M. Sullivan, *Through an Unlocked Door: In Walks Murder* (Jefferson, NC: McFarland, 2018), p. 115.

23. Newton, *Encyclopedia of Serial Killers*, p. 235.

24. Jim Suhr, "Unsolved 1987 Slaying of Illinois Family Haunting," *Northwest Herald* (Crystal Lake, IL), April 13, 2014.

25. Nacek and Abellard, *Dans la Tête d'un Tueur en Série avec Stéphane Bourgoin*.

26. *Most Evil*, "Cold-Blooded Killers."

27. Nacek and Abellard, *Dans la Tête d'un Tueur en Série avec Stéphane Bourgoin*; Diane Fanning, "Conversations with a Serial Killer," *USA Today*, April 18, 2014.

28. *Most Evil*, "Cold-Blooded Killers."

29. Victoria Kim, "The Link Between Serial Killers and Addicts," The Fix, April 14, 2014, https://www.thefix.com/content/link-between-serial-killers-and-addicts.

30. Fanning, "Conversations with a Serial Killer."

31. Tom Jackman and Troy Cole, *Rites of Burial* (London: Pinnacle, 1992), pp. 24–25.

32. Mara Bovsun, "Kansas City Sicko Kept Detailed Diary, Photos of Sex Torture, Bondage and Murder"," *New York Daily News*, July 23, 2016.

33. Ibid.

34. Jackman and Cole, *Rites of Burial*, pp. 46–47 and 183.

35. Jack Rosewood, *Robert Berdella: The True Story of the Kansas City Butcher* (North Charleston, SC: CreateSpace, 2015), p. 8.

36. Bovsun, "Kansas City Sicko."

37. *The Collector*, directed by William Wyler (Culver City, CA: Columbia Pictures, 1965); John Fowles, *The Collector* (Boston, MA: Little, Brown, 1963).

38. *Criminal Minds Wiki*, s.v. "Robert Berdella," http://criminalminds.wikia.com/wiki/Robert_Berdella.

39. R. J. Parker, *Serial Killers Abridged* (Toronto: R. J. Parker Publishing, 2014), p. 219.

40. Jackman and Cole, *Rites of Burial*, p. 231; Orrin Grey, "Robert Berdella, the Butcher of Kansas City," *The Lineup* (*Huffington Post* blog), October 29, 2015, https://www.huffingtonpost.com/the-lineup/robert-berdella-the-butch_b_8426374.html.

41. Jackman and Cole, *Rites of Burial*, pp. 78–79 and 259–61.

42. *Criminal Minds Wiki*, s.v. "Robert Berdella."

43. Bovsun, "Kansas City Sicko."

44. Ibid.

45. *Criminal Minds Wiki*, s.v. "Robert Berdella"; Helen Morrison and Harold Goldberg, *My Life among the Serial Killers: Inside the Minds of the World's Most Notorious Murderers* (New York: Avon, 2005), pp. 196–99.

46. Jackman and Cole, *Rites of Burial*, p. 300.

47. Bovsun, "Kansas City Sicko"; Jackman and Cole, *Rites of Burial*, pp. 268, 271, 289, and 311.

48. Cyril Wecht, Greg Saitz, and Mark Curriden, *Mortal Evidence: The Forensics Behind Nine Shocking Cases* (New York: Prometheus Books, 2007), p. 272.

49. Grover Maurice Godwin, *Hunting Serial Predators: A Multivariate Classification Approach to Profiling Violent Behavior* (Boca Raton, FL: CRC Press, 2000), p. 203.

50. Morrison and Goldberg, *My Life among the Serial Killers*, pp. 200–201.

51. Bovsun, "Kansas City Sicko"; Rogers Worthington, "House of Horrors Shocks Residents of a Quiet Neighborhood," *Chicago Tribune*, July 31, 1988.

52. William Robbins, "Macabre Mystery Surrounding Deaths of 2 Men in Kansas City," *New York Times*, June 25, 1988.

53. Jackman and Cole, *Rites of Burial*, p. 44.

54. Worthington, "House of Horrors."

55. Bovsun, "Kansas City Sicko."

56. William Robbins, "From Bizarre Case, a Bizarre Auction," *New York Times*, November 12, 1988.

57. Richard LeComte, "Pastor Tells of Ministering to Berdella," *Examiner* (Independence, MO), April 1, 1989.

58. Bovsun, "Kansas City Sicko."

59. Grey, "Butcher of Kansas City."

60. Morrison and Goldberg, *My Life among the Serial Killers*, pp. 205–206.

61. Thomas Harris, *The Silence of the Lambs* (New York: St. Martin's, 1988).

62. David Bowman, "Profiler: The Real-Life Model for Thomas Harris; Serial-Killer Expert Psychs Out the O.J., Ramsey and Dahmer Cases—and David Byrne, Too," *Salon*, July 8, 1999, https://www.salon.com/1999/07/08/profiler/.

63. R. Barri Flowers and H. Lorraine Flowers, *Murders in the United States: Crimes, Killers and Victims of the Twentieth Century* (Jefferson, NC: McFarland, 2004), p. 97.

64. Newton, *Encyclopedia of Serial Killers*, p. 112.

65. Ken Englade, *Cellar of Horror* (New York: St. Martin's, 1992), p. 19.

66. Colin Wilson and Donald Seaman, *The Serial Killers: A Study in the Psychology of Violence* (London: Virgin, 2007), p. 198.

67. Frank Stone, *Silence of the Lambs: The True Story of Gary Heidnik* (North Charleston, SC: CreateSpace, 2016), p. 3.

68. *Most Evil*, season 1, episode 5, "Psychotic Killers," featuring Dr. Michael H. Stone and Tim Hopper, aired on August 17, 2006, on Investigation Discovery, https://www.investigationdiscovery.com/tv-shows/most-evil/full-episodes/psychotic-killers.

69. R. J. Parker, *The Basement* (Toronto: R. J. Parker Publishing, 2016), pp. 12–16.

70. Joe B. Warrick, "The Judge in Gary Heidnik's 'House of Horrors' Murder-Torture," United Press International, June 24, 1988, https://www.upi.com/Archives/1988/06/24/The-judge-in-Gary-Heidniks-House-of-Horrors-murder-torture/9996583128000/.

71. Parker, *Basement*, p. 18.

72. Newton, *Encyclopedia of Serial Killers*, pp. 113–14.

73. Parker, *Basement*, p. 34.

74. Harold Schechter, *The Serial Killer Files: The Who, What, Where, How, and Why of the World's Most Terrifying Murderers* (New York: Ballantine, 2003), p. 199.

75. Newton, *Encyclopedia of Serial Killers*, p. 114.

76. Ibid.; Parker, *Basement*, pp. 33–34.

77. *Killer Profile*, season 1, episode 2, "Gary Heidnik: House of Horrors," featuring Christine Nelson, aired October 20, 2013, on LMN, http://crimedocumentary.com/killer-profile-season-1-2013/.

78. Parker, *Basement*, p. 35.

79. Michael H. Stone, *Anatomy of Evil* (Amherst, NY: Prometheus Books, 2009), p. 246.

80. Newton, *Encyclopedia of Serial Killers*, p. 114.

81. *Killer Profile*, "Gary Heidnik."

82. Tom Philbin and Michael Philbin, *The Killer Book of Serial Killers* (Naperville, IL: Sourcebook, 2009), p. 58; Victor Fiorillo, "Inside the House of Heidnik," *Philadelphia*, July 23, 2007, https://www.phillymag.com/articles/2007/07/23/inside-the-house-of-heidnik/.

83. Philip Lentz, "Few Hints of Horror in House Next Door," *Chicago Tribune*, March 29, 1987.

84. Newton, *Encyclopedia of Serial Killers*, p. 114.

85. "Kidnap Victim Jackie Askins Describes Her Struggles Nearly 30 Years after Being Held Captive," *Huffington Post*, August 5, 2014, https://www.huffingtonpost.com/2014/08/05/lisa-ling-kidnapping-victim-jackie-askins_n_5648939.html.

86. *Killer Profile*, "Gary Heidnik."

87. Schechter, *Serial Killer Files*, p. 200.

88. Bill Peterson, "Captives, Body Parts Found in Philadelphia," *Washington Post*, March 26, 1987.

89. *Killer Profile*, "Gary Heidnik."

90. Martin Gilman Wolcott, *The Evil 100: Fascinating True-Life Tales of Terror, Mayhem and Savagery* (New York: Citadel, 2002), p. 287.

91. Parker, *Basement*, pp. 53–54.

92. Nick Vadala, "Philly Woman Recalls Her Terrifying 'Silence of the Lambs' Past for the First Time," *Inquirer* (Philadelphia), April 2, 2014.

93. Parker, *Basement*, pp. 54–55.

94. *Criminal Minds Wiki*, s.v. "Gary," https://criminalminds.fandom.com/wiki/Gary.

95. *Killer Profile*, "Gary Heidnik."

96. Newton, *Encyclopedia of Serial Killers*, p. 115; John Douglas and Mark Olshaker, *Obsession: The FBI's Legendary Profiler Probes the Psyches of Killers, Rapists, and Stalkers and Their Victims and Tells How to Fight Back* (New York: Pocket, 1998), p. 397.

97. Douglas and Olshaker, *Obsession*.

98. Ibid., pp. 398–99.

99. Com. v. Heidnik, 526 Pa. 458 (1991).

100. Jordan Smith, "In Killer's Mind, Counselor Found the Roots of a New Way to Treat Troubled Youth," *Washington Post*, October 21, 2012.

101. *Killer Profile*, "Gary Heidnik."

102. Newton, *Encyclopedia of Serial Killers*, p. 115.

103. Schechter, *Serial Killer Files*, p. 200.

104. A. W. Burgess, C. R. Hartman, R. K. Russler, et al., "Sexual Homicide: A Motivational Model," *Journal of Interpersonal Violence* 1, no. 3 (1986): 251–72.

105. Heather Mitchell and Michael G. Aamodt. "The Incidence of Child Abuse in Serial Killers," *Journal of Police and Criminal Psychology* 20, no. 1 (2005): 40–47.

106. John M. MacDonald, "The Threat to Kill," *American Journal of Psychiatry* 120, no. 2 (1963): 125–30.

107. Stephen D. Singer, "Learning Theory to Childhood and Adolescent Firesetting: Can It Lead to Serial Murder?" *International Journal of Offender Therapy and Comparative Criminology* 48, no. 4 (2004): 461–76.

108. Vadala, "Philly Woman Recalls."

109. Stephen King, *It* (New York: Viking, 1986).

110. Terry Sullivan and Peter T. Maiken, *Killer Clown: The John Wayne Gacy Murders* (New York: Pinnacle, 1983), pp. 256–57.

111. Tim Cahill, *Buried Dreams: Inside the Mind of a Serial Killer* (New York: Bantam, 1986), p. 40.

112. Ibid., p. 21.

113. *Monster in My Family*, season 1, episode 6, "Killer Clown: John Wayne Gacy," featuring Melissa Moore, aired August 5, 2015, on LMN, http://crimedocumentary.com/karen-kuzma-killer-clown-john-wayne-gacy/.

114. Jonah Lehrer, *How We Decide* (New York: Houghton Mifflin Harcourt, 2009), p. 167.

115. Sam L. Amirante and Danny Broderick, *John Wayne Gacy: Defending a Monster* (New York: Skyhorse, 2011), p. 218; Sullivan and Maiken, *Killer Clown*, p. 257.

116. Lehrer, *How We Decide*, p. 167.

117. Newton, *Encyclopedia of Serial Killers*, p. 85.

118. *Criminal Minds Wiki*, s.v. "John Wayne Gacy," http://criminalminds.wikia.com/wiki/John_Wayne_Gacy.

119. Cahill, *Buried Dreams*, pp. 46 and 346–47.

120. Ibid., p. 47.

121. Thomas J. Jurkanin and Terry G. Hilliard, *Chicago Police: An Inside View; The Story of Superintendent Terry G. Hilliard* (Springfield, IL: Charles C. Thomas, 2006), p. 22.

122. Newton, *Encyclopedia of Serial Killers*, p. 85.

123. "John Wayne Gacy Crime Files," Crime & Investigation, http://www.crimeandinvestigation.co.uk/crime-files/john-wayne-gacy-killer-clown.

124. Jurkanin and Hilliard, *Chicago Police*, p. 22.

125. *Monster in My Family*, "Killer Clown."

126. Newton, *Encyclopedia of Serial Killers*, p. 85.

127. *Monster in My Family*, "Killer Clown."

128. Newton, *Encyclopedia of Serial Killers*, p. 85.

129. Sullivan and Maiken, *Killer Clown*, pp. 272–73.

130. Newton, *Encyclopedia of Serial Killers*, p. 85.

131. *Monster in My Family*, "Killer Clown."

132. Sullivan and Maiken, *Killer Clown*, pp. 275–76.

133. Newton, *Encyclopedia of Serial Killers*, p. 85.

134. Wolcott, *Evil 100*, p. 151.

135. Newton, *Encyclopedia of Serial Killers*, p. 85.

136. Michael Fitting Karagiozis and Richard Sgaglio, *Forensic Investigation Handbook: An Introduction to the Collection, Preservation, Analysis and Presentation of Evidence* (Springfield, IL: Charles C. Thomas, 2005), p. 157.

137. Newton, *Encyclopedia of Serial Killers*, p. 85.

138. Cahill, *Buried Dreams*, pp. 123–24.

139. Newton, *Encyclopedia of Serial Killers*, p. 86.

140. Clifford L. Linedecker, *The Man Who Killed Boys* (New York: St. Martin's, 1980), pp. 65–66.

141. Karagiozis and Sgaglio, *Forensic Investigation*, p. 157.

142. Newton, *Encyclopedia of Serial Killers*, p. 86.

143. Morrison and Goldberg, *My Life among the Serial Killers*, p. 93.

144. *Criminal Minds Wiki*, s.v. "John Wayne Gacy."

145. Ibid.

146. Linedecker, *Man Who Killed Boys*, p. 222.

147. Eric W. Hickey, *Serial Killers and Their Victims*, 3rd ed. (Belmont, CA: Wadsworth, 2001), p. 174.

148. David Lohr, "Boy Killer: John Wayne Gacy," *Crime Magazine*, October 14, 2009, http://www.crimemagazine.com/boy-killer-john-wayne-gacy.

149. Newton, *Encyclopedia of Serial Killers*, p. 86.

150. Sullivan and Maiken, *Killer Clown*, p. 301.

151. Newton, *Encyclopedia of Serial Killers*, p. 86.

152. Ibid.

153. Alex Horton, "One of John Wayne Gacy's Seven Unidentified Victims Finally Has a Name," *Washington Post*, July 19, 2017, https://www.washingtonpost.com/news/true-crime/wp/2017/07/19/one-of-john-wayne-gacys-remaining-seven-unidentified-victims-finally-has-a-name/?utm_term=.24927f894b3f.

154. Cahill, *Buried Dreams*, p. 333.

155. Newton, *Encyclopedia of Serial Killers*, p. 87.

156. *Criminal Minds Wiki*, s.v. "John Wayne Gacy."

157. Sullivan and Maiken, *Killer Clown*, pp. 252–56.

158. Stone, *Anatomy of Evil*, pp. 315–16.

159. Sharon Cohen, "Doctor Wants to Unravel Serial Killer Mystery," *Los Angeles Times*, May 23, 2004.

160. Stephen G. Michaud and Roy Hazelwood, *The Evil That Men Do: FBI Profiler Roy Hazelwood's Journey into the Minds of Sexual Predators* (New York: St. Martin's True Crime Library, 1999); Janet Warren, Roy Hazelwood, and Park E. Dietz, "The Sexually Sadistic Serial Killer," *Journal of Forensic Sciences* 41, no. 6 (1996): 970–74.

161. Christopher Berry-Dee, *Serial Killers: Up Close and Personal* (Berkeley, CA: Ulysses, 2007), p. 356.

162. Laura Higgins, "In the Hands of the Father," *Riverfront Times*, March 1, 2000, https://www.riverfronttimes.com/stlouis/in-the-hands-of-the-father/Content?oid=2474998.

163. Linedecker, *Man Who Killed Boys*, p. 226.

164. Vernon J. Geberth, *Sex-Related Homicide and Death Investigation: Practical and Clinical Perspectives*, 2nd ed. (Boca Raton, FL: CRC Press, 2010), p. 557.

165. Jim Fiedler, *Slow Death: The Sickest Serial Torture-Slayer Ever to Stalk the Southwest* (New York: Pinnacle, 2003), pp. 13–16; J. E. Sparks, *Consequences: The Criminal Case of David Parker Ray* (Roswell, NM: Yellow Jacket, 2007), pp. 1–4.

166. Geberth, *Sex-Related Homicide*, pp. 570–78.

167. Ibid.

168. Ibid.

169. Ibid.

170. Fiedler, *Slow Death*, p. 19.

171. Geberth, *Sex-Related Homicide*, p. 581.

172. Ibid., p. 560; Sparks, *Consequences*, p. 34.

173. Fiedler, *Slow Death*, p. 16.

174. Jessica Pacheco-Semenyuk, "FBI Crime Scene Processor Speaks Unvarnished Truth," *I Am New Mexico* (blog), May 7, 2016, https://iamnm.com/fbi-crime-scene -processor-speaks-truth/.

175. Geberth, *Sex-Related Homicide*, pp. 564–67; Fiedler, *Slow Death*, pp. 40–45; Sparks, *Consequences*, pp. 55–62.

176. Geberth, *Sex-Related Homicide*, p. 568; Fiedler, *Slow Death*, p. 38.

177. John Glatt, *Cries in the Desert* (New York: St. Martin's, 2007), pp. 7–14.

178. Charlotte Greig, *Serial Killers* (London: Arcturus, 2018), p. 75.

179. Glatt, *Cries in the Desert*, p. 12.

180. Paul H. Blaney and Theodore Millon, eds., *Oxford Textbook of Psychopathology*, 2nd ed. (New York: Oxford University Press, 2009), p. 659.

181. Glatt, *Cries in the Desert*, pp. 13–20; Geberth, *Sex-Related Homicide*, p. 557.

182. Geberth, *Sex-Related Homicide*, pp. 557–58.

183. Ibid., p. 557.

184. Sparks, *Consequences*, pp. 65–68.

185. Geberth, *Sex-Related Homicide*, p. 557.

186. Sparks, *Consequences*, p. 66.

187. Charles Montaldo, "Profile of Serial Rapist David Parker Ray," Thought Co., December 15, 2017, https://www.thoughtco.com/profile-of-serial -rapist-david-parker-ray-973147.

188. Ibid.

189. "David Parker Ray: New Mexico's Toy Box Killer," *Mountain Voice*, July 21, 2017, https://themountainvoice.com/2017/07/21/david-parker-ray -new-mexicos-toy-box-killer/.

190. Montaldo, "Profile of Serial Rapist."

191. Ann Rule, *The Stranger Beside Me* (New York: Signet, 2001); "Lost Skeleton Could Be That of '74 Bundy Victim," *Desert News*, February 28, 1998, https://www .deseretnews.com/article/616090/Lost-skeleton-could-be-that-of-74-Bundy-victim.html.

192. *Wikipedia*, s.v. "Richard Chase," last edited November 10, 2018, https:// en.wikipedia.org/wiki/Richard_Chase (accessed October 31, 2018).

193. S. S. Hoppenbrouwers, D. R. De Jesus, T. Stirpe, et al., "Inhibitory Deficits in the Dorsolateral Prefrontal Cortex in Psychopathic Offenders," *Cortex* 49, no. 5 (2013): 1377–85.

194. R. James R. Blair, "The Cognitive Neuroscience of Psychopathy and Implications for Judgments of Responsibility," *Neuroethics* 1, no. 3 (2008): 149–57.

CHAPTER TWELVE: CULTURAL CHANGES THAT AFFECT THE PATTERNS OF VIOLENCE IN PEACETIME

1. *Encyclopaedia Britannica*, s.v. "World War I," 2018, https://www.britannica.com/event/World-War-I/Killed-wounded-and-missing.

2. *Wikipedia*, s.v. "Charley Ross," last updated November 12, 2018, https://en.wikipedia.org/wiki/Charley_Ross.

3. Simon Baatz, *For the Thrill of It: Leopold, Loeb and the Murder That Shocked Chicago* (New York: HarperCollins, 2008).

4. *Wikipedia*, s.v. "Lindbergh kidnapping," last updated December 2, 2018, https://en.wikipedia.org/wiki/Lindbergh_kidnapping.

5. *Wikipedia*, s.v. "Bobby Greenlease," last updated November 19, 2018, https://en.wikipedia.org/wiki/Bobby_Greenlease.

6. Becky Little, "The 1927 Murder That Became a Media Circus—and a Famous Movie," *History*, September 24, 2018, https://www.history.com/news/double-indemnity-1920s-murder-crime-tabloids.

7. Mel Heimer, *Cannibal: The Case of Albert Fish* (New York: Lyle Stuart, 1971).

8. *Criminal Minds Wiki*, s.v. "Gordon Northcott," https://criminalminds.fandom.com/wiki/Gordon_Northcott.

9. John Gilmore, *Severed: The True Story of the Black Dahlia Murder*, 2nd ed. (Los Angeles: Amok Books, 2006).

10. Alexis Sobel Fitts, "I Know Who Killed the Black Dahlia: My Own Father," *Guardian*, May 26, 2016, https://www.theguardian.com/us-news/2016/may/26/black-dahlia-murder-steve-hodel-elizabeth-short.

11. *Wikipedia*, s.v. "Charles Starkweather," last updated November 22, 2018, https://en.wikipedia.org/wiki/Charles_Starkweather.

12. *Wikipedia*, s.v. "List of countries by international homicide rate by decade," last updated December 13, 2018, https://en.wikipedia.org/wiki/List_of_countries_by_intentional_homicide_rate.

13. Ibid.

14. Henry Allen, "Book Review: 'The Birth of the Pill,' by Jonathan Eig," *Wall Street Journal*, October 10, 2014, https://www.wsj.com/articles/book-review-the-birth-of-the-pill-by-jonathan-eig-1412974873.

15. Michael H. Stone, "Serial Sexual Homicide: Biological, Psychological, and Sociological Aspects," *Journal of Personality Disorders* 15, no. 1 (2001): 1–9.

16. Natalie Corner, "Serial Killer Ted Bundy Was Motivated by Rejection after He Was Dumped by His First Girlfriend, Expert Claims—and Even Chose Victims Who Were 'Carbon Copies' of the Woman Who Broke His Heart," *Daily Mail*, December 1, 2017, https://www.dailymail.co.uk/femail/article-5125215/Serial-killer-Ted-Bundy-motivated-rejection.html.

17. Christopher Lasch, *The Culture of Narcissism: American Life in an Age of Diminishing Expectations* (New York: W. W. Norton, 1979).

18. Lee Siegel, "The Book of Self-Love: Narcissism," *New York Times*, February 5, 2010, https://www.nytimes.com/2010/02/07/books/review/Siegel-t.html?mtrref=www.google.com&gwh=AE2A872AA7D0BCE4B76FF66607B65C85&gwt=pay.

19. James T. Patterson, *The Eve of Destruction: How 1965 Transformed America* (New York: Basic Books, 2012).

20. Philip Caputo, *A Rumor of War* (New York: Holt, Rinehart, and Winston, 1977).

21. Patterson, *Eve of Destruction*.

22. Ibid., p. 246.

23. William Glaberson, "Parolee Charged with the Killing of 6 in New York," *New York Times*, August 5, 1992, https://www.nytimes.com/1992/08/05/nyregion/parolee -charged-with-the-killing-of-6-in-new-york.html.

24. Alison Gendar, Edgar Sandoval, and Larry McShane, "Rutgers Freshman Kills Self after Classmates Use Hidden Camera to Watch His Sexual Activity," *Daily News*, September 30, 2010, http://www.nydailynews.com/news/crime/rutgers-freshman-kills -classmates-hidden-camera-watch-sexual-activity-sources-article-1.438225.

25. *Wikipedia*, s.v. "Suicide of Audrie Pott," last updated November 17, 2018, https://en.wikipedia.org/wiki/Suicide_of_Audrie_Pott.

26. *Wikipedia*, s.v. "Suicide of Amanda Todd," last updated November 21, 2018, https://en.wikipedia.org/wiki/Suicide_of_Amanda_Todd.

27. Ian Lovett and Adam Nagourney, "Photos Led to Arrest in Abuse of Pupils," *New York Times*, January 31, 2012, https://www.nytimes.com/2012/02/01/education/ former-teacher-61-arrested-in-california-on-abuse-charges.html?mtrref=www.google.com &gwh=5A0084BBBDF9BF9FC440699877CEDA41&gwt=pay.

28. Carol J. Rothgeb and Scott H. Cupp, *No One Can Hurt Him Anymore: The Worst Kind of Murder, the Worst Kind of Mother* (New York: Pinnacle, 2005).

29. Gerald Herbert, "La. Father Found Not Guilty of Decapitating Disabled Son," CBS News, February 14, 2014, https://www.cbsnews.com/news/louisiana -father-found-not-guilty-of-decapitating-disabled-son/.

30. D. T. Hughes, *Lullaby and Good Night* (New York: Pocket, 1992).

31. David Lohr, "Amanda Johnson, Valerie Bartkey Allegedly Sexually Assaulted High School Student with Pliers," *Huffington Post*, February 2, 2012, https://www .huffingtonpost.com/2012/02/02/valerie-bartkey-amanda-johnson_n_1248510.html.

32. Keith Edwards, "Woman Sentenced in Bizarre Sexual Assault Case," WQOW, July 17, 2013, http://www.wqow.com/story/22870624/2013/07/Wednesday/woman -sentenced-in-bizarre-sexual-assault-case.

33. Truman Capote, *In Cold Blood* (New York: New American Library, 1965).

34. Michael Benson, *Murder in Connecticut* (Guilford, CT: Lyons, 2008).

35. Ann Rule, *Bitter Harvest* (New York: Simon & Schuster, 1997).

36. "California Mother Gets Life Term in Baby's Microwave Death," CBS News, December 22, 2015, https://www.cbsnews.com/news/california-mother-gets -life-term-in-babys-microwave-death/.

37. Rachael Bell, "Internet Assisted Suicide: The Story of Sharon Lopatka," *Daily Dot*, February 4, 2013, https://www.dailydot.com/society/internet-assisted-suicide -sharon-lopatka/.

38. Lois Jones, *Cannibal: The True Story of the Maneater from Rotenburg* (New York: Berkley, 2005).

39. *Wikipedia*, s.v. "Murder of Skylar Neese," last edited November 12, 2018, https://en.wikipedia.org/wiki/Murder_of_Skylar_Neese.

40. Marion Collins, *While She Slept: A Husband, a Wife, a Brutal Murder* (New York: St. Martin's, 2005).

41. *Wikipedia*, s.v. "Murder of Annie Le," last updated November 12, 2018, https://en.wikipedia.org/wiki/Murder_of_Annie_Le.

42. Pat Ready, "Elizabeth Smart Describes 'Nine Months of Hell' in Captivity with Brian David Mitchell," *Desert News*, November 9, 2010, https://www.deseretnews.com/article/700080018/Elizabeth-Smart-describes-nine-months-of-hell-in-captivity-with-Brian-David-Mitchell.html.

43. Natalie Kampusch, *3,096 Days in Captivity: The True Story of My Abduction, Eight Years of Enslavement, and Escape* (New York: Berkley, Inc., 2010).

44. Andrew Snell, "Who Was Josef Fritzl? Ten Years on from Capture of Monster Who Kept Daughter as Sex Slave in Basement for Decades," *Mirror*, April 26, 2018, https://www.mirror.co.uk/news/world-news/who-josef-fritzl-ten-years-12431239.

45. *Biography*, s.v. "Phillip Garrido," 2018, https://www.biography.com/people/phillip-garrido-20995807.

46. *Wikipedia*, s.v. "Ariel Castro kidnappings," last updated December 4, 2018, https://en.wikipedia.org/wiki/Ariel_Castro_kidnappings.

47. Peter Davidson, *Homicide Miami: The Case of the Millionaire Killers* (New York: Penguin, 2009).

48. "Relative Says Virginia Tech Shooter Was Autistic," *Fox News*, April 20, 2007 (updated January 13, 2015), https://www.foxnews.com/story/relative-says-virginia-tech-shooter-was-autistic.

49. Christine Hsu, "Adam Lanza's Asperger's, Autism Cannot Be Blamed for CT School Shooting, Experts," *Medical Daily*, December 17, 2012, https://www.medicaldaily.com/adam-lanzas-aspergers-autism-cannot-be-blamed-ct-school-shooting-experts-243927.

50. Adam Nagourney, Michael Cieply, Alan Feuer, and Ian Lovett, "Before Brief, Deadly Spree, Trouble Since Age 8," *New York Times*, June 1, 2014, https://www.nytimes.com/2014/06/02/us/elliot-rodger-killings-in-california-followed-years-of-withdrawal.html.

51. Michael H. Stone, "Mass Murder, Mental Illness, and Men," *Violence and Gender* 2, no. 1 (2015): 51-86.

52. John Cloud, "The Troubled Life of Jared Loughner," *Time*, January 15, 2011, http://content.time.com/time/magazine/article/0,9171,2042358,00.html.

53. "Sikh Temple Shooting Suspect Wade Michael Page Was White Supremacist," *CBS News*, August 6, 2012, https://www.cbsnews.com/news/sikh-temple-shooting-suspect-wade-michael-page-was-white-supremacist/; "Wade Michael Page's Acquaintances Recall a Troubled Man Guided by Hate," *Guardian*, August 7, 2012, https://www.theguardian.com/world/2012/aug/07/wade-michael-page-wisconsin-shooting; *Wikipedia*, s.v. "Wisconsin Sikh temple shooting," last updated November 3, 2018, https://en.wikipedia.org/wiki/Wisconsin_Sikh_temple_shooting.

54. Eric Francis, *A Wife's Revenge* (New York: St. Martin's, 2005).

55. Gary Kinder, *Victim: The Other Side of Murder* (New York: Atlantic Monthly, 1982).

56. John Dean, *House of Evil* (New York: St. Martin's, 2008).

57. Martin Daly and Margot Wilson, *Homicide* (New York: Aldine De Gruyter, 1988).

58. Wensley Clarkson, *Whatever Mother Says: A True Story of a Mother, Madness, and Murder* (New York: St. Martin's, 1995).

59. Charles Hustmyre, *An Act of Kindness* (New York: Berkley, 2007).

60. Rob Preece, "Football Star 'Tortured and Killed Model Who Had His Love Child and Fed Her Dismembered Body to His Pet Rottweilers,'" *Daily Mail*, September 9,

2012, http://www.dailymail.co.uk/news/article-2200537/Football-star-Bruno-tortured
-killed-model-love-child-fed-dismembered-body-pet-dogs.html.

61. Alejandra Pizarnik, "The Bloody Countess," in *The Oxford Book of Gothic Tales*, Chris Baldick, ed. (Oxford: Oxford UP, 1992), pp. 466-477; Valentine Penrose, *The Bloody Countess: Atrocities of Erzsébet Báthory*, trans. Alexander Trocchi (London: Creation Books, 2000).

62. Katherine Ramsland, "Women Aroused by Murder," *Psychology Today*, December 12, 2017, https://www.psychologytoday.com/us/blog/shadow-boxing/201712/women-aroused-murder.

63. Christopher Barry-Dee and Steven Morris, *Online Killers: Portraits of Murderers, Cannibals and Sex Predators Who Stalked the Web for Their Victims* (Berkeley, CA: Ulysses Press, 2010).

64. Brian Masters, *Killing for Company: The Case of Dennis Nilsen* (New York: Pinnacle, 1985).

65. M. William Phelps, *Cruel Death* (New York: Pinnacle Books, 2009), p. 121.

66. *Wikipedia*, s.v. "Erika and Benjamin Sifrit," last updated November 9, 2018, https://en.wikipedia.org/wiki/Erika_and_Benjamin_Sifrit.

67. Desmond Seward, *The Demon's Brood: A History of the Plantagenet Dynasty* (New York: Pegasus, 2014), p. 22.

68. "United States Crime Rates 1960–2016," Disaster Center, 2018, http://www.disastercenter.com/crime/uscrime.htm.

69. Iris Chang, *The Rape of Nanking: The Forgotten Holocaust of World War II* (New York: Basic Books, 1997).

70. *Wikipedia*, s.v. "Luke Magnotta," last updated October 31, 2018, https://en.wikipedia.org/wiki/Luka_Magnotta.

71. "A Criminal Timeline of Travis Forbes, Admitted Killer of 19-Year-Old Kenia Monge," *Denver Post*, September 26, 2011, https://www.denverpost.com/2011/09/26/a-criminal-timeline-of-travis-forbes-admitted-killer-of-19-year-old-kenia-monge/.

72. Louise Boyle, "Texas Man Who Raped Boy and Set Him on Fire Causing Horrific Burns to 99 Percent of His Body Found Guilty of Capital Murder," *Daily Mail*, February 9, 2015, http://www.dailymail.co.uk/news/article-2946738/Don-Collins-raped-boy-set-fire-causing-horrific-burns-GUILTY-capital-murder.html.

73. *Wikipedia*, s.v. "John Couey," last edited July 15, 2018, https://en.wikipedia.org/wiki/John_Couey.

74. *Wikipedia*, s.v. "Murder of Tori Stafford," last edited November 12, 2018, https://en.wikipedia.org/wiki/Murder_of_Tori_Stafford.

75. Annett Schirmer, "Sex Differences in Emotion," in *The Cambridge Handbook of Human Affective Science*, ed. Jorge Armony and Patrik Vuilleumier (New York: Cambridge University Press, 2013), pp. 591–610.

76. Cynthia Stalter Sasse and Peggy Murphy Widder, *The Kirtland Massacre: The True and Terrible Story of the Mormon Cult Murders* (New York: Donald I. Fine, 1991).

77. Ronald C. Naso and Jon Mills (eds.), *Humanizing Evil: Psychoanalytic, Philosophical and Clinical Perspectives* (London: Routledge, 2016), p. 149.

78. John Douglas and Mark Olshaker, *Law and Disorder: Inside the Dark Heart of Murder* (New York: Kensington, 2013), pp. 118–62.

79. Richard von Krafft-Ebing, *Lehrbuch der gerichtlichen Psychopathologie* (Stuttgart, Germany: Ferdinand Enke, 1881).

80. John Borowski, *The Strange Case of Dr. H. H. Holmes* (West Hollywood, CA: Waterfront Productions, 2005); Adam Selzer, *H. H. Holmes: The True History of the White City Devil* (New York: Skyhorse Publishing, 2017).

81. Stephen D. Hart, "Psychopathy and Risk for Violence," in *Psychopathy: Theory, Research and Implications for Society*, ed. D. J. Cooke, A. E. Forth, and R. D. Hare (Dordrecht, the Netherlands: Kluwer Academic, 1998), pp. 355–73.

82. Michael H. Stone, *The Anatomy of Evil* (Amherst, NY: Prometheus Books, 2009).

83. Scott Bonn, *Why We Love Serial Killers* (New York: Skyhorse, 2014), p. 68.

84. Ronald Markman and Dominick Bosco, *Alone with the Devil: Famous Cases of a Courtroom Psychiatrist* (New York: Bantam, 1989).

85. David A. Gibb, *The Camouflaged Killer: The Shocking Double Life of Colonel Russell Williams* (New York: Berkley, 2012).

86. Bonn, *Why We Love Serial Killers*, p. 225.

87. *Wikipedia*, s.v. "Mark Lepine," last edited October 29, 2018, https://en.wikipedia.org/wiki/Marc_L%C3%A9pine.

88. Margaret Cheney, *Why: The Serial Killer in America* (Saratoga, CA: R & E Publications, 1992).

89. Jack Olsen, *The Creation of a Serial Killer* (New York: St. Martin's, 2002).

90. Melissa Moore, *Shattered Silence: The Untold Story of a Serial Killer's Daughter* (Springville, UT: Cedar Fort, 2009).

91. *Wikipedia*, s.v. "Murder, Inc.," last edited December 6, 2018, https://en.wikipedia.org/wiki/Murder,_Inc.

92. Anne Barnard, "Queens Doctor and Cousin Are Guilty in Murder," *New York Times*, March 10, 2009, https://www.nytimes.com/2009/03/11/nyregion/11dentist.html?pagewanted=all.

93. *Wikipedia*, s.v. "Kevin Coe," last edited July 11, 2018, https://en.wikipedia.org/wiki/Kevin_Coe.

94. David J. Krajicek, "She Made Them Killers," *Daily News*, August 16, 2008, http://www.nydailynews.com/news/crime/made-killers-article-1.319258.

95. "Shannon Found Guilty in Death of Army Husband; Sentenced to Life," WRAL, August 31, 2005, https://www.wral.com/news/local/story/119635/.

96. Camila Domonoske, "CDC: Half of All Female Homicide Victims Are Killed by Intimate Partners," NPR, July 21, 2017, https://www.npr.org/sections/thetwo-way/2017/07/21/538518569/cdc-half-of-all-female-murder-victims-are-killed-by-intimate-partners.

97. Alexia Cooper and Erica L. Smith, "*Homicide Trends in the United States, 1980–2008: Annual Rates for 2009 and 2010*" (Washington, DC: US Department of Justice, Bureau of Justice Statistics, November 2011), https://www.bjs.gov/content/pub/pdf/htus8008.pdf.

98. A. L. Kellermann, F. P. Rivara, N. B. Rushforth, et al., "Gun Ownership as a Risk Factor for Homicide in the Home," *New England Journal of Medicine* 329, no. 15 (1993): 1084–91.

99. *Wikipedia*, s.v. "Chester Gillette," last edited September 22, 2018, https://en.wikipedia.org/wiki/Chester_Gillette.

100. Jay Robert Nash, *Murder, America: Homicide in the United States from the Revolution to the Present* (Lanham, MD: M. Evans, 1980), p. 415.

101. *Wikipedia*, s.v. "Elizabeth Ann Duncan," last edited October 30, 2018, https://en.wikipedia.org/wiki/Elizabeth_Ann_Duncan.

102. Thomas Thompson, *Blood and Money* (Garden City, NY: Doubleday, 1976).

103. Bill McClellan, *Evidence of Murder: The Perfect Marriage—and the Almost Perfect Murder* (New York: Penguin, 1993).

104. Joe McGinnis, *Blind Faith* (New York: Putnam, 1989).

105. Joe Sharkey, *Deadly Greed: The Riveting True Story of the Stuart Murder Case* (New York: Prentiss Hill, 1991).

106. Lee Butcher, *To Love, Honor, and Kill* (New York: Pinnacle, 2008).

107. James Ruddick, *Death at the Priory: Sex, Love, and Murder in Victorian England* (New York: Atlantic Monthly, 2001).

108. Linda Rosencrance, *An Act of Murder* (New York: Pinnacle, 2006).

109. John Glatt, *Playing with Fire* (New York: St. Martin's, 2010).

110. *Murderpedia*, s.v. "Carl Coppolino," http://murderpedia.org/male.C/c/coppolino-carl.htm.

111. John Glatt, *Deadly American Beauty* (New York: St. Martin's, 2004).

112. Marion Collins, *Black Widow: The Story of a Beautiful Woman, Two Lovers, and Two Murders* (New York: St. Martin's, 2007).

113. "Man Guilty of Killing Wife with Antifreeze," CBS News, July 2, 2008, https://www.cbsnews.com/news/man-guilty-of-killing-wife-with-antifreeze/.

114. Valerie Edwards, "Missouri Woman, 25, Sentenced to at Least 42 Years for Helping Her Mom Poison Their Family: Killing Her Dad and Brother and Leaving Her Sister with Brain Injuries," *Daily Mail*, March 2, 2016, http://www.dailymail.co.uk/news/article-3472941/Missouri-woman-25-sentenced-two-life-prison-terms-fatally-poisoning-dad-brother-antifreeze.html.

115. Arthur Herzog Jr., *The Woodchipper Murder* (New York: Henry Holt, 1989).

116. John Glatt, *To Have and to Kill: A Loving Wife . . . and a Deadly Plot* (New York: St. Martin's, 2008).

117. "Chef Reveals How He Slowly Cooked His Wife for Four Days and Then Hid Her Skull at Mother's House after Killing Her in Fit of Rage," *Daily Mail*, September 27, 2012, http://www.dailymail.co.uk/news/article-2205371/Dawn-Viens-murder-Chef-slow-cooked-wifes-dead-body-4-days-skull-left.html.

118. *Wikipedia*, s.v. "Marjorie Ann Orbin," last edited July 27, 2018, https://en.wikipedia.org/wiki/Marjorie_Ann_Orbin.

119. *Wikipedia*, s.v. "Winnie Ruth Judd," last edited October 29, 2018, https://en.wikipedia.org/wiki/Winnie_Ruth_Judd; Jana Bommersbach, *The Trunk Murderess* (New York: Simon & Schuster, 1992).

120. Clifford L. Linedecker, *The Murder of Laci Peterson: She Looked Forward to a Child; He Looked for a Way Out* (Boca Raton, FL: American Media, 2003).

121. Kieran Crowley, *The Surgeon's Wife* (New York: St. Martin's, 2001).

122. Linedecker, *The Murder of Laci Peterson*.

123. "Story of the Boy Jones Who Stole Queen Victoria's Underwear," *BBC*, February 2, 2011, https://www.bbc.com/news/uk-wales-12342921.

124. Paul E. Mullen, Michele Pathé, and Rosemary Purcell, *Stalkers and Their Victims* (Cambridge, England: Cambridge University Press, 2000).

125. Robert Beattie, *Nightmare in Wichita: The Hunt for the BTK Strangler* (New York: New American Library, 2005).

126. Doreen Orion, *I Knew You Really Loved Me: A Psychiatrist's Account of Stalking and Obsessive Love* (New York: Dell/Random House, 1997).

127. Samantha Gluck, "Stalking and Obsessive Love," Healthy Place, last updated March 30, 2017, https://www.healthyplace.com/abuse/transcripts/stalking-and-obsessive-love.

128. *Wikipedia*, s.v. "Robert John Bardo," last edited October 30, 2018, https://en.wikipedia.org/wiki/Robert_John_Bardo.

129. Deborah Blum, *Bad Karma: A True Story of Obsession and Murder* (New York: Atheneum, 1986).

130. Ronald Markman and Ron LaBreque, *Obsessed: The Stalking of Theresa Saldana* (New York: William Morrow, 1994).

131. J. Reid Meloy, *Violent Attachments* (Northvale, NJ: Aronson, 1992).

132. "John Hinckley's Last Love Letter to Jodie Foster," *Newsweek*, July 27, 2017, https://www.newsweek.com/john-hinckley-love-letter-jodie-foster -reagan-assassination-484716.

133. *Wikipedia*, s.v. "Perry v. Louisiana," last updated August 26, 2018, https://en.wikipedia.org/wiki/Perry_v._Louisiana.

134. *Murderpedia*, s.v. "Darnell Collins," http://murderpedia.org/male.C/c/collins -darnell.htm.

135. United States Attorney's Office, Middle District of Pennsylvania, "Former Wilkes-Barre, PA. Football Coach Sentenced to 25 Years for Producing Child Pornography, Interstate Extortion, and Cyber Stalking," news release, May 15, 2013, https://www.justice.gov/usao-mdpa/pr/former-wilkes-barre-pa-football -coach-sentenced-25-years-producing-child-pornography.

136. Joseph Cox, "Convicted Child Pornographer Held Victims' Email, Facebook Accounts for Ransom," *Motherboard* (Vice blog), September 15, 2015, https://motherboard.vice.com/en_us/article/9akxn7/convicted-child -pornographer-held-victims-email-facebook-accounts-for-ransom.

137. Ed White, "Adam Savader Gets 30 Months in Prison in Cyberstalking Case," *Newsday*, April 24, 2014, https://www.newsday.com/long-island/nassau/adam-savader-gets-30-months-in-prison-in-cyberstalking-case-1.7811974.

138. Andy Newman, "Stalked: A Decade on the Run," *New York Times*, July 31, 2008, https://www.nytimes.com/2008/07/31/fashion/31stalk.html?mtrref=www.google .com&gwh=8E58E4939D74E38A6FDFC1F44924B828&gwt=pay.

139. S. C. Anderson, "Anti-Stalking Laws: Will They Curb the Erotomanic's Obsessive Pursuit?" *Law and Psychology Review* 17 (1993): 171–92.

140. Ibid.; Robert L. Snow, *Stopping a Stalker: A Cop's Guide to Making the System Work for You* (Cambridge, MA: Perseus, 1998).

141. Sharon Lerner, "Stalking the Stalkers: New York Begins to Prosecute," *Village Voice* (New York), July 3, 2001.

CHAPTER THIRTEEN: SCHOOL SHOOTERS

1. Sara Tenenbaum, "Laurie Dann: Timeline of 1988 Fires, Winnetka School Shooting, Standoff," *ABC7 Chicago*, May 17, 2018, https://abc7chicago.com/laurie-dann-school-shooting-timeline-of-1988-crime-spree/3483715/.

2. Michael H. Stone, "Mass Murder, Mental Illness, and Men," *Violence and Gender* 2, no. 1 (2015): 51-86.

3. Rosa Flores, "Stoneman Douglas' Resource Officer Recommended Committing Nikolas Cruz for Mental Health Issues," CNN, March 19, 2018, https://www.cnn.com/2018/03/19/us/florida-school-shooting-cruz-psychiatric-records/index.html.

4. Mia De Graaf, "Florida Shooter, 19, May Have Had Fetal Alcohol Syndrome That Causes Memory, Learning, and Behavioral Issues, Expert Says," *Daily Mail*, February 15, 2018, http://www.dailymail.co.uk/health/article-5396665/Florida-shooter-19-fetal-alcohol-syndrome; Lynda Cruz, the adoptive mother of Nikolas Cruz, has alleged that the boy's biological mother was a drug addict. See: Max Jaeger, "Alleged School Shooter's Mom Paid $50,000 to Adopt Him from 'Drug Addict,'" *New York Post*, February 27, 2018, https://nypost.com/2018/02/27/alleged-school-shooters-mom-paid-50k-to-adopt-him-from-drug-addict/.

5. FASD played a role, for example, in the case of Richard M. Clark, a juvenile delinquent who raped and murdered a seven-year-old girl in Washington State. See: Burl Barer, *Broken Doll* (New York: Pinnacle, 2004); Another case involving FASD is that of twenty-year-old Dimarzo Sanchez, who strangled a young woman, Roylynn Rideshorse, from Montana's Crow Indian Reservation, and then burned her to death. Sanchez's mother had drunk alcohol copiously throughout her pregnancy, which led to his FASD. Some typical features are poor coordination, hyperactive behavior, small head size, and poor school performance.

6. Carl C. Bell, "Fetal Alcohol Spectrum Disorders and Suicidality," *Clinical Psychiatry News*, December 28, 2017, https://www.mdedge.com/psychiatry/article/155222/addiction-medicine/fetal-alcohol-spectrum-disorders-and-suicidality.

7. *Wikipedia*, s.v. "Sandy Hook Elementary School Shooting," last edited November 13, 2018, https://en.wikipedia.org/wiki/Sandy_Hook_Elementary_School_shooting.

8. *Wikipedia*, s.v. "Seung-Hui Cho," last edited November 12, 2018, https://en.wikipedia.org/wiki/Seung-Hui_Cho; Windrem, "Va. Tech Killer's Strange Manifesto."

9. "Schoolmaster Murdered," *Daily Dispatch* (Richmond, VA) 10, no. 41 (August 16, 1856): 2.

10. "Terrible Shooting Affray at Knight's Ferry," *Daily Alta Californian* (San Francisco) 19, no. 7084 (February 17, 1867): 1.

11. "One Day Last Week," *Nebraska Advertiser* (Brownville, Nemaha County, N.T. [NE]) 18, no. 35 (February 26, 1875): 2.

12. "Tragedy Ends Rivalry for Schoolgirls' Love," *San Francisco Call* 95, no. 129 (April 7, 1904): 4.

13. *Wikipedia*, s.v. "Charles Whitman," last updated December 12, 2018, https://en.wikipedia.org/wiki/Charles_Whitman.

14. *Wikipedia*, s.v. "List of School Shootings in the United States," last updated November 12, 2018, https://en.wikipedia.org/wiki/List_of_school_shootings_in_the_United_States. Another survey in *Wikipedia* covers school and college shootings in other

countries, such as Canada, Australia, and New Zealand, and nations in Europe, South America, the Middle East, and Asia. See: *Wikipedia*, s.v. "School Shooting," last updated November 13, 2018, https://en.wikipedia.org/wiki/School_shooting. As for the primary school, as opposed to college, shootings with the greatest numbers of deaths, these stemmed from Islamic terrorism. One was the 2004 Beslan massacre in the Northern Ossetia part of Russia, in which terrorists stormed the school, took 1,200 children and adults hostage, and eventually killed 330 children. See: "Beslan School Siege Fast Facts," CNN, September 9, 2013, https://www.cnn.com/2013/09/09/world/europe/beslan -school-siege-fast-facts/index.html. Ten years later, Taliban militants broke into the Army Public School in Peshawar, Pakistan, killing 145 students. Regarding the mass-scale kidnapping of girls by the jihadist Boko Haram in northeast Nigeria in 2014, information as to how many were later killed is scanty and unreliable. Not long after, in 2015, the jihadist group, Somali al-Shabaab, killed 147 students at the Garissa University College. See: Michael Pearson, Lillian Leposo, and David McKenz, "Inside Garissa University College Dorm's Scene of Slaughter," CNN, April 3, 2015, http:///edition.cnn.com/ 2015/04/03/africa/kenya-garissa-university-attack-witnesses.

15. Malcolm Gladwell, "Thresholds of Violence: How School Shootings Catch On," *New Yorker*, October 19, 2015, https://www.newyorker.com/magazine/2015/10/19/ thresholds-of-violence.

16. Justin Peters, "Everything You Think You Know about Mass Murder Is Wrong," *Slate*, December 19, 2013, http://www.slate.com/blogs/crime/2013/12/19/mass _shootings_in_america_northeastern_criminologists_james_alan_fox_monica.html.

17. People v. Pisarski, 285 N.E.2d 551 (Ill. App. Ct. 1972), available on Leagle, https://www.leagle.com/decision/19722416illapp3d2351185.

18. Rocha v. People, 713 P.2d 350 (1986), available on Justia, https://law.justia.com/ cases/colorado/supreme-court/1986/84sc100-0.html.

19. Vince Devlin, "1986 Lewistown School Shooting Victim, Family Know Lasting Impact of Gun Violence," *Missoulian*, January 28, 2013, http://missoulian.com/ news/local/lewistown-school-shooting-victim-family-know-lasting-impact-of-gun/ article_11699798-683b-11e2-9f62-001a4bcf887a.html; "Failing Grade Is Linked to Shooting of Teacher," *New York Times*, December 6, 1986.

20. *Murderpedia*, s.v. "Tronneal L. Mangum," http://murderpedia.org/male.M/m/ mangum-tronneal.htm.

21. *Murderpedia*, s.v. "Luke Woodham," http://murderpedia.org/male.W/w/ woodham-luke.htm; "Luke Woodham," Criminal Justice, http://criminal-justice .iresearchnet.com/crime/school-violence/luke-woodham/; C. A. David, "Dare to Be Different," in *Children Who Kill: Profiles of Pre-Teen and Teenage Killers* (London, England: Allison & Busby, 2003), pp. 67–79.

22. Edwin Chen, *Deadly Scholarship: The True Story of Lu Gang and Mass Murder in America's Heartland* (New York: Birch Lane Press/Carol Publishing, 1995).

23. "Slaughter in a Schoolyard," *Time*, January 30, 1989; *Wikipedia*, s.v. "Cleveland Elementary School Shooting (Stockton)," last updated November 11, 2018, https:// en.wikipedia.org/wiki/Cleveland_Elementary_School_shooting_(Stockton); *Murderpedia*, s.v. "Patrick Edward Purdy," http://murderpedia.org/male.P/p/purdy-patrick.htm.

24. David Peisner, "The Ghosts of Jonesboro: Fifteen Years after a School Shooting, a Small Town Is Still Recovering," BuzzFeed, March 25, 2013, https://www.buzzfeed.

com/djpeisner/the-ghosts-of-jonesboro-fifteen-years-after-a-notorious
-scho?utm_term=.xe0NYa5pE#.xyrW03l6Z; *Wikipedia*, s.v. "Mitchell Johnson and
Andrew Golden," last edited November 13, 2018, https://en.wikipedia.org/wiki/
Mitchell_Johnson_and_Andrew_Golden.

25. Michael H. Stone, "Marijuana and Psychosis: The Effects of Adolescent Abuse
of Marijuana and Other Drugs in a Group of Forensic Patients," *Journal of Child and
Adolescent Behavior* 3 (2015): 188.

26. *Frontline*, "The Killer at Thurston High: 111 Years without Parole," produced
by Miri Navasky, written by Michael Kirk and Peter Boyer, aired on January 18, 2000, on
PBS, http://www.pbs.org/wgbh/pages/frontline/shows/kinkel/trial.

27. *Wikipedia*, s.v. "Stoneman Douglas High School shooting," last updated
December 14, 2018, https://en.wikipedia.org/wiki/Stoneman_Douglas
_High_School_shooting.

28. Larry McShane, "Sue Klebold, Mother of Columbine High School Shooter
Dylan Klebold, Reveals She Prayed for Son's Death in New Book 'A Mother's
Reckoning,'" *Daily News* (New York), February 13, 2016.

29. Dave Cullen, *Columbine* (New York: Twelve/Hachette, 2010).

30. Robert D. Hare, *Without Conscience: The Disturbing World of the Psychopaths Among Us*
(New York: Pocket, 1993).

31. Cullen, *Columbine*.

32. John M. Broder, "Student Kills Three Instructors and Himself at U. of
Arizona," *New York Times*, October 29, 2002; *Murderpedia*, s.v. "Robert Stewart Flores,"
http://murderpedia.org/male.F/f/flores-robert-stewart.htm.

33. Sara Left, "A Neo-Nazi 'Angel of Death,'" *Guardian*, March 25, 2005, https://
www.theguardian.com/world/2005/mar/22/usa.usgunviolence1; *Wikipedia*, s.v. "Jeff
Weise," last edited November 12, 2018, https://en.wikipedia.org/wiki/Jeff_Weise.

34. David Kocieniewski and Shaila Dewan, "Police Describe Gunman's Plan
in School Siege," *New York Times*, October 4, 2006; *Wikipedia*, s.v. "West Nickel Mines
School Shooting," last updated October 28, 2018, https://en.wikipedia.org/wiki/
West_Nickel_Mines_School_shooting.

35. John Podhoretz, "Hating a Child Killer," *National Review*, October 5, 2006,
https://www.nationalreview.com/corner/hating-child-killer-john-podhoretz/; Jeff Jacoby,
"Undeserved Forgiveness," *Boston Globe*, October 8, 2006, http://archive.boston.com/
news/globe/editorial_opinion/oped/articles/2006/10/08/undeserved_forgiveness/;
Dovid Gottlieb, "Not Always Divine," *Cross Currents* (blog), October 17, 2006, https://
cross-currents.com/2006/10/17/not-always-divine/.

36. "Report: Cho Hired an Escort Before Rampage," ABC News, April 24, 2007,
https://abcnews.go.com/US/VATech/story?id=3071730&page=1.

37. "Massacre Gunman's Deadly Infatuation with Emily," *Evening Standard*, April 17,
2007, https://www.standard.co.uk/news/massacre-gunmans-deadly-infatuation-with
-emily-7238319.html.

38. Robert Windrem, "Va. Tech Killer's Strange Manifesto," NBC News, April
19, 2007, http://www.nbcnews.com/id/18187368/ns/us_news-crime_and_courts/t/
va-tech-killers-strange-manifesto/#.WvuxQWgvz7k.

39. *Wikipedia*, s.v. "Seung-Hui Cho."

40. David Vann, "Portrait of the Shooter as a Young Man," *Esquire*, February 12, 2009.

41. Ibid.

42. David Vann, *Last Day on Earth: A Portrait of the NIU School Shooter* (Athens, GA: University of Georgia Press, 2011), p. 58.

43. Lisa Wade, *American Hookup: The Bew Culture of Sex on Campus* (New York: W. W. Norton, 2017), p. 19.

44. *Wikipedia*, s.v. "Northern Illinois University shooting," last updated December 11, 2018, https://en.wikipedia.org/wiki/Northern_Illinois_University_shooting.

45. Jodi S. Cohen and Stacy St. Clair, "Gunman Wanted to Punish Illinois University," *Los Angeles*, March 22, 2010, http://articles.latimes.com/2010/mar/22/nation/la-na-illinois-shooter22-2010mar22.

46. Abbie Boudreau and Scott Zamost, "CNN Exclusive: Secret Files Reveal NIU Killer's Past," CNN, February 13, 2009, http://www.cnn.com/2009/CRIME/02/13/niu.shooting.investigation/index.html.

47. Associated Press, "NIU Gunman's Girlfriend: 'I Still Love Him,'" CBS News, February 17, 2008, https://www.cbsnews.com/news/niu-gunmans-girlfriendi-still-love-him/.

48. *Wikipedia*, s.v. "Oikos University Shooting," last edited November 2, 2018, https://en.wikipedia.org/wiki/Oikos_University_shooting.

49. Miva, "Mugshot: Oakland University Shooter One L. Goh First Picture Emerged!!!," FanDaily, April 4, 2012, http://fandaily.info/news/oakland-university-shooter-one-l-goh-first-picture-emerged/.

50. Terry McSweeney, Katie Marzullo, Mark Matthews, et al., "Shooting Rampage Suspect's Motive Was Revenge," ABC, April 3, 2012, http://a.abclocal.go.com/kabc/story?section=news/local/east_bay&id=8605985.

51. Uta Frith, *Autistic Psychopathy in Childhood: Autism and Asperger Syndrome* (Cambridge, England: Cambridge University Press, 1991), pp. 37–92.

52. *Wikipedia*, s.v. "Sandy Hook Elementary School Shooting."

53. Maya Salam, "Adam Lanza Threatened Sandy Hook Killings Years Before, Records Show," *New York Times*, October 26, 2017, https://www.nytimes.com/2017/10/26/us/adam-lanza-sandy-hook.html.

54. Brian Fung, "People Thought Adam Lanza Posted About Newtown on 4Chan. The Official Report Debunks That," *Switch*, November 25, 2013, https://www.washingtonpost.com/news/the-switch/wp/2013/11/25/people-thought-adam-lanza-posted-about-newtown-on-4chan-the-official-report-debunks-that/?noredirect=on&utm_term=.815ffcc53b60.

55. Timberly Ross, "Mom of Mall Shooter Says She's Responsible," *Lincoln Journal Star*, January 7, 2009, http://journalstar.com/news/state-and-regional/govt-and-politics/mom-of-mall-shooter-says-she-s-responsible/article_50377e0d-10ca-5118-8d7d-2e41b45349b6.html.

56. David Kopel, "Guns, Mental Illness and Newtown," *Wall Street Journal*, December 18, 2012, https://www.wsj.com/articles/SB10001424127887323723104578185271857424036.

57. Jana Winter, "EXCLUSIVE: Fear of Being Committed May Have Caused Connecticut Gunman to Snap," Fox News, December 18, 2012, http://www.foxnews.com/us/2012/12/18/fear-being-committed-may-have-caused-connecticut-madman-to-snap.html#ixzz2FRwgXsC3.

58. James Barron, "Nation Reels after Gunman Massacres 20 Children at School in Connecticut," *New York Times*, December 14, 2012, https://www.nytimes.com/ 2012/12/15/nyregion/shooting-reported-at-connecticut-elementary-school.html.

59. Andrew Solomon, "The Reckoning: The Father of the Sandy Hook Killer Searches for Answers," *New Yorker*, March 17, 2014, pp. 34–45.

60. Ibid., p. 37.

61. Kashmir Hill, "The Disturbing Internet Footprint of Santa Barbara Shooter Elliot Rodger," *Forbes*, May 24, 2014, https://www.forbes.com/ sites/kashmirhill/2014/05/24/the-disturbing-internet-footprint-of -santa-barbara-shooter-elliot-rodger/.

62. Elliot Rodgers, *My Twisted World* (CreateSpace, 2014).

63. Laura Shortridge, "In the Mind of a Killer: Not for Sensitive Readers," W24, May 27, 2014, https://www.w24.co.za/Archive/Summary-of-Elliot-Rodgers -manifesto-20140527.

64. *Wikipedia*, s.v. "2014 Isla Vista Killings," last edited November 12, 2018, https:// en.wikipedia.org/wiki/2014_Isla_Vista_killings.

65. Rick Anderson, "'Here I Am, 26, with No Friends, No Job, No Girlfriend: Shooter's Manifesto Offers Clues to 2015 Oregon College Rampage," *Los Angeles Times*, September 23, 2017, http://www.latimes.com/nation/la-na-school-shootings-2017-story.html.

66. Jack Healy and Ian Lovett, "Oregon Killer Described as a Man of Few Words, Except on the Topic of Guns," *New York Times*, October 2, 2015, https://www.nytimes .com/2015/10/03/us/chris-harper-mercer-umpqua-community-college-shooting.html.

67. Anderson, "Here I Am."

68. Given Harper-Mercer's familiarity with previous school shooters, he may have been imitating one of the Columbine shooters. Or at least, he may have believed he was doing so. A widely-circulated story went that one of the Columbine shooters asked one of the victims, Cassie Bernall, "Do you believe in God?" When she said, "Yes, I believe in God," he shot her to death. It was later determined, however, that this story was probably apocryphal. The shooter was more likely the atheistic Eric Harris than the religious Dylan Klebold, but we do not know. David Cullen, "Why Does the Columbine Myth about 'Martyr' Cassie Bernall Persist?" *New Republic*, September 16, 2015, https://newrepublic .com/article/122832/why-does-columbine-myth-about-martyr-cassie-bernall-persist.

69. Max Kutner, "What Led Jayden Fryberg to Commit the Deadliest High School Shooting in a Decade?" *Newsweek*, September 16, 2015, http://www.newsweek.com/ 2015/09/25/jaylen-ray-fryberg-marysville-pilchuck-high-school-shooting-372669.html.

70. *Wikipedia*, s.v. "Marysville Pilchuck High School Shooting," last edited November 11, 2018, https://en.wikipedia.org/wiki/Marysville_Pilchuck_High_School_shooting.

71. Lindsey Bever, "'I Needed to Do This:' A School Shooter's Final Texts Before Gunning Down His Friends," *Washington Post*, September 2, 2015, https://www .washingtonpost.com/news/post-nation/wp/2015/09/02/moments-before-massacre -seattle-area-school-shooter-texted-i-needed-to-do-this-and-i-need-my-crew-with-me -too/?utm_term=.a048c672f358.

72. Max Kutner, Ray Fryberg, Father of Marysville-Pilchuck Shooter, Guilty on Gun Charges," *Newsweek*, September 30, 2015, https://www.newsweek.com/ ray-fryberg-jaylen-father-sentenced-unlawful-possession-guns-378517.

73. Jaeger, "Alleged School Shooter's Mom."

74. Max Jaeger, "Alleged School Shooter's Mom Paid $50K to Adopt Him from 'Drug Addict,'" *New York Post*, February 27, 2018, https://nypost.com/2018/02/27/alleged-school-shooters-mom-paid-50k-to-adopt-him-from-drug-addict/.

75. Dakin Andone, "The Warning Signs Almost Everyone Missed," CNN, February 26, 2018, https://www.cnn.com/2018/02/25/us/nikolas-cruz-warning-signs/index.html.

76. Terry Spencer and Kelli Kennedy, "Florida School Shooting Suspect Belonged to White Nationalist Group," *Northwest Herald*, February 15, 2018, http://www.nwherald.com/2018/02/15/florida-school-shooting-suspect-belonged-to-white-nationalist-group/asqjulw/?fb_comment_id=1603769793074622_1603940556390879.

77. Eric Levenson and Joe Sterling, "These Are the Victims of the Florida School Shooting," CNN, February 21, 2018, https://www.cnn.com/2018/02/15/us/florida-shooting-victims-school/index.html.

78. Paula McMahon, Tonya Alanez and Lisa J. Huriash, "Parkland Shooter Nikolas Cruz During Confession: 'Kill Me,'" *Sun Sentinel*, August 6, 2018, https://www.sun-sentinel.com/local/broward/parkland/florida-school-shooting/fl-florida-school-shooting-nikolas-cruz-confession-20180806-story.html.

79. Paula McMahon, "Odds Are Against Nikolas Cruz Insanity Defense," *Sun Sentinel*, December 15, 2018, https://www.sun-sentinel.com/local/broward/parkland/florida-school-shooting/fl-florida-school-shooting-nikolas-cruz-video-insanity-defense-20180810-story.html; Nicole Chavez and Mike Ellis, "Nikolas Cruz Waives Right to Speedy Trial," CNN, April 27, 2018, https://www.cnn.com/2018/04/27/us/nikolas-cruz-hearing/index.html; Jeremy B. White, "Florida Shooting Suspect, Nikolas Cruz, Willing to Plead Guilty to Avoid Death Penalty, Attorney Howard Finkelstein Says," *Independent*, February 17, 2018, https://www.independent.co.uk/news/world/americas/florida-shooter-nikolas-cruz-guilty-plea-murder-charges-death-penalty-a8215911.html.

80. McMahon, "Odds Are Against," *Sun Sentinel*.

81. Zoe Szathmary, "School Shootings with Female Students," Fox News, February 8, 2018, http://www.foxnews.com/us/2018/02/04/school-shootings-with-female-shooters.html.

82. Timothy D. May, "Girl Admits Catholic School Shooting," ABC News, April 4, 2001, https://abcnews.go.com/US/story?id=93650&page=1.

83. *Wikipedia*, s.v. "Cleveland Elementary School Shooting (San Diego)," last edited November 12, 2018, https://en.wikipedia.org/wiki/Cleveland_Elementary_School_shooting_(San_Diego); Jonathan Fast, "Unforgiven and Alone: Brenda Spencer and Secret Shame," in *School Shootings: International Research, Case Studies, and Concepts for Prevention*, ed. Nils Bökler (New York: Springer, 2012), p. 251.

84. Mark van Vugt, "Gender Differences in Cooperation and Competition: The Male-Warrior Hypothesis," *Psychological Science* 18 (2006): 19–23.

85. V. L. Quinsey, "Evolutionary Theory and Criminal Behavior," *Legal and Criminological Psychology* 7 (2002): 1–13.

86. *Wikipedia*, s.v. "Sex Differences in Crime," last edited September 25, 2018, https://en.wikipedia.org/wiki/Sex_differences_in_crime.

87. J. N. Giedd, "The Amazing Teen Brain," *Scientific American* 312 (2015): 32–37; J. N. Giedd, "The Digital Revolution and Adolescent Brain Evolution," *Journal of Adolescent Health* 51 (2012): 101–105.

88. US Census Bureau, *Statistical Abstract of the United States, No. 70: Live Births, Deaths, Marriages, and Divorces 1950–2002.*

89. David T. Lykken, *The Antisocial Personalities* (Hillside, NJ: Lawrence Erlbaum Associates, 1995), p. 102.

90. Ibid., p. 202.

91. B. D. Whitehead, "Dan Quayle Was Right," *Atlantic Magazine*, April 1993, pp. 47–84.

92. The cases of Dr. Richard Sharpe, James Cahill, Joseph Pikul, and George Skiadopoulos are illustrative.

93. À propos rap music, it is of interest that Jeff Weise, the Ojibwe school shooter from Minnesota, criticized "inter-racial mixing" on the Red Lake reservation and his fellow Native American teens for listening to music of that genre, stating that "kids my age killing each other . . . because of the rap influence." See: *Wikipedia*, s.v. "Jeff Weise."

94. Malcolm Ritter, "Experts Link Teen Brains' Immaturity, Juvenile Crime," ABC News, n.d., https://abcnews.go.com/Technology/story?id=3943187&page=1.

95. G. Di Chiara, "Reward System and Addiction: What Dopamine Does and Doesn't Do," *Current Opinion in Pharmacology* 7 (2007): 69–76.

96. Giedd, "Digital Revolution."

97. Ibid.

98. Eric MacLaren, "The Effects of PCP Use," DrugAbuse.com, last updated September 5, 2018, https://drugabuse.com/library/the-effects-of-pcp-use/.

99. Kathleen David, "Methamphetamine: Facts, Effects, and Health Risks," Medical News Today, last updated June 28, 2018, https://www.medicalnewstoday.com/articles/309287.php.

100. L. Anderson, "Bath Salts Drug: Effects, Abuse & Health Warnings," Drugs .com, September 18, 2018, https://www.drugs.com/illicit/bath-salts.html.

101. A. Serretti and C. Fabbri, "Shared Genetics Among Major Psychiatric Disorders," *Lancet*, 371, no. 9875 (April 20, 2013): 1339–41.

102. Michael H. Stone, "A New Look at Borderline Personality Disorder and Related Disorders: Hyper-Reactivity in the Limbic System and Lower Centers," *Psychodynamic Psychiatry* 41 (2013): 437–66.

103. Brittany Wallman, Paula McMahon, Megan O'Matz, and Susannah Bryan, "School Shooter Nikolas Cruz: A Lost and Lonely Child," *Sun Sentinel*, February 24, 2018, http://www.sun-sentinel.com/local/broward/parkland/florida-school-shooting/fl-florida -school-shooting-nikolas-cruz-life-20180220-story.html.

104. Charles A. Nelson, Nathan A. Fox, and Charles H. Zeanah, *Romania's Abandoned Children: Deprivation, Brain Development, and the Struggle for Recovery* (Cambridge, MA: Harvard University Press, 2014).

105. Michael H. Stone, *The Anatomy of Evil* (Amherst, NY: Prometheus Books, 2009), p. 232.

106. Cullen, *Columbine*, p. 7.

107. *Wikipedia*, s.v. "2014 Isla Vista Killings."

108. Jennifer Shrum and Digital News Desk, "Feline Fun House: Man with Asperger's Builds Ultimate Cat Maze," CW33, September 10, 2014, http://cw33.com/2014/09/10/aspergers-traits-help-man-build-dream-house-for-cats/.

109. Sandra Gall Urban, "Luke Woodham," in *Encyclopedia of School Crime and Violence*, ed. Laura L. Finley, vol. 1 (Santa Barbara, CA: ABC-CLIO, 2011), pp. 529–33.

110. Laura Finley, "Barry Loukaitis," in *Encyclopedia of School Crime and Violence*, ed. Laura Finley, vol. 1 (Santa Barbara, CA: ABC-CLIO, 2011), pp. 273–74.

111. Laura Finley, "Bullycide," in *Encyclopedia of School Crime and Violence*, Laura L. Finley, vol. 1 (Santa Barbara, CA: ABC-CLIO, 2011), pp. 69–71.

112. Peter Davidson, *Death by Cannibal* (New York: Berkley, 2015).

113. *Wikipedia*, s.v. "Dunblane Massacre," last edited November 8, 2018, https://en.wikipedia.org/wiki/Dunblane_massacre.

114. Among 800 "true crime" biographies I have reviewed, for example, mass murderers account for only thirteen, as opposed to 168 for men committing serial sexual homicide and 127 for "uxoricides" (men who kill their wives).

115. Cullen, *Columbine*, p. 70.

116. F. Perry Wilson, "'Deaths of Despair' on the Rise in U.S.," Med Page Today, March 13, 2018, https://www.medpagetoday.com/blogs/themethodsman/71730?xid=NL_breakingnews_2018-03-13&eun=g8819790d0r.

117. E. Fuller-Torrey, "Stop the Madness," *Wall Street Journal*, July 18, 1997, https://www.wsj.com/articles/SB869178650852046000.

118. Cullen, *Columbine*, p. 239.

119. Ibid., p. 169.

120. Ibid., p. 119.

121. Mark Steyn, "Seeking Meaning in the Void," *Steyn Online* (blog), February 16, 2018, https://www.steynonline.com/8462/seeking-meaning-in-the-void.

122. "Mr. President, It's Time to Do Something about Guns," *New York Post*, February 15, 2018, https://nypost.com/2018/02/15/mr-president-its-time-to-do-something-about-guns/.

123. "Quotes on Gun Control," Gun Facts, 2018, http://www.gunfacts.info/gun-control-myths/quotes-on-gun-control/.

124. Nick Allen, "Blood Is Being Spilled on the Floors of American Classrooms: Fed-Up Students Criticize Politicians behind Gun Control Laws," *National Post*, February 17, 2018, http://nationalpost.com/news/world/blood-is-being-spilled-on-the-floors-of-american-classrooms-fed-up-students-criticize-politicians-behind-gun-control-laws.

125. Katie Dangerfield, "Australia Banned Semi-Automatic Weapons after a Mass Murder: Here's What Happened Next," Global News, October 4, 2017, https://globalnews.ca/news/3784603/australia-gun-control-ban/.

126. Hare, *Without Conscience*, p. 242.

127. "Brother of Florida School Shooting Suspect Held on $500,000 Bail," Reuters, March 20, 2018, https://www.reuters.com/article/us-usa-guns-florida-cruz/brother-of-florida-school-shooting-suspect-held-on-500000-bail-idUSKBN1GW2S7.

128. Cullen, *Columbine*, p. 327.

129. Roy Hazelwood and Stephen Michaud, *Dark Dreams: Sexual Violence, Homicide, and the Criminal Mind* (New York: St. Martin's, 2001), p. 88.

CHAPTER FOURTEEN: MAY JUSTICE TRIUMPH OVER LAW: CONTEMPORARY FORMS OF EVIL NOT INVOLVING VIOLENCE, INCLUDING A COMMENTARY ON CHILD CUSTODY CASES AND THE COURTS THAT PRESIDE OVER THEM

1. *Wikipedia*, s.v. "Mens rea," last updated September 2, 2018, https://en.wikipedia.org/wiki/Mens_rea.

2. Lord Kinross, *The Ottoman Centuries: The Rise and Fall of the Turkish Empire* (New York: William Morrow, 1977); Leslie Peirce, *Empress of the East: How a European Slave Girl Became Queen of the Ottoman Empire* (New York: Basic Books, 2017).

3. Kerry McDermott, "'It's Never Too Late to Right Your Wrong': U.S. Daughter Who Sent Her Own Father to Prison for 40 Years after Lying That He Raped Her Pleads for His Release," *Daily Mail*, August 19, 2013, http://www.dailymail.co.uk/news/article-2397002/Daughter-sent-father-prison-40-years-lying-raped-pleads-release.html.

4. Jennifer Gonnerman, "Has Daryl Kelly Spent Twenty Years in Prison for a Crime That Never Happened?" *New Yorker*, December 14, 2017, https://www.newyorker.com/sections/news/why-has-daryl-kelly-been-imprisoned-for-the-last-twenty-years-for-a-crime-that-likely-never-happened.

5. *Wikipedia*, s.v. "Dunblane Massacre," last edited November 8, 2018, https://en.wikipedia.org/wiki/Dunblane_massacre.

6. Michael H. Stone, *The Fate of Borderlines* (New York: Guilford, 1990).

7. Stuart Lavietes, "Richard Gardner, 72, Dies; Cast Doubt on Abuse Claims," *New York Times*, June 9, 2003, https://www.nytimes.com/2003/06/09/nyregion/richard-gardner-72-dies-cast-doubt-on-abuse-claims.html.

8. Colin Wilson, *Rogue Messiahs: Tales of Self-Proclaimed Saviors* (Charlottesville, VA: Hampton Roads, 2000), p. 180.

9. Annett Schirmer, "Sex Differences in Emotion," in *The Cambridge Handbook of Human Affective Neuroscience*, ed. Jorge Armony and Patrik Vuilleumier (New York: Cambridge University Press, 2013), pp. 591–610.

10. *Wikipedia*, s.v. "Jerry Sandusky," last edited December 11, 2018, https://en.wikipedia.org/wiki/Jerry_Sandusky.

11. "Ex-Teacher Gets Over 4 Years on Sex Abuse Charges," *MPR News*, October 4, 2013, https://www.mprnews.org/story/2013/10/04/lynn-seibel-sentenced-to-four-years.

12. Daniel Taylor, "Barry Bennell Branded 'Sheer Evil' As He Is Sentenced to 30 Years," *Guardian*, February 19, 2018, https://www.theguardian.com/football/2018/feb/19/barry-bennell-branded-sheer-evil-as-he-is-sentenced-to-31-years.

13. Fred Barbash, "Decades of Monstrous Sexual Abuse by Psychiatrist Costs Famous Hawaiian School $80 Million," *Washington Post*, February 17, 2018, https://www.washingtonpost.com/news/morning-mix/wp/2018/02/16/decades-of-monstrous-sexual-abuse-hawaiis-famous-kamehameha-school-settles-suit-for-80-million/.

14. Douglas Martin, "Attempted Kidnapping by Coach Stuns Pupils," *New York Times*, April 27, 1993, https://www.nytimes.com/1993/04/27/nyregion/attempted-kidnapping-by-coach-stuns-pupils.html.

15. Cristiano Lima, "Garrison Keillor Fired Over Allegations of 'Inappropriate Behavior,'" Politico, November 29, 2017, https://www.politico.com/story/2017/11/29/garrison-keillor-fired-improper-behavior-268474.

16. Colin Evans, *The Valentino Affair* (New York: Rowman and Littlefield, 2014).

17. *Wikipedia*, s.v. "Stanford White," last edited October 28, 2018, https://en.wikipedia.org/wiki/Stanford_White.

18. Peggy Noonan, "Declarations," *Wall Street Journal* (New York), January 20, 2018, p. A-13.

19. Eliana Dockterman, "'I'm Not Going to Let Him Intimidate Me Anymore.' Kate Upton Speaks Out on Alleged Harassment by Guess Co-Founder Paul Marciano," *Time*, February 7, 2018, http://time.com/5137456/kate-upton-paul-marciano-interview/.

20. Noonan, "Declarations," *Wall Street Journal*.

21. *Wikipedia*, s.v. "Kidnapping of Jaycee Dugard," last edited October 10, 2018, https://en.wikipedia.org/wiki/Kidnapping_of_Jaycee_Dugard.

22. *Wikipedia*, s.v. "Rape Statistics," last edited November 10, 2018, https://en.wikipedia.org/wiki/Rape_statistics.

23. J. P. Hemphill, R. Templeman, S. Wong, and R. D. Hare, "Psychopathy and Crime: Recidivism and Criminal Careers," in *Psychopathy: Theory, Research and Implications for Society*, ed. D. J. Cooke, A. E. Forth and R. D. Hare (Dordrecht, the Netherlands: Kluwer Academic, 1995), pp. 375–99.

24. Rocco Parascandola, Ryan Sit, Ellen Moynihan, and Stephen Rex Brown, "Brooklyn Man Attacks Family Members with Meat Cleaver after Brawl Over 2016 Presidential Election," *Daily News*, November 14, 2016, http://www.nydailynews.com/new-york/nyc-crime/brooklyn-man-attacks-family-knife-fight-election-article-1.2871358.

25. "Serial Killer Clifford Olson Dies: Canada's Most Notorious Dangerous Offender Dead from Cancer," CBC, September 30, 2011, http://www.cbc.ca/news/canada/serial-killer-clifford-olson-dies-1.1110039.

CHAPTER FIFTEEN: A NEW CHALLENGE TO JUSTICE: KIDS WHO COMMIT EVIL

1. Harold Schechter, *Fiend: The Shocking True Story of America's Youngest Serial Killer* (New York: Pocket, 2000).

2. Sol Amaya, "El Petiso Orejudo: La Historia Real Detrás del Mito Que Causó Terror a Principios del Siglo," *La Nacion*, February 17, 2018, https://www.lanacion.com.ar/2107666-el-petiso-orejudo-la-historia-real-detras-del-mito-que-causo-terror-a-principios-del-siglo-xx.

3. *Wikipedia*, s.v. "Leopold and Loeb," last edited November 14, 2018, https://en.wikipedia.org/wiki/Leopold_and_Loeb.

4. David Ovalle, "Life in Prison Again for Southwood Middle Killer Michael Hernandez," *Miami Herald*, February 22, 2016, http://www.miamiherald.com/news/local/crime/article61743422.html.

5. *Murderpedia*, s.v. "Nicholas Waggoner Browning," http://murderpedia.org/male.B/b/browning-nicholas.htm.

6. Andrew Jacobs, "After Telephone Courtship, A First Date Ends in Death," *New York Times*, August 17, 2002, https://www.nytimes.com/2002/08/17/nyregion/after -telephone-courtship-a-first-date-ends-in-death.html.

7. Michael H. Stone, *The Anatomy of Evil* (New York: Prometheus Books, 2009), p. 44.

8. *Criminal Minds Wiki*, s.v. "Craig Price," http://criminalminds.wikia.com/wiki/ Craig_Price.

9. Katie Mulvaney, "Craig Price Refuses to Plead to Attempted Murder Charges," *Providence Journal*, October 12, 2017, http://www.providencejournal.com/ news/20171012/craig-price-refuses-to-plead-to-attempted-murder-charges ; *Murderpedia*, s.v. "Craig Chandler Price," http://murderpedia.org/male.P/p/price-craig.htm.

10. "Citizens' Group Warns Public of Convict's Release from Prison," *New York Times*, August 21, 1994, p. A-44.

11. Jeff Horowitz, Sarah Zimmerman, and Juan A. Lozano, "In Deadly School Shooting, a Confession But No Clear Motive," AP News, May 20, 2018, https://www .apnews.com/cb5e0dca766e4845acf02b6bff8b62c7.

12. David Lohr, "Kirtland Cult Killings Were 'Mandated by God,' Former Member Says," *Huffington Post*, April 17, 2015, https://www.huffingtonpost.com/2015/04/17/ kirtland-cult-killings_n_7088210.html.

13. Burl Barer, *Murder in the Family* (New York: Kensington, 2000).

14. Norman Mailer, *Executioner's Song* (Boston: Little, Brown, 1979).

15. Melissa Jeltsen, "There Were Two Mass Shootings in Texas Last Week, but Only 1 on TV," *Huffington Post*, May 26, 2018, https://www.huffingtonpost.com/entry/ texas-amanda-painter-mass-shooting_us_5b081ab4e4b0802d69caad89.

16. Dana Branham and Sara Coello, "Family's Killer Filed for Divorce, Sought Restraining Order against Ex-Wife, the Sole Survivor of His Rampage," *Dallas News*, May 17, 2018, https://www.dallasnews.com/news/crime/2018/05/17/ familys-killer-filed-divorce-sought-restraining-order-ex-wife-sole-survivor-rampage.

17. Jeltsen, "There Were Two Mass Shootings," *Huffington Post*.

18. "Dr. Michael Stone: The Einstein of Evil," *National Profile Plus* (Uniondale, N.Y.), 2018, p. 36.

CHAPTER SIXTEEN: AN ALPHABET OF "NEW" EVIL

1. *Biography*, s.v. "Beverley Allitt," last updated April 2, 2014, https://www .biography.com/people/beverley-allitt-17162398; *Wikipedia*, s.v. "Beverley Alitt," last edited October 17, 2018, https://en.wikipedia.org/wiki/Beverley_Allitt.

2. John Money and June Werlas, "Folie à Deux in the Parents of Psychosocial Dwarfs: Two Cases," *Bulletin of the American Academy of Psychiatry and the Law* 4 (1976): 351–62.

3. H. D. Symonds and J. Owen, *A Sequel to the Adventures of Baron Munchausen: With 20 Copper Plates, Including the Baron's Portrait* (London, England: H. D. Symonds & J. Owen, 1792).

4. *Murderpedia*, s.v. "China Arnold," http://murderpedia.org/female.A/a/arnold

-china.htm; *Wikipedia*, s.v. "China P. Arnold," last edited September 24, 2018, https://en.wikipedia.org/wiki/China_P._Arnold.

5. Brent Doonan, *Murder at the Office* (Far Hill, NJ: Expanding Horizon, 2006).

6. *Wikipedia*, s.v. "Belle Gunness," last edited November 17, 2018, https://en.wikipedia.org/wiki/Belle_Gunness.

7. Meagan Flynn, "Heinous and Depraved: Man Accused of Brutally Killing Utah Teens, Dumping Bodies in Mine Shaft," *Washington Post*, April 5, 2018, https://www.washingtonpost.com/news/morning-mix/wp/2018/04/05/heinous-and-depraved-man-accused-of-brutally-killing-utah-teens-dumping-bodies-in-mine-shaft-because-they-socialized-with-his-girlfriend/; "Utah Man Forced Girl to Watch Killing of Boyfriend Before She Was Slain, Prosecutors Say," CBS News, April 4, 2018, https://www.cbsnews.com/news/utah-teens-killed-jerrod-baum-forced-girl-to-watch-killing-of-boyfriend-prosecutors; Crystal Hill, "Couple Visited Man's Girlfriend. He Said It Was 'Too Bad' He Had to Kill Them, Utah Cops Say," *Miami Herald*, March 29, 2018, http://www.miamiherald.com/news/nation-world/national/article207379279.html.

8. J. D. Vance, *Hillbilly Elegy: A Memoir of a Family and Culture in Crisis* (New York: HarperCollins, 2016).

9. *Murderpedia*, s.v. "Natasha Wallen Cornett," http://murderpedia.org/female.C/c/cornett-natasha.htm.

10. Alyse Wax, "The Bizarre Story of the San Francisco Witch Killers," 13th Floor, May 25, 2017, http://www.the13thfloor.tv/2017/05/25/the-bizarre-story-of-the-san-francisco-witch-killers/; Paul Elias, "Board Denies Parole to 'San Francisco Witch Killer,'" *Orange County Register*, December 2, 2015, https://www.ocregister.com/2015/12/02/board-denies-parole-to-san-francisco-witch-killer/; *Wikipedia*, s.v. "Michael Bear Carson and Suzan Carson," last edited October 22, 2018, https://en.wikipedia.org/wiki/Michael_Bear_Carson_and_Suzan_Carson.

11. Michelle Gallardo, "Hobart Woman Suspected of Being Serial Killer Gets 65 Years for Husband's Murder," ABC, May 16, 2018, http://abc7chicago.com/hobart-woman-suspected-of-being-serial-killer-gets-65-years-for-husbands-murder/3483351/.

12. Joseph S. Pete, "Documentary: Indian Woman May Have Fed Dismembered Lover to Neighbors at Barbecue, Killed Up to Nine People," *Globe Gazette*, May 14, 2018, http://globegazette.com/news/national/documentary-indiana-woman-may-have-fed-dismembered-lover-to-neighbors/article_912279f3-2e54-5cf7-a2ea-979739f1d953.html.

13. *Wikipedia*, s.v. "Daniel Rakowitz," last edited October 25, 2018, https://en.wikipedia.org/wiki/Daniel_Rakowitz.

14. *Wikipedia*, s.v. "Nathaniel Bar-Jonah," last edited September 21, 2018, https://en.wikipedia.org/wiki/Nathaniel_Bar-Jonah.

15. Mel Heimer, *Cannibal: The Case of Albert Fish* (New York: Lyle Stuart, 1971).

16. *Wikipedia*, s.v. "Fritz Haarmann," last edited November 14, 2018, https://en.wikipedia.org/wiki/Fritz_Haarmann.

17. *Murderpedia* s.v. "Albert Fentress," http://murderpedia.org/male.F/f/fentress-albert.htm.

18. Gary C. King, *Driven to Kill: The Terrifying and True Account of Sex-Killer, Westley Allan Dodd* (New York: Windsor, 1993).

19. Thomas E. Gaddis and James O. Long, *Killer: A Journal of Murder* (New York: Macmillan, 1970).

20. Gary C. King, *Out for Blood: 18 Authentic True Crime Stories of Murder and Mayhem* (Washington, DC: Bleak House Publishing and Gary King Enterprises, 2016).

21. Howard Sounes, *Fred and Rose: The Full Story* (London, England: Warner, 1995).

22. Chris Berry-Dee, *Monster: My True Story* (London, England: John Blake, 2004). Cf. also the movie "*Monster*," made in 2003, about the life of Wuornos, whose part is played by Charlize Theron. *Monster*, directed by Patty Jenkins (Los Angeles, CA: Media 8 Entertainment, 2003).

23. Diane Fanning, *Into the Water* (New York: St. Martin's, 2004); *Wikipedia*, s.v. "Richard Evonitz," last edited June 21, 2018, https://en.wikipedia.org/wiki/Richard_Evonitz; Lauren Burnette, Barbara Cannon, Kim Childers, and Jacob Jones, "Richard Mark Evonitz," (biological summary) (Radford, VA: Radford University Department of Psychology), http://maamodt.asp.radford.edu/Psyc%20405/serial%20killers/Evonitz,%20Richard%20Marc%20-%202005.pdf.

24. John Glatt, *Lost and Found* (New York: St. Martin's, 2010).

25. Gera-Lind Kolarik and Wayne Klatt, *Freed to Kill: The True Story of Larry Eyler* (Chicago: Chicago Review Press, 1990); *Murderpedia*, s.v. "Larry Eyler," http://murderpedia.org/male.E/e/eyler-larry.htm.

26. Matt Birkbeck, *A Beautiful Child* (New York: Berkley/Penguin, 2004); *Wikipedia*, s.v. "Franklin Delano Floyd," last edited December 1, 2018, https://en.wikipedia.org/wiki/Franklin_Delano_Floyd.

27. Birkbeck, *A Beautiful Child*.

28. Janet Pelasara, *The Taylor Behl Story: Love You More* (New York: HarperCollins/Regan, 2006).

29. R. Tyler, "Child Pornography: Perpetuating the Sexual Victimization of Children," *Child Abuse and Neglect* 9 (1985): 313–18.

30. Richard Wortely and Stephen Smallbone, *Child Pornography on the Internet, Problem-Specific Guide Series*, no. 41 (Washington, DC: US Department of Justice, Office of Community Oriented Policing Services, May 2006), http://www.popcenter.org/problems/pdfs/ChildPorn.pdf.

31. John Crewdson, *By Silence Betrayed: Sexual Abuse of Children in America* (Boston: Little Brown, 1998).

32. Jerome Endrass, Frank Urbaniok, Lea C. Hammermeister, et al., "The Consumption of Internet Child Pornography and Violent and Sex Offending," *BMC Psychiatry* 9 (2009): 43.

33. M. William Phelps, *Perfect Poison: A Female Serial Killer's Deadly Medicine* (New York: Pinnacle, 2003).

34. *Wikipedia*, s.v. "Kristen Gilbert," last edited July 17, 2018, https://en.wikipedia.org/wiki/Kristen_Gilbert.

35. *Wikipedia*, s.v. "Arnfinn Nesset," last edited January 30, 2018, https://en.wikipedia.org/wiki/Arnfinn_Nesset.

36. Steven Miller, *A Slaying in the Suburbs* (New York: Berkley, 2009).

37. *Murderpedia*, s.v. "Stephen Grant," http://murderpedia.org/male.G/g/grant-stephen.htm.

38. Adrian Raine, *The Anatomy of Violence: The Biological Roots of Crime* (New York: Pantheon, 2013), p. 77.

39. Ibid., p. 76.

40. Julie Salamon, *Facing the Wind: A True Story of Tragedy and Reconciliation* (New York: Random House, 2001).

41. Raine, *Anatomy of Violence*, pp. 82–83.

42. Ibid., pp. 238–39.

43. Tanya Kach and Lawrence Fisher, *Memoir of a Milk Carton Kid* (Mustang, OK: Tate, 2011).

44. Lynne Hayes-Freeland, "Tanya Kach Tells about Her Time in Captivity in a New Book," CBS News, October 12, 2011, http://pittsburgh.cbslocal.com/2011/10/12/tanya-kach-tells-about-her-time-in-captivity-in-new-book/.

45. Thomas Guillen, *Toxic Love: The Chilling True Story of Twisted Passion in the 'Murder by Cancer' Case* (New York: Dell, 1995).

46. "The Dark Side of Nebraska: Steven Harper," Dark Side of America, https://222.thedarksideofamerica.com/harper-steven-ne.html.

47. "Jealous Woman Killed Lover with Poisoned Curry," *Telegraph*, February 10, 2010, https://www.telegraph.co.uk/news/uknews/crime/7205046/Jealous-woman-killed-lover-with-poisoned-curry.html.

48. Kieran Crowley, "Sal Killed Katie's Kitty and Made Her Watch," *New York Post*, June 23, 1994.

49. "Infamous Child Molester Dies in Jail," NBC News, July 16, 2009, https://www.nbcnewyork.com/news/local/Infamous-Child-Molester-Dies-in-Jail.html.

50. Katie Beers, *Buried Memories: Katie Beers' Story* (Green Bay, WI: TitleTown, 2012).

51. Michael Mendelsohn and Alyssa Newcomb, "Katie Beers: Abduction, Abuse Led to Present Happiness," ABC News, February 8, 2013, https://abcnews.go.com/US/dungeons-katie-beers-girls-held/story?id=18222603.

52. Jessica Schladebeck and Katie Honan, "Woman Kidnapped and Hidden in Underground Bunker in 1992 Reveals Long History of Sexual Abuse," *Daily News*, December 29, 2017, http://www.nydailynews.com/news/national/katie-beers-reveals-history-sexual-abuse-article-1.3726315.

53. E. James Anthony and Bertram J. Cohler, *The Invulnerable Child* (New York: Guilford, 1987).

54. Bob Hill, *Double Jeopardy* (New York: Avon/HarperCollins, 1995).

55. Barry Siegel, *A Death in White Bear Lake* (New York: Ballantine, 1990); *Wikipedia*, s.v. "Murder of Dennis Jurgens," last edited September 13, 2018, https://en.wikipedia.org/wiki/Murder_of_Dennis_Jurgens.

56. Ibid.

57. "*The Child Abuse Prevention and Treatment Act: 40 Years of Safeguarding America's Children*" (Arlington, VA: Children's Bureau: An Office of the Administration for Children & Family Services, March 11, 2015), https://www.acf.hhs.gov/cb/resource/capta-40-years.

58. Arthur Green, "True and False Allegations of Sexual Abuse in Child Custody Disputes," *Journal of the American Academy of Child Psychiatry* 25 (1986): 449–56.

59. Ron Franscell, *Fall: The Rape and Murder of Innocence in a Small Town* (Far Hills, NJ: New Horizon, 2007).

60. Ibid.

61. Ibid.

62. Julia Prodis, "Raped and Murdered 19 Years Ago, Women Returns to Death,"

Los Angeles Times, August 23, 1992, http://articles.latimes.com/1992-08-23/news/mn-7229_1_years-ago.

63. M. William Phelps, *Too Young to Kill* (New York: Pinnacle /Kensington, 2011).

64. Michael W. Cuneo, *A Need to Kill* (New York: St. Martin's, 2011).

65. Michael Fleeman, *Better Off Dead: A Sordid Story of Sex, Sin, and Murder* (Denver, CO: Wild Blue, 2017).

66. Aphrodite Jones, *Cruel Sacrifice: Four Teenage Girls; One Gruesome Murder* (New York: Pinnacle/Windsor, 1994); *Murderpedia*, s.v. "Melinda Loveless," http://murderpedia.org/female.L/l/loveless-melinda.htm.

67. Garry Pierre-Pierre, "94-Year Term in Firebombing in the Subway," *New York Times*, May 3, 1996, https://www.nytimes.com/1996/05/03/nyregion/94-year-term-in-firebombing-in-the-subway.html.

68. Shanna Hogan, *The Stranger She Loved* (New York: St. Martin's, 2015).

69. Janice Peterson, "Martin MacNeill Sentenced to 4 Years in Prison for Identity Theft," *Herald Extra*, August 13, 2009, https://www.heraldextra.com/news/local/martin-macneill-sentenced-to-years-in-prison-for-id-theft/article_3a9954c6-2062-54b2-9221-4af9b7aa836a.html.

70. Hogan, *The Stranger She Loved*.

71. Ibid.

72. Ibid.

73. Mark Green, "Convicted Murderer Dr. Martin MacNeill Found Dead at Utah State Prison," Fox News, April 9, 2017, http://fox13now.com/2017/04/09/convicted-murderer-dr-martin-macneill-found-dead-at-utah-state-prison/.

74. *Wikipedia*, s.v. "Christian Gerhartsreiter," last edited November 10, 2018, https://en.wikipedia.org/wiki/Christian_Gerhartsreiter.

75. Herman Melville, *The Confidence Man* (New York: Dix, Edwards, 1857).

76. Steven Long, *Every Woman's Nightmare* (New York: St. Martin's, 2006).

77. "The Violent Past of the Cannibal Chef," BBC News, October 20, 2008, http://news.bbc.co.uk/2/hi/uk_news/england/7680244.stm.

78. Lindsey Bever, "Cannibalism: Survivor of the 1972 Andes Plane Crash Describes the 'Terrible' Decision He Had to Make to Stay Alive," *Independent*, February 25, 2016, https://www.independent.co.uk/news/world/americas/cannibalism-andes-plane-crash-1972-survivors-terrible-decision-stay-alive-a6895781.html.

79. Gregg Olson, *Bitter Almonds: The True Story of Mothers, Daughters, and the Seattle Cyanide Murders* (New York: Time Warner, 1993).

80. Howard Markel, "How the Tylenol Murders of 1982 Changed the Way We Consume Medication," PBS, September 29, 2014, https://www.pbs.org/newshour/health/tylenol-murders-1982.

81. "Man Guilty of Killing Two in Sudafed Tampering," *New York Times*, April 4, 1993, https://www.nytimes.com/1993/04/04/us/man-guilty-of-killing-two-in-sudafed-tampering.html.

82. John Glatt, *The Prince of Paradise: The True Story of a Hotel Heir, His Seductive Wife, and a Ruthless Murder* (New York: St. Martin's, 2013).

83. Frank McAdams and Timothy Carney, *Final Affair: The Shocking True Story of Marriage and Murder* (New York: Berkley, 2002); Rong-Gong Lin II, "Richard K. Overton Dies at 81; Convicted of Fatally Poisoning His Wife," *Los Angeles Times*, http://www.latimes.com/local/obituaries/la-me-richard-overton7-2009jun07-story.html.

84. Jit Fong Chin, "Richard Overton, Convicted of Poisoning Wife in 1988, Died," *Orange County Register*, June 7, 2009, https://www.ocregister.com/2009/06/07/richard-overton-convicted-of-poisoning-wife-in-1988-dies/.

85. Deborah Hastings, "'Killer Nanny' Yoselyn Ortega Found Guilty on All Counts in Stabbing Deaths of 2 Children," *Inside Edition*, April 18, 2018, https://www.insideedition.com/killer-nanny-yoselyn-ortega-found-guilty-all-counts-stabbing-deaths-2-children-42586.

86. "The Latest: Dad of 2 Slain Children Says Killer Nanny 'Evil,'" AP News, May 14, 2018, https://www.apnews.com/138bbdce6e6b4876b7ab76f4d3520daa.

87. Jan Ransom, "Yoselyn Ortega, Nanny Who Killed 2 Children, Is Sentenced to Life in Prison," *New York Times*, May 14, 2018, https://www.nytimes.com/2018/05/14/nyregion/manhattan-nanny-sentenced-life.html.

88. Elizabeth Rosner, "'Killer Nanny' Carefully Planned Children's Murder: Prosecutor," *NY Post*, August 16, 2018, https://nypost.com/2018/04/16/killer-nanny-carefully-planned-childrens-murder-prosecutor/.

89. Lynh Bui, "A Crying Baby Woke Up a Napping Nanny. So She Force-Fed Her Until the Child Died, Police Say," *Washington Post*, October 26, 2016, https://www.washingtonpost.com/local/public-safety/a-crying-baby-woke-up-a-napping-nanny-so-she-force-fee-her-until-the-child-died-police-say/2016/10/26/efee4b74-9b8d-11e6-9980-50913d68eacb_story.html?utm_term=.7af6b9969261.

90. "Nanny Viktoria Tautz Guilty of Shaking 10-Month-Old Baby to Death," Sky News, June 1, 2017, https://news.sky.com/story/nanny-viktoria-tautz-guilty-of-shaking-10-month-old-baby-boy-to-death-10901081.

91. "Au Pair's Conviction Reduced to Involuntary Manslaughter," CNN, November 10, 2017, http://www.cnn.com/US/9711/10/au.pair.short/.

92. Don Lasseter and Ronald E. Bowers, *Meet Me for Murder: Young Beauties with Hollywood Dreams—a Predator's Deadly Trap* (New York: Pinnacle, 2006).

93. Clifford Linedecker, *Death of a Model* (New York: St. Martin's, 1997).

94. Michael Newton, *Rope: The Twisted Life and Crimes of Harvey Glatman* (New York: Pocket, 1998).

95. Dave Collins and Denise Lavoie, "A Joyful Reunion with Birth Parents Leads to Incest and Murder," *Chicago Tribune*, April 22, 2018, http://www.chicagotribune.com/news/nationworld/ct-katie-fusco-pladl-incest-murder-20180422-story.html.

96. M. William Phelps, *Never See Them Again* (New York: Kensington, 2012); *Murderpedia*, s.v. "Christine Marie Paolilla," http://murderpedia.org/female.P/p/paolilla-christine.htm.

97. Phelps, *Never See Them Again*, p. 182.

98. Michael H. Stone, "Mass Murder, Mental Illness, and Men," *Violence & Gender* 2 (2014): 51–86.

99. Suzy Spencer, *Breaking Point* (New York: St. Martin's, 2002).

100. Matt Nicholls, "Matthew Quesada: The Jason Bourne Fantasies of the Café Killer," Court News UK, http://courtnewsuk.co.uk/matthew-quesada-the-jason-bourne-killer/; "Killer Obsessed with Bourne Trilogy Stabbed Pensioner to Death for Asking If His Crying Daughter Was Okay Before Going on the Run," *Daily Mail*, July 14, 2012, http://www.dailymail.co.uk/news/article-2173571/Killer-obsessed-Bourne-trilogy-stabbed-pensioner-death-asking-crying-daughter-okay-going-run.html.

101. "Divorce Rates Data, 1858 to Now: How Has It Changed?" *Guardian*, January 28, 2010, https://www.theguardian.com/news/datablog/2010/jan/28/divorce-rates-marriage-ons; Ana Swanson, "144 Years of Marriage and Divorce in the United States, in One Chart," *Washington Post*, June 23, 2015.

102. David T. Lykken, *The Antisocial Personalities* (Hillside, NJ: Lawrence Erlbaum Associates, 1995).

103. Patricia Springer, *Mail Order Murder* (New York: Pinnacle, 1999).

104. John Glatt, *Forgive Me, Father* (New York: St. Martin's, 2008).

105. *Wikipedia*, s.v. "Hans Schmidt (priest)," last edited September 20, 2018, https://en.wikipedia.org/wiki/Hans_Schmidt_(priest).

106. M. William Phelps, *I'd Kill for You* (New York: Pinnacle, 2015).

107. *Biography*, s.v. "Siouxsie Sioux," last updated March 11, 2016, https://www.biography.com/people/siouxsie-sioux-17178808.

108. Dale Crowell, "Pin-Up Queen Killer: The True Story of Samantha Scott," in *The Spoiled Brat Killer*, ed. Latty Maravich (Middletown, DE: CreateSpace, 2018); Aram Saroyan, *Rancho Mirage* (Fort Lee, NJ, Barricade, 1993).

109. Ibid.

110. Reuven Fenton, Elizabeth Rosner, and Bruce Golding, "Notorious Child-Killer Still Living in Harlem—and Shows No Remorse," *New York Post*, November 1, 2017, https://nypost.com/2017/11/01/notorious-child-killer-still-living-in-harlem-and-shows-no-remorse/.

111. Sam Ehrlich, *Lisa, Hedda & Joel: The Steinberg Murder Case* (New York: St. Martin's, 1989).

112. Ann E. Imbrie, *Spoken in Darkness* (New York: Plume, 1993).

113. Michael H. Stone, "Serial Sexual Homicide: Biological, Psychological and Sociological Aspects," *Journal of Personality Disorders* 15, no. 1 (2001): 1–19.

114. R. Ronin McDonald, *Secrets Never Lie* (New York: Avon, 1998).

115. Rufus-Jenny Triplett, "Fred Tokars—Where Is He Now—Prison Snitch?" *Cherokee Tribune* (Canton, GA), April 13, 2013.

116. John Leake, *Entering Hades: The Double Life of a Serial Killer* (New York: Sarah Crichton/Farrar Straus Giroux, 2007).

117. Ann Rule, *Every Breath You Take: A True Story of Obsession, Revenge, and Murder* (New York: Pocket, 2001).

118. "Texas Man Guilty in Murder-for-Hire," CBS News, July 6, 2000, https://www.cbsnews.com/news/texas-man-guilty-in-murder-for-hire/.

119. John Tedesco, "Another Trial," *John Tedesco* (blog), January 9, 2000, https://johntedesco.net/blog/another-trial/.

120. Ibid.

121. Phil Hager, "Death Sentence Upheld for Killer Who Showed 'Astonishing Cruelty,'" *Los Angeles Times*, June 23, 1989, http://articles.latimes.com/1989-06-23/news/mn-2460_1_lawrence-sigmond-bittaker-conviction-and-sentence-fair-trial; *Wikipedia*, s.v. "Lawrence Bittaker and Ray Norris," last edited December 8, 2018, https://en.wikipedia.org/wiki/Lawrence_Bittaker_and_Roy_Norris.

122. Michael Fleeman, *Love You Madly: The True Story of a Small-Town Girl, the Young Men Who Would Do Anything for Her, and the Murder of Her Mother* (New York: St. Martin's, 2011).

123. *Wikipedia*, s.v. "Joey Buttafuoco," last edited December 17, 2018, https://en.wikipedia.org/wiki/Joey_Buttafuoco.

124. Kathryn Casey, *In Plain Sight: The Kaufman County Prosecutor Murders* (New York: William Morrow, 2018), p. 178.

125. Ibid., p. 208.

126. Ibid., p. 424.

127. American Psychiatric Association, *Diagnostic and Statistical Manual of Mental Disorders*, 3rd ed., revised (Washington, DC: American Psychiatric Association, 1987), p. 371.

128. Theodore Millon, Erik Simonsen, and Morten Birket-Smith, "Historical Conceptions of Psychopathy in the United States and Europe," in *Psychopathy: Antisocial, Criminal and Violent Behavior*, ed. T. Millon, E. Simonsen, M. Birket-Smith, and R.D. Davis (New York: Guilford, 1998), pp. 9–31.

129. Steve Jackson, *A Clockwork Murder: The Night a Twisted Fantasy Became a Demented Reality* (Denver, CO: Wildblue, 2017).

130. Vernon J. Geberth, *Sex-Related Homicide and Death Investigation: Practical and Clinical Perspectives*, 2nd ed. (New York: CRC Press), pp. 703–39.

131. Roger Scruton, *On Human Nature* (Princeton, NJ: Princeton University Press, 2017).

132. *Murderpedia*, s.v. "Kao Xiong," http://murderpedia.org/male.X/x/xiong-kao.htm.

133. Anthony Holden, *St. Alban's Poisoner: Life and Crimes of Graham Young* (London, England: Black Swan, 1995).

134. H. Andershed, O. F. Collins, R. T. Salekin, et al., "Callous-Unemotional Traits Only Versus Multidimensional Psychopathy Construct as Predictors of Various Antisocial Outcomes During Early Adolescence," *Journal of Psychopathology and Behavioral Assessment* 40, no. 1 (2018): 16–25; P. J. Frick and J. V. Ray, "Evaluating Callous-Unemotional Traits as a Personality Construct," *Journal of Personality* 83, no. 6 (2015): 710–22; S. Pisano, P. Muratori, C. Gorga, et al., "Conduct Disorders and Psychopathology in Children and Adolescents: Aetiology, Clinical Presentation and Treatment Strategies of Callous-Unemotional Traits," *Italian Journal of Pediatrics* 43, no. 1 (2017): 84; L. Arsenault, T. E. Moffit, A. Caspi, and A. Taylor, "The Targets of Violence Committed by Young Offenders with Alcohol Dependence, Marijuana Dependence and Schizophrenia-Spectrum Disorders: Findings from a Birth Cohort," *Criminal Behaviour and Mental Health* 12, no. 2 (2002): 155–68; T. E. Moffitt and A. Caspi, "Childhood Predictors Differentiate Life-Course Persistent and Adolescent-Limited Pathways Among Males and Females," *Development and Psychopathology* 13, no. 2 (2001): 355–75; Michael Stone, "The Psychodynamics of Evil: Motives Behind Acts of Extreme Violence in Peacetime," in *Humanizing Evil: Psychoanalytic, Philosophical and Clinical Perspectives*, ed. Ronald Naso and Jon Mills (London, England: Routledge, 2016), pp. 129–68.

135. *Murderpedia*, s.v. "Graham Young," http://murderpedia.org/male.Y/y/young-graham.htm.

136. Ian Brady, *The Gates of Janus: Serial Killing and Its Analysis, by the 'Moors Murderer'* (Port Townsend, WA: Feral House, 2015).

137. Personal communication quoted in Michael H. Stone, "Narcissism and Criminality," *Psychiatric Annals* 39, no. 4 (April 2009): 194–201.

138. *Wikipedia*, s.v. "Charles Yukl," last edited December 7, 2017, https://en.wikipedia.org/wiki/Charles_Yukl.

139. Robert K. Tanenbaum, *The Piano Teacher* (New York: New American Library, 1987), p. 108.

140. *Murderpedia*, s.v. "Charles William Yukl," http://murderpedia.org/male.Y/y/yukl-charles.htm.

141. Ibid.

142. Keith Elliott Greenberg and Det. Vincent Ferber, *Perfect Beauty* (New York: St. Martin's, 2008); M. William Phelps, *If Looks Could Kill: Money, Marriage, Adultery and Murder* (New York: Pinnacle/Kensington, 2008).

143. Rena Vicini, *Fatal Seduction: Two Women, One Man, and a Shocking True Story of Sex and Drugs, Lesbianism, and Murder* (New York: Pinnacle/Kensington, 1994).

144. Jennifer Hewlett, "Family Fights Parole in '86 Slaying, Among Ky.'s Most Infamous," *Lexington Herald Leader*, February 1, 2011 (updated November 10, 2015), https://www.kentucky.com/news/local/counties/franklin-county/article44077404.html.

145. Jennifer Hewlett, "Board Denies Parole for Elizabeth Turpin in Husband's Murder," *Lexington Herald Leader*, February 22, 2011, https://www.kentucky.com/news/article44080656.html.

FINAL THOUGHTS

1. Peggy Noonan, "The Culture of Death," *Wall Street Journal* (New York), December 7, 2017, p. A-13.

AFTERWORD BY ANN W. BURGESS, DNSc., APRN

1. Susan D. Mustafa and Sue Israel, *Dismembered* (New York: Pinnacle Books, 2011).

2. Michael H. Stone, *The Anatomy of Evil* (Amherst, NY: Prometheus Books, 2009), p. 29; Seth Ferranti, "Having These Personality Traits Might Mean You're Evil," *Vice*, November 10, 2017, https://www.vice.com/en_us/article/3kv7gw/having-these-personality-traits-might-mean-youre-evil.

3. Ibid.

4. Ibid.

INDEX

ABOUT THE AUTHORS

Michael H. Stone, MD, is professor of clinical psychiatry at the Columbia College of Physicians and Surgeons. He is the author of ten books, most recently *The Anatomy of Evil*, and over two hundred professional articles and book chapters. Formerly the host of the Discovery Channel series *Most Evil*, Dr. Stone is regularly featured in media outlets such as the *New York Times*, *Psychology Today*, CNN, ABC News, NBC News, and the BBC.

Gary Brucato, PhD, a clinical psychologist and researcher in the areas of violence, psychosis, and other serious psychopathology, is the assistant director of the Center of Prevention and Evaluation at the New York State Psychiatric Center / Columbia University Medical Center. A regular contributor to the academic literature, he is widely consulted by professionals and patients throughout the country. His research group has received support from the National Institute of Mental Health to study the relationship between early psychotic symptoms, and violent thoughts and behavior.

8/20
T-24 1119
L-6

10/20
T- 24 11/19
L - 6

6/21
T 24 1/19
L 6

1/22/19